Look Back in Hope

Look Back in Hope

An Ecumenical Life

KEITH CLEMENTS

RESOURCE *Publications* • Eugene, Oregon

LOOK BACK IN HOPE
An Ecumenical Life

Copyright © 2017 Keith Clements. All rights reserved. Except for brief quotations in critical publications or reviews, no part of this book may be reproduced in any manner without prior written permission from the publisher. Write: Permissions, Wipf and Stock Publishers, 199 W. 8th Ave., Suite 3, Eugene, OR 97401.

Resource Publications
An Imprint of Wipf and Stock Publishers
199 W. 8th Ave., Suite 3
Eugene, OR 97401

www.wipfandstock.com

PAPERBACK ISBN: 978-1-5326-1855-0
HARDCOVER ISBN: 978-1-4982-4422-0
EBOOK ISBN: 978-1-4982-4421-3

Manufactured in the U.S.A.   JUNE 15, 2017

Grateful acknowledgement is made for permission to use copyright material as follows:

To SCM Press, for citations from Dietrich Bonhoeffer, *Letters and Papers from Prison* (1953) and from Christopher Driver, *A Future for the Free Churches?* (1962); to Oxford University Press, for citation from Thomas Traherne: *Poems Centuries and Three Thanksgivings* edited by Anne Ridler (1966): Extract of 212 words from "century 54" (page188); to the editor of the *Baptist Quarterly* for citation from Clifford H. Cleal, "The Role of the Ordained Minister Today" (1974); to the Beyers Naudé Centre, University of Stellenbosch, for citation from "An Interview with Beyers Naudé" in *Oom Bey for the Future* (2006); and to World Council of Churches Publications for citation from my paper "The Ecumenical Movement: My Vision", in *Reflections on Ecumenism* (2004).

The photograph of Dr Alec Vidler, © Edward Leigh, is reproduced by permission of the Archives Centre, King's College, Cambridge (ref. KCPH/2/2/3/24 (part).

The photograph of the signing of the Charta Oecumenica, Strasbourg 2001, is reproduced by permission of the Conference of European Churches, Brussels.

The photograph of Bristol Baptist College staff and students 1987 is © Bristol Baptist College and is reproduced by permission.

The photograph of Dr Morris West is reproduced by permission of Mr Julian West.

Unless otherwise stated, biblical citations are taken from the New Revised Standard Version Bible, ©1989, Division of Christian Education of the National Council of the Churches of Christ in the United States of America.

For Oliver, Bess, and Tom, and their coming of age.

Contents

Preface | *ix*
Acronyms and abbreviations | *xii*
Prelude: A Journey | *xvii*

Part One: Discoveries 1943–1967
    1   Manse Child | 3
    2   Cambridge Excitements | 23
    3   Oxford Labors | 48

Part Two: Minister and Teacher 1967–1990
    4   Experimental Pastures: The Mid-Cheshire Fellowship | 67
    5   In the Most Ecumenical City:Downend, Bristol | 87
    6   Theological College Tutor … | 109
    7   … and Ecumenical Explorer | 131

Part Three: International Affairs 1990–1997
    8   "His dad's a spy": New Ecumenical Pilgrimage in the Old Unruly World | 165
    9   The Middle East: Conflicts Past, Present, and to Come | 190
    10   Balkan Turmoil | 206
    11   Listening to Africa | 220
    12   South African Pain and Joy | 232
    13   China: A Return Home | 250
    14   Europe Calling | 260

CONTENTS

Part Four: Ecumenical Europe 1997–2005

    15   Making Home in Geneva—and All Europe | 269

    16   Hopes versus Disappointments: Towards the New Millennium 1997–2000 | 274

    17   New Sign-Posts for Unity, New Challenges from War 2000–2003 | 300

    18   Mission, European Integration, Dreams, and Commemorations 2003–2005 | 333

Part Five: Old Interests, New Horizons 2006–2016

    19   A Full Life—At Our Own Pace | 361

    20   Two Troubling Years | 394

Postlude: Still Hoping | 403

Bibliography | 409

Index of Subjects and Places | 413

Index of Names | 417

Preface

THE TITLE OF THIS book is probably both illuminating and puzzling. "Look Back in Hope" suggests a memoir in which the author records experiences which he regards as encouragements to hope. These days however "An Ecumenical Life" might seem a surprising ally of hope. Has not the modern ecumenical enterprise which began with such high expectations, excitement even, in the early twentieth century now had its day? It is not only that the different Christian churches and denomination still seem a long way from unity. The world at large—the "whole inhabited earth" or *oikoumene* from which the term "ecumenical" derives—is still beset by discord and conflict as much as it did a century ago, if not more so. The vision of a Christian fellowship reconciled within itself and empowered to heal a wounded world seems to have little correspondence with reality. I admit as much, but also invite the reader to share what I have seen, heard, and at times experienced at first hand, of transformative changes in relationships both within the churches and beyond, which I feel bound to interpret as signs, parables and foretastes of what Christians are used to calling the kingdom of God or the purpose of God within human history. It is precisely my engagement in the ecumenical movement, at different levels and in many diverse places since student days more than fifty years ago, that has provided me with so many of the experiences on which I look back with hope.

The hope to which I refer is the creation of true community in the world, of people among themselves, with God, and with all creation. That I believe is what the gospel of Christ is all about, what the church is about, and indeed what God who lives and loves as three-in-oneness is all about. It is a hope which appears mightily threatened just now by resurgent sectarianism and nationalism. It will be noted that I have effectively concluded my account with the United Kingdom's referendum decision in June 2016, to leave the European Union. Ensuing political developments in the USA and elsewhere do not feature but my responses will not have caused any surprises in light of what have written throughout most of the book. Many of us are now prompted to speak in apocalyptic terms of what the future may hold, and at a time when so many foundations seem to be trembling it is easy to imagine that all we have experienced and supposedly learnt in our lifetimes hitherto is no longer of any use or relevance. That is doubtless true of much, but not necessarily of all. There may be very important stories to tell and experiences to recall, not all of them grand dramas, some of them very modest and unassuming, which remind us of what the human story is really all about and what matters most of all, and what will remain crucial regardless of changing circumstances. This is, the ever-surprising capacity of grace to touch people's lives and enable them in turn to be gracious towards others and to the world around them, to do justly, to love kindness, and to walk humbly with their God. This is what contains the promise and the hope for our world, and it is in recalling such instances in my lifetime that I find hope for the future.

I have not tried to write a history of the ecumenical movement from my personal perspective, but rather an account of my life as a whole to which ecumenical commitment became central. That commitment is itself an aspect of faith, faith which is not a compartment of life but is the orientation of one's life as a whole. Jesus, wrote Dietrich Bonhoeffer, calls us not to religion but to life, and claims the whole of life for the kingdom of God. So no apologies here for reflections on personal matters, relationships and interests, for which I am deeply thankful. These too are mediums of grace, tokens of, in Dante's words, "The love that moves the sun and the other stars".

The writing of this life, no less than the life itself, owes gratitude to many people, since the first casualty in writing a memoir is confidence in the accuracy of one's own memory. Of first importance is access to actual written records not in one's own possession, and in this regard I am deeply grateful for help received from: Hans von Ruette, archivist of the World Council of Churches at the Ecumenical Center in Geneva, and his staff; Michael Brealey, librarian at Bristol Baptist College; Patricia McGuire, archivist at King's College, Cambridge; and the staff of the Church of England Record Centre at Bermondsey, London, where much of the archival material of the British ecumenical bodies is housed. In addition, a number of friends and colleagues (some of whom themselves feature in the account) have helped me by advising or answering queries on factual detail, or by lending or giving relevant material: the late and sorely missed Gethin Abraham-Williams; Michael Bowker; Christopher Bradnock; Robert Bradnock; John Briggs; David Carter; Alizon Cleal; Donata Coleman; John de Gruchy; Bob Fyffe; Peter Hills; Viorel Ionita; David Lloyd; John Reardon; Paul Renshaw; Alwyn Thompson; David Thompson; Jane Vian; Julian West; Huibert van Beek; Roger Williamson; and Peter Willis. Special thanks are due to Ian Waddington for help in preparing the photographs for publication.

Then of course there is my own family. Above all my wife Margaret, who knows more about this story than anyone else, cast a helpfully critical eye on the content and style of the draft text (reserving her own opinion on some of the matters related!), and our two sons Peter and Jonathan refreshed my recollection of things said and done, in some cases many years ago. Having received the Hebraic blessing of living to see our children's children, I dedicate this book to our grandchildren Oliver, Bess, and Tom.

They and their generation will encounter both challenges and opportunities we can scarcely imagine; may they also draw encouragement from some of the things we have been privileged to learn.

Portishead
Holy Week 2017

Acronyms and abbreviations

AAR	American Academy of Religion
ACTS	Action of Churches Together in Scotland
AEE	Area of Ecumenical Experiment (later termed LEP)
AIF	Association of Inter-Church Families
ANC	African National Congress
AUCECB	All-Union Council of Evangelical-Christians Baptists
AZAPO	African People's Organization
BD	Bachelor of Divinity
BBC	British Broadcasting Corporation
BCC	British Council of Churches
BCSA	Baptist Concern for Southern Africa
BD	Bachelor of Divinity
BEM	*Baptism, Eucharist and Ministry*
BMS	Baptist Missionary Society
BRG	Baptist Renewal Group
BSF	Baptist Student Federation
BU	Baptist Union
BWA	Baptist World Alliance
CAFOD	Catholic Agency for Overseas Development
CCADD	Council on Christian Approaches to Defence and Disarmament
CCBI	Council of Churches for Britain and Ireland
CCC	China Christian Council
CCEE	Council of Episcopal Conferences in Europe

CCME	Churches' Commission on Migrants in Europe
CCOM	Churches' Commission on Mission
CCSA	Christian Concern for Southern Africa
CDU	Christian Democratic Union
CEC	Conference of European Churches
CICARWS	Commission on Church Aid, Refugee and World Service
CICCU	Cambridge Inter-Collegiate Christian Union
CIIR	Catholic Institute for International Relations
CIM	China Inland Mission
CND	Campaign for Nuclear Disarmament
COMECE	Commission of the Bishops' Conferences of the European Community
COSATU	Congress of South African Trade Unions
CRM	Church Representatives' Meeting
CTBI	Churches Together in Britain and Ireland
CTE	Churches Together in England
CUMS	Cambridge University Music Society
CWME	Commission on World Mission and Evangelism
Cytun	Churches Together in Wales
DD	Doctor of Divinity
DPhil	Doctor of Philosophy
EAE	Evangelical Alliance Europe
ECEN	European Churches' Environmental Network
ECWGAR	European Churches' Working Group on Asylum and Refugees
EEA2	Second European Ecumenical Assembly
EEC	European Economic Community
EECCS	European Ecumenical Commission on Church and Society
EKD	Evangelische Kirche in Deutschland
EMPSA	Ecumenical Monitoring Programme for South Africa
ERR	Emergency Relief, Rehabilitation and Reconstruction Programme
EU	European Union
FA	Football Association
FBI	Federal Bureau of Investigation
FCB	Fellowship of Concerned Baptists (South Africa)

Acronyms and Abbreviations

FCFC	Free Church Federal Council
FCO	Foreign and Commonwealth Office
GDR	German Democratic Republic
IALG	International Affairs Liaison Group
ICI	Imperial Chemical Industries Ltd
IRA	Irish Republican Army
ITN	Independent Television News
KES	King Edward VII School
LEP	Local Ecumenical Project/Partnership
LWF	Lutheran World Federation
MCC	Marylebone Cricket Club
MCF	Mid-Cheshire Fellowship (of Baptist Churches)
MECC	Middle East Council of Churches
NATO	North Atlantic Treaty Organization
NCCCUSA	National Council of Churches of Christ in the USA
NGO	Non-Governmental Organization
NPT	Nuclear Non Proliferation Treaty
NUM	National Union of Mineworkers
OSCE	Organization for Security and Cooperation in Europe
OU	Open University
PCR	Programme to Combat Racism
PhD	Doctor of Philosophy
RAF	Royal Air Force
REO	Regional Ecumenical Organization
RHS	Robert Hall Society
RIBS	Runcorn Informal Baptist Society
RSPB	Royal Society for the Protection of Birds
SACC	South African Council of Churches
SADF	South African Defence Force
SCIAF	Scottish Catholic International Aid Fund
SCM	Student Christian Movement
SEEP	South East Europe Ecumenical Partnership
SWEC	South West Ecumenical Congress

UCT	University of Cape Town
UKIP	United Kingdom Independence Party
UN	United Nations
UNA	United Nations Association
UNHCR	United Nations High Commission for Refugees
URC	United Reformed Church
UWE	University of the West of England
VAT	Value-added tax
WARC	World Alliance of Reformed Churches
WCC	World Council of Churches
WMDs	Weapons of Mass Destruction

Prelude: A Journey

DECEMBER 1944. IT IS a bleak morning just outside the village of Gulin in Sichuan, south-west China, and the sun has barely lifted above the surrounding blue-grey mountain ridges. The English couple, accompanied by two Chinese coolies, have turned for a last farewell wave to the group of villagers who have walked with them for about a mile along the road. Now they set their faces northward. The man is carrying some of the baggage; the woman, for part of the way journeying in a litter carried by the coolies, holds a somewhat lighter but perhaps more troublesome bundle, their child, not yet two years old. We (for I am that child) are setting off for England over six thousand miles away, across a world at war.

For their second term of service with the China Inland Mission (CIM) Harry and Fay Clements had been working as missionaries in Gulin since early 1939. Their next furlough was not due for another year but from early 1944 they had been facing a fraught situation. Their two older sons John and Brian, aged nine and six respectively, were away at the CIM school for missionaries' children at Loshan over two hundred miles to the north-west, where it had relocated following the Japanese incursion in the east. The school was sending increasingly worrying reports about John's health. Boarding so far from home in a country at war was evidently taking its toll on him. The advice was to take him out of China for treatment in a more settled environment, and the CIM agreed to the furlough being brought forward by a year. But where could it be spent? In normal circumstances Australia, where Fay had relatives, would have been the answer but that was out of the question with the Japanese occupation of much of south and east China and the war in the South Pacific. The best option seemed to be, if at all possible, to make it back to England. Starting from a remote area of China, and in wartime, was a big gamble, or a venture of faith as my parents would have preferred to say. So a plan was worked out. Harry and Fay with me would leave Gulin in December and we would spend Christmas with fellow missionaries Arnold Lea and his wife in Lushien, about half-way between Gulin and the school at Loshan. My father would then travel on to Loshan and return with John and Brian to Lushien. We would all then travel downriver on the Yangtze River to Chonquing, from where, it was hoped, we could take a flight to Calcutta (today's Kolkata).

So far so good, though it was a great wrench for my parents to leave Gulin where they had been deeply happy, where their work had flourished and where they had made many friends not only in the congregation which grew under their care but in the village at large as well. There, too, I had been born in May 1943 late one night surrounded by smoky oil lamps and clouds of mosquitoes. The birth of a child to the only white woman known for miles around caused a stir throughout the village and I was showered with presents and hailed as "King of Gulin". The last days in Gulin saw long and deeply emotional leave-takings. Well-wishers ranged from the county governor to a beggar boy whose septic foot my parents had treated in the simple dispensary they ran, and who now presented them with six eggs. The final evening was spent with the congregation and it was at this point that the well-rehearsed travel plan started to unravel. Just as the meeting was breaking up the postmaster arrived with an urgent telegram from the CIM office in Chonquing: "Boys proceeding to Kunming direct." My parents were nonplussed. Kunming lay to the south-west in Yunnan province, in the diametrically opposite direction to Chonquing, and while it could also offer flights to India this ran quite counter to the plan for a journey to Lushien and then to Chonquing.

There was nothing for it next morning but to set out northward for the town of Yungning, where there were other CIM workers and which we would have to reach whichever direction we took next. The trek to Yungning took two days, and all that time there was nothing to explain the why and how of that telegram. On arrival at Yungning the CIM colleagues asked, "Did you get the telegram?" "About the boys?" "No," they said, "the one from the British ambassador." It transpired that the Japanese were making a drive through Guizhou province just east of southern Sichuan in a bid to take the American and Chinese airfields in the south-west of the country. Indeed there were rumors that they were only thirty miles from Gulin, and a general evacuation of foreign nationals was being ordered. Although Japanese planes were periodically over Gulin, and Chinese soldiers straggling to or from the front were a frequent sight, suddenly the war now seemed very much nearer. But my parents' concern was to reach my brothers. There was no further word from Chonquing and the advice from the Yungning colleagues was to accept that the CIM telegram was all there was to go on. But how to reach Kunming, over three hundred miles across the mountains to the south-west? The only way seemed to be to hitch a lift on an American army convoy. The Americans were trucking supplies from Kunming up to their airbases near Chengdu, returning on (and laden with) rice alcohol fuel, and so passing through Yungning. One such southbound convoy was due to leave next day. My father persuaded a rather dubious sergeant, who could not easily envisage a mother and infant roughing it in such Spartan vehicles over the mountains in winter, to take us aboard, but he did. So we left early next morning, my father in one truck, my mother and I in the next one. The cabs were partly open and it was bitterly cold. At the Sichuan-Guizhou border the first of many accidents occurred when one lorry stalled on the steep rise from the river bank, ran backwards and smashed the radiator of the vehicle behind. Delays for repairs. By evening the convoy reached the town of Bijie where there was a most welcome surprise: overnight hospitality in a mission center run by German deaconesses who had been allowed to continue their work there despite officially being "aliens". What might have happened to them if the Japanese broke through and discovered they had been traitors to the Axis cause was anyone's guess, but an American officer assured my father the US army would pre-empt any risk and fly them to India. "But wouldn't they be interned there?" asked my father. "We'll take care of them", said the officer, "and not even the whole goddam British Empire will stop us."

Next day my father was in the leading truck, my mother and I in one about halfway down the line. At the top of the next mountain pass the road lay under thick ice and only the first three trucks made it over. The rest of us had to go back to Bijie for the night so for the first time we were separated, my father spending the night in a village inn the other side of the mountain, my mother and I with the German deaconesses again. Next day the rest of the convoy managed to slide itself over the ice, and we were reunited on the road to Weining. The sergeant decided that the three of us should now occupy the same vehicle, which was to prove fortunate. At Weining, by chance, my mother met up with a young English Methodist missionary (how I wish I knew his name now) who gave us hospitality for the night in his bungalow. Next morning, on the road again. By now one truck or another seemed to be breaking down every few miles but the sergeant was determined to reach his destination, a large fighter airbase about sixty miles from Kunming, by nightfall. By the time we reached the high, bleak Yunnan plateau there was no other vehicle in sight—and ours suddenly caught fire. An instant stop, a prompt disembarkation and rapid retreat as everyone waited for the barrels of alcohol to explode. The smoke however did not seem to get worse, the driver bravely crawled underneath and located the source of the trouble in the emergency brake binding on the prop-shaft. Blankets were sacrificed to smother the flames. Back on board again and the journey resumed. It was well after dark when a stationary vehicle suddenly appeared in the headlights. It was the lead truck which had broken down. Ours had to tow it, staggering, to the air-base. These two vehicles were the only ones left on the road out of the eleven which had left Yungning.

We were given generous overnight hospitality at the airbase, but were still sixty miles from Kunming. Next morning my father was told there was no official transport to Kunming for at least another day. But he was pointed to two trucks parked outside the base which looked as though they might be heading in that direction. One drove off as he walked up. The other had an officer sitting in the cab. Yes, they were going to Kunming but they were not allowed to take civilians in a combat zone. My father assured him that we had been living in a combat zone for many months and that all responsibility would be his. "Well," said the officer, "we're waiting for an aircraft tire to take to Kunming. It should have been here an hour ago. Soon as it comes we go. If you can . . . " My father didn't wait to hear the rest but scurried off to collect my mother, our baggage, and me. We arrived at the truck just as the tire was being loaded. My parents always reckoned that the delay in its delivery must have been a case of special providence. We reached Kunming in the afternoon, and after being dropped off from the truck took two rickshaws to the CIM compound. There on the grass, two boys were playing: John and Brian had arrived the previous day. The Americans had heard of their need to get to Kunming, and diverted a two-seater fighter plane (evidently one of the Flying Tigers" whose main base was at Kunming) flying to Kunming from Chengdu to land on a sandbank on the river at Loshan and pick the boys up—John, as he excitedly told his parents, sitting on the co-pilot's knee for the whole flight.

The air-route from Kunming to India lay over the notorious "Hump" of the eastern Himalayas and the Burmese jungles, hazardous for military and civilian aircraft alike because of severe and unpredictable weather. Pilots were told "If you can see the end of the runway, then take off." Accidents were so frequent that to many aircrew it was known as the aluminum route thanks to the wreckage of aircraft that lay along the way. After several days we were booked on a China National Airways DC3 Dakota and took off late in the evening. Though so dangerous the six-hour flight between the mountain tops, punctuated by a re-fueling stop at an RAF forward base in Assam, was in fact the only stage of the whole journey to pass without incident, and we reached Dum Dum airport in Calcutta in the early morning. My parents must have been mightily relieved: not long afterwards a plane filled with children and teachers from Kunming all but ran out of fuel when blown off course in a blizzard, and in Calcutta they attended the funeral of several missionaries whose plane had actually crashed. Much later, they learned that back in Gulin a rumor had been going around that we had been shot down.

Christmas was spent in Calcutta, although the atmosphere there was hardly celebratory. The city was bursting with starving people, sleeping rough, trying to flee the disastrous famine which hit Bengal 1943–44 and in which upwards of three-and-a-half million people died. Added to these were large numbers of refugees from Burma and China. While we waited for news of our onward travel, my father occupied his time helping in the reception office for the continuing flow of evacuees from Kunming. At last, early in January we boarded the train for Bombay (Mumbai as it is called today). The journey took two days and nights, and our entire water-supply for the whole family was contained in a single earthenware jar. "The nights were hot and steamy", wrote my father, "the boys restless, especially Keith who had to share Fay's bunk so that she had very little sleep." After days of waiting in Bombay we were assigned a passage on a Dutch ship the *Johan van Oldenbarnevelt*, which had been chartered for use by the RAF as a troop ship but nearly all the passengers on this homeward run were civilians—nevertheless put under strict RAF discipline. My father served on the passengers' welfare committee. The voyage in convoy via the Suez Canal and Mediterranean took five tedious weeks, relieved by some moments of high tension. At Port Said a newspaper banner headline proclaimed: "Revival of U-Boat Warfare off Crete."

Not long after leaving Port Said and with the convoy steaming to the south of Crete, the welfare committee was suddenly summoned by tannoy to one of the small lounges to be informed that "just to make things interesting" there was a breakdown in the engine room, and the ship would have to heave-to for repairs, alone, while the rest of the convoy sailed on. The programme of quiet evening entertainment was hastily substituted with energetic party games for all by way of distraction from what might happen. After several hours, the vibration of re-starting engines was felt again and eventually the ship gained the relative safety of the convoy. The alarm about U-boats was probably more rumor than fact as it was later established that all U-boats in the Mediterranean had been sunk by then, but that wasn't known at the time. Unharmed by any U-boats still lurking in the Atlantic we reached Greenock on the Clyde in late February. Next evening we were with my mother's relatives in Newcastle-upon-Tyne and a day or two later we made it to her mother's home at Twizell farm a few miles outside the city. Getting there, my parents felt, was oddly like the start of the journey three months and six thousand miles earlier, as it involved a hitched lift on a lorry and walking the last mile on foot. "Grandma Allen" was thunderstruck. Not only had she no idea we had left China, but till then she did not even know of my existence. Such was wartime. Soon we were off to London. "Grandma Clements" at her home in Earslfield, close to Wandsworth, at least had a few days' warning to prepare for our arrival. The flying bomb attacks were continuing, and she insisted that the local council repair her windows, blown out in the last few days, in time for her son and his family who were coming "all this way from China".

My earliest definite memories are of my second birthday the day before VE-day (May 8) and, shortly after, being given sweets at what must have been a victory street party. For me to speak of the journey from China as "our" story, as if I could personally remember it, may therefore seem to be stretching a point. But whether or not I can remember any of it myself is irrelevant because through endless re-telling it became our basal family legend, the saga of what all five of us had been through together, the first really common experience we had—in fact what made us as a family. It was a story of adventure, risk, persistence, being helped by and helping others, a journey of hope. It truly was *our* story, mine included. As a souvenir of the journey the Indian water jar arrived back with us in England. It still stands in the living room of our house today.

PART ONE

Discoveries 1943–1967

On Ben Sgriol, Scotland, 1964

1

Manse Child

LOOKING AT THE EARLIEST photograph of our whole family, taken in Gulin in summer 1943, prompts me to think that to the very young child one's parents simply *are*; they must always have been together! In fact my mother and father had first found their way to China by very different routes.

Gulin summer 1943: Keith's parents present him to the world,
attended by brothers John (L.) and Brian (R.)

Part One: Discoveries 1943–1967

My mother Florence Alfreda Yarwood (hence the acronym "Fay" became her familiar name) was born in 1905 in Newcastle-upon-Tyne and with her family had immigrated twice to Tasmania, first in 1912, returning to England just before war broke out in 1914, and then again just after the war. For a time she worked as companion to a devout Christian lady in Melbourne. She herself, following an evangelical conversion experience, felt the call to go to China as a missionary. She trained for the China Inland Mission (CIM) at the Melbourne Bible Institute, and served in the CIM offices in Chonquing as a book keeper and typist. But she also spent some spells in more isolated posts further up the Yangtze River in dangerous areas of unrest and feuding warlords. "Five feet three inches of courage" is how one senior missionary described her. She was therefore a missionary in her own right, not just a missionary's spouse. Then in 1933 another young recruit arrived in Chonquing.

Harry Clements was born in 1907 in Earlsfield, south-west London. His father was an electrician and his mother a trained cook who in the 1890s had been in service to a lady-in-waiting to the future Queen Mary. From his early teens he was an enthusiastic member of Earlsfield Baptist Church. Keenly interested in history and geography, and well-read (by adult life he seemed to know every line of Dickens), he had set his youthful sights on journalism. But on leaving school at age fourteen he had to be content with working as a clerk in a city manufacturing firm close by St Paul's Cathedral, until he felt the call to the China mission field. He sailed for China in 1931. Apart from his studies as a candidate for the CIM and the requisite language training, he had no formal education after leaving school and no recognized qualifications. Having arrived in Chonquing he soon found that Miss Yarwood was the chiefest of its attractions, but too soon, it appeared, she was moved to another post upriver. He proposed by letter, she accepted and was transferred back to Chonquing where they were married in the autumn of 1933.

As newlyweds Harry and Fay took their first charge together at Ichang just downriver from the Yangtze Gorges and an important staging post for river traffic. Much of their work consisted in facilitating travel arrangements for missionaries and if necessary providing hospitality for them—and often other guests of all sorts of conditions and nationalities. On one occasion in 1935 they were unexpectedly caught up in circumstances of worldwide interest. The brother of T.E. Laurence ("of Arabia") was a medical doctor with the CIM. Accompanied by his mother he was proceeding downriver to start his furlough when news reached Ichang of T.E.'s fatal motor-bike accident in England. Since they were recovering from dysentery when they reached Ichang the Laurences stayed on board their steamer moored in midstream, and it fell to Harry Clements to go out and break the news to them—and then to shield them from the world's press. Having lived that kind of life in their first China spell, and then adventurously from 1939 to 1944 in the remote, mountainous beauty of Gulin, the prospect of life in post-war England, even if thought at first to be only temporary, must have meant a huge psychological adjustment for both parents.

SETTLING INTO AUSTERITY

On arrival in London in 1945 all my parents owned, as well as the clothes they stood up in, comprised three boys and the contents of a trunk and two suitcases. We were effectively refugees. This was not necessarily an extreme privation to my parents since they were regarding England as home only in a provisional sense and were fully intending a return to China once John's health problems had been sorted out. In all likelihood they would eventually have gone back, but by the time John was given the all-clear Mao-Tse Tung was completing his Long March and the Great Revolution was ushered in. Meanwhile a life had to be lived and a home set up. My father soon decided that whatever and wherever the longer-term future for us might be, as an immediate step he should seek to enter the Baptist ministry in England. Not having been through theological college, and with a college course now out of the question for someone with four mouths as well as his own to feed, he decided on the non-collegiate route of taking the Baptist Union Diploma which was duly awarded in late 1945. Soon after, he received the call to be pastor of the Baptist church in West Malling, a village in Kent situated among the hop fields and cherry orchards a few miles west of Maidstone.

Austerity was the code-word for life in Britain in the immediate aftermath of the Second World War. A young child simply accepted this, and rationing of all kinds, as normal while at the same time I was repeatedly informed that that "pre-war" signified quality in everything from toys to furniture to cars (even if acquired second-hand) in contrast to what was now available. Add to this basic austerity the meagre stipend and pinched circumstances of the average nonconformist minister, and the comfort-expectancy of his family dropped still lower.

The congregation at West Malling was a close-knit community, some members becoming lifelong friends of my parents. There was one snag. The church at that time did not have a manse, and there was an acute housing shortage left by the war. After some weeks' lodging with a rather dour spinster we moved into the church premises themselves and lived in the upstairs schoolroom for two years. This was austerity writ large. The schoolroom had a number of alcoves some of which were curtained off as our bedrooms. The central area had to serve as father's study (that is, a desk in one corner), living room (a few utility chairs, table and wireless), bathroom (when a zinc tub was brought in), and playroom for us boys. Today it would seem unacceptable for any family to have to put up with such conditions. At that time, to my child's eye it just seemed to be the place where we happened to be living, home. But at times it was really harsh especially during the bitter winter of 1947, when I can remember being woken at night by the sound of frozen pipes bursting, and one day finding dead birds frozen into the ice on the churchyard wall. But from exactly the same spot I recall the earliest moment when I thought "How beautiful". It was a morning in spring or early summer, and I was coming out of the kitchen to play in the churchyard. The sun shone from a clear blue sky, the green trees seemed to be whispering in delight and the air was filled with birdsong. I was by myself. It felt like a gift, all mine. Later I would think of it as a Thomas Traherne moment. The churchyard made an ideal playground for us children and friends. It was also the place of some pain: physical, when once I fell and badly hurt a knee; emotional whenever, as bedtime drew near, to loud and tearful protests I was summoned indoors at an unjustly early hour while Brian and John happily continued at play. Ours was a family in which, for as long as I remember, there was a lot of mutual teasing between us siblings, between the parents, and between the parents and us. I was expected to give as good as I got, despite the five years' gap between myself and Brian, and three more years between him and John. I looked up to my brothers, John for his ability with his hands and his love of constructing models of all kinds, and Brian for his adventurousness, humor and sociability (he always seemed to collect a gaggle of friends). As for humor, there was always a lot around. My father was well-known and liked for his genial personality. He loved hearing and re-telling jokes. My mother, much less extravert, found humor mainly in the foibles and oddities of people she met and the way they spoke. She could produce quite wicked mimicry of certain preachers, and speakers at women's meetings. My own earliest memory of falling about with laughter is of hearing one of the characters on the famous radio show ITMA talking in a ridiculous way that I never knew adults were capable of. It was probably the bibulous Colonel Chinstrap, well lit up.

If the two years at West Malling were not literally in a manse, the ethos was evidently manse-like. I say evidently, because memories of life before the age of five are somewhat inchoate. I knew my father was minister of the church, and have a memory of sitting beside my mother in a pew during a service, she with her Bible open on her knee. But of my father officiating in any way, I have scarcely any picture. What I do recall quite vividly (evidently I found this much more impressive) was seeing him out on the cricket field playing for West Malling, and one weeknight taking his turn at cutting the grass with a huge motor mower, the main part of which suddenly detached itself from his driver's seat and had to be pursued furiously some distance across the field. My earliest distinctly religious impressions are of bedtime with my mother: a simple prayer, a children's hymn ("Gentle Jesus, meek and mild" and the like), a Bible story (Jesus' birth at Bethlehem a regular favorite) and often, too, stories of our time in China. Indeed, if for my parents (and brothers) China was only just yesterday, for myself even though I had no clear memories it seemed nevertheless to be just around the corner. I was told again and again of the sensation my birth had caused in Gulin, of the queues of people who came to view this offspring of a white woman, of the gifts that neighbors brought for me (beautiful baby shoes and a satin apron, still in my possession). I heard how our housekeeper Lao-ben Yang looked after me much of the time, and how my first spoken words were in Chinese. Gulin, I seemed to be told, was my *real* home, my birthplace and where I had been valued and even honored. I have written elsewhere[1] on the lifelong effect this had on me, of giving me a sense of "living

---

1. Clements, *Ecumenical Dynamic*, 26–28.

in more than one place at once", an almost instinctive awareness of a world much wider than, and just as interesting and important as, the place where one happened to be living at the moment.

MOVE TO THE NORTH: DARLINGTON

Indeed, West Malling itself was soon to become just a memory. The superintendent minister for the Southern Area of the Baptist Union heartily endorsed my father's view that as far as our living conditions went enough was enough, and that a transfer to pastures new was more than justified. In early 1948 my father accepted a call to Geneva Road Baptist Church, Darlington in County Durham, and we moved there in July of that year. Great was the excitement: a proper house at last! It was a three-bedroomed semi-detached, somewhat cramped for a family of five with one of the two downstairs rooms having to double as a study, but nevertheless for us it represented a quantum leap in style. The move of course meant newness all round, including school. Since my fourth birthday I had attended Ryarsh Primary School, a short bus ride from West Malling. It was a pleasant, amiable village school. In Darlington, a middle-sized industrial town noted for its railway works, Dodmire School was bigger, wilder, rather frightening at first. But it provided me with continuity for five years of primary education which, compared with what John and Brian had experienced, made me rather fortunate. For them, John particularly in view of his illness, the conditions of distant schooling in wartime China, the sudden exit, the anxious journey to England, and the unsettled months after arrival in London, were to say the least disruptive of their education at a critical stage. Over the following years I gradually realized just how painful to my parents was this whole aspect of their missionary careers, and they were not alone among missionaries in being made to wonder at the price their children had to pay through separation especially in times of conflict; indeed this is a shadow side of the modern missionary story as a whole. Fifty years later, after both my parents had died, I found among my mother's papers the fraught correspondence from 1944 between them, the mission school and the CIM China headquarters staff. It revealed the heart-wrenching they were going through both on John's account and the decision to come out of China. These letters were almost the only ones my mother had kept from those days. It had been a *very* deep wound. Gradually, too, as I grew up I came to realize that as the privileged youngest one who was spared these set-backs, a very great deal of parental hope was being invested in me to provide some kind of compensation.

Geneva Road Baptist Church stood on the boundary between a pre-war housing area and a new council estate, and the abundance of younger families in the area supplied some three hundred children and teenagers to its Sunday School, youth clubs, Boys' Brigade and Girl Guides. Something seemed to be happening on the church premises every day of the week. The people, were down to earth and friendly, and my father seemed perpetually busy not least because he also took part-time charge of a smaller chapel in Ferryhill, a small mining town about twelve miles north of Darlington. If at West Malling my religious impressions were gained mostly from my mother, here they were much more from my father in his role on Sunday. Interestingly, while he would undoubtedly have described himself as evangelical, hardly any of his preaching that I can recall came over as markedly evangelistic, except perhaps at a baptismal service when he would make an appeal for any who had been moved by witnessing believers' baptism to likewise consider commitment to Christ. What I remember most was the sense of reverence and awe which he breathed when conducting worship, in his prayers no less than his sermons. Essentially he was a pastor and sought to influence people through friendship. At home, meanwhile, there was no mistaking that this really was manse life. Sundays for us all meant the full diet of morning service, afternoon Sunday School and often evening service too, and stern observance of some Sabbath rules (like, no ball games except in the garden). Strict teetotalism of course prevailed (though in later years my mother quite happily took to brewing cider, but perhaps that did not count as it did not involve going into pubs). No playing cards (though the riotous game of Pit was allowed), and no bad language: as an eight rear old I once got into terrible trouble by exclaiming "Damn!" in a fit of temper. There was obviously a sharp line being drawn between school playground behavior and home.

Yet, this was no enclosed, shut-in life. How else at age eight could I have been streets ahead of the rest of my class in general knowledge? One reason is that the manse, compared to the homes of many of my school friends, seemed more like a library than a normal home. We read, all of us. Books that came with Christmas or birthdays were of all kinds, not just children's Bible stories: books about ships, trains and airplanes, about nature, about science, about history and travel, and of course stories—and not just Enid Blyton either. One book above all captivated me for over two years, Stevenson's *Treasure Island*, which I read and re-read till I knew it almost by heart. Love of that story, admittedly, owed much to the Disney film which appeared in 1950 and which fired me to try and write my own stage version (I dreamt of a cast of dozens drawn from friends and classmates). Darlington had an excellent public library and as soon as I was of age I had tickets for the children's section (what an act of national vandalism is now taking place in the cutting back of library services). Nor was all the reading between hard covers. Comics were never frowned upon and, from day one of its appearance in 1950 we took regular delivery of that unequalled boys' weekly, as educational as it was entertaining, the *Eagle*. It was indeed at home, a home that some might have assumed to be a severe, narrow-minded and inward looking coralle, that I started to learn so much about the world. It was as if my parents, having laid down clear markers on what constituted a Christian home, nevertheless regarded the world at large as the place where so much should be taken seriously, and enjoyed too.

At home, too, there was always fun. Cricket and football were followed avidly. Conversation around the meal-table was often lively, and about the news and affairs of the day. It was adult talk, with the assumption that younger ones could and should join in, or at least ask about what they didn't understand. Often those discussions were prompted by the natural history programs which BBC radio used to transmit at lunchtime on Sundays. During holidays in London to stay with Grandma Clements, visits to the Natural History and Science Museums at South Kensington were regular fixtures. Nor was the cinema out of bounds. One day in 1951 or 1952, after school, I overheard my parents talking about "racial prejudice". I asked them what this was all about and they told me they had just been to a special showing for clergy and their wives of a new film, *Cry, the Beloved Country*, set in a faraway country called South Africa. One evening during the 1951 general election campaign we all went to a noisy outdoor hustings in the center of town. Visitors frequently came to the manse. There would be other ministers, or missionaries with tales to tell of life in Africa or South America or India. It often seemed we were open house to servicemen from Catterick Camp or the RAF station at Middleton St. George. Then, too, in a manse there was no escape from exposure to the pains of life, as news of illness, tragedy and bereavement knocked on the front door. Early on I had to learn to answer the phone correctly and politely.

So it was an enriching family environment, the more remarkably so given the financial straits we lived in and at which my mother in particular chafed. Happiness did on the whole prevail. Whatever one did have, was to be enjoyed to the full. As far as I was concerned I never had any doubt that my welfare was my parents' chief concern, and that they wanted me to be happy. Darlington was not a bad place to be in that respect. Lying on the main east coast railway line, in that age of steam it provided a marvelous site for train-spotting boys. The Yorkshire coast at Saltburn or Redcar could easily be reached by train. Richmond on the Swale and Barnard Castle on the Tees were a bus ride away, likewise the villages of Piercebridge and Gainford where we could fish for minnows and bullheads, while Neasham and Middleton-one-Row, downstream from Darlington, could be walked to. On my tricycle, unbeknown to my parents, on a Saturday afternoon or a summer evening, sometimes with a friend or alone, I would venture afield into the countryside as far as Middleton St George or Croft, swing westwards and back home across the center of town. I *think* my parents would have minded, had they known.

Part One: Discoveries 1943–1967

The intrepid tricyclist

If they had found out and objected, would I have had the temerity to ask whether these adventures were any more risky than riding in clapped-out trucks over the mountains of China to Kunming? For China was still part of our conscious scene. My mother would cook Chinese meals whenever she could get the ingredients. By now many stories in addition to those of my birth and the journey to England were familiar to me: of life in the home in Gulin; of the colorful characters in the village and the congregation; of spectacular scenery and fearsome thunderstorms; of Fuh-in-Wan, a place up in the hills which was a center for mission among the Miao tribespeople and a summer retreat for missionaries; of how once on our way to Fuh-in-Wan we were accosted by brigands and only some deft parleying by my father saved the day. In 1949, almost miraculously, a letter from Grace Yang, a young woman who had been left in charge of the congregation in Gulin, found its way to us. It proved to be the last direct contact, but the sense of living in more than one place at once continued.

Compared with what was to happen later, it must be admitted, one aspect of life was decidedly restricted. Although the CIM had recruited missionaries from different denominations it described itself as "non-denominational", not ecumenical.

Confessional differences—Anglican, Baptist, and Plymouth Brethren and so on—were ignored so long as there was commitment to preaching the evangelical version of the faith. In fact even within the CIM a degree of observance of the "comity" principle held, whereby most missionaries within a given geographical area were of the same or similar denomination. Back in England, however, where Baptists were cheek by jowl with Anglicans, Methodists, Roman Catholics and others, the issues of denominational difference could hardly be ignored, and at this stage of their life my parents' attitude was that Baptists were best, and the rest unfortunately in one degree or other in error. Congregationalists were nearly as good, the Methodists were OK but prone to hankering after return to the Anglicans many of whom in turn were dangerously imitative of Rome, the ultimate fount of error and superstition. There were some Catholic families living on Geneva Road, and sometimes insults were traded between their children and us manse boys, and (on one occasion at least) stones as well.

Even here, however, there was a small but gradually opening window onto another world. At about aged eight I began reading about the medieval monasteries, which I found fascinating, and the crusades. At about the same time in history lessons at school taught by our class teacher Mr ("Pop") Bickerstaff we learnt about the Saxon period, about the Danes, St Cuthbert, Lindisfarne and the Venerable Bede. I was captivated by this saga set virtually on our doorstep in north-east England. I talked about it with my mother, and one day in the Easter holidays in 1952 she took me to spend a day in Durham, home to the shrines of Cuthbert and Bede. We went straight from the bus station to the cathedral, paused respectfully by the famous sanctuary knocker and stepped inside. It was the first time I had been in such a church, so different from the Baptist chapels I knew. I would have found it hard at that tender age to put into words what I felt at the sight of those great Norman arches and huge, decorated pillars. I think I would have said something like: "It's huge, but somehow friendly", and "It's very old, but it's as if something strange and wonderful might be *about* to happen here". One Sunday some fifty years later I would stand in the pulpit of that same cathedral to preach during the Week of Prayer for Christian Unity, and recall that first visit. Some wonderfully new things *had* happened in the course of half a century.

Dodmire School helped to open another world. While my brother Brian had piano lessons, for some reason to my regret I was denied these, and instead my mother insisted that I attend Saturday morning elocution classes for children, to counter the allegedly uncouth Durham accent that was creeping into my voice. But music always appealed to me, and at school a young teacher called Mr Seymour, possessed of a clarinet and a large Adam's apple, took us for music appreciation. He began straight away with records of Tchaikovsky's *Nutcracker* suite and that was the birth of my love of classical music. Episodes like that helped to enliven what was mostly a rather plodding time in the middle stream at school. As my tenth birthday approached one was conscious that before long the dreaded eleven-plus exam, which would decide my future schooling, would have to be faced. The head teacher told my parents that it would be touch and go for me. Growing older was producing its challenges whether one liked it or not. In fact as 1953 dawned time was chiming its summons for the family as a whole. Brian would soon turn fifteen and leave school. In March John, who since leaving school had worked as a fitter in a motor lawnmower works, left home to begin five years as a regular serviceman in the RAF. Then, most startling of all, my parents announced that soon we would all be moving, to Lytham St Anne's in Lancashire.

MOVE TO THE WEST: LYTHAM ST ANNE'S

Lytham St Anne's lies on the north side of the Ribble estuary, looking across to Southport. Famed for its golf courses, it is a seaside town that has long worn a genteel air in comparison with its raucous neighbor Blackpool. My parents' advance descriptions of it as a place of beaches and acres of sand dunes made it sound like a child's paradise, and in many ways so it proved. We moved there in June 1953, a week after Queen Elizabeth's coronation, and my father's induction to the pastorate of Ansdell Baptist Church quickly followed. Ansdell is situated between the older town of Lytham and the newer and more extensive residential area of St Anne's. This time the manse was indeed adequate, a four-bedroomed house with three reception rooms downstairs so that for the first time in his life my father had a real study. The church itself was attractively built in the red Accrington Plastic brick in keeping with much of the housing in the area. The congregation, mainly middle-class and in some cases rather well-heeled, had somewhat diminished in number in recent years and my father knew that a great deal of pastoral rebuilding was called for. Instantly we felt welcomed, and I had a sense that life was moving up a gear. We would be there for nine, generally very happy, years. Quite apart from the pleasantness of the place itself—we lived only a few minutes' walk from the shore, the dunes and the Fairhaven marine boating lake—the proximity to Blackpool was a plus not least because at that time Blackpool FC was a power in the soccer world, and that very year had won the FA Cup in one of the most dramatic Wembley finals of all time thanks to the genius of Stanley Matthews, prince of wingers. The ground at Bloomfield Road was therefore to be a place of regular pilgrimage. Not many can boast, as I can, of squatting just a few feet behind the goal line on one of the rare occasions when Matthews himself scored a goal, in September 1955 against Wolverhampton Wanderers. Brian soon got to know Blackpool best of all because he started work as a clerk in a solicitor's office there.

For me of course there was a new school, Ansdell County Primary. Here too there was an upward gear change. Much smaller than Dodmire it was presided over by a remarkable duo, Miss Myles and her deputy Miss Moss, both of them large in stature and formidable disciplinarians; but just as fiercely determined to bring the best out of every child and give him or her a greater confidence in their ability than many others (or the children themselves) would have felt warranted. My own confidence took a knock at first, suddenly finding myself being stared at as a newcomer in class and playground, and it showed when on a first swimming lesson I funked going into the water at all. But the shock therapy of concentrated attention at Ansdell County paid off. At any rate, to considerable surprise in 1954 I passed the eleven-plus exam.

So in September 1954 I started at King Edward VII School, Lytham. "KES" was a direct-grant school, that is, an independent foundation which received financial aid direct from the Ministry of Education for taking a quota of non-fee-paying "county" places, i.e. those who had passed the eleven-plus. I seemed to settle down fairly well at the self-styled "School by the Sea" and made a fair start with all subjects except mathematics with which I always struggled. KES had some outstandingly good teachers. The two I was most indebted to by the end were Peter Carah who taught biology, and J.C Matthews the senior chemistry master. I enjoyed my first taste of rugby more than I expected but presently found it a rather boring business with its endless stoppages for scrum-downs and line-outs. In fact the sovereignty of rugby over soccer as *the* ball-game in winter was about the only form of snobbery that KES manifested. The fact remained that every lunch hour not only was the playground occupied by dozens of impromptu soccer games, but some of us formed our own soccer teams to play on Saturday mornings or afternoons on one recreation ground or another, and moreover wearing our school rugby kit; among the other miscreants was one David Hawtin whom I would meet in later life as bishop of Repton. Cricket I enjoyed much more, becoming a decent wicket keeper but my batting was never good enough to make the school XI. Cross-country running was the sport I was best at, and I regularly ran in the school team in my last three years. In fact long before jogging became the social phenomenon it now is I was often out running by myself along the shore throughout the year.

Lytham meant a fairly contented life for us all, at home, school and at church. At home, some of the strictures were relaxed. John and Brian had, after all, to some extent trail-blazed the way for me. I was given a lot of freedom in my spare time. By age thirteen, sometimes with my best school friend Chris Tagg but more often alone, in a single day I would cycle across the flat Fylde hinterland to the Bleasdale Fells, up the Hodder Valley and through the Trough of Bowland, swinging down and west again through Garstang back to the coast. My parents did not even raise objections when later I took a holiday job which involved some Sunday working. The only restriction which I recall being imposed was not being allowed to join the school Air Training Corps; I found this interdict inexplicable—my parents were not pacifists after all. Perhaps life at Ansdell with its seaside Christianity was slightly too contented at times. The Baptist notion of "fellowship" could mean a genuinely caring community of love and concern, as at times of bereavement, loss or other hardship. It could also be cheapened into a cozy, introspective togetherness with little to differentiate it from that of the tennis club or bowling green (other prominent features of Lytham). My mother at times was resentful of all the unpaid duties that were expected of her as minister's wife and the lack of recognition by some church members of what these imposed upon her in addition to being wife and mother. She was somewhat ahead of her time in threatening on occasion to find a part-time job to supplement the family income and also, I suspect, to make her own life more interesting. My father joined the Lytham Rotary Club and was well-liked in the wider community. But I was reaching the age when parents could become sources of embarrassment as well as objects of respect, and was becoming conscious that being a son of the manse was, in the eyes of many of my peers at school, at best an oddity and at worst an object of mild ridicule. This was made no easier when, for example, in 1956 Premium Bonds were introduced by the government and the main office dealing with these together with the computer "Ernie" which produced the list of lucky prize-winners each month, was opened at St Anne's. A reporter and photographer from the *Daily Express* turned up on the manse doorstep, eager to find a possible clerical objector to the scheme. My father was bounced, against his better judgment I think (and as he himself effectively admitted later on), to pronounce against the scheme as gambling. Once he publicly opposed the building of a new public house in Ansdell. All this meant that by the time of my early teens I was having to think out where I myself stood, not only in relation to my parents, but to church and to faith itself.

This was not easy, as often the case with clergy children. Some of course are happily and genuinely able to make the faith their own, to their parents' delight. Some part company with their parents' religion fairly amicably, while others reject it outright, a rejection which is part of their rebellion against the parental regime and all its works: the anti-clericalism of the French revolution writ small, but sometimes also fueled by grievance that the all-consuming demands of church on their parents have deprived the children of the attention and affection due to them. At the other extreme, the rebellion can take the form of opting for a kind of Christianity thought to be more intense, more exciting, and more authentically evangelical than their parents' version. Or, out of loyalty and not wishing to hurt, the teenager can outwardly go along with the mannerisms of faith and commitment to the church, happily singing the songs and choruses of evangelical joy but inwardly nursing nagging questions and doubts. By my mid-teens, I did not fit any of these categories although perhaps moving towards the last kind. I was not in rebellion, but unlike John and Brian neither had I been baptized. I felt myself to be instinctively Christian, genuinely enjoyed church, the atmosphere of worship and especially hymnody (I sang in the choir), helped in the Sunday school, felt that here was a lot of happiness and goodness, genuine friendliness and mutual caring. Especially, I admired what I saw in certain members. Enid Barclay for example, daughter of a previous minister of the church, Sunday school teacher and in charge of the infants' class at Ansdell County, a strikingly beautiful woman I thought, with a delightful singing voice to match. Always charming and cheerful, she was one of those people who enjoyed appreciating the good in others even when that good was not so obvious. She was a great reconciler, especially when rows broke out between members of the youth club and the rather cantankerous church caretaker. Then there was Harry Fielding who with his wife Margaret had moved from the Rossendale Valley in east

Lancashire and was a company representative. A deceptively laid-back, thoughtful and well-read pipe-smoking man, he was a close neighbor, an almost daily caller at the manse and a regular companion on Saturday visits to Bloomfield Road. He was a great conversationalist on all manner of subjects—including politics where he was a convinced socialist whereas my parents always voted Conservative—and took an avuncular interest in many of my activities, from cricket to cycling. Then in 1957, still in his thirties, he died of a heart attack leaving a wife and two very young children. Harry Morris, the immensely popular church secretary, also died soon after. At the time like the rest of the church I felt the loss of Harry Morris very keenly, but I think Harry Fielding's death may have left an important void in my life in the longer term. A couple of years later, when feeling much more on my own, intellectually and emotionally, he could well have been the significant conversation partner for me, not just on the big questions of belief and politics but, for example, on how could you tell if a girl really liked you or not. That became an urgent existential question for me in 1959 when my parents and I went for a fortnight's holiday at a Christian guest house in Llandudno. There for the first time I fell madly for a girl. She was called Janet, and was also of Baptist parents from another Lancashire town, and I thought her the loveliest girl I had ever seen, or ever would see. I was too coy to do anything about making my feelings known to her. I dreamt of her for months afterwards but beyond sending her a Valentine card dared no attempt at follow up.

FAITH, CHURCH—AND WORLD?

A main problem for me was how the pieties of belief and church life really fitted in with the whole world of thought and experience that was now opening up for me even more widely than before: the world I was learning about at school through history, languages, literature and especially science. From the age of sixteen I was also beginning to experience the non-church world at first hand by taking holiday jobs to supplement my pocket-money, first in a bakery and then, at greater length and far more lucratively, as a hotel porter in the very worldly setting of the Hotel Majestic in St Anne's. There was some irony in the fact that it was my parents who had always encouraged my interest in the wider world, and this was now putting faith and its relevance under question. What for a long while held me to the church was the undeniable quality of life that I saw in many of the members whom I knew personally, a quality that was owed to their faith in Christ. Indeed I was prepared to defend such people publicly from the scorn of juvenile atheists, as when in a school general studies class there was a debate on the motion "Religious belief is obsolete". I led for the opposition (seconded by a Jewish boy). I argued that faith is real for many people today—though if pressed I would have been hard put to say how it was actually relevant to the contemporary world beyond the church. No matter, the motion was defeated. But the relative self-enclosure of church life remained a problem. As far as relationships between the churches went, they seemed detached if friendly.

Part One: Discoveries 1943–1967

My father took his turn as president of the Lytham St Anne's Free Church Council, he attended the Free Church ministers' fraternal meeting, and at Ansdell the Baptist, Congregational and Methodist Sunday Schools attended each other's anniversaries. That is about as far as it went, and there seemed no wish to extend relations further. The word "ecumenical" was as yet unknown to me.

The wider world for me took a markedly outdoor form when shortly before my thirteenth birthday I became a passionate birdwatcher. I had long had an interest in birds (indeed two years earlier I had won the prize of a watch in a national essay competition on the subject of protecting birds' nests) but now I was fired up by an illustrated talk given by a local ornithologist who made me realize just how many species that I had known only in books were in fact to be seen in our area. The Ribble estuary in particular provides the feeding grounds for thousands of migrating and wintering waders. Ornithology became my passion and a lifelong interest. I joined the junior section of the Royal Society for the Protection of Birds (RSPB), and dutifully sent in my quarterly reports of interesting sightings, and in due course also sent my annual records to the Lancashire and Cheshire Fauna Committee. Only one other boy at KES at that time, Richard Wilson who was two years' senior to me, was similarly interested, but together with Peter Carah the biology master we made a pretty effective team which in the course of the years up to 1962 added a lot of information about bird life on the Fylde, especially on migrants. We recorded the first Lancashire sighting of the Barred Warbler which appeared one autumn by Fairhaven Lake, together with such comparative rarities as Grey Phalarope, Little Gull, Dotterel and Buff-breasted Sandpiper, but we were not, to use the current jargon, just "twitchers". It was as interesting to monitor populations and habits of waders like the Black-tailed Godwit, and the dates when migrants came and went, with occasionally some quite unexpected results as when one February I found a party of Curlew Sandpipers wintering on the mudflats at Lytham. By rights these breeders from Arctic Siberia should then have been in southern Africa. Findings like these we published in *British Birds*. But as well as its innate scientific interest ornithology was satisfying a certain romantic streak in me. That birds could be on our doorstep having travelled to and fro for thousands of miles across continents and almost from pole to pole provided me with another dimension of "living in more than one place at once", and the demonstration that where one lived was just but part of a much wider world to which we, like the birds, belonged. That sense was heightened in 1960 when I went with Richard Wilson for a fortnight on Skokholm, the island off the Pembrokeshire coast where one of the most important bird migration observatories and ringing stations was located, and home to hordes of Manx Shearwaters, Puffins and other sea birds. Just how seriously I took all this, and how seriously it was noted by others, was proved in 1960 by a book prize form the RSPB for my recording activity for the year, and in the following year came the highest award of all, the Salzman Prize. Nor was this only a secretive private interest. I wrote a number of articles on bird life for the school magazine, including one piece arguing the case for nature conservation as beneficial for society as a whole. Nearly sixty years on, environmental concern having become the accepted norm, I note with interest the youthful seriousness that moved me to write about the dangers of rampant so-called development and the need for conservation of wildlife, concluding:

> More thoughtful scheming by those in charge would eliminate the result being deserts of bricks and mortar with occasional oases of unadulterated natural habitat. Skokholm is fortunate; barbed wire is not necessary round an island. But not so many other areas, also yielding interesting studies each year, including the Fylde. Much has already gone, some necessarily of course. But let it be hoped that the planners will be able to see in land something besides money. For the art and science of the drama of the natural history can only be studied when the players and the stage are together. But unlike other players, wild birds, beasts and flowers cannot exist without their stage, which, if removed, deprive us and future spectators of the drama forever.[2]

Ornithology as the love of my life drew me towards biology as my main enthusiasm in the school curriculum. At that time there was a powerful drive by government to increase science teaching at secondary level, and at KES there was readiness to accept the funding on offer to develop both staffing and laboratory facilities. There was accordingly a lot of pressure after "O-levels" for pupils to opt for the science sixth rather than the arts (or "modern") sixth. Science was the future. It was an age of tremendous optimism that science and technology could transform the world Although I had done very well in most subjects including English up till then, I needed little persuasion to opt for the sciences (biology, physics and chemistry) at A-level. I was going to be a zoologist, make no mistake. Again, my parents made no demur.

There was however the issue of the e-word: evolution. By then I myself was thoroughly convinced that evolution by natural selection was the explanation for how living creatures including ourselves had come to be as they were. My mother was a literalist as far as the creation account in Genesis was concerned. My father had broadened his outlook to quite an extent and the two of us we had some useful discussions about how the biblical record and evolutionary theory need not contradict each other. But then, so many zoologists from Darwin onwards down to the present, including the ornithologist James Fisher whom I read and admired so much, and indeed whom I once heard give a lecture at Lytham, were evident atheists or at least agnostics. And if indeed the Biblical account could be read in accordance with evolutionary theory that by itself didn't *make God* essential to the story. I spent hours on my bird-watching walks pondering this and wishing that somewhere, somehow, someone would come up with just one satisfying proof that would answer my questions. But answer, for the present at least, came there none.

---

2. Clements, "A Plea for Conservation".

Part One: Discoveries 1943–1967

WARS AND RUMORS OF WARS

There was another world outside to be reckoned with. Those of us who grew up just after 1945 knew well enough that there had just been a war. Our grown-ups talked about it. It was the reason for rationing. The physical signs were still all around to see: the air-raid shelters in our school playgrounds, the gaping, weed-tangled bomb-sites in many of the cities, the iron stubs on walls from which the railings had been purloined to supply the steel for tanks and ships. Still visible on one of the playing fields at KES was the indentation where a Spitfire had crashed, killing its Polish pilot. When I was six years old, hearing Grandma Clements' stories about what it was like during the London Blitz sent me to bed feeling frightened. But in the 1950s came the stream of books and films about wartime heroics: *The Dam Busters*, *Reach for the Sky*, *Cockleshell Heroes*, *Battle of the River Plate* and the like, and the war was invested for us with a kind of glamour. The sand dunes at Lytham were ideal for playing at commando raids or escape from prison camps. But, unlike the generation immediately after the First World War we were also conscious of living already in another kind of conflict on a global scale. The Cold War was part of our culture. In 1956 the Suez crisis and the brutal Soviet treatment of Hungary for a time lit the fears dramatically and by the time of my mid-teens the apparent glamour of wartime derring-do had been well and truly unsettled by the "what if?" anxieties of the nuclear stand-off. In any case, by then I had noticed a rather odd (it seemed to me) phenomenon. In contrast to the popularity and publicity conjured up by war on screen and on pages of comic books, the men I knew who had actually been engaged in combat generally seemed very reluctant to talk about it. It was only incidentally that I discovered that one of the deacons in our church had flown in the RAF and been badly hurt in action. The same applied to veterans of 1914–18. George Cunliffe was a tall, spare Lancastrian in his late sixties who sang in the church choir. One Remembrance Sunday morning as we were assembling in the choir vestry, one of the women remarked how she had just seen the British Legion parading to the Lytham cenotaph, banners held high and medals on display. George glowered and snorted, saying that he didn't hold with all this parading nonsense. Drawing his jacket sleeve up a scrawny arm, he pointed to a long white scar running up to his elbow: "That's what I got from a German bayonet in 1918; that's *my* medal." Silence.

In 1960 the Sharpeville massacre in South Africa shocked us—I say "us" meaning a group of us in the school sixth form looking at the newspaper pictures of black people lying on their faces, dead, shot in the back. Still more to the point, conflict was becoming not just something to read about as history, or to re-enact in juvenile fashion, or even watch our present-day politicians try to deal with. It was something that *we* would have to decide about as adults before long. This came home to me unexpectedly in an extra biology class that Peter Carah laid on for us just after our O-level examinations. It was on genetics, and intended as an introduction to what we would be studying on the A-level biology course. He described the significance of chromosomes and the units of inheritance as then known (this was just before the ground-breaking discoveries by Crick and Watson and others of the make-up of DNA became headline news). He talked, too, about what had become known of the effects of atomic radiation on people in the Pacific following the atomic bombing of Japan and the testing of nuclear weapons, and especially the damage to chromosomes as evidenced by defects in children. As the bell rang for the end of class he stood up and said, "We'll, you're the people who will have the vote. *You'll* have to decide what to about this". The Campaign for Nuclear Disarmament (CND) was growing in strength and the Aldermaston marches were hitting the headlines each Easter. In 1960 (I think) we had a sixth-form debate on the issue. I was unsettled by the whole business and at the time couldn't make up my mind. When was war right or wrong, and could nuclear war ever be right? Canon John Collins was a prominent leader of CND alongside the atheistic Bertrand Russell. But just how did church, gospel, faith, connect with all this? I might sing as piously as I liked about Jesus dying for me on Calvary but what did that have to do with these mighty issues?

NEW NOTES: PROPHECY, ADVENTURE AND NEW HORIZONS

But at the same time during 1960–61 certain things happened, unconnected but sparking off in me a new interest. My father came home from one of the annual Baptist Assembly meetings in London and told us, and then the evening congregation, how impressed he had been by hearing Pastor Martin Niemöller and his account of his seven years in a Nazi concentration camp. This was the first I had ever heard of any kind of Christian opposition to Hitler within Germany. Indeed, I hadn't really given a thought to whether there had been any significant church figure in Germany since Martin Luther. Evidently not all Germans were bad. That put a new slant on the war, and the discovery that the church could enter the political fray and mount a public opposition put church itself in a new light.

Then suddenly, in May 1961, on the very day that my A-level exams began, newspaper headlines were ablaze with the reports of atrocities being committed by the Portuguese military in Angola. I was not only stirred with adolescent rage at the stories of bombardments of villages, and torture and rape inside prisons. I was unbelievably excited that it was first-hand reports from the Baptist Missionary Society (BMS) in Angola, aided by some very vociferous younger Baptist ministers in England, which had ignited the issue and stirred the public controversy that followed. Questions were even asked in Parliament. The BMS had long been part of my upbringing as with any Sunday school child, my father had for some years been a member of the BMS committee and of course I had an innate interest and sympathy with its work, bred from our China background. But for the dear old BMS to be responsible for creating such a furor in the public and political realm was rather like finding one's sober maiden aunt taking to the streets in protest and chaining herself to the railings of Buckingham Palace. Here was a connection no longer to be embarrassed about or apologized for, but rather to be deeply proud of. One's own church did have something to say of real challenge to the world. I hotly argued the issues with friends at school and even persuaded my parents for a time to take the *Guardian*, the paper most strongly supportive of the cause, instead of the *Daily Telegraph* which opted to defend the record in Africa of Britain's oldest ally. That same month Billy Graham came to Manchester to lead one of his evangelistic crusades. I attended his closing rally in the Maine Road football stadium, and in many ways was impressed. But it was the prophetic Baptist voice for Angola rather than Graham's preaching which impacted on me more powerfully.

Soon after this I made an important journey—my first visit to Cambridge. My teachers had for a year or more been recommending me to apply to one of the colleges, but they did not seem able to agree on which one and things had got into rather a muddle. I had therefore decided off my own bat to enquire at King's College about which I knew little except that it had a famous chapel and choir. It was to prove one of the most important choices of my life. The headmaster of KES who was himself a King's graduate was rather sardonic about my prospects as he was about most of my activities (in my termly reports for he for some reason complained about my "lack of obvious participation in school life"). I was summoned for a first interview at King's in late July. John Raven, senior tutor, classics don and (though I did not know it then) keen naturalist, held up the discouragingly short letter from the headmaster and said: "What I'd really like us to talk about is what your headmaster mentions with *astonishing* brevity, that is, your interest in ornithology and that you have published in *British Birds*." So we spent most of the time discussing bird migration. At the end he said King's would make "very strong noises" for me to come provided I took the scholarship exams in December. I spent the evening wandering around Cambridge with another candidate and knew that this was a place I *had* to return to.

Almost immediately I set off on my last adventure of schooldays. During the fortnight on Skokholm the previous year I had learnt that the British Trust for Ornithology had an arrangement with the Meteorological Office whereby an ornithologist could sail with on one of the ocean weather ships in the Atlantic for a month at a time. Accordingly I booked a berth on *Weather Monitor* which would be on Station "Alpha" at 62 degrees north, in Denmark Strait between Iceland and Greenland for the whole of August. I arrived at Greenock on the Clyde at the end of July. Four weeks on a converted wartime corvette rolling on the grey Atlantic was indeed an experience to remember (once I had recovered from sea-sickness) both for the chance to see so many birds rarely seen elsewhere—Great and Sooty Shearwaters from the southern oceans, all four species of Skua, and flocks of the tiny Red-necked Phalarope which had rarely been recorded before at sea at all—and the camaraderie of the officers' wardroom where I was a welcome guest. I returned home something of a hero: "KES Student's Atlantic Adventure" ran the headline in the local press. There was, too, the A-level results to celebrate. The results had come out halfway through the voyage and my father had them radioed to me. I was mightily relieved, for while they were not quite as good as I had hoped for they were enough to award me a state scholarship.

In December I duly sat for the scholarship exams in Cambridge and on Christmas Eve, of all blessed days, heard from King's that while I had not won a scholarship I was welcome to a place there. That was more than enough to celebrate. I spent one more term at school, left at Easter and for five months worked as a laboratory assistant in the botany department at Liverpool University. Quite incidentally but very conveniently, my parents were also moving to Merseyside as my father after nine years at Ansdell accepted a call to Egremont Baptist Church, Wallasey. They might well have left Ansdell a year or so earlier but had intentionally waited until I had taken my A-levels.

It was quite an eventful summer. Grandma Allen, in failing health, had come to live with us at Lytham the previous year, and she died in our Wallasey home in August. The Egremont church was warm and welcoming, the people's humor spiced with ironic Merseyside wit. Much to my relief there was a sizeable and lively group of young people whereas at Ansdell for the last two years I had been in a trough between two generations of teenagers with hardly anyone of my own age and interests. I quickly made some good friendships, with both sexes. But these pre-Cambridge months were also important in that, released from the pressures of exams, I read far more widely and intensively than I had ever been able to previously on the subjects that were most concerning me, particularly science, faith and evolution. C.S. Lewis's *Miracles* was probably the first book of any theological nature that I read. But what I found most rewarding in the long term was to accept the challenge of the scientific and evolutionary humanists themselves and see where they led me. In the end, I found them wanting even on their own terms. Charles Sherrington's *Man on His Nature* for example was a brilliant survey and argument for a materialist, physical basis of the universe and everything in it, including human thought and consciousness. But how, I wondered, could he be so confident that human consciousness could grasp materiality and squeeze it like an orange unless it somehow transcended that materiality? Then there was Julian Huxley, pre-eminent zoologist (therefore to be revered by me) and humanist. He presented the grand vision of evolution "now becoming conscious of itself" and that therefore it behooved humans to take this responsibility seriously and direct the future evolutionary course (included on his agenda for this, controversially, was eugenics). I felt there was a serious contradiction here. If evolution is the be-all and end-all of the universe, the key that explains everything, then why should we bother about moral responsibility? Evolution is going to go on regardless of whether it serves a moral goal or not, whether or not we protest against atrocities in Angola or help elderly or blind people across the road. Put the other way, where do our moral values come from? If we take them absolutely seriously then we can't take evolution with the same seriousness. This is not to deny the fact of evolution, but to argue that doing away with a transcendent source of moral values, or God if you prefer, does not solve the problem. Scientific humanism in effect was sawing off the branch on which it sat. I found notable agreement in the Oxford ornithologist David

Lack's concluding reflections to his study *Swifts in a Tower*: "Various agnostic biologists have sought to show how man's idea of good might have been evolved by natural selection, but the real difficulty is not so much its origin but why, if it has evolved, any value need be attached to it"; and ". . . if truth and goodness have more than an arbitrary value, and most of us act as if they had, this might mean that they are related to what is outside man and nature, to the supernatural."[3] Of course I had to learn that much more needed to be discussed (Teilhard de Chardin also interested me). But this is where I stood on the edge of student years, and I still stand by that basic position. I was also plunging into comparative religion and a good deal of philosophy. Soon after we settled at Wallasey I received as a final accolade from KES the Old Lidunians' War Memorial Prize—a tranche of books to be chosen by myself. Significantly, while one or two of my choices were on science, most titles were on religious or related themes—including some Kierkegaard. I thought I was just broadening my reading, whereas, as later emerged, the overall direction of my academic interests was starting to shift more than I realized.

My parents were thrilled and proud that I was going to Cambridge, the first university place for anyone on either side of the family. For my part I was keen to get away from home, not out of protest or rebellion but simply to explore the wider world for myself. I was aware, I hope, what I owed to home, that interest in the world which my parents had kindled from the start. Looking back, I wonder at times whether my father in particular saw me as the one who might on his behalf, too, manage to achieve that reconciliation between the world outside and inside the church, and to work out a theology that he himself had not quite reached. When, aged 81, he lay close to death in hospital, he asked me to read to him the whole of chapter 1 of Paul's Letter to the Colossians, which speaks of Christ as the firstborn of all creation, in whom and for whom all things are created, and in whom all things hold together and in whom all things are reconciled to God. I was surprised because I did not recall him ever having preached from this passage (though of course he may well have done). But it also happened to be the passage that I too have found most arresting in the New Testament. Then, quite uncannily, sometime after his death I found that he had concluded his own unpublished memoirs with a quotation from the seventeenth century Thomas Traherne: "Never was anything in this world loved too much, but many things have been loved in a false way, and all in too short a measure." I was taken aback, not only because I had never heard him speak of or quote Traherne, but because I, too, had used the same quotation at the end of my book *A Patriotism for Today*. Affinities may run far deeper than ever we imagine.

---

3. Lack, *Swifts in a Tower*, 212.

2

Cambridge Excitements

I NEEDED NO-ONE TO tell me that to be at Cambridge, and at a famous college like King's, was a privilege. I had gleaned as much as I could about Cambridge, its past and present, during the preceding months and so a lot of what I found on arrival and in the weeks that followed was not a surprise but a happy confirmation of what I hoped was in store. I had read in Anthony Sampson's fluent contemporary survey *Anatomy of Britain* that King's was still imbued with an aura of the intellectual and aesthetic elite, combining its historic Etonian connection with an urbane, gregarious humanism typified by the Provost Noel Annan. Further, he said, it was still adorned by its uniquely splendid chapel, its choir probably the finest in the world and its dean, Alec Vidler, "one of the few prophetic minds in the church"—a description which intrigued me at the time and was to mean a great deal to me not long after. What did surprise me about King's was the strength of left-wing socialism in the student body, and that King's cherished a reputation for radicalism in politics as in much else. It was a community of contrasts, in which one was invited to explore one's own way.

SERIOUS ENJOYMENT

Cambridge in 1962 was an excitingly *serious* place to be. What was undeniable about this period was the knocking away of deference to assumed authority and tradition. Just before going up to Cambridge I had seen in London the revue *Beyond the Fringe* and much enjoyed this product of Oxbridge irreverence (most notably Alan Bennett's parody of an Anglican sermon), one of the first waves in the surge of satire that marked the decade. Once in Cambridge I avidly read the fortnightly *Private Eye*, then in its infancy. But such satire was not just a lampooning of the "establishment" for comic effect. There was really serious intent in exposing devious and self-serving politicians, press barons and city financiers for what they were. Indeed the irreverence of the time was mixed with a good deal of idealism and optimism. With the tools of science and technology we were going to make a better world, feeding the hungry, eliminating disease and dispelling ignorance and prejudice. When another King's freshman (who later became a fairly senior Tory figure) asked me, "Have you come to work?" I was somewhat taken aback by the question.

In pre-term interviews with the various tutors and directors of studies it was made clear to us that in King's there was indeed (assuming one's termly bills were paid) only one real crime: failing to attend the weekly hour with one's supervisor and to produce the requisite essay. Apart from that one could arrange or disarrange life as one pleased. But there was a secondary crime in King's: failure or refusal actually to enjoy life in the college and Cambridge as a whole. King's was where you could emerge either from a superb choral service in chapel or an hour's supervision, to find the novelist E.M. Forster (an honorary fellow of the college) shuffling around the quad, or on his hands and knees peering at an advert for a concert low down on the screens outside the dining hall. There was no prescription for enjoyment, merely an assumption that being in such a beautiful, culturally rich and sociable place should be a pleasure and that something was deeply wrong if one was not making the most of it. The gentle checking up on us took place not just in the supervisions but in the sherry parties and evenings over mulled wine, or Sunday lunch, to which dons invited their undergraduates. But they did not force themselves on us, and overall operated with a detached policy knowing that the real social experience for undergraduates lay in the small communities we formed among ourselves. It was a liberality of outlook combined with a subtle notice-taking. One day during my third year, by which time I was reading theology, I was surprised to get a friendly note from Kenneth Polack, a senior tutor and lawyer of Jewish background who—so I had assumed—did not know me very well, passing on some information about a short residential course on social work which looked "as if it might be useful also for ordinands". The King's liberality also meant that the college was ahead of most others at the time in removing the lethal spikes meant to prevent students climbing in or out after hours, and King's was the first of the men's colleges to decide to admit women students, who arrived in 1972.

In Natural Sciences the Tripos (the traditional Cambridge term for an undergraduate degree course and examination) normally required a two year stint in three main subjects for Part I, and a third year in one specialty for Part II. I opted for zoology and physiology as main subjects, with botany and experimental psychology as half-subjects, with the ultimate aim of zoology for Part II. I got down to work as best I could, and my memories of the lectures and practicals (long sessions in the laboratory for all subjects) are positive. It was not however all plain sailing. My zoology supervisor in King's was George Salt: in his fifties, tall, austere both in appearance (whitening hair and trim moustache) and manner, evidently of immense erudition. He mercilessly dissected what he judged the prolix style of my first essays, and I found him frankly intimidating for a time. At student age it is not always easy to distinguish the genuine article from the *poseur*, scientific rigor from pedantry, but in the end I think this exposure was good for me.

King's fresher

I felt no trace of homesickness in the first few weeks at Cambridge, just an immense sense of liberation and coming of age. For the first time in my life I was completely free to dress (more or less) how I liked, play whatever sports I liked and join whatever societies I wanted. I joined the Cambridge Union and the Cambridge Bird Club, played soccer for King's, patronized the cinemas and pubs as I pleased and in college learnt to drink wine. In the summer there would be punting and tennis. Friendships were made as we first year students gravitated into natural small communities each with its own preferred section of table at dinner in hall (one whole table seemed to belong by divine right to the choral scholars). My own immediate circle comprised Alwyn Thompson, another zoologist; Geoff Cubbin a linguist from Bolton in Lancashire, and two mathematicians: Julian Ellis, a zany humorist and good jazz pianist who like me (but a much better player) enjoyed soccer, and Robert Lake. One got to know others of course. Griff Lewis, a Welsh rugby-playing historian, many years later said I was the first person to speak to him at King's. We liked to think we were more down-to-earth than the refined aesthetes and intellectually pretentious figures and those for whom King's was apparently just an annex to Eton or Winchester. In fact even in those days King's seemed deliberately to want to be a home for all types, and if there were snobs they faced at least an equal number of debunkers. So I was basically happy, whether in late-night argumentative sessions over coffee or in the mud of the soccer pitch where I played as full-back in front of a tall, rangy goalkeeper called Michael Scott-Joynt, future bishop of Winchester. Then of course there were the crown jewels of King's, the chapel and its choir. I started going to evensong about once a week.

FAITH: THE SEARCH IS ON

But as well as for work and play I had come to Cambridge hoping for answers to my questions about Christianity and its relation to the whole human quest for truth and the wider world of human activity. I had not had a Damascus road kind of evangelical experience, a sudden conversion accompanied by rapturous floods of joy and certainty. Was this a lack in me, which disqualified me from baptism and church membership? Yet thanks to my upbringing I felt myself to be instinctively on the Christian side. To pretend to have had the standard conversion experience would be spiritual dishonesty for the sake of being counted in. The lack, I felt, was equally on the side of Christianity, as I had hitherto known it, in being unable to be more than an interesting, enjoyable and even uplifting enclave within the modern world rather than embracing that world in a transformative way. Was there a real connection between the two? Was Christianity intellectually up to it in the contemporary world? If, as mentioned in the previous chapter, I found the stance of evolutionary humanism unconvincing and lacking a basis for its apparent moral certainties, was Christian faith from its side able to take seriously the whole human and cosmic quest and give sense to it, or was it to remain an obsolete embarrassment, trapped in its own religious world where it could feel safe? Even so, if it was shown to me that there actually was on offer a Christianity of the type I was looking for, would I be prepared to make a definite act of commitment to Christ?

There was no lack of Christianity, or perhaps one should say Christianities, in Cambridge. There were of course the college chapels which represented a wide range of Anglican lowness, highness and broadness. There was also the decidedly evangelical Cambridge Inter-Collegiate Christian Union (CICCU), which had quite a strong presence in King's. I had a number of good friends who were signed-up members, joined one of the college's Bible-study groups, and on occasion attended the Saturday evening "Bible readings" which were held in the Union debating chamber. But I never felt completely at home in CICCU and less so as time went on. Too many of its members tended to a smiling self-assurance which, I suspected, betokened an avoidance of the trickier questions of belief rather than an honest facing and wrestling with them. Bible study focused admirably on personal faith and experience but at the expense of the taxing social and ethical questions of the hour (such as would be debated in the Union each Tuesday, in the very same chamber where CICCU met!). There even seemed to be relatively little interest taken in *the church*. Of much more importance to me was the Robert Hall Society (RHS), named after the eminent Baptist preacher of Cambridge and Bristol in the early nineteenth century. Forty or so students met for tea at St Andrew's Street Baptist Church each Sunday afternoon when we would be addressed by a wide variety of speakers, from Cambridge or much further afield, on all manner of subjects somehow connected with Christian faith, Baptist or not. It was both earnest and sociable, with not only prayer meetings and weeknight discussion groups but also football matches, theatre visits, parties, punt races, an annual dinner and from time to a time a mission to a local church during the summer vacation. The other Free Church denominations had similar societies. In my first year I was the only Kingsman in RHS. The president that year was Michael Bowker, a medic from Trinity Hall, whom I greatly admired for his friendliness and seemingly imperturbable charm. I quickly made some very firm friendships, several of which remain to this day, especially with two brothers Christopher and Robert Bradnock from Fitzwilliam House (now Fitzwilliam College). Maybe it was significant that Michael Bowker and the Bradnocks were, like myself, offspring of missionaries.

The importance of RHS for me, however, lay in something deeper than mere sociability. Here for the first time in my life I met the whole spectrum of varieties of Christian belief and commitment, from the most conservatively evangelical to the out and out liberal. It would be too much to say that all forms were easily yoked together, and during my second year tensions became apparent and almost disruptive over a matter in which I found myself at the center. But it was a single society in which people for the most part were prepared to accept each other cheerfully while arguing their case, whether on the church steps after a service, in coffee groups or out walking. For me all this was liberation. There were *options* to be explored and tested within a community of people who basically enjoyed and respected each other. Moreover it was encouraging to find that even the most intelligent people could also be Christian, and RHS included people with exceptional minds like David Thompson, historian at Queen's (later to be a Cambridge professor); Alan Brown, a brilliant academic musician and keyboard player from Gonville & Caius who on occasion performed with Benjamin Britten; and Adrian Gill, an Australian post-graduate physicist at Trinity who was to make a major contribution to oceanography before his untimely death in 1986.

Sunday morning fare at St Andrew's Street Baptist was provided by the minister Arthur Jestice, who also served as chaplain of RHS. Quite a few of the more evangelical students preferred Zion Baptist where the preaching was allegedly more biblically sound, but Arthur Jestice was a man of deep pastoral heart and sensitivity whom I grew to like immensely and our friendship was to prove a blessing long after I left Cambridge. There were also two Senior Friends of RHS: Norman Walters, senior tutor at Fitzwilliam, and J.N. Schofield, Old Testament scholar and university lecturer. They were used to casting an ironically amused eye on over-serious undergraduate debates and posturing. Such a society met my need more than any other circle could at the time. The Student Christian Movement (SCM) which for many years had been the most progressive, inclusive and genuinely ecumenical Christian body in British university and college life, was now in process of transforming itself into a "student movement" on the wider social and political scene at the expense of its historic relationship with the campuses. In Cambridge, by the time I knew it SCM was becoming a somewhat ethereal body although its membership card still stood on many students' mantelpieces, and I for one was an avid reader of its periodical *Breakthrough*. As it happened, a significant slice of the RHS membership wore an SCM-type ethos, as did the circle in King's of those who were attached in some way to the chapel, for example David Carter, a first year student and devoted Methodist who became a good friend. So in reality I was very much an SCM type without actually being a paid-up member. Then too there were the Sunday evening sermons given by guest preachers of national and often international standing in the University Church of Great St Mary's, a tradition begun by the former vicar Mervyn Stockwood (by then bishop of Southwark) and being continued by the present incumbent Joe Fison (soon to be succeeded by Hugh Montefiore). The first such preacher I heard was Chad Varah, founder of the Samaritans. The sermons had added value in always being available in print a few days later. I would have laughed in disbelief if a clairvoyant had told me that some thirty years later I myself would be standing in the same pulpit to deliver one of the official University Sermons. That first Michaelmas term in Cambridge was therefore providing me with a rich mix of experience and encounters, whether outstanding preachers or, at the Union, leading political figures: Denis Healey, George Brown and Enoch Powell to name but three.

THEOLOGY A-STIR

Towards the end of that first term in autumn 1962 a particular excitement occurred. The dean of King's, Alec Vidler, suddenly became a figure of public controversy when in a television interview he delivered a hefty attack on what he felt to be the dire state of the Church of England, its intellectual stagnation and stuffy clericalism. Anglican uproar ensued. Questions were asked in the Church Assembly on how and why such a treasonable assault on the church should have come from a figure occupying one of the prime positions in the Anglican world, and why the BBC's Religious Programs Department, of all bodies, saw fit to promote such views. The controversy spilt into the church press and national newspapers as well. But more was to come. Vidler's broadside was but the prelude to the publication of *Soundings*, a collection of essays by liberal Cambridge theologians and edited by Vidler himself. The topics ranged over faith and science, religion and psychotherapy, Christianity and other faiths, the need for a newer understanding of God, and the role of the church in modern society. It was a diverse collection, somewhat uneven in quality (so I reckon now) but united by a conviction that much re-thinking of Christian belief was required if it was to be viable for contemporary people. The book appeared in November, and to conservative minds was further evidence that a conspiracy was afoot in Cambridge to undermine the one true faith and the dignity of the church.

I was intrigued. Theology on this level was well beyond my ken but clearly something was alive and stirring in it, and evidently challenging the very same attitudes which inhibited me from fully declaring myself a Christian believer. I went along to Mowbray's bookshop and bought a copy of *Soundings* as a Christmas present for my father. What he would make of it I did not know, but reckoned that what would appeal would be the signature of its illustrious editor, and accordingly I trotted up to Vidler's rooms in Bodley Court. This was my first really personal encounter with him. With his solid, portly gait ("The only man who can walk down King's Parade by himself and make it look like a procession", someone quipped), closely trimmed white beard and stern expression he looked at first sight an embodiment of what he himself was attacking in the church. But at the same time when not in liturgical dress he preferred a soft white tie to the dog-collar (a Roman Catholic contrivance, he maintained) and a bottle-green jacket to clerical black, while his formidably basso profondo voice (endlessly mimicked by King's undergraduates) was, so one heard, capable of the most iconoclastic utterances on high table. He gladly signed the fly-leaf with a magnificent flourish of his quill-pen (a piece of Victoriana in which he liked to indulge when signing undergraduates' weekend exeats). Hearing that my father was a Baptist minister, far from being dismissive of nonconformity he was happy to talk about Baptist history in Cambridge, about which he clearly knew far more than most Baptists themselves.

Alec Vidler

My father was indeed touched with his Christmas present. I returned after the vacation to a Cambridge in the grip of one of the hardest winters on record, but the intellectual and spiritual odyssey resumed. The first stimulus was the series of four lectures put on by members of the Divinity School on *Objections to Christian Belief*. Again it was Alec Vidler who was prime mover, stating that the times required great honesty of theologians who must "dare to be atheists for the sake of the kingdom of God". I went along on the first evening to hear Donald Mackinnon, professor of philosophy of religion, lead off on moral objections, and was expecting to see a handful of religiously interested hearers. I was staggered to find I had to fight for a place among some fifteen hundred undergraduates crowded into the Examination Schools. The tremendous interest continued for the following three weeks, with Harry Williams (dean of Trinity) speaking on psychological objections, Vidler on historical questions, and J.S. Bezzant (dean of St John's) on theological objections. Of all the lecturers it was Harry Williams who provoked most excitement, weighing into the conventional Christian diagnosis and treatment of sin as promoting even greater guilt and self-hatred, and with cheerful irreverence castigating alike the evangelical appeal to "surrender to Christ" and the translators of the *New English Bible* who with their "fast-flowing ball-pens" were apt to smooth away the more awkward sayings of Jesus. The lectures—later published—had the effect of shaking the standard decks of cards of Christian belief high into the air. Reactions of course varied. Hardened unbelievers were glad to note that even theologians were apparently at last admitting the game was up. Over coffee after the final lecture one sympathetically agnostic Kingsman told David Carter and me that he could not see how anyone could believe after all that. Conservative believers, whether evangelical or high church, were of course angry while many liberals were gleeful at the traditionalists' expense. The main benefit of the lectures was that they made people *think*. For myself, I was glad to see the table shaken but also wanted to see how the cards might be re-arranged once they had landed again.

It was just at this point that another figure came into view who was to prove one of the most formative and long-lasting influences upon me. I had scarcely if at all heard of Dietrich Bonhoeffer (though Alec Vidler mentioned him in his own chapter in *Soundings*), but it was during these weeks that Paul Oestreicher, at that time a BBC Religious Programs producer, spoke at one of the RHS Sunday meetings on "The Abolition of Religion". He spoke of Bonhoeffer's story of resistance and martyrdom, and of his prison writings on "religionless Christianity" to be enacted by a church existing for others, and of how this was a challenge for the contemporary church, in Britain no less than elsewhere. I was arrested. If such as Bonhoeffer, with such unimpeachable credentials in face of the evils of his time, could be so irrevocably committed to following Christ while raising fundamental questions about God and the church, I would have to know more about him. A fresh path seemed to be opening up, with a new mentor in view.

There were other mind-opening encounters during that bitterly wintry term, especially from the pulpit of Great St Mary's, and two sermons in particular. George MacLeod, leader of the Iona Community, thundered mightily (yet also had us laughing) on social injustice, war, and the churches' inaction in face of them. Inwardly I was stirred as I had never been since the uproar over Angola two years before, and as I walked back through the snow to King's Garden Hostel I felt that if the struggle for justice was indeed what Christianity was all about then I certainly wanted to be part of it. I joined Christian CND. In quiet contrast Frank Lake, pioneer of "clinical theology", spoke about the hang-ups, the fear and loneliness in the soul as deriving from subconscious feelings of deprivation which needed to be admitted and owned for healing to take place, and how it was precisely with these that the Christ who knew desolation on the cross came to deal. When I pondered them, both Macleod and Lake in their different ways were helping me to see that belief in God was about an orientation in the real world, the world of society and one's actual personality, not a journey into some other world inhabited by a distant God who vouchsafed some peculiar experience of "religion". It was all about discovering our own real humanity. Then, right at the end of term, Trevor Huddleston came to speak in one of the university lecture halls. The room proved far too small for the crowd trying to get in and so the meeting had to transfer to Emmanuel Congregational Church. I was soon reading his trenchant exposé of apartheid South Africa, *Naught for Your Comfort*.

GOSPEL ENCOUNTER—WITH BONHOEFFER

There was one more decisive influence upon me that term, owing nothing to any theologian or preacher however renowned. I decided to read for myself in just two or three sittings the whole of the Gospel of Mark. Whatever Christianity was about, I felt, it was an encounter with Jesus so wouldn't it be good to expose myself to the earliest, starkest account of his life and ministry, without the aid of any text-book or commentary, and see what happened? I did so, chapter by chapter, making my own notes as I went along. The effect was unpremeditated and unnerving. I suspended judgment on some of the miracle-stories (like the stilling of the storm) but nevertheless was left with an overwhelming impression, of a figure who was a combination of unequalled compassion and courage, who had simply changed people and brought a new way of life into the world. How to account for such impact? Some strange kind of power from beyond had come into the world, confronting it and challenging it to transformation. The crux, literally, came in chapter 8 with the challenge to take up one's cross, to lose one's life in order to find it: a call validated by Jesus' own going to the cross and the irrefutable conviction of the disciples afterwards that he was risen. However it might be explained, all this could not have been just invented. It was too real, almost too frightening in its demands, for that. Whatever else, there was at the heart of this story a real person with a real call to whom I would have to answer.

I went home for the Easter vacation after a brief stop-over in London. On the train from Euston I started on Bonhoeffer's *Letters and Papers from Prison*. It was getting dusk, and the train halted for a few minutes outside Rugby station. In memory I can still see the blue neon "English Electric" sign that glowed on a nearby factory as I read:

> Man is challenged to participate in the sufferings of God at the hands of a godless world. He must therefore plunge himself into the life of a godless world without attempting to gloss over its ungodliness or trying to transfigure it. He must live a "worldly" life and so participate in the suffering of God . . . This is *metanoia*. It is not in the first instance bothering about one's own needs and problems, sins, and fears, but allowing oneself to be caught up in the way of Christ, into the Messianic event, and thus fulfilling Isaiah 53.[1]

And a page or two further on:

> . . . it is only by living completely in this world that one learns to believe . . . This is what I mean by worldliness—taking life in one's stride, with all its duties and problems, its successes and failures, its experiences and helplessness. It is in such

---

1. Bonhoeffer, *Letters* (SCM edition), 122–3.

a life that we throw ourselves utterly into the arms of God and participate in his sufferings and watch with Christ in Gethsemane. That is faith . . .[2]

I wondered whether I should read on. On the one hand it was almost too disturbing in its implications, for this was a vision of God and faith quite other to what a large part of me still hankered after, in wanting a kind of pre-guaranteed certainty, a haven of security beyond all doubts and troubles. On the other hand it was like a re-reading of Mark's Gospel. Beneath it all lay the question of what one wanted life to be: a kind of theorem that had to be proved first, or an adventure on which one could only embark in sheer trust, in which fulfilment lay on the far side of what was present and immediate and conventional, and thus was inseparable from risk? If what Bonhoeffer was saying was true, one did not first have a convincing proof and experience of God, and *then* take on the world. One had to plunge into life in the world, where God was to be found in its sufferings, joys and responsibilities. At Crewe I changed trains. Sitting in the same compartment from Euston had been two senior-looking clerics, evidently travelling further north. Their conversation was low-toned and studious. One of them had placed on the seat beside him a slim paperback. I just caught sight of the title which struck me as interesting, *Honest to God*. It meant nothing to me, and I had no inkling that the following weekend the press and radio would be alive with the controversy unleashed by its author John Robinson, bishop of Woolwich, and his headline-grabbing declaration on the front page of the *Observer*, "Our Image of God Must Go". The storm that erupted over *Honest to God* excited me no end, especially when it emerged that Bonhoeffer, along with Tillich and Bultmann (both names entirely new to me) was one of the major sources he drew upon. It was an uncanny coincidence that I had glimpsed a pre-publication copy of the book just when I was reading one of its major inspirations. There was even some kudos to be gained from the fact that until recently Robinson had been a Cambridge college dean and therefore this London "South Bank" theology was immediately linked in some people's minds with Vidler's Cambridge enterprises (although in fact Robinson had not been part of the *Soundings* group). The first thing I did on returning to Cambridge after Easter was to buy a copy of *Honest to God* and I devoured it at almost a single sitting. For all that I now reckon as its limitations, and perhaps too easy use of very disparate theologians, it is still an astonishingly fluent and captivating read which at the time raised the questions that many in both pulpit and pew had been aware of but had never felt able to express so clearly themselves, and it brought those illustrious German names into the living-room.

It was dawning on me that what church or faith was about was not a fixed, final system of propositions and structures but a living community of people exploring what life might be like under the impact of Jesus Christ. I was not being presented with a take-it-or-leave it religious package, nor with a demand to conform to an obsolete traditional

2. Ibid., 125.

regime, nor to pretend to a dramatically emotional conversion experience that I never had, but was being invited to share in this contemporary adventurous quest. After the end of the summer term, about a dozen of us from RHS spent a week on a kind of work camp billeted at a church in Huntingdon, painting and decorating schoolrooms during the day and reading Bonhoeffer's *Cost of Discipleship*[3] together in the evenings. I myself was equally gripped by *Life Together,* Bonhoeffer's exposition of the theology and practice of community. Christ was the one who brought me out of my isolated self into relationship with himself and others, and the most vital and profound experience of Christ was to be found in the community he was creating, a community of people accepted and accepting each other, and committed to the well-being of the world. In my case it was not a matter of me finding Christ and then finding others who had also found him; rather I had the sense of being found by him in a community where I was accepted and enabled to accept others. But neither was this community a community for its own sake. It was being drawn into God's movement for the world as a whole.

DECISION DAY

That summer I returned to Cambridge for the six-week Long Vacation Term, ostensibly for a course in German for scientists. But I was also reading voraciously in Kierkegaard, comparative religion—and the Bible. I discovered huge tracts of the Old Testament that were quite new to me and far from primitive in outlook were mind-stretching in their reach: the prophets, especially the later chapters of Isaiah, and the wisdom literature too, all of which spoke of God not as confined to a religious area but as the God of all life, all history and the universe. I got excited beyond measure that here was a God who was hidden precisely because of his greatness and majesty (Isaiah 40), beyond human grasp yet to be known in the very earthy matters of justice and compassion and whose rule encompassed every aspect of human life. The same was true of the New Testament, where Paul speaks of a Christ in whom all things hold together, and the kingdoms of this world are claimed for the kingdom of Christ. So faith was after all not an odd corner of life, but the whole of life marked supremely by Jesus in his way to the cross and beyond. It was not a matter of receiving an injection of some esoteric experience of the religious realm. All this reinforced what Bonhoeffer was saying about Jesus calling us not to religion but to life, and that Jesus claims for himself the whole of human life in all its manifestations. Whilst queuing outside the Albert Hall for a Promenade Concert I read George Macleod's *Only One Way Left* and was stirred by his vision of God incarnate being worshipped alike in sacramental liturgy and in the quest for social justice and peace, on the high street no less than on the high altar. Also, on my father's shelves I came across a book just published, *The Pattern of the Church. A Baptist View* in which four progressive ministers—Alec

---

3. That is, the first unabridged English version of *Nachfolge* (Discipleship).

Gilmore, Neville Clark, Morris West and Stephen Winward—set out a challenging vision of the church informed by biblical scholarship and the liturgical and ecumenical movements. I did not fully grasp all the issues, but was delighted to discover that it was not only Anglicans who were wanting to look at their church afresh. Things were indeed happening in the church. An enterprise was afoot, of a church being transformed into the shape of Christ for the sake of the world, and of oneself being transformed by participating in that enterprise. The Jesus of Mark's Gospel was alive and astir and beckoning me to join this adventure of a community on the move with him. After a gap of some years I was praying again. One Sunday evening I took a slow walk round King's Fellows' Garden. To hold back any longer, to want further assurances that this was the way, was impossible. I decided I would be baptized and join the church.

My parents were of course delighted. With two others I was baptized by my father on the first Sunday morning in September. Each of us was invited to choose a hymn for the service. My choice was "Father, hear the prayer we offer" because it expresses so well the view of faith as a costly, risky journey in which one can only trust to be upheld on the steep and rugged pathways as well as in the green pastures, in having to smite the rocks for the living fountains as well as resting by the still waters:

> Be our strength in hours of weakness,
>
> In our wanderings be our guide.
>
> Through endeavor, failure, danger,
>
> Father, be Thou at our side.

Perhaps the mythic power of the story of our family journey from China was asserting itself in my choice of this hymn, and was in turn being reinforced in this poetic expression of faith as a journey, a journey of total immersion into Christ come what may. It so happened that the water in the baptistery was stone-cold, the electric immersion heaters having failed overnight. But my father's face was alight with joy as I stepped into the baptistery, and I had a marvelous sense of liberation as I clambered out: the sense not so much that I had done something, but that something had been done for me, that by grace I really did now belong to Christ and his community and at the same time was free to follow wherever I might be led. For that reason I have ever since counted myself a kind of sacramentalist.

But the question must be asked: how could it be that a son of the manse should have come so late to this understanding of the faith? Why was it that so much of the Bible had until now been virtually a closed book to me? Had I been dreaming through my father's sermons? Or was it that his preaching was unwarrantably narrow even by conventional evangelical standards? I find such questions very difficult to answer. The more important issue concerns that dichotomy under which I had been brought up, between the spheres of church and religious life on the one hand, and of the world at large on the other. My parents had brought me up to believe that the world was fundamentally a good place to be explored and enjoyed, but it still seemed separated from church and faith. Perhaps they felt instinctively that the two were fundamentally connected but did not have a theology that could express this. If so, perhaps they were indeed looking to me to find and articulate it. They had inculcated in me the wish to live in more than one place at once, and I had now been led to find for myself how this was possible in the case of faith and the world.

ADVENT EXPERIENCE

It is Advent Sunday evening 1963, cold, in King's Chapel. In the choir the light from a hundred tapers seems to soar slowly into the fan vaulting and hang there over the waiting congregation, while from the organ flows Bach's prelude *Wachet auf*. Beside me, close to the high altar, sits my guest, mistress of my heart for much of my second year in Cambridge, candlelight glinting in her blonde hair as she smooths her tartan skirt. The organ subsides into the gentler, musing strains of the Brahms *Es ist ein Ros entsprungen*, then silence. Presently a tenor voice echoes from the distant west end, "I look from afar", soon followed by the full choir's urgent cry in Palestrina's rich harmony: "Tell us, art thou he that should come to reign over thy people Israel?" Since Cambridge, Advent has always been my favorite season of the Christian year. This is not only thanks to the Advent processional liturgy in King's Chapel, but feelings of new expectancy in my own life certainly gathered around that *son et lumière* depiction of hope and coming newness, as the choir moved from west to east with a succession of plainchant, carols and hymnody culminating in a blaze of candlelight at the high altar.

Before coming to Cambridge I had never attended an Anglican service of any sort. I started going to evensong about once a week in my first term and soon found that as well as the superb music, at that time under the direction of the dynamic David Willcocks, and its glorious setting in stone and glass, there was something in the pattern of the service itself that appealed to me. My Baptist upbringing had bred in me a second-hand belief that Anglican worship was not only overly formal but priest-dominated, in contrast to that of the Free Churches where we supposedly enjoyed much more lay participation, and where above all far more weight was given to the Bible and its exposition. I quickly realized however that at Anglican evensong, which not only included psalms, the canticles and readings from both Old and New Testaments but also the biblical phraseology of the versicles and responses, I was actually being treated to far more of the Bible than in a typical Nonconformist service of the time. It was the psalms which especially were opened up to me by the uniquely expressive singing of the choir, and that remains my chief spiritual debt to King's. Forty years later I met (Sir) David Willcocks at an international church music festival in Bern, and spoke of the appreciation I still felt. He told me he used to spend *hours* working with the boys on the psalms and, he said, "Above all it's the words that matter, isn't it?" Moreover, while there was indeed a certain formalism about the Book of Common Prayer, it provided a framework which allowed space for private and imaginative devotion of one's own. Nonconformist worship was not only apt to be too conformist to its conventional patterns, but when subject to the singular personality and interests (or hobbyhorses) of the minister it could leave little room for engaging in thought and prayer on one's own terms. There were circumstances in which freedom was provided, not suppressed, by structure.

As well as the Advent service there were of course other especially high moments in King's Chapel. Twice I attended the Festival of Nine Lessons and Carols on Christmas Eve, making a detour while homeward bound from a pre-Christmas visit to Grandma Clements in London, and with other King's undergraduates acting as a steward marshalling the people who for hours had hopefully queued in the fenland cold. On Ash Wednesday 1963 I went along to evensong not expecting anything particularly out of the ordinary apart from the fact that it was to be broadcast live by the BBC. The service however concluded with my first hearing of Allegri's *Miserere* with its heart-stopping, heaven-bound ascent of the treble solo. A few weeks later the choir made its famous recording of the Ash Wednesday service but I was glad to have first heard the *Miserere* live, with an ear unprepared by advance rave reviews. King's Chapel was also the venue for concerts by the Cambridge University Music Society (CUMS), generally also conducted by David Willcocks. Three of those performances were particularly memorable. Heard for the first time, the opening *Kyrie* of the Bach B Minor Mass was stunning: an impact which made one feel "Life will never be quite the same after this". Also unforgettable was the CUMS performance—recorded soon afterwards—of Tallis's forty-part motet *Spem in alium* which seemed to make the chapel's entire fabric shake in a resounding antiphon. Then in June 1964, at the end of my second year, came the CUMS performance of Benjamin Britten's *War Requiem*. Choir, soloists and orchestra were placed in the antechapel whereas I was seated on the other side of the organ screen in the choir. The invisibility of the performers while so close lent even greater poignancy to the sounds of lament and compassion. Close by me were people unashamedly in tears. One final, incidental and uniquely beautiful moment was in store. It was just before ten o'clock that David Willcocks brought it all to a close and, as the last chimes of the tubular bells faded to silence, from far, far away across the city came the sound of a church clock slowly striking the hour. It seemed like an echo from heaven, "Church-bels beyond the starres heard" as George Herbert described prayer.

ECUMENICAL ENCOUNTER

Cambridge was the place where my inbred itch to "live in more place than one place at once" was both satisfied and encouraged still further. It was precisely that longing which made me so susceptible to what was just then gathering momentum as one of the most exciting phenomena of the time: the ecumenical movement. As well as in a Baptist church I was worshipping regularly in my college Anglican chapel, reading the lesson at evensong and taking part in its associated activities and study groups. Then on Sunday evenings in Great St Mary's a whole galaxy of arresting and provocative guest preachers from near and far was on offer. As well as such as George Macleod and Frank Lake, we heard John Robinson explaining to an overflow congregation just what he had been trying to say in *Honest to God*. The saintly Methodist Leslie Weatherhead spoke of healing, mercy and compassion. Mervyn Stockwood, bishop of Southwark, declaimed against "candle-power" as the measure of a church's integrity in comparison with its engagement with social justice. The ringing, incisive tones of the Scottish scholar-pastor James Stewart brought the New Testament compellingly alive. Joost de Blank, recently retired from the archbishopric of Cape Town, carried on his prophetic witness against apartheid and all forms of racism, as did another episcopal exile from South Africa, Ambrose Reeves. And the archbishop of Canterbury, Michael Ramsey, counselled us on prayer. Even public figures like Edward Heath and Dr Richard Beeching (the railway axe-man) addressed us on how Christian ethics may or may not be applicable to society at large. By today's standards the line-up was grossly male and white, but this was not yet today, and in that context it was challenging and liberating. Martin Niemöller, veteran of the German Church Struggle and Hitler's personal prisoner for eight years, also drew a huge congregation but I and some friends were somewhat sobered by what Hugh Montefiore, vicar of Great St Mary's, announced in his welcome to the service. We had hoped, indeed assumed, that the service would include Luther's stirring hymn "A safe stronghold our God is still". Montefiore said that this had indeed been his own intention, but Niemöller had objected: when it comes to those lines about losing everything for God's sake—life, goods, honor, children, wife—he had said, "These young people will be singing their heads off—without knowing what it means." Wim Visser't Hooft, general secretary of the World Council of Churches, spoke of the costly commitment that had brought the ecumenical movement into being, and was still needed, as he recalled Dietrich Bonhoeffer's visits to Geneva during the Second World War.

There certainly was an ecumenical stirring in the world. Shortly before going up to Cambridge I had visited with my parents the rebuilt and newly consecrated Coventry Cathedral, and was intrigued that it included a Chapel of Unity. The very month in which I started at Cambridge saw the opening of the Second Vatican Council in Rome, convened by Pope John XXIII. As with many others, I suspect, my interest was at first lukewarm. Could Roman Catholicism ever change its spots? Then we heard that observers from other churches and denominations had been invited and most were attending (but not from the Baptist World Alliance). Pope John's opening address spoke of the church's duty to work actively for "the full visible unity in truth" among all Christians in a "fullness of charity" which should be extended also to non-Christians. A new rapprochement, at the very least, was being asked for between Rome and Christians generally, and between the church and the modern world. Much more of course was to follow. Among the Anglican observers at the Council was Howard Root, dean of Emmanuel College in Cambridge, and one of the contributors to *Soundings*. Alec Vidler invited him to one of his regular evenings of open discussion in King's and so we had a first-hand account of what was going on, and the implications for renewal of the church. We were evidently entering a new world where almost anything was possible. Alec Vidler at another evening mused, not entirely in jest, that at the present rate the Roman Catholics would be ordaining women before the Anglicans. Then, in the Lent Term 1965 for the first time since the Reformation the pulpit of Great St Mary's was occupied by a Roman Catholic, Dom Christopher Butler, Abbot of Downside and a leading influence on Vatican II. For many of us it was yet another sign of a welcome new day. There came, too, news of a dramatic development at home: the British Faith and Order Conference held at Nottingham in September 1964, attended by 500 delegates from all the main British churches with Roman Catholic observers. Under the theme "One Church Renewed for Mission" it resolved "to covenant together for the inauguration of union" by an agreed date, under obedience to God, and in order to make this commitment decisive proposed the date to be no later than Easter Day 1980. David Thompson, a member of RHS, was a delegate at Nottingham[4] and relayed both the seriousness and the momentous sense of occasion there.

Cheerful RHS group at High Leigh, 1964. Robert Bradnock is holding the tennis ball.

4. He was in fact a delegate of the Churches of Christ.

What all this was disclosing to me was a new image of what *church* meant, a community both embodying and witnessing to true community in the world, a world riven by injustice, Cold War hostility and racism. It was a church being called to challenge and overcome barriers in the world and this it could hardly do unless it was itself likewise becoming united. I found it impossible to separate discipleship from being ecumenical; indeed the meaning of following Christ was only becoming clear and vital to me in terms of being drawn into this movement, a venture from the immediate here and now to the wider there and then. I sensed a web of grace being spun around me, linking me with others past and present and challenging me to help shape the future. What, then, did I now make of being a Baptist? I found much resonance in a book which had also made its appearance in the momentous year 1962, *A Future for the Free Churches?* by Christopher Driver, then a thirty-year old congregational layperson, journalist and writer for the *Guardian*. Avowedly loyal to his nonconformist heritage, Driver was nevertheless pungently critical of much of the current Free Church life and ethos. In face of the complacent if not sentimental reiteration by Free Church leaders and scholars of the importance of "freedom" as represented by nonconformity in English history, he summed up the current predicament of the English Free Churches as their *lack* of freedom: the dull uniformity of much of their worship which, whatever else, was hardly free and imaginative; the introverted piety of individual members and congregations which largely dwelt on personal morality but no longer challenged the wider issues of society; the evident failure of preaching and teaching to be taken seriously by an increasingly educated constituency, whether among its own ranks of younger people or in secular society at large. Unless such issues were radically addressed, he saw no end to the steady emigration of people, especially at the younger end, either into the Church of England or into post-Christian secular citizenship.

Given where I was myself just then, I saw the point of his warning that it was in the loss of students that the Free Churches were proving most vulnerable and no more so than at Oxbridge where, as he put it, they met "the lure of *Ecclesia Anglicana* dressed to kill". Personally I never felt in danger, even at King's, of becoming more than very good friends with her. It was not that I presented myself as a diehard Nonconformist, rather that I was in a circle that believed we were entering into the era of unstoppable ecumenical advance. Undefined, maybe naïve, but it was a feeling that we were all somehow "on the way to unity". We were being welcomed at each other's communion tables and altars, and taking each other seriously as thinkers and activists. Bliss was it in that dawn to be alive, as over our bread and cheese lunches and handling our paperback Bibles we argued and speculated (and joked). In such an atmosphere it did not really seem to matter which denomination you presently belonged to. It made little sense to transfer from one to another because one's real loyalty lay to the Coming Great Church. Driver himself concluded:

> The status quo in British church relations cannot last for ever, and it will be astonishing and catastrophic if it lasts beyond the end of the century. If the rising generation in the Free Churches begins to feel that no significant change can be expected in its lifetime, we expose ourselves to a new stampede out of the chapels, no less injurious than the one that has already occurred. There is no future for the Free Churches, as they are, short of reunion.[5]

Not that I went for much self-analysis, but I imagine that if asked what I was denominationally I would have described myself as an ecumenical Baptist or a Baptist ecumenical. Indeed the Robert Hall Society remained a main focus of my life, and I was secretary for the Lent term 1964. But problems arose just then in an episode which was symptomatic of tensions within the Baptist denomination as a whole, the strength of which I had not till then really appreciated. Each Lent Term RHS elected a president for the next three terms. Normally this was done in a very friendly and informal spirit, only one name being proposed as known to command respect among the members as a whole. This time however a group of the more evangelical members, who had evidently been worried for some time about what they saw as a liberal drift in the society and its leadership, put forward one of their number the moment the nominating process was formally opened, seemingly in the hope of pre-empting any other names. Not everyone was happy with this and soon, not without some misgivings, I was persuaded to stand as well. Inevitably this was now seen as a conservative versus liberal contest, which was by no means wholly true since my main sponsor was a very committed CICCU member from Homerton College. But polarization was inevitable over the coming weeks, some bad blood became evident and when the vote was eventually taken I was not the one elected. This I accepted with such grace as I could muster. All it meant in practical terms was that it allowed me to become more active in Baptist student affairs at national level. A few weeks later, at the annual conference of the Baptist Student Federation (BSF) at High Leigh I was elected to its committee, taking on the roles of representative for the eastern region and organizer for next year's conference at High Leigh. At that 1965 conference I was elected BSF President.

TOWARDS THEOLOGY

Meanwhile in Cambridge a turn in my life was being taken far outweighing the storm in the RHS teacup. Since the Long Vacation Term of summer 1963 I had been pondering whether I really wanted to pursue Natural Sciences for the whole of my three years in Cambridge by going on to Part II of the Tripos in my final year. This was the standard route to the degree. But the Cambridge system allowed a student to take a Part II in an entirely different subject if one wished. It was not so much that I was becoming uninterested in science, rather that my mind was now ranging over the

---

5. Driver, *A Future*, 155.

excitements offered by other areas. To leave natural sciences after Part I was not in itself terribly significant unless one was intending to do postgraduate research. Some students, including medics, occupied their whole three years on Part I. More and more I wondered about . . . theology. I could take the Part IA Theology course which comprised something over half of the standard Part II Tripos compressed into one year. It would mean hard work, but I eventually decided that this was for me. Maurice Hill and Malcolm Dixon, the kindly King's directors of studies in natural sciences, did not bat an eyelid when I put this to them early in 1964. Malcolm Dixon simply asked out of interest, "Do you intend to take orders?" which was standard Anglican terminology for being ordained. But at that stage I was not seriously intending this—or indeed any particular occupation after graduation. I had romantic notions about service overseas in some kind of missionary role where I could use both my scientific and theological education in education or development work. Or maybe I could try broadcasting or journalism. For the moment, it was simply the subject that drew me. Alec Vidler, director of studies in theology, was very pleased to have a recruit from the sciences, anticipating that even if some thought it an unusual move I would by the same token tackle the fresh subject "with great zest". I was equally glad that I would be joined by David Carter who was transferring from history. When the exams came I did not do very badly in the Natural Sciences Tripos Part I, but not particularly well either, with an "II.2". I felt tired.

Alec Vidler was right. Engaging with academic theology did give me a new lease of life. Just before this officially began there came three weeks' camping and youth hosteling in the far north-west of Scotland with Chris Bradnock, Colin Morley (a medic from Fitzwilliam) and his Girtonian girlfriend Ruth Doling (also a medic). Chris and I climbed Ben Sgriol, rising to over three thousand straight up from the shore of Loch Hourn, which gave us fabulous views of the mountainous mainland and coastline, and far across Skye, and my first sight of Golden Eagles. Then came several days under canvas on one of the Summer Isles, Tanera Mohr, which was at that time completely uninhabited, a kindly local fisherman ferrying us there and back. After this healthy reinvigoration I was more than ready for the Long Vacation Term at Cambridge and to be launched into a course of New Testament Greek and a spell of reading in biblical studies, modern church history and theology. Towards the end of the summer two events took me further along the route of the church seeking its transformative role in the world. Another Baptist studying theology in Cambridge, Paul Beasley-Murray, son of the principal of Spurgeon's College, told me about a student conference to be held conjointly with the forthcoming European Baptist Congress in Amsterdam, which he would be attending. I duly signed up for it too and so had my first trip abroad since coming home from China, and my first taste of an international church gathering, with participants from the Soviet Union and other parts of Eastern Europe making it especially interesting. Amsterdam was itself rewarding, with the statutory visit to the Ann Frank House not the only sobering reminder of the recent past. German visitors were often still being met with impoliteness or outright hostility in shops and restaurants. But *the* highlight of the week was the arrival of Martin Luther King, no less, to address the Congress. In fact he preached twice, one of his sermons being on his favorite text Luke 11:5: "Suppose one of you has a friend, and you go to him at midnight, and say to him, 'Friend, lend me three loaves of bread...'" To both see King and to hear his oratory rising to warn that it is *now* nearly midnight in the world and that the knocking that we hear is the cry for justice, was to be in the living presence of prophecy. Not that everyone felt this. Even though this was a year after his famous "I have a dream" speech in Washington DC one or two in the English student contingent couldn't quite see "why he was getting so worked up"; and recently, looking up back numbers of the *Baptist Times* I was surprised to see how little coverage had been given to King even there. It seems as if, yet again, it was safe to acclaim a prophet only after his martyrdom.

The second event had an incidental but nonetheless real connection with the Luther King experience. The Council of Churches in the midlands industrial town of Rugby was wanting a survey to be carried out on community relations, particularly on the situation of West Indian immigrants (as they were called then) and their neighbors. They had invited a team of Cambridge ordinands to help in this for a week in September, and wanted the group to be as ecumenical as possible. About a dozen had been recruited—Anglicans from Westcott House, Methodists from Wesley House and a Congregationalist, the sole woman, from Cheshunt College. There being no Baptist college in Cambridge, enquiries had been made for any Baptist who was studying theology and who might be interested, and so I joined the team. People from the various churches in Rugby hosted us in their homes. It was hard work trudging the streets and door-stepping, and by the end of the week we could not be sure just how valuable were the results for the Council. But it was a learning experience and in those terms it was certainly good. Each evening we met with local churches or immigrant community organizations. It also presented us with a new factor on the English church scene, when we spent a Sunday evening at worship with the New Testament Church of God. The spontaneity and excitement of the worship took all of us aback—and me especially when during a period of mightily vigorous extempore prayer the pastor asked if "one of the Baptist students" would now lead in prayer. Afterwards the other students cheerfully thought this was simply just deserts for Baptist exclusivity. The vibrancy of black Pentecostalism seemed to come from another world, but it was very much here, and here to stay. It was one thing to applaud Martin Luther King. It was quite another to realize just what in practice it meant that the church, to be church, had to be involved in the struggles for justice and racial equality, and it could not do so unless it was itself removing its own internal barriers, whether racial or confessional.

So I started my third undergraduate year with an undoubted sense of vocation—but to what? Oddly, my decision to offer for the Baptist ministry and for further study at Regent's Park College, Oxford, owed as much as anything to the father of the family in whose home I was billeted for the week in Rugby. A very high Anglican, one morning towards the end of my stay he asked whether the week had helped me make up my mind about ordination. I was surprised because I didn't recall ever raising the topic myself. He must have put two and two together from our various conversations, and the way he said it made me wonder if he was an unwitting emissary from above. Soon after the start of the new term a talk with Arthur Jestice, and correspondence with my parents, led to a meeting with Henton Davies, the Principal of Regent's Park College, Oxford, when he was visiting Cambridge and I duly agreed to present myself for interview before the college committee in the coming Christmas vacation.

A ROOM WITH A VIEW

Meanwhile the actual theology course beckoned but so did a continuing and widening circle of friends both within King's and the Robert Hall Society, and beyond. In part this was helped by where I was now living in college. For our second year Alwyn Thompson, Robert Lake and others of our circle had been allotted digs in Newnham Terrace, a somewhat glum relic of Victorian housing backing on to an arm of the Cam near the Mill pub. Now, we had been allocated rooms on W staircase in King's Bodley Court, and Alwyn and I had the topmost sets, W.7 and W.8 respectively. I had one of the most stunning views in Cambridge: from my study room, looking high over the river and the backs to Clare College and beyond, and from the bedroom window along the river behind Queen's. That made W.8 a popular venue for gatherings at almost any time of day, sometimes when I myself was not there (we were far less security conscious in those days). One Sunday I was away all day visiting Loughborough and left a note on the table saying "OK, make yourselves some coffee!" and when I got back about midnight found that a whole posse of RHS people had indeed done just that. Years later, a Girton mathematician confessed to me that during her finals she had often used to decamp there for quiet recuperation after each paper, if the chapel was either closed or too crowded. That it was a "a room with a view" became an even more apt description when one morning there came a gentle tap on the door, a tousled grey head appeared and gently asked if "We might just come in for a moment?" It was E. M. Forster, with an elderly lady in tow. He explained that she was the widow of Hugh Meredith, his close friend of undergraduate days who had lived in this room while Forster himself had occupied W.7 across the landing, and he wished to show the rooms to her. He spent some minutes reminiscing, and went over to the window. Looking down into the court he reflected for a moment then said ruefully: "There used to be two trees there; but they cut them down."[6] He had ever an eye for the apparently commonplace.

There was another advantage to my rooms. They lay directly above Alec Vidler's set which were on the adjacent staircase but had an additional back door onto ours,

---

6. W.7 in fact features as the opening scene in Forster's *The Longest Journey*. The title of his *A Room with a View* refers to an incident in Florence.

used but rarely. It reputedly gave him the chance to escape unwelcome visitors if he spotted them in time, heading across the court towards his official entry. But it meant also that for supervisions I had a very short journey indeed. On Thursday afternoons David Carter and I met with him for our class on the Greek text of Mark's Gospel. Sometimes David would arrive before me, and hearing my knock on the door would open it with a suitably ceremonial flourish declaiming "And enter his courts with praise!" Plied with Earl Grey tea and seated in comfortable armchairs these were relaxed if studious occasions, brought to a halt when the choristers arrived for their weekly tea with the dean on their way to chapel for evensong. Other advantages of the closeness of our rooms were two-edged. Vidler claimed he could tell precisely at what hour I rose each morning because he could hear my alarm clock go off. I did not tell him that I knew whenever he was about to go to bed each night, because he always rounded off his evening with the most guffawing yawns imaginable.

The zest which Alec Vidler had rightly predicted for my venture into academic theology in fact owed a great deal to himself as a teacher and extraordinary personality. He had been dean of King's since 1956. As a church historian and theologian he had impressive breadth as well as depth of learning and was at that time editor of the monthly journal *Theology* which enabled him, as he himself put it, to be a kind of midwife of new theological writing. A high churchman, he nevertheless had a generosity of outlook and could empathize with the different parties within the church and with other traditions, and reckoned that the most significant British theologian of the twentieth century was the Scottish Congregationalist P.T. Forsyth. There was indeed something paradoxical in someone who now provoked controversy by his outspoken criticism of the church while still cutting a very traditional—some said a Victorian—figure. He did not, for instance, attempt to tamper with the worship in King's; indeed in *Soundings* he argued that since only the most radical wholesale changes could save the church, it would be better to leave things as they are for the present rather than attempt piecemeal changes which would only postpone still further the day of reckoning.

It was almost as a matter of course that David Carter and I both took modern church history as our special subject, as Alec Vidler's supervisions in this subject were not to be missed. This was *ipso facto* an ecumenical education. As a supervisor he was diligent in marking and discussing essays, always hoping to find not only accuracy but some independent thinking, and at his most critical when suspecting I had paraphrased one of his own writings: "Why do you say *that*?" he would growl, armed with blue pencil for underlining. He also supervised us in New Testament. I could not know then just how deeply Vidler had been involved in much of the ecumenical social thinking of the previous three decades, and how closely he had been associated with such as J. H. Oldham who thirty years later would be one of my main preoccupations in research and writing. But I got a glimpse of the fruit of that activity by reading his short wartime book *Christ's Strange Work*, an unsentimental study on the applicability of God's commandments to the complexities of social and political life. I am indebted to him more than to anyone else for enthusing me and setting me in the direction of the kind of theology I would pursue ever after. For him theology was always to be viewed in its historical contexts. He further exemplified the style of scholarship—broad in its sweep, well researched and as fair and generous as possible in its judgments—that I have most admired and aspired after; and not least, an intellectuality that remained engaged with the church and issues of the day. For all that he was a stern critic of the contemporary church, he said more than once that what kept our attachment to the church, despite all its failings, was the fact of the saints it had produced. And Alec Vidler himself was a kind man, especially to his students. The Saturday before our final exams, he took David Carter and me by car out into the Suffolk countryside for lunch and to admire the marvelous old churches of Long Melford, Lavenham and elsewhere, inadvertently also amusing us by his endless gruff comments on the shortcomings of other motorists.

Of course there were other notable teachers in the Divinity School. Geoffrey Lampe was there as an influence, but mainly through his writings as far as I was concerned. C.F.D. (Charlie) Moule was the outstanding lecturer in New Testament, Low Church in outlook, as extraordinarily gracious in attitude as he was clear in exposition. Dennis Nineham had just arrived from King's College, London, and lectured on the Gospels. In the Lent term two other series of lectures, not specifically related to any paper but of general interest, I found especially arresting. One was by Owen Chadwick, Master of Selwyn College and Professor of Ecclesiastical History, on the German Church Struggle. Till then I knew very little about the conflict beyond reading a biography of Martin Niemöller and snatches of Bonhoeffer, and indeed as yet hardly anything had been published. Chadwick was superb in recounting the main episodes and developments, and counselled us to look up the contemporary reports in the *Times* for the best available accounts. I went to the university library and duly did so. The other series was by Donald Mackinnon on Barth, Bonhoeffer, Bultmann and Tillich. Mackinnon, everybody knew, was famous for his personal eccentricities and stories were legion of his odd behavior during tutorials and lectures; doubtless some people turned up hoping for samples of his idiosyncrasies as much as insights into modern theology. They were not wholly disappointed, for while Mackinnon was a high churchman his Anglicanism was not Church of England but very much Scottish Episcopal and he was wont to rail against the English establishment in all its forms. This quickly came out in his lecture on Barth during which he ventured to commend his own essay in the Festschrift presented to Barth on the occasion of his seventieth birthday, "in Lambeth Palace, of all places, by the dean of St Paul's Cathedral, *of all people!*" But while people were entertained (or shocked) by Mackinnon, I judged him to be the most *serious* theologian in Cambridge at the time, in that he was wrestling more intensely than anyone else with how theology can be *truth* in face of God who is mystery and of human existence which is ineluctably tragic. His lectures were the ones which made me think the hardest.[7]

FRIENDS AND . . .

At a party towards the end of the final term, someone asked what we most appreciated from our time in Cambridge. I don't recall this, but some ten years later one of those who had been present told me in a letter that I had said "friends", and that at the time he had judged this rather weak as compared with the primarily important academic education. Now, after ten years out in the real world he no longer thought so. For my part, the friendships I had made were an essential part of the academic milieu, and without them I would not have been stimulated, energized and sustained in study. But friendships were also important in their own right and a good number of them, from all backgrounds, continue to this day. What of romance? I had arrived in Cambridge imagining that despite the relative fewness of women the right blue-stocking(s) would appear as if by magic once she/they realized what a gifted and witty, if somewhat shy, freshman had arrived on the scene. All that was required was that I should be given the chance to display what I had to offer, in my own way. It did not quite happen that way. Almost at the end of my first term the annual RHS party, attended by a lot of other students, took place at Girton College. Early in the evening there was a "getting to know you" waltz in which you had to change partners every two minutes or so and in that time you and your erstwhile partner had to find out as many facts about one another as possible. Each time the music stopped one unfortunate couple would be tested on their new knowledge by the master of ceremonies and eliminated if he thought they hadn't done well enough. After several changes I found myself with a Girtonian and as luck would have it we were selected for interrogation. We answered the questions quite well but for some reason were dismissed from the floor. It was quite clear that she wanted to carry on the conversation and invitingly smiled at me for much of the rest of the evening. This was delightful but also unnerving, and not according to the script. Why should she be interested in the peacock when he had not really had a chance to spread and display his iridescent plumage? Later I kicked myself for not responding to the opening gate, really out of fear of an outside claim upon me that I had not anticipated. The fact that I and a girl in the church at Wallasey had been writing to each other did not really enter into it. I had funked the chance. That taught me a lesson. In due course other romantic pulses came and went. Then in my third year there arrived in RHS one Margaret Hirst, a maths graduate of Somerville College, Oxford. She had come for a postgraduate year in statistics, attached to Newnham College. After the King's Advent service, in which I had been a candle-bearer in the procession (a sublime experience), she and others who had been at the service

---

7. For an interesting contemporary outsider's view on the Cambridge theologians and other "radicals" see Ved Mehta, *The New Theologian*.

gathered in my room for coffee. Her main comment was that she had spent the service wondering when I was going to set light to my hair, which in those days culminated in a bunch of curls dangling over my brow. During the Lent Term we saw more and more of each other, and found that as well as humor we almost had in common a shared childhood history, in that she had lived in Darlington when very small, and had in fact been dedicated as an infant at Geneva Road Baptist Church. Had her parents at the end of the war not moved back to Chesterfield we would in all probability have been in the same class at school. By the summer we were definitely an item, and brought the term to a close in style at the Clare May Ball.

Margaret Hirst, Cambridge 1965

Very soon after, the tripos results were declared. In his memoirs Alec Vidler writes of his students: "Their level of performance varied of course: 1965 was notable because of my four pupils who took the tripos that year two got firsts and the other two II.1's."[8] Michael Scott-Joynt and David Carter were the firsts, but I was pleased enough with my II.1 which, so Vidler told me and my parents on degree day, was *very* nearly a first, and for good measure King's awarded me a prize in theology.

Now it was time to head to Oxford and prepare for ministry, whether at home or abroad.

---

8. Vidler, *Scenes*, 161.

3

Oxford Labors

IN LONG RETROSPECT, THE two years I spent at Regent's Park College, Oxford, seem to have been among the least exciting of my whole life. This is not a complaint or criticism of anyone or anything, simply a recognition of circumstances. For everything there is a season, and a time for every purpose under heaven. After the heady, even dramatic, experiences and discoveries of Cambridge there was now to be a time of consolidation and concentration, in preparation for the ministry. Regent's Park College was, and is, part of the university albeit as a permanent private hall: that is, its governing body comprized not fellows of the college but denominational representatives. Its students studied for the university degree. Not all however studied theology with the ministry in view, nor in any case were all studying theology. "Lay students" were for example pursuing law, oriental languages, geography or music. All students, in my time, were male, in accordance with the norm for all colleges being single-sex.

I was certainly busier at Regent's than ever before. In the first place there was the academic challenge of completing the whole of the Oxford theology degree course ("Schools") in two years. Of course having done Theology IA at Cambridge meant that I hit the course running, But as well as the Schools course, for ministerial students there were classes on pastoralia and homiletics (including the dreaded but necessary weekly sermon class). Not only so, but we each worked as a student pastor in one of the smaller Baptist churches around Oxford. For the whole of 1966 with another first-year student Chris Hutt I was assigned to the Baptist chapel at Woodstock, the historically famous village just north of Oxford and adjoining the estate of Blenheim Palace (local people showed us the unobtrusive gate where one could get in for free). This involved preaching regularly there on Sundays, taking midweek meetings and visiting members' homes. At the very least, it provided a reality check with the world as it was. Then there was preaching further afield in the Home Counties or as far as the Welsh valleys. As if this was not enough, until Easter 1966 I was still president of the Baptist Student Federation (BSF) which meant chairing meetings of its committee and the annual meeting of representatives of all constituent societies, and its annual conference at High Leigh, together with the requirement to visit some of the societies at weekends, and a lot of correspondence. All in all it was a *very* busy time, relieved by some sport: soccer in winter, cricket in summer, and for a group of us year-round road-running (we would have been insulted to hear it called jogging).

I already knew several of the Regent's students including Robin Attfield, by now an Oxford double-first in "Greats" (classics and philosophy) and later to be eminent in the area of environmental ethics; and Ed Burrows and David Wilcox who had both preceded me from Cambridge. But in spite of Regent's being a relatively intimate community I found the very intensity of my schedule left little time and space for new friendships of any depth to form. A decidedly compensatory factor, however, was my developing relationship with Margaret who, having completed her Cambridge Diploma in Statistics, began work with Unilever Research at Colworth House near Bedford. She had found there were posts aplenty for statisticians in the defense industry but conscientiously opted for research into increasing food crop yields rather than improving weaponry. This had a certain convenience for us. Bedford and Oxford lay within fairly easy reach of each other: in those days even the delightfully rustic single-track railway from Cambridge through Bletchley still operated, and before long Margaret had a car too. For the next two years rarely did more than a fortnight go by without our seeing each other at weekends either in Oxford or Bedford, or at our respective parental homes in Chesterfield and Wallasey, and in the summer of 1966 we youth-hosteled our way around Scotland. Writing to each other almost without fail by return of post kept us busy too. From today's instantaneous world of mobile phones, texting and email it's hard to imagine ourselves back into that routine of writing, hoping and waiting. We became engaged in November 1966.

SERIOUS MATTERS

Throughout my time at Regent's I kept a journal, recording almost every day not just how I had spent my time but my thoughts, feelings, comments on events in the news, and hopes and plans for the future. For fifty years it lay unread until I began writing this book, and reading it now makes one realize that the past is indeed another country—but by no means a totally unfamiliar one. Turning its pages has produced surprise after surprise (beginning with how legible my handwriting was then compared with now). In some cases the surprise is at how differently I thought or felt about some things then. After a weekend visit in October 1965 to Worthing on behalf of BSF I wrote: "Attended worship at Christchurch Road. Found that [the hymn] 'Dear Lord and Father of mankind' now repels me." Youthful prejudices and judgments should only be expected, along with the introspective and narcissistic tendencies that journal-keeping can easily foster. But I was not prepared for the reminders of just how intensely I felt about many things, and how often these concerns became transposed into highly personal prayers, meditations on Bible passages or sermonic injunctions to myself. Such jottings would not have shamed a seventeenth century Puritan or a

Part One: Discoveries 1943–1967

John Wesley, especially as I confessed to myself how ill-qualified, unprepared and incapable I felt for ministry. But perhaps most surprising of all is where the younger Keith Clements, especially in his comments on ecumenism and the church's role in the world, or the international scene, seems to anticipate the older one by as much as half a century. Of course we might simply be dealing with a Peter Pan here.

Presiding over all at Regent's was the Principal, the strangely gifted Welshman Gwyn Henton Davies ("Henton" for short): a brilliant Hebraist and Old Testament scholar who produced regrettably little in writing, being essentially an oral person who could be mesmerizing alike in the pulpit and the lecture room; a man of uncertain temperament who could both alienate and charm, be willfully dismissive of people yet on occasion unforgettably kind; who in all things walked entirely by his own lights. The story was current that while still Professor of Hebrew at Durham University he had sent his desk to Oxford as a gift "for the Principal at Regent's Park", in all seriousness as a prophetic action in anticipation of his own appointment there, which duly came in 1958. His lectures were rarely dull and sometimes took unexpectedly practical turns as when he took us through the account in Exodus of how the Israelites were commanded to prepare for the encounter with the Lord on Mount Sinai. On coming to the injunction "Prepare for the third day; do not go near a woman", he would pause and with a solemn wagging of the finger say, "Gentlemen, remember: when you're in the ministry and married—*not on Saturday night.*" Doctrine and philosophy were taught by Gordon Pearce, a quietly hedonistic man with a dry wit who had studied under Donald Mackinnon at Aberdeen, and in my view was one of the wisest thinkers and clearest lecturers of that Baptist generation, deserving of more intellectual recognition than his somewhat self-effacing nature would allow. The tutor to whom I related most readily was Barrie White, church historian, of bright-eyed boyish appearance and manner, whose speech whether formal or conversational was always laced with sharp humor but who took the ministry with deadly seriousness. The newest staff recruit was John Morgan-Wynne, tutor in New Testament, who combined a warm heart with devout and dogged scholarship.

But community life in Regent's was not without its problems. In part this was because lay students were resentful of the continual implication that this being a Baptist college they, regardless of their religious beliefs or lack of them, were expected to observe the Baptist mores including attendance at chapel no less than the theologians. And of course relations between the students themselves were hardly always angelic. "Thirty future leaders with no one to lead except each other," quipped Barrie White. Junior Common Room meetings were often rowdy and apt to get inextricably lost in procedural tangles. No doubt there was some useful experience to be gained in all this.

As far as academic theology was concerned Oxford, like Cambridge, could offer a menu far wider than the fare available in one's own college. I enjoyed George Caird's lectures on the Letter to the Hebrews at Mansfield, and Eric Heaton's on Old Testament at St John's. Also at Mansfield I discovered a visiting American lecturer,

Franklin Sherman, giving a course on Bonhoeffer. For some reason, I never found (or made) time to hear Henry Chadwick on modern Christian doctrine at Christ Church. But as far as lectures went, the most unexpected prize came in my final term when, just as an experiment, I went along to a course on "Church and Ministry in the Fathers" being offered by a young Orthodox priest, Timothy Ware. He spoke with infectious enthusiasm and wit and opened up the early church scene in a quite new and exciting way. Many years later on the ecumenical stage I would meet him again, as Kallistos, Bishop of Diocleia. Overall, like many students I spent far more time reading on my own than sitting in lectures. One area that was quite new to me was early Christian doctrine which fascinated me. I was captivated by the second century father Irenaeus and my sole journal entry for May 5 1966, in the midst of working on my essay on him, is his statement: "For the glory of God is a living man; and the life of man consists in beholding God." Reformation history I found less exciting, or at any rate harder to write on, than I had expected. I worked hard at systematic theology, an area which Gordon Pearce, having read my essay on "Creation *ex nihilo*", suggested I might consider as a future specialism. An added bonus at Oxford was being able, when not otherwise engaged on Sunday mornings, to worship at New Road Baptist Church where Eric Sharpe was minister. As well as being a fine preacher with a strong social conscience (as a student at Jesus College before the war he was a close friend of Harold Wilson, the future Labour prime minister). Eric was an accomplished musician and hymnologist and the single most influential hand in producing *The Baptist Church Hymn Book* of 1962. Margaret already knew him and his hospitable wife Gwen from her own time in Oxford, and our friendship was to last for the rest of their lives.

ECUMENICAL LEARNING

It is perhaps no accident that in all my time at Regent's the three particular learning experiences which stand out, for all that they were very different in nature and length, were ecumenical. The first was a four-week pastoral clinical course for ordinands organized by the Hospital Chaplaincies Board, based at Pinderfields Hospital and Stanley Royd Psychiatric Hospital at Wakefield. As well as encountering the realities of illness of all kinds (we worked as auxiliaries on the wards much of the time), the ethical issues of life and death, and the demands of ministering in the hospital scene, as students we were faced with each other. I was one of two Baptists on the course. There were several Methodists but the majority were Anglicans—and very high Anglicans at that from the Anglo-Catholic colleges of Mirfield and Chichester. For the first time, even more than at King's, I was thrown into deep discussion on sacramental theology with those who really believed in it. It seems strange now that at that time we Free Church students were advised not to come forward for communion when it was the turn for the Anglican service in the hospital chapel. But I made some good friends among them, and one evening the Mirfield students took me over to the

Community of the Resurrection a few miles away for an evening with the brothers there. The second occasion, in February 1967, was a day of seminars in which virtually all the theological colleges in Oxford took part, on contemporary pastoral and social issues—a quite novel idea then for Oxford ordination training. I went to Blackfriars for the one on race relations where speakers included David Mason from the Notting Hill Group Ministry and the Oxford philosopher Michael Dummet, a committed Roman Catholic and campaigning socialist. Among the Anglican students attending I found, for the first time since we were at school together at Lytham, David Hawtin who was now an ordinand at Cuddesdon. The third, at the end of my final term, was the course on Christian Education at Westhill College, Selly Oak—a fortnight which took us out beyond the Sunday church scene into contemporary educational issues at large. In their different ways, these experiences reinforced the fact that all churches and Christian traditions find themselves in the same world, and being pulled into that world inevitably challenges and relativizes their own inner group loyalties. A little while after the Oxford seminars, I was summoned to Henton Davies's study to be greeted with the ferocious declaration: "Mr Clements, my picture is hanging up *in the Vatican!*" He had received word (and for some inexplicable reason thought that I was somehow to blame) that he was regarded as disapproving of the seminars on account of his being anti-ecumenical. In order to deny this he wished it be known that he was indeed in a group photograph of scholars taken in Rome. It was all too clear, however, in what he then said to me that he saw the seminars as a threat to his Regent's fiefdom.

Reading my journal of fifty years ago, it is clear that what was important to me was not only the assigned lectures and reading but my own wrestling with questions, trying to develop my own theology and view of ministry and understanding of the contemporary world. Four areas especially stand out.

A BIBLICAL THEOLOGY

Under the guidance particularly of Karl Barth and Dietrich Bonhoeffer I trod determinedly along the path on which I had set out in Cambridge. I ploughed through Barth's *Romans* commentary for much of my first year, surprised that for a book which really marked the start of twentieth century theology the college's library edition seemed little used, and indeed most other students seemed to regard Barth as somewhat *passé* by now. But the "wholly otherness" of God seemed to me axiomatic for all theology and in need of recovery again and again. On December 8 I copied out extensive quotations from Barth's exposition of the righteousness of God in Romans 3:21–22: his magnificent declaration that God's faithfulness stands over against all human activity, including religious, whether of achievements or failures, and thereby is the judgment of everything human yet no less guarantees by sheer grace the promise for humanity.[1] Alongside Barth I relied on Bonhoeffer, especially his *Ethics*, for the insight that it is precisely in God's worldliness that his otherness is manifest, in the incarnate Christ. In Christ God and the world are united, and we cannot truly have God without the world or the world without God.

By now the tide of "secular theology" which John Robinson had done much to encourage, though not actually to initiate since much of it was coming from the USA, was in full flood, and being avidly debated in theological colleges. "I am more secular than thou", someone in Regent's quipped in satire of what could easily have been just a passing fad. Paul van Buren's *The Secular Meaning of the Gospel* (1963) and Harvey Cox's *The Secular City* (1965) would soon be followed by the "death of God" theologies of William Hamilton, Thomas Altizer and others. On a January evening in 1966 Margaret and I went to hear John Robinson address a meeting in Oxford on "Faith in a society without religion". This was the fourth time I had heard him in the flesh, and once again I was sympathetic but this time more uneasy about his use of Bonhoeffer. I noted: "He dealt very well with the subject of religion as an entity being eroded by secularization, using Bonhoeffer as the basis of his argument. But he did not do full justice to Bonhoeffer in that he did not mention Bonhoeffer's critique of religion 'from the other side', from the theology of the Word of God (Barth et al). Not to mention Bonhoeffer's *twin* approach to secularity/religion seems to me to lead to a state of imbalance." It was from Robinson that evening that I first heard the name of Ronald Gregor Smith, the Scottish theologian who was also exploring the theme of secularity. Meanwhile, Bonhoeffer with his emphasis upon God's revelation taking concrete worldly form, and upon faith as participation in this worldly form in Christ, remained my chief mentor. Of course there were dangers in such a devoted attachment to a figure who had attained a cult-like status. I believed I was aware of this. In the midst of a study of his *Ethics*, in particular his section on "Christ, reality and good", I reflected:

> *Why* does he influence me so? Is it the example of his life? Or just that I want to be "radical" too? Or what? But the more I study him, the more perplexing I find his life, and its conditions so different from my own. And the more I read of his works, the more surprisingly "orthodox" in several respects, I find him. And yet his thought continues to have a hold on me. More than most writers, he is a man of such extraordinary depth of thought and breadth of vision, and who is at the same time so personally aware of the living Christ, and whose sole aim is to witness to him. Bonhoeffer is a true witness to the Christ: he wishes to witness to him throughout his life and thought, which includes so much of the life and thought of the whole of Western man.

This true kind of worldliness in faith was indeed what I had been seeking since my later teen years. Bonhoeffer in fact was not the only stimulus in this direction. One evening at home, quite by chance, I heard on the radio some words which both

---

1. Barth, *Romans*, 96–97.

arrested me then and haunted me for long afterwards: "You never enjoy the world aright, till the sea itself floweth in your veins, till you are clothed with the heavens, and crowned with the stars..." This was the start of what was to grow into a greater awareness and major interest in the seventeenth century priest and poet Thomas Traherne.

ADEQUATE FOR MINISTRY? WHAT MINISTRY?

For ordinands in the 1960s secular theology was not just an intellectual game, insofar as it was bound up with how we saw the role of the church in society, and therewith the kind of ministry we envisaged for ourselves. These were hot issues at the time. The fortnightly journal *New Christian* edited by Trevor Beeson was one of liveliest forums of debate in liberal or radical circles and was essential reading for many of us in the Regent's common room. Traditional ministry in the local church was under fire. In 1965 a stir was caused when Nick Stacey, Rector of Woolwich, who had sought—controversially—to develop new forms of urban mission and ministry in Southwark Diocese, out of a sense of failure resigned his living to become Director of Oxfam. Three years later he was appointed Director of Kent Social Services. His however was only the most high-profile case of those who felt that the traditional roles of pastor or priest had had their day and that if the aim was to help people cope with life and its problems other professions were now more relevant. This was not only affecting Anglicans but increasingly the Free Churches too. At Regent's one was aware of a steady stream of Baptist ministers opting for teaching, the probation service or other forms of social work. This to say the least was contributing to a climate of uncertainty. "I want to think about the role of the ministry in a way rather different from those being pursued at present—scriptural, traditional etc": so I wrote soon after entering Regent's. The questions, at least, were registering with me. But so too was a certain kind of experience. On a Sunday evening in February 1966 I reflected on having just conducted the communion service at Woodstock:

> .... the communion service is still fresh and vivid in my mind. The first one I've ever led—I don't think I shall ever forget it. Having participated in it as the minister, I've seen it in a completely new light, and somehow it was rather devastating. Being able to say the words of institution is wonderful enough—"For I received from the Lord what I also delivered unto you..." but it was the moment of actually breaking the bread which hit me most of all. It struck me—here one was doing what *Christ himself* actually did in the Upper Room, what the apostles did, and what the whole Christian church has done and always will do. Somehow I was intensely aware of the congregation as never before, especially those in particular need—the couple who have lost their child, the man who is losing his job because the plane factory is closing down, the woman who has been a widow for several years and is desperately trying to find another husband, and so on. One also becomes conscious of oneself so

much, and how one stands in at least as great a need as the rest of the congregation. I think I learned more about the ministry in that single moment, than a whole library of text books could ever teach me.

We were at Emmaus, on the evening of the first day of the week.

The minister, in other words, really has significance only in relation to the community. The prime question is how that community relates to the world in which it is set. It seemed to me that to make the main question of how the *minister's* work is of direct relevance to the world was to deny the priesthood of all believers, and to clericalise the church which in fact comprises the whole people of God. The real question is how the people are to be equipped for *their* secular ministry in the world; and this enabling is a prime task of the minister. Bonhoeffer's statement that the church is truly church when it exists for others was to be applied to the whole community, not just its pastor who must therefore not rush to make himself the one who is most conspicuously relevant to the world. For me therefore the concept of ministry as that of word and sacrament and pastoral care had to remain central, and was not to be diverted into other kinds of professionalism however tempting. But "word and sacrament and pastoral care" would themselves need reorientation in the present context, for a truly worldly church.

This would of course have immense ecumenical implications. But there was also the question of just *where* I thought my ministry might lie. I was still thinking of work overseas although I felt, and was also counselled in this direction, that I would be of more use as an export if I had first gained experience and perhaps further qualifications at home. In addition however, missionary service was now under question as much as ministry at home. By the 1960s the missionary history was losing much of its innocence, especially when seen in the context of the story of western colonialism and imperialism, the gospel following the flag (or gunboat) scenario. Stephen Neill's panoramic yet remarkably detailed *A History of Christian Missions* had just appeared (1964) and helped put this aspect of the missionary story in truer perspective. I myself, as I have related in chapter 1, had been stirred by the Baptist stance in Angola as a *counter*-narrative to the colonial one. Nevertheless the suspicion was there and had to be faced, not least in relation to that part of the story with which my own was personally entwined: China. I appreciated an editorial by Lesslie Newbigin in the *International Review of Missions* critical of opposing to one another the preaching of the gospel and technical aid. There must be preaching for conversion, he stated: "But conversion is not the turning of a man to Christ for his own sake, or simply to increase the size and power of the Church . . . Conversion in the Bible is the turning of a man to Christ so that he may become a partner in Christ's work and a witness to God's kingdom. It is the enlisting of men in God's service for the fulfilment of His purpose for the world."[2] We are not, said Newbigin, to be reporters only, but also signs of the resurrection, living out in our flesh the experience of victory over the powers of

---

2. Newbigin, "Editorial".

evil. "An escapist is not a sign of the Resurrection. The relation between the word and the deed is that both must be visibly rooted in the same reality; *namely, in that new community which is created and indwelt by the Holy Spirit.*" (My emphases). That, I felt, expressed exactly where I was on the route towards ministry.

BIBLE AND NEWSPAPER, PRAYER AND POLITICS

"The election campaign is hotting up. Labour has a clear lead, and I hope they maintain it . . . Basically, it is to be fought on the record—of 13 years of Tories, 17 months of Labour—and the present situation. That is why Labour will win it. I think that the Liberals will also do better—I hope so. Whether to vote labour or liberal here in Wallasey [a safe Conservative seat] I've not yet finally decided." So I wrote on March 15 1966. I did not record, nor do I now remember, how I actually voted in that election which returned Harold Wilson's government to a secure Labour majority. By now I was trying to follow Karl Barth's dictum about reading the Bible in one hand with the newspaper in the other. As far as the newspaper was concerned it was mainly the international pages which drew me. This was the age of the Vietnam War, the intensifying struggle against apartheid in South Africa, the confrontation with Rhodesia's racist unilateral bid for independence, and the renewed Arab-Israeli conflict. The Campaign for Nuclear Disarmament had passed its peak but the Cold War had not. For many these were the issues that shaped the public conscience, and as a child of that time I was no exception. I was not a marcher or demonstrator but followed these issues assiduously. I wrote to Ernest Marples, MP for Wallasey, about the US bombing of Vietnam and heard Ambrose Reeves report on his recent visit to North Vietnam. In May 1966 (having just come from the Baptist Assembly in Westminster Chapel) I watched from the public gallery the House of Commons debate on Rhodesia. I argued with other students who seemed oblivious of the scale of Israel's US-supported military power and who on the eve of the war in June 1967 were praying that God might "yet stay Nasser's hand". I was chronically impatient at the churches' apparent failures to speak a prophetic word, but rejoiced at the stand being taken in South Africa for instance:

> The news of the students' strong protest in S.A. strikes a note of cheer in the growing twilight of that part of the world . . . It is too much to hope that the students' sharp and courageous reply will spark off a flame of anti-government movements. But it does give one heart, to know that young people are taking a stand. They are the prophets. Perhaps they will make more people think in S.A. One hopes so. And especially, that the churches will more and more stand up.

> The Church seems tragically paralytic in her silence at the moment. Resolutions on Vietnam from the leaders of the Councils—but little else. The mass of the churches seem to be sharing in the general apathy and acquiesce in the brutal American policy. We are scared we might be in the wrong. But this

is no time for such self-concern; it is the moment to declare God's word of judgment, which ought to be resounding at least as devastatingly as the bombs in Vietnam. Our declaration, if it is to be truly prophetic, cannot be simply one of "moral indignation"—otherwise it will lapse into effete sentimentality. Prophecy points to deep realities within the political order; these realities are being ignored in the Vietnam situation. We must warn of the annihilating consequences for *all* in Vietnam, if escalation continues. *The* political reality in this situation is that present policy will lead nowhere, destroy all, and its own purpose, and being everlasting shame on the West.

In the Middle East [June 7 1967], a complete Israeli victory in Sinai seems imminent. Doubtless relief here in the W. But what of the long-term results? The war will only have aggravated the root problem of Arab versus Jew. True, Nasser may topple—but who may come in his place?

But I was glad to see some strong ecumenical impulses at work. In April 1967 I strongly approved of the British Council of Churches' (BCC) resolution to abolish the British independent nuclear deterrent. "It is an issue conveniently forgotten just now. I hope we all in the churches will have the courage to stand by this lead: it is genuine prophetic judgment upon the hour, and judgement is very much in season just now." I also welcomed and devoured the BCC 1967 report *World Poverty and British Responsibility*.

CHRISTIAN UNITY: TIME FOR ACTION?

Those last remarks, coupled with those about the three significant ecumenical learning experiences, point to the fact that however concentrated were my studies and concerns it was hope for the ecumenical movement which, overall, determined my perspective during these two years. During my first two terms at Regent's these questions were coming close to home for me as president of the Baptist Student Federation (BSF). Not only had attendance at the annual conference been falling for several years but questions were increasingly being asked about the place of a national denominational student body—in relation to the constituent Baptist student societies on the one hand and to the ecumenical scene on the other, and to bodies like the Inter-Varsity Fellowship (IVF) and the Student Christian Movement (SCM). Was a body like BSF a help or hindrance to ecumenical relations? But this did not answer the basic question of whether, at campus level, there was need for separate denominational societies or whether at the very least they could come more close together under the umbrella of Joint Christian Councils. Such attempts as had been made at both Cambridge and Oxford, however, were not exactly encouraging. I felt myself more and more led to argue that denominational societies, at whatever level, could in the end be justified only if they were working ever more ecumenically together and shared the goal of visible Christian unity. In my presidential address to the BSF conference at High Leigh in Holy Week 1966 I stated:

> This issue . . . of the ecumenical movement is one in which I believe Baptist students and their societies must find their true place. Our attitude to it is positive, and there is no going back from it. Our experience of the contribution we can make in Joint Christian activity on the student level, whether in worship, study, or mission, is itself inherently worthwhile because this is the way God is leading His Church; and our experience as students should prepare us to do all we can in the local churches to further similar aims when we take our place as responsible church members, in pew or pulpit.

It was not easy, however, to make this point without it sounding like yet another justification for the status quo of division. I feared that this was how I was being interpreted in some quarters, not least in the report of the conference in the *Baptist Times* where what I had said about ecumenism was made to appear very secondary, implying (I noted in my journal) "that I thought denominational societies could be justified at all costs—whereas my point is that they must be justified in the context of a positive ecumenical contribution."[3] In retrospect it became evident that I was making a big assumption about the ecumenical commitment of the Baptist denomination and its leadership. BSF, linked so closely to the youth departments of both the Baptist Union and Baptist Missionary Society, was liable to be held hostage to the level of ecumenical commitment in those bodies.

But ecumenism at the global level was certainly still in the air during 1965–67. An American Southern Baptist professor, Morgan Patterson, who was an observer in his individual capacity at Vatican II, spent several weeks at Regent's and shared his reflections with some of us. But the more immediate interest lay at home, with the follow up to the 1964 Nottingham conference and its call to work for a united church by 1980. As part of this the BCC sponsored a study programme for local groups, *The People Next Door*, and I was glad to see my parents now enthusiasts for the cause in Wallasey. Then in March 1967 the Baptist Union Council received and adopted for study by the churches the report of its working group, *Baptists and Unity*. The report could not exactly be described as anti-ecumenical. But it was hardly enthusiastic for closer unity either. Safety-first was its motto. It asked Baptists to consider three main points: whether it was a rigid insistence on believers' baptism ground that made for separation from other churches; how far their present church organization was to be regarded as an essential expression of the gospel; and whether the modifications and safeguards which episcopal churches had proposed went far enough to meet the hesitations of non-episcopal churches. These sounded like neutral questions but negativity was deeply embedded in them. Then, as regards the Nottingham 1964 resolution: "It would be a mistake for the Baptist Union (and perhaps for some others) to pursue

---

3. Cf. *Baptist Times* April 14 1966.

the idea of organic union by 1980, lest it endanger denominational unity and thereby seriously weaken the witness Baptists have to make." Nevertheless, it stated, continuing study of the issues was of great importance and links should be maintained with the British and World Councils of Churches.

It could have been worse, but at best the report was reactive if not passive, with no hint of any initiative to be taken. Baptists were no further forward than they were forty-five years earlier in their responses to the 1920 Lambeth Conference "Appeal for Reunion of All Christian People". The Baptist Union was effectively saying that it would watch with some interest the efforts for unity being made by others rather than fully participate itself, still less offer any lead on its own terms. Invoking denominational unity, whatever that might mean, as the trump card was the same as saying "nothing doing". I was among those who found this appalling, and wrote in my journal:

> Whatever the actual substance, it can only appear as a negative shirking of the issues. It is going to make Baptists themselves even more complacent than they are now. It threatens to cut us off from the mainstream of Christian thought and action in this country. To say that "we are not ready to negotiate for unity yet" is to admit that we shall *never* be ready for it. Should the archangel descend from heaven and announce the Last Day, doubtless the Baptist denomination would plead for a few more years "until we're ready". "Nonconformists"! "Free" Church! No prophetic quality in all this. Simply "Peace, peace."

I also wrote, I recall, in such terms to Baptist Church House. One felt deeply sorry for Ernest Payne, retiring general secretary of the BU, lifelong ecumenist and for eight years a president of the WCC. He was clearly disappointed, saying that the Council being the body it was had done the only thing it could do. But he pointed to more positive developments elsewhere—the continuing conversations between Anglicans and Methodists, and between Presbyterians and Congregationalists in England, and the new possibilities opening for local ecumenism especially in the new towns now being built. These indeed offered some continuing hope, but the heady optimism of my Cambridge days was starting to dissipate. I was glad in a sense that the report had not come out in the autumn of the previous year. Had it done so then, I might have been so depressed as to consider not being ordained to the Baptist ministry at all. As it happened, by March 1967 the process of seeking my first pastorate was well under way and was about to reach the point of no return.

A FIRST PASTORATE

One morning in October 1966 I had my first meeting with Douglas Hicks, large and affable Area Superintendent of the Central Area of the Baptist Union, who had come to interview students who would be leaving for the ministry the following year. He was to become a long-standing friend. He listened carefully to my thoughts and promised we would meet again in due course. Over the coming three months I was put in touch with two churches, visited them and, in that coy Baptist phrase "preached with a view". Neither church wished to pursue possibilities any further, in one case because I seemed too young and inexperienced and in the other case I was not evangelical enough for one section of the congregation. By March the following year time was getting on. It was not only that finding a pastorate was becoming urgent, but Margaret and I had set our hopes on getting married in the late summer—and the question of her work loomed large in all this.

Then one morning after prayers an excited Henton Davies accosted me in the quad with a letter from Douglas Hicks in his hand. An enquiry had come from the recently formed Mid-Cheshire Fellowship of Baptist Churches, a grouping of four small churches in the area of Tarporley and Northwich, asking if someone fresh from college would be prepared to work alongside the minister Clifford Cleal for two or three years, and Douglas Hicks had thought of me. I needed no encouragement to take this up—I had already heard about the Fellowship which was not too far away from Wallasey and in the same Baptist association (Lancashire and Cheshire) as my father's church. Not only so, but Clifford Cleal's own reputation had already reached me well before him. He had been Director of the Christian Citizenship Department (what would soon be called Social Responsibility) of the Baptist Union for eleven years, and was known as one of the most socially committed and imaginative players on the Baptist stage. Leaving that BU post at the age of 59, instead of going for an easy ride into retirement he had wanted to try something new, experimental and visionary. Norman Jones, area superintendent for the North West, was himself a forward-looking strategist and saw the possibilities of linking smaller churches in both urban and rural areas so as to be able to support a ministry not for survival purposes but for new forms of mission. The Mid-Cheshire Fellowship was one of these, and he had invited Clifford Cleal to consider it as a means of what he was looking for in his final years of ministry. He became its minister, based in Tarporley, in 1964. Douglas Hicks quickly set up a meeting for me with Clifford Coleal at Baptist Church House in London, and so for the first time I met this tall, winnowy man of extraordinary vitality, sharp mind, compassion and humor with an eager expression on his open, honest face that was always looking for an excuse to smile (yet who also, I had been warned, did not bear fools too gladly).

Clifford Cleal

He walked with a slight limp, legacy of a youthful rugby injury. We went to a nearby café and spent most of the afternoon there. He talked about his vision not just for pastoring the churches but for developing a socially oriented ministry into the whole area on an ecumenical basis and involving social services, voluntary agencies, trades unions and schools. Nearby, the new towns of Runcorn and Winsford were being built, and the possibilities, he said with bubbling enthusiasm, were endless. But he could not lead this all on his own. Three of the four churches had been without a minister for many years and a lot of pastoral rebuilding needed to be done. Would I be prepared to give it a go working alongside him? He made clear that it was a high-risk venture, with no guarantee of success, and on a minimal stipend with no promise yet of longer term financial support. The regional Baptist Association had promised a grant though only for two years at present, and a manse would have to be found somewhere in the area. I was excited but also nervous. Would I really be up to it, and what would Margaret feel about it? On the other hand I had told myself often enough that life in discipleship was an adventure, not a safe seat, the steep and rugged pathway rather than the green pastures the desirable way. Moreover the prospect of working alongside this man as senior minister was magnetic. That afternoon we talked long and widely about Bonhoeffer and Teilhard de Chardin, about trades unions and church attitudes to industrial relations, about sport and science. He had a first-class mind (a Regent's man himself and an Oxford first to boot) and a thorough ecumenist.

He had been among the pioneers of industrial mission during the war, had attended the inaugural assembly of the World Council of Churches at Amsterdam in 1948, and worked at the social affairs desk of the British Council of Churches from 1948 to 1953. He was deservedly famous for speaking his mind.

By mid-May it was all settled. I had visited and preached in all four churches of the Fellowship. Clifford Cleal reckoned my sermon on Jeremiah's message to the Hebrew exiles, "Seek the welfare of the city where I have sent you into exile, for in its welfare you will find your welfare" a first-rate word for the church in present-day society (I was no less gratified by my mother's response when during the Easter vacation she came with me to hear me preach in a church in New Brighton: "Just like what the People Next Door meetings were all about"). The formal invitation came on behalf of the whole Fellowship and I gladly accepted. Soon, too, Margaret was able to negotiate a transfer within Unilever Research from Colworth House to Port Sunlight on the Wirral, a fair distance from the Northwich area where we would be living but manageable by car each day, and so we were able to plan for a wedding in early September. Meanwhile came the marathon of final work for the week of Oxford Schools exams in June, and when they were over I was fairly exhausted. Then followed the end of session events at Regent's, with Ernest Payne speaking to the point on not giving way too easily by changing theological fashions and the need to keep a sense of history. Then came the education course at Westhill College.

A VERY NEAR THING—AND A GOOD THING IN THE END

All seemed to be going smoothly towards the new life starting in September. A small two-bedroom house had been found for us in the village of Barnton on the northern edge of Northwich, and Clifford Cleal and I had been to see it. It was obviously desirable for Margaret likewise to inspect it, and it so happened that on July 6 she would be coming by car with three colleagues from Colworth House for a meeting at Port Sunlight. They would be staying overnight at a hotel in Chester. On arrival there she would phone me, I would drive down to pick her up and we would go over to Barnton and back. Evening drew on, no call came and I was getting restive. When at about half past eight the phone did ring it was not Margaret but the casualty sister at Chester Royal Infirmary. There had been accident, she said, and your fiancée is here. . . . Hearing my intake of breath she told me not to panic, her life was not actually in danger but she had some injuries. My father drove me down to Chester, and there we learnt the full horror of what had happened. North of Whitchurch the car had collided head-on with a lorry. Margaret's colleague at the wheel was killed outright. She herself had a nasty laceration across her forehead but, much more seriously, a broken neck, in fact two vertebrae were fractured. One of the other passengers was also badly injured. Mercifully the spinal cord itself was undamaged and there was no sign of paralysis anywhere. But it was a very near thing. Relief vied with visions of the nightmare scenarios of what could so easily have

Oxford Labors

happened one way or the other. After several days in hospital she was returned home to Chesterfield with her neck encased in a cumbersome plaster cast, presently replaced by a softer removable collar which could be worn as necessary, and she worked out her last few days at Colworth House. When the accident happened Margaret's mother had been on the point of sending out the wedding invitations. She was persuaded to hold her hand for only a short time, and our plans went ahead.

The day after the accident, I received a summons to Oxford for a *viva voce* exam. Evidently my papers had put me on the borderline for a first. I duly went, and found that Henton Davies, who had of course been informed of the accident and was distressed as much as anyone, had been kind enough to call the chairman of the examiners to alert them to whatever trauma I might still be in. The red-robed professors were indeed sympathetic and gentle with me, but that did not stop George Caird neatly filleting my answer on the historicity of the passion narrative in the Fourth Gospel. Once again, as in Cambridge, the final verdict was "a very good second." For the next four weeks I earned some money and incidentally extended my experience of the industrial scene as a laborer at Spiller's flourmill in Birkenhead, most of the time emptying bags of surplus or second-grade flour down a chute to where, I was told, they would be used in the making of dog-biscuits.

Chesterfield September 2 1967

Our wedding duly took place on September 2, a bright and gusty day, at Cross Street Baptist Church in Chesterfield, conducted by the minister Geoffrey Ellis with my father also taking part. Chris Bradnock was best man, Margaret's sister Kate the bridesmaid. We honeymooned at Reeth in Swaledale, one of Margaret's favorite spots, and a week later moved into our new home in Barnton. My ordination, and induction to the Mid-Cheshire Fellowship, took place at Tarporley on September 16. Henton Davies preached. For such occasions he was in the habit of choosing a biblical text which he judged appropriate to the person being ordained. My father and I speculated that for me he would choose Philippians 4:3, " . . . and Clement also". We were right. But what none of us had expected, and which thereafter was recalled with never-ending amusement by the Mid-Cheshire folk, was his constant, quaint reference to me and my "beloved Margaret".

PART TWO

Minister and Teacher 1967–1990

Bristol Baptist College staff and students 1987

4

Experimental Pastures: The Mid-Cheshire Fellowship

IT WAS OFTEN SAID, with reason, that a first pastorate was where you went to make all your mistakes. In the days leading up to my ordination in 1967 I had certainly been full of misgivings about my own competencies, as my journal entries make clear: Such sentiments can of course be the pessimist's insurance premium against ultimate disappointment. But they were at least resonating with the reality of what I had been told often enough would be an experimental situation with so many unknowns. It was some comfort, if a strange one, to know that I might not in any case be there for more than two years. In fact I was to stay for just over four, and basically very happy, years for both myself and Margaret. What is more, the time in the Mid-Cheshire Fellowship (MCF) proved to be much more than a stage from which I "moved on" to supposedly better or more important things. Indeed, much in my later engagements, both ecumenical and academic, actually had their genesis in Cheshire and can be seen as outcomes of what I experienced and learnt there and then.

In simple geographical terms Mid-Cheshire was reckoned as that part of the Cheshire plain lying north of Crewe and between the M6 motorway to the east and Chester to the west. Largely rural and agricultural, it was famous for its dairy-farming (alluding to a butter advertisement of the time, locals boasted that it had the most contented cows in England). But thanks to extensive subterranean salt deposits the industrial giant Imperial Chemical Industries (ICI) Ltd also had a major presence in the center of the area, with its Brunner-Mond Division chemical works based around Northwich while Winsford, slightly further south, had the largest rock-salt mine in the country. The River Weaver Navigation, the Shropshire Union and the Trent and Mersey Canals, historic waterways dating from the early industrial revolution, were not only still vital connections with the Mersey estuary but also added much to the charm of the landscape. In the Northwich area the mix of industry and agriculture

PART TWO: MINISTER AND TEACHER 1967–1990

made fun of the conventional sociologists' divide between urban-industrial and rural-agricultural society. Many of those who worked as charge-hands or clerks at ICI, or crewed the motor barges on the canals, regarded themselves as country folk.

THE MID-CHESHIRE FELLOWSHIP

The village of Tarporley lies about nine miles south west of Northwich, and its Baptist church, dating from 1717, was the largest in the group with 66 members.[1] Here Clifford Cleal and his warmly hospitable wife Rene lived, in a large manse (which we knew often rang with vigorous arguments between two equally strong-minded people) adjoining the church on the high street. The other three churches, Anderton, Little Leigh and Milton, all much smaller in membership, lay on the north-west fringe of Northwich. Anderton chapel in fact was virtually in the village of Barnton which perched on a ridge overlooking the ICI works at Winnington and Walliscote. Anderton itself is famous for that remarkable piece of Victorian hydraulic engineering, now restored, the Anderton Lift which can transfer vessels between the Weaver Navigation and the Trent and Mersey Canal, at that point lying immediately adjacent to each other but on different levels. Barely a mile further out lay Little Leigh, a more decidedly rural village with its Baptist chapel, built in 1820, set at the end of a row of council-built housing.. A mile further out to the north-west was the Milton church at Acton Bridge, a hamlet straddling the main west coast railway line. None of these three churches had had a full-time minister for many years, largely being served on Sundays by lay preachers or by students from the Baptist College in Manchester. To a degree they had done well to survive thus far, but the future for such small causes throughout the denomination was increasingly doubtful. The formation of the MCF was thus undoubtedly in part a survival exercise for them, but not necessarily one they had welcomed unreservedly. It was bringing new challenges and demands as well as opportunities; and now to receive a novice minister was in itself a challenge, and the risk in the operation was no less for them than for me. At least, with there being no ministerial predecessor in living memory for many of the members, I could hardly suffer from comparisons. Even with the relatively small membership of the Fellowship as a whole and within each individual church, there was huge variety, in background and occupation—farmers, ICI manual and clerical workers, technicians, computer programmers, teachers, doctors, council workers. There was also the whole spectrum of Baptist outlook. The Tarporley church included an ultra-Protestant Welsh family who would not countenance having a lighted candle in the church at Christmas, nor a symbolic cross at any time; while in the same congregation Derek Walley, progressive dairy farmer at Whitegate (and secretary of MCF till 1968) and his wife Jean, a biology teacher, were as theologically radical as they come and at times made John Robinson

---

1. In practice attendance at Baptist churches is typically larger than the formal membership of the church.

and his *Honest to God* seem mild by comparison. But diversity and tension on issues of belief were rarely, if ever, beset by rancor. The monthly Fellowship magazine *Neighbours* opened its pages to often lively but respectful views and debate. Its purple and white cover strikingly depicted the context of the world in which our Cheshire churches were set: either side of a cross were silhouetted a tractor at work and an industrial skyline of factory roof and chimney. Very soon after our arrival, in October 1967 this whole scene was swept by disaster in the epidemic of foot-and-mouth disease that broke out in Shropshire and quickly spread northwards with devastating results. A total of 149,642 cattle had to be destroyed in Cheshire alone, including those on at least one farm belonging to MCF members. At night, the pyres of burning carcasses lit up the distant countryside to ghastly effect. The damage was colossal not only in economic terms but emotionally and socially too. An entire herd that had been built up and cared for over many years had to go if a single case was discovered in it. One of the Little Leigh farming families told how last thing each night a reluctant visit had to made into the shippon, in fear and trembling lest a fatal tell-tale cough be heard from one of the animals. Socially the plague was disruptive because of the need to quarantine farms that had been, or might be about to be, affected. But equally there was a solidarity in suffering that united in spirit the whole area, farming or not, directly affected or not.

CLIFFORD CLEAL: HIS VISION

A decisively influential factor in my whole time in mid-Cheshire was Clifford Cleal himself. He was a man of rigorous thought as well as energy and compassion. Shortly after retiring in 1972 he wrote an article "The Role of the Ordained Minister Today". It reflects a lifetime of experience in local pastorates, his pioneering of industrial mission in wartime Swindon, his ecumenical collaboration on social and industrial ethics with such eminences as J.H. Oldham, and his work in social responsibility both for the British Council of Churches and the Baptist Union; and no less conveys the vision which animated his leadership of the Mid-Cheshire Fellowship, and therewith what he was able to offer me in following up the understanding of ministry which had begun to animate me while at Regent's.

In this article he acknowledges that the ministry is a high calling, but insists that it is not the *only* calling that deserves to be called noble. Laypersons too shoulder huge responsibilities for human welfare in, for example, health care or town planning. There is no ladder of prestige: "The whole people of God are called out of the world to witness in the world, and to proclaim that those who repent in faith can inherit the Kingdom . . . Whether we consider the minister's role, or his employment, or his calling, it must be in the context of the whole Christian community . . . all are ministers, the servants of Christ who came 'not to be ministered unto but to minister.'" Ministry is therefore a team affair. Even in Word and Sacrament the minister requires the help of qualified people if preaching and worship are to be related to the workaday world and the complexities of society. Cleal draws on the arguments of the ecumenical missionary thinker Henrik Kraemer and the work of the Ecumenical Institute at Bossey in Switzerland, and this extended citation puts his case cogently:

> Grouping can mean a more realistic cross section of the community as for example where a farming community is linked with a nearby industrial district and both are aware of the needs of an expanding population. Ministerial oversight would then include bringing together for regular fellowship and discussion the members of these communities. This naturally leads to a strategy of approach to the whole area, and this must be ecumenical. For surely help to the handicapped, relations with the police, approaches to industry are matters of concern to all the churches. Where the ministers involved have worked out a basis of mutual understanding, the deployment of resources is more efficient and real co-operation with Social Services departments, Trade Unions, etc, can be developed. If ministers cannot or will not cultivate a fellowship based on common obedience to Christ keen laymen tend to become disillusioned with the organized church.[2]

The role of the minister can therefore be as supporter and counsellor, and facilitator of the networks that can enable lay people to work together for the kingdom in the world. But ministers, by virtue of their "apartness" can also be the people who can initiate such ventures as happened in the early days of industrial mission. The same can apply in the area of family life and education. But no less he emphasizes the importance of the minister's spiritual life. Clifford Cleal was an intensely spiritual person who had no inhibitions about wearing his devotional heart on his sleeve at times, and insisting on and the need for proper rest and time for reflection. I was supremely fortunate in being his associate for four years.

MY WORK IN THE CHURCHES

Clifford Cleal and I met together regularly, fortnightly if not weekly. The allocation of work was clear: Sunday preaching around the four churches was shared fairly equally between us (it often meant conducting three services on Sunday). Pastoral work at Anderton and Little Leigh fell largely to me. Joint activities of the Fellowship would be our shared responsibility. This would give Clifford time and space for his wider work in the community, which I would also be able to see at close quarters. So I was soon immersed in the normal round of pastoral care. At Anderton we embarked on an additional new building for the church, which meant a lot of extra work from 1969 to 1971. With Margaret having the car most weekdays for her travel to and from Port Sunlight, by day I purred along the Cheshire highways and byways on a moped,

---

2. Cleal, "The Role", 197.

pleasantly breezy in summer and often numbingly cold in winter. An additional responsibility came with the formation of what called itself the Runcorn Informal Baptist Society (RIBS): a collection of about twenty younger Baptists, mostly professionals, who had recently moved to Runcorn New Town, where there was no Baptist Church but a desire for Baptists to work ecumenically. RIBS served as a place of lively weeknight encounter for them while most of its members worshipped in various churches of different denominations in Runcorn. RIBS was also linked to the MCF and was served by Roy Jones, Baptist minister appointed to the ecumenical team in Runcorn. I labored at my sermons, and perhaps too often the congregations evidently had to labor to understand them. We tried some new forms of worship involving greater congregational participation and a variety of forms of preaching and teaching, often with much acceptance. Pastoral work, I discovered, was essential if people were to be given the sense that they and their feelings counted when they were being presented with changes and new challenges.

But also seeing Clifford Cleal's wider vision taking flesh was instructive and inspiring, as I shadowed for a while a probation officer at work, attended the lunch meetings he organized for local authority social services people and those working in the voluntary sector, and his larger gatherings which focused on industrial issues for both managerial and trades union people. Two of these meetings stand out in memory: one in December 1968 addressed by John Garnett, director of the Industrial Society, an independent organization promoting good working conditions and better human relations in industry (I remember the day well because it was also the day news came of the death of Karl Barth); and in April 1969 when Lord Collison, general secretary of the Agricultural Workers, spoke on the government white paper on industrial relations "In Place of Strife". Such events illustrated well what a non-religious Christianity could look like as Christians, humanists and others of goodwill sought to identity what good behavior meant in the community of work—yet it was notable how appeal to the Bible could be heard from some quite unexpected quarters. Enabling such encounters to happen was what a modest, but enterprizing, facilitating ministry was all about. Years later, I would appreciate just how much the J. H. Oldham influence had been at work here, and how bereft of memory (and good sense) are so many of today's tortuous debates about faith in the public square.

Part Two: Minister and Teacher 1967–1990

ECUMENICAL VILLAGE

Anderton Chapel 1970

With such heady visions of ecumenism as had accompanied me from Cambridge onwards, settling in Mid-Cheshire and modest Barnton in particular might have proved a come-down. Quite the opposite. Barnton, within its own context and limitations, was a lesson in local grassroots ecumenism in its time. Partly this was due to the compact nature of the village itself and its four thousand or so population, in which even if one did not wish to meet one's neighbors it was hard to avoid doing so. This applied to the churches too. There were five churches in all. In addition to our Anderton chapel, there was the Anglican parish church, Christ Church; two Methodist churches (relics of the original three varieties of Methodism that had persisted into the mid-twentieth century, and now in process of uniting as one congregation); and on the council estate the Our Lady of Fatima Roman Catholic Church. As soon as I had arrived I found that I was *expected* along with the other clergy to play a part in the life of the community. In my case I was first of all invited (almost ordered) to sit on the committee planning the dedication and inauguration of the village Memorial Hall, formerly a school which stood almost opposite our house in Lydyett Lane. This taught me a lot about the subtle hierarchies at local level, not least in planning the service of dedication for the hall which, being a war memorial, was to take place on Remembrance Sunday. Delicate questions: who should perform the laying of wreaths and the unveiling of the plaque? The president of the local branch of the British Legion, a veteran of 1914–18, was on the committee and should obviously have a prominent role, but was invited to suggest others who might also take part. "Well, he said, there's our vice-president Mr X. He's Second World War, *but quite a good chap.*" I continued to serve on the monthly Memorial Hall Management Committee, most of the other members being either on the parish council or the burial board, or all three committees and it was rumored that some were in the habit of turning up on Monday evenings not sure which of the bodies had its turn that night and on occasion finding that none of them were. But these were all good people with a sturdy commitment to their community and a recognition of the place of the churches in it. The same view was taken of the importance of clergy presence when a local authority elderly people's home, Oakwood House, was opened by the (Conservative) MP for Northwich Sir John Foster, a humane, scholarly (sometime fellow of All Souls) and courteous man who had served as a diplomat and was lawyer at the Nuremberg War Trials. I had friendly correspondence with him, albeit in disagreement, on such matters as arms sales to South Africa. The old people's association once a year had a kind of service-cum-tea-party in the Memorial Hall and the parish priest Albert Brookes, the Methodist minister David Le Seelleur and I were lined up on the platform and dubbed Faith, Hope and Charity (I being the youngest was Hope). Likewise I found a ready welcome in the Barnton junior and secondary schools—not just to add clerical decoration to Christmas or Harvest services but to hear the head teachers' views on what they thought their school was for in the community. They seemed surprised and gratified that anyone from outside was taking such an interest in them.

In such a community, it was inevitable that church members, certainly among the Anglicans, Baptists and Methodists, in many cases knew each other well as neighbors and workmates of long standing, indeed often having been at school together, not to mention crossing denominational barriers or transferring allegiances on marriage. As a result there was a ready-made sense of togetherness quite independent of any conscious planning to be ecumenical. There was for example an informal custom of generous inter-church loaning of choir members when on special occasions a choir needed a bit of reinforcing in one voice part or another. Over the year churches were careful to avoid clashes of dates for their major anniversaries and seasonal fairs not only to avoid competition but also to enable attendance and support at each other's festivities. Understandably this sort of relationship applied less to the Roman Catholics but Father Hoskins of Our Lady of Fatima was starting to respond, if nervously, to invitations to joint services and was warmly received especially at the annual service for the Week of Prayer for Christian Unity. For him, a priest whose formation had been long before Vatican II, this was a real step of faith. Such occasions were part of a more conscious and intentional ecumenism. Christian Aid Week collections were a regular feature. Ecumenical Lent Groups were held in 1971, Margaret being a leader of one of them. Serious consideration was given to how a former church school in Barnton might be turned into a permanent youth center for that side of Northwich as a whole. On Whit Sunday 1970 there was a joyous open air service, singing led by the Barnton brass band, on the town green. Most notably of all, during the winter of 1970–71 the Anglicans, Baptists, Methodists and Roman Catholics made a joint visitation of homes on the newest estate in Barnton, going out in denominationally mixed pairs on behalf of all the churches and finding a ready welcome on the doorsteps precisely for that reason. In short, Barnton provided me with a modest but real experience of ecumenism in practice at immediate local level. I look back on it, gratefully, with a kind of nostalgia but also with hope because it shows what *can* happen regardless how ordinary and parochial it might appear to be.

Serving the town as a whole was the Northwich Council of Churches, well organized and with strong lay as well as clerical leadership. In 1968 Bishop Kenneth Sansbury, soon to retire as general secretary of the British Council of Churches, came as speaker at its annual meeting, and fresh from the recent Fourth Assembly of the WCC at Uppsala, Sweden. I served on its committee and also as minutes secretary. Its regular meetings saw lively discussions on both local (e.g. affordable housing and youth services in the area) and wider issues (like racism). At the last meeting I attended in 1971 I proposed a resolution, which was adopted, calling on the government to address more urgently the plight of refugees from East Pakistan, welcoming its response so far but calling on it also to bring pressure on the wider international community. There was also still in existence a branch of the Free Church Federal Council (FCFC) of which I became President in 1970. But I shared the feeling that in a truly ecumenical age such an independent existence was an anachronism, and successfully pushed for it to be integrated into the Council of Churches. Another regular meeting ground was the Northwich clergy fraternal which met about monthly and included the young Roman Catholic priest Father George Brown with whom I got on well, as likely to meet him on Witton Street in the center of town, or indeed in Woolworths, as in his presbytery. One day in April 1971 my journal records:

> Called on George Brown . . . Christian Aid Week. Spent best part of 2 hours there. Talked about ecumenical relations, theology of the sacraments, celibacy, problems of ministry, etc. Showed me round the Church. Agree that ecumenical things in Northwich at moment are not using to the full the fund of goodwill there is already—e.g. fraternal not making much progress. Also 2 glasses of excellent Scotch!

Our comments reflected the way in which at levels just higher than the immediate neighborhood ecumenical relations had to be more intentionally based and required harder work. But there was no denying the stratum of good will to be exploited. There was also the sense that our ecumenical life was indeed part of a much bigger movement, as seen in the post-Vatican II excitements and the radical calls coming from the WCC. There had to be both push from the local and pull from the international levels—or from other intermediate levels. An interesting example of the latter surfaced early in 1971. I was deputed by the Lancashire and Cheshire Baptist Association to attend a consultation convened by the bishop of Chester Gerald Ellison. The bishop entertained us liberally with beef stew and beer and shared the idea being mooted by a number of dioceses in the Northern Province of the Church of England on a proposed Northern Crusade. This sounded promising if nebulous and I agreed to be the Baptist representative on the coordinating committee for the Cheshire area. There were two difficulties to be addressed. One was the need to define the aims more clearly. The other, related to that and which was for some months to prove very problematic, was to get the Anglicans to see that if this was indeed intended to be ecumenical they couldn't just expect other denominations to jump on board a bus whose destination and route they had had no part in deciding—a besetting Anglican sin, I fear. Some rather heated discussions on the coordinating group ensued but to good effect. The arrival on the scene of Francis House, archdeacon of Macclesfield, former religious broadcaster and seasoned international ecumenist (for some time associate general secretary of the WCC) helped to improve matters greatly. By the time I left in late 1971 what was in view for "Call to the North", as it was now called, was certainly a much more inclusive and participatory programme both to renew the life of the churches and open their doors to the outer world, and I heard good reports afterwards of some results of this locally, at least in Cheshire.

ECUMENICAL SET-BACKS

There was no mistaking the ecumenical buzz around at that time, much of it lay-led and inspired and certainly encouraged by many church leaders. But there were also questions on unity to be faced at denominational level, and for us Baptists that meant dealing with the report *Baptists and Unity* which, as I said in the previous chapter, I regarded as a dispiriting response by the Baptist Union to the 1964 Nottingham proposals for a united church if possible by 1980. The MCF discussed this fully at a Sunday afternoon conference including members of the Runcorn RIBS group. Obviously one could only expect a wide variety of views from any cross-section of Baptist opinion at local level, and I was slightly surprised when Clifford Cleal himself took me aside beforehand to warn me that his own opinion was likely to be less critical than my own, and that the BU Council had probably gone as far as could reasonably be expected. My own view was that that might be true of the BU Council as such, but the report itself might at least have suggested various much more positive options to that of merely treading water. But I was pleasantly taken aback by the scorn with which key parts of the report were met by some in the gathering, most of all the report's expression of fear lest denominational unity be imperiled. "Chicken!" shouted Ron Jones, one of the most respected members of Little Leigh, who had come from Methodist upbringing, and had newly taken on the secretaryship of the MCF. One of the Runcorn members. Andrew Stunell, whose later career took him into politics (he became a Liberal Democrat MP, was a junior minister in the 2010–15 coalition government and is now a member of the House of Lords), declared caustically "This 'denominational unity' is a *myth*." Our submission, as I recall, tried to reflect these views as well as more cautious ones but the final Baptist debate took place at the Baptist Union Assembly in May 1969. Some conservative voices called for the report to be referred back, and some moderate voices asked for more light than heat on the issue of unity. But the sharpest voices were those dissatisfied with caution, above all Michael Taylor, minister of Hall Green, Birmingham and about to become principal of the Northern Baptist College. He spoke for the disappointed among us: "Are we as Baptists going to continue in the mainstream of Christianity or are we going to opt out into a backwater?" The report, he said was "an exercise in offending no one and maintaining the *status quo*. . . . We have talked for five years and changed nothing . . . We seem to be paralyzed by fear."[3] Hear, hear.

As an attempt to respond to this and other challenges in the denomination there was formed the Baptist Renewal Group (BRG), its prime movers being Michael Taylor, Robert Brown of Coventry and Roger Nunn, youth secretary of the British Council of Churches. The BRG certainly provided for some years a good meeting place, both at its autumn conferences and its entertaining fringe meetings during the Baptist Assembly, for the ecumenically and radically minded among us. But it (or we) never really solved the problem that it was one thing not to care about dividing the denomination but quite another nevertheless to influence the denomination in the desired direction. Almost inevitably BRG became an in-group for the likeminded with little wider impact. The same went for the umbrella grouping for similar bodies in all denominations, One for Renewal, which, again, provided useful support for the elect but was ignored by the churches at large. Further, by the later 1970s the term "renewal" had been virtually hijacked by the burgeoning charismatic and newer evangelical movements. A new kind of sectarianism was creeping in from all sides

The sharpest body-blow to ecumenical hopes, however, came in 1969 with the failure of the scheme for Anglican-Methodist reunion. Or more precisely, its rejection by the Church of England; more precisely still, the failure in the Church Assembly by the House of *Clergy* (in contrast to the bishops and laity) to approve the scheme by the required majority. The fateful votes were taken on July 8. The Methodist Conference approved the scheme. The Anglican answer to nearly twenty years of study and discussion and, more recently, formulae worked out with great care and sensitivity, was a shock and a disappointment to most (though not all of course) Methodists. One society steward in Northwich, the day afterwards, told me it felt like being jilted at the altar. The pain was no less among many Anglicans, not least the archbishop of Canterbury Michael Ramsey. My Cambridge Methodist friend David Carter later told me that the father of a close Anglo-Catholic friend at King's, himself a noted high churchman and theologian, instructed his son in no uncertain terms that as a matter of *duty* he should at the first opportunity attend a Methodist communion service with David and receive the sacrament with him, so ashamed was he that the Anglicans had spurned the sincere

---

3. *Baptist Times* May 8 1969.

and far-reaching Methodist moves to accommodate Anglican wishes on episcopal ordination. So too, by implication if not association, all ecumenically minded people in the other Free Churches were likewise brushed aside. The impression was received that conservative forces in the Church of England, high or low, would brook no change regardless of the wider Christian fellowship and the needs of a changing English society. That was demoralizing. But the ecumenical buzz was not wholly quietened, not even when the scheme was again rejected by the General Synod in 1972. There were too many ecumenicals in all the churches for the spirit to be quenched completely.

EXEMPLARS OF RECONCILIATION

There was another kind of experience which gave me hope, and still gives me hope as I look back to that time. Not only was much of the ecumenical enthusiasm of that time lay-led, but the heart of what it means to be ecumenical was often shown by so-called ordinary lay people in their very personal attitudes and actions, and from these I learnt a good deal. I give three examples, the first two being associated with tragedy.

First, Harold and Amy Riding, members at Anderton, almost at retiring age when we arrived there. Harold was a vehicle painter at the ICI Winnington works, with a forbidding face like crumpled steel. A strong-minded man, he was once sent to Coventry by his union for disagreeing with a strike call, but volunteered to take on the unpopular job of sick-visitor for union members, so in the end they had to talk to him again. Usually he had a cigarette in his mouth which meant he was typically last into church before the service began, and first out afterwards. I don't remember ever seeing a book in the Ridings' home but what they knew was worth a whole library, for they had a remarkable story to tell. I had heard it from several people but once morning heard it from Harold himself one snowy morning as we waited, shivering, for a building surveyor to turn up at the Anderton chapel. Harold and Amy had had two sons, and the older one was killed in the Second World War. A navigator in the Fleet Air Arm, he was lost in an attack on the huge German battleship the *Tirpitz*. Harold said that when he received the dreaded telegram he was so smitten with grief and anger that he swore that the first German he met, he would break his neck. May 1945 came and therewith not only the end of the war in Europe but, at least as important to a Baptist chapel in the north of England, the Anderton Sunday school anniversary. That Sunday afternoon Harold was standing outside the chapel door, no doubt finishing off his fag, as children in their Sunday best and proud parents and grandparents were turning up. Two young men in drab uniforms also wandered up, asking in thick accents and broken English what was happening here? "Children's service—singing—come on in!" Harold replied, before he realized what he was saying. These were his first Germans, now let out from the nearby prisoner of war camp at Marbury. He had broken not their necks but his own vow, and invited them into his church. Having been told about the youth fellowship they turned up again one weeknight evening soon after, bringing some others from the camp, and beating everyone roundly at table tennis. Soon the news was going round Barnton: Harold and Amy were the first in the village to have these German lads round to tea, sitting at the same table where their own lost son had sat. Harry told all this without any sense of virtue, rather a sense of wonder that it had simply happened, inexplicably, graciously on both sides. He discovered that one of the Germans, Siegmund, belonged to a Baptist church in Dortmund. I reflected that just over a month before that first encounter, Dietrich Bonhoeffer on the day before he was executed gave a message to an English fellow-prisoner for his friend George Bell, bishop of Chichester, assuring him that he still believed in the reality of the international Christian fellowship that rises above all national conflicts and interests, and that "our victory is certain". That did not need to wait for high-level conferences and sophisticated theological debate, it was already being put into practice by the Harolds and Amys and Siegmunds of this world. In fact the friendship continued long after the war, with mutual visits between Dortmund and Northwich, down to the generation of grandchildren and, as far as I know, the links continue still. This kind of thing happened many times just after the war, as Jürgen Moltmann for example movingly testifies from his own experience as a young and bereft prisoner of war kindly treated by Scottish mining families.[4]

    The second instance arose in the context of perhaps the most tragic event of our time in Mid-Cheshire. One evening early in May 1970 Rebecca, the six year-old daughter of one of our Little Leigh families who lived in Weaverham, died suddenly at home in a choking fit while suffering tonsillitis. I need not recount the desolation I had to sit with in their home late that night, nor my foreboding as next morning I drove out to Little Leigh to inform the grandparents. Seeing in the distance the small house I was approaching, it I felt like I was a bomber pilot about to shatter and destroy the peace and happiness of that home which would never be the same again. So it proved, and the grief was felt by the whole church fellowship. It was Ascension Day and it was the Little Leigh Baptists' turn to host that evening the annual united service for all the Barnton and Little Leigh churches. The prayers of intercession were taken by the vicar of Barnton, Albert Brookes. Of course he had been informed of the tragedy and included prayers for Rebeca's family, but he went further and concluded with a prayer for Rebecca herself using the wording of the traditional requiem: *Grant her eternal rest O lord, and let light eternal shine upon her*. I wondered how some of our folk, inured against "Catholic" practice such as praying for the dead, would react to this—I would scarcely have dared to use it myself. Yet after the service it was Barbara, farmer's wife, mother of three herself and the most decidedly evangelical of all the Little Leigh members, who came up to the vicar, tears in her eyes and grasping him by the hand, to say "Thank you for your beautiful prayer". There are occasions of crisis and need to which only certain words are adequate, regardless of their source, and they leap like electric arcs across traditional boundaries—and thereby relativize those divides.

    4. See Moltmann, *A Broad Place*, chapter 3.

The third was on one of the two occasions when the MCF linked up with the Baptist church in Moss Side, Manchester, and hosted a camping weekend for the young people of both fellowships at Brassey Green, the picturesque site of a very old but not totally disused chapel. Much of the practical work at our end fell to the Tarporley church and its members were encouraged to help and welcome the Moss Side visitors who included young Afro-Carribbeans. I was a bit nervous about how one prominent member at Tarporley, the organist in fact, would react. He was of uncertain temperament, prone to complain about Clifford Cleal's preaching (and mine) whenever we ventured onto social topics including race relations. Yet when the visitors actually arrived, no-one was more eager and delighted than he to show them around and take them out to enjoy more of the beauties of the Cheshire countryside in his car, and even (I think) to join in the football match with them. "Really?" exclaimed Rene Cleal in disbelief when I told her, "Bless him!"

These, too, are the kinds of memories of Cheshire on which I look back in hope whenever I think of the ecumenical future. Things can happen in actual meeting which don't always happen in meetings.

PUBLIC ISSUES

There was no shortage of issues, at home and on the world scene, to tax the alert Christian mind during these years. The Cheshire foot and mouth crisis itself, as well as its human costs challenged us to think of suffering afflicting the whole created order. Then what a year was 1968: the assassination of Martin Luther King; Enoch Powell's speeches on immigration; student revolutions at home and abroad; the papal Encyclical on birth control *Humanae Vitae*; and the Soviet invasion of Czechoslovakia dashing the hopes of the Prague Spring. Then too, there was the 1967–70 Biafran war with its resultant humanitarian crisis, and the continuing devastation in Vietnam spilling over into Cambodia. At home there was yet more industrial unrest, among power workers (resulting in some electricity cuts), postal workers, newspaper workers, and refuse collectors among others. British accession to the Common Market was on the agenda again. In 1970 we faced a general election. The pages of *Neighbours* were full of comment and discussion on these topics. Equally, Clifford Cleal and I did not shy away from them in our sermons, provoking both agreement and argument at times.

Of particular relevance to the Cheshire context was the whole question of conservation and farming (including fair prices for farmers), and its relation to industry and town and country planning. But the environmental movement as a whole was only just coming onto the wider public agenda, thanks to such pioneering works as Rachel Carson's *Silent Spring* (1962) and the widening appeal of the World Wildlife Fund (as it was then called). Margaret and I, still with our respective enthusiasms for botany and bird-watching intact, joined the Cheshire Conservation Trust of which Jean Walley at Tarporley, with a her professional biological interest, was a keen advocate. In fact I found in the Fellowship as a whole that the human relation to the environment touched a nerve more than any other public issue. For the harvest festival at Anderton in 1970, including the children's afternoon service, I culled from my own biology days an illustrated talk on "what makes beans grow—or not"; and then in the evening preached on the dangers of idolizing technology for its own sake. I had more firm handshakes of gratitude than I can ever recall before then.

On the international scene it was South Africa which, as it did for so many others, focused most of my attention not least, as I have mentioned, the question of arms sales to the apartheid regime, and its use of the Simonstown naval base. Friends who had gone to work in Uganda reinforced our concern when they told us of the effect of British policy on opinion in that country and elsewhere in Africa. But the issue of apartheid came closest to home in the sporting arena and above all on the cricket pitch. The matter became very controversial in 1968 when Basil D'OIiveira, South African born "Cape Colored" but naturalized British citizen, although an obvious choice for the English squad due to tour South Africa the following winter was excluded by the MCC[5] selectors evidently in order not to cause offence to the South African authorities and its rigorous policy of racially segregated sport. There was uproar in much of the British media, and David Sheppard, notable test cricketer himself, now an Anglican priest in east London and about to become bishop of Woolwich, led a spirited through unsuccessful protest at a special meeting of the MCC itself. But when Tom Cartwright of Worcestershire had to withdraw from the squad through injury the selectors had no option but to include D'OIiveira. The South African Government declared this unacceptable and the tour was cancelled. In 1970 the South Africans were due to tour England and by now for many in this country apartheid in sport represented if not the most serious then the ugliest face of apartheid, and widespread protests were building up led by ex-South African Peter Hain and his Stop the Tour Campaign. Serious disruption was threatened by some. Of course there were other views, including the ridiculous notion that objectors were "bringing politics into sport" as if that had not already been done by the apartheid regime. All this coincided with the continuing concern over helicopter sales to the South African government, not to mention the slow process on Rhodesia. The whole issue of southern Africa spilled into Baptist quarters in the spring of 1970. At its meeting in April 1970, the BU Council decided that there would be no public resolution on South Africa at the forthcoming Assembly, merely one couched in the blandest terms about "great concern at the continuation of political and religious liberty in so many parts of the world" and disquiet at "discrimination of color, race, nationality and religion". Ernest Payne, now three years out of office as general secretary but still forceful when roused, had proposed a special resolution on South Africa but to no avail. When the Assembly met in May, the President Sir Cyril Black, Conservative MP for Wimbledon, remained adamant in

---

5. The MCC (Marylebone Cricket Club) was until the early 1980s the governing body of English cricket.

not accepting any further motions. I joined in cat-calls from the gallery. Sitting next to me was Norman Fairburn, another minister from the North West, who jumped up shouting "If the Baptist Union has nothing to say about apartheid it has nothing to say at all!" It was evident that many abstained from voting, or voted for the main resolution out of sheer frustration that anything said was better than nothing. That I felt was a dubious line to take and with others left before the vote was taken. Coming out of Westminster Chapel I bumped into Gordon Hastings, minister of the prestigious Sutton Baptist Church, who was muttering angrily, "Damn shambles! Damn shambles!" Matters did not quite end there, however, and the controversy over the cricket tour spilled into the *Baptist Times*. One correspondent urged Baptists to *support* the tour financially. I replied:

> Far from paying towards the expenses of a tour to which they are opposed, many Baptists will want to do something definite, if small, to show their opposition to apartheid and all its works, including racially segregated cricket. I would therefore commend Baptists to support Linton house, which is being built by the North West Baptist Housing association in Manchester to accommodate needy overseas students, particularly married couples. Those opposed to the tour could send a donation, say the price of a day spent at a test match, or more—and encourage others to do the same.[6]

Norman Jones, area superintendent for the north-west, told me that quite a bit of money did come in. As it happened, the tour was called off before the end of May. Later in the summer of 1970 the issue of racism in Africa boiled up still further with the controversial decision by the WCC, as part of its new Programme to Combat Racism (PCR) to commit part of its Special Fund in support of the non-military and humanitarian work of liberation movements in Southern Africa. There were lively arguments at all levels in the British churches, even in the Northwich fraternal. In *Neighbours* I tried to put the case for the WCC action in as measured a way as possible in face of all the understandable misgivings or objections to it.

FAMILY, FRIENDS, FUN AND LEISURE

Mid-Cheshire was not all work and no play. Margaret and I enjoyed the Cheshire countryside, and the proximity of Chester, Liverpool (especially for the Liverpool Philharmonic and a marvelous Chinese Restaurant, the Yuet Ben) and Manchester. We holidayed mostly in the Yorkshire Dales and Scotland, but in 1969 with some other Baptists went on a glorious two week package tour, of Italy including Florence, Rome, Venice, Pisa and Assisi. Most of our family circle remained in easy reach of Northwich: my parents at Wallasey until 1969 (also enabling convenient overnighting at times for Margaret when winter weather disrupted travel to and from Port Sunlight), Margaret's

6. *Baptist Times* May 21 1970.

parents at Chesterfield just over the Cat and Fiddle pass, my next eldest brother Brian and his family at Chorley, and Margaret's sister Kate and her husband Philip, both now social workers and living near Wolverhampton. Then one day in April 1969 my parents turned up unexpectedly at Barnton bursting with the news that they were moving. We knew that for a year or more they had been looking for a new pastorate and that many ministers coming within sight of retirement age had increasingly difficult prospects. But this was different and their excitement knew no bounds for they were moving to Sri Lanka (or Ceylon as it was still called then). My father had been offered and accepted an appointment to take charge of the Baptist Missionary Society field office in Colombo, effectively to see to the transfer of all BMS properties to the Sri Lanka Baptist Union, in itself the arrangement proper to an age of partnership rather than patronage in mission, but which would also ensure that this could be done before the Sri Lankan government made any moves to expropriate all foreign assets. The opportunity to take on another overseas post, twenty-five years after the return from China, gave them a new lease of life. They flew out to Colombo in July that year.

Of course, too, we made friends in Mid-Cheshire itself both with older folk and people of our own age, and from the Runcorn group, with some of whom we are still in touch. Above all, we got to know Michael (Mike) and Elizabeth (Liz) Jackson of Winsford, just slightly older than us. Mike had come fresh from the Northern Congregational College to the pastorate of Over Congregational Church a year before we arrived, and their wedding had been just two weeks' before ours. Both were Manchester theological graduates and Liz was now a lecturer at Crewe Teacher Training College. We instantly struck a rapport which is as strong today as ever, made up of mutual sympathy, confiding in difficulties and frustrations and much laughter and mutual hospitality. We were also able to keep up with a good number of Cambridge friends including Chris and Robert Bradnock, and wedding invitations were a source of joy. We were much blessed.

STUDIES

For all his activist bent Clifford Cleal insisted that I should maintain my studies and keep open the possibility of an academic future. I continued to read widely. Chester had an excellent Students' Library with a well-stocked theological section. Margaret groaned slightly whenever she arrived home to see another volume of Karl Barth on the table. But I also dug into Jürgen Moltmann, John Macquarie, P. T. Forsyth and T. F. Torrance whose address at the Baptist Assembly in 1968 greatly impressed me with its argument that Jesus' vicarious action included being *believer* on our behalf—an elements of reformed theology that had never struck me before. I also started reading for the first time the Scottish theologian Ronald Gregor Smith, prompted in part by the news of his untimely death in 1968, partly because he was known to be a major advocate and interpreter of Bonhoeffer, and partly because I had read both approval and disapproval of him in the secular theology debates. In his *Secular Christianity* and *The Free Man* I indeed found much emphasis on the secular but, in contrast to other radicals, an apprehension of the *mystery* that confronts us in the midst of human relationships. This interest in Gregor Smith was to come to full blossom a few years later.

But meanwhile it was church history that continued to appeal to me, and I wondered whether this area might provide a topic on which I could write a thesis. On my last day at Regent's Park in 1967 I had had a last browse round the college library and came across the bound editions of the *Baptist Times* of 1914. I turned to the editions that had come out at the onset of war, and was immediately arrested. Here was a living account of the shock and horror that war had brought in August 1914 and of how in the subsequent weeks the churches of all denominations had tried to respond ethically and theologically to it. I determined that this would be my first subject for original research—very little had been written on it so far. For much of my time in Cheshire therefore, whenever opportunity allowed whether at Oxford or in the library at Baptist Church House in London, I would pore over these back numbers. I gradually came to the conclusion that Baptists, like most others, for all their pre-war pacifism or near-pacifism, had joined in the war initially on moral grounds because of German violation of Belgian neutrality, and thereafter were sucked into the overall commitment to the war effort come what way.. But it also led me into studying more of the pre-1914 background of the churches' peace movement, especially the exchange visits and joint councils set up by the British and German churches in 1908–09, an interesting and little-regarded part of the genesis of the modern ecumenical movement. And of course all this chimed in well with my current interests in the international scene. To this must be added that Ernest Payne, with whom I talked at the BRG conference in December 1968, expressed his personal interest in my project. Just how encouraging he was emerged a few weeks' later when he wrote to me saying that he had obtained for me a handsome grant from the Dr Williams Trust for the purchase of relevant books.

My interest in Bonhoeffer continued, and was given a boost in a quite unexpected way. One day in March 1970 Clifford Cleal phoned to say that he had been due to speak at a weeknight devotional meeting at the Methodist church in Kelsall, a little village on the edge of Delamere Forest between Northwich and Chester, but was having to cry off at short notice, and could I go instead? In fact he'd already told the church that I would go if free, and that I would speak about young people and especially students today. I suppose I was not too pleased at this confidence thus placed in me, but as I did happen to be free that night I agreed to go. I found a gathering comprizing the minister John Wright, who was nearing retirement, and no more than eight or so mainly elderly people, and wondered whether this outing really was really worth the time and effort. But I duly spoke on what I knew and thought about contemporary student attitudes, protests and demonstrations and the like, and what lay behind them. I concluded by remarking that the real question for all of us in society was what we meant by freedom, and read out Bonhoeffer's poem written in in prison, "Stations on the Way to Freedom". Mr Wright rose to thank me for my talk, and then mused about my reference to Bonhoeffer—"*the man of our time*", he said, and proceeded to tell an astonishing story. Reflecting on how memory lapses over time, he told us that when moving house a few years earlier he had come across a notebook which he had used as a daily journal while a student at Richmond College in London in the early 1930s. He was astonished to read of things he had long completely forgotten, and no more so than when he read of one day in 1934, when they had had a had a visit from a young German theologian and pastor, Dr Dietrich Bonhoeffer, who had given the students a splendid talk on Karl Barth's theology and the situation of the church in Nazi Germany. John Wright had himself acted as the visitor's host and guide round the college. Only now had there come back to him the picture of this very polite, softly spoken young German with ruddy face and fair hair. A few weeks after my visit to Kelsall there appeared the English edition of Eberhard Bethge's monumental biography of Bonhoeffer, which I quickly read. Bethge gave some account of Bonhoeffer's visit to Richmond College during his time as German pastor in London. I wrote to John Wright mentioning this, and in turn he sent me not only his full diary record of that now-memorable day, but his notes on the lecture that Bonhoeffer gave. It was an astonishing discovery. The notes lay in my files for some time, but in due course they were to prove my entry ticket to the circle of serious Bonhoeffer studies including a personal acquaintance with Eberhard Bethge, and eventually found their way into the new edition of all Bonhoeffer's works. And all because I did agree to take on a seemingly unpromising weeknight engagement in a tiny Methodist chapel on the edge of Delamere Forest.

MOVING ON

By mid-1970 I was beginning to look for pastures new. Clifford Cleal himself was reaching retiring age (in fact he remained part-time at Tarporley until 1972) and I believed that the primary need was for me to make way before long for a more experienced but still energetic pastor to lead the Fellowship. My future direction though was not entirely clear. Should it after all be with the missionary society overseas? I had several more conversations with the BMS but nothing suitable seemed to be in the offing. Meanwhile I was still hoping for the opportunity for some concerted postgraduate academic work but not as a full-time student. I was in fact coming late to writing, and had not so far tried to publish anything in any journal, beyond a sermon in the *Expository Times* based on the calling of Moses, drawing parallels between his youthful (and violent) protest against the oppression of his fellow Israelites and youth's protests against injustice today, and how God calls the protestor into his own project of liberation.[7] Through late 1970 and early 1971 Margaret and I considered a number of churches looking for a new minister. None seemed to gel on either side: some were

---

7. Clements, "God's Concern".

very pleasant and were genuinely hopeful of my acceptance but it was never clear to us what they were looking for in me. Others were not interested, as was their right, or were actively hostile. In one case the thought of a minster's wife being a working woman (as distinct from unpaid curate) was unthinkable. In another, a church in Sheffield to which I had been inexplicably (and unfairly both for me and the church) commended by the then area superintendent for the North East, my admission of readiness to cooperate with Roman Catholics put a full stop to the conversation.

At the Baptist Assembly of 1971, marked by Principal Michael Taylor's controversial address "How Much of a Man was Jesus Christ?" which stirred up a Baptist storm for the next two years or more, I was among the newly accredited ministers presented to the incoming President who was none other than Henton Davies. Regent's men received from him a commendatory hand on the shoulder (a second blessing?) as well as a handshake. At the end of that meeting Clifford Cleal came up to me to say that he had just spoken to one Jack Knight, secretary of the Downend church in Bristol, whom he had known for some years and whom he had once accompanied to Bossey for an ecumenical lay conference there, and that my name had been sent to the church. At once this sounded more interesting. Indeed it so proved. Later in May I went to meet a gathering of deacons and representative members at Downend, following which Margaret and I spent a weekend there in June and I preached with a view. A strong call came from the church meeting, and having finally heard "nothing doing" from the BMS, readily accepted. What really appealed about the church was its embrace of a wide range of views, an accepting sense of fellowship and, particularly, an imaginative approach to both Junior Church and adult educational work, and willingness to experiment in worship. Moreover, Bristol itself appealed, with its reputation as the most ecumenical city on the country, and with both a university and a Baptist college a most promising context for academic interests. We would move in November. This would of course mean Margaret leaving Unilever.

The main task to be carried out before then was the completion and opening of the new Anderton building, for which I was effectively acting as clerk of works and which meant a lot of blood, sweat and (almost) tears to meet the opening date, already once postponed, of October 3. It was a joyful event, and deeply gratifying in that many came from all the other churches in Barnton, and all the other clergy too. The press photograph shows Father Hoskins in the group at the church door, looking much more at home than on his first visit to a united service three years earlier. A crowning gem to the day was the arrival of a card of greetings and prayerful good wishes from the St Nicolas Church, Dortmund, sent via Harold and Amy Riding's fiend Siegmund, inscribed with the text Second Corinthians 5:17, "So if anyone is in Christ, there is a new creation . . . " How apt, not only for a church embarking on a new venture, but for the recollection of that story of how at Anderton twenty-five years earlier a new creation was born through hospitality and reconciliation.

That evening Margaret and I went out to Liverpool to celebrate in the Yuet Ben restaurant. We had additional cause for happiness at a new creation. That morning we had received confirmation that Margaret was pregnant. Our first child would be on the way with us to Bristol.

My final and farewell Fellowship service was, appropriately, at Anderton on October 31. Bearing in mind my misgivings four years earlier I preached on the story of Jesus reaching out to Peter who was fearfully sinking in the waves: "You of little faith, why did you doubt?" (Matthew 14:31). I have said enough, I hope, to convey what I gained from the time in Mid-Cheshire. How did the folk estimate me? Comments in *Neighbours* included:

> My first impression was, "He's just a boy, the responsibility will be too much for him". During these years K.C. has proved how wrong I was. The minister who looked "just a boy" has proved himself capable of carrying out his duties with a strength of purpose that belies his years. In four years Minister and Congregations have learnt quite a lot from one another. If we have learned well, then we shall be a stronger Fellowship of Churches and K.C. will leave us a better minister.

And:

> We appreciate all the help he has given us in various ways. We do thank Mr Clements and his wife for the very happy fellowship we have shared with them. It is not possible to say that *all* his sermons have been appreciated by *all* the congregation, but we feel but we feel sure there has been a message for someone each and every time he has spoken.

Graciousness and honesty—what more could one wish for as a Godspeed?

5

In the Most Ecumenical City: Downend, Bristol

DOWNEND, ORIGINALLY A VILLAGE in south Gloucestershire, was by the early twentieth century effectively a residential suburb of Bristol on the north-east fringe of the city. Its chief claim to historical fame lay in being the birthplace in 1848 of the giant of English cricket, W. G. Grace. Downend House in which he was born still stands today, appropriately renamed Grace House. Directly opposite on Salisbury Road stands what must have been the first building the young W. G. would have seen each morning—the Baptist chapel dating from 1786, founded by Caleb Evans, Welsh preacher, minister of Broadmead Baptist Church in the center of Bristol, principal of the Bristol Academy for educating future ministers, and slave-trade abolitionist. By now seamlessly part of the north-eastern Bristol sprawl and subsumed with its neighbor Mangotsfield under Mangotsfield Urban District, Downend nevertheless retained something of its village character, certainly as far as attitudes went.

My predecessor at Downend, Bill Dixon, had after ten years of solid pastoral ministry left a congregation of just over one hundred church members, plus children, young people and other attenders. Like Jack Knight the church secretary and his family, a good number hailed from South Wales having come over shortly before the Second World War to work in the burgeoning aircraft industry at Filton and Patchway, where respectively the British Aircraft Corporation and the Rolls Royce aero division were now located. Their prize achievement was the supersonic Concord which made its maiden flight in 1969 and was being produced in numbers to enter service in 1976. As well as the aircraft-related people we had a wide variety of professions and trades represented in the congregation including teachers (John Bacon, for example, church treasurer, was head of a junior school), health professionals, and workers in the construction and retail industries and insurance companies. Ken Jessop, chief planning officer for Chipping Sodbury in South Gloucestershire was a member. There was one farming family, witnessing to just how close Downend still lay to the northern green belt. And of course we had a sizeable number of retired and elderly people. Margaret and I felt very welcome. Not least the news soon went round that we would in a few months be not two, but three, in the manse.

We were very soon relishing much that Bristol as a city had to offer, too, with its music, theatre, libraries and shopping, as well as its good communications and proximity to some of the most beautiful countryside in the West Country and Wales. As far as being the most ecumenical city in England was concerned, this was certainly an attraction but for a time a matter of reputation rather than actual experience for me. On arrival I knew personally none of the chief actors, preeminent among whom was Oliver Tomkins, bishop of Bristol since 1953, formerly associate general secretary of the WCC and then successively secretary and chairman of the Commission on Faith and Order. Rupert Davies, principal of Wesley College and leading Methodist ecumenist, I had once heard speak in Cambridge on the ecumenical movement. Leonard Champion, about to retire as principal of the Baptist College, had been a member of the Faith and Order Commission as was Morris West who had just arrived as his successor, and both of whom I had also speak at student gatherings. But I had not made personal acquaintance with any of these and initially theirs was a level of ecumenical activity beyond my reach. But Bristol ecumenism was also manifest at local levels. Following the 1964 Nottingham Faith and Order Conference there began the process of setting up local Areas of Ecumenical Experiment (AEEs), later to be termed Local Ecumenical Partnerships (LEPs), enabling congregations of different denominations to cooperate in the sharing of ministries, buildings and as much common life as possible. The area covered by the diocese of Bristol soon had more AEEs than anywhere else in the country—owing a lot, it was felt, to Oliver Tomkins's personal leadership. The Downend area had no AEE within it, but the Mangotsfield and District Council of Churches (MDCC) was very active with good cooperation between Anglicans, Baptists, Methodists, Roman Catholics and the Salvation Army. The Methodists were especially heavily involved, and among the new friends made were Jean and James Hanmer, schoolteachers and members of the Staple Hill Methodist Church, who were outstanding alike for their commitment, vision and creativity in mobilizing the churches towards a more prophetic role in the community. Likewise Arthur Milroy, vicar of Downend, accepted me as a (younger) brother in Christ from the word go, and I was very sorry that he moved away to Derby soon afterwards. But Ray Price at Mangotsfield proved a most valuable and supportive colleague, not least in 1975 when the new vicar of Downend made an extraordinarily virulent attack on the annual united service of the MDCC which, as president for that year, I had largely devised and at which I preached.

DOWNEND BAPTIST CHURCH

I find it hard to imagine how any minister could not have been fundamentally happy to be pastor at Downend during those years. It was a fellowship of quite diverse (and in some cases very strong) personalities and manifesting a wide spectrum of theological outlook. As in any community there were some grumblers but overall it was imbued with a generosity of spirit. People who took themselves too seriously or self-pityingly were liable to be cut down to size with shafts of humor. Jack Knight the secretary, I felt, typified the best in the Free Church layperson of his generation: deeply devoted to his church and giving of his best to its administration; committed also to the wider scene both in the Bristol Baptist Association and the Free Church Council, and the ecumenical area generally; and not least, out of his experience at the Rolls Royce works, taking seriously the role of Christian laypeople in industry. He could be argumentative and stubborn but was never incapable of final persuasion, and he usually could smile at the end of the day (or argument). Our relationship with one another was central to my work there. Also essential to the work of the church was Phyllis Thomas ("Mrs T") whose official role was that of caretaker, but in the best sense in fact took care of just about everything that took place on the premises, not least the youth club. I gave as much as I believed I could to pastoral work, worship and preaching. One of the best things about the church was its outward-looking character, as could be seen in the items in the monthly church magazine, covering everything from news from the Baptist Missionary Society, to Vietnam, to the needs of Ugandan Asian refugees (we had a collection of urgently needed items for such families), and to reports on ecumenical matters both locally and nationally. Twice the youth leaders organized a week-long summer holiday club for young people from Bill Dixon's church at Small Heath, Birmingham. The young people themselves in 1972 joined in the "Green Sabbath" promoted by the Baptist Union Youth Department to raise awareness about world poverty, involving a twenty-four hour fast and some street drama outside the shops in Downend. Our worship likewise often reflected concern for the wider world, especially on Sunday evenings when we had a series on social issues including alcoholism, juvenile delinquency, and Christians in Parliament (with a local MP). For one such service on race relations we invited Carmen Beckford, Afro-Caribbean chair of the Bristol Community Relations Council to speak. Not finding any hymns in our hymn book which adequately reflected this concern in a contemporary way I set about writing one myself, "Father of glory, whose heavenly plan". In due course it found its way into the hymn book supplement *Praise for Today* (1974) and then in revised form (by then more inclusive language was the order of the day) in *Baptist Praise and Worship* (1991). But whenever I hear it sung today it is still with a twinge of regret. We lost one family from the congregation that night. The father was a police officer and they had been upset by the speaker's comments on police attitudes to young blacks in Bristol. I could not persuade them to return (though they did, apparently, after I left Downend). For me the high points each year were the all-age festival services we arranged at Easter, Harvest Thanksgiving and Christmas in which children, youth and adults could take part and celebrate on equal terms whether using material supplied by the British Lessons Council or of our own devising. For two of the Christmas occasions I wrote a play. So I was not short of attempts at creativity.

 The safe arrival of our first child Peter in May 1972 was a thrill not just for Margaret and myself but for the whole church family. My parents having returned home from Sri Lanka in April that year, my father was able to conduct the service of infant dedication. For Margaret herself the move from Cheshire and into maternity meant the transition from paid employment and it was not easy. Keeping the peace among the factions of the women's organizations in the church and keeping the youth club accounts made for an occupation but not a compensation. For a while she took on some part-time maths coaching. Then in 1974 came a welcome change when she became a tutor in maths with the Open University—a post which she maintained for the next forty-one years—and not long after also began lecturing in statistics on courses for local authority weights and measures inspectors. All this also of course provided some extra income, but these years were the most financially straitened of our lives. Some health issues also arose for Margaret, resulting in three stays in in hospital during our time at Downend. We insisted on regular although not frequent theatre and concert outings for ourselves, but holidays were mainly shoe-string weeks in a rented cottage with Margaret's parents, or in a seaside home or caravan kindly loaned us by cousins or church members. And like everyone else, we had to cope with power-cuts in the early months of 1972, and the miseries of the three-day week in 1973 which affected church activity too.

A SIGNIFICANT YEAR: WRITING AND LAY EDUCATION

In addition to Peter's birth, the year 1972 opened up a quite new and unexpected horizon. In the first place it saw my first serious and successful attempt at getting into theological print. My work on the churches and the First World War which had occupied me during our time in Mid-Cheshire, had also given me food for thought on some wider theological issues. Since the mid-1960s there was a vogue among theologians of "secular" bent to speak of God being "at work in the world" and the role of Christians and churches as being to share in that work. Thus Harvey Cox in his best-selling *The Secular City* (1966): "The Church is first of all a responding community, a people whose task it is to discern the action of God in the world and to join in His work."[1] This was a very appealing mode of theology, but it seemed to me to be rather redolent of much of the preaching of pre-1914 liberal Protestants who saw the hand of God in the progressive movements of civilization, peace-building and extensions of freedom over the globe. But had not such optimistic theology at times been guilty of virtually identifying God with human progress (above all in the ill-fated "New Theology" of R. J. Campbell)? And had it not been dealt a death-blow by the catastrophe of 1914–18? Was not therefore a similar judgment likely to fall on contemporary secular theology? I wrote an essay on this question, "God at Work in the World: Old Liberal and New Secular Theology", which was published in the *Baptist Quarterly* for July 1972. I argued that the more discerning of both the old liberals and the current secular

---

1. Cox, *The Secular City*, 105.

theologians did maintain the theological distinction between God and the world. The real mistake of the old liberals, and potentially that of their contemporary counterparts, lay elsewhere: "If our theology claims to take the world seriously, *then it must do precisely that*. We must look at the world as it is. The uncomfortable complexities must be faced, and not short-circuited by a superficial moralizing of the situation (let alone theologizing)".[2] I drew attention to Alan Booth's warning that, in international relationships, to moralize about a situation of conflict rarely contributes to a solution and that in a curious way the task of moral earnestness is "to deflate the moral pretensions of nations as a contribution to peace"[3]. It might, I suggested, be claimed that the caution and humility to which the truly secular style drives the Christian could be the type of reverence for today. Looking back on the article from more than 40 years of experience, I think I now understand more fully what I wrote then.

Second, as far as the primary subject of Baptists and the First World War was concerned, I had by this time virtually completed as much research and reading as I had wanted to do. I gave a paper, "Baptists and the Outbreak of the First World War" at a Baptist Historical Society summer school in 1974. Earnest Payne was laudatory ("Well worth waiting for!"), it was published in the *Baptist Quarterly* in 1975 and ere long references to it were appearing in other and weightier studies on the churches and that conflict, which was very gratifying. Much more has been written on the subject since then but I still think of it as a useful contribution in the field, and one that provided me with a good deal of the intellectual equipment for engaging with international affairs and conflict later on.

During the Baptist Assembly meetings in London at the beginning of May 1972 Morris West buttonholed me and asked if I would come to see him at the Baptist College where by now he was Principal-in-waiting during the concluding weeks of Leonard Champion's reign there. I had already heard him speak about the future of the college at the annual West of England minsters' conference at Sidmouth in February. In 1970 the college had celebrated the bi-centenary of the Bristol Education Society which had been a defining moment in the history of ministerial training in Bristol, and one of the projects adopted as part of the celebrations was the development of the college as a resource center for the education of lay people as well as ministers, and to provide for this the L.G. Champion Fund had been created. What Morris West wanted to know was whether I would be interested in the new, part-time post of Lay Training Organizer that was being created. Yes, I was indeed interested (I was also asked to teach some introductory New Testament Greek to ministerial students) and with the agreement of the Downend deacons soon accepted, and began work on the program during the summer. It was this appointment which more than anything else set the direction which my entire life and work took thereafter.

---

2. Clements "God at Work", 358
3. Booth, *Not Only Peace*, 45.

Part Two: Minister and Teacher 1967–1990

Morris West

Morris West, at first sight somewhat austere in appearance and demeanor (Margaret used to say he was modelled on Badger in *Wind of the Willows*) was in fact very approachable and had a mischievous sense of humor. Quite apart from his first-rate intellect he was the shrewdest judge of character I have ever known, the more so because his perception was always infused with humanity, not cynicism. He used to comment that, as in *Hamlet*, every drama needs a Horatio, someone of sound wisdom and common sense to hold things together when everything seems to be falling apart. That describes his own role on many occasions of evident crisis whether for an individual student or minister, the college or even the denomination as a whole. His own career was illustrative of a concern for a ministry focused on the local church, but a church very much in the world. He himself had studied at the Bristol College and at Regent's Park, and went on to postgraduate study in Zurich under the eminent theologian Emil Brunner and the New Testament scholar Eduard Schweizer. He was increasingly drawn to church history and, significantly in view of his subsequent ecumenical interest, his doctoral thesis was not on a Baptist or other figure from the dissenting tradition, but on the sixteenth-century Anglican bishop and martyr John Hooper. While at Zurich in 1952 he was a youth delegate at the third World Conference on Faith and Order at Lund, Sweden, an event famous for posing the question, endlessly cited as an ecumenical principle ever since, whether churches "should not act together in all matters except those in which deep differences of conviction compel them to act separately?" He returned in 1953 to Regent's Park as tutor where he taught for six years. In 1959 he took up the pastorate of Dagnall Street Baptist Church, St Albans where he served for twelve years, becoming ever more prominent in Baptist denominational affairs but also in ecumenical life, being appointed to the WCC Plenary Commission on Faith and Order in 1964 and the Standing Commission in 1971. Moreover it was during this time that a close friendship developed with the then bishop of St Albans, Robert Runcie, later to be archbishop of Canterbury. Not only so but his social concern found expression in an almost unique form for a minister at that particular time, in his appointment as a Justice of the Peace, a role in which he continued to serve after moving to Bristol. Indeed while at Bristol during the early 1990s he was leader of a national delegation of JPs to the then home secretary Michael Howard, to register concern at the consequences for sentencing of his "tough" approach to crime. Morris West thus brought an unusual range of personal gifts and experience. I was to be a special beneficiary in all kinds of ways in the coming years. In that first interview I quickly grasped what he wanted—and that included his wanting me to use my own imagination and initiative as far as possible. I was being given a rare challenge and gift, in one.

THE LAITY MOVEMENT

A main attraction in the Bristol College post was the opportunity it would give me for connecting with one of the most vital and creative streams in the modern ecumenical scene: the laity movement. Indeed, a considerable part of the ecumenical movement had been a lay concern and was lay-led, especially in the early SCM and Student Volunteer missionary movements in which John R. Mott and J. H. Oldham had been so prominent and of which the 1910 Edinburgh Missionary Conference had been a fruit. Later, a more intentional and considered theology of the laity emerged, seeing the whole people of God (clergy included, in their appropriate place but not necessarily in control) engaged in mission in the world. Oldham, author with W.A. Visser't Hooft of one of the preparatory books for the major ecumenical Oxford 1937 conference on Church, Community and State, emphasized the role of the laity as the main bearer of Christian mission and witness:

> . . . if the Christian faith is in the present and future to bring about changes . . . in the thought, habits and practices of society, it can only do this through the living, working faith of multitudes of lay men and women conducting the ordinary affairs of life. The only way in which it can affect business or politics is by shaping the convictions and determining the actions of those engaged in business and politics. It remains inoperative and unproductive, except in so far

as it becomes a principle of action in the lives of those who are actually carrying on the work of the world and ordering its course in one direction or another.[4]

At the international ecumenical level the main impetus was given by the Dutch missionary and theologian Hendrik Kraemer, from 1948 the first director of the Bossey Ecumenical Institute near Geneva. His 1958 study *Theology of the Laity* became a bible for everyone concerned for what he called "the spiritual mobilization of the laity" and, aware of this but not having read it for myself till then, almost the first thing I did having accepted the college appointment was to get it out of the library and devour it in almost in one reading. After the Second World War it was Germany that led the way in much of the laity movement, with the setting up of the Evangelical Academies, and the two-yearly Kirchentags, great gatherings bringing together Bible study, theology seminars, and political and social debate. In Britain a main advocate was Kathleen Bliss, ecumenist, educationist and associate of Joe Oldham, and whose book *We, the People* came out in 1963. The most widely influential works were those co-written by Ralph Morton, deputy leader of the Iona Community, and Mark Gibbs, an ex-schoolteacher and founder-director of the Audenshaw Foundation set up by Gibbs to advance lay education and participation in Christian witness in the world and which produced the lively series of *Audenshaw Papers*. Above all, Gibbs's and Morton's book *God's Frozen People* (1964) became an international best-seller and was followed in 1971 by *God's Lively People*. The first title took its cue from Hendrik Kraemer's remark that in face of near-despair at the institutional church it should not be forgotten that it has considerable "frozen credits and dead capital" waiting to be liberated and used in the form of the laity.

I drank deeply from Gibbs and Morton, and realized also that here I was reconnecting with the spheres in which Alec Vidler and Clifford Cleal had been active in the 1940s, both of them having been collaborators with Joe Oldham, Vidler in fact being an executive officer of the Christian Frontier Council for a time. A start had been made by the Bristol College staff with courses in 1971–72 and a programme had already largely been devised for 1972–73. In the latter series I was relieved that Morris West's influence was apparent in the outward-looking topics of, for example: an evening course on Christians and Broadcasting, led by the broadcaster and sports commentator Alan Gibson, and Peter Firth, senior producer of religious programs at BBC West of England; a weekend conference on world poverty; and, especially, a weekend conference for managerial people on decision-making in industry. In the actual logistics and organization of content for these events I had a great deal to do, which was a good learning experience. The conference on decision-making in industry was a highlight. The main speaker was Norman Macleod, deputy chairman of ICI Ltd, a member of Morris West's former church at St Albans. Some twenty people attended, mainly from Baptist churches, from a cross section of industries and public bodies in the Bristol area. For some it was their first experience of confronting human and ethical issues, such as

---

4. Oldham, *The Church and Its Function*, 117.

handling redundancies, beyond pietistic platitudes. Others, assuming that the chief of a multinational such as ICI would simply amplify their own bullish anti-trades union attitudes, discovered a much more nuanced approach to the complexities of industry and human relations on that scale. Still others were simply relieved to find themselves in a setting where doubts and difficulties about being a Christian at work could be admitted rather than pretended out of existence. Also present was Ray Taylor, himself a product of the Bristol College, and now chaplain in the Newport Industrial Mission just across the Bristol Channel, where much of his time was spent in the large Lanwern steelworks. I had previously heard and met him at student gatherings and was much impressed by his basic conviction that "If God wants people to make steel then in the light of the gospel he also wants them to make it in some ways rather than others, and it's our Christian calling to find out what that means".

The college provided me with an advisory group of both lay people and ministers to reflect on the work being done and to help with suggestions for future programs. Morris West took a continuing close interest in the work, giving me a considerable amount of freedom and responsibility but always available for comment and advice when needed: an object lesson in the art of delegation. One of the first things I did was to take soundings from a number of ministers in the Bristol area on how they saw this new role the college was taking on. It was as well that I did, for the views were mixed. Some were welcoming—in fact one looked forward to transferring his mid-week Bible study meeting en bloc to the college evening courses. Others were suspicious or indeed critical of what they saw as empire-building by the college. This last reaction was countered, I hoped, by the result of a survey by questionnaire which I conducted of lay people in churches over a wide area of the West Country, on their own views of what they felt they needed and would value in Christian education. The results were clear: the area in which they felt most in need was in discerning Christian obedience in their secular work; and the area in which they felt they actually received least help from their local church was the same. The most effective way to a more positive relationship with the clergy, I found, was to involve them personally in the lay training work when it was judged they did have a particular contribution to make. This certainly paid dividends. But then, too, there were odd voices to be heard on the college committee complaining that this new attention to lay education was not so much an extension of the college's work as an inherent devaluing of the ordained ministry, the training of which was the central role of the college. So it was not all plain sailing, and the case had repeatedly to be made. But I relished the sense of leading a venture onto untrodden ground and over time, I think, there were many more supporters than detractors. Soon a pattern developed for the programme each year. In the autumn, there was usually an evening biblical course, the lecturer being Harry Mowvley, college tutor in Old Testament, accompanied either by John Ziesler from the university Theology and Religious Studies Department, or Ivor Jones of Wesley College, and usually in conjunction with the university Department of Extra-Mural Studies. But the topics overall covered an enormous range, everything from World Christianity to Faith and the Scientific Outlook, from Women and Men in the Church to educational issues, from Eastern Europe to the Inner City. For input or leadership we recruited people from Bristol and many other parts if the country with a special contribution to make out of their expertise and experience, not only theologians but scientists, doctors, psychiatrists, educationists, social workers or whoever else could be of use.

Out of the first meeting on decision-making in industry grew the Industrial Group which met three or four times a year and soon, at my insistence, became inclusive of trades unionists as well as managerials. Ray Taylor served it continually as counsellor, and we had input from a variety of visitors and also from John Ware, Anglican priest and leader of the Bristol Social and Industrial Mission. It varied in size but was to continue meeting for over ten years, and its membership became both multi-denominational and non-church. Discussion was often vigorous. One regular member said it was "a place where I can speak my heresies without fear." Some found it a little too challenging. Following the 1973 three-day week and then the electoral defeat of Edward Heath I received an irate letter from a senior company figure in Bath declaring that he refused to sit down with representatives of a movement that had brought down a democratically elected government. Nor did all events in the lay program work well. A Saturday conference on Christians in Local Politics for example proved a notably damp squib. But each year at least two hundred people were coming into the college for one part of the program or another, and not all from Bristol either but as far afield as South Wales, the Midlands or deeper down in the West Country. In addition on occasion we tried taking the programme out to churches well beyond commuting range for participants. By 1975 the college committee was appreciative and congratulatory.

ECUMENICAL—BY DEFAULT

Not only were some of the courses and events on specifically ecumenical topics, but the program as a whole became increasingly ecumenical in scope and participation, as was bound to be the case when the agenda was that of the one and the same world, the *oikoumene* in which the people were trying to live out their faith. As mentioned already, a good deal was done through the University Extra-Mural Department, overseen by its full-time staff tutor in humanities and an advisory panel chaired by Professor Kenneth Grayston, head of the university Department of Theology and Religious Studies, which was of course a very ecumenical, indeed interfaith, group. Another collaborative group was the Avon Ecumenical Training Group which brought together church-related bodies including the Anglican, Baptist and Methodist theological colleges, departments of religion in colleges of education in the region, and which met three times a year in the library of Bristol Cathedral with the encouraging presence of the dean, Horace Dammers. In addition there was a new and very promising lay group, the Ecumenical Order of Teachers, in which Rupert Davies had a founding role and which for more than thirty years proved to be a powerful and enriching adult education network over much of the West Country.

But no group was more important for me than the ecumenical body for the whole of Bristol, the Bristol Council of Churches. Its secretary was Donata Coleman. Born into an aristocratic Austrian family (with the actual title of Prinzessin Elizabeth-Donata Reuss) but very down-to-earth and determined in a non-aristocratic way, she served for many years as a German-English interpreter at international ecumenical gatherings, and felt no compunction about taking her knitting in her translator's booth whenever she felt she already knew by heart what the next portentous speaker was going to be saying. She gave much publicity to our college lay training work, fed in ideas for new work, and helped to resource it with contributors. She and her husband, Peter Coleman, had from early on impeccable ecumenical credentials: they had met at a post-war international SCM conference. Peter as a young priest in London had in fact been an assistant secretary of SCM, taught for some years at King's College, London (numbering Desmond Tutu among his students), making a name for himself as an engaged scholar especially on ethical subjects, and arrived in Bristol in 1966 as vicar of St Paul's, Clifton, and chaplain to Bristol University. By the time I was on the Bristol scene, he was a canon of Bristol Cathedral with responsibility for ordination training in the diocese. Donata and Peter made a formidable ecumenical team, especially through their extraordinary wide range of influential contacts both in the UK and throughout the world. Not least of the benefits of knowing them was their ownership of a cottage, Boxenwood, in the heart of the Quantock hills in Somerset. In a very primitive state when they bought it, it required in effect a series of student mini-work camps to make it habitable but before long it provided them with a family country retreat which they generously let to church and ecumenical youth groups for weekend conferences—and for short family holidays for friends. Their visitors' book from the early days onwards read like a *Who's Who* of the scholarly and ecumenical world. I owe a huge debt to both of them. Years later at WCC or Conference of European Churches gatherings Donata would ask me how I was coping with the sea of problems (and problem people) surrounding me, and I would comment both ruefully and gratefully, "Well, you as much as anyone else got me into all this!"

SOUTH WEST ECUMENICAL CONGRESSES, AUDENSHAW—AND THE KIRCHENTAG

Soon after arrival at Downend I was made aware of a large ecumenical event brewing in Bristol for April 1973, the South West Ecumenical Congress (SWEC). It was the brainchild largely of Peter Coleman, who during the 1960s had been taking groups of students to the continent to take part in work-camps and to experience places like the Taizé community in France. In 1966 his group had gone to the German Kirchentag in Stuttgart, and Peter was stimulated to see if such an event, if not as large nor on as national a scale, might be possible in England. This was the genesis of SWEC 1973. By 1972, my first full year in Bristol, preparations were well under way. Crucial to the vison was the hope that many local ecumenical groups would work on the themes—unity, spirituality, race, social justice, international relations and so forth, and feed in their thinking to the big event itself which would take place over the weekend April 6–8. In the event two thousand people turned up from all over the West Country, from all age-groups and denominations. The climax came on Sunday afternoon when the Colston Hall was packed to capacity to hear Archbishop Michael Ramsey and Cardinal Suenens of Malines, Belgium. I commented in the Downend church magazine:

> Suffice it to say that the days when to be a Church "leader" meant to say smooth things to keep things as they are, are gone for good (in the Church of England and Roman Catholic Churches, anyway). Dr Ramsey warned against the dangers of complacency and expressed disappointment with the slowness of progress towards unity. The phrase which will always stick in my mind from his address is: "The heart of the Church may have to be broken." Only with complete and utter humility dare we hope to offer ourselves to God for his service.
>
> As for Cardinal Suenens, what can one say? Only that no Baptist who calls himself an "evangelical" would be quite the same person after hearing him. For patent simplicity, simple love of Christ, true humor and a concern for brotherly love, God has given us Cardinal Suenens as a great example to our age.

One change that SWEC did bring for me, was pretty soon afterwards to be recruited by the Colemans onto the planning group for the next SWEC, scheduled for 1976. At the same time however I made two moves of my own into the bigger picture. The first was to get in touch with Mark Gibbs who among all his other activities was Chair of the Association of Lay Centers in Europe, chair of the Ecumenical Committee of the German Kirchentag and general secretary of the Christian Frontier Council. I discovered that he lived in a cottage at Muker in Yorkshire, just a few miles up from Reeth in Swaledale where Margaret and I holidayed each summer with her parents. From Reeth I phoned him and he agreed, slightly reluctantly it seemed, to give me half an hour of his time. He was indeed a somewhat brusque figure on first meeting (par for the course I was told), and somewhat skeptical when he heard that I was working at lay education from a theological college context. But he knew that the Northern Baptist College was thinking along similar lines, listened to what I had to say, and took notes. The upshot was that he invited me to the next annual meeting of the British laity centers, in Stockton-on-Tees in November that year, and I duly went, as also to the next one in Coventry the following year. So there I was in a network which included such as Ralph Morton and other figures from Iona and, from the continent, Werner Simpfendörfer, pioneer and by now veteran of ecumenical social thought and peacemaking. Mark Gibbs, I found, once he was convinced you really meant business and were prepared to learn from others in the laity centers' network, became a good and supportive friend and colleague and was very appreciative of some of my later writing. Indeed, Michael Taylor once had to warn me that the danger-point with him came when he reckoned you could be very useful to *his* agenda and if not careful you would find oneself working almost full-time for him. I was glad to heed the warning which came just in time for me in the early 1980s. But I was deeply sorry at his death from cancer in 1986 at the age of sixty-six.

My second move, encouraged and supported by the Baptist College, was to go and experience for myself the next German Kirchentag in June 1975, at Frankfurt-on-Main. It was my first visit to Germany, and as the train raced past the vineyards along the Rhine valley towards Mainz there was a sense of "here at last!" As with most novices at their first Kirchentag it was a mind-blowing experience: fifteen-thousand full-time visitors, ten thousand day visitors and thirty-thousand at the closing rally together with hordes of volunteer helpers (mostly in adolescent T-shirts), with nearly everything taking place in the huge Frankfurt *Messegelände* exhibition complex, all made for a logistical miracle. The theme that year was "In Anxieties—and behold we live" summarizing the Pauline acclamations in Second Corinthians 6:1–10 and symbolized by the logo of a hand pierced by a flowering red rose. This Kirchentag was an exploration of the tensions of modern human life, between self-assertion and self-denial, between security and freedom, between power and powerlessness, between preservation and change. After opening services in different churches there was a large outdoor rally at which tensions were already apparent: anti-government protestors confronted by a large contingent of riot police; a demonstration by Chilean refugees against repression by the Pinochet regime at home, and a group with a banner declaring "The church must not become Marxist". But there was also lots of music, hymn-singing, the sending of a message to Beyers Naudé who should have been there from South Africa but had been placed under house arrest, liberal distribution of *Apfelwein*, and people of all ages, colors and nationalities. For the next three days it was largely up to oneself as to which of the many Bible studies, happenings and services to attend, all aiming to delve further into the problems of the age in the light of faith. Central to it all was the Market of Possibilities, with over a hundred stalls and cubicles set up by groups from all over Germany demonstrating needs and possibilities of hope and renewal in church and world. Much of it represented active political and social concern with race, housing and environment high on the agenda, but with prayer and new forms of worship, catechesis and evangelism also evident. A highlight of the larger events was the three-night ecumenical dialogue between leading Protestant theologian Heinz Zahrnt and progressive Catholic Hans Küng on "Who is Christ?", "Who is God?" and "Who is a Christian?" and it got more gripping each time. I could hardly have imagined six thousand people spending three hot, sticky evenings listening to theological exploration of Christian faith at this level. As it was, the ecumenical evening "On the Way to Nairobi" (the Fifth WCC assembly, to take place in December that year) had to be repeated later the same night for the hundreds of us who could not get in to the Matthäus Kirche for the first time, and poor Philip Potter, general secretary of the WCC, had to preach his sermon again at 11.00 pm. It was in an outdoor café that I had my first meeting with Potter: Donata Coleman had given me a letter to pass to him personally, underlining the invitation to attend SWEC 1976. But the Kirchentag, then as now, did not attract only senior church figures. Hurrying to one of the evening sessions in the Messegelände I came across a group of well-suited dignified men being escorted into a side-entrance: Chancellor Helmut Schmidt and his entourage were arriving. The Kirchentag had become too important a public occasion for politicians to miss. Afterwards I reported fully to the college and the other relevant groups in Bristol.

Over the next thirty years I was to go to more Kirchentags. It has grown even bigger since then. The international contingents have grown hugely too—in 1975 I think the British visitors were just about in double figures, well-shepherded by Mark Gibbs. Now they probably number hundreds. Among those I met for the first time in Frankfurt was Mike West, at that time senior chaplain in the Luton Industrial Mission and whom I was later to meet again in very different contexts. But there was also one real gem of a new friendship. International visitors at the Kirchentag are offered free accommodation with local families. I was joyously welcomed by Henry and Barbara Jakob and their two young sons in their Praunheim home on the northern edge of the city. Between them Henry, computer specialist and Lutheran, and Barbara, Manchurian by birth and Russian Orthodox by faith and fluent in at least six languages, constitute an ecumenical community of their own. We have been friends as families ever since, with their Frankfurt home an ever-open door for us, and telephone calls at Christmas and on birthdays.

SWEC 1976—AND MORE ECUMENICAL STUDIES

We worked hard on the planning group for the second SWEC 1976 which duly took place March 26–28 1976. Materials for local group study were prepared (I wrote two of them I recall). We had people of stature like Bishop Colin Woods, Father John Coventry, and the Abbot of Downside. The literally towering presence this time however was Philip Potter who, as well as Stuart Blanche, archbishop of York, preached at the Sunday morning televised service from Broadmead Baptist Church. By this time, controversy over the WCC's Programme to Combat Racism was if anything higher than ever. Potter, together with the Methodist Pauline Webb, dealt with the matter calmly but cogently at the final meeting in the Colston Hall. Even Mark Gibbs was impressed by the weekend—he had been main speaker at one of the seminars on commitment to justice and peace. But while the attendance was good it was but not as high as in 1973, the Colston Hall being little more than two-thirds full for the concluding session. What was happening? Something of the earlier excitement was draining away. In retrospect some of us felt that too much reliance had been placed on local study groups to provide input and impetus, or at any rate that the linkage between the local scene and the final event had not been thought through enough. Or was it simply that the ecumenical movement as we had known it was already losing the interest of the churches? SWEC had been envisaged as a kind of Kirchentag. But a half-way Kirchentag is no Kirchentag, In the evening after the final session, at a splendid party in the Colemans' house for remaining speakers, eminences and helpers (Philip Potter proved excellent and jovial company) I shared with Peter Coleman my own thoughts: SWEC 1973 had been mainly church talking to church; this one had been church talking about the world; a next one would have to be church talking with world about the world. Peter thought this a useful analysis. But there was to be no further SWEC. It seemed that what the Kirchentag did, namely to mount a truly *public* event for the whole public arena, politicians included, was simply beyond the capacity of us in the UK churches (or the English ones at any rate). Large gatherings are still the order of the day of course in the shape of festivities like Greenbelt and Spring Harvest, but these in their different ways still seem to be more like consumer occasions for the faithful rather than gatherings for all.

GIVING ACCOUNT OF HOPE—AND UNITY

At the opposite end of the scale, I found nothing was more rewarding than two small ecumenical study groups we ran at the college during this time. The WCC Faith and Order Commission had begun a study programme focusing on the place of *hope* in the Christian message, "Giving an Account of Hope", referencing the text 1 Peter 3:15. In part of course this was echoing the new emphasis on hope and the critical role of eschatology that had been brought into theology by the likes of Jürgen Moltmann and Wolfhart Pannenmberg, both of whom were members of the Faith and Order Commission. Faith and Order was inviting local groups in different parts of the world to contribute to the study, and I suggested to Morris West that we might involve the Lay Training programme in this. He agreed and we formed a study group which started meeting in late 1973. Nearly wholly lay, it comprized Anglican, Baptist, Methodist, Quaker, Roman Catholic and United Reformed members, and one Orthodox—Father Nicolas Behr, priest of the Russian Orthodox Church close to the college, who in fact earned his living as a carpenter for the university. We met monthly for most of 1974, each session consisting of informal conversation about what really mattered to us in our faith, where we found hope in the gospel for ourselves and society, and what it should mean for Bristol. The result was not systematic theology but was profoundly theological for all that, and I wrote up the record of the meeting, citing actual exchanges of conversations and the reflections and prayers that members had written. Soon after our document was produced Morris West and I arranged an open evening at the college on the Faith and Order Plenary Commission which had just met in Accra, Ghana, where the Giving Account of Hope project had been prominent. As well as Morris West, from the Bristol area Rupert Davies, Raymond George and the Anglican theologian Mary Tanner had all been at Accra, as had Donata Coleman. They—Mary Tanner especially—welcomed our paper, which I had also sent to Martin Conway, secretary for ecumenical affairs at the BCC who took me aback by praising it to the skies and said it was the best thing that had come out on the project from the UK. No less was I surprised when not long after he was asking me whether I would consider being his successor at the BCC, but I hardly felt ready for such a move just yet. The paper "A conversation about hope" found its way to Geneva where likewise it created a lot of interest and was published in *Study Encounter* in 1975.[5]

The second group was of similar composition and looked at the WCC report *What Unity Requires* as recommended by the Fifth WCC Assembly at Nairobi (1975) and especially its concept of *conciliar unity*. The notion of unity not as uniformity or homogeneity but based on a common understanding of the apostolic faith and on eucharistic communion, and manifest in an equal belonging to common decision-making bodies, was a very creative and promising one. Members of the group, none of them professional theologians, were able to relate to it and to see how it might work at local, national and international level. It seemed to herald a way out of the logjam that had blocked British ecumenism since the failure of the Anglican-Methodist scheme and to offer a means of re-energizing the dialogue that had stymied (at least as far as Baptists were concerned) the post-Nottingham 1964 proposals. In 1976 came the "Ten Propositions" produced by the Churches' Commission on Unity in an effort to keep the post-Nottingham process moving. At Downend we devoted two full mid-week sessions to them, at one of them inviting the vicar of Downend to be guest speaker on "Ministry and Sacraments—a Non-Baptist View", followed by a church Sunday afternoon conference. We tried to be as positive as we could, and were certainly more so than the majority of the 55% of Baptist churches who responded. The Baptist Union Advisory Committee on Church relations recommended to the BU Council in November 1977 that it was not possible proceed further.

Indeed it was obvious by now that *as a whole domination* the BU would never be able to move towards visible unity with other traditions. Surprisingly, very few (Paul Rowntree Clifford was one) requested that more note be taken of the differing opinions among Baptists. Given the congregational basis of Baptist ecclesiology, should not opportunity have been given for those congregations who felt more passionate about unity to proceed according to their lights? For myself, the excitement was no longer in what was being solemnly discussed in denominational headquarters but in the more personal encounters about hope and unity and the difference that could be made in the world. A huge rift was growing between what was being discovered in local contexts—in official Local Ecumenical Projects but not only there—and the supposedly normative, dully denominational control of the whole unity process. Which tail was wagging which dog? "Living in more than one place at once", I was

---

5. "Clements, "A conversation about hope".

discovering, increasingly meant going against the stream. Of course one wasn't alone in this and as a minster it was important to find like-minded company. This need was well met by joining a group of younger ministers who met regularly with Ron Cowley, minister of Tyndale Baptist Church, for theological conversation and mutual support. It continued to meet after 1975 when Ron became Superintendent of the Baptist Union Western Area.

NEW THEOLOGICAL PROJECTS: THE BETHGES, BONHOEFFER AND RONALD GREGOR SMITH

My visit to Germany in 1975 had not been solely to attend the Kirchentag. On the way home I stopped at Koblenz for two nights, in order to meet for the first time Eberhard Bethge, the friend and biographer of Dietrich Bonhoeffer, and his wife Renate (née Schleicher), Bonhoeffer's niece, who were then living at Rengsdorf bei Neuwied. There, Bethge was director of the Pastoral College of the Evangelical Church of the Rhineland, a center for in-service training courses, conferences and seminars for pastors. With the assistance of Edwin Robertson, Baptist minister, friend, and long-standing translator of Bonhoeffer into English I had contacted Bethge a few weeks earlier and sent him the notes that John Wright had given me of Bonhoeffer's lecture at Richmond College in 1934[6], and asked if he I could see him briefly on my way back from Frankfurt. He readily agreed. Renate Bethge, youthful looking, bright-eyed and eagerly conversant, met me off the train at Neuwied just outside Koblenz and drove me at speed up the winding roads into the hills above the Rhine to the little village of Rengsdorf. I had been told of the Bethges' friendliness but nothing quite prepared me for the welcome they gave me—and I was just one of countless people who over the years had wanted to make their acquaintance. Eberhard, then in his mid-sixties, strode into the living room with a broad smile on his face and an outstretched arm, and soon we were sitting down to tea. During 1974–75 Morris West had asked me to sit in on a seminar he was running on Bonhoeffer for final year university students and so I was able to relay a number of the questions which the students had raised, and the Bethges were very interested in these not least because of the seriousness which several students had paid not just to the famous *Letters and Papers from Prison* (for most of which Eberhard was the recipient of course) but Bonhoeffer's earliest works *Sanctorum Communio* and *Act and Being*. It was an enthralling Sunday afternoon. The Bethges talked about Bonhoeffer as if he'd just gone out of the room and would be back again any moment, so real he still was to them; but at the same time never as if they alone owned him. It was not on that occasion but a later one that I asked Eberhard where the originals of the prison letters were now housed and he replied, "Oh here, still in my desk". He pulled open a large drawer and asked if there was any

---

6. See above, chapter 4, p.54.

one in particular that I'd like to see. Without hesitation I said, "The one of July 21 1944"—the famous one he'd written to Bethge the day after the failed bomb attempt on Hitler, when he effectively knew what his fate would be. So there it was, on rough paper protected by a waxed overlay but still decipherable: "*Lieber Eberhard—Heute will ich Dir nur einem kurzen Gruss schicken*—"Today I will send you only a short greeting. . . "followed by those extraordinary sentences about faith, the this-worldliness of Christianity, and sharing the sufferings of God in the world and so being taken beyond all concerns about success or failure.

As for the notes of Bonhoeffer's Richmond College lecture, these, said Bethge, were being forwarded to the editors of the new collection of all Bonhoeffer's works. It was not however only about Bonhoeffer himself that I had gone to talk with the Bethges, but about one of Bonhoeffer's most important British interpreters, Ronald Gregor Smith. Early in 1974 I had decided finally to go for postgraduate research on a theological topic, for an Oxford BD by thesis. I had wondered about a Bonhoeffer subject but—oddly now in retrospect—there was a prevailing skepticism just then about whether there was anything more to be said about Bonhoeffer after the use made of him by the radical theologians of the 1960s. I was however intrigued by Ronald Gregor Smith who had died in 1968 at the early age of fifty-five, and who was by many reckoned to be among the radicals himself, yet standing somewhat on his own ground and in whose writings there breathed a sense of mystery, or at any rate a caution about saying *anything* too hastily about God. Gregor Smith had been editor of SCM Press before taking up the chair of divinity at Glasgow in 1956 and was instrumental in seeing much of Bonhoeffer into English print, together with Rudolf Bultmann and other leading theologians and biblical scholars. But it was his treatment of Bonhoeffer in his *The New Man* (1956) that intrigued me. Taking up Bonhoeffer's call in his prison writings for a new understanding of God's transcendence in a "world come of age", he saw this as taking "this-worldly" form in a new responsibility for history: history as the sphere which in the Bible is where God in Christ meets humankind and is in turn the sphere into which faith, in contrast to "religion", leads the believer into full responsibility for society.

For the purposes of doing an Oxford BD I had to find an Oxford-based supervisor, and Barrie White at Regent's Park enabled me to contact John Macquarrie, Lady Margaret Professor of Divinity, canon of Christ Church and perhaps the most esteemed Anglican theologian of the 1970s, whose *Principles of Christian Theology* I had read and re-read several times. We met in his rooms at Christ Church and he was encouraging in my interest in Gregor Smith whom he had known well for many years not only as a colleague at Glasgow University when Gregor Smith was professor there, but earlier still when they had both been army chaplains in the latter part of the Second World War. But in probing into his relationship with Bonhoeffer it would be the Bethges who would be crucial, for Gregor Smith and his German wife Käthe had been their closest friends in Britain from the time when Eberhard Bethge had been pastor of the German Church at Forest Hill (Bonhoeffer's parish during 1933–35) from 1953 to 1961, and Bonhoeffer would have been top of the agenda for many of their conversations.. The Bethges, still in touch with his widow Käthe now living in Kiel in northern Germany, encouraged me to make contact with her and in fact wrote in advance telling her about my visit with them.

So from 1974 working on the Gregor Smith materials became my main academic preoccupation. It was an education in itself for it introduced me to a whole sweep of continental theology and philosophy, and in greater depth than I would ever have known otherwise. For three years I scoured theological and university libraries, and the British Library, for obscure journals and German monographs (students in the digital age don't know they are born). But it was above all Käthe Gregor Smith who was the key helper. At first diffident about approaching a still recently-bereaved widow for information and advice, I found her overwhelmingly kind and enthusiastic, sending me samples of his correspondence and diary extracts, and helping me to plot in detail the course of his life and engagements. Ours grew into a voluminous correspondence and it became clear that she was as keen on the thesis as I was.

Then in the summer of 1976 I spent a week in Glasgow University Library where the bulk of Gregor Smith's unpublished materials, including his university lectures, were housed. It was only on my final morning there that I came across the most remarkable discovery of all: his reflections written in the summer of 1944, just after he had left his Church of Scotland parish in Selkirk to become a chaplain in the Scots Guards. In Selkirk he had passed through something of a crisis, unable any longer to maintain his poise as scholar-priest, a modern day George Herbert, in a world at war, and had eventually opted to "get into the same boat" as other people. While at Pirbright Camp he penned some highly personal thoughts on the change he perceived himself having to make, and the church too, in seeing "the historical Jesus without prejudice" and "discarding much of the accumulated dogmas of the church" and thereby coming nearer to "proper faith". He confesses to being bowled over by the startling humanity of Jesus: "The despair of the proper; the perplexity of the sinner; the undoing of the wise. What is this life? What is here that is not in the Churches? What is the secret of this freshness, gaiety, abandon, which characterizes his whole handling of people and of problems? In one word, I should call his secret *humility*. That is the startling gift of God". Such humility has been smothered in the entrenched pride of the churches—they have not understood the humility of God and "all those other magnificent dialectical insights of Jesus which flow from this teaching, about strength in weakness, wisdom in folly, victory by means of the death of the cross, gain through loss, life through death."[7] Not only was all this so Bonhoefferian in tone but, almost uncannily, it was being penned during the same weeks as Bonhoeffer was writing in such similar vein in Tegel prison. I wrote to Eberhard Bethge with samples of those reflections. He replied from New York where he was lecturing on Bonhoeffer at Union Seminary: "This is really astonishing parallel that you have found out. And

7. Clements, Theology of Ronald Gregor Smith, 40–41.

I am specially pleased that your work shows now to Käthe more clearly where the roots are of what we had later so much in common . . . The figure of George Herbert is of course not familiar to me. But I have a feeling for what you found about Ronnie's relation to this 'church-father' figure for him. And the parallel dates in August 1944 are fascinating indeed."[8]

John Macquarrie was a kindly and patient supervisor, despite all the other demands on him willingly giving of his time for several visits to him each year. By mid-1977 I had all the material to hand and was giving thought to how the thesis might be shaped.

THE 1970s—WHAT CONTEXT?

The 1970s, politically and culturally, get a bad press these days. Some portrayals of the decade give an impression of almost unrelieved disruption, gloom and cynicism. I suppose at times it was so, particularly during the power shortages and three-day weeks of 1973. But we cannot choose the time in which we live and I think like most people Margaret and I simply got on and made the best of it. I do remember it as a time of increasing anxiety for the churches. The numerical downward slide was continuing, and no-one of whatever tradition or theological hue seemed to have the overall answer. Some put their faith in the new thinking about church growth coming from across the Atlantic. Akin to this but by no means always allied to it were the gurus advocating the application of management techniques to church life. "Management by objectives" became a useful tool provided it was just that, a tool and not a dominating cure-all. The single most useful nugget of wisdom I gained from one of the many manuals was the simplest: the advice once given to the head of the Bethlehem Steel Corporation in the USA, which was at the end of each day to list the things to be done next day, put them in the order in which they have to be done—*and stick to it*. Then do the same for the coming week. After three months he reckoned the advice had been worth fifty-thousand dollars. It didn't make me a millionaire, but it did answer the question when people commented that I seemed to be able to get so many things done in a single week. It was in fact a strong component in one's spirituality, concentrating the mind wonderfully. As Whittier's hymn—which I *did* now count as among my favorites—puts it, "And let our *ordered* lives confess/The beauty of thy peace." A disciplined devotional life was therefore important. I stuck to the Daily Office produced by the Joint Liturgical Group.

Nor did the busyness act as a shield away from the wider context but interacted with it. The Mangotsfield Council of Churches arranged public hustings for the general elections of 1974. In June 1975 just before the referendum on British membership of the European Economic Community I preached on the issues of Europe as they should be viewed by Christians.[9] I enjoyed a good relationship with Terry Walker,

8. Letter from Bethge 22.12.76.
9. See below, chapter 20, pp402f.

Labour MP for our constituency (Kingswood). He was an active Anglican and indeed served as Second Church Estates Commissioner of the Church of England, and willingly participated in a number of our local ecumenical meetings on social and international issues. But the political climate was changing. Margaret Thatcher became leader of the Conservative party in 1975. In July 1977 a *Times* editorial lauded her spiritual values with the enigmatic statement that while she was no Calvinist she was "a better Lutheran than Luther." I responded with a letter, published on July 12, suggesting that her unequal emphasis on each man having to play his part in working out his own salvation "is a distortion of the truly evangelical position, and leads not to the truly personal freedom of love, but to an individualism based on merit, a religion of 'works'", and thereby a reversal of Luther's teaching. Such a tiny pebble thrown into the current now flooding public life could hardly make a difference but I felt it needed saying—the more so as time went on.

A (PARTIAL) CHANGE OF SCENE

By summer 1997 I had been at Downend nearly six years. Our son Peter was now five years old, and in June of that year was joined by his brother Jonathan—the five-year gap between them quite unintentional. In fact it was a case of change all round. Bristol Baptist College had decided to appoint a fourth full-time tutor and I had applied. My appointment was no foregone conclusion and after the interviews in February it was not until Easter that the decision to appoint me was made. It would mean both continuity and change, continuity in that my work would include maintaining the Lay Training Program as well as overseeing the work of the student pastorates and taking on a share of the academic teaching. But it would mean leaving Downend where attachments and friendships had grown very strong. We would move from Downend and live closer to the center of the city, in Westbury Park, close by the famous Bristol Downs. Peter would start his schooling in Henleaze nearby.

We were farewelled from Downend at the start of September. During the ceremonial tea Peter made his mark on the occasion by complaining loudly during my response to the several speeches, "Daddy, this is going on for a *very* long time!" There was much to remember gratefully at Downend and, as in Mid-Cheshire it was above all the signs of grace, often unexpected, among so-called ordinary people that were the most memorable. Willie Trotman was a product of the Christian Endeavour movement, a straightforward evangelical of the old school and of strong opinions, intensely loyal as a deacon of the church, and now nearing retirement from his work as a factory time-keeper. One evening at our mid-week prayer and Bible study meeting we were discussing how we should regard people of other faiths. Willie was clearly bursting to say something and when he eventually had a chance to speak it was not what I was expecting. He told how the previous week a Muslim man who had arrived to do some maintenance work came into his little office and asked if he might unroll his prayer mat there and then, and offer up his morning prayer. Almost indignantly Willie said: "I would have regarded it a complete denial of the divinity of our Lord Jesus Christ if I had *not* said 'Of course!'". He had seen instinctively what many others laboriously fail to see, that the incarnate Christ had come not as a Christian but as truly human, to enable, not prevent, all who seek God to reach God—or if one prefers, to open heaven's ears to all who call to God on earth. Mind you, Willie's wife Winnie could also surprise us. A registered blind person, she once won the prize for darts at the church garden party.

6

Theological College Tutor . . .

It is December 7 1977, and at the Advent communion service in the chapel at Bristol Baptist College I am preaching on the text John 1, verse 5: "*The light shines in the darkness, and the darkness has not overcome it.*" Actually it is not only I who am preaching. The setting is also the sermon: the chapel is in complete darkness save for a single candle on the communion table. But this is what I say:

> What are you most conscious of, as you sit here? It is dark, yes. But what about the candle-glow? Isn't that what is most noticeable? Just one small light, true. But it's there, an arrow-head of light defying the darkness, captivating in its beauty. No matter how dark the room is, it can't take away the beauty of the candle-flame which will go on burning as bright as ever.

I cite the contemporary happenings that are emphasizing the darkness of the world, from terrorism in Europe to the murder of Steve Biko on South Africa. But the light of hope stemming from the cross and resurrection defies the darkness.

> Some of you will someday have to witness to this hope, in very real darkness. In a grief-stricken home. In a hushed hospital ward. In a twilight inner-city area. In a church stumbling through shadows of seemingly hopeless problems. You may yourself wonder where the light is. You may yourself have to be the light for your people—you, in your own staggering faith and trembling hope, when the only light you can see is Jesus himself. Remember how you once sat in a dark chapel looking at a single glowing candle. Jesus is light now and promise of light to come. There is darkness, yes; but remember the candle; look through the dark to Jesus. And remember the word: "*The light shines in the darkness, and the darkness has not overcome it.*"

I look back on that scene and that service as a source of hope not least because it did give hope. Many years later, more than one former student told me how he or she during difficult times in their ministry had recalled the candle in the darkness—or indeed had used the same symbolism themselves. Much too in that sermon embodies what I was trying to do all through those thirteen years as a college tutor: to root the expression of Christian faith in the actual context of the contemporary world, both at home and afar, both in teaching and no less in worship. For that reason the college chapel in all its simplicity where morning prayers were said and the weekly eucharist (yes, we did use that term) was celebrated on Wednesday evenings, came to mean as much to me as King's Chapel had done.

Indeed the whole life of teaching and learning in community was an extraordinarily rich, many-layered experience for which I never ceased to be thankful. "The best job the Baptists can ever give anyone", is how Ernest Payne, himself tutor at Regent's Park College before becoming General Secretary of the Baptist Union in 1951, described being a college tutor. At Bristol, I never found reason to disagree. A community of students keen (for the most part) to learn with their vocations in mind, very congenial colleagues, opportunities for study and writing of one's own, all in the context of shared prayer, discussion, humor, and sport all made for a daily *life together* as Bonhoeffer called it. I resumed playing football again, and even cricket; running too but that was mostly an individual recreation (including the full Bristol marathon in 1984 if that could be called recreation—never again). But it was not, for me at any rate, to become a closed-in existence. It was precisely while college tutor that my horizons and activities widened dramatically, as illustrated by the fact that whereas in the thirteen years before my appointment I had (apart from a holiday in Italy) been abroad only twice, in the thirteen years I was at the college (in addition to holidays) I was to visit no less than seventeen countries in continental Europe, North America, Africa, the Middle East and East Asia. This was not accidental; the reasons for these new involvements lay to a great extent in what I was been studying and writing as well as teaching.

HOME?

One undoubted attraction of being a college tutor is that the college can provide a community in which one can be at home. At least in my case there was no need to look to the college as a *substitute* home, for Margaret and I were much occupied with our own still in the making. The one problem with accepting the tutorial appointment was whether the college could or would afford to pay for the housing of the fourth tutor. We came to the rescue (somewhat to the disappointment of one of the staff who had hoped our coming would "send the balloon up" on the need for greater generosity by the college to its tutors generally) by just managing, thanks to some savings and proceeds from Margaret's working, to afford the deposit on a three-bedroomed semi-detached house in Westbury Park. This was much nearer to the center of Bristol than Downend, not much above a mile from the college and just a few minutes' walk from the pleasant Bristol Downs. We transferred our church membership from Downend to Tyndale Baptist on Whiteladies Road. The house was in a reasonable condition but needed some major interior repairs and redecoration. It would be our Bristol home for the next thirty years, the first home that Peter—now just turned five and starting school at Henleaze Infants—could ever really remember clearly and the only one that Jonathan, just three months old when we moved, would know at all until he went to university. Margaret continued her work for the Open University and Weights and Measures Inspectors. In 1978 she started lecturing part-time in statistics at Bristol Polytechnic (as it then was). She was working full-time there by early 1982 and had her post made permanent in 1983. Peter meanwhile was making his mark in music, excelling at piano and also playing violin in Bristol junior orchestras, and in 1982 won a choristership and music scholarship at Bristol Cathedral School. This meant that for the next four years we were an ecumenical family much involved as choir parents in cathedral life (and the tribulations as well as delights which that entailed). Jonathan started school in 1981. It was, then, a very busy and not always tidy household with a lot of organization required to keep the burgeoning activities of all four of us in some kind of synchrony. But there was time for enjoyment too. From 1981 we began camping holidays abroad, first in France and then Germany, Switzerland and Austria, though not to the neglect of the Yorkshire Dales, the Lake District and Scotland. My parents on returning from Sri Lanka in 1972 had settled first in Shakespeare country at Henley-in-Arden from where my father gave part-time pastoral help to the Baptist church in Alcester, then in 1979 moved to Tewkesbury to act as wardens in the historic Old Baptist Chapel, set in a narrow court almost opposite the large and famous Abbey. This provided them with an adjoining cottage, described by a visiting John Betjeman as the most desirable residence in the whole of Tewkesbury. In 1983, at the instigation of their old ministerial friend of Darlington days Arthur Francis and his wife Thea (widow of Norman Jones), who lived at neighboring Bourton-on-the-Water, they moved to the delightful Cotswold village of Naunton, where my father had his last retirement pastoral charge in the chapels of that village and nearby Guiting Power. Wherever they went, my parents were warmly received for their friendship and ministry—and from our point of view were conveniently near to Bristol.

COLLEGE LIFE

Collegiality with Morris West as Principal in charge was more than a word, and in the previous chapter I have already indicated why he was an outstanding senior colleague. His quiet but plain-speaking Yorkshire-born wife Freda was a trained teacher but gave herself to overseeing the domestic scene in the college. Senior Tutor was Norman Moon, now approaching retiring age, scholarly, teaching church history, ethics and philosophy of religion, immensely kind to all and sundry with a record of delightful absent-mindedness, a sort of Monsieur Hulot as played in the Jacques Tati films, whose wayward antics as a car-driver caused endless amusement (or moments of terror) for all and sundry. He was also immensely devoted and hard-working. It was thought that in his twenty-seven years as tutor he had never taken a day off for illness. The third tutor was Harry Mowvley, a contemporary of Morris West in the first post-war student generation of Bristol students and who like Morris had also gone on to Regent's Park. The top Hebraist of that generation, he had returned to Bristol in 1960 to pastor the Cotham Gove Baptist Church. Under his ministry, the congregation united with the nearby Methodist and Congregational causes to become in all but name a Local Ecumenical Partnership, re-named Christ Church and Cotham. After part-time work at the college he had become full-time tutor in 1963, teaching Old Testament and Hebrew in both the college and the university. As superbly clear in diction (a Yorkshire West Riding woolen accent honed to even greater effectiveness by speaking and singing tuition) as in thought and exposition. he had an unrivalled ability through informed scholarship to bring the biblical narrative alive to all levels of audience, whether in university or college, or for lay classes or in Sunday worship; and all with a vigorous personal warmth and humor. I was very much the junior colleague (soon after arrival I was dubbed by some students "the boy wonder") but never felt treated as one, and as far as working context and relationships were concerned these particular years were to prove the happiest of my whole life. Neville Clark, impressively intellectual tutor and then principal of the South Wales Baptist College, also came over once a week to take a class, and Morris West reciprocated at Cardiff.

But the community was of course essentially the students, in 1977 forty-two in number, in age ranging from late teens to mid-40s, eleven of them women, most intending for the ministry but several "option-option" students among them, i.e. studying theology but not necessarily (or not yet) with ordination in mind. Over the years they came from a wide range of backgrounds: only a minority straight from school, some already graduates from university, others having been in business, or in nursing or teaching, some having served overseas as missionaries, or some from the armed forces. In personality and aptitude they were a fascinating mix. Some were obvious academic high-fliers on the university degree course, others struggled with even the rudiments of New Testament Greek; some were hearty sporty types, others poets and musicians; theologically they ranged from the very conservative (though hardly ever fundamentalist) to the flamboyantly liberal. In the course of time the numbers of women grew, both as option-option and ministerial students, reflecting a degree of change in Baptist attitudes to women's ordination—but only a degree because some inconsistencies remained. At least one woman came with the required recommendation from her home church for ministerial training yet the church made known that they themselves would not be prepared to call a woman as minister to the pastorate! A very positive feature was the number of students from overseas, a tradition which in fact dated back to the nineteenth century. In my years as tutor, for longer or shorter periods of time we had students from Bangladesh, Canada, Germany, India, Italy, Kenya and Switzerland.

The college was affiliated to the Department of Theology and Religious Studies of Bristol University. In fact the Department had first grown out of the Baptist, Wesley

(Methodist) and Western (Congregational) Colleges.[1] This meant in practice that a number of students read for the University BA in theology, and college staff taught certain courses in the university, a mutually very fruitful arrangement. Students not on the university course studied for the Cambridge Diploma and Certificate in Theology. My own work comprised several responsibilities. First, some nine students, mostly married men who needed a roof over their families' heads, looked after some small churches in and around Bristol, in some cases in challenging council estates. These "student pastorates" needed to be made into a genuine source of learning experience for themselves and for one another. I shared with Morris West the classes in pastoral theology with a special course for first-year students too. I took on some of the Cambridge Diploma teaching from Norman Moon—at first modern church history, philosophy of religion and ethics, and later on Christian mission. In 1984 I started teaching courses for the University in modern Christian theology. And until about 1985 I maintained the continuingly flourishing lay training work. Margaret too became involved, leading with Freda West the monthly weeknight meeting for students' wives.

The college occupied a site on Woodland Road, just opposite Bristol Grammar School and virtually surrounded by university buildings and departments. Within a quarter of a mile radius were not only the university but the busy shopping area of Park Street, a hospital, a factory, offices and a wide range of housing, in fact a cross-section of modern urban society. Relationships with a statutory and voluntary agencies gave students opportunities of first-hand experience of the probation service, the courts, and inner city community projects (some shared in the work of a refuge in the St Paul's area, for women seeking to get out of prostitution). The Commission for Racial Equality in Bristol prepared a course on issues in multi-racial society. Nor were a mosque, a Hindu temple and a synagogue far away.

Also just ten minutes' walk away, on Whiteladies Road, were the BBC West of England and Radio Bristol studios. Soon after arriving full-time at the college, in December 1977 I was invited by Peter Firth, at that time senior producer of Religious Programs for BBC West, to contribute to the BBC World Service a series of short talks in the "Reflections" series. So started a long-running relationship with the BBC where it was evidently thought I had an aptitude for preparing and delivering talks, and in due course some longer documentaries too. For a time I took a regular slot on the Saturday evening "Ten to Ten" devotional slot on Radio 4, on the (very) early morning "Prayer for the Day", and wrote and presented several series for the Sunday evening "Seeds of Faith" programs. In early 1981 the Lay Training programme was effectively put on the air with Radio Bristol's first "Lent Line series", pioneered by the college, in which house groups used material prepared beforehand and could phone comments for discussion with invited guests and speakers in the studio. For my own part I found broadcasting not only enjoyable but highly useful too now that I was a college tutor.

---

1. Western College moved to amalgamate with other Congregational colleges in Manchester in 1968.

PART TWO: MINISTER AND TEACHER 1967–1990

Being responsible for helping students to communicate more effectively, especially in preaching, it was good to be under critical professional scrutiny oneself. Working with both the producers and technical staff was instructive, not least in how to stay calm especially when going live. On a bitterly cold Sunday morning in December 1979 I was at Brown Street Baptist Church in Salisbury to preach the third of an Advent series of sermons on The Four Last Things, my subject being "Hell". It very nearly turned into just that, as with about three minutes to go before going on air a technician wandered into the church from the outside broadcasting van whispering, "Anyone here got a 13-amp plug?" They had blown the fuse with their electric heater. Fortunately a plug was found just in time from the vestry and the waiting millions were not spared hell at all.

HISTORY—AND NOW

Bristol Baptist College was not only located in a very specific spot in space, but in a particular point in time. It could lay claim to being the oldest Free Church college or academy in the world since it was on June 3 1679 that a wealthy Bristol businessman, Edward Terrill, elder of the Broadmead Church, signed a deed of gift in favor of his church to be used for the support of a minister at Broadmead who could teach the biblical languages and prepare young men for the ministry. It was made at a time of persecution of dissenters, which debarred them from the universities of Oxford and Cambridge. Such was the origin of what became the college. The sense of past legacy was increased by the college's holding of perhaps the most splendid collection of historic English Bibles in the country, including the most prized possession of all, the only complete copy of William Tyndale's New Testament of 1525, acquired and then bequeathed to the college with other gifts by Andrew Gifford (1700–84), tutor and antiquarian. An impressive stained-glass window in the stairwell commemorated Tyndale's life and martyrdom. We had a lot of history behind us. Was that history in danger of becoming a prison?

The tercentenary of Terrill's gift was fast approaching for 1979 and so much of our time in my first two years was taken up with preparing worthy celebrations. These included a Sunday morning television broadcast, recorded a few days previously, of a college communion service in which we told the story of the college's founding and subsequent history and its contribution to the life of the churches today, and included the re-enactment of a baptismal service in the Broadmead Church. The programme made quite a big impact. Most viewers were impressed (apparently it prompted a sudden spate of baptisms in Wales). In addition there was a live radio broadcast on Pentecost Sunday morning, which actually fell on the anniversary date of Terrill's bequest, June 3, from the Broadmead Church at which Morris West preached, and for which I had written a hymn especially for the occasion with a tune composed by one of the students, Bill Longley. Later in the autumn there was a splendid lunch in the university dining hall with the Lord Mayor of Bristol and the University Vice-Chancellor as honored guests, and Morris West was awarded an Honorary Doctorate of Laws.

In terms of linking the past and, present, however, and still more importantly the vision that been the genesis of the college and that which must now be its vision for the future, nothing was more significant than the series of four open evenings, which counted as the lay training programme for February that year, on "What Has Happened to . . . " Eric Sharpe led the evening on hymnody, taking his cue from the role that Bristol men like John Rippon and John Fawcett in the eighteenth century had played in stimulating and developing this central feature of Free Church worship, and looking at the state of the art-form today. Kenneth Grayston, with William Tyndale in mind and also Terrill's wish for biblical language study, looked at where New Testament studies were now heading. Derek Winter, former Baptist missionary in Brazil, now lecturing at St Paul's College, Cheltenham and a foremost British authority on Liberation Theology, explored the changed and newly changing concepts of world mission since the days of William Carey and the founding of the BMS, in which Bristol-trained pastors had taken a leading part. All the evenings were well attended, but the really full house was drawn by none other than Tony Benn, at that time MP for Bristol South, and minister for technology in the Labour Government. We had invited him to speak on "What Has Happened to the Nonconformist Conscience?" He lived up to his reputation of being a real charmer, as I found when entertaining him to dinner beforehand, and of being well informed on church and theological issues, coming as he did from a prominent Congregational background and, through his parents' connections, having known personally such theological stars as the American Reinhold Niebuhr. At the meeting itself, characteristically he spoke without notes on what he considered nonconformity to mean today, quoting Thoreau's dictum that every man must march to the beat of the drum as he hears it for himself—though bearing in mind the need for true solidarity (see miner and, trawler men for example) as a counterweight to individual, entrepreneurial acquisitiveness. Challenged as to where he personally stood as regards Christian faith, he told, quite movingly, how he had once visited the Soviet atheist propaganda museum in Leningrad, and how he was left feeling at the end that despite all that could be said against Christianity, there was no getting away from the impact made by the life and teaching of Jesus of Nazareth. It was a remarkable evening. Not surprisingly we took flak from some ministers and churches who wanted to know why we had invited such a partisan left-wing speaker.

The sense of historicality and historic responsibility became even more real as from 1980 to 1985 I was editor of the Baptist Historical Society and thus had responsibility for the *Baptist Quarterly*, selecting and commissioning articles, organizing reviews and writing some twenty editorials myself. So it was in a context of a lively communal life, a conscious indebtedness to the past, and no less responsibility to the future. that I was now living and working. This was not incidental to the theology which I was now searching out and writing on, for personal life, for the church in society and for the wider world, as I now hope to show.

RONALD GREGOR SMITH, FAITH, FACING SECULARISM

By the time I started as tutor at the college in 1977 I had assembled and analyzed all the available published and unpublished writings of Gregor Smith, and by late 1979 had completed the writing of the thesis. It was structured in three parts: an account of his life and work in outline; his treatment of his major sources, Buber, Kierkegaard, J.G. Hamann, Bultmann, and Bonhoeffer; his theological vision of the task and method of theology, man, faith and God. In later life as the Glasgow professor he could still state in his introductory course in theology: "My whole understanding of the theological task might well be summarized as the attempt to grasp what the reality of the presence of God's Spirit in history means"; and "The new man is man in community with man in the strength of the given grace which meets him as tasks and responsibilities and opening freedoms in actual situations in their wholeness . . . "[2] There are ambiguities in Gregor Smith's thought, allusive and elusive as it is. The true theologian cannot be too comfortable with God, and Gregor Smith was too much infected by the mystery ever to be at ease with the divine. But what most intrigued me was that while he had no illusions about the human condition (he came, after all, out of a Scottish Calvinist background), and its seemingly inherent tragic tendencies towards self-destruction, his was essentially a theology of *hope*. Humans are constituted by their relationships in community. So long as there is encounter between persons, there lies the "between", the realm of spirit (or Spirit), the vapor ready to be ignited by the Word of God. Christ as the end of history, the omega as well as alpha, is ever present and ready to re-ignite the human story and impel it further towards its great consummation. In fact his final work, *The Doctrine of God*, not quite completed at the time of his death, having cited First John 3:2 concludes on a strongly eschatological note: "As he is: this we shall see in the indescribable end, not the collapse of history, not the loss of time and significance, not the static 'isness' of an indifferent principle, but the endless fulfilment in an endless movement of reciprocity, which we already glimpse and see in a mirror, darkly."[3]

This was indeed for me a theology of hope which enabled me to see myself anew in my particular situation, outwardly so insignificant and unpromising in the world of the late 1970s which was still frozen in ideological division and confrontation in the world at large and in cynicism at home. Many theologians have talked much about history, about God at work in history. Jürgen Moltmann had excited us with his theology of hope based on the resurrection of Christ as the signal of God's future. But few explored as deeply as Gregor Smith the nature of history, not as a process to be

2. "Introduction to Theology." Unpublished lecture, Gregor Smith papers, Glasgow University Library. See citations in Clements, *Theology of Ronald Gregor Smith*, 202.

3. Smith, *Doctrine of God*, 183.

observed externally or simply an object of hope, but as a drama to be experienced *from the inside*, what it actually means *to live historically*, as a recipient of grace and in free responsibility in one's specific situation.

It was well before my thesis was completed and submitted that I wrote and presented a documentary on Gregor Smith for BBC Radio 3, *Still Point*. The title—a phrase from T.S. Eliot's *Four Quartets*—was in fact that of Gregor Smith's first book, written in his wartime parish in Selkirk. Indeed the programme focused much on his wartime spiritual struggles and writings in parallel with those of Bonhoeffer[4], and their bearing on his later thought. We had two actors reading the parts of Gregor Smith and Bonhoeffer, together with a clutch of notable interviewees whose comments we in Bristol recorded downline: Gregor Smith's former colleagues John Macquarrie and Alan Galloway, John Bowden (the then editor of SCM Press), Eugene Long (former research student in the USA), Lady Collins of William Collins and Sons publishing house and, most important of all, Käthe Gregor Smith who reminisced most movingly. In weaving it all together I was helped immensely by Chris Mann, assistant producer of religious programs at BBC West, a person of boundless energy, imagination and sometimes audacious ideas. It involved some lengthy days and almost all-night sessions in the studios and cutting rooms in order to get it finished (just) in time for transmission on September 26 1978, the exact tenth anniversary of Gregor Smith's death. Not only so, but just at that time I went to Germany for the biennial meeting in Hamburg of Baptist theological teachers in Europe and went on from there to Kiel where I at last met with Käthe Gregor Smith face to face, stayed as her guest overnight and was able to present her with a tape cassette of the programme. The thesis itself was awarded the Oxford BD in April 1980 (some claim that the Oxford BD at least rivals the Oxford DPhil. in status but I would not count on that, and in any case the degree gown and are hood are no match for the doctoral garb.) It was published as *The Theology of Ronald Gregor Smith* by E.J. Brill, Leiden, in 1986.

Whatever else Gregor Smith had done, he had made the *personal* element in faith central: personal response to the reality of grace which claims us in Jesus Christ in the midst of all our present historical claims and invites us to trustful response in communion with and for others. In the autumn of 1979 I led a study weekend for the Baptist and United Reformed Church Society of Bristol University at Boxenwood, the cottage in the Quantocks belonging to Peter and Donata Coleman. The topic was "Faith", and out of the notes of my talks and the subsequent discussions grew my first book, *Faith*, published by SCM Press in 1981. Relatively short (126 pages), its aim was simple, namely, to present faith as neither acceptance of a package of doctrinal propositions, nor a conjuring up of esoteric religious experiences, nor a round of hyperactive activity in good causes: rather, as something very human, as trust, gift, decision, confession, commitment, freedom, understanding and exploration, all in response to grace which comes to us from outside of us. John Bowden's ready welcome to it at SCM

---

4. See above chapter 5, p.107f.

Press was some compensation for his declining of the Gregor Smith thesis, but there was a fair amount of Gregor Smith echoing through my text. There was a wide and generally gratifying reception in reviews and correspondence, both from evangelicals like Bryan Green and from such as Maurice Wiles, figurehead of the Oxford *Myth of God Incarnate* liberals. The one sniffy review appeared in *Theology* with the complaint that it was all so *sound* and gave the impression of being delivered as sermons to a congregation that did not expect to be disturbed. But I was trying to help people who were *already* disturbed and confused whether by the fundamentalisms burgeoning even on the campuses, or the more wildly extravagant claims of the charismatic movement, or even some distorted versions of liberation theology which were making everything hinge on a rather joyless and moralistic social activism (and thereby rather less than liberating). Looking back on it after thirty-five years, it is not quite the book I would write now but I believe it was right for that time. I was surprised recently to hear from an Anglican priest that it was still recommended reading on a training course for hospital chaplains that she had just attended.

The Gregor Smith studies bore another fruit. In 1979 I was invited by Roger Hayden, at that time minister in Ealing, to join a small group of Baptist ministers wanting to formulate a theological basis for Baptist life and mission more thoughtful than the repeated calls for ever more strenuous evangelism. This was a response to Leonard Champion, former principal of the Bristol College, who had that year had issued a challenge to the younger generation to work out "a clearer, more coherent and more widely accepted theology than prevails among us at present". The other members of the group were Paul Fiddes, Brian Haymes and Richard Kidd. We met six times during 1979–80 and the result was a short book *A Call to Mind. Baptist Essays Towards a Theology of Commitment*[5] to which each of us contributed a chapter. Fundamental to all our approaches was a stress on the sovereignty and universality of God in Christ, and the primacy of human relationships, both in the church and in society as a whole, as the sphere of faith and obedience. My essay, the first in the book, was on "Facing Secularism", and argued that faced with their marginalization from an increasingly secularized society, the churches by trying to stress their distinctive religiousness were putting themselves ever more firmly into a religious ghetto and thereby contributing ever more to a dominant secularism. God and the world were to be distinguished, yes, but God's presence in all the world has to also to be recognized and upheld. Here, very much on Gregor Smith lines, I argued for the actual experience of "Spirit" as the realm of the interhuman:

> In meeting another person, in genuine openness and mutuality, we also encounter this mysterious realm of "Spirit" which is not simply ourselves, but enables us to be ourselves in relationship. That is, if we look at what it is that makes us human, or enables us to be human, the mysterious reality of Spirit

---

5. The group also produced *Bound to Love* (1985) in which my own contribution was "The Covenant and Community" (chapter 4).

which is not simply ourselves, both disturbing and gracious. Here is one sign of a mystery at the heart of life—really at its centre, not in some freakish, peripheral concern of humanity: a sign that we are indeed transcended by a mystery which is very present.[6]

On that basis, we are open to perceive the reality of revelation in Christ in whom surrender to the Spirit was total, "the consummation of this experience of transcendence."

This, then, was where my theology was leading me by the late 1970s: the interhuman as the place where God is always encountering us, the place of our responsibility and the place where the full revelation of God in Christ is made known. But on the larger scale, from apartheid South Africa to Cold War Europe, in the world of the late 1970s the interhuman realm was in a parlous state. Could such a theology be adequate to it?

OVER THE WALL TO EASTERN EUROPE

It is late on a Saturday night in November 1978. In East Berlin the great thoroughfare of the Unter den Linden, wrapped in freezing fog, is almost deserted. We are a group of ten people, recruited by the British Council of Churches, on a week's study visit to the German Democratic Republic (GDR). Having been warmly received by our hosts and well fed in a top-class restaurant we have decided to take a stroll, and literally take the air. A slightly nervous humor typically accompanies those abroad for the first time in a largely unknown environment. In a kind of glass-enclosed sentry box outside one of the government buildings sits a uniformed guard. "Do you think he has central heating?" someone asks. "He *is* the central heating!" someone else quips.

Of course, as well as with physical fog such a visit to such a country was wreathed in ambiguities. Its official sponsor was the Great Britain-GDR Friendship Society which on the GDR side could only act with the imprimatur of Erich Honecker's government, and therefore even before we set out we invited the charge that like it or not we would be part of a propaganda exercise by the regime and its project of demonstrating "socialism with a human face". But equally, like it or not, we were there as representatives of the British churches to learn more of what life was like for the people and churches of the GDR. We would ask our own questions, make our own reflections on the answers and come to our own conclusions. I had been invited as a Baptist representative, and beforehand talked much with Donald Black, social responsibility secretary at the Baptist Union, and with Ernest Payne who in his ecumenical work had visited the GDR several times, and read up what Trevor Beeson had to say in his chapter on the GDR in his highly useful book on Christians in Eastern Europe, *Discretion and Valour*. What's more, at the meeting of European Baptist theological

---

6. *Call to Mind*, 19.

teachers in Hamburg in September I had met and talked with two members of staff of the East German Baptist seminary in Buckow, Christian Wolf and Klaus Fuhrmann, I had arranged to meet with Klaus Fuhrmann at some point in Berlin, and he had given me contact details for the Baptist pastor in Erfurt where we would be spending much of our time. Before leaving London our group as a whole was well briefed by Paul Oestreicher at the BCC, and moreover two of the group, our leader Mike West of the Luton Industrial Mission (whom I had met at the Kirchentag in 1975) and Roger Williamson, Human Rights Officer of the BCC, had themselves been in the GDR before. So on no account were we total innocents, although one or two were doughty left-wingers determined to find everything to praise in the socialist miracle, to the detriment of the West. My own motivation was sheer curiosity and excitement at the opportunity, at last, to see life on the other side and to see first-hand—I hoped—some of the historic sites of the Lutheran Reformation.

The fog cleared overnight. Sunday dawned bright and crisp and we took ourselves to morning service at the historic Marienkirche, now standing almost alone in the Alexanderplatz and dwarfed by that symbol of East German technical prowess, the enormous television tower. It was cold inside the church—the heating had broken down. But we heard a remarkable sermon from the pastor, Jürgen Henkys, who preached from the Book of Daniel. The exile Daniel, the apparently hopeless and helpless person under the tyrant Belshazzar, was not in fact powerless: he knew the secret of history, he could read the writing on the wall, he knew who was in charge of history, and therefore had the real power, the power of hope. Delivered firmly but cheerfully, within a stone's throw of the huge Soviet embassy, for those with ears to hear his exposition needed no application.

After lunch we boarded the small bus assigned to us and set out south for Erfurt in Thuringia. After a couple of hours bumping along the unevenly concrete autobahn the bus chugged to a crawl, and we had to stop in Dessau to wait for repairs to its alternator. Out of earshot of our two minders the driver muttered that he wished he had a West German, not a Polish, bus. We eventually arrived at the Erfurter Hof Hotel towards midnight. Erfurt was our base for the next five days, and a full programme had been arranged for us in the city itself—hospitals, a factory, party officials, and the city center shopping area, musical concerts and so forth. The welfare system was indeed in many ways impressive. It was made clear to us that welfare like every other national policy was firmly in the hands of the main communist party, the Socialist Unity Party. Other, smaller parties were allowed including the Christian Democratic Union (CDU), a representative of which met with us, which allowed committed Christians some share in political life but even the CDU would not be allowed to debate the main premises of Marxist social policy. We met with some pastors, one of whom said quite openly that he would not join the CDU because having grown up in the Third Reich he never wanted to see the church in uniform again (an allusion to the Nazified so-called German Christian movement). His father had been a Confessing Church pastor who had suffered not by imprisonment but out of sheer nervous exhaustion under harassment by the local Nazi gauleiter, and wondering who in his flock was the informer. It was evident that churches and Christianity were allowed and even welcomed as part of the GDR social fabric—within the limits prescribed by the SUP. Indeed churches in the GDR wielded a surprising amount of muscle in their own welfare work, especially their hospitals and old people's homes and in collecting for overseas aid. In March that year there had been a much publicized meeting between the presiding bishop of the Evangelical Church in the GDR Albrecht Schönherr (one of Dietrich Bonhoeffer's students) and Erich Honecker, other church leaders and government officials, with agreement to allow some more freedoms to the churches including more broadcasting time. Yet very soon after came a government announcement of compulsory military education in schools, with which the church leaders were much less happy. One had the impression of a steady and only slightly ameliorating pressure for conformity, seen for example in the *Jugendweihe*, the state-sponsored rite of passage into citizenship for young teenagers which was clearly intended as a rival to church confirmation. No outright persecution, but the message was clear: "You'd be wise to conform because our Socialism is the future and religion will wither away." While at Erfurt we had a short informal communion service in one of our hotel rooms, and one of our minders came along. He said that he had been brought up a Roman Catholic, and still deep down felt himself to be a Christian.

But how much were we being allowed to see beneath the surface? On our second day in Erfurt I called the Baptist pastor whose name had been given me, Heinz-Dieter Hirsekoorn, and in the evening took the tram out to the suburb where he lived. I was warmly welcomed and talked long with his wife and his assistant, a deaconess. There were no specific complaints about life in the GDR from a political point of view (would I expect anything else, a stranger in a police state?) but an undoubted sense of sadness and hardship. Frau Hirsekoorn had an aged mother in the West, and she had been refused permission to visit her for many years. Good clothes were hard to come by. Yet the work of the church went on. Soon there would be a baptismal service in their church, and prayers were asked particularly for a young woman who would be a candidate. The implication was clear that her decision might prove a costly one for herself and her family. But they were as eager to hear about churches in the UK as I was to hear about theirs. Then, towards the end of the evening, the pastor took me upstairs to his son's room. The shelves were well-stocked with scientific textbooks, a microscope and other laboratory instruments were on a table, the walls were covered with charts. "He wants to be a biochemist," said his father. "So he will be going to university?" I asked. After a pause, Heinz-Dieter Hirsekoorn shook his head sadly. "No pastor's child will get a university place." Back at the hotel I confided with some of the others that I at least had met with real unhappiness in the GDR.

Next day Roger Williamson, with whom I was sharing a room, and I misbehaved. He wished to visit friends in Halle. I was annoyed that despite being in the historic heartland of Protestantism there was nothing scheduled on our program for visiting any of the sites associated with Luther—not even in Erfurt where he had been a friar in the Augustinian monastery. We got up well before dawn, stole away to the railway station and caught a northbound train. Roger got off at Halle, I continued north towards Wittenberg. The sun rose over frosted fields and I got into conversation with a woman sitting opposite me. I explained why I was in her country and where I was going. She turned out to be a member of the Moravian *Herrnhuter* community. Limitations of our respective German and English notwithstanding we talked softly and at length. On the opposite side of the aisle sat a heavily built Soviet Red Army officer complete with impressive briefcase. I wondered what was in his mind as he stared impassively ahead. Were faith or the churches even on his horizon, preoccupied as he must have been with the assumptions of power and control? Who could lay claim to the future? My Moravian companion gave me details of how to contact the Provost of Wittenberg, Hans Treu, when I got there.

I reached Wittenberg mid-morning. It was a beautiful day and I seemed to have the historic core of the town, its cobbled streets and squares, almost to myself. I made a bee-line to the Lutherhaus where the reformer had lived and taught, and spent an hour there; then to the Castle Church, long since rebuilt but still marking the spot where he had mailed his ninety-five theses to the door in 1517. Inside I duly paid respect to his tomb. I ate sausage and sauerkraut in a Gasthaus on the main square, then called on Provost Treu who was agreeably surprised to find an unexpected visitor from Britain (he knew the offshore islands, and had a map of them on his study wall) on his doorstep. We talked about the situation since the March Schönherr-Honecker meeting, and about theological education in the GDR and England. Back to the train, and in Erfurt I found the rest of the group at an organ recital in one of the main churches. It was practically full, with a lot of young people too.

Next day, Thursday, for all of us was a day outside Erfurt: to Jena in the morning where we spent some time in the theology faculty and met both staff and students, a pleasant but somewhat disappointing meeting since no-one seemed really able to open up on what they thought theology was about in the GDR. Then in the afternoon, to the winter sports center at Oberhof, and Weimar just a few miles away with its historic church where Bach played, which Goethe loved and Herder too; the city that gave its name to democracy, civilization and culture until the darkness fell in 1933.

And just five miles from Weimar is . . . Buchenwald, as if the devil had been given permission to argue the closeness of the demonic to goodness, truth and beauty. One's first encounter with a concentration camp is, perhaps inevitably, emotionally traumatic. It is not so much that it makes the *enormity* of evil so apparent (over two hundred and forty-thousand imprisoned in Buchenwald since 1937, over fifty-six thousand done to death, are easily stated statistics), but rather it brings evil down to size, one's own size, and that is disturbing. Through *these* iron gates bearing the cynical motto *Jedem das Seine* ("To each his due") new arrivals had been marched inside the barbed wire, like the young Hungarian Jew Elie Wiesel whose scarifying account *Night* had provided my first vivid account of life and death in both Auschwitz and Buchenwald. Wiesel says that on arrival at Buchenwald, exhausted and deadened from the long march from Auschwitz, he scarcely glanced at the crematorium and its billowing chimney. All this was done not by some monstrous, mechanical abstraction of evil, but by human persons. That was the disconcerting thing. That SS officer's uniform jacket draped over a chair in the guardhouse might well fit oneself. It was human beings who dumped men down a chute to be hanged or shot in the back by the score each day, their remains shoveled into the ovens. Of course we were given lectures on how this demonstrated the evil of fascism which the socialist system brought an end to in 1945. So much in the GDR was in fact justified by "Back in 1945 . . . " Our noses were also rubbed in Western guilt for what was happening in Southern Africa. But no matter, what was on display here went deeper than any political scapegoating could. As Mike West said on coming out of the crematorium "It's *sin*, isn't it?" We laid a wreath in the cell dedicated to Paul Schneider, first martyr of the Confessing Church who was beaten to death there in 1939. "Father, forgive us", was the simple prayer uttered by Mike West. A place like Buchenwald will reduce us to tears and will make us angry, but if it only leaves us self-righteous then it has not done its job of reminding us that we each stand in constant need of heaven's mercy and help.

Back in Erfurt that evening I was able to squeeze in a private visit to Luther's Augustinian monastery. Next day we journeyed back to Berlin, in time for some afternoon visits at various government ministries including their office for overseas development. It provoked some humor by its very humorlessness. A po-faced official solemnly and at length discoursed on how many tons of cement the GDR had shipped to Yemen in the past two years; and how they were also producing educational material on their work including a film entitled (honestly) *Pilots in Pajamas*. Heads down all round, stare at the table in front of you, tummy muscles tight and *for goodness sake no eye-contact* . . . Mercifully, dignity was maintained. We had a sumptuous farewell dinner with our hosts and minders.

On our next and final morning Klaus Fuhrmann met me at the hotel and drove me out to see parts of East Berlin I would not otherwise have seen, including the Baptist church at Lichterberg where a meeting of ministers was taking place with the President of the Baptist Union, Herbert Moret. I had brought a couple of English Bibles with me for use in the seminary at Buckow and Klaus Fuhrmann took them gratefully (also carefully covering them up with a coat on the back seat of his car). He in turn left me with perhaps the most memorable and thought-provoking saying I heard throughout that week. He told how all his upbringing and contacts had been in the West, but he had been working in the East when the Wall went up in 1961. His first thought was "How could I, or should I, get back to the West?" Yet in the course of time, he said, he had come to think of the Wall going up as a blessing from God. It had made clear to him where his place of ministry and witness now had to be, and for that he was grateful. That remained for me the defining thought on how to assess the churches in the GDR who, however great our concern for them, were neither to be pitied or patronized, nor romanticized, but accepted as partners with important things to teach us. "Critical solidarity" was the phrase being used by Albrecht Schönherr and others to describe their stance as a church within socialist society and it merited immense respect.

The group met up in London early in 1979 for final debriefing and reflections. I wrote an account for the *Baptist Times,* in the following months gave talks to local groups, and made and presented three Reflections for BBC World Service. Then in the summer of 1979 I gave a twenty-minute talk on Radio 3, "What Luther Says to Marx" which was then published (slightly abridged) in the *Listener*. I suggested that the GDR for obvious reasons was fairly short on historical monuments of Marxism, whereas Christianity's history was everywhere visible, from the Luther sites to the onion-towers of churches in every town and village. It was therefore a question for the regime of how it could give Luther his historical due while keeping the churches fairly well under control and in their proper place on the side-lines. But might in fact the past keep the future open, or at least put questions to it? I made the point that there were church leaders and theologians who, for all the restrictions placed upon them, were not prepared to be put into the otherworldly, pietist slot but would at least watch the public sphere very closely, drawing their inspiration from such as Dietrich Bonhoeffer who decisively rejected the way of "thinking in two realms". The talk received much appreciation—at first anyway. Some months later however I heard from Peter Firth, who had produced the programme, that Ian McIntyre the Controller of Radio 3 and others were critical of its "naivety". This I judged could only have come from people who had not heard or read the talk as a whole, and had understood me as saying that just because there is a lot of religious history on view in the GDR this would safeguard the churches' future. That alone, I was quite clear, would not be enough. It was simply that there was too much of Christianity in German history for it to be written out of the country's heritage and what mattered was what the churches would make of any opportunity that would come their way to reclaim and assert that heritage; and the churches were in fact alive and *there*, however restricted. Finally of course history, far more than any argument I might have adduced, delivered its own verdict. When change began to stir in 1989 it was above all the churches of the GDR in the "revolution of the candles" that stimulated protest and debate and channeled them into peaceful forms and ensured that the end of Soviet rule took place with exemplary peacefulness. They had indeed been sufficiently alive.

BONHOEFFER, PATRIOTISM AND BRITAIN

The visit to the GDR, brief as it was, had stimulated me to think harder about what it meant to live historically and responsibly. At the same time my interest in Bonhoeffer was continuing. In April 1980 there took place in Oxford the Third International Bonhoeffer Congress. I attended and gave a seminar paper, derived from my BD thesis, on "The Issue between Bonhoeffer and Bultmann as Seen by Ronald Gregor Smith." But my main interests at the event, the overall theme of which was "Dietrich Bonhoeffer and the Church in the Modern World" lay elsewhere. So much of the congress programme was occupied with the wider scene, past and present. Eberhard Bethge gave his pivotal paper "Dietrich Bonhoeffer and the Jews" which brought Holocaust studies into the center of Bonhoeffer scholarship in a new way. East-West relationships were bound to feature also, not least with the presence of a number of participants from the GDR with one of whom, an enthusiast for the official party line, some of us had lively debate on the Soviet incursion into Afghanistan, Then, too, there was my first experience of meeting leading Bonhoeffer scholars from afar, like Clifford Green, Pat Kelley, Geff Kelly, John Godsey and Bill Peck from the USA, Hans-Dirk Hoogstraten of the Netherlands and—to become especially important for me—the South Africans John and Isobel de Gruchy. With all such there was a disposition towards critical engagement with the socio-political realities in their own contexts. What, then, in my own context called for critical engagement?

At this distance in time I cannot reconstruct the exact sequence of thought, and maybe it was a case of chicken-and-egg, but during 1980–81 I was thinking more and more about "patriotism" as a feature of Bonhoeffer's life and thought (Edwin Robertson had aptly entitled his third selection of translations of Bonhoeffer's collected works *True Patriotism*, and likewise Mary Bosanquet her *Dietrich Bonhoeffer: True Patriot*). Equally I was troubled by the *lack* of any serious attention—least of all in the churches—to what national loyalty might mean in Britain today, and how the Bonhoeffer aspect and the British scene might be brought together. It was striking how readily people were prepared to hail Bonhoeffer as a patriot, while in Britain patriotism was now a somewhat embarrassing idea believed to have been hijacked by the National Front, the likes of Enoch Powell ranting against immigration, or in its more benign form the assumed property of the Conservative Party. During 1981 I read intensively not only on Bonhoeffer but on British social and cultural history and contemporary analyses of British notions of identity, and by Christmas that year had the outlines of a book worked out. This needs stressing. *A Patriotism for Today* had been conceived, its argument laid out and its contents largely decided upon well *before* the Falklands war broke out in April 1982. That war immeasurably heightened interest in patriotism and made the book highly topical when it first appeared in the spring of 1984. But the book was not actually a response to that war and Margaret Thatcher's exploitation of the patriotic impulses it released. Rather, the war and its accompaniments showed the book's relevance and for that, in a peculiar way, I should be grateful. When Collins published its second edition in 1986, the cover picture was of the Falklands task force returning to Portsmouth to cheering crowds bedecked with Union Jacks and red, white and blue balloons.

I cannot deny that the Falklands conflict lent urgency and edge to the writing. I was on study leave from the Baptist College from May to September 1982 and most of the writing was done in that time, including some days in solitary at Boxenwood Cottage. In September I attended the European Baptist theological teachers' conference in Turin and on the way home spent much of a day with the Bethges, now retired from Rengsdorf and living in Wachtberg-Villiprott, a village the other side of the Rhine near Bonn. Eberhard and I went through my outline and notes, he as usual with as many questions to me as answers. As a useful adjunct to this main work I had also written a paper for a Baptist Historical Society summer school at Malvern in July, on "A Question of Freedom? British Baptists and the German Church Struggle". But at a time of concentrated work it is always good to have the foil of a rather different theme, and during that summer I wrote and presented a series of six Sunday evening Radio 4 programs on Thomas Traherne's meditations and poems. It evoked a wide response from listeners (not least because Gerald Finzi's music inspired by Traherne was used as background). Traherne's delight in creation and his passionate sense of the presence of Christ in all people and all things, clearly resonated with the kind of theology and spirituality many people were searching for. In fact, as I have argued much more recently, the seventeenth-century Traherne and the twentieth-century Bonhoeffer are rather close neighbors spiritually. Both advocate a "worldly holiness".[7] The BBC repeated the series the following year. Some people were surprised that a Baptist should be a devotee of an Anglican metaphysical writer; stereotypes die hard.

In February 1983 the MS of *A Patriotism for Today. Dialogue with Dietrich Bonhoeffer* was completed in ten chapters. I began with looking at the situation of patriotism in contemporary Britain, the way it was a vague sentiment attaching to a Britain no longer in existence, or a right-wing ideology, or just an embarrassment to "progressive" minds. Then I moved on to Bonhoeffer's own life and death as a study in patriotism comprising and holding together different elements in a creative whole. In an age when nation and loyalty to it is liable to take on an absolutized (and therefore demonic) value—"I vow to thee, my country, all earthly things above"—Bonhoeffer's distinction between nation as an unalterable "order of creation" (see the Nazi German Christian movement) and "an order of preservation" helps keep nationhood in a proper biblical perspective, allowing it real but qualified importance.

> A true love of country . . . will view it as part of this world which is God's creation, which has sinned and stands under his judgement, and which God nevertheless wills that it should experience the new creation. Thus, in all its particular human features, it will be loved. As it is, before God, it will be loved. Not as we would like it to be, clouded in mists of illusory grandeur, but as it is—it will be loved. Nor as we imagine might become once is has conformed

---

7. See below, chapter 19, p.39 on my lecture to the Traherne Association in 2014.

to our utopian blueprint, but as it is—it will be loved. Patriotism, so often associated with pride, therefore really begins with gratitude . . . [8]

But this, to be truthful, also means a readiness to accept guilt when this is required by the country's record—the most difficult, sensitive and taxing aspect of all true patriotism. It means challenging the militarization of the country's identity—this was being written at the height of the Cold War and the nuclear stand-off between East and West—and the self-destructive effect on national identity of the means of total annihilation. Then (almost) finally, the book looks at the relation between true patriotism and true ecumenism, and the significance for Britain and its churches of what Bonhoeffer to the very end held to so passionately: the church as one universal body of Christ in and for all nations, to be neither domesticated nor nationalized. The true church will ever qualify and if necessary counter prevailing forms of national loyalty. Christian citizenship ultimately lies elsewhere.

Nevertheless the particular issues raised by the Falklands conflict could not be avoided. I had no quarrel with the need to free the Falkland's/Malvinas from Argentina. It was the impression that this achievement by itself was the answer to all Britain's questions about its identity and its place in the world that was problematic. As if dispatching a task force to the ends of the earth to liberate two thousand white islanders could be rejoiced over when Britain itself had displaced the two thousand inhabitants of the island of Diego Garcia in the Indian Ocean to make room for a US military base. It seemed that military adventurism was being seen as the psychological panacea for Britain's ills, providing a distraction from its declining status towards being a mediocre, middle-ranking power in the world; a belief that only by such displays of power could it merit love and loyalty. A patriotism for today would have to be of a very different order, and Bonhoeffer could help supply the clues as to what that might look like and what the churches' contribution to it might be.

OF PRESSING INTEREST? NO . . . THEN YES

So too, I hoped, others would see it this way but I was to be disappointed. John Bowden at SCM Press returned the MS saying that it was no longer feasible to publish anything on Bonhoeffer. His time had evidently gone. Next I tried Collins, along with SCM the major English-language publishers of Bonhoeffer, and after a long delay came the reply: very interesting and original but regretfully . . . Come the autumn, after a talk with Morris West we decided that the Baptist College would itself bring it into print. We had the book professionally type-sent, printed and bound in time for the launch just after Easter 1984. We sold over 1a thousand copies in less than two years, not bad for any religious book in those days and it went for a reprint.

---

8. Clements, *Patriotism for Today* 71.

Summer 1984 was Bonhoeffer-dominated in a number of ways. In June the Fourth International Bonhoeffer Congress was held in the GDR, at Hirschluch bei Storkow about an hour's drive out of Berlin, in a remote church conference center, somewhat Spartan as far as conditions went but delightfully situated amid extensive pine forests. I gave a seminar paper on "Barmen, Bonhoeffer and Anglo-Saxon Individualism". Not surprisingly, being in a self-contained conference there was much less interaction with the GDR scene than on my first visit six years earlier. But I did get out to visit the Baptist seminary in the little lakeside village of Buckow. The Bonhoeffer conference itself provided a taste of another seminary and its life, that of Finkenwalde, where Bonhoeffer had been director 1935–37. Among Bonhoeffer's former students attending Hirschluch, as well as Eberhard Bethge (accompanied of course by Renate) was Albrecht Schönherr, now retired from being presiding bishop of the Evangelical Church in the GDR. He conducted morning and evening prayers following the same pattern as at Finkenwalde. Of all the Bonhoeffer congresses I have attended, I recall Hirschluch with particular affection thanks to its idyllic setting but also its relaxed camaraderie. Perhaps it was also because I was able to stimulate further interest in *A Patriotism for Today*, copies of which had already found their way to a number of participants including John de Gruchy who with his wife Isobel was there. One afternoon John and I went for a walk and agreed that, with both of us coming from a Free Church (John was a minster of the United Congregational Church of South Africa) at the next congress we should both present papers on Bonhoeffer and the Free Church tradition. Four years seemed a long time ahead, then. Little did we know that events were to bring us together again several times, and sooner than expected, before 1988.

In fact it was through John that a positive twist was given to the fortunes of *A Patriotism for Today*. Early in 1986 he contacted me about a series of volumes he would be editing for Collins, on key figures in modern theology, and would I do the one on Schleiermacher? I agreed. But he also mentioned my name to the editor of Collins Liturgical, Sue Chapman, with whom he was dealing and told her that I had produced an interesting book on Bonhoeffer. She asked to see a copy and almost by return asked if Collins could bring it out in a new edition, commenting that if the MS had crossed *her* desk in 1983 it would have been accepted instantly. So with the subtitle slightly changed to *Love of Country in dialogue with the witness of Dietrich Bonhoeffer* there reappeared in October 1986 the second edition of *A Patriotism for Today*. This of course was gratifying. For all the talk of the Bonhoeffer industry being over, bells had been rung far and wide, both in Britain and overseas. Reviews spoke of freshness and originality, of new insights both into and from Bonhoeffer. Pauline Webb on the radio said that good timing makes for prophetic writing. Trevor Beeson in *Theology* said that as an exercise in practical theology it could hardly be bettered. In *Contact*, the journal of the Clinical Theology Association and other pastorally-oriented bodies, Alan Wilkinson, historian of the British churches in two world wars, could hardly have been more fulsome:

The Falklands War showed how much jingoism and imperialist nostalgia lurks below the surface of British life. It is as though (Clements remarks) that Britain has had no history since 1945. And British Christianity is still painfully ignorant of the transnational character of the church. British Christians have this much to learn from Bonhoeffer.[9]

From the *Expository Times* to the evangelical *Third Way* similar echoes sounded. Of course there was the odd dissent. But one of the most interesting responses came from the mother of a boy with severe learning difficulties. I remarked in the book that the biblical injunction "Let love be genuine" (Rom. 12:9) when applied to country meant "Love what is genuinely there" as distinct from what we would like to be there, and she commented that that was also the challenge facing a parent in her situation, who had to learn to love the child that actually was, not the child she wished had been born. No less significant than the reviews and correspondence however were the invitations which came in steadily to address the theme or related issues at clergy fraternals, study conferences of parishes and dioceses, classes in extra-mural studies departments, the Cambridge Theological Society, the sixth form at Ashville College in Harrogate, the annual conferences of the Industrial Mission Association, and of cathedral deans and provosts, to name but some. I was becoming known as the Bonhoeffer-patriotism-nation-national-loyalty man. Indeed I have to say that while I have written other and more substantial books, in some respects I still regard *A Patriotism for Today* as my most important effort. It was entirely on my own initiative, it raised major issues in theology and public life and indeed broke new ground. I cannot say that it was this book that created a new interest in Bonhoeffer at large, as I think that revival was bound to come anyway, but it was an early wave on that new current. As for me personally, it placed me in a definite, albeit not prominent, position in contemporary theology and, still more important, was to be influential in leading me into new engagements with the international and ecumenical scene. The web of grace was certainly spinning me along. The family was being drawn into it as well. Shortly after the Hirschluch congress we went on holiday to camp in the Black Forest and Switzerland. En route to our first night in Frankfurt with Henry and Barbara Jakob, we had been invited for lunch with the Bethges at their home in Wachtberg-Villiprott. While Peter entertained us on the piano seven-year old Jonathan worked his way steadily through the proffered box of toys, ending up with the clay pieces of a model village. Dating from the the late 1890s at least, they had originally belonged to Renate's father, Rüdiger Schleicher, another member of the resistance and victim of Hitler's revenge in 1945. As Jonathan sorted out the buildings to his own satisfaction on the patio, one could imagine that a new generation was indeed picking up the past.

9. *Contact* 87 (1985:2), 35f.

Part Two: Minister and Teacher 1967–1990

With Eberhard Bethge, Wachtberg-Villiprott 1985

One last question, in fact one I've been asked at intervals over the years: would I revise *A Patriotism for Today* for *today*? No. It would require too much re-writing to give it a truly contemporary feel. Better to let it stand, and it has in fact been republished in 2011 by the American house Wipf and Stock. I believe its main thesis still holds: that Britain has still to come to terms with itself in a world where the language and clothing of imperialism no longer make sense, yet where military adventurism now even more than ever is clutched at by saber-rattling politicians who want to "defeat evil" and "project our values" onto the rest of the world, eager to parade gestures of strength and power rather than actually make things better.

7

... and Ecumenical Explorer

IF I HAD TO choose an image as an icon for the mid-1980s it would be a shopping trolley parked outside the entrance to our local supermarket in Bristol, into which shoppers were dropping items of food bought not for themselves but for the families of striking miners. The coal dispute, one of the longest and bitterest industrial conflicts in British history, began early in March 1984 and ended in March 1985, with the National Union of Mineworkers admitting defeat and Margaret Thatcher's government claiming a victory not just over the miners but over generations of trade union power throughout British industry. It was a deeply divisive episode—but divisive in more ways than one. Most people habitually did not like strikes and in this case some of the methods of the strikers, but neither did they like the thought of families with young children or elderly dependents going hungry, hence an innate sympathy manifest in the trolleys collecting food for them.

A PIVOTAL YEAR

If 1985 was a pivotal year for Britain, so it also proved for myself. Thanks in large measure to *A Patriotism for Today* I found myself being drawn ever more closely and in a public way into theological engagement with issues of the day, at home and abroad. Just after Easter that year I was invited to preach in the church of St Mary de Crypt, Gloucester, on Christian responsibility in politics. I repeated my familiar theme about Britain succumbing to a nostalgia for the imagined past, whereas the resurrection of Jesus—who identified with the poorest, the nobodies in society who are therefore raised to prominence with him—poses questions about the values that lie behind every political enterprise and decision:

> Some put their faith in Victorian values, some in revolutionary ideologies, but we are called to trust in the future which God offers us, the God of resurrection. If we believe in the God who raises the dead, we should be able to face the future and have a vision for our society for the twenty-first century, instead of invoking the ghosts of the past. This means that Christians should be among those who raise the questions which come from the future, questions which no one else or

few others seem to be asking at the moment. Is it not incredible that after twelve months of bitter conflict in the coal dispute, involving so much expenditure and leaving such a legacy of mistrust, no word has been heard yet on an energy policy for the whole nation? How are our God-given natural resources to be used for the benefit of all? How are the human resources of the mining communities—dismissed as "the enemy within"—to be enabled to make the contribution they want to make for the welfare of all? Or what about Britain's place in the world today? If we believe in the reign of God signaled by Jesus' resurrection, then we believe that we cannot postpone indefinitely the day of justice between north and south, the day of recompense in southern Africa.

St Mary de Crypt was not only historic in the sense of being medievally ancient. Its present congregation was largely the creation of David Paton, former China missionary, author of the trenchant critique of much of the western missionary effort *Christian Missions and the Judgment of God,* for two years successor to Ronald Gregor Smith as editor of SCM Press, sometime canon of Canterbury Cathedral and withal a stern critic of all accepted orthodoxies especially about the church and its forms of ministry. He had enjoyed *A Patriotism for Today* and here again I was conscious of that web of grace being spun in that generation of J.H. Oldham, Gregor Smith, Alec Vidler and not least Bill Paton, David's father, India missionary, successor to Oldham as secretary of the International Missionary Council and a first associate general secretary of the WCC. We had a good long talk after the service. He did not bear fools gladly but if he felt you had something worth saying he was all encouragement. The following year I was invited to lead a weekend conference for the St Mary de Crypt congregation in the Forest of Dean.

Just over a week after that Gloucester service came the fortieth anniversary of VE-Day, and I was the preacher at the commemorative civic service in Bristol Cathedral, at the same time as the dean of Bristol Horace Dammers was preaching at a similar service in Hanover, Bristol's twin city. *A Patriotism for Today*, more than I had imagined, was turning into a diary-filler. But my mind was not running entirely on the socio-political as the only business of theology. That same summer I wrote and presented a series of six Sunday evening programs on Radio 4, "There's Music in God". It comprised readings, with my comments, and appropriate music, from five past theologians on the spiritual significance of music: Augustine, Luther, P. T. Forsyth, Barth and Bonhoeffer, plus one living theologian, John Macquarrie, whom I had interviewed for his reflections. The producer was Ernie Rea who had succeeded Peter Firth as senior producer for religious programs at BBC West and was destined to become controller of Radio 4.

Working simultaneously on such apparently disparate themes in fact brought home to me still more what Bonhoeffer in his prison letters had described as the necessary "polyphony" of life. The college and university teaching was continuing. In the university as well as lecturing on modern theology in general I gave a course on English theological controversies, starting with the pre-1914 "New Theology" of R.J. Campbell and continuing through to contemporary controversialists like Don Cupitt and David Jenkins. These I developed into a substantial book *Lovers of Discord* published in 1988 which had a quite wide and appreciative readership. I also gave a course on Theological Responses to the Jewish Holocaust, which I think may fairly count as one of the earliest treatments of the subject at degree level in the UK. Meanwhile in rather different vein the Psalms and Hymns Trust of the Baptist Union had decided the time had come for a replacement of *The Baptist Hymn Book* of 1962 and I accepted to become secretary of the committee deputed to produce it. "Oh well, "said Morris West when I consulted him about it, "it'll be as good a way as any other of losing friends." This was to be pretty time-consuming right up until the book *Baptist Praise and Worship* appeared in 1991. At the wider level, I was appointed to the Doctrine and Inter-Church Co-operation Commission of the Baptist World Alliance (BWA) which meant attending meetings of the BWA in Singapore (1986), Amman, Jordan (1987), Nassau, Bahamas (1988) and Seoul, South Korea (1990). At the most exalted ecumenical level, I joined the Plenary Commission of the WCC Commission on Faith and Order.

Any assumption that I might have had that foreign travel was all pleasure was rudely and literally shaken after the biennial meeting of European Baptist theological teachers held in Warsaw in July 1985. Complications of flight availability and costs meant that the most feasible itinerary was to fly to Berlin and then take the train to Warsaw, and vice versa on return. This worked well on the outward journey, and I met up with Paul Fiddes and Bruce Keeble of Regent's Park at the Berlin Zoo station to board the eastbound train. The dining car was excellent. The main impression of Warsaw itself was of poverty. We arrived bearing gifts of tinned food, sweets and toiletries for our Polish hosts. The meetings were good. Interest was shown in *A Patriotism for Today* with one Swede exclaiming "But is this systematic theology, or ethics, or history, or pastoral theology—or what?" The meetings over, Paul Fiddes, Bruce Keeble and I caught the, midday train bound for Berlin. Seated in the rearmost coach, about an hour out of Warsaw we were pleasantly contemplating lunch and about to move to the dining car when there was an awful screeching of brakes, the train juddered to a stop amid clouds of dust and voices shouting. Further up the train some passengers were trying to climb out of the windows. We had collided with a tanker train that had jumped the rails at a level crossing. Fortunately no one had been injured and the tanker trucks were evidently empty or there might have been a fearsome conflagration. The accident had happened at a tiny village called Bednary, a name that would be forever etched on our memory, as we disembarked with our baggage and sat for four hours by the track in the hot sun waiting for word from the railway officials on what would happen next. Eventually a rescue locomotive arrived and hitched the serviceable coaches, including our own, for a long trail back to Warsaw and then head westwards again by a longer and more southerly route through the night. The worst thing was that the dining car had had to be left with the other damaged rolling stock at Bednary, and all that the three of us had between us was half a packet of ginger nut biscuits. It was a long night, and we finally reached Berlin Zoo about breakfast time next morning.

That, however, was not the end of unexpected journeys that year.

SOUTH AFRICA

All through the summer of 1985 the news was full of mounting crisis in South Africa. TV screens showed townships alight and demonstrators confronting heavily armed police and military vehicles. International pressure for change in the apartheid state was being ramped up, not only with boycotts of South African exports and calls for disinvestment, but with major US banks like Chase Manhattan declaring they would no longer provide loans to the private sector in South Africa nor roll over old loans, so plunging the country into deeper economic crisis. Yet the government's only response was to declare a state of emergency with ever more rigorous clampdown on protests. Mass arrests took place. On August 15 President P. W. Botha made a speech in Durban which made no concessions nor any significant policy changes, yet could claim that "we are today crossing the Rubicon". Such a statement was at worst vacuous, at best highly ambiguous. The future looked ever more ominous. People were talking of an inevitable bloodbath. In all this the South African churches and their leaders opposed to apartheid were themselves highly exposed and vulnerable.

Early in September I received a call from Don Black at the Baptist Union: the British Council of Churches had received an invitation from the South African Council of Churches (SACC), of which Beyers Naudé was now general secretary, to send a group to visit their country, and would I be willing to go as BU representative? The visit would take place at the end of September and last ten days, its main objects threefold: to express the goodwill and fellowship of the British churches to the SACC, its member bodies, and the people of South Africa; to enter as deeply as possible into the political predicament of the country and seek understanding from a Christian perspective of how healing of the nation for a society of peace and justice in society might prevail; and to help and advise British Christians to a better understanding of the problems and of appropriate responses to adopt in encouraging an end to apartheid. I needed little persuasion, although it would mean shifting or cancelling some diary engagements and missing the events at the start of the new college year. Morris West was wholly in favor. The family too was agreeable, admittedly with some nervousness at the prospect of my going to a setting of which the predominant media image was one of violence. September, as always already a busy month, was taken up with preparatory reading and digesting briefing material supplied by Brian Brown, South African Methodist minister in exile from his country and now Africa secretary in the BCC Division of International Affairs. There were also media enquiries as to what I was expecting from the visit. The rationale for my own inclusion in the group was stated to be "particular expertise on questions of the relationship of church and state", and I told the *Baptist Times* that as a theologian I was hoping to hear a truly prophetic word from the South African churches.

We were due to leave on Sunday September 22 and all arrangements seemed to be going to plan when on the Saturday morning everything was suddenly put under question. The plan had been for a delegation of twelve, but the South African authorities now insisted that it be reduced to nine. Which three should be ejected from the balloon? By phone I eventually tracked Don Black to a conference in a remote part of North Wales and suggested that he call Brian Brown or Paul Oestreicher and put the argument that as I was the only Baptist on the list if I were to be dropped it would mean a significant slice of the British church constituency no longer being represented. By lunchtime the matter was resolved. I was among the fortunate nine.

We assembled at Heathrow on Sunday afternoon, in the airport chapel, with Brian Brown, Paul Oestreicher and the moderator of the BCC Division of International Affairs Elizabeth Salter whom I was meeting for the first time in what was to become a long and happy friendship. The tension was palpable. The South African government's displeasure was all too evident and it was not clear what would await us at the other end. But we had weight on our side. The two most senior church figures were John Taylor, former Uganda missionary and general secretary of the Church Missionary Society, and recently retired as bishop of Winchester whose writings such as *The Go-Between God* I so much admired; and James Monaghan, auxiliary bishop of St Andrews and Edinburgh and President of the Justice and Peace Committee of the Roman Catholic Bishops' Conference of Scotland. The most publicly high-profile figure however was Gerald Priestland, famed journalist, broadcaster, sometime BBC religious affairs correspondent, and a Quaker. Only two women were in the group but they were of major standing: Mildred Nevile, general secretary of the Catholic Institute for International Relations (CIIR, later known as Progressio) and Margaret Cornell, formerly of the Royal Institute for International Affairs (Chatham House) and chairperson of the International Affairs Committee of the Church of England General Synod. Jim Wilkie, Scotsman, a former missionary in Malawi, was now an executive secretary of the Church of Scotland Board of World Mission and Unity. Leon Murray, layman, was Vice-President of the Methodist Church and the one black member of the group. Philip Morgan, general secretary of the BCC, was already in South Africa. We had further briefing from the BCC trio who, after prayers led by the airport chaplaincy team, wished us Godspeed at the Terminal 3 barrier.

Next day we landed at Johannesburg mid-morning. Very grudgingly, it seemed, after two hours we were finally allowed through the barrier and met by a much relieved Byers Naudé and others from the SACC. Naudé had long been one of my heroes, and I had never envisaged him insisting on himself heaving Margaret Cornell's and my baggage into his modest car for the drive to our hotel. In the afternoon we all met with Naudé and staff for a briefing at Khotso House, famous headquarters of the SACC in the center of Johannesburg, and heard from him first-hand of the critical situation in the country, and why an international visit such as ours was important at this time. From Khotso House we were taken straight to an evening reception at the home of the bishop of Johannesburg, namely Desmond Tutu, who played host to us and a posse of church leaders, mostly white. I at least was expecting this to be a somewhat solemn gathering, even if the supply of drinks on the table looked promising enough. But I had not reckoned with Tutu whose idea was that this should be a real *party*. He began by pointing out to everyone that John Taylor, to those who knew him, was loved for his humorous songs, and asked him to take us through the one about the dangerous hippopotamus he had once composed and taught to a scout camp in Uganda. This had to be sung by everyone, accompanied by the most undignified actions even on the part of the sober dark-suited dignitaries. What an ice-breaker. At least if we were all prepared to make ourselves look ridiculous it ensured we would all start on the same level. Nor, a little later, was the bishop himself allowed to get too episcopal. "Desmond," interrupted his wife Leah at one point, "this is not the time for one of your sermons!"

Next morning another assumption was jolted. We joined the SACC staff at Khotso House for their morning prayers. News was shared about latest developments, people in particular need, detainees named, and so on. The service concluded with a hymn, sung in the Xhosa language but the tune of which I instantly recognized: "Blessed assurance, Jesus is mine." This was a surprise to me, to say the least. Where I came from this was a hymn associated not with the struggle for peace and justice but with Billy Graham evangelistic rallies, a marker of other-worldly revivalism, an embarrassment to social activists. Yet here it was being sung with gusto, with even Beyers Naudé himself bellowing it out at full volume. What was happening? It gave me cause to reflect that, if in fact I had been a young detainee in the police cells, facing possible or actual beating and torture, would I really be just wanting to sing defiantly about the coming of freedom and justice? Or would I in fact be wanting a blessed assurance that no truncheons or electric shocks could take away? Change the context, and the relation between piety and politics, prayer and protest may well be reconfigured. Why else did Dietrich Bonhoeffer in *his* prison cell turn again and again to the hymns of the seventeenth-century pietist Paul Gerhardt? Later that day we were taken out to Soweto and saw all that was to be seen there, from poorest squatter families living in abandoned trucks, to the Casspir and Hippo armored vehicles patrolling, and to the valiant community and medical work being carried on. One was conscious of trying not to have all one's prejudices confirmed but South Africa at that time painted everything in vividly contrasting color.

To say that next day was to prove memorable is an understatement. I may have told the *Baptist Times* that one of my hopes was to hear a prophetic word, but I had no idea how soon this was to be realized. On our arrival in Johannesburg Philip Morgan told us of rumors circulating that a radical and highly controversial declaration called the *Kairos Document* was about to be released from a group of "contextual theologians", mainly black, calling for a new level of political opposition and civil disobedience, and that many church leaders were nervous about it. It was due to be launched this very day, September 25. Our group was scheduled to visit Pretoria for the day but Mildred Nevile and I decided to stay in Johannesburg for the launch event in the afternoon at Khotso House. I was glad we did, for very rarely if ever have I been able to claim I was present at a truly historic event. The conference room was packed, with journalists and media people in plenty including Mike Wooldridge, BBC correspondent for South Africa, and his tape-recorder. The atmosphere was tense, there having been warnings beforehand of a possible police clampdown. From the very opening of the first chapter it was clear that *Kairos* was speaking a language never before heard from the churches even in South Africa:

> The time has come. The moment of truth has arrived. South Africa has been plunged into a crisis that is shaking the foundations and there is every indication that the crisis has only just begun and that it will deepen and become even more threatening in the months to come. It is the KAIROS or moment of truth, not only for apartheid but also for the Church.
>
> The Church is divided. Both oppressor and oppressed claim loyalty to the same Church and its day of judgment has come.[1]

So the scroll of prophetic judgment was unrolled with its critiques of "State Theology" and "Church Theology", rejecting calls for reconciliation which ring false unless established on the basis of repentance and justice, the need for a prophetic theology which recognizes that God sides with the oppressed, and a "Challenge to Action":

> And finally the moral illegitimacy of the apartheid regime means that the Church will have to be involved at times in civil disobedience. A Church that takes its responsibilities seriously in these circumstances will sometimes have to confront and disobey the State in order to obey God.

This was clearly explosive stuff. It was not only yet another attack on apartheid, but a massive indictment of the church, calling the church to admit its dividedness along the oppressor-oppressed fault-line, and the need to take sides. Was it, as some were to think, an unwarranted stab-wound on the church, or was it a necessary surgical incision for the sake of the church's true healing? What struck me was the calm, matter-of-fact, almost dead-pan tone of voice in which the document was read out, for all its explosiveness, its potential for fierce dissension and the risk that it might incur from the authorities. No flamboyant rhetoric or histrionics. Just a case of "That's it". That in fact befitted the way in which the document had been produced. It was from the heart, but not off-the-cuff. An initial draft had been produced by these largely Soweto theologians, widely circulated for comment and subsequently revised and in its final form issued over some one hundred and fifty signatures from many confessions, and from both black and white. Moreover it was to a large extent stating what was already being acted out by many in the

---

1. *Kairos*, 4.

churches and beyond. I cannot now actually recall who presented the document apart from the Roman Catholic Albert Nolan whose book *Jesus before Christianity* I had reviewed not long before and with whom I talked at the end of the gathering. I also spoke with Mike Wooldridge who encouraged me to call the BBC in London and offer them an interview about it, which I did that evening from my hotel room. I phoned home too, got Peter and told him about possibly being on air next morning. But I don't think the interview was ever broadcast. Perhaps I had sounded a little too excited. After all, I felt, this is what it must have felt like at Barmen in 1934 when the Theological Declaration of the Confessing Church was proclaimed.

Next day, Thursday 26, the group divided into three. Mildred Nevile, John Taylor and Jim Wilkie flew to Port Elizabeth; James Monaghan, Philip Morgan and Leon Murray to Durban and Pietermaritzburg; Margaret Cornell, Gerald Priestland and myself to Cape Town. At Cape Town airport we were met by Lesley Liddell of the Western Cape Council of Churches who drove us straight away to meet Allan Boesak, just released from detention. Founder and leader of the United Democratic Front, prophetic Reformed preacher and theologian and President of the World Alliance of Reformed Churches, we found him impressive both in his undaunted spirit and in his eloquent analysis of the present scene in which he called the recent actions of the government "the last convulsions of the beast", saying that deep down the government surely knew too. Asked if he thought his methods of non-violent protest really offered hope, he said that it was precisely non-violent action which the government feared since it was only violence they knew how to deal with. Over the next two days we spent time with economists and social scientists of the Universities of Cape Town and the Western Cape, and theologians like Margaret Nash and Charles Villa-Vicencio, and of course John de Gruchy who joined us for dinner on our first evening. I was struck by how amid the heat and dust of conflict there were people who at the same time could be such hard-headed, rigorous analysts whether in sociology, economics or political science, not to mention theology. We toured the (in)famous Crossroads squatter camp and Mitchell's Plain. Another image had to be revised: I had imagined a squatter camp to be a scene of unmitigated squalor. In fact while the poverty was dire, rarely had I seen such a tidy place. There was no litter because litter as such does not exist: it has to be put to use, somewhere, somehow, in one's makeshift building. Signing the visitors' book in a community center, we found that compared with international visitors very few names and addresses came from Cape Town itself. And it was all set between the stunning beauty of the shore and the stern splendor of Table Mountain. We met with a number of church leaders including the Anglican archbishop of Cape Town Philip Russell, at his beautiful residence Bishopscourt, under Table Mountain. Actually, on that occasion the "we" comprised only Margaret Cornell and myself. Gerald Priestland declined to spend half a morning there: "One archbishop is much like another", he mused. We discussed the *Kairos* document with the archbishop. He expressed reservations about it, and wondered if it was really necessary. But until I offered him a look at my copy he confessed he had not actually seen it.

I spent late afternoon and evening of that day with John and Isobel de Gruchy and other theological colleagues from the University of Cape Town. One of the rooms in the de Gruchy household was filled with young people on a protest fast against conscription. On our last day there, Saturday, there came quite a surprise. We were introduced by a Baptist layman, Errol Nourse, to a group of Cape Colored Baptists in one of whose homes we had lunch and who told me about an organization recently founded, the Fellowship of Concerned Baptists (FCB). They were deeply unhappy with the quiescent stance of the (largely white) Baptist Union of South Africa, and the way in which the (largely black) Baptist Convention existed only as an affiliate of the Union with no equal voice at national level and no independent representation in the Baptist World Alliance. They agreed that I and they should keep in contact.

We flew back to Johannesburg that Saturday evening and met with the other two groups in the hotel to share our experiences from the three different locations. Aware that we were very likely under surveillance we found a secluded alcove at the far end of a corridor. Our mood was somber, in human terms pessimistically realistic. We had been inspired by many of the people and groups we had met. Yet, faced with an intransigent regime that understood only repression as a policy there seemed no way out of a spiraling descent into a violent outcome. At the end John Taylor quietly led us into a moving meditation and extempore prayer, reminding us that even in the Bible situations arose in which words and declarations no longer carry meaning, and events take over. Moses finally tells the utterly intransigent Pharaoh "You will see my face no more." In such a scenario we can only pray in fear and trembling that God's will be done. Sometimes, it seems, hope can only arise when we dare to look into the abyss.

Next day, Sunday, we spent with churches of our respective denominations. I was almost entirely with white Baptists of two congregations. The one I attended in the morning in the Sandton district was at least trying to build bridges with the black community—and had lost several disaffected members as a result. The minister and his wife were former missionaries in Zambia, and after the service she drove me around the nearby Alexandra Township, reckoned to be one of the poorest urban areas in the whole of the country. We didn't dawdle—"Just duck if a rock comes through your window," she said cheerfully, "at least then you can say you've really been here!" I was entertained to lunch by two elderly white couples, charming and gracious but in the midst of the meal as we talked about helping people of different races to live together came the ultimate in conversation-stoppers: "Now Hitler, he had the right idea, didn't he?" It so happened that my lift to the other church in the evening was a pleasant gentleman who was one of those who had left the Sandton church on account, as he put it, of the pastor becoming "too black-oriented."

Our final two days were occupied mainly with northward trips to Pretoria and surrounding districts, on which for some reason I was required to be driver of our minibus. We visited the so-called homeland of Bophuthatswana which was more like a dumping ground for unwanted people; had meetings with a wide range of church figures and Dutch Reformed theologians including missiologist Dr Karl Bosshoff whose views on race and nationality sounded just like those of the "German Christian" theologians of the 1930s; and the British ambassador. Some were able to meet that courageous member of parliament Helen Suzman but our hopes for at least one or two being allowed to visit Nelson Mandela in Pollsmoor Prison had already been dashed. We met with Louis Le Grange, Minister for Law and Order, for an interview in which I acted as moderator. It was a surreal experience as we tried to quiz him on the reputation of the South African police for brutality and the hatred and fear they evoked among the black population. He acted all innocence, saying that of course "Our police have the same job as yours in England." "You mean," said Gerald Priestland glaring down at him from his solid height, "that ours also load young people into vans and beat them up as a matter course?" We were also hosted to lunch by the Anglo-American Corporation with bankers and high-flying businessmen (including two blacks) for whom naturally, sanctions and disinvestment were touchy issues to say the least.

Farewelled with prayers and thanks by SACC staff we flew from Johannesburg on the evening of October 2. Elizabeth Salter and BCC staff were there to meet us at Heathrow next morning and took most of us straight to a press conference. Then home. Back at the college I received something like a hero's welcome. But then began the hardest part of the whole experience—trying to assess what it had all meant and communicate to our constituencies the reality of what we had witnessed. We put together our report *Whose Rubicon?* published jointly by the BCC and CIIR early in 1986. I wrote most of the section on the *Kairos Document* and its significance.

I should two odd little postscripts to the visit itself. The first was a case of benign spookiness—through perhaps some psychological explanation can be supplied. On the flight down to Johannesburg, for about an hour as we cruised towards the Limpopo in the morning light I was half dozing and seemed to hear in my head African singing—fervent, rhythmic, joyous and insistent. I knew it was African but was quite sure I had not heard this particular chorus before. When we got to Khotso House, in a room on the ground floor a trades union protest meeting was taking place, with much clapping and singing . . . and it was *exactly* the same as I had been hearing in my head on the plane. Some years later at a German Kirchentag I was in conversation with a black South African and for some reason mentioned this to him. "Ah, "he said smiling, "you were being welcomed!" The second concerned my phone call home on the evening when I had spoken to the BBC about the *Kairos* launch. Peter had taken the call and I was puzzled because for half a minute I could hear him but he could obviously not hear me. When I got home I asked him about this. In turn he asked me, "What was all that I could hear about the police on the line?" The surveillance had evidently been real enough, if somewhat clumsy. Had my room been searched by the security police, comments might well have been made as to why a grown man should bring a little teddy-bear with him. But Jonathan with the solicitude of an eight-year old had insisted that "Little Ted" should accompany me as a mascot.

A CONTINUING IMPACT

The main impact of South Africa upon me was twofold. The first, shared by all of us on the visit, was the overwhelming reality that the main actor on the scene now comprised black South Africans themselves who for good or ill were taking their future and that of the country as a whole into their own hands. The apartheid regime was totally discredited and constitutionally incapable of making any significant change without ceding power. The white, western lenses through which we habitually viewed the South African scene had to be discarded. President Botha claimed that the country had crossed its Rubicon. The majority population had certainly crossed theirs—in a very different direction. Second, following on from this was the question of sanctions and disinvestment. Before the visit I was by no means sure about economic sanctions, either their moral justification or their practicability. Seen from the black perspective, the questions became drastically revised and in their original form irrelevant. We (I mean people like myself) had thought it was a question of how people in the west could ourselves change the situation or "help" the anti-apartheid struggle as if it was all up to us. But time and again the blacks we spoke with regarded our heart-searching with bemusement. The struggle was *theirs* and if we wished to be alongside them that was fine but make no mistake: it was *their* protests, boycotts, strikes, and marches that would in the end carry the day. Yes, our solidarity would be welcome but we were not to agonize too much over whether sanctions would be hurting them (as they undoubtedly would) because they already knew more than enough about suffering and did not need any lessons from us. So I came back believing that sanctions were a moral and practicable necessity, because notwithstanding all the questions they raised I had entered into relations of trust and friendship with certain people in the struggle and in my guts felt I had to be alongside them. At the end of the day, decisions that matter are determined by who it is we feel personally related and responsible to, not morality considered as abstractions of right and wrong. We presented our report to the BCC Assembly in November. Among the responses of the BCC was the recommendation that BCC policy "will be strong advocacy of and full support for carefully targeted sanctions."

Pretty soon I was into a round of speaking engagements in and around Bristol and well beyond, and quite a bit of correspondence. In October the rugby correspondent of the *Guardian* stated that the only question raised by the British Lions' forthcoming tour of South Africa was the matter of their safety and security. I penned a letter which appeared a day or two later, stating that as one who had recently been in the country I could assure him that the safety of the team would be no problem since that would be a matter for the South African police who were adept at dealing with troublemakers in their vans and interrogation cells, and the players would be kept not only out of harm's way but out of sight and sound of the victims of police brutality—the only question that night trouble them would be their consciences if they had any. The editor of the *Bristol Evening Post* called me soon afterwards and asked if I could write some columns in similar vein for the paper, but I was just too busy. I reported to the Baptist Union Council in November, warning against any assumption that South African Baptists, white ones certainly, were against apartheid in practice hoever much verbally they may denounce it as unchristian, which raised some eyebrows.

The Baptist Union invited Allan Boesak to address the Baptist Assembly in London in May 1986, but he was refused permission to travel by the South African government. "Tell them I am with them in spirit", was his message. I was asked instead to speak briefly and introduce a time of silent prayer. This was no substitute for Boesak but I recalled for the assembly what he had told us during our BCC visit the previous September about the South African government's fear of *non-violent* protest. The *Baptist Times* reported that for more than five minutes the congregation in Westminster Chapel sat in silence, a spiritual call to end apartheid in South Africa, and continued: "Baptist minister Keith Clements had introduced the prayer for the assembly because 'We British are in South Africa economically as the largest trading partner. We are in South Africa historically as the country whose past actions did much to shape the structures on which apartheid was built' And above all, he said, 'We Christians are there spiritually as members of the one body of Jesus Christ, the church which in South Africa is being tested as to its faithfulness to the truth of Christ.'"

BAPTIST CONCERN AND DIVISION OVER SOUTH AFRICA

It was later in 1986 that two other ministers Philip Smith, ecumenical chaplain at South Wales Polytechnic, and Paul Walker, minister of Highgate Baptist Church, Birmingham, and I myself strongly supported by Don Black at the BU, set up a small network, Baptist Concern for Southern Africa (BCSA). Set within the wider and flourishing ecumenical stream of concern our primary aims were modest and specific: to give support to the Fellowship of Concerned Baptists in South Africa (FCB), to make known their activities to our UK constituency and to raise some funds for them. In November 1986 we brought Errol Nourse over and arranged a speaking tour for him beginning in Bristol, and he made quite an impact. Just before Christmas we invited Baptists nationwide to fast for twenty-four hours as a gesture of solidarity with the victims of apartheid and to make a donation to raise funds for the FCB. In some ways we were knocking at an open door. At one of the meetings I addressed in Bristol an old age pensioner came up to me and said she had £200 from some savings interest that she didn't know what to do with—how could she donate? We got support for the fast and funding from a wide range of ministers and laypeople across the county. Then in April 1987 another Cape Colored member of the FCB, John Daries, minister of Rocklands

Baptist Church on Mitchell's Plain, Cape Town, arrived and after a weekend with us in Bristol visited the Baptist Assembly and spoke with great effect at a fringe meeting arranged by Don Black. Tall, wiry with a laid back sense of humor but a very sharp mind and force of expression, John was to become our main contact in the FCB for the next few years, feeding us with information in a continual stream of personal letters and more public bulletins. Don Black and I thought it essential that he be brought into the arena of the Baptist World Alliance, which was due to hold the annual meetings of its council and commissions in Amman, Jordan, in July 1987. Don and I were both going to Amman, and arranged his accommodation accordingly. He would see to his own travel—what that meant we didn't quite know and for a couple of days after the start of the BWA meetings we were in growing anxiety as to how, or if, he was going to make it. But turn up he did, having flown into Tel Aviv and then hitched his way as far as Jericho where he met a farmer who offered him a ride on his camel and gave him a bed for the night, and next day he negotiated his way across the Allenby Bridge. Once in the setting of the BWA meetings he had opportunity of making all kinds of informal contacts but of course he had no official status. Don Black and I wanted something more. So we got the agreement of the BWA general secretary, Gerhard Claas, to hold an open meeting one evening after the official programme for the day was over, on "Baptists and the Future of South Africa", featuring John alongside Trevor Swart, secretary of the South African Baptist Union. Over a hundred people turned up. I moderated and began by inviting the two South Africans in turn to respond to two questions. First, is there any alternative to a violent outcome in South Africa? Second, what role will be played by the South African Baptists in this scenario? Both spoke fairly briefly. Then it was open to the floor and the questions came thick and fast, most especially from blacks from elsewhere in Africa, from the Caribbean and the USA but also from Europe. Trevor Swart behaved with dignity under the skeptical barrage but it was obviously John Daries who was carrying the day. It was one of the most inspiring meetings I have ever chaired. At last, the black Baptist community of South had taken the international Baptist stage and become really visible. John Daries was on the way to being lionized and a number of important friendships especially with Germans and Scandinavians began for him in Amman. Back in South Africa later that year the Baptist Convention voted to disaffiliate from the Baptist Union and to seek full membership of the BWA in its own right.

Part Two: Minister and Teacher 1967–1990

Mt Nebo, Jordan: John Daries points to the Promised Land in hope.

In May 1988 the Standing for the Truth campaign was launched in South Africa, with mass protests, boycotts and civil disobedience largely by the black population but with support by concerned whites too. For us in BCSA and ecumenical circles the next twelve months in this scenario proved critical and indeed quite fraught. The Baptist Union of South Africa, by now worried about its image in the UK and elsewhere, had invited the general secretary of the Baptist Union Bernard Green and the editor of the *Baptist Times* Geoffrey Lockes to visit South Africa for two weeks in February 1988. They reported to the BU Council immediately on their return, and gave themselves extensive coverage in the *Baptist Times*. It would be unfair to describe their visit and itinerary as wholly stage-managed by the white Baptist Union since they were able to visit representatives of the Convention, the FCB and indeed the SACC too. But what emerged was essentially a public relations exercise for the Union, praise for its "moderate" stance and rejection of the idea that they were in any way condoning apartheid. Their reports were largely impressionistic with no attempt at analysis of the political scene and the role of the churches within it. It was as though *Whose Rubicon?* had never been written. Indeed Geoffrey Lockes caused huge offence, not just to us in BCSA but to many in the ecumenical circuit, for some remarks about an unjustified industry of attacks on South Africa. Moreover, articles by a number of us putting another point of view were refused publication by him. It was not that anything specific in the reports of Green and Lockes was in itself incorrect, it was rather the incomplete and very partial nature of their account as a whole that was found wanting. More than our own criticism, it was the response of the FCB people that was most telling. Kevin Roy, a white South African Baptist, wrote with genuine appreciation of the purpose and spirit of the visit and the value of the discussions the visitors had with South African Baptists. But Geoffrey Lockes had written in the *Baptist Times* of how Baptists there were "right in the forefront working for the victims of the country's history, playing their part in pressing and working for social justice and political change", and sought to discount the "myth" that Baptists were pietists uninvolved in social and political issues. Roy confessed with sorrow that this was not an accurate portrait:

> There is a fundamental principle that applies almost across the board to white Christians in South Africa, and it is a principle which was only very imperfectly grasped by Bernard and Geoffrey in their visit. It can be formulated as follows. While apartheid and racial discrimination are genuinely and sincerely deplored by the, majority of South African Baptists, yet they continue to support and defend the status quo out of fear for what the alternative might be, and this fear is built up and strengthened by the subtle but powerful propaganda of the state controlled media.

Kevin Roy went on to spell this out in terms of wide Baptist support for the Nationalist Party and military service. He had submitted his article to the *Baptist Times* but it was rejected without explanation. During 1988–90 however we in BCSA published three issues of a newsletter *Concern* which I edited, giving prominence to news and views from the FCB members themselves. We published Kevin Roy's article in *Concern* no. 1.

I myself crossed swords with Bernard Green who stated in the *Baptist* Times of April 7 1988 his "fear of the power of polarization" in South Africa as in other situations of conflict, and argued that with the ANC and the South African government being on a dangerous "collision course", the middle ground of compromise and negotiation was the key to reconciliation. By contrast it seemed to some of us that since the ANC represented no more than a demand for a truly unitary, democratic state with one vote per person regardless of race this was in fact the middle ground, and it was therefore a very strange argument that the ANC and United Democratic Front should be the ones to compromise. Angry, I wrote to the *Baptist Times* that one could never generalize about conflict situations, and while polarization was regrettable it could not be decided in advance that one side did *not* have a more just claim than the other. Each case had to be examined on its merits. I continued:

> My own experience in South Africa in 1985 brought home to me how misleading it is to categorize the "extremes" as "left" and "right" as though these were options chosen with equal freedom. Yes, reconciliation through negotiation is the only way in which South Africa's tragedy can finally be overcome. But such negotiation is precisely what the political leaders of the black majority

have been demanding for decades, and it is what the white Nationalist regime has been intransigently refusing them. When the government's only answer to such aspirations has been imprisonment, banning, torture or even death, where do you expect the oppressed to go?[2]

Clearly some of us and the BU secretariat were ourselves on collision course and the annual Baptist Assembly was fast approaching. Bernard Green and Geoffrey Lockes agreed to a meeting with Don Black and myself in Baptist Church House. There was frank speaking on both sides, and it grew heated with Bernard Green at one point standing up and threatening to walk out. But we did come to agreement on the form of words for a resolution on South Africa which laid out the area on which there was at least consensus: condemnation of the South African government for apartheid and its persistent attempts to discredit the opposition, calling on the British government to reconsider its economic policy towards South Africa, and expressing support for the Christian leaders there. I agreed to move the resolution at the Assembly where it was overwhelmingly passed. In July that year the BWA meetings took place in Nassau, Bahamas. Not only was John Daries there, but so too were Gideon Makhanya and Peter Mhxlope, secretary and president respectively of the Baptist Convention. The membership application of the Convention was accepted by the BWA Council with acclaim. Something had happened to which we had given a push, even if only a minor one, to make a difference. But it was not all plain sailing for us in BCSA. We had raised quite a substantial amount from individuals and churches in the UK for the FCB. It emerged however that the person at the South African end to whom we had entrusted the transmission of the funds to the FCB had betrayed that trust. We had to admit to an error of judgment and informed our constituency accordingly. It was however an instance of grace that the FCB people continued to show their trust in us and to use us as channel of communication to the wider world. There were deeply impressive people among them, John Daries included. He could even make light of his experience on returning from one of his visits to Europe, being taken off the plane by security men and arrested, made to stand naked for twenty-four hours, and beaten intermittently. Among the whites there was Ivor Jenkins and his wife Karin in Pretoria. Ivor was director of the Koinonia organization and took a leading part in the Standing for the Truth campaign and efforts to desegregate transport in Pretoria. They had had shots fired into their home. Ivor and Karin visited the UK in 1988 and spent twenty-four hours with us in Bristol. Two days later I got a phone call from Don Black, whom they had just visited in London. Don's voice was shaking with emotion: "Keith, I think I must resign . . . ", so outpaced he felt in commitment and discipleship by this young couple, and the risks they undertook. I persuaded Don to stick with his post, for ours was the privilege and duty of making such costly witness known to our community. Then there was the stalwart Gisela Nicholson of Pretoria, secretary of the

---

2. *Baptist Times* April 21 1988.

FCB. The black leaders like Gideon Makhanya and Peter Mhxlope were memorable for their heart-warming evangelicalism combined with a mighty commitment to justice. Then too there were the black young people whom we assisted financially and with hospitality in coming to the UK in summer 1988 for the BWA Youth Congress in Glasgow. Their comments on the ethos of that event occasion were not only appreciative but sharply critical at some points—and were not wholly welcome to the BWA.

There is much, much more that could be said on how in BCSA we tried to create an informed and committed awareness of the realities of South Africa as experienced by concerned Baptists there, and many more people and incidents that could be recounted. One day Ian Linden of CIIR phoned me to say that a black activist, a Baptist in fact, had just arrived in London having had to flee literally for his life from Bophuthatswana. Could we give him hospitality for a day or two in Bristol? So at the college we received John Lamola who shared his story, and the wider scenario of what was now happening in South Africa, with staff and students. Eventually joined by his wife and family, he went on to study for a doctorate at Birmingham University. The whole South African engagement from 1985 onwards was for me profoundly educative. It brought together my Bonhoeffer interests and my contemporary international concerns, and this bore fruit in a paper I presented to several groups during 1988-89, "Taking Sides: South Africa and the Cost of Confession", later published in my 1990 collection *What Freedom? The Persistent Challenge of Dietrich Bonhoeffer*. It also put me more deeply than anything else previously, into consciously "living in more than one place at once". Indeed, at home it was sometimes teasingly remarked that my address was as much Cape Town as Bristol. At a more general level, when twenty-five years later the struggle against apartheid tends to be seen only in the large and distant picture and somewhat romanticized, it is important to recall just how taxing, stressful and frustrating the nitty-gritty work could be. But the victory was eventually won in South Africa and so this period is one on which I can look back—notwithstanding all the political and economic problems South Africa faces today—in hope.

AND THE CHURCH? VISIBLE UNITY

However much issues like South Africa may have been a preoccupation for me they did not usurp an equal concern for the visible unity of the church. Indeed from student days it had never occurred to me that what in ecumenical circles could broadly be called "Life and Work" issues on the one hand and "Faith and Order" on the other, should ever be in competition even if at some points there was a certain tension between them. Life and Work rightly claimed that Christian unity was never an end in itself since the gospel was for the whole world in its need of reconciliation. Faith and Order rightly claimed that Christian witness for justice, peace and reconciliation in the world was vitiated if the churches themselves were not at peace with each other and seen to be on the way to being visibly one. During my time as college tutor I became ever more involved in the quest for visible unity as well as in peace and justice issues.

This really began in 1982 with the transmission to the churches of the now famous "Lima text" *Baptism, Eucharist and Ministry* (BEM) by the WCC Faith and Order Commission. All churches and denominations were invited to respond, and it quickly became the most widely distributed, studied and discussed ecumenical text of modern times. Morris West as a member of the Faith and Order Standing Commission had been at the meeting in Lima where it was finally and unanimously accepted as ready for transmission, and obviously had a personal interest in it. We had seminars on it with college students, and there was also a lively study group set up by the Bristol Baptist Association to prepare a response to be included by those from the Baptist Union. The Lima text undoubtedly helped to foster a common language between different confessions. In retrospect from more than thirty years on, one cannot help but feel we all could have gone much further by now in working out and implementing the implications of these insights.

In 1984 I was appointed to the British Council of Churches Board of Ecumenical Affairs (BEA) which met twice a year, and the reception of BEM and the churches' responses to it were high on its agenda. Donata Coleman, now living in Exeter as her husband Peter had become bishop of Crediton was also a member. I went to several local ecumenical meetings to speak on BEM during 1984–86. One in the diocese of Guildford was at Redhill where I was on a panel with Mary Tanner. We were asked by one Anglican priest whether in face of the current ecumenical lethargy we could offer him any remedy for the pain he felt at the slowness of progress towards visible unity. My reply was no: the pain you feel is a necessary part of the Spirit's prompting. Two of the other meetings, in Exeter and Barnstaple, were at Donata's instigation as she was also serving as ecumenical adviser for Devon.

In one sense my contact with the WCC Faith and Order Commission went back to 1973–74 and the "Giving Account of Hope" project.[3] But my first direct involvement came in August 1985 when I attended the meeting of its Plenary Commission in Stavanger, Norway, as a consultant. In a way I was following in Morris West's footsteps as he was bowing out of Faith and Order, though unlike him I never became a member of the Standing Commission. Stavanger was an eye-opener for me on just how far the ecumenical scene had moved from being gatherings of people *from* different contexts around the world to being dialogue *about* those contexts and the way they shaped the specifically theological concerns of the dialogue. Faith and Order certainly was no longer a theological ivory tower, for a major part of its programme was precisely the relation between the unity and renewal of the church on the one hand, and the renewal of the human community at every level on the other. Theology could not be compartmentalized away from social, political and cultural issues, including

---

3. See above chapter 5, p.103f.

the relations between women and men. For example, one group at Stavanger looked specifically at the implications of the Lima text for racism.

Beforehand I had known hardly any of the participants at Stavanger apart from Mary Tanner (who was a Vice-Moderator of the Commission), Martin Conway who acted as minutes secretary, and Oliver Tomkins who with his wife was present as a guest father-figure of Faith and Order. But I quickly got to know many more, some of whom became lasting friends like Günther Gassmann, Geneva-based secretary of the Commission; Horace Russell, Jamaican Baptist scholar; Jean Tillard, Dominican French Canadian and person of mercurial passion and humor; Paul Crow of the Americans Disciples of Christ; Duncan Forrester of New College, Edinburgh; Robert Smith of the United Church of Canada with whom and his wife Ellen I spent a lot of time; and Gennadios Limouris, Greek Orthodox on the WCC staff. Theological eminences were there like Wolfhart Pannenberg of Munich, very much the Herr Professor; Raymond Brown the leading Roman Catholic biblical scholar of New York; Geoffrey Wainwright, British Methodist theologian now an emigré at Duke University, USA; and Dietrich Ritschl of Heidelberg, descendant of the great nineteenth-century Protestant theologian Albrecht Ritschl.

As well as reviewing the past work of Faith and Order, the main themes at Stavanger were BEM, the programs "Towards the Common Expression of the Apostolic Faith Today", and "Unity and Renewal". I was willingly attached to the Apostolic Faith project, which had emanated from a resolution at the Fifth WCC Assembly at Nairobi in 1975 asking the churches "to undertake a common effort to receive, reappropriate and confess together, as contemporary occasion requires, the Christian truth and faith, delivered through the Apostles, and handed down through the centuries"[4], and it was given further impetus at the 1982 Lima meeting. Basic to this programme would be an explication of the Niceno-Constantinopolitan Creed both in its historical context and in a contemporary expression. I enjoyed the group discussion, especially the vigorous but jovial arguments with Vlassios Pheidas, Greek Orthodox professor, on the relation between scripture and the language of the creed, and indeed the meaning of the word "apostolic". Did this mean only repeating what the apostles had said? Or did it also mean—as I hoped—that we in our generation would also be apostolic in the sense of being led and enabled by the Spirit to express the gospel appropriately for today? Behind these and similar arguments about context at Stavanger there was however lurking a question: had Faith and Order, in taking onto its agenda the relation between unity of the church and unity and renewal of the human community, in fact presumed that this relationship was clear when in fact it was not, and was it possible therefore that what was happening was an invasion and take over by the Life and Work agenda? This was my first in-depth encounter with the Orthodox at a *corporate* level, although a course we ran in the lay education programme at the Bristol College in early 1984, "Meet the Orthodox", was for me an important taster, not to mention the participation of Father

---

4. Best, *Faith and Renewal*, 115

Nicholas Behr in our study groups on hope and unity[5]. There was a massive theocentricity in the Orthodox, an apprehension of the mighty, overflowing divine presence which overrode into triviality our western intellectual hang-ups about the distinction and relation between God's transcendence and immanence. I came away from Stavanger feeling that while I could not be Orthodox, I could not be Christian without them.

I came away from Stavanger with many new friendships with people in all continents and many confessions. I also heard moving and inspiring stories. Like, for example, from Ulrich Kühn, Lutheran professor in Leipzig in the GDR. At lunch one day he told how as a boy towards the end of the Second World War he was living in a village near Dresden. Once in February 1945 he went with his parents to visit the city. They knew that a night or two previously there had been an allied air-raid but had no idea what it had meant until they reached the outskirts of the city, and saw the utter devastation wrought by the firestorm. He said that there and then, in his boyish but sincere way, he had prayed and made a vow to God that he would devote his life to peace in the world. Fulfilling that vow was easier said than done in the conditions of the GDR, but there was to be a sequel four years after our meeting.

There was also work to do in follow-up to Stavanger, especially as I was also on the Doctrine and Inter-Church Cooperation Commission of the Baptist World Alliance. For the 1988 meeting of the commission in Nassau, Bahamas, I wrote a paper on the Apostolic Faith project and its significance for Baptists, later published in the *Baptist Quarterly*.[6] At the next meeting of the Plenary Commission, in Budapest in 1989, a discussion arose about the distinction between "creedal" and "non-creedal" churches. I intervened to say that this was an unhelpful basis for ecumenical discussion. Rather, it would be more creative to invite non-creedal churches to explain how even though they may not use creeds regularly or formally in worship and teaching, the content of the apostolic faith is nevertheless preserved and transmitted by other means in the life of the churches, in worship, hymnody, preaching and so forth. Conversely, creedal churches could be invited to explain just how what is formally confessed in their use of creeds is actually translated into effective personal faith in the lives of their members and communities. As well as the Plenary Commission in Budapest, during 1989-90 there were smaller consultations on the Apostolic Faith project which I attended in Würzburg, Oxford and Venice. The Würzburg meeting was especially enjoyable, being in such a beautiful city in June, even if there were contrasting mood swings among the participants. There was a long and protracted argument between the Orthodox and others (especially the Roman Catholics) over the *filioque* clause in the traditional western form of the creed, which states that the Holy Spirit "proceeds from the, Father and the Son", whereas the Eastern form states only that the Spirit "proceeds from the Father": a severe bone of contention between Orthodox East and

---

5. See above, chapter5, p.103f.

6. "Towards the Common Expression of the Apostolic Faith. Baptist Reflections on this Faith and Order Project", *Baptist Quarterly* 33, 2 (April 1989), 63–71.

Latin (including Protestant) West for centuries. No-one expected this consultation to resolve the issue, but matters were inadvertently not helped by our attendance at an evening choral concert in Würzburg Cathedral in which a Mozart mass was the main item. Of course the form of the text of the Credo was the western one, and as (mis)fortune would have it, when it comes to "filioque" Mozart in this version brings in all his trumpets and drums with a triumphalistic flourish. There was Orthodox annoyance and both Günther Gassmann and Jean Tillard had to deny strenuously that this was not a conspiracy on their part. The Venice consultation just before Easter 1990 was also memorable not least for the hospitality of the nuns in the convent where we met. Margaret and Jonathan, who was then aged twelve, were able to come with me. The sisters were delighted to have a *bambino* to mother and he got an equally warm welcome from the Roman Catholic Cardinal Patriarch of Venice Cardinal Marco Cé, on whom the group made a ceremonial call during the week. The Venice meeting was also memorable for the presence of Ulrich Kühn, five years after Stavanger. Now he was able to tell us about how Leipzig just months earlier had been a center of peaceful change in the "revolution of the candles" in which with other pastors he had played a leading part. His boyhood prayer amid the ruins of Dresden had been answered.

Confessing the One Faith. An Ecumenical Explication of the Apostolic Faith as it is Confessed in the Nicene-Constantinopolitan Creed (381) was published by the WCC in 1991. Has it ever been put to actual use as a basis for common confession of the faith by the churches? Time and again it appears that the churches, once an agreed basis for unity seems to have been reached, find other reasons or excuses for not venturing further. But at the time it showed well what could be done—and done again if need be—and therefore is a sign of hope.

BONHOEFFER—AND OTHERS

From 1986 the flow of speaking and writing on Bonhoeffer continued unabated, largely it has to be said in response to requests and invitation. In 1986 I wrote and presented a thirty-minute documentary on BBC Radio 4, *Striking the Serpent's Head* which narrated Bonhoeffer's role and motivation in the conspiracy against Hitler but with extensive inputs from Eberhard and Renate Bethge whom I had interviewed and recorded again the previous year. This also allowed Eberhard to tell much of his own extraordinary story of friendship with Bonhoeffer, his own arrest and interrogations after the failure of the July 20 Plot, and how both he and the prison letters managed to survive the Gestapo and the last days of the war. Then in 1988 came the Fifth International Bonhoeffer Congress in Amsterdam, at which John de Gruchy and I presented our papers on Bonhoeffer, the freedom of the church and the "Free Church" concept. That summer I was on sabbatical study leave from the college and made my first visit to the USA, primarily to teach an elective course on Bonhoeffer at Eastern Baptist Seminary, Philadelphia, and managed to see New York, Washington

DC and Baltimore also, before flying on to Nassau, Bahamas, for the BWA Council and Commission meetings. The following year came the start of a new and prolonged venture: the translation into English of the entire range of Bonhoeffer's works in their new definitive German editions. I joined the English-language editorial board at its first meeting in Chicago in September 1989. The transcript of my interviews with Eberhard and Renate Bethge was included in my collected essays *What Freedom?* published in 1990.

But on my 1988 visit to the USA I had also gone armed with a BBC tape recorder, as I did also to the Bonhoeffer Congress, for the making of a radio documentary on Karl Barth, *Against the Stream* which was broadcast on December 10 1988, the twentieth anniversary of his death. By September I had the recorded inserts by theologians who had known Barth or were indebted to him including contributions by Paul Lehmann of New York, Eberhard Bethge, Tom Torrance and Duncan Forrester of Edinburgh, and Allan Boesak from South Africa. Then in November accompanied by the BBC producer Stephen Oliver I went to Tübingen in Germany and Basel in Switzerland to interview Germany's most well-known theologian Jürgen Moltmann, plus Hans Küng, one of the first Roman Catholics to take Barth seriously and now a thorn in the side of the Vatican, and Jan Milic Lochmann the Czech successor to Barth's chair at Basel whom I had met in the Faith and Order meeting in Stavanger. The experience proved to be a study not only on how Karl Barth had been such a varied influence on these theologians of the next generation, but also on how so very different personalities these figures were. Jürgen Moltmann, polite and softly spoken, received us for a morning visit in his home and we all sat down in easy chairs having been given the impression we had all the time in the world. It was quite a moving conversation, as Moltmann made clear that while he had in the course of his own theological journey taken a long farewell to Barth, Barth in some respects remained indispensable: his doctrine of God's election of humankind in the crucified Christ meant that no one ultimately was without God, no one was ever to be completely written off. He told us he still kept a photo of Barth in his study, and I asked him. "What question if any does Barth seem to ask of you as you look at him?" He replied, "All this theology you are writing, are you doing it for your sake, or for God's?" A long silence. Hans Küng's large house was on a hill above Tübingen, and inside it looked like a large library and a high-tech office rolled into one. A portrait of his favorite saint, Thomas More, hung on the turn of the stairs. He said he could only give us half an hour as he was racing to finish and dispatch a lecture he was shortly to give in the USA. In an upright chair he spoke crisply and somewhat edgily, with frequent glances at the clock, and at his secretary busy on her computer, about Barth's continuing relevance today not least for the Roman Catholic Church (now "more Roman than Catholic"). But it was good. Next afternoon we were in a cold and drizzly Basel, recording descriptions of the scenes and street sounds outside Barth's former house and the university area, then as darkness fell turned up at the appointed hour at Jan Milic Lochmann's modest house down a side-street, with a taxi waiting at the door as our flight back to London was in little over an hour. The door opened, we stumbled over a large fleeing cat and found ourselves in a kitchen hung about with washing and a distressed Mrs Lochman toiling over her ironing board: "Oh, I am so sorry. He has *forgot*! I do not know. This has *never* happened before!" In a small study piled high with books stuffed with slips of paper (clearly a rather different filing system from Küng's) it was our turn to look nervously at our watches . . . and wait. Presently the door opened and in burst a breathlessly apologetic Professor Lochman. None of us even bothered to sit down as Stephen Oliver hand-held the microphone to his face, and we were treated to a marvelous five-minute, off-the-cuff eulogy to his famous predecessor. Barth's greatness, he said, lay in his vision of God as the God of *grace* and this informed his life too. For example the only Basel congregation he would preach to was that in the city gaol because there, he said, not in the respectable churches where people would only want to hear the famous theologian, were the people who really wanted to hear about grace. (I was later reminded of this by an Australian friend who once heard Barth say he was fed up with people who came to Basel "to see the Zoo and Karl Barth.") Hurried but ecstatic thanks, a dive into the taxi and we just made the flight. *Against the Stream*, judging by the audience postbag, was well received, though there was a sneering review in the *Independent* and even Ernie Rea thought that at times it was a "hard listen" for Radio 4 (or had BBC dumbing down already begun?). I was gladly surprised to get a letter from Henton Davies. I recalled him at Regent's Park telling us how while studying in Germany in the early 1930s he had heard Bultmann lecture, and also a rather unpleasant pro-Nazi theologian, but now he told me he had also heard Barth in Bonn and witnessed him facing down a protest against him by Nazi students. I wished I had known before making the programme, and it put me in mind of collecting an anthology of recollections by such as Henton and others from Britain who had studied theology in Nazi Germany. It would have made an interesting booklet (title: "Swatting under the Swastika"?-I hardly think so); but it never came high enough on an increasingly crowded list of priorities. The most touching letter of all came from a listener who was evidently struck by Lochman's remark about Barth preaching to the prisoners, and told me about his brother, who oddly happened to have the same name as myself, now serving a long prison sentence. I wrote to my gaoled namesake and we had an interesting exchange. For good measure, for several years I would hear of recordings of the programme being used in theology departments as an introduction to courses on Barth.

CAN CHANGE BE REAL—AND PEACEFUL?

In February 1987 I visited the Soviet Union for the first time. The All-Union Council of Evangelical Christians-Baptists (AUCECB) were holding a five-day pan-Soviet conference on the theme of peace, and a good number of international guests had been invited. Douglas Sparkes, Deputy General Secretary of the BU, and I went there to represent British Baptists. We were cheerfully informed just before leaving Heathrow that the temperature in Moscow had risen to minus 10 Celsius. Suggestions of other possible thawings were also in our ears. Mikhail Gorbechev had become general secretary of the Soviet Union Communist Party in March 1985. By 1986 we were starting to hear from Russia terms such as *glasnost*, denoting greater transparency in government, and *perestroika* indicating restructuring or re-grouping of the economy and possibly even some kind of democratization. Soon, more interestingly still, rumors spread of Gorbachev's desire to reduce the nuclear stand-off between East and West. Was all this real, would it prove a change as dramatic as that of John XXIII at the Vatican nearly thirty years earlier? Or was it largely cosmetic? And was this conference itself, obviously held by permission of if not at the behest of the state, part of the window-dressing or part of a genuine attempt to encourage greater dialogue with the West? At any rate, it was a most interesting and encouraging week. On the Sunday morning Douglas Sparkes and I were driven out in ever deepening snow to a village amid the birch forests called Vestrokovo, where we both (via an interpreter) preached as did a pastor from Georgia.

Preaching in Vestrokovo Baptist Church

It was as a small but very warm-hearted and welcoming congregation of all ages, and after lunch at the church we had a two-hour discussion with the elders about Baptist customs, worship, discipline, the second coming, sin against the Holy Spirit, repentance, angels . . . In the evening we were welcomed with other guests into the vestry at the famous Moscow Central Baptist Church about which we had heard so much and I was looking forward to being part of a packed congregation of over a thousand, fervent singing led by a crack choir and above all powerful preaching-until just before the vestry prayers began I heard the pastor Michael Zidkhov informing us, "Brother Clements will be preaching." My notes for my sermon at Vestrokovo in the morning had been scanty enough. Now I did not even have those with me. But at least I had a Bible text in my head, "See what love the Father has given us, that we should be called children of God." (1 John 3:1). In fact standing in that pulpit, whatever it meant to the congregation, was inspiring for myself. Preaching through a good interpreter can be an asset. It gives time to recollect one's thoughts between each sentence and phrase and a kind rhythmic partnership builds up the rhetorical effect.

The conference as a whole took place in the Central Baptist Church during the week. Much speechifying and lecturing. Alexei Bichkov, president of the AUCECB, put me on a panel of overseas guests one morning, wishing me to speak on some of the themes in *A Patriotism for Today*. I had brought several copies with me, and when the officials at the customs desk at the airport went through our bags I was a bit disappointed that they didn't display any suspicion towards them but were far more interested in Douglas Sparkes' copy of the *Baptist Union Yearbook* which they took away to examine and presumably photocopy parts of it before returning it to him. Lists of names and telephone numbers apparently were much more significant in their eyes. There were cultural events. We saw the usual sights of Red Square and the Kremlin, were taken to the ballet and museums, and shopped in the famous GUM store. There were choral concerts and poetry recitals in the church in the evenings. The gathering had other useful purposes. I was able to talk at length with Denton Lotz, assistant secretary of the BWA, about South Africa, as also with Knud Wumpelmann of Denmark, general secretary of the European Baptist Federation. We were addressed by the Chairman of the Soviet Council for Religious Affairs Cosntantin Harchev, and towards the end we international visitors were hosted by the government at a lavish lunchtime reception. It might have been window-dressing but I believed that within it there was a genuine desire to open doors more widely to the world. There was very little self-justifying propaganda. Three memories of non-verbal communication remain vivid from that week. The very old lady at Vestrokovo who after the service pointed to my heart and then mine. The elderly pastor with worn, lined face and gnarled hands who was sitting next to me at the concluding communion service in the Central Baptist Church, and on whose wrist as he passed the common chalice to me I glimpsed a tattooed number, witness no doubt to the long cruelty of the gulag; often in my mind's eye I see it again when at communion I similarly hold the common cup of Christ's sufferings. Then, wandering around the cathedrals and churches of the Kremlin—the Dormition, the Deposition, the Annunciation—now all museums, I saw the frescoes of multitudes of saints and angels, a silent congregation but in their silence seeming to be not mourning but *waiting* for the time when once again the air would be filled with incense and glorious, harmonious chanting, and they too would sing again.

Though we did not know it at the time, just before this Moscow conference, on January 27 Mikhail Gorbachev had stated bluntly to a meeting of Central Committee members that glasnost and perestroika were the only solution to the problems of the Soviet Union. But we were well aware that something new was also under way in East-West relations. Ronald Reagan who had been calling the Soviet Union an "evil empire" had catching up to do on the race towards nuclear downsizing, and Margaret Thatcher believed Gorbachev was someone "she could do business with". It was not until the summer of 1989, however, that change in Eastern Europe really began to impinge on me, at the Plenary Commission of Faith and Order in Budapest, August 9–21. There we could hear government ministers talking about the impossibility of their country surviving economically without from being linked into the new electronic communications systems emanating from the West—and what then? We learnt too of the beginning of migration from the GDR via Hungary to the West. And actual change was afoot within Hungary. A new Baptist theological seminary was being built, and a few months earlier the local authorities had objected to the inclusion of a baptistery in it on the grounds that this represented an attempt to build a new church in the guise of a seminary. By the time of my visit the authorities had lost interest but problems had arisen from another quarter. The newly-formed local Green Party was objecting to the cutting down of some trees to make way for the new building. From communist bureaucracy to Green democracy in a matter of months!

I have to confess that in writing and academic work I was ever more deeply into peace issues yet like most other people was not aware of the full significance of what was actually happening in Europe and indeed globally. From early 1989 I was a member of the British Council of Churches Peace Forum. We produced a thoughtful booklet on the arms trade. In October we visited Northern Ireland, trod the sectarian streets of Belfast, met members of ecumenical peace groups and local churches (I preached at Bangor Presbyterian), and stayed at the Corrymeela Community. Among the most interesting members of the Forum was General Sir Hugh Beach who, starting off as a Second World War artillery officer, was by now an expert on "smart" weapons and a vigorous opponent of landmines and British nuclear policy. For a book edited by the theologians Richard Bauckham and Roger Elford, *The Nuclear Weapons Debate: Theological and Ethical Issues*[7] I wrote a chapter ,"Nationalism and Internationalism: A Theological Critique". In 1989 I became President of the Bristol and District Association of Baptist Churches, and took as my presidential theme "Christ our Peace". In June we had a whole day of meetings at Weston-super-Mare devoted to the theme, with speakers from Bristol and further afield, on issues including disarmament, world mission and liberation theology, poverty and the environment. In retrospect, knowing what soon came after may prompt the question "Was it all

7. SCM 1989.

necessary?" My answer is yes, because so many of the issues are still with us. History did not come to an end, as Frances Fukuyama triumphantly proclaimed after the fall of the Soviet Empire, but in its darker aspects re-emerged in new ways. But more importantly, at that particular time in the early autumn of 1989 *nothing* still seemed certain or safe. Then came November and the excitements in Berlin. For the autumn rally of the Baptist Association I had invited Paul Oestreicher, now Director of International Ministries at Coventry Cathedral, to be the guest speaker. Broadmead Baptist Church was packed. The dance group from Tyndale Baptist Church performed a musically accompanied mime of Bonhoeffer's poem "Stations on the Way to Freedom". Paul Oestreicher spoke movingly on Jesus in the midst of his suffering on the cross bringing his mother and John the Beloved Disciple to care for each other in their mutual need, and the significance of community-building in the world today. It was almost exactly the fifty-first anniversary of the horrors of *Kristallnacht* in Germany when he and his parents on account of his grandfather's Jewish ancestry had to flee and hide before their eventual escape to New Zealand. He spoke of the churches' efforts to build bridges with the East, recalling with much affection Archbishop Michael Ramsey's comments to a GDR official who was complaining about the "Cold War", "Well, don't you think we should try warm peace?". He spoke of hope in what was happening. We concluded the service with that rousing hymn of missionary optimism, "There's a light upon the mountains" with those telling lines:

> He is breaking down the barriers,
> > he is casting up the way;
> He is calling for his angels
> > to build up the gates of day.

Prophetic? Next evening, the Berlin Wall was opened.

SOUTH AFRICA AGAIN

Then, South Africa! We had John de Gruchy with us in Bristol in November 1988. He addressed students both at the Baptist College and in the university theology department. They were somber occasions. At that time there still seemed no exit from confrontation and repression. John was asked at the college, "What is the main hindrance to change" and he answered "Self-justifying politicians". He also had to admit that the churches had their own sins of apartheid to confess and be liberated from. The atmosphere was similar in early July 1989 at a conference hosted by the Divinity Faculty in Cambridge with South African theologians including Charles Villa-Vicencio and James Cochrane. Later, in December 1989 John de Gruchy came to Bristol again, en route home from New York with Isobel, to preach at a BBC Radio Sunday morning Advent service from St Paul's Clifton, the Anglican university chaplaincy church. As if to illustrate just how sensitive even then was the subject of apartheid in the British context, at the end of the rehearsal on the eve of the broadcast the BBC producer took issue with John because his sermon was so critical of the apartheid regime, calling on people in Britain to welcome the prospect of change in South Africa as much as they were welcoming the changes in eastern Europe. Fortunately John did not budge and after a long phone call to Stephen Oliver in London got his own way. But John too was now optimistic. On meeting him and Isobel at Heathrow I had found him as excited as he was surprised at the latest news: the de Klerk government was initiating conversations with the ANC. That could only be taken seriously.

On Sunday February 11 next year I was preaching at a church anniversary in Luton, on the text I Peter 4:17, "For the time has come for judgment to begin with the household of God". I pointed out that with the end of communist rule over so much of Eastern Europe, it ill behooved us to assume complacently that all would be well with us in the West. But members of the congregation were excited, the black members especially, about something else and wanting to hurry home to see live on TV Nelson Mandela coming out of prison. But nothing could yet be taken for granted. It is a measure of how uncertain, still potentially dangerous even, at that time the South African situation still seemed that I found myself completing an assignment on sanctions against the still-apartheid government. This had arisen out of a small caucus of us British theologians during the Cambridge conference in July the previous year, and our felt need for stating a theologically based ethical argument for sanctions. For some reason this task finally fell to my lot, though I did send round the draft for comments from various parties both in the UK and South Africa. Taking for the main title a cue from Luther I called the booklet *God's Angry Love. The theological case for sanctions against South Africa* and it was published by Christian Concern for Southern Africa (CCSA) in the spring of 1990. In thirty-six pages it highlighted the real, structural nature of apartheid and its devastating consequences for poverty in South Africa, with biblical and theological reflections on economic injustice and the applicability of economic coercion on those in power, and on structural sin and repentance. Were all the arguments *passé* by now? CCSA did not think so, since the discussion about whether sanctions had or had not already been an effective or ethically justifiable strategy still needed rehearsing and as Elliott Kendall, executive secretary of CCSA stated in his commendation: "The issues are far wider than the South African question. There are moral and spiritual matters which are of profound importance to the Christian and to the Churches." This was to become all too true in later cases such as Iraq—and it was important to understand that while South Africa was one case, other situation and circumstances could pose quite different questions.

CHANGE—ME TOO?

The last two years of the 1980s brought changes at all levels. In 1988 both Margaret's father and my father died, in May and November respectively. Even when we ourselves have reached middle-age, parental loss can have a profound effect in pushing us into a sense of who we are and acceptance of responsibility for ourselves, something that, however mature we think we are, we have long perhaps subconsciously feared. From the early 1980s at intervals I had had a recurring dream, not quite a nightmare but nonetheless scary, of entering a house partly resembling one of my childhood homes, partly not, at night, dark, cold, and utterly empty. On my father's death, the dreams stopped. The dream had become reality, loss no longer to be dreaded.

At the same time, changes in the world at large were being mirrored at other levels nationally and locally, affecting the churches too and not least in Britain, and were now to affect me and the family. In 1987 Morris West had retired as principal of the Bristol College. Under his leadership and encouragement I had enjoyed a decade of the most productive and enriching life an academically inclined yet outwardly engaged minister of my age could ever have hoped for. He was succeeded by John Morgan-Wynne who came from twenty-five years as tutor at Regent's Park College. I assured John that I fully supported his appointment, but having now been ten years at Bristol I thought that it was time for me to move on within the next two to three years. This was in the first place for the college's sake. Harry Mowvley had retired in 1984 and in his place had come Michael Wotton who after serving fourteen years with the BMS in Brazil brought outstanding skills as a biblical language teacher. But this meant that now there was none of us on the teaching staff who had had full-time experience of pastoring a local church in this country during the past ten years. The local church scene was rapidly changing and there was a danger, I felt, of a growing isolation of the college in relation to its church constituency. I therefore felt free to explore whatever paths might open up for using more widely what I had been learning and experiencing while at Bristol. In early 1989 I was invited by the appointments committee at Regent's Park, Oxford, where Barrie White was having to retire through ill-health, to be interviewed for the principalship. I did so, though with some misgivings but at least it would be a sensible way of testing the waters. In the event both Margaret and I felt that it was not quite the place for me or us, and as events proved Paul Fiddes, already tutor there, good friend and immensely able scholar with a real vision for the college, was eminently the right person for the post. Some upset came to the Bristol college scene in the later summer of 1989 with the separation of Michael Wotton and his wife Jill, and Michael was due to leave the staff at the end of the summer term in 1990. By early that year a new possibility was coming into view for me, though very tentatively at first. British ecumenism was about to undergo a radical structural overhaul. The British Council of Churches (BCC) would be replaced by four national (English, Scottish, Welsh and Irish) bodies and an overall four-nation

Council of Churches for Britain and Ireland (CCBI). Much of the executive work of CCBI would be undertaken by "coordinating secretaries" responsible for, respectively, church affairs, public affairs and international affairs. It seemed to me that I might offer both my academic interests and my recently widening international experience for the international affairs post. The job would be mainly desk-based in London, but Margaret and I having done our sums worked out that the price of a season rail ticket on the fast Bristol-Paddington line would be just about financially and logistically comparable with moving to London—and in any case she could continue working at Bristol Polytechnic. I applied, was interviewed and appointed in April. The news actually came while Margaret, Jonathan and I were in Venice for the Faith and Order consultation mentioned earlier. In the middle of lunch I was summoned to the phone by one of the sisters, to hear Bernard Thorogood, chair of the appointing committee, tell me the news. Good news? Yes, but the implications of such a move into what was in effect a very new experimental ecumenical situation, totally different from a college existence, were somewhat daunting. Next day was Palm Sunday in Venice and we attended the passion narrative service in St Mark's Cathedral, on the way back having to dodge children in the streets waving full-size palm fronds, not our usual English book-mark crosses made of the odd leaf. We returned home in time for me to preach in another cathedral, Gloucester, at the Good Friday ecumenical service.

Family holiday, Austria 1989

That year brought change not just for me however. At Bristol Cathedral School Peter's musicianship had flourished, In 1989 he was awarded the organ scholarship at Clare College, Cambridge, and after a gap year working in an insurance company would be going up to read music at about the same time as I started work at CCBI. And my almost daily commute to London, and a good deal of travelling around the country and abroad, would have effects upon home life for us all. On June 13 I preached my last sermon in the college chapel on the text Psalm 84:5: "Happy are those whose refuge is in you, whose hearts are set on the pilgrim ways". Pilgrimage was the watchword for the new ecumenical venture coming out of the "Not Strangers but Pilgrims" process of the past few years and I tried to say what this biblical concept meant for all of us, as individuals, churches and indeed the world (Jürgen Moltmann: "Has modern society a future? Its future is conversion".) But amid all the uncertainties, excitements and anxieties of the new way ahead I also looked back for a sign of hope to my own earliest journey, from China to England. Out on display by the communion table stood the earthenware jar that had been our water-supply across India: small, simple, frail and vulnerable but our source of life. By grace we can travel in hope.

Before finally departing from the college there came an eastward journey in August: attending in Seoul, South Korea, the congress of the Baptist World Alliance, and at the end of that my first visit to Hong King to see something of the church scene there and how Christians were shaping up to the impending reversion of the territory to China. A useful transitional exposure. While bird-watching on the shores of the New Territories I looked longingly towards the distant hills of mainland China and wondered if indeed I would be able someday to tread the land of my birth.

PART THREE

International Affairs 1990–1997

Roses in the rubble: Beirut 1991

8

"His dad's a spy": New Ecumenical Pilgrimage in the Old Unruly World

SATURDAY SEPTEMBER 8 1990 in Liverpool was a bright day in every sense. A great congregation assembled in the Anglican Cathedral, enlivened by the alleluias resounding from hearty communal singing led by John Bell of the Iona Community. The inauguration of the Council of Churches for Britain and Ireland (CCBI) replacing at four-nation level the British Council of Churches (BCC), had begun. The Methodist John Newton, who with Bishop David Sheppard and Catholic Archbishop Derek Worlock formed the notable Merseyside ecumenical trio of church leaders, preached. To those who still equated Christianity with divisiveness and conflict, either in despair or approval, he warned, "Peace has broken out!" We poured out of the nave to process to the Roman Catholic Cathedral along the appropriately named—as it seemed to us—Hope Street, led by four giant pilgrims on stilts, clad in walking gear with knapsacks. To the fore, Archbishop Robert Runcie and Cardinal Basil Hume were walking arm in arm, joining in the singing of "Bind us together". It was a pleasant surprise to find myself alongside my Lytham schoolmate David Hawtin, now bishop of Repton. To his left was the Dominican Timothy Radcliffe. We gathered again in the great octagonal sanctuary of the Catholic Cathedral for the acts of commitment by the participating churches, and the commissioning of those of us who had been appointed as staff of CCBI.

The day was the staging-post on a much longer journey than just along Hope Street. The BCC had been founded nearly half a century ago in 1942 with a membership of the Anglican Churches and most of the Protestant denominations of the British Isles, plus in due course a number of the Orthodox diaspora. Not until the Second Vatican Council did significant relations with the Roman Catholic Church begin. The papal visit of John Paul II to Britain in the summer of 1982, however, had a huge and decisive public impact, and the sense quickly grew that some form of new organization was required to do justice to the rapidly changing ecumenical scene in Britain. Nor was the Catholic reality the only factor. The rapidly growing presence of the Black-led and Pentecostal churches who also found features of the BCC ethos uncongenial had to be acknowledged. Moreover that BCC ethos was also now under increasing scrutiny within some of the mainline churches which had been in it from the outset. What did it mean to be a council *of* churches? What was the relation between it and the member churches? Some felt that the BCC was prone to act as a body apart from the churches, claiming to act and speak on their behalf, sometimes controversially so in the socio-political sphere (like the World Council of Churches) but with uncertain representative validity.

What was needed, many believed, was a means by which the churches in all their diversity could nevertheless *as churches* come together in increasing fellowship, joint action and witness, and themselves make the decisions on what further to do and say together. This became clear in the initiative launched in 1985 by the BCC and churches across the whole spectrum, the "Not Strangers but Pilgrims Inter-Church Process", involving study and discussion at every level from national conferences to local house-groups. Out of this was born a set of proposals for new ecumenical instruments to replace the BCC. CCBI would be the body at four nation level. England would have an entirely new national body, Churches Together in England (CTE); Wales would have a like body, Cytun; the Scottish Council of Churches would be replaced by Action of Churches Together in Scotland (ACTS), while in Ireland the Irish Council of Churches (actually the oldest ecumenical body in the British Isles, founded in 1922) would continue, along with the Irish Inter-Church meeting (which included the Roman Catholics) set up in 1973. The "churches together" model had arrived. At every level, these instruments would not be agencies "doing ecumenical work for the churches" but rather enabling the churches themselves to work together on the tasks they considered essential. This embodied the spirit of the Inter-Church Conference at Swanwick in September 1987 which gathered up the Not Strangers but Pilgrims process and set out the proposals to be put to the churches. The Swanwick declaration rang with new hope and confidence:

> We now declare together our readiness to commit ourselves to each other under God. Our earnest desire is to become more fully, in his own time, the One Church of Christ, united in faith, communion, pastoral care and mission . . .
>
> It is our conviction that, as a matter of policy at all levels and in all places, our churches must now move from co-operation to clear commitment to each other, in search of the unity for which Christ prayed and in common evangelism and service of the world . . . [1]

Ecumenism not as an extra but as a dimension of all we do, became the watchword of the hour, and at Liverpool this vision was confirmed in hope and joy. A truly inclusive fellowship of Christian churches was being created. It was Basil Hume who for many of us embodied the commitment to this vision as he had indeed inspired much of it. Not that everyone was 100% confident that the future of ecumenism was sound and clear. Was inclusivity being bought at the price of losing the prophetic edge which the

---

1. *Churches Together in Pilgrimage*, 7.

BCC had brought *to* the churches? Would the pilgrimage have to be at the pace of the slowest and most cautious walkers? But on September 8 1990 it was the vision rather than the questions which predominated, certainly for myself as one of the appointed coordinating secretaries, though the questions certainly were there. Like the other co-ordinating secretaries I would, at first, have nothing but a support group to guide and advise me personally, but not to relate to the churches or even the governing bodies of CCBI. The guidelines in the job descriptions for coordinating secretaries spoke of a required capacity to live with insecurity and I already knew what that meant. Five weeks before the inauguration, on August 2 Saddam Hussein had invaded Kuwait. The last public statement issued by the BCC was to condemn the action. CCBI as yet did not even have a mechanism for issuing or even formulating an ecumenical response of any kind. But there would undoubtedly be pressure for some kind of response. With a world in burgeoning turmoil especially in the Middle East it felt a bit like being a David facing a Goliath with not even a sling to propel the few pebbles at his disposal. But that was all part of the excitement. One was joining a new enterprise, writing a new chapter in the ecumenical story. My very last lecture at Bristol Baptist College in May that year had been on the modern ecumenical movement in Britain up to the present day. I was able, with tongue only partly in cheek, to conclude by putting my notes aside and telling the class that having taught the history I was now looking forward to help making it. Accepting the uncertainty and risk was all part of the privilege.

A NEW LIFE

CCBI certainly meant a new way of life for me, first of all on the immediate practical level. Instead of a few minutes' drive to college every morning there was now a commute of two hours in total each way door to door, three or four days a week, between our home in Westbury Park and Inter-Church House in Lower Marsh close by Waterloo Station. But the First Great Western InterCity service from Bristol Parkway to Paddington was generally very efficient and after a while that and the dash along the Bakerloo underground line to Lambeth North seemed quite routine; and one could always do some work on the train. Some days when there was disruption on the suburban rail network I was able to get in to the office more easily than London-based colleagues. Looking back as a septuagenarian, however, it now looks like an unwarrantably strenuous existence for seven years.

Then too there was a world of difference between a college tutor and a coordinating secretary. Instead of lectures to prepare and deliver there was an office to run, and really I had had little administrative experience beyond organizing my own and students' time, and very little need of secretarial help apart from what the principal's secretary and her assistant provided. Now, rather than encouraged I was at first somewhat disconcerted to find I would have a full-time personal assistant (PA), which seemed to signal how big and complicated the work was liable to prove. That feeling however dissipated within minutes of my first meeting with Eva Namuganza (later, Kisitu on her marriage) who had been PA to Michael Smart, secretary for International Affairs at the BCC, and had a good deal of know-how to share with me. Eva was Ugandan by birth, her family having escaped from the regime of Idi Amin, and so there was an international dimension and experience right in our office itself. Enthusiastic, energetic, eager to tackle any job given her (she was especially adept at coaxing or bullying lazy embassy staff into action when a visa was needed in a hurry), and with an infectious humor, Eva as a colleague proved a blessing without whom I could never have done whatever was useful at CCBI.

A CREATIVE TEAM

So Eva and I were a team, but of course within a larger staff-team at CCBI. John Reardon, URC minister, for a good number of years secretary for Church and Society and Deputy General Secretary in the URC, had been appointed General Secretary for the new CCBI, and brought considerable experience of ecumenical life and a calm, wise demeanor which was much needed in a new ship of untried seaworthiness venturing into uncharted waters. Coordinating Secretary for Church Affairs was Colin Davey, Anglican priest who had been serving as secretary for Ecumenical Affairs in the former BCC and so brought an important layer of continuity as well as a deep commitment to the new way of working. Ermal Kirby, Methodist from the Wesleyan Holiness Church background, had been appointed Coordinating Secretary for Public Affairs, and soon showed considerable skill in identifying and analyzing the *processes* by which the new ways of working ecumenically could, or could not, be effective; this impressed me greatly, tending as I did to move more by instinct than by the rational plotting of a route. CCBI inherited the BCC's Unit on Community Relations which became the Churches' Commission for Racial Justice with David Haslam, radically campaigning Methodist minister, as its secretary. Then during the first year of CCBI as first appointee to the women's desk[2] there came Lavinia Byrne, Catholic nun of the Institute of the Blessed Virgin Mary, writer and broadcaster and delightfully outspoken on many issues, above all as an advocate of women's ordination; and in 1991 Carmel Heaney, a Roman Catholic from Northern Ireland was appointed associate secretary for youth affairs.

For my work in international affairs, however, one clutch of colleagues was to be especially important. The Conference for World Mission, descendant of the Conference of British Missionary Societies, had been a division of the BCC. With the advent of CCBI it became in cooperation with the National Missionary Council of the Roman Catholic Church the Churches' Commission on Mission (CCOM) headed by Donald

---

2. The agenda of the Women's Desk was largely that of helping the CCBI churches to engage with the Ecumenical Decade of Churches in Solidarity with Women, launched by the WCC in 1988. Lavinia Byrne was succeeded at the desk by Jean Mayland in 1996.

Elliot, URC minister who had worked in Malaysia and then with the URC division on World Church Mission. Gordon Shaw, Methodist minister who after serving thirteen years with the Church of South India was regional secretary for Asia and the Pacific for the Methodist Church Overseas Division, had come to the Conference for World Mission with a similar brief but extended also to the Middle East. He was a mine of information and wise counsel. Some staff changes in CCOM soon brought new arrivals: Edmund Tang, a Catholic Hong Kong Chinese, came to the China desk and Gillian Paterson, a London area organizer for Christian Aid, took over as Mission Education secretary. It was natural and essential that CCOM and my International Affairs agenda should be closely related. As often as not, for ecumenical work international issues had a world church dimension, and conversely world mission issues had to be seen in the context of political and social developments on a global scale. I was thus very well served, and in addition to all these resources there was Christian Aid, the major occupant of Inter-Church House, then under the directorship of Michael Taylor whom I knew well from our time as Baptist theological educators. In addition to Christian Aid, the Catholic Agency for Overseas Development (CAFOD), and the Scottish Catholic International Aid Fund (SCIAF) became agencies of CCBI. A number of bodies that had been closely associated with the BCC continued in existence and became "bodies in association" with CCBI, such as the Churches' Human Rights' Network, the Churches' Peace Forum and the Churches European East-West Relations Network, which were important nodes of expertise and insight on international affairs. Immensely important was Quaker Peace & Service as a source of information and advice about just any part of the world where there was conflict, actual or potential. Then there were other organizations not formally related to CCBI in any way but important resources on international issues of justice and peace: for example the Council on Christian Approaches to Defence and Disarmament (CCADD) on whose committee I soon found myself, and the Royal Institute of International Affairs at Chatham House of which I became a member. There were individuals like Sydney Bailey, the Quaker writer on peace and human rights, immensely and widely respected for his non-partisan pacifism and wisdom on conflict resolution, who was anxious to meet me and offer some very welcome advice in face of the crisis in the Gulf. Suddenly I found myself being invited by Foreign Office officials and senior clergy to meet over lunch at places like the Athenaeum, that most patrician of London clubs. If that was flattering to one's vanity, it also became apparent that my full job title "Coordinating Secretary for International Affairs in the Council of Churches for Britain and Ireland" was a rather indigestible mouthful. I was phoned one day by a young journalist who was doing a survey of the opinions of "significant persons" on various topics and who first wanted to confirm that I was the "secretary for eternal affairs". No such luck, I informed her.

During these early days of CCBI life one had to be steer a course between two contrasting attitudes: there were those who were simply mourning the end of the BCC, and those who were rejoicing at its demise. The former had to be told that the ecumenical movement was indeed continuing but with a new methodology which should be given a good try because the churches had clearly said that this was what they wanted. The latter had to be told that the acquired wisdom of the BCC era could not simply be discounted and that much of the agenda if not the methodology was obviously the same, especially in international and public affairs, since that was written not by the churches but by the world which was pursuing its way regardless.

FIRST TEST: THE GULF WAR

Clearly some kind of pragmatism was needed in the move from "doing things on behalf of the churches" to "getting the churches to work together". Saddam Hussein was in illegal and brutal occupation of Kuwait, and the US-led coalition was amassing its forces in the Gulf, public anxiety was mounting, and there were calls from individuals if not churches for some kind of ecumenical response. Philip Crowe, principal of Salisbury-Wells Theological College, had commented adversely in the press on the lack of a church voice so far. I talked with a number of sympathetic people in church social responsibility departments—Don Black at the Baptist Union, Rachel Stephens of the Methodists and Chris Wigglesworth at the Church of Scotland, and went to work on a briefing paper which at least set out some facts about the Gulf region, factors behind the crisis, the role of the UN and so forth, together with information about churches in the region. This was welcomed by the CCBI Steering Committee at the end of October, and with its blessing was distributed to the member churches. But something more was needed—an actual discussion of the issues by those in the churches charged with responsibility for international affairs. I therefore organized a colloquy on the Gulf Crisis for concerned people with an international affairs brief in their respective churches. Some thirty attended the colloquy at Bloomsbury Central Baptist Church November 15–16. It consisted mainly of inputs from invited contributors from the Middle East churches, the Foreign Office, CCADD, the Bradford School of Peace Studies and other bodies, and individuals such as the archbishop of York John Habgood, Philip Crowe and Sydney Bailey. The moderator was the bishop of Bury St Edmundsbury and Ipswich, John Dennis. Both the listening and the questioning were exhaustive but illuminating. It ended on the Friday afternoon and I spent most of the weekend at home writing up the discussion and recommendations, just in time for the meeting of the CCBI Church Representatives' Meeting (CRM) at Swanwick on the Monday. I presented the report which was attentively received. Basically the report pointed out the huge uncertainties and potential costs, in human terms, of actual war against which the resort to arms must be weighed. There was hesitation over a specific response by the CRM but at least it was informed hesitation. The constitution of CCBI, however, also allowed for the six Presidents to issue statements. In early December the growing likelihood of war made a total silence from the churches seem irresponsible, even if all that could be said was an indication of the consequences of war for the Middle East region and beyond, and the need to emphasize that for a war to be just it must be a last resort and the minimal requirement must be that all other avenues had really been explored. That meant a frantic few days' presenting and modifying a text which would be agreeable to all six presidents, who included a Quaker pacifist and a Just War archbishop, a task made no easier by the fact that just then I was on my way to a meeting in Cyprus. These were still pre-mobile phone days, and there were fraught efforts to get the text finalized on an inter-city train payphone and then from a hotel bedroom in Limassol. But eventually it was agreed and went out early in December.

Come the New Year, and despite several meetings with guardedly optimistic officials at the FCO there was a general sense of the inevitability of full-scale war to repel the Iraqi invasion. Saddam Hussein had been given a deadline of January 15 to withdraw from Kuwait and showed no sign of complying. On January 9 we had an ecumenical delegation to meet with the Foreign Secretary Douglas Hurd at the FCO. Putting together a delegation of eight persons as representative as possible of the main spread of denominations, the four nations and gender had proved at least as taxing as preparing an agreed statement. But we went and the Foreign Secretary listened. On January 17 my support group was to meet for the first time, at Inter-Church House. That morning I was woken at about 3.00 a.m. by the phone ringing. It was a *Guardian* reporter: against a background noise of frantic voices and teleprinters the caller told me that "Desert Storm" had been launched and she wanted to know what the churches' response was. This seemed as far away as it was possible to be from the studious discussion in a college ethics class on the Just War. I asked for and was given a few minutes' grace to reply, put the phone down and tried to wipe the sleep from my brain. What in due course I told the paper was that in the churches there was a spectrum of views on war in general and on this one in particular but that all were concerned about the human and environmental cost. On arrival at Paddington station six hours later I was able to read my comments— "churches have doubts" ran the headline to the report—in the later edition of the paper. It so happened that my support group was to meet with me for the first time that morning. We listened to the reports still coming in on the radio. Later that afternoon I gave a live interview on the phone to the PM radio programme. At least we were doing our best to counter any gung-ho mentality. In the radio interview I was asked "Do the churches support our troops?" A tricky one. I said that whatever the views of churches and Christians on the war itself, clergy and others would be ready be alongside and assist all who would be injured or traumatized in any way by their experiences.

COORDINATING MADE REAL

That day marked in more than one way an important stage in my CCBI work. My support group comprised extremely able colleagues and friends: Don Black of the Baptist Union; Rachel Stephens of the Methodist Church; Pamela Gruber, of the international affairs desk of the Church of England, immensely well informed, incisive and sometimes acerbic; Father Sergei Hackel, genial Russian Orthodox priest, scholar and broadcaster; Andrew Clark of Quaker Peace & Service; Leslie Morrison, one of my former students and now Congregational minister in Scotland; Jenny Borden, Deputy Director of Christian Aid; Peter Brain of the URC; Bob Beresford, Roman Catholic deacon of cautious temperament but with a deliciously droll sense of humor; Myriel Davies, President of the Union of Welsh Independents and also of the United Nations Association; and Chris Wigglesworth of the Church of Scotland. It met with me twice a year throughout the rest of my time at CCBI and provided much counsel, advice and constructive criticism on my working methods and priorities. At any rate, I always felt encouraged by the end of each meeting. Most of the members themselves carried important responsibilities on international affairs within their own churches or organizations, and therefore would be crucial in facilitating the "working together" model of ecumenism. But the support group as such did not have that role, and at that first meeting I was told in no uncertain terms that I ought to get moving in creating just such a mechanism. I did, and the result was the International Affairs Liaison Group (IALG) which comprised designated persons (often, but not necessarily, staff) from the churches and appropriate organizations in association with CCBI. It had its first formal meeting in October 1991 and thereafter met quarterly. It enabled the sharing of important information on geographical regions or themes of concern, formulating lines of joint action and resourcing of the churches and, when appropriate, assigning particular pieces of work to one church or body on behalf of all. It was the very embodiment of the working together model and as such I believe it was very effective. Mostly the meetings were held at Inter-Church House but as far as possible I tried to ensure that we had a residential meeting each year outside England. We met in Scotland (Dunblane) twice, and once each in Ireland (Rathgar near Dublin) and Wales (Coleg Trefeca). But the work of ecumenical coordinating was not limited to the IALG. The large number of networks and bodies in association with CCBI, many originating in the BCC days, on issues ranging from South Africa to the Arms Trade, from Human Rights to East-West European Church Relations, and the need to ensure that they could feed in their insights and challenges to the churches, meant that my diary was always full. Reading my notebooks from these years, filled with notes of meetings, travels and visits, induces a sense almost of exhaustion which I rarely felt at the time although I was aware of the temptation of at times actually enjoying just *too* much the adrenaline-induced excitement when dealing with crises, at the expense of the hum-drum work of networking, preparing routine meetings and communicating. In fact much of what I relate in this chapter no doubt reads like an intensely bureaucratic existence, far removed from the heady vision that had caught me in my student days of what the ecumenical movement was all about. But here I was dealing with the cogs and levers which made the movement possible.

Each of the four national instruments had deeply committed and able secretaries: Maxwell Craig (ACTS), Noel Davies (Cytun), David Stephens (ICC); and not forgetting Martin Reardon for CTE who inhabited an office on the ground floor of Inter-Church House, his desk a chaotic jumble of papers but belying a very wise, calm and orderly mind (he was always to be seen in a red shirt and straw boater in order to demonstrate, so his friends said, that the age of eccentric but brilliant Anglican clergy was not over). But above all I came to appreciate just how valuable for international affairs work was the diversity of perspective and expertise of the churches at four-nation level. The Church of Scotland, for example, through its missionary history had close and long-standing relationships with central and southern Africa and the Middle East, and also had important partnerships with the Reformed churches of central and Eastern Europe. Wales had a special consciousness of the role of smaller nations on the world scene and pressed their cause vigorously on the international ecumenical stage. The Irish churches for their part were still going through bitter experience of coping with sectarian conflict and violence, and this was being turned to good account by linkages with churches in contexts of violence elsewhere in the world, including South Africa, Israel-Palestine, Cyprus and Sri Lanka. In short, there was a wealth of insight and experience among the churches of the British Isles and it was a privilege to help this to become a shared resource. I fear this has been dissipated by developments, or rather degradations, in recent years.

GENEVA AND BEYOND

There were coordinating links to be built and maintained further afield. Two months into CCBI, at the end of October 1990 I made my first visit to Geneva which was not only important educationally for me but was necessary to help communication with the World Council of Churches (WCC) and the other organizations in the Ecumenical Centre. Elizabeth Salter, now working in the International Affairs Department of the WCC, arranged my three-day programme of meetings with staff persons of the WCC, Conference of European Churches (CEC), Lutheran World Federation, World Alliance of Reformed Churches and so forth. Emilio Castro, general secretary of the WCC, was I think away at the time. But I had my first encounter with Jean Fischer, general secretary of CEC, in an office which all unbeknown to me would become *very* familiar to me seven years later. I continued to visit Geneva at least once a year, and not least significant for my interests in the longer term was the acquaintance I made with the WCC library and its archivist Pierre Baffe.

Other opportunities for networking beyond the home scene were plentiful. I attended the German Kirchentags in the Ruhrgebiet (1991), Munich (1993) and Hamburg (1995)—at this last one in fact we had a team from CCBI staff and supporters and staffed a British ecumenical stand in the Market of Possibilities. It was also convenient (not meant cynically) that I continued on the Baptist World Alliance Doctrine and Inter-Church Co-operation Commission, which met in Montreal in 1991 and Montego Bay, Jamaica, in 1992. Just prior to the Montreal meeting I spent several days in New York, staying with Larry and Nyla Rasmussen at Union Seminary, which enabled me to visit the National Council of Churches nearby on Riverside, and also the UN building where I had a conducted tour and met with the Anglican representative to the UN, Bishop Sir Paul Reeves of New Zealand. The BWA Montego Bay meeting was memorable for the perspective it gave on the fight against slavery, particularly one evening at a large open-air meeting. Baptists have been accustomed to telling the story of the leading roles taken by abolitionist missionaries such as William Knibb and Thomas Burchell—roles never to be discounted. But as I listened to my fellow Regent's Park alumnus Burchell Taylor preaching I realized I knew barely half the story, and to my shame Sam Sharpe, the Baptist who led the actual *rebellion* of slaves in 1831, was barely more than a name to me. From Montego Bay a number of us including several from the UK flew to Managua in Nicaragua. The Nicaraguan Baptists were hosting an international Baptist peace conference at La Boquita, a small resort on the Pacific coast. I was delighted to find Gideon Makhanya and several other Baptist Convention pastors from South Africa there. A highlight was a visit from the famous socialist opposition leader Commandante Daniel Ortega whom each of us met personally. This was opportune for me, because next day I was leaving in order to be home in time for a major weekend festival in Bristol, "Rise Like the Sun", sponsored by Christian Aid and CAFOD to mark the problematic five-hundredth anniversary of Columbus's arrival in the Americas. At the closing event in Bristol Cathedral I was able to convey Ortega's greetings and thanks for solidarity with the Nicaraguan liberation movement. My Latin American experience was extended in 1995 when the BWA Congress was held in Buenos Aires and I used the time to meet also theologians in the Anglican, Pentecostal and Methodist churches including the liberation theologian José Miguez Bonino.

FAITH AND ORDER

While at CCB I also continued as a member of the WCC Faith and Order Plenary Commission. This meant attending the Fifth World Conference on Faith and Order held at Santiago Compostela, Spain, in August 1993, and the Plenary Commission meeting in Moshi, Tanzania, in 1996. The Santiago conference had been preceded by growing doubts and tensions, especially since the WCC Assembly in Canberra in 1991, about the quest for visible unity, and even the status of Faith and Order within the WCC. But expectations were higher than doubts. For the opening service in the great Cathedral of St James the *botafumeiro*, the huge censer that swings to spectacular effect over the transept, was put into operation. But was it, someone mused to me as we left the cathedral, meant to symbolize the frustrations of ecumenism, continually oscillating between hope and despair? I felt that the conference itself was very fruitful, pursuing the theme *On the Way to Fuller Koinonia*. The emphasis on *community* as the heart of unity in Christ, mirroring the life of the divine Trinity, opened up promising avenues away from the arid exchanges between received confessional positions. Notable input was given by, among others, Frances Young of Birmingham (who led Bible studies each morning), Desmond Tutu, Wolfhart Pannenberg, Rowan Williams, John Zizioulas, Elizabeth Templeton of Edinburgh, and Nelida Ritchie of Argentina. But there were also warnings that even much of this kind of discussion was far removed from the concerns of many people all over the world, and that moreover new challenges were coming from on-European, non-white regions of the world which were likely to demand a redrafting of the ecumenical agenda entirely. In a place like Santiago, goal of pilgrims for centuries "ecumenical pilgrimage" easily becomes a cliché. I wrote an account of Santiago for the *Tablet*, concluding:

> I came away from Santiago with a wild, irreverent dream that one day the *botafumeiro* will in mid-swing break loose from its mounting, crash through the cathedral wall and soar triumphantly into orbit. An eschatological vision perhaps, but I do believe that grace being stronger than gravity, the swing in the hopeful direction is even now more pronounced than in the other.[3]

I had also said in that report that "The integral link between Faith and Order on the one hand, and the concerns for justice, peace and the integrity of creation on the other, were settled (I hope) once and for all." This proved slightly premature. At the Moshi meeting of the Plenary Commission in 1996 there was a disconcerting move by some cautious Lutherans (and perhaps others) for the project on Ecclesiology and Ethics to be ditched. This would have been ironic given that at the start of the meeting we had listened to a splendid address by the President of Tanzania, Benjamin William Mkapa, a committed Roman Catholic, who himself had emphasized the importance of Christian unity being manifested in concern for the whole of human society, justice, peace and welfare. I had also shared in a panel discussion with two others on this programme.[4] In the debate on the future of the programme I staggered to a microphone to argue strongly against such a move, and the proposal was defeated. I say "staggered" because like some others I had been laid low for the previous couple of days by a nasty stomach bug. (The Lutheran sisters in charge of the hostel where about twenty of us were being housed miles out in the bush and banana plantations, had insisted I swallow a huge purple-colored tablet which resulted in my knowing nothing more for the next twelve hours). I wondered if I had been a bit heavy-handed but Alan Falconer, director of Faith and Order, and others such as Martin Cressy of Cambridge told me they had been really worried by the possibility of what would have been a decidedly retrograde step for Faith and Order.

---

3. "Faith and Order Pilgrims", *Tablet* 28 August 1993. "Irreverent" in the first sentence of this citation was wrongly rendered "irrelevant" in the publication.

4. See Falconer (Ed.), *Faith and Order in Moshi*, 159–162.

PART THREE: INTERNATIONAL AFFAIRS 1990–1997

WORLD ISSUES, HOME QUESTIONS AND HELPFUL CHURCH LEADERS

Change and crisis in several regions and countries of the world made the international agenda especially challenging for the churches during my time at CCBI. Five contexts were particularly significant: the Middle East beset by the first Gulf War and the continuing sore of Israel-Palestine; the break-up of the Former Yugoslavia and the ensuing conflicts in the Balkans; the crisis of growing poverty in much of Africa; the final stages of the anti-apartheid struggle and the transition to democracy in South Africa; and China, including its relations with Hong Kong in the lead-up to the hand-over of the colony in 1997. For different reasons my personal engagement with each of these situations was particularly challenging and transformative, and in order to do justice to each I am next devoting a chapter to each of them especially since a key common factor was the first-hand experience gained through travels and visits.

But there were important matters where the main target of concern lay in British actions at home, in government policy and in public opinion. The arms trade was a prime concern, not only as regards the dubious and oppressive regimes to which British firms were still being allowed to export weaponry and related technology, but also the extraordinary level of economic privileges which the government uniquely gave to the arms industry to guarantee the viability of its export trade. An excellent workshop led by Roger Williamson at the CCBI Assembly in February 1992 highlighted the issue and the need for international church cooperation too, and this was confirmed by a consultation hosted in Brussels in February 1994 by the European Ecumenical Commission on Development (EECOD) at which Roger Williamson also spoke and where Archbishop John Habgood, was present. In February 1996 we in CCBI launched a full report and study pack *Countering the Arms Trade: Churches Count the Cost*, publicized with a press conference in the Jerusalem Chamber in Westminster Abbey, with Cardinal Hume and John Battle MP, Labour spokesperson on defense, as speakers. No less important were efforts to ensure British support for the Nuclear Non-Proliferation Treaty (NPT). Few people, either in government or at large, seemed to be aware that the NPT which came into force in 1970 committed the UK, as with the other then nuclear powers (USA, USSR, France and China) to pursue cessation of the nuclear arms race and nuclear disarmament. In February 1995 we organized a delegation, led by John Habgood and including Sir Hugh Beach, to the Foreign Secretary Douglas Hurd to present the case for further action. Human rights also remained high on the agenda—the Churches' Human Rights Forum remained active, there was involvement in the meetings of the Conference on Security and Cooperation (CSCE) as it then was, and frequent briefing meetings at the Foreign Office for non-governmental organizations. Implicit in all such concerns was the need to maintain governmental and public support for the United Nations, which celebrated its fiftieth anniversary in October 1995 with a service in Westminster Abbey at which Desmond Tutu preached. In CCBI we enjoyed good and mutually supportive rapport with the United Nations Association (UNA), its director Malcolm Harper, and its President Myriel Davies who was in fact a CCBI President and a member of my support group. To mark the anniversary, our International Affairs Liaison Group produced a substantial study and discussion guide *The United Nations Fifty Years On: The Churches and Hope for International Order*. As an accompanying leaflet said, "The UN is often criticized; when there is a failure it hits the headlines. The proper response to its difficulties is to realize the still greater need there is for its values, and for commitment to its aims, and for deeper understanding of humanity's problems." It was largely the work of Roger Williamson with help also from Myriel Davies, but was also discussed in draft by the Liaison Group and specialists in the field, presented for approval to the Church Representatives Meeting and issued over the signatures of the six CCBI Presidents.

Mention of Basil Hume and John Habgood is not accidental. As two of the six presidents of CCBI they were outstandingly committed to the new instruments. For Basil Hume, who in many ways was the chief spiritual impetus behind the Inter-Church Process, the new understanding of ecumenism centered on a shared exploration into the mystery of the love of Christ and he gave himself heart and soul to the venture—as he did to everything he believed in. "Let's kick up a real fuss!" he told me when we were preparing to issue a call to the government on the need for better reception of refugees from Bosnia. One of my abiding memories is of him sinking utterly but happily exhausted into an armchair at the end of the barn dance which concluded an evening at a CCBI Assembly at Swanwick. One would hardly expect the same of John Habgood who conveyed the much more dignified air of a cautious—some would feel aloof—academic archbishop but he cared sincerely and deeply for all that we were trying to do. At that time it was "York" who was specifically designated as the senior Anglican figure for ecumenical relations (itself a sign of the Church of England's serious ecumenical commitment in those years). Not least was he a superb and sensitive moderator of gatherings like the Church Representatives Meeting. Very soon I felt I'd got the knack of getting statements out of the six presidents: first of all get Basil Hume's support in principle, then send John Habgood a draft of what might be said, which would always come back with thoughtful emendations. Following the cardinal's enthusiasm and the archbishop's perception and clarity the rest was usually plain sailing, albeit with a bit of trimming of the sails here and there (whether this procedure was strictly according to the rules I never knew, but there is a saying in the gospels about being as wise as serpents and innocent as doves.). John Habgood did not in fact stand on his dignity. Our son Jonathan, then a young teenager who often had to answer the phone if Margaret and I were not yet home from work, was impressed by the fact that it was always simply "John Habgood" not "the archbishop of York" to whom he found himself speaking (he remarked similarly about Paddy Ashdown when he called about a delegation being planned to Former Yugoslavia). In those early days we were indeed blessed with church leaders of quality and commitment.

Part Three: International Affairs 1990–1997

THE ECUMENICAL LEVIATHAN: VISION AND STAFF ROLES

As well as being a time of enthusiasm, however, the early years of CCBI also began to throw up some real questions. Some of these were sternly practical, which of course usually denotes a financial element. The budgeting for CCBI had not been as thorough as first thought. In particular, nothing had been earmarked for a communications desk. This was quickly recognized as a serious weakness, at least by us staff. Under the new dispensation whereby work could be shared or undertaken by one church on behalf of all, it was suggested that the communications desks of one or more churches might take on the media work for CBBI. This was tried with the staff of both the Church of England and the Roman Catholic Bishops Conference for England and Wales, taking six-monthly turns. But it proved barely satisfactory, not so much because such staff were unenthusiastic but because with the best will in the world their responsibilities to their own churches were always bound to take priority, and after a while these arrangements were discontinued. Eventually in 1997, just after I left CCBI, Mary Houston was appointed to a new role in the general secretariat to assist the general secretary in communications with the churches and media work generally. The absolute necessity of an ecumenical organization having its own communications department was something that fortunately I stored up for future reference

In addition to such immediate questions, however, as CCBI approached its fourth birthday some rather deeper issues were surfacing concerning the relationships between the churches and the formal and informal networks through which much of the ecumenical work was to be carried out—and with the staff too. In 1994 Gill Paterson and I wrote two papers, primarily for our CCBI colleagues, *Fishhooks for Leviathan? Staff Perspectives on Leadership within the Ecumenical Instruments* and *Facing Leviathan. Networking and the Role of Staff*. The first paper focused on what was meant by leadership in the ecumenical movement today. Was it a narrowly conceived managerial role of keeping the machinery of the organization intact and running smoothly, or was it to include a dissenting role which sought a vision and looked to the future? We pointed out that in the so-called Marigold Book, *Churches Together in Pilgrimage*, founding document of the new instruments, the coordinating role of staff was certainly seen as creative and not just enabling a relating together of what was already happening in the churches. Indeed it involve a readiness "to imagine and suggest" which patterns of work would be appropriate, and we were to be "deliberately set free to explore where the priorities for Christian obedience now are and how they can best be served". In our papers we suggested that "it may be our task to help the churches identify where prophecy is taking place—within, on the margins of, or beyond the churches themselves". Maybe it was the role of staff to safeguard the element of anticipation. In the second paper we took a hard look at the catchphrase of the hour, "networking", where all too often, we felt, the emphasis was too much on "net" and not enough on "working". Networks could not just be for exchange of views and information, but must have a sense of aim and purpose for the ecumenical vision. What is more, how were the churches of CCBI relating to each other? Was it truly a common journey they were undertaking? Or did the relativities of size, power and financial resources determine churches' attitudes towards each other? How at home and fairly treated did the African and Afro-Caribbean churches, for example, feel? Was policy basically being determined by the bigger churches? We identified a basic problem in the anxiety which was being manifest all round, for the loss of identity and control, especially as financial belts were gradually being tightened. That fear was likely to extend to ecumenical staff too. Moreover, such fear would affect networking: "fear and insecurity will encourage a networking style that seeks to guard information, to confine power and influence to one's own or like-minded bodies, to avoid the sense of risk which is endemic to creativity and change".

Reading these papers just over two decades later, I think we can claim to have been more prophetic than we realized at the time, and not just about CCBI but much else in the ecumenical movement. The questions were nevertheless real and relevant, especially as moves towards a review of CCBI, to which a commitment had been made at the very start, began in 1995.

"DO YOU MISS THE COLLEGE?" BROADCASTING AND WRITING

Several times after moving to CCBI I was asked if I did not miss the academic and community life of the theological college. The short answer was "I'm too busy to miss it!" Some people expressed concern, on the assumption that my writing days would be over—Eberhard Bethge for one, and for another the writer and broadcaster Colin Morris who buttonholed me at a Christmas drinks party put on at Broadcasting House in London by BBC Religious Programs. I have to admit that occasionally when life got just *too* hectic or problems seemingly intractable, I thought wistfully of the relatively quiet study overlooking Woodland Road in Bristol. But having put my hand to this plough, there be could be no looking back from the ecumenical furrow however tricky it proved at times. As it happened, my pen (or rather, word-processor) remained active on much else besides my CCBI work.

For one thing I continued broadcasting on radio. Just after starting at CCBI, I wrote and presented another Sunday evening series titled "Fight the Good Fight" which comprised reflections, accompanied by music, on four historic sites of battle which I had visited in the past few years, focusing on the human cost of war and on the whole range of emotions that it engenders, from courage to fear and grief. It was ironic, or providential, that the programs went out on Radio 4 in November 1990 during the build up to the first Gulf War. We began in 1066 on the site of the battle of Hastings, and Battle Abbey. The second programme took us to the twelfth century and the crusader castle of Krak in Moab, which I had visited when in Jordan in 1987. For the third we went to the USA, to Valley Forge in Pennsylvania, where in 1777–78

Part Three: International Affairs 1990–1997

George Washington had fought against bitter cold and adverse circumstances to consolidate his army for final victory in the War of Independence. For the fourth and final one we were in twentieth-century Germany, at the Möhne Dam, which Margaret and I and the boys had once visited on our way back from holiday. The epic story of the RAF Dambusters raid of 1943 of course hardly needed an introduction, but the programme reflected not just on the courage and ingenuity involved but also on the scale of loss—one third of the aircrews and some twelve-hundred civilians, mostly non-German slave laborers. Not unexpectedly it prompted quite a large postbag from listeners always glad of tales of wartime derring-do. But the letter which touched me most was the shortest. Written on a slip of paper, it requested a copy of the script of the programme and continued: "I was fiancée to one of the men actively involved in the raid depicted, who did not return", and it was signed "Miss Marguerite S——". *Miss*. After nearly fifty years, a witness to the pain of irreplaceable loss so often side-stepped in easy adulation of heroics. I also started presenting the Saturday evening "Ten to Ten" devotional slots on Radio 4. Because they often had to refer topics or news of current interest they were recorded on the immediately preceding Friday afternoon, which worked out very well for me, since having faxed in my script the previous day or that morning, I could get the tube from Lambeth North to Oxford Circus, slip up to Broadcasting House, record the programme (usually on one take) and then be on my way to Paddington and home without trouble. I also did similar programs for BBC World Service which provided some surprises for friends and acquaintances who happened to have their radios turned in far places.

But more literary ventures beckoned. In early 1990 while still at the college in Bristol, I had been 'phoned by Duncan Forrester, Professor of Practical Theology and Christian Ethics at New College, Edinburgh. We had known each other since the Faith and Order Commission meetings in Stavanger in 1985, and I had just sent to him for comment the draft of my booklet on sanctions against South Africa, *God's Angry Love*. He noted that in it I had quoted the remarks of J. H. Oldham (1974–1969), undisputed pioneer of Christian social and ecumenical thinking and a founding figure of the WCC, to the effect that "Christianity is not primarily a philosophy but a crusade". Duncan explained that he was the literary executor of the late Kathleen Bliss, ecumenical educationist and powerful advocate of the role of the laity, who had begun to write the biography of Oldham. She had amassed a hefty collection of Oldham's papers and correspondence but at the time of her death in 1989 she had made only a relatively modest beginning on the writing. Would I be interested in taking it on? I was immediately interested, since while I had as yet no specialist knowledge of Oldham it was apparent that this was a task that both needed doing and would take me into the heart of the modern ecumenical story. At Duncan's invitation I flew up to Edinburgh to discuss it further, and deep in the bowels of the New College library he showed me the dauntingly huge and as yet uncatalogued archive that Kathleen Bliss had collected. That was somewhat unnerving, since before any significant writing could be undertaken the papers needed indexing—a task that would take far more expertise (and time) than I possessed. On the other hand a substantial sum had been raised (interestingly, mostly from the German churches) to help fund the project. I decided to accept the invitation, despite knowing that soon I would be leaving academia for an ecumenically activist post. I judged that living with Oldham and drawing on his story and insights would provide further inspiration for my CCBI work. The matter of cataloguing the material was solved when we recruited William Naphy, an American research student working in Scotland, who did the work superbly. Nevertheless the writing took much longer than any of us, especially Duncan Forrester who I suspect had some anxious moments, had initially hoped. I was not able to make a real beginning until 1995, and finding any extended spaces in the diary for concentrated writing was obviously difficult. Quite a lot of the writing was done on my lap-top on the InterCity train between Bristol and London: not the ideal environment but I was not without the odd willing helper, as shown once by the person in the seat behind me who tapped me on the shoulder to say, "Hey, you've spelt 'disappointed' wrong". More rapid progress was made in the sabbatical study leave I enjoyed in the summer of 1997 between leaving CCBI and going to work in Geneva. It was eventually completed in the spring of 1998 and published in 1999 as *Faith on the Frontier. A life of J. H. Oldham*. The numerous trips to Edinburgh and the New College library were turned into a real pleasure by the hospitality that Duncan and Margaret Forrester afforded me in their Murrayfield home. There were also lengthy sessions in the British Library and the India Library, a lot of correspondence and several interviews with people who had known Oldham. Among the latter there was a memorable afternoon spent with Eric Fenn, then in his nineties, who had been Oldham's assistant at the pivotal 1937 international conference at Oxford on Church, Community and State. Then, while working for BBC Religious Programs, he had diligently recorded the minutes of the Moot, Oldham's remarkable study group of thinkers as diverse as T.S. Eliot, Karl Mannheim, John Baillie, Walter Moberly, John Middleton Murray and Alec Vidler, which met from 1938 to 1947. Eric Fenn's mind and memory were crystal clear as he recounted conversations with key figures from both the Oxford conference and the Moot. I was also very grateful to Oliver Tomkins, whom I had known as bishop of Bristol till his retirement in 1975 and who as a leading ecumenist himself saw the importance of the Oldham biography. He wrote with helpful comments and he it was who not only allayed my fears about approaching the nonagenarian Fenn but wrote to him with the stern command, "You are *not to die* before Keith Clements has interviewed you on Oldham!" In fact I was struck by how the Oldham work was re-connecting me with previous mentors like Alec Vidler who had not only been a member of the Moot but had co-edited with Oldham the wartime *Christian Newsletter*, and Clifford Cleal who had worked with Oldham on employment issues in the early days of the British Council of Churches. Then, still very much alive, there was Marjorie Reeves of Oxford and Ronald Preston of Manchester who had been involved with some of Oldham's groups towards the end of the war and afterwards. They added their own memories of the almost totally deaf Oldham shuffling around the room to each person in turn, so as to get the trumpet of his hearing device pointing straight at the speaker. Another fund of personal memories and insights was Bishop Lesslie Newbigin, whom Oldham in the late 1930s had regarded as his protégé and had tried to recruit into some of own schemes, but had chosen to go to India instead. My first dealings with Lesslie Newbigin were in fact in March 1988, when we were joint leaders at a study conference for Irish Presbyterian ministers, on mission and reconciliation, at the Windermere Centre in the Lake District. Not only on Oldham but on many other subjects I came to respect his wise counsel (by his trenchant criticism, he once saved me from publishing a lecture I had just given which was, I had to admit, not very good). In the 1990s there were still other survivors from the Oldham era but nothing prepared me for the shock of answering the phone at home one day in 1993 and hearing a stentorian voice last heard in Cambridge nearly thirty years earlier: "This *is Donald Mackinnon* here . . . " Calling from his Scottish home he wanted to know if I was aware of the importance of the *Christian Newsletter* which Oldham had handed over to Kathleen Bliss in 1945, and which continued to appear "until Kathleen Bliss", he boomed, "*suddenly* and *unexpectedly* became *pregnant*!" We continued the conversation later that year during a symposium in Aberdeen, on P. T. Forsyth.

If the Oldham biography shadowed my footsteps at CCBI without coming to full fruition till later, it was nevertheless an important factor in the writing of the one book which did see the light of day during that time, *Learning to Speak. The Church's Voice in Public Affairs*. The promptings and influences were several. During my last year at the Bristol college I had found myself growingly puzzled and irritated by what seemed to be the wish of the churches—not least my own Baptist denomination—to confuse witness to Christ with self-publicity, and the frenetic desire to advertise all the good things they could claim to be doing in society. True, Jesus said, "Let your light so shine before others that they may see your good works". But the object of this is, he said, is that they may give glory to your Father in heaven—not increased status and admiration for the church itself. What is more, later in the Sermon in the Mount Jesus enjoins a form of *secrecy* on his followers. They are to beware of practicing their piety before others to be seen by them, and "when you give alms, do not let your left hand know what your right hand is doing, so that your alms may be done in secret, and your Father who sees in secret will reward you" (Matt. 6:3–5). Several times during 1989–90 I found myself preaching on this theme and warning against the churches succumbing to the self-promoting and publicity-at-all costs culture of the day. One such sermon I preached at a Sunday morning service at Bloomsbury Central Baptist Church. Afterwards an elderly gentleman who had been listening very carefully in the back pew thanked me for my "very refreshing" words. It was Daniel Jenkins, eminent United Reformed Church theologian who–yet another!–had been in Oldham's Moot. Then, during my first two years at CCBI, as I have made clear, a frequent concern was the issuing of statements, and while I was in no doubt about the necessity of this in principle I was increasingly troubled about the assumptions of many people who assumed that the churches should "speak out" on this issue or that. Did loquacity always make for prophecy? We wanted to speak *to* the world, but *from what* did our speaking come? It was sometime in the spring of 1992 while standing on Vauxhall station on the way home from a CCBI staff away day that the thought occurred to me: maybe the church would acquire more authenticity and credibility if it was prepared to be known as a *learner* before it spoke to others. Here Oldham was indeed important.

In the book, after surveying the current scene and the pressure to speak, I drew upon the case-studies of the Barmen Declaration and the *Kairos* document, and critiqued what I called the chattering culture of our time. I looked at the biblical motifs of prophecy and discipleship—emphasizing that the Hebrew prophets were all learners before they were speakers—and sought to be positive about what the church *does* know and learns afresh through humble service, drawing upon the experiences of the churches in three contemporary contexts of transition: South Africa, the Middle East, and Eastern Europe, all of which exemplified the prophetic stance of "those who are taught" (Isaiah 50:4). The book concluded with a survey of different modes of "speaking", and a check-list of points by which the churches can test their motivations and expectations when wishing to speak.

Learning to Speak was published by T. & T. Clark in February 1995. Most reviews were appreciative, though in *Theology* Hugh Montefiore, bishop of Birmingham, was somewhat dismissive on account of its "somewhat Barthian" tone, and feared that it would not help him answer a recent request for an episcopal comment on a critical issue of medical ethics (a remark which, I felt, ironically exemplified the very attitude I was criticizing). One of the warmest responses came in a long telephone call from Ian Linden, director of the Catholic Institute for International Relations[5] who felt that what I was saying was very significant indeed but that some people might miss its profound implications, and wanted to know how it might be promoted further. To my surprise, more than twenty years later I discovered that it was still being used in the USA and Australia in classes on Christianity and public ethics, and was being reissued by Wipf & Stock in the USA.

BONHOEFFER—AND OTHERS

As mentioned in the previous chapter, in 1989 I had become involved in the Dietrich Bonhoeffer Works English translation project, and was now on the Editorial Board. Further, I was assigned the task of editing the English edition of Volume 13 in the series, which comprised all Bonhoeffer's known correspondence, lectures and sermons from his period as pastor in London 1933–35. It seemed very appropriate that this

---

5. Now "Progressio".

particular volume should be dealt with by an English editor and translators based in the UK. For a variety of reasons little progress was made during my CCBI time beyond recruiting Martin Conway, at that time President of the Selly Oak Colleges, as consultant to the translators, and the work only really took off after I moved to Geneva in 1997. In the meantime however the Editorial Board for the whole project, in collaboration with the Minneapolis-based Fortress Press, was meeting each November during the American Academy of Religion (AAR) meetings and so I started attending the AAR and Bonhoeffer Editorial Board meetings, beginning with Philadelphia (1995) and New Orleans (1996), and I was in regular contact with the Executive Editor of the whole project, Clifford Green of Hartford, Connecticut. In addition, there were the four-yearly International Bonhoeffer Congresses which took place in New York (1992) and Cape Town (1996). By now the International Bonhoeffer Society was a growing and intensifying international network of scholars and other people with a deep interest in Bonhoeffer, held together by common interest and friendship. I was particularly glad to get to know as friends many of the American members. Chicago college professor Burton Nelson (like me, a child of China missionaries), wore a delightfully innocent, humorously saintly air and had amassed a huge collection of photographic transparencies of people and places associated with Bonhoeffer's life. Also of Chicago were Geff Kelly, Roman Catholic, formerly of the Christian Brothers, of rumbustious, irreverent humor (and language), now teaching at La Salle University, and his English-born wife Joan and their daughter Sue who was afflicted from a very early age by a brain tumor. Pat Kelley, at that time teaching at Lynchburg, Virginia, had written a thesis on Karl Barth that I would rank as the best unpublished piece of theology I have ever seen, and was accompanied by his wife Connie. Cliff Green I have already mentioned. John Matthews was an astute Lutheran pastor at Apple Valley, Minnesota. Then must be mentioned Jack (an FBI agent) and Elinor Neel; Larry Rasmussen of Union Seminary and his wife Nyla; Alice Bond, a nurse of Lynchburg, Virginia, Southern Baptist to boot but very different in stance from that other inhabitant of Lynchburg, Jerry Falwell; Jim Burtness, Lutheran professor of systematic theology whom in fact I had first met some years before while he was a visiting scholar at Mansfield College, Oxford, and his wife Dolores; and Barbara Green, translator of Bonhoeffer's *Discipleship*, who had worked with the churches in East Berlin during the communist time, a close friend of Albrecht Schönherr and much involved with the German Kirchentag. The International Bonhoeffer Society had become more than an association of scholars. It was a fellowship in which not only ideas but joys and sorrows and serious mutual concerns were shared, from Scandinavia to Latin America, from South Africa to North America, from Japan to Australia: a form of what Bonhoeffer called life together, on the international scale.

The Bonhoeffer Congress in Cape Town in January 1996 was the first time such an event had moved out of the global north, and was a triumph of organization for John de Gruchy and his colleagues, whose assurances that South Africa was now a safe country for international visitors had been vindicated. Its theme was "Bonhoeffer for a New Day: Theology in a Time of Transition" which obviously related well to the context of newly-democratic South Africa aspiring to leave apartheid behind. The overall motif was provided by Bonhoeffer's question to his friends and family in the resistance shortly before his arrest in 1943, "Are we still of any use?"—a question facing anyone or any group facing new challenges in a changing world. There was an array of major international speakers including Konrad Raiser, general secretary of the WCC, and the South Korean feminist theologian Chung Hyun Kyung who in 1991 had caused major controversy at the WCC Assembly in Canberra. Desmond Tutu, Beyers Naudé and Frank Chikane were among the South Africans bringing testimony of what Bonhoeffer had meant in the struggle against apartheid. I gave a paper which for me marked some new ground to tread: "Dialogue with the Orthodox World: A Further Journey for Bonhoeffer". I had long been intrigued by the way Bonhoeffer's theology, especially his understanding of the incarnate Christ, and of salvation as the restoration of the image of God in humankind, showed strong affinities with certain Orthodox approaches, and especially an indebtedness to the second-century Greek Church father Irenaeus. This new attention to Orthodox theology on my part was to prove timely in ways I could not then have foreseen but were to be very apparent in the ecumenical journey that beckoned in the coming months.

The previous year, 1995, had seen the fiftieth anniversary of Bonhoeffer's death and of course there had been a plethora of commemorative events around the actual anniversary of his execution on April 9 which that year fell on Palm Sunday. In the morning, at Lincoln, I gave a lecture on the significance of Bonhoeffer's prison experience, at the annual conference of prison governors and chaplains, hosted by the bishop of Lincoln. By the afternoon I was at Coventry Cathedral to deliver a sermon at evensong, to the annual conference of Secondary School Heads. It was impressive, how each event testified to the appeal of Bonhoeffer for people in crucial areas of public responsibility. Next evening I was back in Bristol to address an ecumenical evening, at which the German pastor for the south-west of England also spoke.

PULPIT AND LECTERN

Whether on Bonhoeffer-related or other topics, while I was at CCBI interesting pulpit invitations included: Gloucester Cathedral on Remembrance Day 1992: evensong twice each at Oriel College, Oxford, and Clare College, Cambridge; weekday addresses in Worcester Cathedral and Westminster Abbey; and a Sunday evening service in St Giles' Cathedral, Edinburgh in March 1996. There was also a symposium on the theologian P. T. Forsyth at Aberdeen in June 1993 at which I have a paper on Forsyth as a political theologian; and in January 1994 a colloquium on the wartime "Baillie Commission" at New College, Edinburgh, at which I spoke on John Baillie and Oldham's "Moot". What with my interest in Gregor Smith, J.H. Oldham,

Baillie and Forsyth it seemed that as far as British theologians were concerned it was Scottish figures whom I found most interesting. An accident? My Scottish friends, naturally, think otherwise. There was also in April 1996 an interesting high-powered weekend conference at Chartridge in Buckinghamshire, organized by the Inter-Faith Foundation, with lectures by Jewish, Christian and Muslim scholars, and eminences including the Duke of Edinburgh, Crown Prince Hassan of Jordan and Sir Evelyn de Rothschild in attendance. I had been invited to give a paper on "Religion as Critique of Nationalism".[6]

But of all preaching or lecturing sites and occasions, none could exceed in sentiment finding myself in October 1993 in Great St Mary's, Cambridge, to deliver the University Sermon, from the same pulpit where as an undergraduate thirty years earlier I had heard the likes of Martin Niemöller, George Macleod, Wim Visser't Hooft, John Robinson, James Stewart . . . and many more. It may have been to save me from too great elation at this honor that, in the manner of St Paul, I was given a thorn in the flesh in the form of a dose of 'flu two days' previously. I had to forgo the Vice-Chancellor's Saturday evening dinner and overnight hospitality, but Margaret drove me to Cambridge. On Sunday morning it was a still somewhat groggy preacher who just about managed to remain upright in the pulpit. My theme was "Secular Power and Christian Unity" and the biblical text was John 18:36, "My kingdom is not from this world . . . " Jesus' words to Pilate, I pointed out, were often wrongly taken to mean a kingdom not *of* this world, a project unrelated to political power and social righteousness, whereas a kingdom not *from* thus world indicates the reign originating in the power and love of God which challenges and breaks into the power-structures of this world. Noting that it was almost exactly the sixtieth anniversary of Bonhoeffer's arrival as pastor in London, I said that the issues which he and his contemporaries like George Bell wanted the churches to face were still with us—and in some ways even more so when unreal claims were made for example in the idea of a national church. At the core of the sermon I quoted from the annual report of the Association of Friends of "a certain English cathedral" (Bristol, actually):

> Not for the Church of England an introverted congregationalism; to sink into that would be to abandon the mandate we have been given. Those who are beyond the congregation are as much our concern as those within. We are concerned to minister to people in society as in their privacy; in their corporations as in their individualism; in their secular life as in their ecclesiastical professions. That is what it means to be a national and established church.

To which I rejoined:

> Amen, brother! And that is also exactly what it means to be one of the Free Churches in Britain today, not to mention the Roman Catholic Church as well. No church has a monopoly of public and national concern. We all invest

---

6. Subsequently published in *European Judaism* Vol. 31, No 1 (Spring 1998) Issue No 60, 90–104.

considerably in social responsibility... The assumption that all else apart from the established church is ipso facto introverted sectarianism is a delusion.

Today, I would still say, and have said, the same, only yet more angrily.

FAMILY ON THE MOVE

By chance the occasion at Great St Mary's became something of a family affair. Peter had graduated from Clare College that summer after three good years as organ scholar, and also that year had gained his Fellowship of the Royal College of Organists (FRCO) with high distinction, being awarded the Limpus Prize for the best performance marks, and the Read Prize for the highest marks overall. He stayed on for another year at Cambridge to do some postgraduate research and earned his keep as organist at Great St Mary's. For the University Sermon it was the recognized duty of the organist of King's to play, but Stephen Cleobury for some reason did not appear so it fell to Peter after all.

My mother had died early in September that year aged eighty-eight. In the summer of 1991 she had moved from Clevedon to live at Pembury near Tunbridge Swells, in Cornford House, a home for former CIM missionaries. I conducted the funeral at Cornford House, attended by all the residents which made it the most appropriate way of acknowledging that she, like they, had first been a missionary in her own right and not just as a "wife". This left Margaret's mother our one remaining parent. She had had surgery and radiotherapy for cancer in 1984 but had recovered well and remained in Chesterfield after her husband's death in 1988. We and all her grandchildren celebrated her eightieth birthday in fine style in October 1995. By the end of the following year her health was beginning to fail again and she moved to live with Margaret's sister Kate and family at Whitley Bay near Newcastle-upon-Tyne. She died in a hospice there in April 1997.

Margaret at about the time I went to CCBI was promoted to principal lecturer at Bristol Polytechnic which in 1992 was renamed University of the West of England (UWE). It was a time of unprecedented expansion in higher education, the numbers at UWE rising from 12,000 to 20,000 within a few years, which brought all the added pressures on teaching time and space. She continued tutoring in maths for the Open University, including tutorials for a number of students in Horfield Prison in Bristol, and at Leyhill Open Prison. Not all tutors were evidently so willing to make such visits, and her readiness to do so was to stand her in good stead with the OU as time went on.

After his extra year at Cambridge Peter was appointed organist and director of music at St Peter's Church, Bexhill-on-Sea. This was a congenial environment, and the church had a strong musical tradition but of course he needed extra income and soon began teaching music part-time at Hurstpierpoint College, and was appointed full-time in 1997. His other activities included conducting the Hastings Choral Society, and thereby another dimension to his life was added through meeting Laura Epton, a music graduate of Reading University who had returned to live in her native Hastings, and they became engaged at Christmas 1997. Jonathan meanwhile was working his way through Bristol Cathedral School, and already turning his attention to journalism of a certain kind (an alternative publication to the official school magazine that he and some friends started while in the sixth form, was eventually banned as too subversive). In 1995 he started at Birmingham University where he read history which he greatly enjoyed, not least when in his final year as a special topic he studied the role of leading German scientists and their relations to the Nazi state. This involved some original research, an area in which Eberhard Bethge was glad to help in supplying background on some of the scientists in the Bonhoeffer family circle.

For a while we still managed to holiday aboard as a whole family, the last time being in 1992 when once more we camped in the Black Forest and Austria. We saw the Bethges again, and stayed with Henry and Barbara Jakob in Frankfurt. There was, too, an especially memorable, unexpected encounter on our outward journey. As usual, having disembarked from the overnight ferry at Vlissingen we drove non-stop across Holland to find breakfast at the first likely place over the German border. This happened to be a small town called Kerken. After coffee and rolls in the first café we could find, Peter wandered off to look at the local Catholic Church while the rest of us did some shopping. Peter returned to say that he'd found the church open, there was a good-looking organ and a friendly priest, and that we would be very welcome to look around. The priest was indeed friendly and wanted to discuss with me why I as an *evangelisch* only would only believe in a *geistlich* ("spiritual") understanding of the Lord's Supper. I didn't wish to get drawn into this as there was much else to see in the church, and meanwhile Peter was enjoying himself with Bach's St Anne fugue on the organ. That over, the priest collected us all in the entrance foyer of the church where he showed us three memorial plaques from 1939–45. One was for those in the town who had died in uniform. One was for those who had been killed in the bombing during the last days of the war. The third was a list of names of the Jews who had been deported from Kerken to the death camps. What a poignant trio of memorials. We bowed our heads and together, in English and German, said the Lord's Prayer. Ecumenism flowers in most unexpectedly beautiful ways.

There is one picture, however, which I suspect all of us will especially treasure from our holidays. In 1991 we had three weeks in Ontario, Canada, as guests of our American Baptist friends Bill and Kitty Brackney who lived at Hamilton just outside Toronto. Part of the time we stayed in a big log cabin belonging to friends of the Brackneys, on the shore of Lake Boskung. It was quite remote, an idyllic spot for bathing, boating and sunbathing, and exploring the surrounding forests and river valleys, while just a little further afield was Niagara Falls. Our nearest neighbors were beavers. One night we went out in canoes, as quietly as possible to try and see them in motion. It was a dead calm, moonlit night. Presently we could just glimpse their snouts surfacing in the moonlight, the minutest silvery wakes trailing behind them, the utter quietness every so often punctuated by the thunderous *thwack* of a tail hitting the water as a warning sign to others that humans were getting close. An unforgettable experience, the kind in which one knows that the world is not just beautiful but *meant* to be beautiful. Such moments point beyond themselves, to a hope for the whole creation.

One day at the Cathedral School a new boy arrived in Jonathan's class. When the teacher who was making the introductions came to Jonathan, he said, "This is Clements. His dad's a spy." Such were the youthful rumors, evidently reaching the staff room, prompted by reports of Jonathan's father visiting unlikely, far-distant and in some cases dangerous places. It is time now for some account of these travels during the CCBI years, what led to them and how they affected me. Some judgment can then be made as to whether indeed in some senses I was a spy.

9

The Middle East: Conflicts Past, Present, and to Come

> There is the widespread feeling that what has happened can only deserve the name of "tragedy". The suffering in Kuwait and Iraq is immense. At present there can only be speculation about the full extent of casualties among the Iraqi forces and, still more pertinently, among the Iraqi civilian population as a result of the intensive aerial bombardment. The damage to the Iraqi infrastructure of basic amenities, communications and energy supplies will itself create its own tally of victims for some time to come. Moreover, the full consequences in human attitudes are as yet unknown. The complexities of the damage to relationships between Arab societies and the west, and within the Arab world itself, have still to be assessed. A war, brief as this has been yet prosecuted on such a scale, is a deep wound in the flesh of the human family of the region.

THIS IS ONE PARAGRAPH from the briefing paper *The Gulf Crisis. Time for Reflection* which I prepared for the churches in early March 1991 following the expulsion of Iraqi forces from Kuwait. An immediate issue for the churches was the appropriateness or otherwise of a national service of thanksgiving following the end of the conflict. The Churches' Peace Forum reflected on this and I summarized the Forum's anxieties in a discussion paper (April 4 1991). No Christian service could regard national interest as paramount, nor disregard the sufferings of the Iraqi people, nor overlook the existence of Iraq's Christian churches, nor the impression in the Middle East that the Gulf war had been largely waged by "Christian" nations on Muslim peoples . . . and so forth. Was there any real cause for thanksgiving? The issue became controversial when, without any consultation with the churches as a whole, or the Scottish churches in particular, the government announced that the service would be held in Glasgow (Roman Catholic) Cathedral on May 4. I sent my paper to John Habgood as the Anglican president of CCBI, who had been invited to preach at the service. He strongly supported the thinking of the paper which, in calling for restraint, penitence and reconciliation, he saw as "an expanded version of some thoughts I put to the Prime Minister long before the present service was planned". The service when it took place was described in the *Tablet* as "dignified and muted", with John Habgood himself emphasizing the suffering of innocents in this "wretched business".

TO LEBANON 1991

There was however a longer-term need for renewing and strengthening our relations with the churches of the Middle East and to take seriously their experiences and perspectives on the conflict and its aftermath. Already, towards the end of January a delegation of four Iraqi church leaders led by His Beatitude Patriarch Mar Raphael I Bidawid, had visited the UK, meeting with a number of church leaders in London, and also with CCBI staff and church representatives at Inter-Church House. But it was clear that signs of initiative from our side would be welcome. Although I had met with some of the church leaders at a CEC-MECC meeting in Cyprus the previous December, my only first-hand experience of the Middle East proper had been in Jordan at the BWA meetings in 1987. But a new opportunity was presented by forthcoming meetings in Beirut of the Middle East Resource-Sharing Group of the WCC Commission on Church Aid, Refugee and World Service (CICARWS) and the MECC's Annual Meeting of the Emergency Relief, Rehabilitation and Reconstruction Programmer (ERR), in May. Clearly a visit to Lebanon at this time would offer unusual learning opportunities, and Gabriel Habib, general secretary of the MECC and Ghassan Rubeiz, Middle East secretary of CICARWS, encouraged me to come and make whatever use I could of the presence in Beirut of workers from several countries in the region as well as Lebanon itself. Lebanon, racked by civil war and occupation since 1975, and now breathing in a draught of peace with the start of the implementation of the Taif Agreement reached in 1990, was at a most critical point in its own history; equally, the wider problems of the region, compounded still further by the recent Gulf War, were being reflected in specifically Lebanese agonies. There was of course a certain nervousness about such a visit just then. "Going to Beirut? Must be mad," said the woman at the Middle East Airlines desk at Heathrow when I checked in on May 3. "Only joking", she continued, "it's much safer now." The security situation was in fact still fragile, and MECC/CICARWS had warned of possible last-minute changes of plans. Terry Waite and other western hostages were still being held underground somewhere in the country.[1] I had been helpfully briefed, though with the standard warnings about going at all, by Foreign Office officials on Middle East affairs Stewart Eldon and Edward Glover. A sad omission from my preparation came with the sudden death of John Lyttle, the archbishop of Canterbury's Adviser on Public Affairs from whom I was due to get advice based on his unique experience of involvement in attempts to obtain the release of the British hostages.

---

1. In fact a few months after my visit there was a brief bout of further hostage-taking in Beirut. One British newspaper headline declared: "Beirut stares into the abyss again." All hostages were released by the end of 1992.

PART THREE: INTERNATIONAL AFFAIRS 1990–1997

There was only one other obvious westerner on the nearly full flight to Beirut. Douglas Soutar of Christian Aid would be flying out a few days later. I spent most the flight trying to finish Robert Fisk's dramatic and personal account of Lebanon's fifteen-year war, a tale of atrocity and massacre, *Pity the Nation.* Descending over Beirut, it was an almost eerie experience to shut the book and look down at where so much of "it" had happened in 1975: the shattered apartments and hotels near the beach, the sports stadium, the all-too visible sites of Sabra and Chatila and of course the airport area itself. On landing, Syrian troops, hardly friendly in appearance, seemed to be all over the airport. The MECC staff in Beirut had been told of my coming but in the bustle and confusion of the primitive baggage reclaim hall I felt totally alone and anxious as to how and where to find my way next. Then came a soft tap on my shoulder: "Reverend Clements? I am Mike Nahhal": sheer relief at hearing my own name, and to meet this tall, slightly stooping, gentle man, the Communication and Relief Secretary for the MECC in Beirut. A Greek Orthodox layman, Mike was to be my guide, mentor and guardian angel for the next eight days. We drove along the notorious airport road through Syrian and Lebanese army checkpoints, past the site of the US Marines base destroyed by a suicide bomber in 1983, and straight into down town Beirut. It was a healthy piece of acclimatization to see right away the acres of shattered, skeletal apartments and high-rise blocks, walls sprayed with pock-marks left by the sheer profligacy of ammunition; yet here and there, several floors up, signs of occupation by families determined to find anything remotely like a home. I checked into the Hotel Mayflower, an oasis of hospitality for journalists and the few other western visitors throughout the years of conflict. The owner greeted me like a long-lost nephew, doubtless seeing me as a foretaste of the return of the good old days of western business and tourism. With the welcome came a free drink—and a candle and a box of matches since electricity from the grid was on for only up to six hours a day. For *some* of the rest of the time there was reliance on generators, hence the characteristic smell of diesel in so many buildings. Having telephoned the British embassy (the Foreign Office had told them of my visit) I ate out with Mike Nahhal who briefed me on much of the current situation in the country and the relief work of the MECC. Next morning at breakfast concepts of normality were revised yet further. As well as some European aid workers arriving, a young man was standing at the hotel door with a pistol in his back trouser pocket, while a yet younger guy dressed in black sauntered in with a Kalashnikov rifle and disappeared upstairs. This was somewhat disconcerting as I was expecting the British ambassador or one of his staff to call briefly. But it was simply, the reception staff explained to me, that the PPS—a pro-Syrian political party—was holding meetings in the hotel and it was customary for such groups to see to their own security in case of assassination attempts. Presently a large car with Union Jacks a-flutter on its wings did roll up in front of the hotel and almost as quickly drove on again. I was called to the reception desk and handed a card from the ambassador, David Tatham, inviting me to a dinner party at his residence the following Wednesday evening. He apologized for not having proper invitation cards any more, but the message concluded: "Ties." Much of Beirut might be in ruins, the supply of diplomatic stationery might have run out, but . . . ties would be worn. *Some* standards were being maintained. By the afternoon I was adjusting to being in a city of alarming sights yet also of reassuring gestures. Throughout the week, as a white westerner I was conscious of being something of a novelty on the streets or in restaurants, especially if I was by myself, but by and large the surprised looks were welcoming rather than suspicious. Just once, Mike Nahhal bustled me into a side-alley as we approached a group of men coming in the opposite direction whom he evidently judged to merit precautions.

Mike Nahhal

Mike Nahhal, despite the many demands on his time, had organized a full exposure programme for me. On the Sunday morning I worshipped with the Anglican congregation (in Arabic the cadences of the Book of Common Prayer are almost as recognizable as in English) and was invited to give the final prayer and benediction. I spent a lot of time with staff in the MECC offices in both West and East Beirut and saw at work their centers for health and community projects and youth. The evening at the ambassador's residence (in a heavily fortified compound) drew together quite a gathering of business and professional people with an interesting range of views on Lebanon, its past problems and future prospects. (One question of etiquette I had not expected: how does one politely remove the Praying Mantis that has just landed on one's plate?) On another evening I was at the home of Wa'il Kheir, an academic jurist who was Greek Orthodox by confession, executive director of the Foundation for Human Rights (Lebanon), and who had gathered a group of colleagues in the Foundation—industrialists, academics, businessmen, a judge and social worker—to meet me. In three hours I heard a great deal about their concerns for Lebanese life especially in the wake of the Taif Agreement. I made two visits to the Near East School of Theology (NEST) and talked with its president, the Armenian Evangelical Hovhannes Karjian. I had interviews with a number of academics, journalists, newspaper editors and politicians, both Christian and Muslim (in the latter case both Sunni and Shia). I had an hour with Khatchig Barbican, Minister of Justice and Deputy for Beirut, and as well as issues like the future of Lebanon we discussed the situation of the British hostages. I joined other visitors at a meeting with Archbishop Aram Keshishian of the Armenian Orthodox Church, whom I knew from the Faith and Order Commission.

There were two memorable trips outside Beirut. On my third day there, two visitors from Swiss Inter-Church Aid and I were taken by car up the Bekaa valley to visit MECC projects. Doubts about the wisdom of venturing up the Bekaa notwithstanding (it was a Hezbollah stronghold), the most obvious presence was that of Syrian army checkpoints. Mostly we were waved though on the nod, but my nerves did prickle slightly when at one of these a soldier stuck his head inside the car window and demanded to know if there were any English inside. When I raised my hand he just said politely, "Good morning sir. How are you? I learning English. Have a nice day!" In a small town where Mosque and Catholic Church coexisted happily we were entertained to coffee by a Muslim family. After the fertile stretches of vines, grain and vegetable fields (also white opium poppy plots) the landscape turned to semi-arid, we left the main road and reached the village of Hermel where the MECC had sponsored a school for mentally handicapped children. Later on in the village of Kah we visited the Catholic Church which also housed a school, run by a Sorbonne-trained nun. We found time to see the famous Roman temples at Baalbek, and on our homeward way called at another school for handicapped children at Bichout on the eastern slopes of the valley. After dark, the drive back to Beirut was an adventure in itself, with oncoming lorries showing varying degrees of illumination assuming the right to the middle of the road. The second trip was south from Beirut to Sidon. Two Japanese visitors and I were taken by Robert Nicolas, ERR coordinator for south Lebanon. The journey was through a scene of contrasts: Mediterranean blue to the right, while less than a mile or so inland stretch after stretch of whitening rubble where whole villages had been laid waste. We spent time at the MECC's physiotherapy center which had narrowly escaped during the recent fighting as witnessed by the rubble outside and the bulletholes in the office furniture of the director Hussein Kurdich. Here victims of bullets and landmines were being fitted with prostheses and given hydrotherapy. We were sorry there wasn't time to visit any of the displaced persons' camps, merely a quick glance at the crusader castle on the shore then back to Beirut.

WHEN IS A WAR "OVER"?

Typically, the outside world breathes a sigh of relief on hearing that a war is "over" and can turn its mind to other things. But for the people left amid the rubble peace is something that has to be rebuilt piece by piece, act of trust by act of trust, and often literally brick by brick. Hope has to be nurtured. One day Armand Georgevitch, ERR coordinator at the MECC East Beirut office, took me by car on a tour of East Beirut and the mountain to its rear, where the beauty of the deep, wooded valleys and gorges contrasted vividly with the wreckage of so many homes and buildings in what had traditionally been a summer residence area for better-off Lebanese. Much of the damage had occurred in the previous year's fighting between General Michael Aoun's forces and the Syrian military. It was touching to find, in the garden of one gutted house, the children's swing, slide and climbing frame twisted into a tangle of rusting metal. Yet out of the rubble, like a symbol of hope, roses were again blooming, while across the street young men were busy sawing and hammering. One could only wonder, too, at instances of resilience and determination. Lamia Shkeiban, ERR project coordinator at the MECC West Beirut office, told me: "My parents' home where I lived was bombed, not too badly but my car was destroyed. The only thing to do was forget about a car and move to an apartment a few minutes' walk from the office." Right on the old "green line" which had represented the divide between East and West Beirut was Ain Baida, a kind of island of apartments which had remained more or less intact, where the people had refused to allow militias of any side to mount their weapons and where, after they had lost their water-supply, the MECC had sited a dispensary and sunk an artesian well with piping for water so that this brave community could stay together; and where the residents had determinedly kept an open space free from interference as a recreation ground for their youngsters.

PART THREE: INTERNATIONAL AFFAIRS 1990-1997

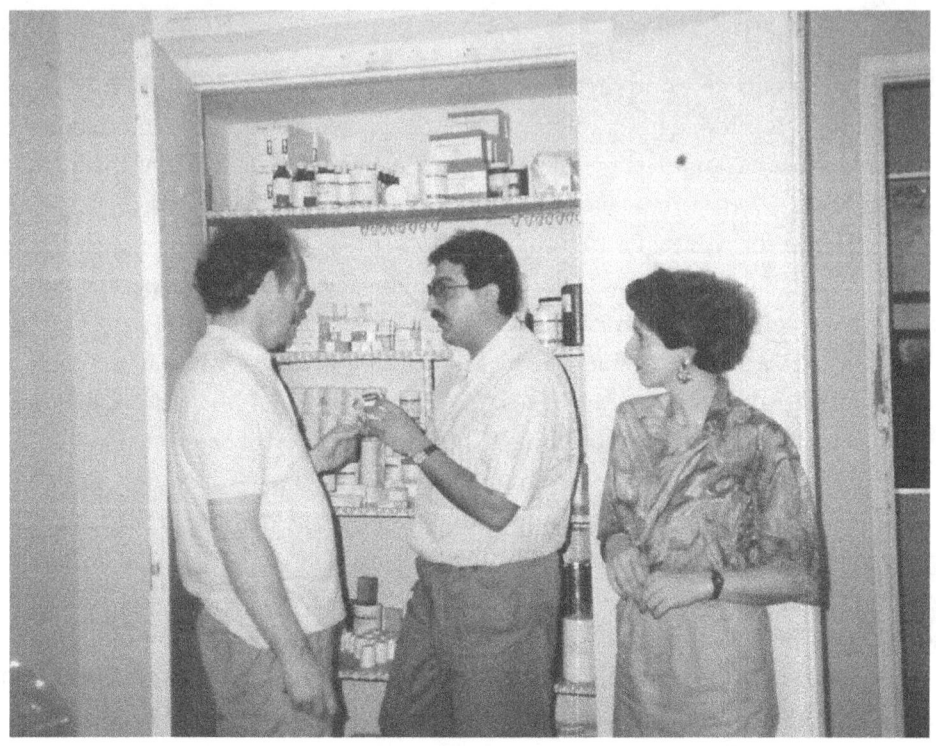

In the MECC clinic, Beirut

But having endured their own war, and then trying to rebuild their peace, the Lebanese now had the Gulf War of 1990 to contend with. There were direct economic consequences, not least with the loss of remittances from the many Lebanese working in the Gulf, and the loss of the Gulf markets for Lebanese exports. But there were serious political consequences too. No-one had a good word for Saddam Hussein but there was no less contempt, indeed outright anger, for the oil-rich rulers of the Gulf seen as self-indulgent autocrats enjoying lavish comforts with sublime indifference to the hardships of the mass of people in the Arab world. There was mistrust of the West's handling of the crisis, not least because President Hafez al-Assad of Syria's support for the anti-Hussein coalition earned him favors from the USA and almost a free hand in northern Lebanon. His invasion and attack on Beirut, involving murders of unarmed Lebanese troops and rape of their wives, in the autumn of 1990 made Syria despised and feared by many. At least, the Taif Accords were requiring Syria to withdraw, as likewise Israel from southern Lebanon, but the likelihood remained of the continuing sway of Damascus. Then there was the Palestinian issue which, thanks to the large presence of refugees from Palestine since 1948, and the defining moment of the Sabra and Chatila massacres of 1982, was of all sores in the region the longest running, with no sign of healing. One afternoon I spent two enjoyable hours at a tea-party in the home of Dr and Mrs Nabib Jamal, members of the Anglican congregation whom I had met the previous Sunday. They had invited a number of friends to meet me. Like the

Jamals, they had all left Palestine in 1948. It was indeed like the archetypal vicarage tea-party until someone dropped the word "Israel" into the conversation and there was an outburst of anger. Why, as many others asked in Lebanon, was the international community not taking as much trouble to ensure compliance with UN resolutions about the illegal occupation of Palestine, as about the occupation of Kuwait? The latest war had heaped another layer of suffering and frustration on an already wounded region and the Palestinians still felt left at the bottom of the international pile.

This is the context in which the Lebanese churches were now having to determine their priorities in concert with the churches of the whole region. The MECC, already including the Catholic family, had just received the Maronite Church into membership, potentially a very significant step given that the Maronites had usually been seen as parenting the Phalangist party which was so deeply embroiled in the sectarian events of 1975 and after. Ecumenism had to be a *sine qua non* of witness to the gospel in a region where the need is for reconciliation, where the Christian presence is numerically in steady decline due to emigration and where in a number of countries the threat of Islamicisation is felt. Yet leaders like Gabi Habib in the MECC believed that in terms of their divine calling their survival—and indeed their unity—was not an end in itself but was for the sake of the gospel of justice, peace and reconciliation for all the peoples, not only Christians but Muslims, Jews, Druze and whoever, in the societies of which the churches are part. The nature of such witness was brought home to me above all when seeing projects like Foyer de la Joie, the school for mentally handicapped children I had seen at Hermel in the Bekaa valley. Here was not just another project to help the needy, of which countless more could have been set up especially in the limelight of publicity in Beirut. Rather, it had been asked, "In the most out-of-the-way, liable-to-be-forgotten areas, who are the most vulnerable, and how can they be served in a way which helps to integrate the different communities, Muslim and Christian especially?" This was a servant mode of being church, the church for others. Such work of course depended greatly on funding through CICARWS and other WCC-related agencies and it vitally illustrated ecumenical solidarity in action.

In such a situation the church does not need consciously to take risks. It is already at risk simply by being there, in a largely Muslim environment and a fragile social structure both nationally and regionally. But we must not, said one Orthodox layman, project onto Islam our own images. "Islamic fundamentalism is a phenomenon of despair", he said. "We do not yet have the solution to Christian-Muslim relations but we know it will not come by confrontation. Equally, Arab Christians must recover a true sense of their own identity. We Christians must impress on Muslims that we are Arabs—and we were there before Muslims were! We are not remnants of the Crusaders, but are oriental Christians. We want neither to be enemies of Islam nor stooges of 'western' Christians."[2]

2. For a remarkable theology of being Christian church in Lebanon, see Frieda Haddad, "The Christian Community as sign and instrument for the renewal of human community: a Lebanese

There is not space to narrate all the examples and instances of faithful witness in that fraught and uncertain environment. But I think again of Mike Nahhal, steady, gentle, compassionate, unassuming and, almost otherworldly in his self-effacing desire just to get things done: not a do-gooder but a good doer; and withal someone who always had time for enjoyment of the best in life, as once he showed just before getting back into his car, bending down to pick some flowers from the dusty verge to put in a jar in his desk, "To remind me of the beauty of God's creation." And if, as the Orthodox remind us, the mark of sainthood is joy then there was true sainthood in Lebanon. One evening several of us visitors from abroad were taken by Ghassan Rubeiz and other Lebanese to a seafront fish restaurant where we dined on that marvelous Mediterranean delicacy of large sardines baked in their own oil. Such conviviality in the face of besetting problems and potential dangers was a gift of grace and a sign of hope. By the time we were finished night had fallen, and the still lampless streets of Beirut were pitch dark but Ghassan Rubiez shepherded us unerringly back to the Hotel Mayflower. We learn most about a country from those whose friendship and guidance we accept and trust and whose enjoyments we can share.

On my return home there was plenty to report on to CCBI colleagues and the International Affairs Liaison group—and the Middle East staff in the Foreign Office who seemed no less grateful for my lengthy report "Eight Days in Lebanon". Barely a week later I was with Gabi Habib again, at a conference on the post-Gulf War situation called by the Italian Baptists and other Protestants at Santa Severa near Rome, attended also by Joan Brown Campbell, general secretary of the National Council of Churches USA (NCCCUSA) and several other Americans. Elizabeth Salter was also there from the WCC. The wisest word was spoken by Gabi Habib who summed up his impressions of the meeting by saying of Middle East and European churches, "We have begun a journey of mutual discovery". I was glad in a small way to be part of that process.

In terms of military action the Gulf War might have been over but the misery of large sections of the Iraqi people continued. The issue of sanctions against Iraq stayed top of the CCBI international affairs agenda for many months. It was in some ways a paradox that we who in relation to South Africa had advocated sanctions as an alternative to war should now be querying these measures which the international community, and above all the USA and Britain, were adamant were necessary to force Saddam Hussein's compliance with the terms of the ceasefire and—it was now being said—to ensure his eventual removal from office. The Church of Scotland later produced a highly useful report on the whole question of sanctions in the so-called new world order.

---

perspective", in. Best, *Faith and Renewal*, 184–191. I have cited this paper elsewhere, e.g. in my *Dietrich Bonhoeffer's Ecumenical Quest*, 298f.

WITH THE IRISH IN THE HOLY LAND

In October 1991 I was back in the Middle East again, this time in Israel-Palestine with an ecumenical party of twelve clergy and lay people from the Irish churches, Anglican, Protestant and Roman Catholic. Gordon Gray, Presbyterian minister from Lisburn in Northern Ireland, was the leader of the group and had much experience of similar ecumenical visits to the region and to other contexts of inter-communal conflict. Sam Poyntz, bishop of Connor, was the senior Anglican and Tony Farquhar, bishop of Down and Connor, the senior Roman Catholic. A main object of the visit was to enable mutual sharing of experience and perspectives between the churches and peoples caught up in the two contexts of conflict in which religion was a factor. This, it should be borne in mind, was well before the IRA ceasefire of 1994, not to mention the 1998 Good Friday agreement. We were there for nine days, seeing all the usual historic pilgrimage sites but also with a good deal of time in Gaza and the occupied territories of the West Bank. We met with church leaders including the Latin Patriarch of Jerusalem His Beatitude Michael Sabbah and the Anglican bishop of Jerusalem, Samir Kafity, and Jewish academics like Rabbi David Rosen in Notre Dame University. There were sessions with Palestinian community leaders in Gaza—some of the Irish Protestants conscious of their own context were nevertheless taken aback by the fierceness of the anger they encountered—and victims of Israeli military action there, and we saw the impressive work of a Christian (in fact Baptist) hospital. In Jerusalem we had lunch with the director of the Council of Jewish Communities and so heard at first hand the advocacy of Jewish settlements in the West Bank, "a frightening disregard of history, international law and plain justice" my diary reads, noting that not even in apartheid South Africa and not even from a die-hard Afrikaner politician had I heard such sheer blinkered prejudice. But equally we saw the impressive work for reconciliation of the Centre for Rapprochement (Palestinian/Israeli/Muslim/Jewish/Christian) in Beit Sahour near Bethlehem. In France Square in Jerusalem we talked with the courageous Israeli Women in Black at their weekly demonstration against the Israeli illegal occupation. In Tel Aviv we met with the director of International relations in the Likud Party, and saw where some of Saddam Hussein's Scud missiles had landed during the Gulf War. One was conscious all the time of the fragile context. At midday on the Sunday after a church service by the Garden Tomb I was walking near the Damascus Gate when a shot rang out from the other side of the crowded road. A Palestinian woman had tried to pull a knife on an Israeli soldier and was now lying wounded on the pavement. Yet there was poignancy in the evening by the Dome of the Rock, as one heard simultaneously the prayers of Jews at the Wailing Wall, the bells of nearby churches and the call to prayer from the minaret of the Al Aqsa Mosque.

"Have learnt a lot about Ireland!" I noted in my diary and indeed the visit was as much about Ireland as Israel-Palestine, as I realized in the conversations among our group. Both in Ireland and the Holy Land the struggle was on to find a shared narrative, a common understanding of history among divided peoples bound to the same land. That was far from easy, in either context, but still necessary as was made clear at the Tantur Ecumenical Centre where we had a final day of prayer, meditation and reflection on the whole experience. It was good, too, to experience something of the spirituality that a group such as this brought with them. "Pilgrimage" can sometimes appear to be a form of escape from the often brutal realities of the scene. In Bethlehem of course we went into the Church of the Nativity. We were almost the only people there and we stood silently around the image of the star in the floor, by tradition the spot where stood the manger in which the infant Jesus was laid. Someone started singing, softly, "Away in a manger". I thought, "Oh no, here we go on a sentimental piety trip". But others, and soon all of us, joined in. When we had finished someone offered a prayer about what we had seen in the past few days. Others followed, and before long all the misery of Gaza, the struggles for justice against settlements in the West Bank and the disputes over water supplies to Arab communities in the north, the courage of peacemakers in Beit Sahour and among the Women in Black, and the hopes and fears of all the years that met there at the first Christmas now crowded into the manger scene. There could, I realized, be a point where pilgrimage and the mission for justice and peace coincide and reinforce each other. The point was brought home to me even more forcefully in the Church of the Holy Sepulcher in Jerusalem. The actual shrine of the tomb is very confined, taking no more than three persons at a time. I was third in line to go in, behind Gordon Gray and Sam Poyntz. Just as I was about to stoop down and enter I felt a slight tap on my shoulder. It was Tony Farquhar who whispered, "Keith, do you mind if I go in before you?" Of course I agreed for it was obvious what he wished: to kneel with his Irish brothers so that Anglican, Protestant, and Catholic could pray together at this holiest Christian shrine and bring with them for forgiveness the sins of divided Christianity and its complicity in a conflict-ridden world.

AN UNKNOWN REGION

> Paradoxically, the region which is the historic birthplace of their faith is almost opaque to western Christians, an area of seemingly alien cultures and intractable political problems baffling in their complexity. It is a world which is simply "there", to be reacted to with emergency measures applied from outside whenever a particular crisis erupts with obvious implications for the wider world, especially for its oil supplies . . . Bouts of urgent concern alternate with longer periods of indifference and refusal to engage with the deeper issues from within . . .

That is what I wrote in a discussion document *Counting the Cost: The Middle East Three Years after the Gulf War* in early 1994 for the CCBI Assembly that year. It drew together the reports and thinking of aid agencies, ecumenical bodies including the MECC, and the Council of Christian Approaches to Defence and Disarmament. It covered the topics: Kuwait, destruction and reconstruction; Iraq and the continuing regime of Saddam Hussein and the continuing suffering of the people; environmental damage; re-militarization of the region; enforced population movements especially of Palestinians and Asians since the Gulf War; the Arab-Israeli peace process; human rights and democracy; questions about a new world order; Christian vulnerability in the Middle East; and priorities for the western churches. "What is required . . . is a venture at seeing the life, suffering and potentialities of the Middle East from within. The fact that for twenty centuries the Christian communities of the Middle East have themselves been doing just that is, ecumenically, both a challenge and an invitation to the churches of the west."

ANGER AND PAIN: IRAQ 1994

Not long after this document was produced, in spring 1994 there came just such an opportunity for me to further my own experience of the region from within. Invitations were received by CCBI as by other ecumenical bodies and churches in various parts of the world, to a symposium being sponsored by the churches of Iraq on "The Church in the Service of Peace and Humanity", and focusing on the effects on the Iraqi people of the continuing UN sanctions. Such an event, we realized from the outset, could only be taking place with the permission, if not desire, of the Iraqi government (the invitations came via the Iraqi Ministry of Religious Affairs). So a lot of consultation took place within CCBI and the Middle East Forum of CCOM, and with NCCUUSA and the MECC. It was eventually decided that all the factors notwithstanding, CCBI should be represented as a sign of solidarity with the Christian communities of Iraq and should take the opportunity of listening to them at first-hand. The NCCUSA people came to the same conclusion. The Vatican too would be sending a delegation, and the MECC was also supportive and would be represented at it. At the request of the CCOM Middle East Forum I agreed to attend on behalf of CCBI and also, at the invitation of the Churches' Commission on international Affairs in Geneva, to represent the WCC. Foreign participants would assemble in Amman, Jordan, on June 9 and next day travel by coach to Baghdad where the opening session would take place on the morning of June 11. The rest of the symposium would take police in Mosul, concluding on June 14.

On arrival at our hotel in Amman I found Dale Bishop, Middle East Coordinator for NCCCUSA, whom I knew from visits to New York, waiting somewhat anxiously and saying that he had decided not to proceed to Baghdad if I failed to appear! The coach journey next day was uneventful and in Baghdad we joined the whole party of participants in the Al-Rasheed Hotel (at the entry to the foyer one had to walk over Georgie Bush's face in a mosaic inserted into the floor). The other members of the non-Iraqi contingent included Dr Albert Aghzarian from Beir Zeit University in Jerusalem,

Nina Hallah from MECC Cyprus, Archpriest Victor Petluchenko from the Moscow Orthodox Patriarchate, Bishop Michael Fitzgerald from the Pontifical Commission on Inter-religious Affairs, and others from Sweden, Germany, Netherlands and USA. But I was also delighted to find again Mike Nahhal, now working as MECC Coordinator for relief work in Iraq. All told there were about two hundred participants, the great majority of course being Iraqi church leaders and representatives.

We were bussed north to Mosul in the afternoon and evening of June 11. The sun was sinking as we passed Tikrit, Saddam Hussein's hometown, and nearby was the huge oil refinery ringed with anti-aircraft guns. In Mosul we were housed in the Nineveh Oberoi Hotel close by one of the president's palaces and overlooking the Tigris. Next morning the symposium began in earnest. Presiding overall was His Beatitude Mar Raphael Bidawid, head of the Chaldean Catholic Church, the largest Christian community in Iraq, whom I had met on his visit to London in 1991, and it was also good to meet again Father Yousif Habbi, also of the Chaldean Catholic Church, and Archbishop Assadurian of the Armenian Orthodox Church who had likewise visited in 1991. The formal sessions were largely occupied with set-piece speeches by the Iraqi church leaders, but also including Dr Abdyul Menb'am Ahmed Saleh the Minister of Religious Affairs, Bishop Marian Clish the Vatican Ambassador to Baghdad and Dr Abdul Rezzaq Al Sadim, a Muslim. Several of the visitors including myself spoke briefly and I also read a message from the WCC. By and large the Iraqi contributions were strong declarations of the Christian commitment to peace, justice and human rights to be applied to all people without discrimination, and denunciation of the UN embargo as a continuing act of war against the Iraqi people. Set pieces they may have been, and obviously aimed at least in part at the ears of the government, but they were also marked by a deep and unmistakable anger at what was perceived as sheer injustice committed by the international community. Some employed the demonizing language about the "forces of evil and darkness" bent on murdering the country. Given the highly-charged tone of many of the speeches, and what could be dismissed as rhetoric intended for home consumption, the final statement of the symposium was remarkably factual and prosaic, calling for world attention to the sufferings of the people as a matter of human rights and dignity, though some from the floor called for stronger language to be used.

There were many occasions for private and informal conversations. On two afternoons we visited historic churches and mosques (including the prize exhibit of the tomb of the prophet Jonah) and the site of ancient Nineveh. Some of us attended Sunday evening liturgy in the Syrian Orthodox Cathedral where there also took place concluding ecumenical and inter-faith prayers for peace. Michael Fitzgerald and I enjoyed a supper party in a Chaldean Catholic home where we were joined by a Muslim family. In the course of the time in Mosul we heard many accounts underlining the nature and extent of the humanitarian crisis: of the average wage of government employees being the equivalent of three US dollars per month and the cost of a bag of flour or millet being one dollar; of many families having only one meal per day on an almost entirely carbohydrate diet (with particularly serious implications for infants); of the elderly and young being especially vulnerable; and of the acute shortage of even basic medical supplies. The churches knew well enough about the shortages since they were all involved in regular food distribution programs including help via the MECC. There was no pretense that *all* Iraqis were suffering extremes. The well-to-do were still able to cushion themselves. But quite apart from the physical and health hardships, all of us as foreign visitors were struck by the psychological trauma brought about by the continued embargo. This came over both in the speeches and in many private conversations. The population as a whole was feeling totally battered, isolated and helpless. The Iran-Iraq war had bled them mercilessly in the 1980s, they felt the Gulf War had been inflicted on them and now they were having to endure sanctions which were humiliating them socially, emotionally and spiritually, without redress: an ominous parallel with the effects of the British blockade of Germany after World War I. A people with a long and proud cultural history—Iraq being one of the cradles of civilization is not just a truism—who until recently had enjoyed a relatively sophisticated cultural life with a high standard of social welfare, now felt disowned and pilloried by the world outside. It is not as though these people felt able to exercise any political leverage and the sanctions, in contrast to those on apartheid South Africa, were no inducement to seek such change but were felt to be one more burden heaped on an already helpless people and consigning them to yet more bitterness, resignation or despair. As one person said to me: "We don't matter to anyone anymore. Nobody cares about us. And we don't care about politics." People privately were prepared to express their dislike of Saddam Hussein, but how to get rid of him? There had been attempts, I was told, including one by a brother of the president who had paid the price by being thrown to a pack of the president's voracious dogs. At least one plot, another said, had been prevented by intervention by the CIA, no less

Then there were foreigners from Third World countries trapped in Iraq. By chance in Baghdad I came across a young Christian man from South Sudan who handed me a document on behalf of the "Sudanese Christian Association Baghdad" appealing for financial help for South Sudanese migrant workers who were wanting to leave Iraq. The devaluation of the currency and the closure of many embassies in Baghdad meant that they could neither afford tickets not obtain visas easily. Some had tried to get out via Jordan but found themselves trapped by inability to afford accommodation or to get visas to travel further.

Part Three: International Affairs 1990–1997

A welcome from the Syrian Orthodox in Mosul

Pain layered upon pain . . . Yet also one met faith, cheerfulness and resolve, as in the Syrian Orthodox congregation in Mosul, so outgoing and welcoming and glad at any sign that they were not forgotten. One just hoped that our visit did convey to such people that they were not alone. On the final day of the symposium I and Mike Nahhal with about thirty other participants inadvertently made a gesture of solidarity in suffering by succumbing to salmonella food poisoning. There was no medication or relief apart from water. We were still in a weak condition when we set out next morning for our return to Baghdad and thence to Amman. On leaving Baghdad late in the evening we were already several hours behind schedule and certain to miss our flights home. To make matters worse, this bus was long past its use-by date. In the grey light of dawn, still in the desert many miles from the Jordanian border, I was awakened by a juddering noise beneath my seat at the rear of the coach and we crunched to a halt. A tire had blown. The driver and his mate established there was a spare, but no jack. "Sanctions, you see." It was about two hours before they were able to hail a passing truck possessed of the right tools and eventually we continued on our way. At the Jordanian border there was an unconscionably long delay for passport checks by the Iraqis. By then it was early afternoon, it was searingly hot, and to make matters worse we could see just on the Jordanian side a refrigerated drinks machine stacked with Coca-Cola. When eventually we were let across there was a desperate raid on that machine. By now Mike Nahhal was suffering severely from dehydration and was in a semi-comatose state. The bus ploughed on. In mid-afternoon in Azrak, of Laurence of Arabia fame, we once more ground to a halt, this time with gear-box trouble. Reduced to a crawl, we finally made it to the hotel in Amman but not before stopping on the edge of the city to transfer Mike Nahhal to an ambulance for hospital treatment. He did recover, we learnt later. At the hotel reception desk I was met by "Phone call for Mr Clements!" It was Eva at CCBI where she and other staff, not to mention Margaret at home in Bristol, were getting frantic about our apparent disappearance somewhere in Iraq. Contact was restored with home and London. After such a meal as my battered innards could take I thankfully collapsed onto clean sheets, and was home next day. There was a full report to share with CCBI, and I went to Geneva to report to the WCC.

There still hangs on our study wall an alabaster bas-relief of Mary and child Jesus. After the service at the Syrian Orthodox Cathedral in Mosul I went into their gift shop and spotted it as an appropriate souvenir. Asking how much it cost I was told quite firmly, "No cost. This is gift for you." I tried to insist that I should pay, that after all their church was badly in need of money. But no, it had to be a gift. This was of course the East, the land of Abraham and Sarah where hospitality to strangers was at the heart of life. For over twenty years now it has been a precious reminder of faith and generosity under privation. Today, bearing in mind what has since happened to Mosul and its population, Christians included, under so-called Islamic State it is nothing short of priceless to me. Its image of simplicity and vulnerability is a reminder of what incarnation, of love seeing and experiencing the world from within, is all about.

10

Balkan Turmoil

ON A MORNING AT the beginning of February 1993 I stood in the town square of Karlovac, about thirty miles south-west of Zagreb, Croatia. Buses were rolling into the square and disgorging scores of weary and ragged passengers, mostly men. They were refugees arriving from detention camps in Bosnia. Soon they were mingling with the huddled groups waiting silently around the square. People were moving from group to group, anxious for any news of relatives who might have arrived already, or of whom there was as yet no news, or perhaps never would be. It was a somber ballet of the physical and emotional wreckage wrought by war.

OPENING ENGAGEMENTS

As late as the spring of 1991 I was as unprepared as anyone for what was happening in the Balkans. Yugoslavia and its constituent parts, like the Balkans as a whole, were largely unknown to me. I had met some Serbian Orthodox theologians in the Faith and Order Commission, and some Yugoslav Baptists at meetings of European Baptist theological teachers. Some friends spoke of the pleasures of holidaying on the Dalmatian coast. Moreover, while most of us hailed the 1989–90 changes in Eastern Europe as embraces of the unquestioned values of independence and self-determination these were mostly seizures, by recognized states, of freedom from the hegemony of an external power, in this case the Soviet Union. We were not ready for the impulses towards self-determination of ethnically-defined communities which wished to *become* recognized states. Therefore it was with some bemusement, then puzzlement and finally alarm that we watched events unfold in the first half of 1991. The first violent incidents and exchanges between Croatian and Serbian forces were followed in May by declarations of independence from Yugoslavia by Slovenia and Croatia despite calls for delay by the European Union—which nevertheless (and controversially in some eyes in the West) was supportive of their independence. Escalation was apparent in clashes between the Serb-dominated Yugoslav army and Croatian forces, and suddenly the whole Yugoslav scene—soon to be called "Former Yugoslavia"—was manifestly explosive with ominous implications for the Balkans as a whole.

Early in September I set about writing a briefing paper on Yugoslavia for the CCBI churches, which put on me on a steep learning curve as I struggled to study, set down and outline the historical and political background, the composition of the country as established under Tito, the complex mix of ethnicity and religion in a country which was, as one commentator put it, "the despair of tidy minds", the latent factors in the current tensions, and pointing to the future likely flash-points. These latter were Bosnia-Hercegovina and the hitherto "autonomous provinces" of Vojvodina and, especially, Kosovo. It warned that historical experience showed civil wars to be typically the most brutal. I drew upon a number of sources including the UN and Human Rights Watch, and was particularly helped by Stella Alexander, a noted historian on Yugoslavia, and Chris Cviic of Chatham House, himself Croatian by birth. Some members of my support group complained about my devoting time and effort to this. Was a squabble in a corner of Europe really worth attention? But the paper was widely welcomed in the church constituency and also found effective use by WCC staff. Not quite so welcome was the impression created that I was now the expert on Yugoslavia, but soon this work needed little further justification as the Serbian-Croatian military conflict escalated and included the three-month Serbian siege and bombardment of Dubrovnik. The very fact that the divides in Yugoslavia were largely along religious lines, especially between Catholic Croatia and Orthodox Serbia, together with the substantial Muslim presence in Bosnia, presented an inescapable challenge for ecumenical work. The Conference of European Churches (CEC) and WCC, working together with the Roman Catholic Council of Episcopal Conferences in Europe (CCEE) obviously had prime responsibility here. It was quickly apparent that despite the very long-standing close proximity of the main churches and faith-groups in Yugoslavia there had been practically no ecumenical or inter-faith co-operation developed there even after the end of the Tito regime. That was a grim realization, and once the fighting began it was logistically and diplomatically impossible for any ecumenical meetings to take place except outside Yugoslavia, on neutral territory. The development of any ecumenical and inter-faith dialogue between the parties depended on the ecumenical world outside. Thus, a round table of high-level representatives of the Serbian Orthodox Church and the Conference of Roman Catholic Bishops in Former Yugoslavia met under CEC and CCEE auspices in St Gallen, Switzerland (the headquarters of CCEE) in late January 1992, and in September that year Patriarch Pavle of Serbia and Cardinal Kuharic, archbishop of Zagreb, actually met in Chateau Bossey, Geneva. The round table approach was to be developed by CEC with larger meetings, in particular at Pecs, Hungary in December 1993, including Muslim and Jewish representatives.

Geneva was the hub of the ecumenical enterprise in relation to the conflict, and that enterprise included the efforts of churches and national ecumenical bodies as far afield as Germany, France, the Netherlands, Scandinavia, the USA—and ourselves in Britain and Ireland. I visited Geneva several times each year and met with Jean Fischer, general secretary of CEC, and WCC staff for informal consultation, or attended more formal meetings of the Coordinating Group on Former Yugoslavia. These often included staff from the major aid agencies as the humanitarian crisis grew, and on one visit in 1993 I spent a whole morning at the UN High Commission for Refugees (UNHCR). Back home, in CCBI we set up a Balkans Working Group which met regularly, drawing upon the expertise of people involved in peace work, the UN, the aid agencies Christian Aid and CAFOD, as well as from our member churches.

In January 1992 Croatia and "Yugoslavia" i.e. the Serbian-dominated remainder of the Yugoslav Republic, signed an armistice (though military exchanges, as well as serious tensions, were to continue), and attention was now turning to Bosnia-Hercegovina which declared its independence in March, and the long siege of Sarajevo by the Serbs began. Meanwhile in CCBI, in conjunction with the Churches East-West European relations network we were busy preparing a two-day consultation on Yugoslavia and the role of the churches there, which took place at Bloomsbury Central Baptist Church May 5–6, chaired by David Bleakley, Northern Ireland politician with a fine record on promoting reconciliation and a leading lay Anglican. Its aim was to generate more information for the British churches on the Balkan conflicts, and their religious dimensions; to offer a sign of solidarity for the suffering peoples there and to encourage their pursuit of peace; and to consider what particulars contributions our churches might make in in partnership with other churches in Europe in the search for a just peace. Serbian and Croatian representatives came together with a number of experienced diplomats, political scientists and church figures. But the Serbian Orthodox representatives did not seem in any mood for serious reflection, and were frankly dismissive of the presentation by Carmel Heaney, CCBI Youth Secretary and herself Irish, on the dangers of sectarianism. Nor could they answer the question of the sole Bosnian representative: "Just how are Serbs being threatened in Bosnia?" It exemplified the difficulty that people had of seeing a conflict from any perspective than that of their own inherited assumptions and interests. Perhaps the greatest value of the meeting was the resourcing it gave to David Bleakley himself, who was about to go on a visit with Huibert van Beek of the WCC to Serbia and Croatia on behalf of CEC and WCC. It was maybe significant that very soon after this meeting the Holy Synod of the Serbian Orthodox Church, meeting May 14–27 issued a long statement distancing itself from the Milosevic government's war policy and condemning every act of violence committed by whomever—though at the same time protesting the unique level of suffering, past and present, being experienced by the Serb people. Shortly after this Synod, two bishops, Stefan of Xica and Dositej of Scandinavia and Britain, came to London accompanied by Graham Doyle, the Anglican Apokrisarios and chaplain in Belgrade. I went with them to meet officials in the Foreign Office, and they also came to Inter-Church House to meet a number of church leaders and CCBI staff. The overall message was becoming familiar: please beware of one-sided accounts of the conflict. From our side, it was evident that we needed much more understanding and clarity on what the attitude of the Serbian Church actually was in the present crisis.

A NEW STAGE: BOSNIA

During the summer of 1992 the violence in Bosnia escalated in a quantum leap of horror: not just the siege of Sarajevo, brutal enough as it was, but the practice of ethnic cleansing of whole communities by Serb forces involving destruction of homes, mass rape and murder. There was no shortage of comment in Britain. The archbishop of Canterbury and Cardinal Hume each issued statements on the unacceptability of what was happening and pleading for protection of delivery of humanitarian aid; likewise the bishop of London, the Moderator of the Free Church Council and the bishop of Coventry (chairman of the International Development Affairs Committee of the Church of England General Synod) made clear their concern as did the General Assembly of the Church of Scotland. In great haste one Friday the CCBI Presidents addressed a strong plea to Prime Minister John Major for a much more generous reception refugees (I had the task of personally delivering it to 10, Downing Street in the evening and it received media coverage next morning). At the international level a most significant statement was the oral intervention made by WCC general secretary Emilio Castro to the special session on Yugoslavia of the UN Commission on Human Rights, in August. It was a stark and specific detailing of the horrors of ethnic cleansings and incarcerations in camps of civilians in Bosnia (most but not all being committed by Serbs), but also included a confession that no less than the UN and the world community as a whole the churches "have thus far been unable to address the issue with any effectiveness", and called for a genuine, renewed commitment to the protection of human rights. In August I wrote an article "Lights in Bosnia's dark" for the *Tablet*, stating:

> The last few weeks have suddenly frightened people into realizing that what is taking place in the former Yugoslavia, especially in Bosnia, is indeed right on the doorstep of their own responsibility. It is now dawning on people that this conflict might be unravelling towards fearful consequences—not least for Christian-Islamic relations across the world. Whatever action is finally decided upon it will be important to keep in mind the larger context within which the Churches have been involved.[1]

I therefore gave an account of the ecumenical work both in Britain and at the international level and the efforts to create and sustain dialogue between the religious communities in Former Yugoslavia. In November I produced a second briefing paper, "The Churches and the Former Yugoslavia", detailing recent ecumenical and church leadership initiatives and statements on the conflict, international relief and refugee

---

1. *Tablet* August 22 1992.

work, British and Irish church initiatives, reflections, likely future issues, and sources of further information.

SERBIA AND CROATIA: THE CCBI VISIT 1993

Meanwhile feeling was growing that a corporate CCBI initiative should be taken in the form of an actual delegation to the Former Yugoslavia, in the context of the overall international ecumenical engagement with the scene. During a two-day visit to Geneva in December I conferred at length with Jean Fischer, general secretary of CEC, and other ecumenical staff. Convening another round table was proving difficult, I was told, as it seemed that Cardinal Kuharic of Croatia was either unable or unwilling to attend a meeting either in Novi Sad (Serbia) or somewhere in Croatia. As for a delegation, it was proving ever more difficult to get into Bosnia itself, certainly to Sarajevo which was now extremely dangerous. The President of the French Protestant Federation Jacques Stewart was seeking approval from the French defense ministry to go to Sarajevo on an exploratory visit with a French foreign office minister but he would need clearance to go on a UNHCR flight and this was far from certain. In any case, said Fischer, he himself was rather skeptical of visits which could at best be described as ecclesiastical tourism to crisis areas. Within Serbia itself however it might be a different story. How about trying to see and assess the situation in Kosovo, the historic birthplace, it was claimed, of Serbian identity and national pride, and now highly sensitive because of its large Albanian-speaking Muslim population?

A CCBI visit to Serbia and Croatia was therefore planned at short notice. No more than a week would be available, January 26—February 2. And it would have to counter the logistical difficulties posed by the almost complete isolation between the two conjoined countries. The group comprised John Biggs, (Moderator of the Free Church Federal Council), Patricia Cockrell (a Quaker with much previous experience of Eastern Europe including the Balkans); Andrew McLellan (Convener of the Church of Scotland Church and Nation Committee), John Neil (bishop of Tuam in the Church of Ireland and a President of CCBI), Kevin O'Connor (Auxiliary Bishop in the Roman Catholic Archdiocese of Liverpool), John Oliver (bishop of Hereford) with Richard Marsh (Adviser to the Archbishop of Canterbury on Ecumenical Affairs) and myself as staff. John Biggs and John Neill acted as co-leaders. We assembled at Lambeth Palace for a four-hour briefing on January 25 which included input both from the Foreign Office Adriatic desk and Dr Shabbir Akhtal, a Muslim scholar and writer highly critical of the western policy on Bosnia. Next day we flew to Budapest where we were met by the Anglican chaplain in Belgrade Graham Doyle and the British Embassy bus for the drive to Belgrade where we were housed in the British residence. We were now in a very different world from anything we had known before as next day, January 27, was St Sava's day, the great date in the Serbian calendar of national commemoration. Sava, first archbishop of the Serbs in the thirteenth century, was the leader who achieved the independent jurisdiction of the Serbian Church and was greatly instrumental in integrating the Serbian kingdom. He is therefore the historical embodiment of the traditional religious and national sentiments of Serbia, and their fusion in one patriotic emotion. In the morning St Sava's Church was already packed to the doors when we arrived to attend the Mount Sinai Liturgy, celebrated by Patriarch Pavle. Our specially assigned place close to the altar enabled us to appreciate the splendor of Byzantine celebration to the full, in its rich blend of superb choir, clouds of incense, dazzling vestments and above all the obviously deep emotion of so many people present, from the young mother quietly weeping as she held her child up to see what was going on, to the older women who came forward to kneel and clutch the priestly vestments as the gospel was read. TV cameras were much in evidence, and they had clearly been briefed to zoom in on us from time to time. This was followed by a visit to the Orthodox theological faculty and then a meeting with Archbishop Perko, head of the Roman Catholic Church in Serbia, followed by a session with the British Military Attaché Colonel Moody and other embassy staff for discussion on Bosnian atrocities. Two of us visited the weekly anti-war demonstration of the Women in Black—shades of South Africa and Jerusalem again—and were invited to a meeting of the Women against Rape group. A minority maybe, but there was significant non-nationalist, anti-war movement in the city. In the evening it was back to St Sava's Day as we attended the official celebration in the huge St Sava Centre, essentially a concert of patriotic poetry and music. Next day, the major part of the morning was spent at the Patriarchate where Patriarch Pavle received us for conversation lasting over an hour. Pavle, a frail, diminutive figure, every bit the ascetic and devout monk, was gracious and to all intents sincere in deploring the war but perhaps inevitably his answers to our questions were couched in generalities of regret: a genuine but other-worldly soul. In marked contrast Archdeacon Father Radomir Rakic who sat in on the discussion and helped with translation, was thoroughly outgoing and jovial in manner but left us in no doubt that he thought our and other westerners' concerns were misplaced and irrelevant to the situation there. We saw other religious leaders. Alexander Birvis, a Baptist pastor, told us of his extensive refugee relief work. At the Mosque the Imam Revzo cj. Nukce on behalf of the Mufti who was visiting Cairo, received us. Rabbi Cadik Danon and other Jewish representatives received us similarly.

There was one major set-back. We had hoped that two or three of us could go into Kosovo but Graham Doyle was adamant that for some unexplained reason this would just not be possible. We were left to judge whether the reason was mainly logistical, or political, but either way it was a disappointment. As we were preparing for our drive back to Budapest on January 29, which would take us through the former autonomous province of Vojvodina, we were also strongly discouraged—indeed almost prevented—from making any contact with the Hungarian-speaking Reformed Church there. I had however the telephone number of Bishop Imre Hodosy of that church, and while John Neill kept reluctant officialdom talking in the dining room of the residence I surreptitiously made a call from a desk in the hall and, in German, managed to get through to the bishop's secretary and arranged for us to stop for lunch with him in the village of Feketic, just off our route to the Hungarian border. That worked. Heavy snow made it a somewhat arduous drive and we were glad of the warmth both of Bishop Hodosy's welcome, and the meal. We heard, ominously, of a low-level but increasing process of intimidation against the Hungarian and non-Orthodox population of Vojvodina. Back in Budapest we were put up overnight in the guest house of the Hungarian Ecumenical Council.

Next morning we made a dawn start by train to Zagreb, along the frozen shores of Lake Balaton, and then over the border into Croatia where bright winter sunshine bathed a gentler landscape of hills and quiet villages. As we drew near to Zagreb the railway sidings were piled high with huge containers of UN relief supplies. At the station we were met by Boris Peterlin, a Baptist layman who ran the Christian Information Service (CIS) and Carolyn Boyd, a young Scottish artist who had made her home in Zagreb and also worked for CIS. In the Hotel Dubrovnik where we were to stay they briefed us on our programme. In the evening we had a formal meeting with Cardinal Kuharic and the president of the Episcopal Committee for Ecumenical Affairs, followed by an hour at Hotel "I" with the British delegation of the European Community Monitoring Mission. Then to conclude the evening we were back at the Cardinal Archbishop's House for supper with him and other clergy. Next day was a Sunday and for morning worship we divided ourselves between the Roman Catholic Cathedral, the Lutheran Church and the Baptist Church. I preached at the Baptist Church, through an interpreter, to a congregation not only of Croatians but Serbs and refugees from Bosnia. So cosmopolitan had that community become that the pastor had recently been asked by a nationalist Zagreb politician, "Are you still a Croatian church?" to which of course the answer was, "We are still a church of Jesus Christ". In fact, in both Serbia and Croatia it was in the minority congregations that we found the most hopeful signs of non-nationalist Christianity with outgoing concern to the whole community. In the afternoon we all gathered at the Muslim Centre and met with its director Dr Serko Omberbasic for discussion of refugee issues. Then came one of the most telling and poignant experiences of the whole week: Camp Resnik, on the outskirts of Zagreb, which had been set up the previous summer largely on the initiative of Bosnian refugees themselves and now housing about five thousand people, mostly women and children. We visited and spent time with several families in their crowded wooden huts, and met with the camp president. We spent a good deal of time in the small clinic, housed in a caravan, where some of the group interviewed the doctor who was carrying out therapy for rape victims, and collected information on what was needed in the way of surgical equipment.

Next morning, out on the streets of Zagreb John Neill in his episcopal purple cassock was accosted by several men in army camouflage dress who knelt at his feet, heads bowed, to receive a blessing. He was so attired because he, John Biggs and I were on our way to a televised press conference. This was followed by a visit to the headquarters of the UNHCR in Zagreb, and a briefing with Manuel de Almeida y Silva, external relations officer to the Special Envoy of UNHCR José Maria Mendelici whom we also met briefly. So by road to Karlovac to where, as I have described, Bosnian refugees were arriving. Karlovac in fact lay close to the frontline with the Serbs of the Krajina. A few days previously there had been renewed shelling of the town center. Two churches stood on opposite sides of the square, one Catholic, the other Orthodox. The Orthodox Church had been gutted by fire (some had attributed its destruction to the Serb artillery mistaking it for the Catholic church}. We visited and toured the UNHCR center, under the charge, interestingly, of a young theology graduate from Rome, Alessandra Morelli. It was handling over one thousand people at a time. She warned against the danger of underestimating the damage to morale of the refugees who, once out of Bosnia, might manifest an appearance of relief and cheerfulness. "These are battered people, in every way", she said. It was difficult to envisage how such people could ever return or feel able to live with the very people who had evicted them. A further experience was in store for us. We drove the short distance to the village of Turanj, right on the frontline with the Serb forces of the "pink zone" and were shown round by a Croatian soldier. The village was completely empty. House after house had been destroyed by Serb militia early in the war and still lay blackened and empty. The Serb positions now were just a few fields from us, fortunately not active that day but from further away there sounded the thuds of artillery fire. We returned to Zagreb for final de-briefing with Boris Peterlin and Carolyn Boyd, then began the long rail journey back to a now frozen Budapest, largely occupied with preparing a communiqué to be faxed to London in advance of our arrival back there next day.

At Heathrow we held a brief press conference. The reaction of one church press officer, affecting lack of interest, was, "But you haven't condemned anyone" as if much of what we had described wasn't condemnation in itself. I flew on to Geneva and reported to WCC and CEC next morning. Several of us over the next week or two gave radio interviews. Patricia Cockrell and I were interviewed by Jenni Murray on the BBC *Women's Hour*. Then it was a matter of collating the various written contributions from members of the delegation and editing them into our report *Churches, Nationalism and Conflict*. As well as detailing our itinerary and programme it covered the massive refugee crisis, media communication in Serbia and Croatia, sanctions against Serbia, religion and nationalism, comments on the Catholic and Orthodox Churches, minority churches, and peace and women's groups, and concluded with overall conclusions and recommendations.

A BIG BUT WEAK CHURCH: IMPRESSIONS AND REFLECTIONS

It was admittedly a very short visit, with diverse encounters and impressions compressed into a tight programme. But if one's antennae are on full alert such a brief exposure is not necessarily superficial. Some perceptions were very specific and capable of exact description, others were more subtle, barely conscious but no less significant for all that: for example the almost instantly different feel to being in Serbia and to being in Croatia. In Serbia we were certainly made welcome but with a subtle defensiveness which seemed to say, "Being strangers and from the West, you will not really understand our situation", compounded with the economic effect that international sanctions were having at every level of life there. In Croatia with equal subtlety, but no less evident, was the sense conveyed, "You and we belong together as Westerners—what did you make of the Serbs?" This was not accidental, for we had been travelling back-and-to across the ancient fault-line of Europe between Latin West and Byzantine East dating effectively from the death of the Emperor Theodosius I in CE 395, a line which not only divides Serbia from Croatia but runs through Bosnia-Hercegovina

I went to Belgrade expecting to see the full panoply of the Orthodox Church on display as the bearer of the nation's identity and destiny. So indeed it appeared, in that magnificent St Sava's Day liturgy. But in the evening at the national celebration in the St Sava Centre it was a very different picture as Patriarch Pavle appeared alongside other national figures. This frail, diminutive figure was dwarfed by the sharp-suited ministers of state and the barrel-chested military top brass. This symbolized the reality that was already dawning on us: the church, for all its outward display and claims to national significance was in fact a very minor player with hardly any practical leverage on the political scene or, even more unfortunately, any real weight on public opinion. It was little more than a useful emblem of national identity when it suited the politicians so to use it. This was a paradox which one had to come to terms with if, as ecumenical visitors, we were to have realistic expectations of that church. The long years of communist subjection during which, for example, there had been no religious teaching allowed in schools and there had been exclusion of any church interaction with government, had left it lacking any experience of teaching socially relevant ethics or attempting to mobilize public opinion. The church leadership had called for people to reject any "materialist" party programme in the general election of 1992 but what guidance in more specific goals did this indicate? The Holy Synod in May 1992 had condemned all violence in Bosnia, including by Serbs. But how to influence public opinion at large seemed an impossible task—made extremely difficult, it has to be said, by the almost total control of broadcasting media by the government. Some of us had a discussion with a senior cleric about the church's attitudes to those in society who were opposed to the war, such as Women in Black and the Anti-War Campaign in Belgrade. The church, it might be felt, should surely be relating to such movements in civil society and, as far as was possible, be building alliances with them. Interestingly, the priest was not so much critical of their aims as their methods, for example their use of candles in public vigils. Candles, he said, were for use in worship in church, or in intimate dinner-parties, not in such public events. There was here an assumed chasm between the sacred and secular. That sacred symbols might become vehicles of powerful public prophecy was apparently beyond comprehension, and how to link the church's life and mission with what was already stirring outside was just not perceived. The church may have been distancing itself from aspects of the Milosevic government policies but it was hardly *confronting* them, and at the same time it was distancing itself from the public sphere altogether. That was the real problem. Critical comparisons were made in some quarters with the church scene in Nazi Germany, or the anti-apartheid struggle in South Africa, with demands that the Serbian Church take on a "confessing stance" or else be suspended from membership of the WCC and CEC for acquiescing in the brutalities taking place in Bosnia. I myself was to write to Jean Fischer in 1994 arguing that the scale of atrocities in Bosnia constituted a *status confessionis* not just for the Serbian Church but for all churches in the ecumenical movement. But to have expelled that church from the ecumenical scene would have been like condemning an athlete with a broken leg for not running a fifteen-hundred-meter race, and would merely leave ourselves with a glow of moral righteousness. Our report stated:

> The symbolic identification of the church with the ideals of the Serbian nation may have the effect of smothering the undoubted protest that many in the church wish to articulate. It would seem that the Serbian Orthodox Church needs the contact and critical dialogue that the ecumenical movement can provide if it is not to lose the independence that is demanded for a prophetic witness. At the very highest levels in the Serbian Orthodox Church, there are voices of condemnation for Serbian policies, as indeed for those of other states as well but these words of protest need to be linked to a very deep evaluation of the witness that the church can have in the nation.

There was, I came to realize, no one-fit-all template for ecumenical engagement with situations of crisis and conflict and this was one of the most significant things I learnt from this visit.

In Croatia the sense and sensibility were rather different from Belgrade. In Zagreb we had the impression of a Roman Catholic Church that had emerged from years of communist domination to a scene not so much one where the church could be used by the state, but where the church was itself a very powerful force within the state (an impression borne out by some of the Protestant minority voices that spoke of enjoying *less* freedom now than under a communist government). Yet, despite this much more confident position there was little critical, prophetic engagement: no questioning of Croatia's role in the conflict, a total identification with national aspirations and no sense of guilt at what was perceived in Serbia as a reversion to World War II attitudes to the extent of using the fascist *Ustashe* emblem on its flag. Again, as in Serbia, there had been a vigorous propaganda campaign by the state media. Both the Croatian Catholic and Serbian Orthodox Churches were in urgent need of interpretation to one another.

Of course we discussed among ourselves the question of further intervention by the international community to bring pressure to bear upon Serbia, to maintain the integrity of Bosnia and to especially to protect the Muslim community. We came to no consensus on a definite position, and not only because our group included a whole range of views from pacifist to Just War adherents. One thing we were agreed upon was that however hard the sanctions were hitting Serbia (and we heard many tales to that effect), to lift them now would send entirely the wrong signal to the Milosevic regime. As far as military intervention was concerned, most felt that in terms of Just War doctrine "it is a genuinely weighty consideration that the effects of concerted military action in one part of the region may stimulate outbreaks of conflict elsewhere in the region, far worse than we have hitherto seen". And we were further agreed that the work of UNHCR, engaged in the biggest relief operation anywhere since World War II, needed far more appreciation than it was receiving hitherto and also needed to maintain its strict neutrality.

Through 1994–96 the ecumenical engagement with Former Yugoslavia, including Bosnia, continued. In 1994 Paul Johns, on the staff of the Methodist Church Division of Social responsibility and a member of the CCBI Balkans Working Group, was able to get into Bosnia and report on humanitarian needs and priorities for the churches. Richard Marsh went to Sarajevo to prepare the way for a visit by the archbishop of Canterbury George Carey. It continued to be a messy situation through which none could pass with a clear conscience, certainly not after the Srebrenica massacre of July 1995. But wars so often end through exhaustion and in November 1995 the Dayton Peace Agreement, brokered largely by the USA, was reached, and signed the following month. Meanwhile on November 10, virtually simultaneously with the final Dayton negotiations, CCBI in conjunction with the Council of Christian Approaches to Defense and Disarmament, (CCADD) held an intensive one-day ecumenical hearing, "Former Yugoslavia: Prospects for a Peace Settlement and Reconstruction" at Vaughan House, Westminster. Over seventy people attended, mainly from the churches with speakers representing a wide variety of perspectives of involvement: British, US and Russian diplomats; the UN, UNHCR and other humanitarian agencies; the WCC, Christian Aid and CAFOD. Specific recommendations were made for follow-up on many aspects of humanitarian aid, refugees and asylum seekers in the UK, confidence-building and the role of the UN, and much else, together with recognition of the urgent questions still to be dealt with, on intervention and policing in situations of violence.[2] Then in February 1996 CEC held an international consultation on reconciliation, in Belgrade, which I attended. Patriarch Pavle was the official host. There were frustrating discussions on questions like acceptance of corporate guilt—frustrating because in that situation so much was at the mercy of participants' personal experience. Discussion of Serbia's record for example was stymied by the Orthodox priest for whom the argument was settled by, "My uncle was killed by Croats in 1944". But at least we were sticking with the issues.

2. CCADD in particular followed up with studies on "humanitarian intervention", prompted both by the Former Yugoslavia case and the Gulf War of 1991.

SERIOUS CRITICISM

For all who had been seriously engaged since the start of the conflicts in 1991 it was a tiring and at times bruising slog. It became more so with the ferocious criticism launched at our efforts from one British quarter in particular. Adrian Hastings, professor of theology at Leeds University (he retired in 1994) was an outstanding church historian who described himself as a Protestant Catholic—he had been a Catholic priest but with typical and robust independence of mind married in 1979. In earlier life he had been a member of the White Fathers missionary order in Africa, and in 1973 became internationally famous for exposing Portuguese army atrocities in Mozambique. A burning passion for justice marked him no less thereafter, and above all in the early 1990s on behalf of the Bosnian Muslims and indeed for Bosnia in its entirety as a multi-ethnic state. He launched an impassioned and well publicized personal campaign for international military intervention or at the very least the exemption of Bosnian Muslims from the arms embargo on Former Yugoslavia. Anything less would mean complicity in genocide. Concomitant with these views was his fury at what he saw as the pusillanimous silence of the churches on Bosnia and inaction of the ecumenical bodies.[3] In September 1994 several of us in CCBI and the Balkans Working Group had a meeting with him and the bishop of Barking, Roger Sainsbury, who was one of his chief supporters but much more conciliatory in attitude. It was evident that Adrian Hastings was not as fully informed as he believed about the ecumenical initiatives. After this meeting we were largely left alone apart, as I recall, from some sniping in the odd radio interview. Nor did we allow the Dayton Peace Accord to provide an excuse for dropping Bosnia from our agenda. In CCBI we were involved in recruiting and briefing volunteers to go and monitor the Bosnian general election in September 1996.

For me personally Adrian Hastings' criticisms—often virulent—were particularly painful because for several years we had been high in each other's esteem. He had reviewed my *Lovers of Discord* with high praise, was very generous with my work on Bonhoeffer, and I had been no less grateful for his writings especially *A History of English Christianity* 1920–1985. At any rate our differences during 1993–95 did not outlive our mutual regard. Shortly before he died in 2001 he was fulsome in his review of my biography of J.H. Oldham and equally I gave a very positive commendation of his *The Construction of Nationhood* (1997) in *Theology*. As his *Times* obituary said, "He was generous in giving praise, if scathing in rebuke, and never held a grudge."[4] I must be one of the few people who personally experienced all three characteristics in equally large measure. The central issues with which we were both concerned was the relation between reconciliation and justice, which had been central in South Africa too. Can these be totally set at odds with each other, or in terms of actual

---

3. Cf. K. Clements and A. Chandler. "A Live Bishop Bell in 1994?"
4. *Times* May 31 2001.

implementation can one be neatly prioritized over the other?[5] Shortcomings of course there were and I still have an uneasy conscience whenever I think of Bosnia. In mitigation I would say that whatever the faults, they at least came from engagement, not detachment. As Bonhoeffer observes in his *Ethics*, there is no attempt at responsible action which does not incur guilt in some form. *Kyrie eleison*.

THE WIDER BALKAN SCENE

From late 1994 I found myself involved on the wider Balkan scene. In December that year I went to represent the WCC at the fifth anniversary of the Romanian uprising against the Ceausescu communist regime. This had been triggered in December 1989 by the revolt in Timisoara led by the bishop of the Hungarian-speaking Reformed Church there, Lazlo Tökes. I flew to Bucharest and took the night train to Timisoara accompanied by Matti Sidoroff, a priest and academic of the Orthodox Church of Finland who was working for Aidrom, an ecumenical humanitarian agency set up with the assistance of the WCC after the events of 1989–90 and serving the newly-formed Ecumenical Association of Churches in Romania. In Timisoara we sat in on the final sessions of an ecumenical conference which was part of the anniversary events. After the previous day's lengthy travel and the far from comfortable overnight train I struggled to stay awake but was jolted into uprightness by the forthright and welcome remarks of the Orthodox metropolitan bishop of Timisoara Nicolae Corneanu, to the effect that the concept of a national church was contrary to Orthodoxy: "The church is a universal community but found in different situations", and as such the church had a vital role to play in the unification of Europe, he declared. That evening the actual commemoration of the 1989 uprising took the form of a four-hour service in Bishop Tökes' church, enlivened by spirited choral singing (it could almost have been in the Welsh valleys) and several addresses. In mine, on behalf of the WCC I told the congregation: "Five years ago you did not simply call for freedom. In speaking out courageously you *became* free already." Back in Bucharest Matti Sidoroff introduced me to a number of church figures and I learnt a lot more about the revolution and the present political and church scene. On a dull, snowy day Matti also took me by car to the eastern, Germanic part of Transylvania. I was much impressed by Aidrom's emphasis on ecological issues and education for environmental responsibility, the need for which was underlined by the numerous oil-wells in inhabited areas and even, in some villages, placed in people's gardens. That evening I learnt something more in this regard, when Matti Sidoroff and

---

5. In fact Hastings recognised a problem in being consistent here. In 1989 he had been critical of the South African *Kairos Document* for its call to put justice before reconciliation, and he stated that justice "is not an alternative to liberation, but rather each is internally part of the other". By 1998 however he was stating in relation to Bosnia: "Without a serious beginning to justice, an appeal for reconciliation is neither Christianity nor humanism. It is merely opium." (Adrian Hastings, "Reconciliation in Bosnia", in Butler, *Open Hands,* 340. In actual practice as distinct from theory, pursuit of the goals of justice and reconciliation cannot always be neatly disentangled. How can we ever be sure that, in Hastings' own words, there may not be a serious *beginning* to justice?

I were guests at the dinner table of the abbot of one of the Orthodox monasteries just outside Bucharest. One of the huge unfortunate legacies of the communist era was the state of agriculture in Romania as forty-five years of collectivization had ended traditional methods of farming and the knowledge that went with them. After the 1989 revolution land was redistributed to local farmers who were provided with tons of fertilizer—but had little idea of how to use it effectively. Collectivization however had not been total. The monasteries with their own lands had been largely left alone, and had preserved the traditional ways of organic farming, fishponds and so forth. They now came into their own as teachers of responsible land use, an instructive example of the economic and social use of acquired wisdom. It recalled the gospel saying: "Therefore every scribe who has been trained for the kingdom of heaven is like the master of a household who brings out of his treasure what is new and what is old." (Matthew 13:56)

In the spring of 1995 Huibert van Beek at the WCC asked Matti Sidoroff and me to team up again and visit several Balkan countries to explore, in view of what was happening in Former Yugoslavia, the possibilities of a regional conference or series of conferences of churches on their role in peacebuilding. Accordingly in late April and May we went to Macedonia, Bulgaria and Romania, and in September visited Greece. We met with leaders of nearly all the churches in these countries, Orthodox, Catholic and Protestant and also in several cases with Jewish and Muslim representatives. We reported that there was no outright rejection of the proposal but actual enthusiasm varied widely. It was indeed a complex scene both between and within churches. Churches in some cases had hardly begun to discover each other. Macedonia in particular was a sensitive piece of the whole, both as regards Albanian-Christian relations and intra-Orthodox disputes between the Orthodox Church of that country and the Serbian Orthodox Church. But it notably extended my knowledge of the churches and the interconfessional issues of the region. Most fascinating of all I found the situation in Cluj-Napotica in northern Transylvania where I flew from Bucharest to find a unique mix of Reformed, Lutheran, Orthodox, Baptist, Pentecostal and Unitarians (and where I discovered that it was the custom to drink cognac as an aperitif rather than as a digestif, even on a very empty stomach). CCBI, too, became engaged in the wider region by sending a delegation to Albania in April 1995, which brought back some very concrete recommendations on resource-sharing in theological education. More than I could have realized at the time, my Balkans exposure was to prove a vital preparation for the next stage of my career.

11

Listening to Africa

DURING THE 1990S IT was commonplace to speak of Africa in hyperboles of disaster: famine, debt, corruption, civil war, genocide. As a whole continent apparently unravelling at every level it could be dropped, so some international finance experts were saying, to sink without trace from the world economic scene. But what of the churches' involvement in Africa? In February 1992 CCBI, prompted mainly by its affiliated aid and development agencies Christian Aid, CAFORD and SCIAF, devoted a main session of its biennial assembly at Swanwick to Africa. Two guests from Africa were the main speakers: Bishop Samuel Tilewa Johnson of the Anglican Church of Gambia and Josphat Mulyungi, a Roman Catholic development worker from Kenya. Both made a moving appeal for the churches of Britain and Ireland to enter with them into a new kind of partnership. In fact rarely can the voice of Africa have been heard so powerfully, yet so winningly, in Britain. Their appeal made a big impact. The Assembly resolved to make Africa a major priority of ecumenical concern and action, to be focused in two main thrusts: a rigorous commitment to Africa's struggle for economic justice, and a new and deeper relationship of genuine partnership with the churches and peoples of Africa, at every possible level.

SOLIDARITY IN CRISIS: MALAWI 1992

Sooner than expected this commitment was presented with a challenge from one country in particular. On March 8 1992 a critical situation in Malawi arose—or rather, an already critical situation became explosive when the Roman Catholic bishops of that country issued a pastoral letter protesting against the increasingly autocratic rule of President Hastings Banda. This prompted a yet further crackdown by the government which pronounced the document seditious. The bishops were for a time put under house arrest and there were threats against their lives. Soon the other Christian leaders, notably the Anglicans and Presbyterians, together with Muslim leaders and a variety of lawyers and opposition groups, formed an insistent platform calling for an end to abuses of power and repression of free speech. Malawi had become a police state, seeming to buck the trend towards democracy over much of Africa elsewhere, and the churches there suddenly looked very vulnerable. CCBI resolved to send a delegation of three prominent church figures from Britain as a gesture of solidarity and to report on the situation at first-hand. Robert Davidson (a former Moderator of the General Assembly of the Church of Scotland), James O'Brien (Roman Catholic bishop in Hertfordshire) and Mark Santer (Anglican bishop of Birmingham), accompanied by Jim Wilkie of the Church of Scotland, agreed to go. But how to arrange their reception in Malawi by the churches there which were under such strict surveillance by the regime, when even preliminary contact with them might bring trouble and jeopardize the whole mission? What in fact happened became for me a parable of what true ecumenism means, and in a way amusingly so. In May I was in Helsinki attending the annual briefing meetings on human rights of the Conference on Security and Cooperation in Europe (CSCE)[1]. While there I called in on Jaakko Rusama, secretary for ecumenical affairs in the (Lutheran) Church of Finland. We shared a common debt to Cambridge—he had got his PhD there for a thesis on George Bell supervised by my friend David Thompson. In the course of conversation about what was on our respective agendas just then, I mentioned the problems we were having in setting up our delegation to Malawi and the sensitivities about contacting the leaders of the churches there in advance. He looked thoughtful for a moment or two and then said, "I've a Finnish friend who's a missionary in Malawi. Nobody apart from him in the country probably understands Finnish . . . " (Finnish, of course, along with Hungarian, is about the most impenetrable language even to most Europeans). He told me to write down what we wanted to say to the Malawian churches. I did so, including the names of the delegation members, and within minutes it was translated into Finnish and being faxed to Jaakko's friend. Next day Jaakko handed me an English translation of the reply. All was well, the contacts had been made and the welcome to the delegation would be warm. Jaakko's friend had taken some extra precautions in his reply. He had spelt the names of the delegates backwards so as to disguise them (thus for example "Mark Santer" became "Kram Retnas" which looks suitably Baltic at least), and in addition the names of the three churches were transformed into "The Big Church on the Big Island", "The Papal People" and, best of all, "The Bagpipe Church". With such a demonstration that even the uniquely unusable language of Finland could play a role, this was indeed ecumenical resource-sharing and this little piece of cloak-and-dagger work might be cited in support of Clements's Dad "being a spy". In fact yet another extra precaution was asked for by Jaakko Rusama's friend, namely, not to use him as a conduit again. The delegation did go ahead, and very successfully. Hastings Banda conceded the opposition's demands for a referendum in June that year.

---

1. Later renamed Organisation for Security and Cooperation in Europe (OSCE).

PART THREE: INTERNATIONAL AFFAIRS 1990-1997

LISTENING TO AFRICA

Meanwhile a somewhat bigger project was underway in CCBI and CCOM as a follow-up to the commitments made at Swanwick. Much of Africa was in the grip of drought in 1992 and, in some areas, real famine. Christian Aid and CAFOD proposed high-level visits from the British and Irish Churches to the churches in some of the worst most affected countries, as a way of highlighting their needs and those of their people. This took a great deal of organization both at the CCBI end (we were asking people with very full diaries to clear up to ten days in their schedules) and in Africa where the churches or ecumenical bodies were being asked to organize the programs. The visits were originally planned for the second half of 1992. In fact they had to be delayed until early 1993 (by which time the worst of the drought was over). Not only did the problems of communications and logistics have to be overcome but it transpired that not everyone, especially if they had not been at the Swanwick Assembly, was happy with the way the visits appeared to be agency-driven; indeed the international affairs desk person in one of the largest churches complained angrily about the churches being hit over the head by the aid agencies. That was somewhat unfair since the agencies were at least underwriting the costs of the visits and were supplying staff to accompany them. The visits did take place in January 1993. The countries visited were Ethiopia, with John Rawsthorne (auxiliary bishop in Liverpool Roman Catholic archdiocese), and Leslie Wallace (Irish Methodist Missionary Society); Kenya, with Father Olu Abiola (Council of African and Afro-Caribbean Churches and a President of CCBI), Pauline Webb (Methodist Church) and Meurwyn Williams (Union of Welsh Independents); and Mozambique, with David Coffey, (general secretary of the Baptist Union of Great Britain) and Bruce Cameron (bishop of Aberdeen in the Scottish Episcopal Church). The delegates came back both challenged and inspired, and at their overall debriefing identified five major priorities: continued advocacy for just terms of aid and trade; faith partnership, i.e. the British and African churches learning from each other about their common tasks of evangelism and development of spirituality; sharing in theological exploration; examination of what democracy means in Africa; and developing relationships with the African Independent Churches (i.e. those that did not owe their existence to Western missionary work or being set up by western-originated churches). It was not long after this that I visited for the first time an African country other than South Africa. In April 1993 I was in Johannesburg for a meeting of a working group of the WCC Programme to Combat Racism (PCR)[2] and afterwards was able to add on five days in Zimbabwe, based mainly in Harare with an intensive programme arranged by the Zimbabwe Council of Churches (ZCC) whose general secretary just then was Murombedzi Kuchera.

In April 1994, any assumption that we were learning how to relate to Africa was massively jolted by the news of the massacres in Rwanda. At first it seemed as if the

---

2. See next chapter (12) on South Africa.

violence triggered by the deaths on April 6 of Rwandan President Juvenal Habyarimana and the President of Burundi Melchior Ndadaye, when their plane was shot down by unknown assailants on approach to Kigali airport, was simply another stage in the ongoing, mostly low-level, conflict between the Hutu and Tutsi peoples in the Great Lakes region. Quickly it emerged as more than that: upwards of eight hundred thousand people, nearly all Tutsis, massacred by the Rwandan army, Hutu militias and Hutu civilians, within twenty days. This was mind-numbing. What could one say? Small wonder that the first reaction of CCBI churches and the various Christian agencies was to hold a candle-lit vigil outside St Martin-in the-Fields in London for the dead and bereaved. But we had to try, learn, and think, and during the rest of the year there were meetings and seminars drawing together people, churches and organizations with links to the region. Rwandans themselves came to visit and speak to us at Inter-Church House. There was no lack of analysis of the historical roots of the conflict, of the role of European colonial policy in fostering division and rivalry between two so closely related and similar peoples as the Hutus and Tutsis, of the too-slow implementation of the Arusha Accords agreed the previous year which were meant to encourage power-sharing between Hutus and Tutsis in government; of the failure of the UN peace-keeping presence in Rwanda; of the complicity even of some of the Roman Catholic hierarchy in Rwanda in encouraging Hutu hostility towards the Tutsi population. It was a grim scenario, aptly summed up in a short book published by the WCC, quoting a young survivor of the genocide, *The Angels Have Left Us*.

RWANDA AND BURUNDI: CHURCH, GENOCIDE AND RESPONSIBILITY

I did not realize at the time that Rwanda and its neighbor Burundi were to provide my own next personal encounter with Africa. The events in Rwanda and the low-level genocide against Hutus in Burundi, were raising profounder questions about what was involved in encountering Africa than we were facing in 1992. In the summer of 1994 I was asked in my Support Group to try and find some time to reflect on how as Christians in the north and the British Isles in particular we should relate to a continent where the scale of the problems seemed so immense as to overwhelm our capacities for thinking morally. Was there really any point in engaging with issues of such magnitude? Is it in the end a trivial game? Can conscience be realistic? Or was it better to be honest and switch off? At the same time however Africans themselves were still asking us to see the positive, life-affirming aspects of Africa: its tremendous human and natural potential, the vibrancy of communal life and not least the vitality of much of its Christianity. But everyone seemed to agree that Africa was almost synonymous with "crisis". I was glad to accept this challenge but felt that the reflections should if possible be informed by some more first-hand experience of an African context. The opportunity for such came in the spring of 1995, with an invitation from the WCC to join a team which would be visiting Rwanda and Burundi as part of its Joint Africa Consolidated Programme, aimed at encouraging "the African ecumenical movement to examine systematically the role of the Church of Christ and that of the international ecumenical institutions such as the WCC and the National Councils of Churches in Africa in support of the struggles of Africans for peace, justice and sustainable development". Rwanda and Burundi would be a serious test of such grand aims.

The organizer and leader of the visit was Daniel Ntoni-Nzinga, an Angolan Baptist on the staff of WCC Unit III whom I had already met in Geneva. We flew together from Brussels to Kigali on June 23. Kigali at first was an odd experience. Hundreds of thousands had died the previous year yet in contrast to, say, Beirut there was very little obvious sign of physical damage. Machetes and rifles, rather than bombs and rockets, had done their work. It made talk of genocide almost unreal at first. The most cynical physical reminder was to be seen on the plate glass entrance door of the Hotel des Diplomates, where we stayed. It was plastered with the stickers left by the news teams who had covered the violence of a year before: all the world's media, it appeared, had been there, from ABC News to Wiltshire Sound. They had been—and gone. On busy, jostling streets it was hard to imagine the eight hundred thousand absences. But they hit me next day when I went to Sunday morning worship at the Baptist Church. At home in England empty pews or rows of chairs betoken holiday time of year, or perhaps just numerical decline. Here they were witnesses to the recent dead or to those who had been able to flee. But it was a marvelous service aided by fine singing by two children's choirs. The pastor, Samuel Rugumbage, preached. Two people from the congregation led the prayers of intercession. I was invited to give a message which I duly did and it was touchingly well received. Afterwards I heard more of what had happened in the violence. The church building and its adjoining language school had been looted and damaged. Many members had been killed, though not on the actual site of the church. A layman, Mark by name, who had conducted part of the service that morning told how he had had to hide (helped by Hutus in fact) and though his car was destroyed had managed to get to Zaire for a time. But his brothers, their wives and children had all been murdered. I talked also with Samuel Rugumbage, his wife and three delightful children. He had had to adopt the six orphaned children of his brother who with his wife had been killed. In the midst of death, the African extended family was as alive as ever. Back at the hotel other members of the ecumenical team were arriving. What made this African visit unusually significant for me was that most of the seven-person team, two of whom were women, were themselves African, from Angola, Cameroun, Sierra Leone and Ghana, not white and European. It was not another visit from the north but from the ecumenical family weighted mainly from Africa itself, and its main object was to help the *African* ecumenical movement. Brussels-based Father Francis Boedts of the Catholic Commissions on Justice and Peace in Europe and I were the only members from Europe. I was particularly impressed with Dr Louise Tappa from the Baptist Union of Cameroon, and Canon Kodwo Ankrah from Ghana.

The three days in Kigali were certainly intense. We met for five hours with leaders of the churches in membership with the Conseil Protestante du Rwanda. We saw the Apostolic Nuncio (a defender, but gently so, of his church's role in the conflict), staff of Church World Action and other agencies and human rights organizations. We were received by Colonel Epimague Ruhashyai, Acting Director of the Cabinet Office of the Rwandan government and adviser to the Prime Minister on security. Appropriately the building in which his office was located was heavily guarded, but the mounted Bren gun round which we had to step on our way in looked dangerously dilapidated. One afternoon we were driven out to the Masaka Orphanage, home to some two hundred children, from toddlers to teenagers, who had lost parents in the massacres. Bereavement, it was borne in on us, involved much more than just the loss of parents as individuals. In that context it made such loss into an ever-widening reach of collateral emotional damage. Loss of parents in many cases meant the loss also of money for school fees which meant loss of education and, in turn, career prospects. Such loss could in the course of time breed bitter resentment and the desire for revenge. Not much there to interest the happy-snappy news teams who thought it was all over and were safely back home. I briefly visited the Anglican diocesan office and delivered a parcel of mail and medicines from London. Wherever we were, whether on the road or at table back in the hotel, we talked endlessly about Africa, theology, development and the churches. It was like one long seminar.

We flew to Burundi on the morning of Wednesday June 25, in a small twin-propeller plane that hill-hopped over the beautiful Great Lakes scenery down to Bujumbura. As in Kigali our programme was a mix of meetings with church and political leaders but also more with lay people including women and youth. We also found time to hippo-watch on Lake Tanganyika. In Bujumbura we had two lengthy meetings with leaders and church representatives of the Conseil National Protestante du Burundi, and met with the secretary of the Catholic Bishops' Conference, Bishop Budaudira. We had an evening with State President Sylvestre Nkbantungany, a most intelligent and restrained figure, at his residence up in the hills. He knew all about violence, his wife having been assassinated a year previously. We saw leaders of the two main political parties and the President of Parliament, the UN representative Ouid Abdullah, the Belgian and US Ambassadors, human rights organizations, women's groups, students and business leaders. The Christian Aid representative in Burundi Eliane du Toit, was particularly helpful to us and I was to meet her again in London when she visited Christian Aid headquarters in Inter-Church House. We visited two large camps for displaced persons, in tents and school buildings but the deteriorating security situation ruled out any journeys further afield. In addition I myself was able to meet with the UK diplomatic representative in Burundi, Kay Oliver, and with Carl and Solveig Nielsen, Danish Baptists with long missionary experience of the country and now working with Dan Church Aid. From his office Carl took me in his land rover to see a ruined Baptist church and its ancillary buildings out in Ngura, a somewhat scary journey, he warned, since it was still the site of frequent violence and one had to expect the whine of the odd rifle bullet. Bujumbura itself was under curfew at night. In the late evenings I sat in my hotel room reading Charles Marsh's study of the younger Bonhoeffer's early theology *Reclaiming Dietrich Bonhoeffer* which explores how relationality, sociality and "the other" are central to his thought, and his focus on "Christ existing as community". Outside, the otherwise quiet night was punctuated by rifle shots and now and again a grenade explosion, telling reminders of the threatening *breakdown* of community.

WHOSE RESPONSIBILITY?

In such scenes as we found in Kigali and Bujumbura where did the responsibilities of the churches lie and how could the ecumenical fellowship assist them? First of all, our group felt, the outside ecumenical bodies might observe some basic courtesies. It was not a good experience to find on our arrival in Bujumbura that the report of a team visit by the WCC and the All Africa Conference of Churches in April that year had not reached the Council of Churches there and did not do so until we had photocopied one of our own copies. Then there had to be much listening, without being biased in advance by the kind of comment that "The churches are deeply compromised . . . ". Such a line by itself conveys very little — or at least, once we sat down and talked with church representatives it was immediately refracted into several different hues. If one looks for obvious saints or villains, they do not readily stand out. What are to be found are real, flesh and blood human beings, devoted to their official tasks, very busy and indeed often over-worked, and carrying burdens in everyday circumstances of great difficulty and danger beyond what most of us in Britain, at any rate, could imagine. Time and again, moreover, we found ourselves caught in the crossfire between the churches and some of the aid and development agencies. Soon after landing in Kigali Daniel Ntoni-Nzinga and I were having coffee in the open air with some staff of a European agency who were simply dismissive of the churches there as being both compromised and incompetent at doing anything useful. I was shocked. Supposing the churches in war-ravaged Europe at the end of the Second World War II, some of which were also deeply "compromised" as well as bereft of resources, had been treated with like contempt by the American and Swiss partners in inter-church aid? Not surprisingly we heard complaints from the church side: too many NGOs ignored the churches who were, after all, part of the grassroots communities the NGOs were supposedly here to help. I have to say that Christian Aid and CAFOD were not so regarded. They had a very good press among the churches. Christian Aid for example in the aftermath of the catastrophe of 1994 helped to fund meetings for Baptist leaders inside and outside of Rwanda, manifesting a perception that such meetings were not just ecclesiastical affairs but had a vital part to play in rebuilding community.

To say that the churches, anywhere in the world, are deeply compromised by itself says very little. The yardstick by which church leaders typically measure their own work, whether in Rwanda, Burundi (or Britain), is what is happening locally. The church, they say, is *not* discredited there. In Rwanda and Burundi, people were still attending church in large numbers. It is there, in the villages, where reconciliation needs to be taught, where people need to be trained in community-building and suchlike, and certainly a great deal was happening in that respect. Anglican bishops in Rwanda and the Catholic Bishops' Conference in Burundi affirmed that this was where peace-building work needed to be done, and their own commitment to this was not in any doubt. Clearly a lot of energy was going into such work at diocesan and parish level. Nor were the church leaders wanting to shift all the blame onto others. In Rwanda we did hear the odd complaint that the denominationally and ethnically divided church was a product of the colonial-missionary era but this was a minority view. As anywhere, church leaders measure their effectiveness by what is happening under their supervision: in other words, the pastoral criterion, the state of their flocks. What they find it less easy to talk about is their relation to the powers outside (or above?) their remit as ecclesiastical shepherds. Here in both Rwanda and Burundi is where a quite startling contrast lay between what they expected of themselves and what others in society were hoping from them. In Rwanda, it was a prominent government minister, a Catholic layperson, who said to some of us: "One does wonder, just what gospel has been preached in Rwanda all these years"—about the most seriously theological question I heard in all Kigali. In Bujumbura it was the foreign diplomats who lamented most severely the churches' silence and divisions in face of the drift into chaos, and no-one was more definite in this regard than the UN Special Representative Oud Abdullah, a Muslim. Coming as I did from a European—or perhaps especially British—scene in which the churches seem ever more discounted by political authorities it was certainly a change to hear so many demands from those at the center of public life that the Christian community address the realities of the situation with moral imperatives. In other words, while the church leaders see themselves in a pastoral role others long from them also to adopt a prophetic stance. From whom, in their history, did these churches learn this imbalance in their vocation? In fact given that so many of the crimes in 1994 were committed by people at least nominally in their churches, the pastoral and prophetic role should have been inseparable. In such a situation, neither blanket condemnations nor flannelling compliments serve any purpose in our relations with the indigenous church leadership. Rather we need to explore with them precisely where the problems lie, and to converse with them about identifiable priorities and tasks.

It was quite a different sort of experience, especially in Burundi, to sit with leaders of women's groups and with students and other young people. It is a truism to say that women are the main victims of violent conflict in Africa. But we found that they were also feeling a special responsibility in countering violence since the violence was—at an immediate level—largely a youth phenomenon. In Bujumbura the main targets were Hutu young people, the main killers gangs of armed Tutsi youth. The anguish of mothers was all too apparent. They had a very definite expectation that the churches should declare resolutely against the culture of violence and death that was taking over. In our meeting with the National Protestant Council it was a woman who provided the most trenchant critique of why it was that the church leadership was largely stymied in its engagement with political leaders. We asked a group of about twenty women with whom we met, whether any work on Bible-study from women's perspectives was being undertaken in Burundi, the reply was simply and wistfully, "We have no women theologians here". We had the impression of a large section of the church membership both deeply committed and frustrated. This was even truer when we met a large group of mostly Hutu students with whom we spent Sunday afternoon in Bujumbura, and the small group who asked for another and less public meeting with us the following night. Here there was real fear. Some of their friends and fellow-students had been butchered in a massacre on the campus earlier in the year. But there was also bewilderment and anger at the nonsensical way that minute ethnic differences had been absolutized and politicized in the interests of power elites (one woman said that when she had been "told she was Hutu" she spent a long time looking at her face in the mirror trying to see what this meant). They were demanding that the church counter this by word and example. As visitors we had a role to play in acknowledging the need for this debate within the church, especially between people and leaders, and to encourage it in our address to the leaders.

CHURCH AND POWER

In Rwanda some Catholic bishops had no problem admitting that church members were involved in the killings, "but this has a longer history than what happened last year". Was this last comment a symptom of a relapse into fatalism or a recognition, at least, that some *analysis* of society, both its history and its structure, was required? In fact it was the African members of our team who pressed on the Rwandans and later the Burundians the need to analyze why it happened. One response from our hosts in Kigali was that people were still too traumatized to cope with such analysis, and that traumatized people need time to adjust to reality. We had long, long discussions with both our hosts and among ourselves on this. My own contribution to this discussion was to refer to the European experience of the Holocaust which well over half a century later still haunts the consciences of Christians no less than others and has revealed both the necessity and great difficulty of facing the truth. It is quite correct to say that apprehension of the truth takes time when the truth is so ugly and appalling. We should be suspicious of shot-gun confessions. Facing the truth and confession are not single, over-and-done-with events. They are processes in a new direction of existence, and as such they require a *beginning*. There are also two distinct elements in facing the truth.

One is the personal existential question of guilt and responsibility: *mea culpa*. The other is the analytical question of what happened as a social, political event, and why. The two levels are of course connected and it is important that they remain so in thought. We might not expect more than a beginning to be made, but nor should we expect less. I was surprised, and gratified by how often the discussion returned to the European case as a kind of reassuring and instructive example. How moving it was, over twenty years later, to hear Dr Pascal Bataringaya, President of the Presbyterian Church of Rwanda, lecture at the Twelfth International Bonhoeffer Congress in Basel (2016) on what has been learnt from Bonhoeffer and his understanding of guilt, confession and reconciliation, in its bearing on the Rwandan experience and the role of the churches there.[3]

One refrain ran throughout our discussions in Rwanda and Burundi: the tragedies that had taken or were still taking place were the outcome of political power being sought and clung on to as an end in itself and at all costs. The combination of democracy and tribalism too easily produced a dictatorship of the majority. The resulting impasse, when politicians refused to engage in engage in dialogue or seriously consider power-sharing, led down the hardline path to confrontation and violence. If however we describe this is an inevitable process we may be falling into the trap which so many of the politicians had set for themselves. "Please," said the UN Special representative in Bujumbura, "don't buy their stories. No more history. No more 'explanations.'" The crucial matter is how to *change* the story, and that is a matter of political *will* for peace. It was here the churches were faced with their severest test. In Rwanda, church leaders were ready to concede that many Africans are too deferential to authority, and that "While 98% of the people do not want a new cycle of violence their leaders want to hold on to power". This prompted impatient reactions from the Africans on our team who detected yet another symptom of the endemic acquiescence of Africans in their own manipulation and exploitation by others. As one of them put it, colonialists have long told us, "I can't help it if you're stupid". The stock answer of church leaders about concentrating on the grassroots where people need training in greater responsibility and initiative, left to itself, can be an opt-out unless the church-leaders themselves provide role-models of civic courage and witness in relation to the political authorities, so breaking the chain of subservience. But it was precisely here that the real problem lay: the willingness of African church leadership to become subservient coalition partners of people in power, for the sake of protection or status or privilege, or all three. As such they become part of the power-structure rather than a challenge to it. It was, according to one of our team, yet another manifestation of the way whereby in Africa Christianity again and again created the aspiration to becoming an elite rather than serving and energizing the people as a whole. A context in which power is regarded as an absolute right and good, determining all the values in human transactions, becomes destructive of all relationships at every level in society.

---

3. "Wege zür Versöhnung: Die ruandischen Kirchen und die Arbeit der Versöhnung nach dem Genozid—Impulse der Friedensethik Dietrierch Bonhoeffers". Unpublished at time of writing.

The tragedy is that in this cyclic process of death and despair so many other people get hurt. My African colleagues saw this clearly: the church in Africa is surely to be a community publicly concerned for the whole people yet free from the destructive power-systems at work, and continually calling power to account. This is why *the church as church* is of immense significance in Africa, politically and culturally, and cannot be set aside as inconsequential compared with, for example, narrowly defined developmental work. Nor now, in looking back to that visit of over twenty years ago, do I feel that the Rwandan and Burundian church scene is so totally removed from my own British situation. The churches are always prone to being slotted in to a pre-determined pattern of power instead of challenging it.

We in Britain do not have the excuses, or should I say forbidding challenges, that the churches of the Great Lakes region had in 1995, for hesitancy in accepting public responsibility. There, even to recognize the scale of the problem was a matter of civic courage. As a representative of Africa Rights Watch said in Kigali, there was so little *trust* in this society. One might say that was because human rights were not being observed. Equally, one has to say that human rights observance requires trust: trust that cases will be judged fairly, that people will give honest testimonies, that political leaders (at least sometimes) will tell the truth. Part of the difficulty in measuring a society by the plumb-line of codes of human rights is that they cannot operate in isolation from the fabric of civil and communal life as a whole. A basic requirement is an independent and effective judiciary. That in turn posits some severely practical and material requirements. In 1995 Rwanda's judiciary was hampered by lack of such basics as paper and typewriters, as well as judges and lawyers so many of whom had perished in 1994; not to mention reasonably reliable, objective and independent media. Then there are the almost intangible but vital elements that make for a feeling of community: a sense of belonging, knowing who one's neighbors are, and a respect for the dignity of the other person. Human rights observance, like democracy, requires a soil in which to grow and become rooted.

RETURNING HOME: REFLECTIONS AND GRATITUDE

I came home therefore with much to share on the situation of these two countries and the churches within them, and many of the questions they prompted are still live ones today and not just in Africa. To be partners with churches in Africa, I had come to realize, could be far more demanding, yet no less enriching, than had even been envisaged at the Swanwick Assembly three years earlier. I was glad to be liberated from the assumption that as a European I must be among those with ready answers. After all, how would I have felt about a mostly African delegation coming to sort out the problems of Former Yugoslavia? Being trusted to hear the stories, the heartaches the fears, the anger even, and yet also the hopes of people especially at the younger end, was an experience of grace. And speaking of grace, I must mention one further encounter. It occurred while we were in Kigali, on our visit to the orphanage at Masaka. We were on the forecourt of the building talking to the deputy director and social worker of the orphanage, both of them Baptists whom I had met at the Sunday morning service in Kigali, and watching the children playing, and teenagers gossiping. As I was standing there, camera in one hand, wondering just what traumatic experiences these youngsters had gone through, and what might still be giving them nightmares, I felt something or someone catch hold of my free hand, gently but firmly. I looked down, and it was a little girl, about two years old. She was not obviously attention-seeking, was not asking for anything, but simply stood there for several minutes. Her name, I was told, was Natasi. A child of the chaos, her parents were probably a pile of bones somewhere. It seemed as if she was saying, "Welcome here. It's quite safe, you know. I'm glad you've come. Welcome to Africa!" Literally touched by this, somehow with my free hand I managed to take a picture of that hand-clasp. It felt like the touch of the future of a whole continent, an opportunity and a responsibility which I was being invited to share.

Africa's hand of welcome

12

South African Pain and Joy

For the British Council of Churches (BCC) South Africa and the struggle against apartheid had been one of the most central and long running concerns in international affairs. It was natural that the international affairs desk at CCBI should inherit and continue this commitment, albeit with no specialist Africa staff beyond that of agencies, such as Christian Aid in particular, and the network of CCOM. It was in any case a major concern of my own since my 1985 visit to South Africa, and I continued my connections with the Fellowship of Concerned Baptists in South Africa ((FCB) and the majority-black Baptist Convention of South Africa. From John Daries I continued to receive a stream of letters and bulletins on the South African scene in general, the Baptist constituency in particular and his own activities. Yet what a time it was, in 1990, to become engaged at a new ecumenical level. Nelson Mandela had been released on that memorable day in February and also let loose was a tide of euphoria around the world, as in South Africa itself. In the UK Mandela, it seemed, was being lionized even by people who lately had still been calling him a terrorist. But presently it was clear that fears as well as hopes abounded on all sides. Many blacks in South Africa were deeply distrustful that President de Klerk would really be willing, even if able, to deliver the non-racial, truly democratic society that had always been the stated goal of the ANC. Equally, many whites were fearful that that was what he would indeed concede in the end. Would the heads of the South African Defense Force (SADF) go along with this? And even if they did, what about the secretive, extreme right-wing armed militia groups? It was truly both the best of times and the worst of times. Nothing was guaranteed, nothing was inevitable.

Warnings there were a-plenty. On February 26 1991 the South Africa Coalition held a large conference at Church House, Westminster. It was moderated by Simon Barrington-Ward, bishop of Coventry, who spoke of illusions being held by both government and public opinion in Britain that apartheid was really now over. The current secretary of the South African Council of Churches (SACC) Frank Chikane was a main speaker and warned against speaking too soon of irreversible change. Some voices in the international community were calling for the lifting of sanctions as a due reward to the de Klerk regime. But as yet the mass of South African people were still not allowed to be part of the political process. Only a tiny minority of political prisoners had as yet been released. Political trials were still continuing. The repressive security legislation remained in place. Exiles had still not been allowed to return. Violence, especially in Natal, was rising. Freedom will come, Chikane said, but it would be costly. There was need of a fully inclusive Constituent Assembly (hitherto opposed by de Klerk) to take the political process forward, as proposed by the SACC and the Roman Catholic bishops. Other speakers from South Africa spoke in similar vein. Michael Taylor, director of Christian Aid, recognized the remarkable progress that had been made so far but much still remained as before. Apartheid could not be said to have ended until there was economic justice for all. The progress thus far had largely been in response to pressure from outside and this must be maintained, and Taylor recalled the emphasis of the *Kairos* document that reconciliation could not be real before justice was secured. At the Baptist World Alliance Council meetings in Montreal in July that year I heard much the same from Gideon Makhanya of the Baptist Convention, as we drew up a resolution asking the BWA and its member churches to continue to call and press for irreversible change in South Africa. The end was not yet.

MARCH 1992: THE REFERENDUM

Just as my first visit to South Africa in 1985 had coincided with a significant, even dramatic, event in the launch of the *Kairos* document, so too my second visit in March 1992 fell in with a major step, if very different in kind, on the long march out of apartheid: the white referendum called by President de Klerk in which he sought a mandate to continue the negotiating process. The question which was put to the white voters was simply: "Do you support continuation of the reform process begun on February 2 1990 and which is aimed at a new Constitution through negotiation?" Although part of my visit was dominated by this event and its significance, the referendum was not even on the horizon when I started to plan the trip several months earlier. My main stated purpose was to renew contact on behalf of CCBI with the SACC, to visit the Baptist Convention and Fellowship of Concerned Baptists, and to find out what was happening in theology in the new and changing situation. I would spend about six days based in Johannesburg as guest of the Baptist Convention, and then have four days in the Western Cape hosted by John and Isobel de Gruchy in Cape Town.

I landed at Johannesburg on March 17, the actual day of the referendum vote. Jan Smuts airport was a much more relaxed placed than in 1985 and entry procedures seemed actually friendly even before Diba Madolo, secretary of the Baptist Convention, greeted me at the barrier. Another comment on the changing scene, however, was provided by the airport car-park where it seemed that almost every parking bay had its pile of smashed glass, witness to the rising level of common criminality. Even if one had not been told, it was obviously referendum day. In and around Johannesburg practically every lamp-post and telegraph pole had its posters urging (in the main) a yes vote "for South Africa", "for peace and prosperity", "for the future". Only a few said

"No to the ANC". Diba Madolo drove me straight to the Baptist Convention offices where at mid-morning a simple yet moving service of intercession for the referendum was shared by the staff of the Convention and the Presbyterian Church in South Africa which occupied the same building. Midday we drove out to the Madolo home in Dawnpark to the east of the city, a small residential suburb which until the repeal of apartheid legislation was a wholly white area, now about 20% black. Not everyone was evidently happy with this. Once when we were returning to Dawnpark Diba's car was deliberately slowed down by a car in front of us bearing the slogan "Armed Commando Response". One of his fellow black neighbors, Diba pointed out to me, was Chris Hani, secretary of the South African Communist Party and leader of the armed wing of the ANC, Umkhonto we Sizwe. He had supported suspension of the armed struggle once negotiations began. Just over a year later his name, and Dawnpark, would become tragically famous. By evening the television news was getting excited about the turn-out for the referendum, estimated as high as 75% in some areas.

Next day was referendum result day. Diba Madolo dropped me off at SACC headquarters, a new Khotso House (the one I had become familiar with in 1985 had been bombed) on Marshall Street, and I spent the morning with Mary Mxadana and William Smith of the International and Ecumenical Relations Department, and then with Frank Chikane and his assistant John Lamola whom I was glad to see again, he having returned from the UN[1]. We watched the first referendum results come in on a small TV set in Frank Chikane's office. The early signs were of a clear "Yes". Evident relief all round. "God is on our side", murmured one staff member. After lunch in Khotso House came what for me was *the* most dramatic event of the day. As well as referendum result day it was budget day and COSATU[2] and ANC supporters staged a massive demonstration against continuing economic hardship and discrimination, in particular the effect of VAT on basic necessities. Twelve thousand people, nearly all black, marched through the center of Johannesburg and we watched from the steps of Khotso House as they passed along Marshall Street, a vibrant, joyous yet disciplined surge of singing, toyi-toying and dancing with banners and posters. John Lamola raced down the steps to join in for a time. There was no reference to the white referendum—it seemed an irrelevance to these people, just like the half-dozen or so police who were tagging along awkwardly at the rear with nothing to do. This and the similar demonstration in Cape Town received about ten seconds' coverage on TV that evening. What did occupy the TV screens of course was the decisive (nearly 69%) "Yes" vote. President de Klerk told the world, "We have closed the book on apartheid." "Not yet, mister!" said the black voice in the next armchair in the Madolas' sitting room. There was indeed ambivalence among the black community. In engineering terms, the result was a necessary but not sufficient condition for progress. Frank Chikane expressed both the relief (an overall "No" vote would wrecked the negotiating process) but also the realism:

1. See above chapter 7, p.149.
2. Congress of South African Trade Unions.

> The much-publicized referendum must be seen in the context of South Africa's total population—most of whom had no vote on March 17—and of the demands of their varied representatives. We remind the National Party that negotiations are, by definition, an open process and that "bottom line" positions in negotiations are but a starting point. Such an open process is integral to the democratization of the country.

There was moreover real hurt that for all de Klerk's talk of closing the book on apartheid there had been no note of sorrow or apology for apartheid itself. Desmond Tutu regretted that the President "had not uttered any note of contrition for the unspeakable pain and damage that apartheid had inflicted on the majority of South Africa's people". Bishop Wilfred Napier, President of the South African Catholic Bishops' Conference, likewise noted: "The furthest [the President] will go is to say that apartheid was abandoned because it couldn't succeed, rather than it was an evil in itself"; and insisted that the negotiations must now lead to a democracy for all the people.

A lot was crowded into these few days in Johannesburg with SACC staff and Baptist Convention officials, although the new Khotso House was a lot quieter place than that of 1985. There no longer being quite the sense of crisis, still less the successive states of emergency, overseas financing of a number programmers had been reduced; but also a number of former staff had been opting into the more secular social schemes of social reconstruction now on offer. But there was no doubting the continued deep commitment of Frank Chikane and his staff. Soweto, too, was changing: no armored vehicles patrolling, some more middle-class housing appearing, and improvements to roads, not to mention fewer adverts for alcohol but many posters about the dangers of AIDS: "Don't womanize, condomise". I also went to Pretoria twice to meet Justice and Peace staff of the South African Catholic Bishops' Conference and, in the home of Gisela Nicholson, the executive of the Fellowship of Concerned Baptists. I had a memorable morning at the home in Mamelodi Township of Nico Smith, radical Reformed theologian and founder of the Koinonia organization (he had refused to vote in the referendum on account of its being whites-only). Also in Pretoria at the University of South Africa (UNISA) for the first time I met Louise Kretzschmar who taught systematic theology and ethics. A white Baptist, she was strongly identified with the Baptist Convention as well as the FCB, and was writing a dissertation on the privatization of Christian faith in South Africa as exemplified by the white Baptists. On my final morning in Johannesburg, a Sunday, Diba Madolo took me out to the colored township of Ennerdale, south of the city, where Diba had a preaching engagement in the Baptist Church. The pastor, Desmond (Des) Hofmeister, I already knew, having met him at the BWA Congress in Seoul two years earlier. The worship occupied most of the morning, from about 9.00 am till just before midday, though much of the first half was spent in learning songs to be used later on, and in all-age Sunday School. I was asked at no notice to take the adult class. This proved in fact to be one of the most rewarding experiences of my whole visit, leading an impromptu Bible study on my choice of text Luke

13:10–17, the story of Jesus healing the crippled woman in a synagogue on the Sabbath day. The group responded well, interpreting for themselves and for their own context this story of healing, liberation, challenge to repressive authority and new acceptance into community. Even here the ambivalence towards the referendum surfaced, as when a very gentle, evangelical woman wondered if a "No" vote might not have been better since it would have brought into the open the underlying issues which were still not being faced. After the service much of the fellowship resorted to the home of one of the members for a hearty communal lunch—and to root for South Africa against England in the cricket world cup semi-final being shown live on television. They were even very forgiving at the pitiful way the match ended in an English win. There followed a time of informal discussion on the life and future of the Convention. Then Diba Madolo drive me to the airport for my flight to Cape Town.

CAPE TOWN: THEOLOGY FOR RECONSTRUCTION

John de Gruchy met me off the plane at Cape Town and he and Isobel hosted me for the next five days in their Rosebank home, close by the famous cricket ground and with the stunning backdrop of Table Mountain. Here too signs of change were all around, notably in the now more commercially active harbor and waterfront developments. But what of theology? What had happened to the *Kairos* of 1985? Did the present scene mean a new "Kairos"? Or was that sort of talk appropriate anymore? Where things stood out sharp and clear in 1985, 1992 seemed to present a misty scene with some very dense patches of fog indeed. But many of those in the churches who took a strongly critical line against apartheid were at pains to deny any lessening of their prophetic stance now, but the pastoral and educational aspects of leadership were now being consciously and deliberately embraced.

There was a corresponding theological move now apparent as was made clear in discussions with John de Gruchy and other theologians at the University of Cape Town (UCT), such as Charles Villa-Vicencio whom I had first met there in 1985 and subsequently at the 1989 Cambridge conference. "It was easy in the old days," said Charles. "Suddenly we're in a situation where we need to know what it means to say 'yes', not just 'no'." They were into ambiguities now, especially in the economic sphere and, he went on, "We are looking more like you! All your [British] complexities are ours." In this confusing scene the theological task was to discern the signs of God's kingdom in the struggles for human rights, in the building of civil society , the search for a common culture, and a preparedness "to get our minds confused in these debates" otherwise the church would become totally marginalized. People were again speaking (I was glad to note) of J.H. Oldham's "middle axioms" in Christian social thought. One thing was certain according to Charles—the church itself was at a point of transition in South Africa and "we don't know what it will become". I was powerfully reminded of Bonhoeffer, writing from prison about the challenges that would face a post-war, post-Nazi world where instead of being put under the spotlight as in the Church Struggle and the oppression by the Nazi state, the church was more likely not to be noticed in society at all. Hot from the press, Charles' questions and vision were already set out in in his book *A Theology of Reconstruction*[3]. Flesh was also being put on such thinking in, for example, a conference to which I was invited at Stellenbosch, that lovely city of historic buildings and surrounded by vineyards, on "Church and Development: An Interdisciplinary Approach" held by the Ecumenical Foundation of South Africa. Nabs Wessels of the Western Cape Province Council of Churches described "development" as the buzzword fast replacing "liberation", but in fact a continuation of it in attempting to develop human potential. The role of NGOs was a main item on the conference agenda. The exercise had to be a move from anti-apartheid to nation-building. Some rather tricky questions also arose. For example, was there now to be a role for such bodies as the Development Bank of South Africa which had been formed by the apartheid government to deal with the notorious "homelands"? Was such a creation of apartheid to be simply ditched, or was it capable of being adapted for just ends? It was a nice theological question: is anything so depraved as to be utterly unredeemable and unusable? Perhaps this was the social dimension to sanctification.

Such was the atmosphere in which I was briefly but deeply immersed in the Western Cape: refreshing, invigorating engagement with the re-creation of society. There was also the chance to make new friendships and renew old ones. At the Stellenbosch conference it was a privilege to meet again the white Anglican priest and social activist Michael Lapsley whom I had last seen at the 1988 Amsterdam Bonhoeffer Congress where he had moderated the session at which John de Gruchy and I lectured. Only, now he was minus both hands and the sight in one eye, having been sent a letter-bomb while in Zimbabwe in 1990. Jim Harris, a white Baptist pastor who was writing a PhD thesis on Baptist identity in South Africa, showed me around some Baptist causes including the Baptist Theological College where I met its principal, Peter Holness. At UCT I attended a lecture by a visiting British academic, James Barber of Durham University, on British policy towards South Africa (interesting to learn that the British Foreign Office was even then providing diplomatic training for the ANC). Then it was good to meet up with John Daries on his home territory. I spent an afternoon with him visiting squatter camps on the Cape Flats, Khyelitsha and Mitchell's Plain, and the church at Rocklands where he had been minster till recently, and Pastor Oswald Tshuka and his family. Perhaps most memorable was the Nomsa Makaphonsi School, opened in 1990 and named by the local people in memory of the activist woman and her husband assassinated that year, and vividly illustrating the under-resourcing of black education-but also the commitment of those dedicated to teaching. At least one classroom had over a hundred children to one teacher. They were also very pleased to show me the desks provided by the British Embassy. And as always in Cape Town, there was a wonderful fish restaurant where the de Gruchys took me one evening.

3. Cambridge: Cambridge University Press 1992.

Dietrich Bonhoeffer, sometime in the winter before his arrest in 1943, wrote of the "experience of incomparable value" of seeing "the great events of world history from below", from the perspective of the oppressed and suffering.[4] This visit to South Africa had given me a glimpse of such an experience, albeit briefly, particularly in Johannesburg where I had been largely among the black community, a guest in a black home, while viewing the referendum which was indeed an important step towards the liberation of South Africa yet about which many blacks were reserving judgment, in contrast to the world at large who viewed it euphorically as unmitigated success. That was instructive for me, and a real privilege to see it from that angle. Equally in Cape Town and Stellenbosch I had met with theologians and other academics wrestling seriously and creatively with the hard choices facing the changing society and the churches within it. It was an engagement, I had to confess, which in its quality and depth of seriousness had no parallel as yet back home in Britain. I therefore had much to share of both hope and cautious realism on returning home.

NEW WORK: ECUMENICAL MONITORING AND RE-THINKING THE PROGRAMME TO COMBAT RACISM

Back home in fact a new, very practical phase of ecumenical engagement with South Africa was calling. By April 1992 it was being judged that the negotiating process had now sufficient momentum to justify hopes for truly democratic elections within a year or two, given that the Constituent Assembly now coming into being would set up the long-awaited constitution for post-apartheid South Africa. But in a country with no experience, for the vast majority, of such elections, and in conditions where violence and intimidation were always background fears, the voting would require for its credibility independent monitoring by the international community. The SACC and the Catholic Bishops; Conference invited, via the WCC, the ecumenical community abroad to take part in the monitoring programme leading up to and during the elections whenever they should take place. So was born The Ecumenical Monitoring Programme for South Africa (EMPSA). CCBI became involved in this early on, with Paul Renshaw, Christian Aid's Africa Secretary, the lead person in charge of the recruiting and briefing programme. EMPSA planning group meetings feature regularly in my diary and notebooks from April 1992 onwards. Soon after, in June 1992, another line was thrown to me which was to connect me again to South Africa, when I had a phone call from Barney Pityana in Geneva, who was in charge of the WCC's Programme to Combat Racism (PCR). Pityana, black South African Anglican priest, theologian and human rights lawyer, had had his own struggles as a banned person under the apartheid regime, and after serving as a priest in exile in England had been director of the PCR since 1988 but was about to return to South Africa. The PCR had

---

4. Bonhoeffer, *Letters*, DBWE 8, 52.

of course been heavily involved with South Africa—though also in many contexts elsewhere—and was now having to consider its own future. A small working group was being formed to look at racism anew in theological terms but particularly taking the economic aspects into account, and would I join it? We had a first meeting at Cartigny near Geneva at the beginning of July, to which Charles Villa-Vicencio came, along with the American Jewish liberation theologian Marc Ellis and engaged academics Philomena Essad of Amsterdam, Jacquelyn Grant from Atlanta, Father Antoine Sontag of Paris and South African contextual theologian Itemelung Mosala, at that time teaching in Cambridge and a leader in AZAPO (African People's Organization). A second meeting was fixed for April next year, in Johannesburg.

APRIL 1993: TRAGEDY, VIOLENCE AND ITS REDEMPTION

The second meeting however was overshadowed by other and more immediate issues, because yet again my going to South Africa coincided with an unforeseen and, this time, tragic event. We were scheduled to arrive and assemble on April 12. On April 10 Chris Hani was assassinated by a white gunman outside his home in Dawnpark where I had stayed with Diba Madolo the previous year. We each arrived therefore in an atmosphere of, to say the least, trepidation in view of what this act of violence on a key figure in the anti-apartheid struggle might mean. A violent reaction from the black communities? The wrecking of the whole negotiation process? Our group was nine in number. Barney Pityana had now left the WCC and was succeeded by Debbie Robinson of the USA as director of the PCR. Charles Villa-Vicencio was unable to attend, but South Africa was well represented by Itemelung Mosala. Even in the relatively secluded setting of Kempton Park (a Lutheran conference center) the event was bound to focus our thoughts still further. The recurring and overriding image was of an earth tremor opening up a fearsome fissure in the ground, of people struggling to decide whether to leap across, or to allow themselves to slide into an abyss of violence. This was a *Kairos* at least as dramatic as that of 1985. Nevertheless in our group we did our best to work through our agenda. We were surprised to find the (white) administrative staff of Kempton Park in a state of denial of the reality of what was happening, as we tried (unsuccessfully) to persuade them to allow their (black) staff to attend any memorial events that might be happening that week. We were grateful for their warning that a Black Mamba had recently been seen in the grounds but we felt that something still more deadly was afoot and had to be dealt with.

The black political leadership had designated Wednesday April 14 as a national day of mourning for Chris Hani, and a work stayaway. As a group we had no hesitation in deciding to attend the main memorial service in the Central Methodist Church in downtown Johannesburg. We arrived first thing in the morning to discover that the service had been rescheduled for midday, and the building was being checked by the police for bombs etc. At least this ensured we were able to find seats in good time, about ninety minutes before the service officially started. By noon three thousand people were crowding the church and ancillary rooms downstairs, while over ten thousand were jamming the streets outside. The congregation was overwhelmingly black. Most of the whites present (except for special guests like foreign diplomatic staff seated in the choir above the pulpit) were women—I noticed one in the gallery wearing her black sash. Liturgy began long before the official opening of the service, with spontaneous communal chanting and singing: waves of emotion rising and falling in those typical African rhythms and harmonies.

The service, perhaps as befitting its Methodist setting, combined the formal and the spontaneous, the solemn and the celebratory. Frank Chikane preached the sermon, "The Death That Was No Ordinary Death". It was an absolute tour de force, not only with solemn and powerful rhetoric but in humorous asides and witticisms (yes, we were laughing at times) with which he sharpened the significance of what he was saying. It was only after joking that of course the media would incorrectly be reporting him to be comparing Chris Hani to Jesus Christ that he went on to say, as the heart of his message:

> In the same way that those who crucified the Lord Jesus Christ did not understand the implications of their act for the whole created reality, so it is with Janus Waluz [Hani's assassin]. He pulled the trigger to end the life of Chris Hani but in this act he has pulled the trigger to end the life of the racist apartheid regime which he wanted to save. In pulling the trigger he has released unstoppable energy, which will destroy apartheid and usher in a new non-racial and just South Africa.

The whole message turned on the perception of Hani's death as itself provoking a crisis, an either-or, in South African history: a slide into destructive violence or a rapid move to a settlement and a new, democratic government. The concrete demands were clear to Chikane—transitional mechanisms now, joint control of all the security forces, and an earlier election date. But this sermon was far more than a shopping list of political demands. It was a genuinely prophetic utterance in enabling people to see where both the judgment and the hope lay in this crisis-"Chris Hani is dead, but his death has opened the eyes of many and has given us an opportunity to make a choice". As well as repeating the indictment of continuing enslavement of so many under apartheid, Chikane recalled the ANC's commitment to fight racism but *not a racist war*. He reminded us that it was through "a simple human act of a gallant white woman [Hani's neighbor in Dawnpark who noted Waluz's car number] that the assassin had been arrested, and therefore "South Africa cannot continue to think in terms of just black and white". So to the final peroration, as positive as could be: "Now is the time to make peace. Now is the time to reach a final settlement. Now is the time for South Africa to be free." This was *performative* utterance, bringing about what it proclaimed; not just telling people to leap across the fissure but by its very content doing so itself and calling others to follow. It was truly one of the most outstanding declarations I have ever heard.

Addresses by political party leaders Tokyo Sexwale (ANC) and Geraldine Fraser-Moleketi (South African Communist Party) followed and were equally incisive in seeing Hani's death as a futile attempt to block the moves to justice. The clergy present were asked to exit from the church and address an overflow meeting in the nearby gardens. Meanwhile messages of sympathy and solidarity from many parts of the world were announced. It was heartening to hear those from the UK—Christian Aid, Anti-Apartheid and Trevor Huddleston. We ourselves were recognized and welcomed. Almost at the end Walter Sisulu, veteran leader of the ANC, arrived in a wheelchair and gave a short greeting. Prayers were led by the Anglican and Catholic bishops of Johannesburg and the whole service concluded, inevitably, with a fervent rendering of the anthem *Nkosi sikelele Afrika*. (God bless Africa).

This occasion was a dignified response to tragedy. There was anger but not a hysterical outburst; grief but not a mindless lapse into sheer accusation. There was an acceptance of the responsibility of using this moment, in face of all its potential for unprecedented disaster, as a moment for rapid, decisive and constructive change. It was a determination to channel the anger into a rage for peace. At the same time as the service was taking place Nelson Mandela was addressing a rally in the Jabulani Stadium in Soweto, and likewise calling on the youth to channel their anger and turn their enemies' into friends. The black leadership were determined to meet the inhumanity not with a like brutality but with a greater humanity, a greater vision, and a greater courage to press towards the only answer which could save the country from utter chaos. This was not exploitation of a tragedy for political ends. It was the attempted *redemption* of a political and moral folly for the greater good of all. It is still something that renews my hope whenever I look back on it.[5]

Chris Hani's actual funeral and interment were scheduled for the following Sunday and Monday. In the PCR group we managed, as hoped, to complete our work by the middle of Sunday morning, and after a brief act of worship which I was asked to lead, we transferred from Kempton Park to the Holiday Inn Garden Court in central Johannesburg. We were not alone as new arrivals there: Mohammed Ali and his entourage, on tour in South Africa, were also checking in. Itemelung Mosala had arranged for us to spend the afternoon in Soweto in the home of some of his AZAPO colleagues where we had a meal with other AZAPO people who had also come for the funeral. Our hosts lived quite close to the FNB stadium where Chris Hani's body had arrived earlier in the day for the lying in state and the start of the ceremonies. Dusk was falling as our minibus approached the stadium. The area for a quarter of a mile radius around was jammed with cars, minibuses and all kinds of vehicles as thousands

---

5. More than one hundred rallies were held all over the country. Most passed entirely peacefully. There was a bit of window smashing and looting in Cape Town, with ten people reportedly killed in the country overall, and such incidents received far more TV coverage (not only in South Africa but also, I learnt later, in the UK) than the real story of overall peaceful, dignified commemoration. In Pretoria fifty thousand people gathered outside Protea police station from where the police fired, killing five and injuring many more.

Part Three: International Affairs 1990–1997

from all over the country were converging. Under the darkening sky the atmosphere was vibrant with emotion, as crowds of young blacks, many wielding symbolic but rather forbidding-looking axes, toyi-toyied their way into the stadium. Only once was verbal abuse spat at us whites in our group as we waited for entry but our black sisters and brothers were protective and insisted on forming a human shield around us. In fact the uniformed officials acting as marshals welcomed us as comrades and the frisking for weapons seemed as much an embrace as a precautionary duty.

Once in the floodlit arena, now filling towards its eighty-thousand capacity, it was time simply to contemplate a scene quite unlike anything I had ever witnessed before. It was, once again, both mourning and celebration, expression of loss yet affirmation of what must not be lost. Here in Africa spirituality was about being large enough and deep enough to cry and sing at the same time, just as in the Hebrew Psalms, and wherever in the Bible death and resurrection are conjoined. History was being made before our eyes, not just because it was such a large gathering with a lot of noise (the largest such gathering hitherto in South Africa, larger even than at Steve Biko's funeral in 1977) but because a critical decision and affirmation was being made here, that leap across the fissure which had opened up, a determination not to be intimidated or brutalized in return; a resolve to wring still more rapid progress to justice out of the tragedy that had sought to halt it. Such decisive moments of commitment are the great points in human history.

A motorcade swept across the green turf and to huge applause an unmistakable figure, arm raised, stepped out into the floodlights. Nelson Mandela was being welcomed not just as the President of the ANC but effectively as the President-in-Waiting of the whole country. It was as just such a statesman that he had spoken a few days earlier, calling for all South Africans to stand together against those who from any quarter wished to destroy what Chris Hani gave his life for, whether black or white. Standing in that stadium, in that gathering of prayer and protest, it was quite clear where by now the real mantle of moral strength and leadership for South Africa lay.

The early evening saw the start of the all-night vigil. Chris Hani's body lay in an open casket in a tent to one side of the arena, with his family seated by it. Our AZAPO friends used their good offices to good effect—we were invited to join the group of church dignitaries led by Desmond Tutu as they entered the arena and proceeded to the tent to present their condolences to Mrs Hani and her daughters. Sitting with then was Mrs Tambo, soon herself to be widowed. Debbie Robinson spoke to Mrs Hani on our behalf. It was a privilege to be so close to Desmond Tutu and the mourners at that moment. We had to leave the stadium before the end of the evening and I was not able to attend the funeral service proper next morning as I was leaving for Zimbabwe that day. But the impact was being felt everywhere, it seemed, including in quarters normally resistant to encounter with social reality. Of course there was blindness and deafness in some circles, as ever. Gisela Nicholson of the FCB whom I was able to meet briefly at Jan Smuts airport told me that at her Baptist church in Pretoria the previous day the only prayers that had been offered in relation to the Hani events were pleas that "all the people in that stadium might be converted to Christ". But many whites interviewed in the street for TV sound-bites showed real distress at the incident. Before leaving the hotel for the airport I watched on TV in my room Desmond Tutu preaching the final address. The same arms that had gently embraced the Hani family in comfort the night before were now windmilling in excitement as he proclaimed the certainty, through God's grace, of the triumph of justice, righteousness and peace. Later, in one of the hotel bar lounges, I watched the interment ceremony. It was moving in its dignity and symbolism, culminating in the sight of white doves of peace flying out of the grave. Some Afrikaner whites were also watching from the bar. A woman in the group walked over to the set and as she fumbled with the buttons I thought she was switching it off. But no, she was wanting the sound turned up. I hoped and prayed that that, too, was a symbol if what might be happening at large. People were at last paying heed to a largely black event being interpreted in black terms. From Harare I faxed to Eva at CCBI a press statement. Back home a week later I found muted interest. One church press officer asked if I was "really convinced about Nelson Mandela".

TOWARDS DECISION DAY 1994

There was however much to be done. Paul Renshaw was doing splendid work on the EMPSA programme and eventually by 1994 out of the international total of three hundred no fewer than forty-seven volunteers had been recruited and sent from Britain and Ireland. The programme was officially inaugurated in September 1993 by a visit of international Eminent Persons whom we farewelled from Heathrow, led by Sir Paul Reeves, former archbishop (and governor) of New Zealand and sometime Anglican Observer at the UN (where I had met him in 1991). All this of course signified the now decisive momentum towards the elections of April 1994 and EMPSA played a real part in helping to ensure that intimidation and violence did not hold sway. One EMPSA monitor was told by a South African Communist Party member: "We sometimes do not want to understand the other side, so the intervention of international monitors can sometimes achieve something that seems to have the touch of a miracle."[6]

At another level I had academic contact with the South African scene, as an external examiner for the successful doctoral theses of Louise Kretzschmar and Jim Harris.[7] Then at the end of January 1994 I was in South Africa again, first of all attending part of the WCC Central Committee meeting in Johannesburg (I served as proxy on the last two days for my fellow British Baptist John Briggs), and then in Cape Town

---

6. Quoted in Paul Renshaw, *The Touch of a Miracle? Report of the CCBI in the Ecumenical Monitoring Programmer in South Africa September 1992—May 1994*

7. Louise Kretzschmar's thesis was published as *Privatisation of the Christian Faith: Mission, Social Ethics and the South African Baptists* (Legon Theological Studies: Legon, Ghana, 1998). Jim Harris is now an Anglican priest involved in ordination training in the Western Cape.

where John de Gruchy had organized one of his theological summer schools for clergy and laypeople. John was capitalizing on the presence of international attendees at the WCC meeting as a source of speakers on the theme of ecumenism, so as well as Mary Tanner (Anglican), Elizabeth Welch (United Reformed) and myself from the UK, Konrad Raiser (WCC General Secretary) and Larry Rasmussen (Union Seminary, New York) joined the party to augment the input from a strong team of South African speakers. Larry Rasmussen and I stayed with the de Gruchys, and I was also able to spend time with John Daries again. He had taken two major decisions, as he explained in a letter written about this time under the heading "God and I Are Squatting":

> I've always known that the only way to really understand the experiences of people living in squatter conditions (informal housing as it is now called) is to become one. For this reason I have erected a shack in Die Bos, a squatter community near Somerset West. I have also severed my ties with the Baptist Church and joined the Anglican Communion. So what better place to test and see whether my call to the ministry is still valid. So I am living here, as a person of faith. The community of Die Bos is a very special community. Now I'll just be living here, as an ordinary person. Some of my experiences I'll be sharing with you, via these letters. All of my experiences I'll be sharing with God, through prayer, through argument and debate. After all . . . God and I are squatting.

John took me to Die Bos one afternoon. It was indeed a vibrant, welcoming community of about one hundred and fifty homes, with ninety-six children and led by a remarkable woman, Dinah Smith who acted as mayor. It needed, said John, a woman's passion to get the people together and energize the community's development in face of addictions of all kinds, water shortage and desperate needs of the children, bouts of violence, and harassment by the municipal administration. John was obviously regarded as the community's pastor. Worship services were held in the community room. Just recently he had taken the funeral of a man stabbed in a drunken brawl. Dinah had just come back from a meeting with Nelson Mandela in Parl. She was a woman of faith as well as energy: "Pray for us" she told me with a broad smile. This was a heart-warming visit and of some encouragement to John himself. John de Gruchy remarked a little while afterwards how important it was that concerned people from overseas should relate to and support such "little ventures" as well as the bigger and more publicized programs.

SOUTH AFRICAN PAIN AND JOY

At die Bos, Dinah Smith next to KC

After several days of high-level ecumenical deliberations and then the theological seminars in Cape Town it was a relief for Larry Rasmussen and me to get away with John and Isobel for a weekend at their country retreat at Vermaaklikeid, some one hundred and eighty miles south-east of Cape Town on the Indian Ocean coast, where the de Gruchy family had built themselves a thatched cottage close by the little Duiwenhoks River. Whenever I went to South Africa I always took my binoculars with me and had added quite a long list to my tally of birds identified, but bird-watching had always had to be in hurried moments between meetings or when travelling at speed along the highways. Now at last here was a whole weekend in a kind of Eden, with hours of relaxed walking, boating, and swimming. It was indeed an ornithological Paradise especially as there were so many raptors on display. Sitting around at a barbecue on the Saturday evening our conversation got round to that topic of perennial interest to visitors to Africa, snakes. "No, "said John, "they may be around but you won't see them."

"And talking of snakes . . . " .L. to R. Larry Rasmussen ,John de Gruchy, KC, Isobel de Gruchy

Next morning we were all swimming in the river, and as I was hauling myself out of the water I spotted a sinuous line of ripples advancing upstream towards us. It passed close by, a large Puff Adder. Apparently they don't strike when in the water, but we were glad to leave it to enjoy the river by itself. That afternoon we returned to Cape Town, I to be dropped off at the airport as I was to fly on to Durban. In the entrance foyer it was a nice surprise to find John Daries waiting for me, to wish me Godspeed and to pass on to me some further contact information. Had we but known it, it was our last farewell.

From Durban I was taken by car to the university town of Pietermaritzburg where I stayed two nights and met and talked with theologians much involved in contextual theology. My final day was spent in Durban where among other appointments I saw at first hand the work of the Diakonia organization in the squatter camps and also met a group of our EMPSA monitors from the UK. Not all were quite happy with the arrangements at the Durban end. Those who had had no previous Third World experience of any kind found conditions in the squatter camps emotionally hard to take on board at first. Being in Natal, where the threat of violence from the Inkatha movement was real, they had perhaps the toughest assignment of all. But overall they seemed resolute and cheerful. I called Paul Renshaw as soon as I was back home to give him some feedback but by then I was practically voiceless, having succumbed to that curse of long-haul flights, the fluey cold.

KEEPING WATCH

The South African elections were now a little over two months away, to be held on April 27. In CCBI we prepared information to brief our churches, and provided material commended by the CCBI Presidents for use in services and in prayer vigils on the very eve of the elections. This was much appreciated and widely used. In South Africa itself there were of course continuing anxieties about possible disruption, even violence, on the day or just before. I was annoyed by an article in the *Guardian* on April 11 by Gary Yonge, which described the assassination of Chris Hani the year before as having "unleashed violence that plunged South Africa into chaos at a delicate stage in the negotiating process". This was, as I have recounted earlier, quite untrue. I wrote to set the record straight and cited the political and church leaders who had ensured that chaos did *not* result. We could therefore pray in hope rather than just anxiety. The letter was published. The weekend before the elections it was my turn on the Saturday evening Ten to Ten devotional slot on BBC Radio 4 and of course I spoke about the elections and the fact that so many people in Britain and around the world would be watching with and praying for South Africa. A hymn was always included in the broadcast and for this one I had chosen the well-known "The day Thou gavest, Lord, is ended". Sometimes dismissed as a piece of imperialist-inspired Victorian sentiment, it is in fact a fine expression of belonging to the worldwide ecumenical community, and never before had I felt a hymn come alive with such fresh meaning as this one did as an accompaniment to our vigils for South Africa, above all in the verse that speaks of the church which, unsleeping around the clock, "Through all the world her watch is keeping/ And rests not now by day or night." Vigils were held throughout the day on April 26. In London the major focus was at St Martin-in-the Fields which so often during four decades of the anti-apartheid struggle had been a center of protest—the more so as it stands so close to the South African embassy which had often been provoked to anger by the demonstrations. That day, however, the ambassador himself came to join in the vigil, a marvelously fulfilling moment for all concerned. In the evening several of us CCBI staff were present in the church for the final few hours which would conclude at 11 pm British time, South Africa's midnight when her day of decision and destiny would begin. Few were present by now, all was quiet, the silence profound. With about half an hour to go, four black women came in and sat in one of the front pews. The final chime of eleven fading away, as one they rose and sang *Nkosi sikelele Afrika*. Past suffering, endurance and present hopes were gathered up and were greeted by the new day.

"I voted for the ANC," writes John de Gruchy, "which won by an overwhelming majority. But irrespective of who we voted for, we were all proudly South African."[8] Equally, many of us from outside were proud to have South African friends. Six months after the elections, Desmond Tutu paid one of his visits to London on a thank-you mission and preached in St Martin-in-the-Fields. His visit was short and he was

---

8. de Gruchy, *I Have Come a Long Way*, 188.

not entirely well, but I managed to secure an interview with him which I recorded so that parts could be transcribed for a leaflet for use in our CCBI Listening to Africa programme. He spoke about Europe needing to listen to Africa for Europe's own sake. "You have a culture where success is everything, where there is nothing worse than to fail", he said. He questioned our emphasis on "independence", as distinct from "interdependence": be prepared to *receive* from one another, and from God, was Africa's message; and, lowering his voice almost to a whisper which he typically does when making his most important points, "Give *grace* a chance". But of course he spoke specifically about South Africa too, and of the times of darkness into which the country seemed to fall during the long years of struggle, including that most recent tragedy of the death of Chris Hani. But when was it, I asked that he felt hope was going to win the day? He had no hesitation: when the great people's movement, the "Standing for the Truth"[9] campaign, was launched in 1988; that was when the people showed that they were unconquerable. And what about the threat of chaos? "Our God," he said, "is a God who knows all about chaos, from the story of creation through to the crucifixion. Ours is a death and resurrection faith."

I had good cause to remember those words a few months later, at the end of March 1995 when during the CCOM Africa Forum at the College of the Ascension in Birmingham a fax arrived for me from Wilma Jakobsen, Desmond Tutu's chaplain and a close friend of John Davies. John had died of a heart attack. "He spoke often of you," she said. I was able to call her and give a message to be read at his funeral. I recalled my memory of him in 1987 in Jordan, standing where Moses had stood on Mount Nebo, pointing towards the Promised Land. He had once told me how difficult he found it when watching the Olympic Games on TV, whenever the flags of the medal winners were hoisted above the podium, and he felt it hard not to weep because at that time there was no flag for his country that he could identify with. At least, he had seen the new day and the new flag, and his memory will always be inspiring and a source of hope.

CAPE TOWN 1996: REMEMBRANCE, SUFFERING AND HOPE

My fourth and final visit to South Africa during my time at CCBI was to Cape Town in January 1996, for the Seventh International Bonhoeffer Congress which I have already described[10]. Wilma Jakobsen was chaplain to the Congress. We found time to talk about John and she took me out his mother's home to meet her and other members of the family. The Congress itself of course was greatly in tune with its South African context.[11] We spent a memorable day on Robben Island, its prison now a kind of shrine (too sanitized say some) to the endurance of Nelson Mandela and the other long-term prisoners who had been held there. I brought back as a souvenir some

---

9. See above, chapter 7 p.
10. See above, chapter 8 p.187.
11. See de Gruchy (Ed.), *Bonhoeffer for a New Day*.

stones from the quarry in which they had been forced to labor. I also had with me a BBC tape-recorder and made interviews with a number of people Including Frank Chikane, Russel Botman and Bishop (soon to be Archbishop) Njongkulu Ndungane) who had been in the forefront of the struggle, and some younger people who were still struggling with issues of justice and reconciliation. Particularly memorable were a young Afrikaner and a colored man of similar age, who at first were finding it hard to talk to each other because of their contrasting backgrounds and experiences but were finding a way towards common ground. I also held the microphone up to contemporary theologians like Charles Villa-Vicencio and Denise Ackerman who were concerned that the church should urgently address the current scene.[12] But the highlight was the interview with the veteran Beyers Naudé for whom Bonhoeffer had been an inspiration and model since his pioneering days with the Christian Institute in the early 1960s. His most interesting comments were in response to my question about what, for him, had been the hardest aspects of the struggle. He said:

> I think what I found it hardest to cope with was the suffering which was created especially to innocent blacks in South Africa, especially the young people, who came to me, sometimes one by one, who shared with me the detention, the agony, the torture, and what they went through. And then I said to myself, especially when they were black and the people who inflicted on them were mostly, as I was, white, that I constantly said, "But God, why can't you let more whites suffer this way, so that the danger of the future racial conflict and the resurgence of a form of black racism, that that would be balanced in what was happening? It was not an easy time.[13]

It is important, I believe, that today under the heading of "the ending of apartheid" we do not forget or elide such experiences out of the story in a false triumphalism. It was so costly. But Naudé remained above all a witness to *hope*. He spoke about the *surprise* at the turn which events eventually took in 1989–90, about the need to be more humble in our assumptions about the ways God works in history: " . . . I constantly marvel at the way in which we believe we've got the wisdom, but that God creates a totally new situation, and out of what seemed the impossible comes a new and glorious reality. And this is to my mind, you know, also part of the gift of grace of God—what it means to be one of his children . . . "[14] One of my treasured recollections of the Congress is of Beyers Naudé standing on the quayside on Robben Island—laughing, seemingly at the miracle of it all. Yes, I look back on those South African experiences with hope.

---

12. The programs went out on Radio 4 on Sunday evenings in March 1996.
13. Clements, "An Interview", 169.
14. Ibid. 168.

13

China: A Return Home

ANY ENGAGEMENT IN INTERNATIONAL affairs must inevitably reckon with the largest country on earth, with well over a billion inhabitants and thereby about a fifth of humanity: a country moreover which is not only a major political and military player in its region but since the 1980s has seen an economic miracle of stupendous growth. Of all the major national and regional engagements during my time at CCBI, it was China which also touched me in the most personally challenging way. It was the land of my birth and the country which, as I have described earlier, while growing up in England I felt I was still mentally and emotionally living in, and in a real sense belonged to. In childhood that gave me a sense of privilege over friends and schoolfellows who only knew England. What is more, being part of the missionary story added a touch of glamour. When in the 1950s Alan Burgess's book *The Small Woman* made famous the English missionary Gladys Aylward (whom my father had known while training for the CIM in London), and Ingrid Bergmann in her starring role in the film *The Inn of the Sixth Happiness* made her more famous still, some of the kudos seemed to wash over oneself. But such innocence was eroded by what one learnt in later years: about the Western imperialist and commercial inroads into nineteenth-century century China, the iniquitous opium wars and the Treaty of Nanking, and the ways in which the massive missionary enterprise had largely followed, benefited from, and often been protected by, the gunboat. Still later, through studying missionary history, came the revelation that in the first half of the twentieth century many Chinese Christians themselves were resentful at the paternalism of the Western missionary presence which they saw as hindering the growth of a genuinely Chinese church. The missionary exodus which followed the Great Revolution was by no means wholly an expulsion by the wicked communists. In many cases the departure was encouraged by the Chinese Christians who viewed a continuing Western presence as a hindrance to their witness in the new situation. One had been told that, following the revolution, the patriotic Three-Self movement (for a self-supporting, self-governing and self-propagating church) was simply a front for the communist-controlled church while the "true church" was underground. Now it appeared it was not as simple as that. "Three-self" thinking in fact dated from such nineteenth century missionary pioneers in Asia as Henry Venn and Adoniram Judson. Then of course there was David Paton's sharp critique, born out of his own China experience, in his book *Christian Missions and the Judgment of God*. Hardly surprising, then, that I had grown to be somewhat ambivalent about owning my China missionary connection. As literally a child of the missionary movement in China, had I in fact been born out of a huge mistake? Was I fated to be a tiny, personal embodiment of the whole problem of being a Westerner faced with the guilt of generations of exploitation of Africa, Asia and Latin America?

RETURN TO GULIN?

In CCBI the Churches' Commission on Mission (CCOM) China Forum was a focus of much expertise, and resolved to send a study group to China in May 1994. I was invited to join the group along with three other CCBI/CCOM staff, Edmund Tang of the China desk who was largely responsible for planning the visit, John Reardon and Gill Paterson. John Pritchard, General Secretary if the Methodist Church Overseas Division and moderator of the China Forum, acted as leader. The group, lay and clergy, Anglican, Protestant and Catholic numbered fourteen in all, from all quarters of the British Isles. It included Tommy Murphy, an Irish Catholic missionary who had worked in Taiwan and with whom I shared a room for much of the trip. My presence in the group lent a particular opportunity—or challenge. The itinerary as planned by Edmund Tang, after our entry via Hong Kong, included several days in Sichuan province and the big question was whether this would include Gulin. Getting to my birthplace would be a prize not just for me but the whole group, since it would mean seeing a remote rural area largely closed to foreigners for over forty years. Edmund Tang did not want to build our hopes too high. For one thing the journey from Chongqing to Gulin would be two days of pretty tough travelling by road; for another, Gulin was in an area under the very strict thumb of local communist cadres, and special permission would have to be sought. We would not know for certain until we were in Hong Kong, at the earliest. As well as Chongqing, and elsewhere in Sichuan, we would be visiting Wuhan, Nanjing and Shanghai, beginning and concluding the whole experience in Hong Kong again.

During our two days in Hong Kong I was glad of the opportunity to see more of the territory than on my visit in 1990, and we had useful briefings on the situation of the churches in China, most notably by the missiologist Philip Wickerei, and on the Hong Kong scenario as 1997 approached. On the afternoon of May 7—my birthday—we were getting ready to leave for the airport when Edmund Tang brought us the news: we *did* have permission to go to Gulin! We landed at Chongqing in mid-evening. The officials at immigration were at first intrigued, and then delighted, to notice both my place and date of birth as given in my passport. The celebratory mood continued with our reception by our local hosts in the China Christian Council, for no sooner had we arrived at our hotel and sat down for our welcome meal than a massive birthday cake with candles arrived on the table. Next morning, a Sunday, I became conscious of another sense of welcome, of a slightly uncanny sort. We were taken by coach to an outlying small town, Beibei, to attend morning service there. One night about a week before the trip I had had a dream. I was standing in a bright green field, surrounded by mountains, and along the sides of the mountains ran parallel stripes of a pale gold color. The image was still vivid in my mind when I awoke, and I was puzzled because I couldn't recognize the scene nor ever recall seeing such mountains even in photographs. But on our way to Beibei we passed hills . . . just like those I had seen in my dream. The horizontal stripes, I was told, were wheat terraces. Had the bright green field of my dream been a rice paddy field? Had the dream resulted from some long-buried memory, prompted by excitement at imminent return to Sichuan, breaking surface in my subconscious?

ARRIVAL!

Our two days in Chongqing included some sight-seeing and visits to local churches and pastors there, and I was able to visit the site of the old CIM house where my parents had met and married in 1933 Then we set off south on the two hundred mile journey to Gulin, two bone-shaking and at times hair-raising days in a coach of uncertain temperament through spectacular mountain country, just as my father had described it—though for my parents and brothers in 1938 the same journey by junk and on foot had taken many days (and was far more perilous). Overnight we stopped in Luzhou, a town familiar to my parents, where we were hosted in the church for dinner, the members apologizing profusely for being able to provide a meal of "only" twelve courses. Next afternoon we arrived in a widening valley and there was Gulin, looking much as my parents described it (and perhaps as I half-consciously remembered?), a nondescript market town, buildings with grey cylindrical roof tiles, the river swishing slowly through, and a distant surrounding frieze of jagged mountain tops. In the somewhat run-down hotel we were warmly welcomed by the local Christian leader, Mr Yang and a small group of other Christians, together with a reception committee of Gulin County officials (we were of course to be well minded by the cadres). It was certainly a joyous encounter but we were eager for news of whatever church remained here and first it seemed disappointing. There were very few Christians left in Gulin itself and the church had been closed for many years on government orders. I was particularly sad to hear that Grace Yang, the woman who had taken over pastoral leadership of the church when my parents left, and from whom they had a last letter in 1949, had died only the previous year. Had the last living link of memory been broken? Not quite, Mr Yang's father, now very aged, was there too and his eyes began to light with recognition when I showed him our family photograph taken in 1943 when I was still a babe in arms. Not only so, but Mr Yang Junior presently recalled my father, known in Chinese as "Pastor Tsen". We were taken on a walk through the town, provoking much curiosity from the locals most of whom had never seen Westerners before. On the way back I, with Edmund Tang and a few others, was offered a diversion. Led by Mr Yang we

CHINA: A RETURN HOME

were taken off the main street, up a flight of steps through some recently rebuilt shops and apartments, to what remained of an old courtyard, set against a high stone wall at the back. This was it: the site of the compound into which my parents transferred in 1942 and set up a new church building, mission dispensary and their own home. Here is where I was born, to the joy of my parents, the puzzlement of Brian my next older brother, and the excitement of the villagers. Here is where I had been a stranger, and taken in. Now I was taken in again. Mrs Yang-lu, a young mother who occupied the house now standing closest to the old compound wall, was charming and invited me in. She, too, had been born on this site and was intrigued to hear my story and tell it in turn to her little boy Yang-li, also born there. So there we were, two nationalities, three generations in age for whom this spot on earth was uniquely special.

Home for all three of us

Back at the hotel came another surprise. Three elderly men, travel-stained and weary in their blue peasant clothes, were waiting to see us. They were Christians from

Part Three: International Affairs 1990–1997

the Miao tribespeople in the hills. Thanks to Mr Yang Junior, word had got around the area that we were coming and they had been walking seventy miles over three days to see us. This was humbling and moving beyond words. Clearly something extraordinary was happening. After our evening meal I was asked to lead a short meditation (with effusive thanks of course to the local officials who were keeping a watchful eye on proceedings). I thought nothing could be more appropriate than to refer to T.S., Eliot, about arriving home and knowing the place for the first time. Late that evening I sat alone on the balcony outside my room overlooking the river, listening to the crickets and frogs, the other sounds of Gulin settling down for the night, and fending off the mosquitoes. It must have been just like this on that other night fifty-one years before; and yes, close by, a baby's crying rose into the still, warm air. This was the place, with all its poverty and wartime dangers, where my parents had wanted to be and into which they were prepared to bring me too.

If that day had been remarkable, next day was even more so. My parents had often talked about Fuh-in-wan, about twenty miles from Gulin up in the hills. It had been a center for the mission among the Miao tribespeople, and every summer my parents would spend the hottest weeks of the year there and share in the annual convention for the Miao Christians. So that was where in infancy I had spent my first two summer holidays. On our way there in 1944 we had briefly been captured by brigands and only some quick-thinking arguments by my father had extricated us. Now, Mr Yang Junior, determined that our party should get to Fuh-in-wan, had spread the news around the Christian communities in the hills and persuaded the local officials to let us make the journey. It was even rougher than getting to Gulin. Twice on the deeply rutted road the bus had to disgorge us to walk for a mile at time. Finally we reached the footpath leading down the side of the mountain. As we descended single file we caught the distant sound of singing and the green bay of Fuh-in-wan opened between the forested slopes. We reached a little clutch of wooden buildings and a crowd of upwards of a hundred and fifty people of all ages, from little children to old people with creased, toil-worn faces. Many were wearing their beautifully embroidered Tibetan-style costumes. I was pushed forward to lead the way through a kind of guard of honor as they sang in Miao what we were informed was "Hallelujah! Jesus Christ is come again". This may not have done much for my modesty but it was the most moving welcome I have had ever experienced. Gathered from many miles around they had in fact been waiting for us for over twenty-four hours. After more than forty years since the last missionaries had left they were saying "We still belong together". Wide-eyed with curiosity they jostled around. As I talked to them about my parents' love for Fuh-in-wan. I produced the hand-sewn baby shoes and clothes given me in Gulin, the new-born child in their midst those many years ago (even one of the local officials was impressed, remarking of the quality of the clothes, "These would have been for a *very* important person!"). There was one heart-stopping moment when a message was relayed to me: "Your sister's grave is here!" It was a mistake, but no less moving for all that. For a child's grave was indeed there, that of Gladys Bird, child of another CIM couple, who had died in 1930 aged three, "The, loneliest grave in all the world", commented Tommy Murphy, deeply touched as we all were. Then came the inevitable banquet, after which we were all gathered in front of the old church building, now long since commandeered by the government as a school, for prayers and more singing. This was also a clear message to the local officials: as in many other parts of China we want our churches and meeting-places to be given back and re-opened.

"We still belong together."

So Fuh-in-wan was a place of poignant memory but also of hope. The faith which missionaries had brought was now that of the people themselves, else how could they have survived in such isolation and much oppression all those years, and still sing "Hallelujah" so joyfully? In Gulin the previous evening I had asked one of the three men who had come so far to see us, how they were able to share their faith and win new disciples. "Well," one of them said, "for example when a family is short of hands to get in the rice or wheat crop, Christians come and help them. People are impressed, and want to know why." We eventually took our leave with the air resounding to "God be with you till we meet again", sung in Miao. Many of them came with us up the steep mountain track. There were tears on both sides. One old lady, weeping, would not let go of one of the women in our party saying, "You have brought the grace of God to us", to which the only reply could be, "Today *you* have given the grace of God to *us*". In real meeting, grace abounds to all. Edmund Tang remarked to me. "We have seen a retrieval of the missionary history". Trudging back up that steep hillside

I mused, too, on the fact that notwithstanding all the severe question marks about the modern missionary story and its imperialist tie-ups, on the individual and local level it had also been one of selfless devotion and love to the point of sacrifice, and my parents had been part of that side of the story in poor, half-forgotten Gulin, ridden by opium and gangsterism on the ground and with Japanese planes often overhead. Our journey continued back to Chongqing via Luzhou, where next morning there was yet another surprise. Not only had our leave-taking from the local cadres in from Gulin and Fuh-in-wan been very friendly, but in Luzhou two officials badly wanted to meet with myself and Edmund Tang. One was the local director of the government Foreign Affairs Department, the other an ex-mayor of Luzhou whose father was from Gulin and a Christian, and who said he remembered my father and other missionaries. We had a very constructive talk about the problems facing the Christians in the area, and could only hope that it would bear fruit. A young pastor in Luzhou told me, "Now you too are a pastor of Gulin!"

A NEW PARTNERSHIP BECKONS

From Chongqing we cruised down the Yangtze, through the famous gorges, still then in their full grandeur before the great damming took effect, to Ichang where my parents had served their first term together. The great urban centers of Wuhan and Nanjing were our next destinations. At Wuhan we spent much time in the large and thriving theological seminary, and at a service for students I preached on John 12:24: "Unless a grain of wheat falls into the earth and dies. . . . ", reflecting on my parents' story and our experiences at Gulin and Fuh-in-wan. Chinese students, we found, were very deferential even in a small seminar, and somewhat reluctant to ask questions although among some there was a real interest in contemporary Western theology, especially at Nanjing. There we were hosted at a reception given by leaders of the China Christian Council and its President Bishop K.H. Ting, by any reckoning one of the outstanding Christian leaders of the twentieth century. In his little speech he made clear that China's Christians would forever be in debt to the missionary era and those who had brought the gospel. The "Three-Self" motto which had given so much offence to many Western Christians after 1949, was no longer a slogan of willful independence rejecting all outsiders, but was being re-thought as the basis for a new era of *partnership* in the gospel. But it had to be true partnership. Helpers from outside would be welcome, but only as co-workers with the Chinese churches with whom the initiative and leadership now lay. I felt that not only had I been able to retrieve and own my personal relation to the missionary story, but had witnessed a healing of a major historical wound, thanks to the grace and humility of the Chinese Christians.[1]

1. I have written elsewhere of this aspect of the visit to China in relation to Bonhoeffer's theology, in "Healing the Wound: A Return to China with Bonhoeffer". See Clements, The *Churches in Europe*, 61–68.

Next morning, John Pritchard, John Reardon, Edmund Tang and I were invited to have a private conversation with Bishop Ting and his colleague Dr Han Wenzao, in which we went further into these and other matters, in particular the recent government law om registration, on human rights and religious freedom, and relations between the CCC and regions and local areas. The most sensitive area of concern for us was that of human rights and religious freedom. Ting was wholly agreeable to churches and bodies outside China saying what they believed to be necessary about human rights but at the same time we had to recognize that the situation of the Chinese churches was that of a very small minority, between 1 and 2 % of the population and if they spoke in similar terms about human rights in general they would simply not be listened to—or would have things made more difficult for them. Their own approach was to work on specific cases of non-compliance by the authorities—especially at local level where the attitudes of officials could vary considerably from region to region— with the actual laws pertaining to religious activity. This contextualizing of the voice of the church—indeed a matter of "learning to speak"—I found very helpful. The social witness of the Chinese churches was indeed to be extended, but in ways that actually related to and could make a real difference in their situation.

We saw much else in China: the work of the Amity Foundation in Nanjing including its Bible-printing press in Nanjing; church-related training of nurses and doctors; and small-scale medical centers and rural development projects. We saw the phenomenal development of Shanghai rising before our eyes. In Shanghai too we attended a packed Sunday morning service. From my view in the gallery I estimated that 40% of the congregation were in the 25–35 age range. Chinese Christianity had a burgeoning younger membership but a still ageing leadership, which presented a growing challenge as the church faced a modernizing China.

GETTING THE PICTURE RIGHT

We had plenty to report on our return home. For my part I wrote substantial articles for the *Baptist Times* and *Tablet* and some smaller pieces for other journals, and having taken a tape-recorder with me on the trip wrote and presented three BBC Radio 4 programs, "The Sichuan Road". Six years later they were re-broadcast on BBC World Service. For the International Affairs Liaison Group and other interested parties I wrote a report on the implications of what we had seen for wider socio-political issues and the churches' approach to them: the sheer immensity of scale in all things Chinese; economic development; regional growth and rural poverty; China and the outside world; human rights and the churches. Some of us who had been on the visit took issue publicly with what we felt to be persistently distorted views of Christianity in China. Later in the summer the archbishop of Canterbury, George Carey, also visited China and on his return, having given positive impressions, provoked some controversy on his return when at a press conference he appeared to condone a ban on sending Bibles into China. The *Times* reported him as coming under fire from missionary circles who alleged that as his visit was under official sponsorship he would not have been allowed to visit the rural areas where most Christians live, with the implicit assumption that it was only the "unofficial" churches, i.e. those not in membership with the CCC, that represented true Christianity in China. I responded in a letter pointing out that as a child of China missionaries I too had been on a recent "official" visit and that as a group we had been allowed to visit my birthplace in one of the remotest rural areas and see for ourselves both the vitality and problems facing the Christian communities there, where both the registered churches of the CCC and unregistered groups were actively cooperating. I concluded:

> Any assumption of a sharp dichotomy between "official" and "unofficial" Christian groups does not do justice to the complex and changing reality of the Chinese religious scene, which forbids easy generalizations. It is, after all, little more than ten years since virtually *all* churches were still closed after the dark night of the Cultural Revolution. Western Christians, rightly concerned to help their Chinese counterparts, must beware of projecting on to them their own interests and even rivalries, which would promote a new divisiveness rather than the strengthening of Chinese Christianity as a whole. To do so would repeat some of the most unfortunate aspects of the missionary era.[2]

Alongside my letter was a pithy one from John Pritchard saying that Chinese Christians were making a better job of evangelism than we in Europe, that their church was growing by 10% a year and that they "need British missionaries like Chinese cuisine needs burger chains".

The main ecumenical reflection on the visit took place at the CCOM China Forum in October, with a careful allocation to different churches and organizations of the tasks that should be followed up, whether in the areas of development, sharing of resources in theological education, mission education at home, or whatever. I suggested, having floated the idea with Edmund Tang, that for the sake of raising wider awareness about China-related matters we should mount round table meetings on China which would attract a cross-section of people from varying specialisms and concerns but with a common interest in China, whether journalists, mission organization staff, political scientists or theologians, and anyone seeking ideas and information. This did indeed transpire, and during my remaining time at CCBI four such meetings took place in London: "China's Growth: implications for its neighbors" (November 1995); "Human Rights in China" (March 1996); "Hong Kong: its struggle for selfhood" (October 1996); and "Does China Need Development Aid? The role of NGOs" (March 1997). They were well attended and appreciated by specialists and generalists alike. It was a very satisfying expression of ecumenism under the new model. I could also imagine J. H. Oldham, ever seeking to bring together "the best minds" on important issues, watching and nodding in approval.

2. *Times* October 7, 1994.

HONG KONG: HAND-OVER TO THE FUTURE

The Round Table on Hong Kong was not an isolated sign of concern. One of the last pieces of international affairs work by the BCC in 1990 had been a high-level church delegation to the colony. Its report *Searching for Roots in China, Planting Roots in Hong Kong, Taking Root in Eternity* was one of the first publications issued by CCBI; and my very last act for CCBI was to farewell from Heathrow another delegation to Hong Kong in May 1997. I had used the opportunity of my own first visit there in 1990 to meet with leaders of the Hong Kong Christian Council and others concerned with the implications of the handback in 1997. In turn in CCBI we welcomed visitors from the Hong Kong churches, notably in May 1996, and in July that year I attended the BWA Council meetings in Hong Kong and used the opportunity, once again armed with a BBC tape recorder, to interview a number of Hong Kong church figures—Baptist, Methodist, Anglican and Catholic—on their views about what would happen after 1997 and the attitudes of the churches. Among the most concerned were Kwok Nai Wong, leader of the Hong Kong Christian Institute, Peter Cheung, secretary of the Catholic Institute for Religion and Society, and the Baptist ecumenical theologian Raymond Fung. I also interviewed some Buddhists. While there was a range of opinion on the dangers presented to Hong Kong society by the handover, the main concern was that the Hong Kong churches themselves were not sufficiently prepared to face the responsibilities presented by the coming changes and that too many Hong Kong Christians would be content to continue in their worship services and individualistic piety which would probably be tolerated by the authorities. Not entirely cynically, it might be argued that whatever the stated fears about ownership of Hong Kong passing to China, British colonial rule had in fact been a good preparation for living under the Beijing regime.

But the main message was nevertheless one of hope, hope born out of taking the widest and longest-term view of history possible. Kwok Nai Wong, having analyzed stringently the problems now facing Hong Kong and its churches, and the need to arouse the public at large, came down finally to insist that the future of Hong Kong and China lay in no human hands, but in God's. This resonated very much with what had long been the faith of Bishop Ting in Nanjing who, speaking of the devastatingly bleak years of the Cultural Revolution, could say:

> We were, to use and expression in King James' version of Hebrews, made a gazingstock both by reproaches and afflictions. But it was a great period for Christians and the church in all our powerlessness to win the quiet sympathy and good will of the people around. The Church in China is weak and powerless, but the gospel itself is strong and full of power.[3]

We had seen and heard that, too, at Gulin and Fuh-in-Wan.

---

3. Unpublished lecture. Cf also Ting, *A Chinese Contribution to Ecumenical Theology.*

14

Europe Calling

It was late one Friday afternoon in November 1995. I was at my CCBI desk trying to sort out my commitments for the following week (Africa Forum, Middle East Forum, Ecumenical Staff Association and the like) when I took a phone call from Keith Jones, deputy general secretary of the Baptist Union at Didcot. What he said was so unexpected that at first I couldn't quite grasp what he was saying: would I agree to the BU nominating me for the post of General Secretary of the Conference of European Churches (CEC)? I was totally taken aback. In the first place, while in principle I knew that I was unlikely to stay at CCBI forever and had from time to time toyed in imagination with future possibilities including other ecumenical organizations CEC, for all that I had had frequent dealings with Jean Fischer and his colleagues especially over Former Yugoslavia, had never featured on that horizon. Moreover, for some reason I was not even aware that Jean Fischer was about to retire. All I could do was express my surprise and instant misgivings, agreeing to mull it over and call him back in a few days, with no encouragement that I would be positive. Back home in Bristol that evening, with some bemusement I told Margaret about the phone call. To my surprise her reaction was, "Well, why not let it run and see what happens?" Misgivings notwithstanding—especially about the domestic upheaval that a move to Geneva would entail—I eventually decided to do so. After all, while I was in no hurry to leave CCBI where I was happily at work and where my contract had been renewed that year, I *would* eventually have to seek pastures new and couldn't assume that the when and where of this would come calmly and of my own choosing. Might the very unexpectedness of the suggestion coming from outside lend seriousness to the possibility of its being a *call* in the profounder sense? It is foolish of course to look for the hand of God too early in one's affairs; equally it can be disobedience to shut the door too early on a possibility simply because it is unexpected, unsought and somewhat discomfiting. On the more rational level I could see that this appointment would be an extension of my ministry consistent with all I had been doing thus far, and a sensible use of my accumulated experience as pastor, academic and ecumenical worker at many levels. The only way clarity would come would be to say "Yes", as I did to Keith Jones the following week, agreeing to the BU submitting my C.V. to the CEC powers-that-be and so set the process in motion with no expectations as to the outcome in the New Year.

THE WHEELS TURN... AND SLOW DOWN

In February I received a fax from Professor Alexandros Papaderos, chair of the CEC search committee, informing me that I had been shortlisted for the post and inviting me to be interviewed. Things were now looking serious. I talked with friends and colleagues who knew CEC well such as John Arnold, dean of Durham Cathedral and at that time President of CEC, and Rachel Stephens who was on its Central Committee, and dug deep into the recent reports and literature produced by CEC. I had of course known in general terms about its history: how it had originated as an offshoot of the WCC (with a Welsh Baptist, Glen Garfield Williams as its first general secretary) during the late 1950s as a bridge between the churches of East and West. In divided Cold War Europe this gave it its main *raison d'être* at that time. Now in the post-1990, rapidly changing Europe its agenda likewise was changing and expanding, covering theological dialogue, human rights, social and diaconal work, women's issues and the environment; and with the growth of the European Union the relationship between CEC and the European Ecumenical Commission on Church and Society (EECCS), based in Brussels, was now of prime concern with discussions underway on an integration of the two bodies. With CEC now numbering some one hundred and twenty member churches—Anglican, Protestant, Old Catholic and Orthodox—right across Europe there was lively debate about what the regional ecumenical organization should now be and how it should work. European ecumenism was therefore in for an exciting if unsettling time.

In the paper I was asked to submit to the search committee I tried to show my awareness of these challenges and to state my convictions of the priorities for CEC in the coming years. The interviews took place in late May in a secluded villa near Salzburg belonging to the family of Roland Siegrist, a member of the committee and Director of the Austrian Red Cross. It was a very friendly and hospitable occasion. There were two other short-listed candidates, a Danish Lutheran and an Orthodox priest of the Ecumenical Patriarchate. I was perfectly satisfied with the whole occasion including the interview itself. But the CEC Central Committee meeting at Bossey soon afterwards could not come to a decision, which would have to be delayed until its next meeting early in 1997. So began six months of extreme uncertainty and frustration, barely relieved by hints now and then that "it's really all very positive". More relieving that summer were the interesting travels to Hong Kong for the BWA Council meeting, and to Tanzania for the Faith and Order Commission meeting in Moshi, and above all our wonderful holiday with Elizabeth Salter in her mountainside house at Doucy-en-Bauges in the Haute Savoie. From there we made a day visit to Geneva so that Margaret could at least see the Ecumenical Centre and meet some of my friends there.

PART THREE: INTERNATIONAL AFFAIRS 1990-1997

Elizabeth Salter

In fact, so far as I could gather the problem was less about the merits or otherwise of us three candidates as individuals, than about inter-confessional (and maybe intra-confessional) politics, and had I known all that was going on in the Central Committee I might have been tempted to withdraw. As it was, another approach was made to me during the summer with regard to the vacant post of director of the Ecumenical Institute at Bossey. This would have attractions if the CEC process ran aground completely. I let my name go forward and was in fact short-listed in December. Those weeks were made no easier by Margaret having to go into hospital for a hysterectomy. But very soon after the Bossey short-listing came the call from Alexandros Papaderos: mine would definitely be the sole name brought to the CEC Central Committee at its meeting in Geneva early in January. So I presented myself for interview by the whole Central Committee. The only fierce questioning came from one of the Orthodox bishops who wanted my assurance that I would "condemn proselytizing by Protestants". By a large majority I was elected. Next day I attended for the remaining business of the Central Committee and was presented to the public at a press conference next morning.

IN TRANSITION

So it had all become real. I was committed, excited, yet somewhat nervous and not knowing quite was in store, just as at all the other major passage-points of life. The big difference this time of course was that I really would be in charge of an organization, accountable to its governing body but with overall responsible for its direction and implementation of its policies. What would this mean for me? More important was the process of induction into the current CEC scene itself. In late February I attended the meeting of the Presidium (effectively the executive of the Central Committee) at Sigtuna, Sweden and so got a feel for the preparations being made both for the Second European Ecumenical Assembly and the CEC Assembly to take place in Graz, Austria in just four months' time. Soon after, I participated in a weekend consultation at Celakovice, near Prague, on religious freedom and state law. At the end of March Margaret and I visited Geneva where for the first time I met all the executive staff of CEC and those of EECCS too, now in serious discussion on the means of integration of the two bodies. We also prospected in preliminary fashion for a place to live and tried to get more idea of the practicalities of living in Geneva, although for the present at least Margaret would keep her lecturing job at UWE and we would retain our house in Bristol. These weeks were more than somewhat stressful for Margaret, still recovering from her recent surgery, and with her mother now close to death in Newcastle-upon-Tyne. She died at the beginning of April. Just before the funeral we both went to Graz for a weekend where with help from CEC staff I was brought a little more up to speed on what would be happening there in the events in July. All this was good and necessary but I still felt very much the new boy.

Meanwhile there was a leave-taking from CCBI to be gone through. It proved quite a wrench to leave people with whom I had worked so closely over seven years, especially such as Eva Kisitu who had been such a part of my work. It was gratifying and encouraging to find that despite all the question marks over the "new method" of working in CCBI, our international affairs work was truly appreciated. My final meeting of the International Affairs Liaison Group was a residential twenty-four hours session at Coleg Trefeca in Wales which included a review of the previous seven years. One person commented that we had been able to do so much because I "had not quite kept to the rules" laid down for Coordinating Secretaries. I would interpret this as saying that I had not *broken* the rules, but had done a little more than they required. Certainly I had sought to work in a basically coordinating way but also making my own contribution through writing and involvement in visits and travels. Formally, I would not start at CEC until September but CCBI generously allowed me sabbatical level from the beginning of May in order to work intensively on the biography of J. H. Oldham. So effectively I left CCBI at the end of April, farewelled with a big lunchtime party at Inter-Church House, following straight on from a final, truncated meeting of my Support Group, and attended by friends and colleagues across the whole range of CCBI churches and related organizations. Margaret and Peter were able to be there as well. I was presented with a large briefcase, a small CD-player and a selection of classical CDs. In other words I was expected both to work and to go on enjoying the good things of life. There was also an enormous card, signed by scores of well-wishers including Cardinal Hume, and carrying some elegant turns of phrase like Sergei Hackel's "For lack of cloning facilities, they have to hold on to you, not we. For all that, their gain is our common gain, and we take pleasure in that"; and some nuggets of wisdom like Martin Conway's "And when they come in twenty-seven languages . . . ! Here's wishing you good colleagues, an untroubled digestion, with courage in face of challenges and the faith that moves mountains—for starters: the rest will be given on the pilgrimage". There had also come—and continued for much of the year—a welter of well-wishing letters not only from Britain but from around the world, including from the Ecumenical Patriarch Bartholomew and Patriarch Alexei of the Russian Orthodox Church, and from many who were old friends and just as many who would soon be new friends and colleagues. More than one said that they thought the whole of my previous experience had been leading up to this appointment.

For the sabbatical period the CCBI International Affairs desk was occupied most ably by Rachel Stephens of the Methodist Church, the financing of the arrangement being secured from the fund raised in Edinburgh for the Oldham project as a whole. Working at home and helped by further time in the library at New College Edinburgh, the British Library and the Selly Oak Colleges library I was indeed able to break the back of the most complex and demanding section of the Oldham life, namely his work on Africa in the 1920s. Right at the start of the sabbatical, however, came another rewarding event. Bristol University had a scheme whereby people who had taught part-time in any of its departments could submit for the PhD on the basis of their published works. This I did, and on May 2 (the day after Tony Blair's landslide election victory) was examined orally by Rowan Williams and Duncan Forrester, and was duly awarded the doctorate. Three weeks later it was nice to be greeted as "Dr Clements" by John Arnold in Canterbury Cathedral where on behalf of CEC Margaret and I attended the service marking the fourteen-hundredth anniversary of the arrival of St Augustine in England. I was seated immediately behind Prince Charles in the nave. Margaret was placed among the wives of bishops and deans somewhere in the choir. Beforehand we had been amused by the directives enjoining Anglican clergy of whatever rank to wear only "choir habit", presumably to prevent *manqué* popes, cardinals, and heads of orders from over-indulging themselves sartorially. Margaret reckoned afterwards that the millinery of the spouses more than compensated for this discipline.

THE GRAZ ASSEMBLIES: AN INDUCTION

I flew to Graz on June 21 for the Second European Ecumenical Assembly (EEA2), which opened two days later. This together with the Eleventh CEC Assembly which followed immediately was my real induction experience. Like its predecessor at Basel in 1989, the Graz EEA2 was a genuinely pan-European venture and, sponsored jointly by CEC and CCEE, a fully interconfessional event. But whereas Basel had taken place just on the eve of the fall of the Iron Curtain and had celebrated its theme "Peace with Justice" as a *hope* for change in Europe, Graz was celebrating the fruit of the changes that had come about in 1989–90. That was evident in that so many of the 10,000 participants had been able to travel freely from eastern Europe—fifteen hundred came from Romania alone by train—in their own right and not just being represented by the officially sanctioned few. It was, in the words of former WCC general secretary Philip Potter, genuinely a people's gathering. In its combination of colorful and creative worship, multitudinous workshops, seminars and plenary debates all taking place in the Graz exhibition park it had something of the atmosphere of a Kirchentag. At the same time not all that had happened since Basel was cause for celebration. The disasters of Former Yugoslavia for example had wounded the hopes enlivened at Basel, hence the significance of the headline theme at Graz: "Reconciliation-Gift of God and Source of New Life." Nor was it all about Europe, but about Europe and the wider world. On the opening day in the registration area I bumped into my South African Baptist friend Reuben Richards. Asking what he was doing here I got the reply, "Telling you guys about reconciliation!" He was now working with Desmond Tutu on the Truth and Reconciliation Commission. Many church leaders were there including archbishop of Canterbury George Carey. Plenary addresses were given by Chiara Lubich, famous founder of the ecumenical and renewal Focolari Movement, head of the Armenian Church Katholicos Karekin I and Brigalia Bam, current general secretary of the South African Council of Churches. But unlike a Kirchentag, the EEA2 aimed to be more than study, debate and celebration. It aimed to set out definite commitments and guidelines for action by the European churches for their united life and action on the issues of the hour, especially peace, economic justice, human rights and the environment. This proved more difficult. It was not as though everyone was starting from scratch, since from months before the actual meeting all churches and participants had been able to study a preparatory document on the issues. But it was the near-impossible task of the various drafting committees to shape and hone down the welter of proposals (or demands) into concrete recommendations which, after debate in plenary could find consensus among the seven hundred official delegates of CEC and CCEE. Some issues proved controversial, especially that of the role of women both in church and in society. There were also some underlying reservations on the Roman Catholic side on what kind of status any pronouncements by the Assembly could have (the Vatican was keeping track of the outcomes rather anxiously).. The final message of the Assembly was positive in its affirmation of united witness by the churches in all the fields of concern that were challenging peace, justice and human rights.

I greatly enjoyed the EEA2, being helped in this by having hardly anything to do except attend whatever I liked turn up as a guest at formal and informal receptions with church dignitaries and Austrian government figures and, for most of the time, simply talk with people who wanted to meet the next general secretary of CEC, and gave a number of press and media interviews. Within the (relatively large) goldfish bowl of ecumenism I found myself for a time a kind of celebrity. One WCC staff member of Middle East background addressed me, in all seriousness, as "Your excellency". It was a time of being among friends old and new. The Assembly concluded on Sunday morning June 30 with an outdoor service of thanksgiving and commitment, culminating spontaneously in a riotous, dancing rendition of the American traditional sung "Amen!"

The CEC Assembly which followed was of course smaller in numbers and low key by comparison. Much of the six days was occupied with the formal business of setting up the new CEC Central Committee and various other statutory groups, which gave me an eye-opener into the political machinations of different confessions seeking to maintain, or enhance, their power in the governing bodies. I had however a particular assignment having been asked to be on the Policy Reference Committee, which had the task of bringing recommendations to the plenary Assembly on future priorities and directions for CEC arising from sections of the Assembly. In fact much of this process was really a continuation of the outcomes of the EEA2 but now to be interpreted as the agenda for CEC over the next six years. It was therefore another stage in giving me ideas and a feel for what my responsibilities would soon be. It also meant experiencing long late-night sessions arguing over wording of resolutions, such as I had met before in Faith and Order meetings but never quite so intensely as here. As incoming general secretary I was also presented to the Assembly and gave a short presentation on who I was, where I had come from and what I was expecting. In face of varying pieces of partisan advice I flagged up that I was not interested in narrowing CEC's inclusive vision of its mission into either the purely socio-political or the internal ecclesiastical and "spiritual" area. But I did speak about the spirituality which was needed to undergird all our work, and concluded with yet another reference to my baptismal hymn and its final verse:

> Be our strength in hours of weakness,
>   in our wanderings be our guide;
> through endeavor, failure, danger,
>   Father, be there at our side.

Margaret and I flew out to Geneva in late August. Our domestic pad there for the first eighteen months was a very small ground-floor flat in chemin Francois-Lehmann, a few minutes' walk from the Ecumenical Centre. Such household items as we were transferring to Geneva, and most of my books, arrived by road transport soon after. On August 31 Margaret flew back to England. Next day I was at the CEC General Secretary's desk of CEC. A new life had begun.

PART FOUR

Ecumenical Europe 1997–2005

CEC Assembly, Trondheim, Norway 2003

15

Making Home in Geneva—and All Europe

"Welcome to the menagerie!" is how Philip Potter, general secretary of the WCC for twelve years up to 1984, used to welcome new staff or visitors to the Ecumenical Centre in Geneva. It was still an appropriate greeting in 1997. This collection of conjoined rectangular 1960s buildings, set in pleasant flowered and shrubberied grounds conveniently close to the airport and barely two kilometers short of Geneva's northern border with France, was the daily workplace for scores of people of widely diverse nationalities, mother-tongues, ages, and of course Christian confessions—not to mention personality and temperament. The largest presence was that of the WCC itself but closely followed by the Lutheran World Federation (LWF). CEC shared a second-floor corridor in the "Jura" wing with the World Alliance of Reformed Churches (WARC)[1]. A number of much smaller agencies and organizations working under the ecumenical umbrella also had their offices in the Centre, as did international representatives of the Russian Orthodox Church, the Ecumenical Patriarchate and the World Methodist Council. It all made for a stimulating and enriching environment in which to work, especially as staff in the different organizations had many interests and concerns in common, with information, ideas, and insights to share in the overall ecumenical task. Close by, the imposing presences of such UN-related bodies as the World Health Organization and the International Labor Organization added to the internationalist ethos, not forgetting the fact that the ILO also had a very good restaurant, at that time open to the public, which offered a more relaxed and intimate ambience than the Ecumenical Centre cafeteria when entertaining distinguished visitors (or at any rate those whom one wished to impress).

VISION AND REALITY

Sometimes in my early days in Geneva I was asked about my "vision" for CEC. In one sense I could say little more than what was already, and to my mind very clearly, set out in the preamble to its Constitution which stressed the common confession of Christ, the

---

1. In 2010 WARC united with the Reformed Ecumenical Council to form the World Communion of Reformed Churches.

quest for visible unity through conciliar fellowship, commitment to the wellbeing of all humankind, the renewal of spiritual life, and peace in the world. But of course one also had to say that this foundational vision had to focus on the particular challenges and opportunities now facing Europe and its churches, summed up in the key-word of the assemblies at Graz in 1997: reconciliation. In Europe the Cold War was long over but the continent remained divided between relative affluence and poverty, much of it along the old East-West lines. Violent conflict was still simmering in the Balkans. All over Europe minority communities such as Roma, Sinti and Sami were still subject to discrimination and marginalization, as were refugees and uprooted peoples generally. Both in society at large and in the churches themselves the role of women still needed recognition and affirmation. The likely enlargement of the European Union would bring new stability but also new challenges especially on its eastern frontiers. The churches themselves, meanwhile, still had a long, long way to go among the path of visible unity before they could justly claim to be both a reconciled and reconciling community. I therefore had to say that my vision focused on a willingness to be *changed* by engaging with these challenges. At the opening service of the first meeting of the new CEC Central Committee in Morges, near Lausanne, in November 1997 I preached on the story of the risen Jesus' conversation with Simon Peter by the lakeside, focusing on his words: "Simon, Son of John, do you love me?" (John 21:15–22). It was one thing to say, as was said at Graz, that reconciliation is the gift of God and source of new life; but the love seen in Christ, who washes feet like a servant and whose love is consummated on a cross, is to be seen in a community motivated by that same love, and that will be costly.[2] Moreover, I concluded, Jesus' remark "What is that to you?" in response to Peter's question about the "other disciple", had a special relevance when it came to the work of the Central Committee itself. "Some will be elected to particular, prominent positions. Others will not. But what is that to us? All of us matter."

This was said in all innocence. A few hours later such idealism received a severe jolt. One of the first tasks of the committee was to elect from its forty members the new President, Vice-President and Deputy Vice-President. It was accepted practice for the presidency to rotate around the Protestant, Anglican and Orthodox traditions. It was now the turn of the Orthodox, and there was widespread consensus that the ideal candidate would be the Romanian Metropolitan Daniel of Iasi, who had had long involvement in the ecumenical movement (in fact for some time on the staff of the Bossey Ecumenical Institute). At the Graz Assembly, indeed, he had made an outstandingly eirenic gesture during the fraught process of elections to the new Central Committee, beset as always by the need to meet the quotas of confession, age, gender and region in order to arrive at the most balanced representation overall. In order to allow a more just tally of minority churches and youth, Daniel moved to cede the second place allocated to his own Romanian Church in favor of a young Romanian Lutheran pastor, Elfriede Dörr. This was warmly welcomed by the assembly overall, but not by a number of other

---

2. Sermon "Called by Name—To Be More than Ourselves" in *The Churches in Europe*, 23.

Orthodox especially the Russians who were infuriated at what they saw as confessional disloyalty. At Morges the displeasure of the three Russian Orthodox members was made very evident (they were clearly under orders from Moscow) and they gave notice they would simply not accept Daniel as President. Other Orthodox were embarrassed. Phone calls were made to Moscow but the Russians made clear that grave implications might follow if their views were overridden: not that this would precipitate the Russian Church leaving CEC but that it might add to their case for an eventual withdrawal later. After a long, late-night session of the nominations committee I had the task of rousing Daniel from his bed and explaining the situation to him. With a mixture of irritation and amusement he accepted the news with good grace. A day or two later when the committee transferred to Geneva for the day, he led the morning meditation in the Ecumenical Centre chapel on the theme of saintliness, making the point that according to Orthodox tradition the supreme sign of saintliness is *joy*, and throughout the next six years he was a most loyal and supportive member of the Central Committee. In his stead, Metropolitan Jérémie Caligiorlis, representative of the Ecumenical Patriarchate in Paris, was elected President. *Oberkirchenrätin* Rut Rohrandt of the Evangelical Church of German (EKD) and Professor Jean-Marc Prieur of the University of Strasbourg were elected Vice-President and Deputy Vice-President respectively. And the Russian Orthodox stayed on board.

GENEVA TEAM, EUROPEAN TRAVELS AND GENEVAN HOME

This one incident and its workable if not ideal resolution gives a flavor of much of what it was like to be General Secretary of CEC: keeping the boat moving in the right direction despite all the buffetings without and within. But to be general secretary of CEC was to be part of, and to lead, a team. At that time the executive staff in Geneva in addition to the General Secretary comprised six highly able and committed people. Hans Schmocker, Secretary for Finance and Administration, had worked most of his life in international and church organizations concerned with social care and development and was still of indefatigable energy. He was a native of Schaffhausen in northern Switzerland and it was always a delight to overhear him whenever on the phone to someone of similar background he lapsed into the lilting *Schweizerdeutsch* dialect; and no less endearing to many was his flute, his constant travelling companion all over Europe. Robin Gurney, an English Methodist, was Communications Secretary who had worked in journalism in England and also had had a spell with the WCC. It is odd to recall that at the time of my arrival email was only just coming into general use, and Robin had the task of upgrading all our computers (and ourselves) to cope with this. Viorel Ionita, Romanian Orthodox priest and professor of the Orthodox Faculty of Theology in Bucharest, was Study Secretary and brought a solid theological mind to bear on all our work. Rüdiger Noll, a pastor of the EKD, ever-energetic (he had been a professional basketball player a few years before) was Secretary for Peace, Justice and Human Rights and had been heavily involved in the EEA2 programming at Graz. Irja Askola, a pastor of the (Lutheran) Church of Finland, covered both Inter-Church Service and the desk for the Decade of Churches in Solidarity with Women. Her cheerful demeanor and positive attitude in all things were in clearest contradiction to the stereotypes of Baltic gloom. John Taylor, English, a specialist in interfaith relations and formerly secretary-general of the World Conference on Religion and Peace served as consultant and Associate Secretary for Inter-Church Service. He had been responsible for much of the work on reconciliation in Former Yugoslavia, together with servicing the European Churches Working Group on Asylum and Refugees (ECWGAR). One of the first things I did was to arrange a twenty-four hour residential retreat for the executive staff in a house up on the Salève just over the French border, to enable us all to get to know one another better, how we saw our work, and what had led us to ecumenical activity in the first place. One interesting feature that we discovered we had in common as we shared our life-histories was that each of us had experienced some kind of upheaval or deprivation in early childhood. This was a great team but in turn none of us could have worked without our administrative and support staff. My PA Françoise Maxian, Austrian born, whom I inherited from Jean Fischer, had an enormously important role not only as far as my secretarial help was concerned but in seeing to much of the organizing of meetings of the Central Committee and Presidium, and dealing with all sorts of queries—sensible or otherwise—from church leaders and others wanting information on this or that. On the 'phone she was the human voice of CEC.

That was all the more important as so much of my time was spent travelling. As well as the governing bodies of CEC (Central Committee and Presidium) the General Secretary had to attend meetings of the various committees, commissions and working groups which might be held anywhere from Barcelona to Moscow, not to mention meetings of associated ecumenical organizations and synods or assemblies of member churches. There were many and varied invitations to preach or lecture, and a good number of these presentations were collected and appeared in my book *The European Churches as Witnesses to Healing*. In the course of my eight years I visited at least once every European country apart from Malta, Latvia, Slovenia, Ukraine and the Asiatic republics of the former USSR. I would return laden with souvenirs presented to me, especially from the Orthodox world, and my shelves were soon replete with icons and medals and ornaments of all kinds. On one occasion I had deliberately flown to Transylvania with only minimal hand baggage in order to save precious time at the airports—only to find myself presented with an enormous facsimile edition of a seventeenth-century century Bible. But such visits, I believed, were as much pastoral as bureaucratic. At the WCC Assembly in Harare in 1998, a worker from the Ecumenical Humanitarian Association in beleaguered Vojvodina came up to me and said simply, *"You came!"* In fact one was always operating on several levels at once. There was the ongoing administrative work in Geneva and staff affairs to be seen to. There was what I would call the creative and developmental aspect, the thinking ahead to what further issues would need to be addressed and what new projects might be developed. And there were the unexpected and often unwanted crises requiring some kind of emergency response—which might turn into new opportunities for CEC to fulfil its mandate. All this added to the intensity of life, and ensured that it was indeed *life* and not mere existence: never entirely free of friction or tension (and just on occasion seemingly at breaking point) but for that very reason always generative of new possibilities.

Such an intensely active life required some kind of still point, or at least counterpoint of relaxation and refreshment. This was admittedly not easy. There was obviously no normal sort of home life with Margaret being in Bristol but we did our best to meet up either there or in Geneva fairly often. For me the National Liberal Club in London made a convenient place for stop-overs or small meetings while transiting through London. Life became much easier once Easyjet started a Bristol-Geneva service. Holidays became even more precious, and Margaret was able to get out for a few weeks at a time during her university summer vacations. Robin Gurney and his wife Ruth had a small apartment on the French Mediterranean coast at Argelès-sur-Mer just south of Perpignan which we, as other CEC staff, made welcome use of several times. Each Easter we would also head off south into France for a few days in the valleys and gorges south-east of Grenoble. But nor did we neglect the Lake District and Scotland during the summer. Geneva itself afforded three main blessings contributing to our sense of home there. One was the larger, sixth floor flat in Chemin Taverney which with the help of Hans Schmocker we found and rented from January 1999. To the south it gave us splendid views to the Alps (to watch Mont Blanc turn pink with the rising sun was a regular breakfast treat) and to the north across the airport the skyline was commanded by the Jura. It was ideal for entertaining, and for putting up visiting family and friends. As with the first flat, it was in Grand-Saconnex and therefore conveniently close to the Ecumenical Centre and the airport. The second blessing was the English-speaking Lutheran Church which met in the old city of Geneva and which we soon joined. Its pastor was the Canadian Stephen Larson and its worship, following the order of the Evangelical Lutheran Church of America, was very much to our taste, combining as it did the regular eucharistic liturgy with a great deal of creativity especially in the music which was under the imaginative direction of Terry Macarthur of the WCC. The congregation was a real mix of people either Anglophone or for whom English was second-language (including Japanese, Indonesian, Indian and various Europeans). While English predominated, it was instructive also to have to sing the Agnus Dei in Arabic, or the Sanctus in Portuguese, or to learn a hymn with African speech-rhythms. Third, there were friendships, too numerous to detail, made with others in the Ecumenical Centre. Geneva for both of us did become a home, with its music, theatre and surrounding scenery as extra bonuses.

16

Hopes versus Disappointments: Towards the New Millennium 1997–2000

THE UPSET OVER THE Orthodox nominee for the presidency notwithstanding, the meeting of the CEC Central Committee at Morges in November 1997 did good work. The Graz Assembly had recommended that much of CEC's work be organized through three commissions, respectively on Dialogue, Church and Society, and Solidarity. Central Committee endorsed this decision and appointed membership of the commissions from names proposed by the member churches. The largest commission would be that on Church and Society in view of the impending integration of CEC and the European Ecumenical Commission on Church and Society (EECCS), with ten people to be appointed by CEC and ten by EECCS as presently constituted. The appointment of the Solidarity Commission proved more problematic because the very concept of such a commission, covering as it did diverse forms of diaconic work and inter-church service, remained unclear. It was therefore called an "Interim Commission on Solidarity", to which nine persons were appointed. Appointments were also made to the various statutory committees dealing with finance, personnel and so on. All bread and butter work, but essential. One quickly learned that people could arrive on a Central Committee with all manner of motivations and understanding of their role. Some were seasoned ecumenical veterans like John Arnold, now discharged from his CEC presidency but ever the wise and diplomatic counsellor for whom I was eternally grateful; or his contemporary from ecumenical student work-camp days in the 1950s, Alexandros Papaderos who was as deeply devoted to CEC as to his Orthodox Church and, having chaired the committee which nominated me for the general secretaryship, continued to regard me as his protégé. By and large Central Committee members grew into their proper roles, and most valuable were those who in discussion presented appropriately the perspectives of their own church and region but who also back in their own churches would determinedly argue the ecumenical case—and not least for the funding of CEC. It is invidious to mention particular names, but outstanding examples were people like Antje Heider-Rottwilm of the EKD and Margarethe Isberg of the Church of Sweden. In addition, this Central Committee as elected at Graz met the requisite youth quota with a clutch of very committed and enthusiastic younger women and men.

At CEC Central Committee, Iasi, 2000. L. to R. Hana Tonzarova, Isabel Best (foreground), Metropolitan Daniel, KC, Metropolitan Jérémie Caligiorlis, Professor Jean-Marc Prieur, *Oberkirchenrätin* **Rut Rohrandt**.

THREE PATRIARCHS

If my first few months at CEC meant a welter of organizational and administrative work this did not exclude the relational side of the job, especially as regards the Orthodox world. In September I went with Jean Fischer to Serbia as he wished to take his leave of Patriarch Pavle and also of Bishop Irenij of Novi Sad. Our meeting with Pavle was cordial and he was much as I had found him in 1993: acknowledging criticism of the Serbian Orthodox Church but saying "We Serbs had to defend ourselves" and that no side was without guilt. He assured us he valued the fellowship of CEC and agreed that mutual love meant being open to one another and listening to each other. We met with Bishop Irenij and two Reformed Church leaders at Novi Sad in the evening. I went on from Belgrade to Novi Vinodolski on the Dalmatian coast of Croatia where the European Baptist Federation was having its annual council meeting. Then, at the end of November, I went with Jean Fischer and Father George Tetsis (the Ecumenical Patriarchate representative in Geneva) to Istanbul to be formally introduced to the Ecumenical Patriarch, Bartholomew whom in fact I had met in his pre-Patriarchal days in the Faith and Order Commission. It was a friendly and gracious meeting. A week later one was made aware just how precarious was the situation of the Patriarch in Istanbul when there was a bomb attack on his residence.

Third, in late January Metropolitan Jérémie and I went to Moscow to pay our respects to the head of the Russian Orthodox Church, His Holiness Patriarch Alexei, and to meet other church leaders. We were there over a long weekend, with abundant hospitality (vodka and champagne flowed freely) which was as well as it was bitterly cold weather. We had extensive talks with members of the Church's Department for External Affairs, including Father Hilarion Alfayev and Archbishop Vladyk Longin of Klin, a member of CEC Central Committee. The matter of the CEC Presidency seemed forgotten. We learnt (and saw) a lot about the problems of present-day Russian society and of how the Church was trying to cope with them pastorally and educationally. I visited the Moscow Baptists and was warmly received. It was evident that the leadership wished to remain in CEC. But, with the dismemberment of the previous All-Union Council of Evangelical Christians-Baptists into separate, mainly regional, groupings, it was not clear just who could now represent Russian Baptists in CEC and that would have to be a debate among themselves. I was invited to preach in the Central Baptist Church at their Saturday 5.00 pm service. I did so, perforce extemporaneously as in 1987, on the text Romans 8:26: "The Spirit helps us in our weakness" (or at any rate it was from memory—the previous Sunday I had preached on this text in the Scottish Church in Geneva for the Week of Prayer for Christian Unity, so it was still fresh in my mind). The congregation was smaller than in 1987, and for good reason. As the Baptist pastors told me, since the big changes of 1989–91 there had been genuine liberalization of religion and so several new Baptist churches had been opened in and around the city. From there it was culture-change as I joined Jérémie, Longin and other guests at the Bolshoi Theatre for a performance of the opera *A Bride for the Tsar*. Next morning, Sunday, came what was for me the highlight of the weekend, the Divine Liturgy in the Church of the Domitian in the Kremlin, celebrated by Patriarch Alexei himself. Here was my dream and prayer of 1987[1] fulfilled: what had then been a silent, empty museum was now thronged with worshippers, clouds of incense, the sonorous, haunting harmonies from the choir echoing all around. It was indeed a witness to resurrection, and Patriarch Alexei received me personally in front of the iconostasis. Afterwards Jérémie and I joined other guests at a special "tea" for university staff and students as it was the Feast of St Tatiana, patron saint of students. The "tea" was well supplemented by vodka and much singing of the traditional student song *Mnogaya lyeta* ("Many Days"). Then we resorted to the Patriarch's residence for a long, positive discussion followed by lunch in mid-afternoon.

Was all this mere junketing, at the expense of "real" ecumenical dialogue? No. In the culture of Eastern Christianity things take time, must be allowed to grow, unlike the obsession with immediacy in the largely secularized West. It is around the table and in conviviality that relationships are nurtured, or healed, and some serious ecumenical

1. See above chapter 7 p.157f.

mistakes have been made by people who can only think in terms of set agendas, fixed deadlines and precise "outcomes". It is worth recalling that that pioneer of the early ecumenical movement, John R. Mott, in building up the YMCA spent much time in the 1890s travelling across Russia, meeting students and singing *Mnogaya lyeta* (though I doubt if he touched the vodka). But this visit was nearly twenty years ago. Relations between the Russian Orthodox leadership and other churches, even Orthodox ones, not to mention the ecumenical bodies, are not now so convivial.

CRETAN STORM, ROMAN PROGRESS

In January 1998 I sent a general epistle to all the member churches if CEC in follow-up to the Central Committee meeting of November. It sounded a thoroughly encouraging and optimistic note, telling how the spirit of Graz was still flowing in many kinds of new initiatives all over Europe, of how the Central Committee meeting had started the implementation of the Graz recommendations and how the new commissions were already getting down to work. I especially highlighted the significance of the new Church and Society Commission:

> Being the result of the integration of the European Ecumenical Commission on Church and Society (EECCS) with the Peace, Justice and Human Rights work of CEC . . . [this] Commission will continue the special role of EECCS in monitoring the European institutions in Brussels and Strasbourg, and the CEC role in peace and human rights concerns, including relating to the Organization for Security and Co-operation in Europe (OSCE) and the UN. The potential significance of this integration cannot be overestimated: the new Commission will be a *pan-European ecumenical* instrument on a scale not known before, with a unique access to the centers where decisions on the future shape of Europe, its peace and security, its economy and social justice, are shaped.

There was indeed, I concluded, much to look forward to in the coming year. There was movement and direction. That proved literally the case in a somewhat unexpected way when the Presidium met at the end of March, by invitation of Alexandros Papaderos at the Orthodox Academy in Crete. We only *just* met there because our visit coincided with the worst storm to hit the southern Aegean in living memory. Athens airport was already awash when Robin Gurney, myself and others in the advance party took off for Chania, and we learnt later that we were almost the last plane allowed out of Athens that evening and aircraft had to be tethered to the ground. The short flight to Chania at the western end of Crete was, to say the least, extremely turbulent and scary. As we neared the island I sought to reassure Robin by looking out through the window and saying that I could actually see the sea. "Oh, *can* you?" he responded gloomily. But eventually we did land safely if bumpily and were soon inside the solid buildings of the Academy at Kolympari. For days the whole sweep of sea in the Gulf of Chania was one white mass of surf. In due course the full complement of the Presidium did make it from Athens, the winds died down and we carried through the business of the meeting. Much was made, of course, of the fact that that it was in setting sail again from Crete that St Paul had his own experience of a disastrous storm.

Of special interest to report on was the first meeting of the CEC-CCEE Joint Committee, which had taken place in Rome in February, the first since the EEA2 at Graz. A key recommendation from Graz, endorsed by the CEC Assembly immediately afterwards, was that:

> ... the churches develop a common study document containing basic ecumenical duties and rights. From this a series of ecumenical guidelines, rules and criteria could be developed which would help the churches, those in positions of responsibility and all members, to distinguish between proselytism and Christian witness, as well as fundamentalism and genuine faithfulness, and help to shape the relationships between majority and minority churches in an ecumenical spirit.

Already a meeting to evaluate the outcomes of Graz had taken place in October at the Loccum Evangelical Academy in Germany and had looked further at this proposal. Clearly it would somehow fall within the remit of the CEC-CCEE joint committee. Our meeting in Rome in January took place literally in the shadow of St Peter's, in the St Martha's Guest House used for participants in prestigious meeting in the Vatican. Very comfortable the setting may have been but I was not the only one feeling somewhat nervous at the prospect of the meeting. Not that I had any doubts about the quality of our CEC delegation: Metropolitan Jérémie, John Arnold, Metropolitan Daniel, Antje Heider-Rottwilm and Bishop Finn Wagle of the Church of Norway, plus several of our staff. Nor was any problem anticipated with any of the persons as individuals on the CCEE side. The President of CCEE, Cardinal Miloslav Vlk of Prague, carried both weight and integrity as one who had endured long and great deprivation during the Communist period. Vincent Nichols, at that time auxiliary bishop of Westminster, I knew well from my CCBI days. Starting at Graz, I had begun a very cordial friendship with my opposite number on CCEE, its secretary the Italian Don Aldo Giordano. It was rather the anticipation of a collective conservatism on the Catholic side that loomed large. At the close of the EEA2 at Graz disquiet had evidently been transmitted from the Vatican about the direction taken by the assembly and the status to be accorded to its recommendations and message. Would similar dampers be applied to attempts an actual follow-up to Graz on a joint CEC-CCEE basis? At any rate the reception was cordial, and a highlight was the morning we had in private audience with Pope John Paul II. We were each introduced personally to the Holy Father. When my turn came he looked at me keenly: "*Deutsch?*" I wasn't sure whether he was relieved or disappointed when I confessed to being an *Engländer*. There followed a positive address by him on the significance of our work.

Hopes versus Disappointments

Meeting Pope John Paul II, introduced by Cardinal Vlk.

Three matters on the agenda were of special concern. The first was the common study document of "guidelines, rules and criteria" as called for at Graz. There was approval that this should be furthered. Thus was officially set in motion what came to be the *Charta Oecumenica*. Second, there was agreement to hold an Ecumenical Encounter to mark the new millennium in 2001. Ecumenical Encounters had been a feature of CEC-CCEE cooperation over the years. They had been relatively short (three-or four-day) but intensive gatherings of church leaders and theologians focusing on a particular theme. The first had taken place at Chantilly, France, in 1978, the second in Logumkloster, Denmark, in 1981, and the third at Riva del Garda, Italy in 1984—this last one being of special ecumenical significance as it highlighted the Niceno-Constantinopolitan Creed as a basis for united Christian witness. The most recent Encounter had been at Santiago Compostela in 1991 on the theme of common mission. There was agreement at our Rome meeting that an Encounter to mark the millennium would indeed be appropriate. Here is where I am tempted to raise my own trumpet. The message from the EEA2 at Graz had included the commitment "to involve young people, entrusting to them the ecumenical vision for the future and also to take forward the conciliar process concerning justice, peace and integrity of creation". Pondering this, the idea had come to me while at home in Bristol over Christmas that a meeting marking the start of a new era should not only be an encounter between the confessions but between the generations. Should not therefore the gathering be one of equal numbers of senior church figures and of people under the age of thirty? I put this in private to Aldo Giordano who was supportive, and when it came to the CEC-CCEE committee as a whole it was endorsed. It was also agreed that it should be held as close as possible in date to Easter which in 2001 would happily fall on the same date in both Western and Eastern calendars; and Vincent Nichols' suggestion was accepted that the theme be "I am with you always, to the end of the age". It is worth noting that the concept of the *Charta Oecumenica* and the proposal for the Encounter were quite independent of each other, even though the signing and launch of the *Charta* which took place at the Encounter in 2001 was a very appropriate ingredient in that event.

The third issue had also been highlighted at the Graz EEA2, in several commitments made by the churches, "to cooperate in seeking to outlaw all forms of violence, especially against women and children", and "to promote the status and equality of women in all fields, including decision-making processes, while preserving the distinct identities of men and women". In close cooperation with Irja Askola at the CEC women's desk the Ecumenical Forum of European Christian Women—which included Roman Catholics—had been to the fore in highlighting the issue of violence against women especially in the home, and the growing problem of the trafficking of women in Europe for sexual and economic exploitation. CEC therefore brought a proposal to the Rome meeting that CEC and CCEE should jointly support a letter of church leaders to all European churches on the issue of violence and trafficking, and likewise help to promote a booklet on violence being prepared by the Women's Forum. Following the Graz experience there was some anxiety that on the Catholic side there might be hesitation in focusing on violence against women in particular, especially if this meant turning a critical eye on the church itself. We need not have worried, because to the fore came Karl Lehmann, bishop of Mainz, with an informed and impassioned plea that this be taken seriously, born out of his recent conversations with a leading hospital consultant detailing the horrific nature of injuries to women that he had had to deal with. From his intervention there was no looking back.

It was possible to be critical of the Rome meeting as still being too hesitant. Rüdiger Noll for example pointed out that in follow-up to Graz overall there were still not many truly ecumenical (i.e. involving Roman Catholics) groups at work, although the setting up of the European Ecumenical Environmental Network (EEECEN) was to prove very significant. But things on the whole seemed to be looking good as we moved further into 1998. In May the Dialogue Commission had its first meeting in Münster, during which I preached on Ephesians 1:22, "And he has placed all things under his feet", at the Ascension Day eucharist in the Apostelkirche.[2] The process towards completing the CEC-EECS integration was going well, and it was with some confidence born out the sense of the churches' role in Europe that I preached ten days later at the Sunday morning service, broadcast on BBC Radio, in the Norwegian Sailors' Church in Cardiff, during the summit of EU leaders taking place in that city[3]. There had been some hope that Prime Minister Tony Blair might come and read the lesson (I recall Harold Wilson, when prime minister some twenty years earlier, being only too willing to do so at a Baptist service broadcast from Liverpool) but word came that his minders and spin-doctors were not in the habit of allowing him to perform in occasions where the whole script was not under their control. I certainly was not going to let my sermon be subject to political scrutiny (the BBC itself could prove difficult enough at times). Ten days later, the first full meeting of the new Church and Society Commission met in Poland. We, like Europe as a whole, were on the move. Or so it seemed.

ANOTHER STORM BREAKS

Out of a seemingly blue sky, in August a financial cloudburst hit us. In fact it came from a storm long brewing but one from which we had good reason to hope we would be spared. Ecumenical organizations are habitually fragile as far as their finances are concerned and CEC was no exception. CEC's basic funding came from member churches' subscriptions, gauged according to their size and with the overall economic situation of their respective countries somehow factored in. By no means all churches met their stated annual obligations. Additional grants might come from churches or organizations for certain aspects of the work or particular programs. But always there was little safety margin, and no reserves to fall back on. At the Central Committee in January 1997 at which I was appointed, there had been discussion of the staffing levels that might be sustainable following the Graz assemblies. One member of the committee, a bishop of the Church of Cyprus, stated that he was associated with a charitable fund from which he could secure a donation to CEC of one million US dollars within the next twelve months. Gasps of delight and gratitude around the table. Jean Fischer said that if such a gift materialized this would secure the present staffing level well beyond Graz. Amid the general sense of relief only one voice, I seem to recall, cautioned against basing plans on a fortune not yet acquired. But who could doubt the solemn word of a bishop? After my arrival in office the promise and guarantee were repeated on the bishop's visits to Geneva and many times by phone. Once I stayed all day in London where I was told the person in charge of the foundation would meet me, but my mobile phone stayed

2. See "Who Rules—and How?" in Clements, *The Churches in Europe*, 35–38.
3. See "Europe is Meeting" in Clements, *The Churches in Europe*, 25–28.

silent. In February 1998, in fact during a meeting of the Budget Committee, a small amount did arrive in Geneva. But CEC was already seriously in deficit. In March, at the Presidium meeting in Crete the auditors' comment was noted: "The ability of the CEC to continue as a going concern is dependent on its ability to cover the accumulated deficit and/or to obtain additional financial support." Helmut Weide, moderator of the Budget Committee, had also pointed out that the present staffing level could *not* be maintained without considerable improvement in the finances. Weeks and months rolled on, hopes and anxieties vied in equal measure. Then, one day in August Margaret and I spent a day with Elizabeth Salter at her alpine retreat in Doucy-en-Bauges. She had somehow got a copy of that day's *Guardian* and browsing through it I came across the report of a financial scandal being uncovered in Cyprus involving large sums being laundered—and the bishop's name appeared as one of those associated with it. I immediately called Robin Gurney to follow this up. It was as we had feared. There was no suggestion that the bishop was personally responsible for the malfeasance but it was enough that his name was associated with it for his church to suspend him from office. Clearly we could not now expect anything more from this source, and CEC was in much deeper trouble than anyone could really have foreseen. In the ensuing weeks Hans Schmocker, Helmut Weide and I tried to think of all manner of ways expenditure could be cut without making any redundancies, but to no avail. The CEC officers met in Geneva. One suggestion was, do we actually need a communications office? I squashed that one flat. It was not only my CCBI experience but a growing knowledge of how things actually worked in the ecumenical world, which made me realize that it is precisely the smaller an organization is that makes its communications work more essential. It was eventually and inescapably clear to us that a whole desk of one executive and support person would have to go. One desk in a small tightly-knit staff community is a big cut. It would be painful. Central Committee would have to decide.

The Central Committee meeting in Valbeek, Belgium, was a grim affair and not only because it was cold and wet and the former monastery in which we stayed and worked was forbiddingly austere. Much of the meeting was dominated by the financial crisis and how to meet it. After long and searching discussion it was decided that it was the Associate Secretary for Inter-Church Service (Asylum Seekers and Refugees) post, occupied by John Taylor, which should be ended as soon as possible and no later than end 1999. This was of course deeply hurtful for one who had done so much in this area and in the programmatic work on reconciliation in the Balkans, and it was also upsetting for the staff as a whole. But it was quite clear that we could not go on living beyond our means, and the writing had in fact been on the wall for some time. There was also, understandably, a storm of protest from those in the churches and associated associations who were vitally concerned with the whole era of refugees and migrants. Was this not typical, it was asked, of the way that church bodies marginalize the already marginalized and most vulnerable people? The rejoinder to this was that this was also the area in which so much activity was already taking place beyond the formal confines of CEC, and presented a prime example of what the Graz CEC Assembly had called for: a methodology in which CEC supported and helped to coordinate what was already going on, rather than doing the work for the churches. But this episode was about the most painful of my whole career.

Valbeek was not all doom and gloom however. EECCS had its own final General Assembly there, at one session of which the President of the EU Jacques Santer gave a notable address, and to which CEC Central Committee members were invited. There was also a joint session on the work programme for the new Church and Society Commission, during the discussion of which I noted that the questions and comments hardly differed from one organization to another, which I thought augured well for the future.

ECUMENICAL SERVICE INCARNATE

Nor did the crisis prevent or distract from the ongoing work of CEC. For one thing it intensified the search to find an effective and viable "Solidarity" commission for diaconic work. The other commissions and projects moved on. The first meeting of a group mandated to initiate work on the *Charta Oecumenica* took place at Cartigny near Geneva in October. Most significant of all in maintaining the impetus was the pull of the wider world and the need and opportunity for cooperation with other bodies. In November I made my first visit to Albania to share in meetings of the WCC-sponsored diaconal Round Table for that country, a meeting of church-related NGOS from different European countries and the USA with their local partner organizations in Albania, organized by Alex Belopopsky, WCC Europe secretary with whom I came to work very closely throughout my time in CEC. That visit also provided my introduction to His Beatitude Anastasios, head of the Autocephalous Orthodox Church of Albania and one of the most outstanding church leaders I was ever to meet. Greek by nationality but cosmopolitan in experience and outlook, he was a scholar of wide erudition who in earlier life had researched in Africa on missions and religions, worked for a time on missionary studies in the WCC, and was later professor in the University of Athens. He was appointed to the archbishopric of Tirana, Durres and All Albania in 1992 and—as befits his name—oversaw the veritable resurrection of Orthodox Christian life in Albania following the grim forty-six years of communism which under the brutal Enver Hoxha was the most ruthlessly anti-religious of all European Cold War regimes. "A wonderful man, unusual blend of vision and realism", I wrote in my diary having sat next to Anastasios at the welcome dinner for the Round Table participants. At that time, a visit to Albania was almost like experiencing the Third World in Europe. The roads in much of Tirana were appalling, rainwater was sloshing everywhere without drains or gutters, out in the countryside donkey carts were still normal sights on the road, while on the verges every kilometer or so was marked by the small, concrete mushroom-like bunkers, relics of the Hoxha era when a western military invasion was allegedly the main threat. We visited Durres, saw the impressive Roman amphitheater and, more significantly for the present-day, the new theological seminary which Anastasios had initiated and was being attended by both men and women. We saw a great deal of the social and educational work being supported by the main church organization Diakonia Agapes, led by Nina Gramo, a member of CEC Central Committee. We heard from UNHCR about the exodus already under way from Kosovo in the north, and how the refugee effort was having to contend with much sheer gangsterism in that border area.

There were also lively discussions. Some NGOs, as one had found in Africa in 1995, seemed to manifest a we-know-best attitude ignoring the wisdom and experience of the local nationals, and not always seeing the importance of support for the church itself. One important issue, as always, was who should be the main recipients of aid? It was easy to identify who were the poorest of poor in a poverty-stricken country. But who were the people best placed to help them? Diakonia Agapes had faced criticism from some quarters for channeling some aid, such as educational aids and school equipment, regarded as middle-class benefits. But one of Albania's problems was the steady drainage of professional people from the country to more stable environments abroad. The country badly needed competent indigenous people to stay and be encouraged to build its society and economy and to resource its own social care. On the Sunday morning some of us attended Divine Liturgy in the Church of the Annunciation. I recorded: "Church crowded, all ages, lovely singing. Anastasios celebrating. At no notice, was invited to give short message to congregation, which went down well." That evening Anastasios invited me to meet him for an hour's conversation and then dinner. Anastasios was bringing to the Balkans an almost unique quality of church leadership, eirenic and truly ecumenical, afflicted by neither national nor ethnic nor confessional myopia. For myself, and in due course for Margaret too, he became a personal friend, wise and supportive.

With Archbishop Anastasios in Sarajevo 2001

While in Tirana I was also able to meet the local Baptists who were being helped by the Italian Baptists (the US Southern Baptists had pulled out of Albania when a spell of violence threatened) and among them it was especially good to see once more Saverio Guarna whom I had known well at meetings of the Baptist World Alliance.

HARARE, ORTHODOX AND TENSIONS

Just a few weeks later, December 4–13, I met Anastasios again, along with some five thousand other people attending the Eighth Assembly of the WCC in Harare, Zimbabwe, under the theme "Turn to God—rejoice in hope". This was the largest WCC assembly to date, but despite its theme title it was neither the most joyous nor hopeful though it certainly did seek to turn to God. Ever since the previous assembly in Seoul (1991) there had been a swelling current of Orthodox discontent about the nature of ecumenism as manifest in the WCC, particularly as regards common worship and what was considered to be a too-western style of decision-making and voting, which obviated a truly representative kind of gathering. More broadly, there was dissatisfaction with what was seen as too great acquiescence in western secular and liberal trends—including, most potentially explosive of all, feminism. In May that year there had been a consultation of the Orthodox at Thessaloniki at which these concerns were articulated, and which was surrounded by rumors that the Orthodox might even refuse to attend Harare. Particularly in conversation at Harare with some Russian delegates whom I had come to know well I was disturbed to find just how deeply these concerns ran even though I was repeatedly assured that their target was the WCC, not CEC. The main outcome from Harare was the creation of the WCC Special Commission on the Participation of the Orthodox Church in the ecumenical movement which ensured that the anxieties and questions could be faced by all sides in a more creative fashion. There was also much good within the Harare gathering itself, a highlight being the appearance, to rapturous acclaim, of Nelson Mandela who in his address spoke graciously and movingly not only of the support given by the WCC in the struggle against apartheid but of the significance of the churches' long missionary involvement in Africa especially in the provision of schools and colleges, of which he himself was glad to admit being a notable beneficiary. By contrast President Robert Mugabe's speech to the Assembly included a lengthy rant against past and continuing colonial oppression. There was also the "Padare" (the Shona word for meeting-place) which gave opportunity for numerous groups to make presentations and initiate discussions on a variety of themes. I was involved in two if these: one on the Graz EEA2 and its follow-up; and a better-attended one on the theme of my book *Learning to Speak*, on how the church should address public issues, which I shared with Larry Rasmussen. I made one intervention in the Assembly plenary when the future programme of the WCC was being discussed. One delegate had suggested that given the tightening financial resources of the WCC, could not some of the programmatic work be handed to the regional ecumenical organizations (REOs)? I was highly critical of the suggestion if it assumed that REOs such as CEC could find additional funding not available to the WCC when in fact we were all drawing from the same financial well in the churches. This was to anticipate by a few years the discussion on a reconfiguration of the ecumenical movement.

KOSOVO 1999

Not only was CEC the regional body with the largest Orthodox presence, but in Europe relations between the Orthodox and other communions had not just interconfessional but big geopolitical implications too, across the ancient and still potent East-West fault-line. That had been very evident in the conflict in Former Yugoslavia which, despite the Dayton Peace Accords of 1995, was now moving towards a denouement in Kosovo. Though small in area, Kosovo was the emotional heartland of Serbian identity. For the Orthodox, especially, Kosovo had sacral significance as the site of Serbia's most revered historic churches and monasteries. Yet by now ethnic Serbs were only a minority in Kosovo, the Albanian (and largely Muslim) population having risen from about 50% at the end of the Second World War to about 80% by the mid-1990s. The Kosovo Liberation Army (KLA), formed in 1991, had from 1995 initiated an armed campaign targeting Serbian police-stations and other landmarks of Serbian authority, with large amounts of weapons looted and smuggled in from Albania. From 1998 Serb regular military units and paramilitaries launched a campaign of retribution and a cycle of violence and counter-violence ensued. In July 1998 the Orthodox monastery at Zociste was razed to the ground by the KLA. It was just after this that a three-person delegation from CEC went to Former Yugoslavia. Professor Karsten Fledelius (Danish Lutheran, Denmark and a member of CEC Central Committee), Sister Mother Maria Rule (Russian Orthodox in the UK) and OKR Klaus Wilkens (EKD Germany) were able to visit Belgrade, Novi Sad, Montenegro, and parts of Kosovo including Pec, Decani and Pristina. Karsten Fledelius reported to the CEC Central Committee:

> A multi-ethnic society is seen as the only possible choice for people to live peacefully together in this part of the world. A solution through violence was totally counter-productive . . . In relation to the government, the Serbian Orthodox Church is a dissident. The delegation returned very worried about the situation of refugees and displaced persons.

Just how dissident was the Serbian Church in relation to the Milosevic government was of course a matter of interpretation, but enough was being said by the hierarchy to provide a basis for dialogue and a scrutiny of accountability.

In CEC and WCC we were having almost weekly meetings on Kosovo. Meanwhile diplomatic efforts were continuing to find a solution to the crisis. On September 23 the UN Security Council passed Resolution 1199, expressing grave concern at reports that over two-hundred and thirty thousand people had been displaced by the use of indiscriminate force by the Serbian and Yugoslavian military and calling on all parties to cease hostilities and maintain a ceasefire. Shortly after, an activation warning (i.e. threat of military intervention, in this case by air power) was issued by NATO. Richard Holbrooke, US Ambassador to the UN, was shuttling back and forth and in October his efforts succeeded in an agreement to a ceasefire, to be overseen by the Kosovo Verification Mission of the Organization for Security and Cooperation in Europe (OSCE). The ceasefire however unraveled with breaches by both sides in December, and by early January 1999 not just the rural areas but urban centers also were beset by bombings and murders. In western eyes, a turning point came on January 15 with the massacre of forty-five Albanian farmers at Račak. But diplomatic efforts continued, and on February 6 a peace conference convened at Rambouillet just outside Paris, with NATO Secretary General Javier Solana as mediator. The nations of the "Contact Group" believed that the restoration of Kosovo's pre-1990 autonomy within Serbia, plus the introduction of democracy and supervision by international organizations, constituted a non-negotiable set of principles, the Status Quo Plus. Unlike the Dayton negotiations on Bosnia of 1995, however, Slobodan Milosevic did not attend in person, which created the suspicion that while Serbs might be present at the Rambouillet table the real decisions were being made in Belgrade. There was criticism of this not only abroad but in Serbia too—and not least within the Orthodox

Church. Bishop Artimije of Prizen in Kosovo and Father Sava of the Decani monastery, who had most certainly distanced themselves from the Milosevic policy and spoken clearly against it, actually went to Rambouillet to protest that the Serbian presence there did not properly represent Serb opinion, even in Kosovo itself. Learning of this visit I wrote on behalf of CEC to Robin Cook, the British Foreign Secretary, and to the French Foreign Minister, with a copy to the UK Permanent Representative to the UN in Geneva, pointing out the significance of their stance: "In recent days both Father Sava and Bishop Artimije have repeated their prophetic calls for the true basis for a settlement to be recognized, prompting their denunciation by certain nationalist circles in Belgrade as traitors to their people." They therefore merited serious attention by the international community.

On March 23 the CEC Presidium was concluding its meeting in the Marti Codolar Seminary in Barcelona. As some of us were enjoying the afternoon sun before leaving for the airport Margarethe Isberg came out to tell us that the Rambouillet talks had finally failed and that NATO was about to begin air attacks on Serbia. Before leaving Barcelona Metropolitan Jérémie and I had just enough time to issue a short statement, warning that to refuse the search for reconciliation would bring judgment to pass and, again, warned of an immense scale of suffering especially among those who would be uprooted in the conflict. Next day began the aerial bombardment which was to last until June 11. On March 29 a joint statement was issued by the General Secretaries of the WCC, the LWF and WARC and myself on behalf of CEC. Because this gave prominence to a call for an end to the NATO bombing and less explicit mention of violence against the ethnic Albanian Kosovars this statement received strong criticism from some quarters including two member churches of CEC. The statement however was actually a letter addressed to the UN Secretary-General appealing for him to take an initiative both to end the bombing and to bring about an end to violence being committed by all sides. Of major concern to us was the evident marginalization of the UN, the supreme authority in international conduct, from its rightful position in arbitration and mediation. It was in fact only under UN auspices that an end to hostilities in fact was eventually agreed.

We were also bearing in mind that not only the Serbian Orthodox Church but also the minority member churches of CEC in Serbia (Lutheran, Reformed, Methodist) were all opposed to the NATO action. In the CEC *Monitor* I tried to summarize the role of the ecumenical family in such a time of conflict: "It is, first, to stand with the victims, to feed the Christ who is hungry, naked and sick in the refugee camps. It is, second, to call for the observance of human rights, dignity and international law by *all* parties involved, and to call to account those who violate such principles, on whichever side. Third, it is to set an example of persistent search for resolution through encounter and dialogue, however hard at times it may seem. We might at times feel hopeless. God never is."

BELGRADE UNDER FIRE

In Geneva I was having almost daily meetings with my colleagues in WCC, LWF and ARC and also the representatives of the Ecumenical and Moscow Patriarchates. It was eventually decided that three of us—Alex Belopopsky of the WCC, Olli-Pekka Lassila at the LWF Europe Desk, and myself, designated as leader—should if possible visit Serbia and literally sit with the churches there. It took a long time before we were assured of visas but on April 17 we flew to Budapest and were driven to the border on transport provided by the Yugoslav embassy in Budapest. After an unconscionable delay we were allowed through. On the way to Belgrade were signs of war: bridges for example lined with tires which could easily be set alight to confuse air-to-ground missiles. We stopped in Novi Sad to meet with Protestant leaders there, and with staff of the Ecumenical Humanitarian Association, and viewed the destroyed bridges across the Danube (a feature of the bombing which not only distressed but bewildered the inhabitants of Novi Sad as to its military purpose). It was evening when we arrived in Belgrade. There was a noisy demonstration on one of the bridges—against the bombing but, we noticed, not pro-Milosevic. I asked our Serbian companion if we English-speakers should keep our voices down. "Of course not," he said, "you will not be regarded as enemies here." Darkness fell. In the distance a stream of orange anti-aircraft tracer climbed into the night sky. On our returning back to the foyer of our hotel a sharp explosion reverberated across the city, and two waiters leaped up with a shout, clenched fists joyously waving: a missile had evidently been hit in mid-air. Next morning at the breakfast buffet I found myself with a familiar figure from the TV screen, the BBC World Affairs correspondent John Simpson. He had incurred some displeasure from the government at home for allegedly showing too much sympathy for the Serb population in his reports on the effects of the bombing. We had a short conversation and I thanked him for reporting what people outside might not want to see and hear, and hoped he felt encouraged. He said he was, and in return he wished us well on our mission which he found very interesting. Half an hour later we were on our respective ways, he with a film crew to make a feature on how Serbian families were coping with nights under bombardment, and we to the patriarchate. He is undoubtedly one of the most courageous people I have ever met—and cheerful with it too, as his wave and smile made clear as he was driven off.[4]

We spent most of the morning with Patriarch Pavle and his staff. Some days earlier I had sent a fax to his assistant for External Affairs, Father Andreas Cilerdzic, an impassioned plea that the plight of the Kosovar Albanians who were mostly fleeing not the NATO bombing but the ethnic cleansing going on in Kosovo, must be addressed by the church leadership in Belgrade. We followed this up in conversation

---

4. In his *Not Quite World's End. A Traveller's Tales* (London: Macmillan, 2007), Simpson speaks openly about his beliefs and his return to Christian faith, which owed much to what he saw of the Christian anti-apartheid church leadership in South Africa.

and there were honest exchanges when we made clear that to most of the outside world there were very definite and informed perceptions as to the immediate causes and responsibility for the flight of refugees from Kosovo into Albania. We were heard carefully, and our hosts reaffirmed to us their commitment to the right of return for all refugees, and for Kosovo to continue as a multi-ethnic community. On our way out of the Patriarchate building we were accosted by microphone-wielding reporters: "Do you oppose the bombing by NATO?" Answer: "We oppose all violence in Serbia."

"Do you oppose the bombing by NATO?"

We had hoped that a simultaneous visit would take place to Albania and Macedonia, the countries bearing the brunt of the refugee crisis. This was delayed, however, at the request of Archbishop Anastasios in view of the immense pressures under which the churches and its humanitarian partners in Albania were laboring just then.[5] (Anastasios, incidentally, ordered the students from his Durres seminary to go and help in the refugee camps. Some of them protested, "But they're Albanian Muslims. Once they know we're Orthodox they'll probably want to kill us." "Well," said Anastasios, "show them Orthodox love.") By late April it was evident that churches and national ecumenical bodies throughout Europe, and beyond, were deeply concerned about the Kosovo situation and a variety of perspectives were apparent in their statements, though all of course wanted an end to the war. It was decided therefore that CEC and WCC, with the

---

5. The visit, by Sylvia Raulo and Wilhelm Nausner, in fact took place 17–24 May.

collaboration of LWF and WARC, should convene a meeting of a representative cross-section of churches to exchange views and perceptions, and identify a strategy not only for the present but also the longer term. This meeting was scheduled for Budapest, May 26–27, to be hosted by the Hungarian Ecumenical Council.

Meanwhile another initiative was brewing under the aegis of the Russian Orthodox Church for a high-level group of church leaders (and maybe some respected political figures) to attempt some kind of mediation. There was some skepticism about this in Geneva, suspicious that it was a ploy to rival the official ecumenical bodies and gain some kudos for the Moscow Patriarchate. While alert to these misgivings I nevertheless felt that it was important enough to be in touch with it and at least to know what was going on, especially as the Moscow Patriarchate was likely with the aid of the Kremlin to have some channels to Belgrade not open to Westerners. I therefore accepted the invitation at short notice to fly to Moscow on May 5 for an initial meeting with Metropolitan Kirill of Smolensk (at that time in charge of the External Affairs Department of the Patriarchate), Father Hilarion Alfayev, Bishop Rolf Koppe from Germany and *Praeses* Jürgen Gohde, head of the German Diakonical Service. Two weeks later on May 18 we met again in a hotel in Vienna, joined by: Celistino Migliore, Under-Secretary for the Holy See's Relations with the States; Richard Marsh, Ecumenical Secretary to the archbishop of Canterbury; Jacques Stewart, leading French Protestant pastor and President of the World Conference for Religion and Peace; Paul Wilson, Director of the Europe Office of the National Council of Churches in the USA; Brother Luc of the Taizé Community; and Ivan Jurkovic, official of the Secretariat of State in the Holy See. The Vienna Group as we were henceforth self-styled drew up a short memorandum. After voicing deep concern for the victims of the tragedy and the dangers it posed to the unity of both Europe and its churches, and affirming the nature of Christian responsibility for peace, it stated the need for a peace process with legitimate representation by all sides. "The best way to initiate such a peace process would be the adoption of an appropriate resolution by the UN Security Council. The priority is to stop the present military activities including the NATO bombardments and to introduce an immediate and verifiable end of violence and repression in Kosovo accompanied by the withdrawal of the military and paramilitary forces. This needs to be monitored by international observers. Human and political rights and liberties should be guaranteed to all people. All refugees and displaced persons, should be given the right to return to their homes in the Former Republic of Yugoslavia, of which Kosovo is an integral part."

MEETING THE INDICTED WAR-CRIMINAL

The suggestion also arose that a small group from those attending the Budapest meeting to take place the following week might go from there to Belgrade and if possible meet with President Milosevic. I said I could be available for such a visit but did not think I was essential to it and did not expect to be involved. The Budapest meeting itself convened on May 26 and was remarkably useful. More than forty representatives of churches and ecumenical bodies from all over Europe, East and West, and from the USA and Canada, came. Representatives of the Serbian Orthodox Church, including Bishop Irenij, and the Protestant Churches of Former Yugoslavia were also present. I was asked to lead off with a survey of the range of positions taken by churches, which by and large tended to mirror those of their respective governments. Of course the Orthodox in Europe and all the churches of the Balkans were opposed to the NATO action. The Methodists of Britain and the Netherlands churches however had called for intervention by ground troops. Many churches were asking for greater UN involvement. All were according highest priority to the plight of refugees and the maintenance of human rights. But the first afternoon and evening were to see the limit of my involvement. Next morning came the news that Slobodan Milosevic had been indicted as a war criminal by the International Criminal Tribunal for Former Yugoslavia. For the next stage in the story let my hurried diary account, which I shared with family and friends soon afterwards, albeit it in all its raw note form, take over for a moment:

> At that stage [evening] I was still assuming that the sub-group of our Vienna Group would be going as planned to Belgrade next morning—Metropolitan Kirill and his side-kick Hilarion Alfayev, Jürgen Gohde of EKD and the RC Archbishop of Vienna (Schönborn). However at breakfast next morning came an urgent summons to meet with Alfayev and Kirill in Alfayev's room. Main problem was that Vatican had put last-minute stoppers on Schönborn going: apparently he's connected with some sort of allegations about a scandal. But also was news that Milosevic likely to be indicted by the Hague Tribunal as war criminal. Could we then get another RC at short notice? Aldo Giordano makes phone calls to Vatican. No go. Seems they are having cold feet due to the indictment business. No suitable RC in Budapest either. So group has to be reconstructed. Decide that Fr Leonard Kishkovsky (US) who is at the Budapest meeting anyway, was on the Jesse Jackson visit to Milosevic 3 weeks ago, and was among those who talked with Bill Clinton after that visit, should go. And the group SHOULD go precisely because with the indictment business, contact might v. soon become difficult. Then question of balance: group now looking overweighted with Orthodox. Need wider European representation so everyone looks at me. I re-join the main meeting in its first session of the morning. Then Alfayev comes in and whispers: we've got to go—now! Hasty farewells. We are whisked off down to the Yugo. Embassy in the city, passports stamped with visas in no time. Polite coffee and slivovic. By 11.30 we are on our way in the same minibus and with same driver as before. A Yugo. official accompanies us to the border—a nice chap, a mad-keen soccer-buff fascinated by the Man. United victory in the Eur. Cup and keen to discuss English soccer back to the year dot.

At the border nothing like the delay of last time. We are met by a Yugo. Foreign Office car filled with officials, which drives ahead of us, the whole motorcade led by police car with flashing lights and siren whenever required to clear everything else off the road. We drive non-stop at top speed all the way. Police at every intersection or traffic lights clearing the way for us. Suddenly realize *they* are taking this very seriously and probably also worried about security from the air. Reach Belgrade. Check into Intercontinental. Told that Milos. will see us later that evening. After 30 mins to freshen up we sit down to dins. Halfway through the soup one of the minders turns up to say the Pres. will see us NOW. So off we go, swished off in posh cars.

Across the Danube, up into the leafy suburbs in the hilly part, huge iron gates swing open and we sweep up to the official Presidential palace, one so far not attacked. Two mins later we are sitting down with the big man in his magnificent reception room. He is welcoming, v. affable, excellent English; a very complex personality, I suspect, consistently shifting his vulnerability around inside himself.

Kirill presents our memo, prepared in Vienna. M. reads it, nods: "Gentlemen, I agree with this completely". So I invite him to say what then are the main difficulties from his point of view in reaching agreement? He talks at length, length, length. So we press him on a) verification of end of hostilities in Kosovo, b) withdrawal of forces from Kosovo, c) composition of peacekeeping force (NATO etc). It's great that Leonid Kishkovsky is there, because he relays what Bill Clinton said to HIM about the NATO presence which is not quite "what the papers say". M. looks interested. Seems he *is* prepared for independent verification of end to violence, withdrawal of 90% of his forces, and even a NATO contingent in the peacekeeping force—even a "core" of NATO. Does he mean it? At least he's said it.

We go on to human rights abuses in Kosovo, ethnic cleansing etc. Much denial, explanations, "shock" at allegations of rape etc: "any crimes are already being dealt with by our police." It lasts well over an hour. At the end I present him with Brenda Fitzpatrick's World Vision report on crimes against women and children, drawn from the refugee camp stories. Before leaving, photo and TV shots, as expected. I say to him, "Mr President, things may get even more difficult soon for diplomatic contact. If ever you feel that what you are saying is not getting through, we invite you to use channels of communication through the churches." He asks for my card.

So it was. We then go off to the Patriarchate for session with Pat. Pavle and other bishops (by now Irenij and Andreas have also returned from Budapest). Lasts over an hour. Sirens go. Lights go out, presumably a power station hit. Candles brought in. Back to Intercontinental. Half the electricity is off but the hotel has a private generator. Dins at last. Try to call home but no go—seems communications been hit again.

Bed. Sleep. Wake up to beautiful morning. Have to trot down 7 flights of stairs because lifts not working. Meet the others over breakfast. I say, "Well, a quiet night after all, then." They look at me and say, "Where were you at 4.30?" Apparently there were four loud missile bangs and the whole place shook. This may be bad news for me as far as judgment day is concerned.

Call Richard Marsh back at Lambeth Palace-phones working again it seems. Brief him because he is off to the Foreign Office later in morning. Then we are off again in the polished cars to the airport because Chernomyrdin [Russian Foreign Minister] is about to arrive. It's a ghost airport, almost totally empty since the NATO action started. We wait in the VIP lounge. Eventually the white RUSSIA plane lands and taxis to the apron. Huge bevvy of press, TV cameras and sound booms appears from nowhere. Mr C. comes down the steps. Kirill among the welcoming party. Few mins later we are sitting down with him, telling him our impressions of M., encouraging him to take up the points we thought positive in M's remarks.

Then back into town. We visit the Russian Orth. Church which is very close to the TV building which was blasted [on April 23], and saw damage to the church roof etc. Then to coffee with the "Karic Foundation", a sort of academic outfit run by two Serb brothers, one of whom in the government, the other with strong business connections in Moscow. Then off in the minibus again—except that Kirill and Alfayev are flying back to Moscow with Mr C.

High speed and escorts again, all the way to the border. Reach Budapest about 4.30 pm. At the airport the friendly Yugo. Embassy people are there again. They had provisionally re-booked me for Zurich-Geneva next morning as we thought we wouldn't be back for the 5.30 evening flight. That anyway turns out to be fully booked but the nice Swissair lady gets me onto the Austrian Airlines Vienna flight so all is well, and so back to Geneva. Next step, contacts with the NATO countries.

So that's it. What will come of it? I don't know, but I'd rather we tried than not at all. Should we have shaken hands and sat down with an indicted war-criminal? Depends what you think more important—keeping one's hands "clean" or trying, even against the odds, to end this bloody (in every sense) business. As Trevor Huddleston once said re. South Africa, better to have blood on one's hands than water.

Or, as Bonhoeffer puts it, the "structure of responsible action involves both willingness to become guilty and freedom"[6].

My most telling image of the whole visit remains that of carrying on the late-night conversation with Patriarch Pavle in the darkness by candlelight, once again a symbol of hope but now in a scene very different from either King's Chapel at Advent or the Bristol College chapel. Two further points can be added. The first is relatively trivial but possibly revealing. When Milosevic first greeted us and sat down he lit a cigarette.

---

6. Bonhoeffer, *Ethics*, 275.

Then he noticed a TV camera was already there and he stubbed it out saying "It's not a good example for the young people". I suspect much more likely was that he realized it was bad for the image of himself since as a result of the economic sanctions cigarettes were generally unobtainable in Belgrade except on the black market. The second is to repeat the question, did our visit have any effect? The received historical opinion is that it was ultimately the threat of the use of ground troops, strongly advocated by Tony Blair, which persuaded Milosevic to climb down; that he finally realized that the Russians despite their anti-NATO rhetoric would not come to his aid; and that it was a Finnish-Russian mediation team which finally formulated an acceptable military presence for Kosovo incorporating NATO troops but under UN authority. We do not know if we had added so much as a milligram of influence towards this outcome, but we had tried to speak peace to power. Appropriately enough, having got back to Geneva I was off next morning to Bienenberg in northern Switzerland for the fiftieth anniversary assembly of the organization Church and Peace, at which I had been asked to preach on the theme text, "Therefore, love truth and peace" (Zechariah 8:19b).[7]

CONTINUING CRISIS

Kosovo continued to occupy us for the rest of the year. The Vienna Group remained in existence and we had a number of telephone conferences. A CEC-WCC delegation visited Kosovo at the end of June. With the plethora of peace groups wanting to get involved in the region ("Should there not be peace between the peace groups?" we asked), CEC with WCC convened a meeting at Bossey in mid-August for church related peace groups to identify priorities and attempt some co-ordination of their efforts, and it pursued further the reflections on longer term needs for the region which had begun at the Budapest meeting in May. There was a poignancy in that the meeting of the CEC Central Committee in September in Nyborg Strand, Denmark, celebrated the fortieth anniversary of CEC's origins in meetings at that very same place in 1959, in an age when Europe was cruelly divided; and now CEC was once again having to accept the challenge of bridge-building in a conflict situation. Once the period of emergency relief and humanitarian aid was over, the churches and church-related agencies had to co-operate and commit themselves to long-term support and development in the region. The WCC Europe desk became the coordinating instrument for this joint initiative known as the South-East European Ecumenical Partnership (SEEEP). At a meeting in late 1999 three priorities were agreed upon: capacity-building; return or integration of refugees and displaced persons; and peace and reconciliation. CEC became the lead agency for the peace and reconciliation hub, with the Peace and Human Rights Desk under Rüdiger Noll taking the responsibility. Then in November a two-day conference was held in Oslo hosted by the Church of Norway and the Norwegian

---

7. See Clements, *The European Churches* 53–60.

government on "Europe after the Kosovo Crisis: Implications for the Churches" with participants from across Europe and representation from the USA. It was addressed by, among others, Knut Vollebaek, Norwegian Minister for Foreign Affairs and Chairman of the OSCE. It produced a final message, "The Crisis is Not Over!" with very specific and strong recommendations to the churches and their agencies, political leaders and the UN, on the wider and continuing lessons to be learned from the Kosovo conflict.

ECUMENICAL POLYPHONY

There was an amazingly rich polyphony in the life that was CEC at the end of 1999, to which I cannot do justice here. For three weeks in September 1999 the Synod of European Bishops met in Rome. CEC had three delegates: Finnish Orthodox Archpriest Veiko Purmonen, Reinhard Frieling of the EKD and co-moderator of the CEC Dialogue Commission, and myself. I found the atmosphere open and welcoming, presided over by Pope John Paul II, but the tone of the bishops' interventions somewhat hesitant and confused as well as conservative, and ecumenical relations did not feature in a major way. Only Cardinal Carlo Maria Martini of Milan seemed to challenge the status quo of conformity, with an impassioned plea to restore the true collegiality of bishops which had been called for at Vatican II. Each of us ecumenical delegates were invited to make an intervention. In mine I drew attention to the *Charta Oecumenica* then in course of preparation, but also suggested that the theme of the Synod, "Jesus Christ alive in His Church—Hope for Europe" needed not contradicting but complimenting by "Jesus Christ Alive in Europe—Hope for His Church". Reinhard Frieling made mention of the recent Lutheran-Roman Catholic Agreement on Justification which had not been noted by the Synod until then. Once again there was a personal meeting with Pope John Paul II, this time at lunch when Aldo Giordano and I were guests of the Holy Father and Cardinal Edward Cassidy, head of the Pontifical Council for Promoting Christian Unity whom I had known since meeting him at the Irish School of Ecumenics in Dublin seven years earlier. The Pope seemed to have aged much since our encounter at the CEC-CCEE meeting in Rome the previous year. At one point he had to be reminded who Aldo Giordano was, and indeed what CCEE was.

Then, too, a shared concern with Roman Catholics was the issue of violence against women, violence and human trafficking. In 1998 the Decade of Churches in Solidarity with Women came to a conclusion, but 1999 saw the fruition of two most important pieces of CEC work in this area. The decisions of the February 1998 CEC-CCEE Committee in Rome, on violence against women and the trafficking of women, were truly followed up. In 1999, following the CEC-CCEE Committee in Guernsey, the Presidents of CEC and CCEE signed a common letter to their member churches alerting them to the growing phenomenon of violence against women, urging that church leaders "declare publicly that any kind of violence against women is a sin for it is an offence against their human dignity" and calling for all churches to encourage more open discussion of the issues within their communities and name the attitudes and structures which nurture this violence. In addition CEC produced a brochure on violence against women written by Lesley Orr McDonald of the Church of Scotland with Irja Askola, the cover design underlining *It happens everywhere—including your community*. Second, the EU having named 1999 as the Year against Violence against Women, with trafficking of women as a priority issue, trafficking was taken up as a major theme by the CEC Women's Desk in close collaboration with the Ecumenical Forum of European Christian Women and others. The result was a major consultation over Advent weekend in Driebergen, Netherlands which brought together seventy women and men from twenty-seven European countries. The statement of the consultation brought to the awareness of the churches just how far-reaching and complex was the issue right across Europe, and challenged the churches to break the silence surrounding prostitution, sexual abuse and violence. I look back upon this programme as especially important because while today human trafficking is no longer headline news but appallingly all too well-known, at that time it was the churches who were pioneers in highlighting the issue. Sadly, from CEC's point of view, 1999 also saw the departure of Irja Askola back to her native Finland. In 2010 we rejoiced with her and her church when she was .appointed the first woman bishop of the Church of Finland, with charge of the diocese of Helsinki. She was succeeded at the CEC Solidarity and Women's Desk by Eva-Sybille Vogel-Mfato of the EKD.

PAST, PRESENT—AND TO COME?

As the 1990s neared their end thoughts naturally became both reflectively reminiscent and forward looking to the new millennium. I experienced some particular promptings to look both behind and ahead. In July 1998 there was the unveiling by Queen Elizabeth of the statues of ten twentieth-century Christian martyrs above the west door of Westminster Abbey. They included Dietrich Bonhoeffer and Martin Luther King, and while still at CCBI I had been involved in the discussions about the occasion with Canon Anthony Harvey of Westminster Abbey and Dr Andrew Chandler, historian with a special interest in Bishop George Bell and the German resistance. The moving service inside the Abbey included a Bach cello suite played by Dietrich Bethge, Bonhoeffer's grand-nephew and godson. Both Eberhard and Renate Bethge were present too, and it was the last occasion on which I was with Eberhard, now nearing his ninetieth birthday. To us as a family joy arrived later that month with the wedding of Peter and Laura Epton at Hurstpierpoint College. Also in 1998, at long last, and much to the relief of Duncan Forrester too, I finished the writing of the J. H. Oldham biography. So *Faith on the Frontier* was published jointly by T. & T. Clark and the WCC in September the following year, with three launch parties in appropriate places: in the WCC library in Geneva, close by the Oldham memorial sundial; at New College, Edinburgh where Oldham had studied, next door to the Assembly Room of the Church of Scotland where in 1910 he had masterminded the World Missionary Conference; and at the Athenaeum in London where he had earned the reputation of recruiting and maneuvering people into his programs ("Find out where power lies and then take it to lunch at the Athenaeum" was the probably apocryphal but nevertheless appropriate motto attributed to him). Philip Potter had generously written the foreword, describing Oldham as "my model in all my ministry since 1948". Reviews were more universally complimentary than for anything else I had written, though I was not quite sure what the veteran American ecumenist Paul Crow meant when he described the book in the *Ecumenical Review* as "the most important thing" I had ever done for the ecumenical movement. But it was good to have this wily prophet of the ecumenical story highlighted, for he still has much to say. It was not easy to have completed the book when I was still in the thick of my work, but on the other hand not a few people including David Edwards remarked that perhaps it could only have been written successfully by someone who was wrestling daily with the contemporary versions of the questions Oldham had to face.

I was also prompted to reflect on where I had come and where I—and the ecumenical movement—might be going when in January 2000 at the invitation of John Arnold, at that time the dean, to preach in Durham Cathedral at Sunday morning choral eucharist during the Week of Prayer for Christian Unity, I could not help recalling the nine-year-old boy who had been awed and impressed by the place forty-eight years before.[8] The gospel reading for that Sunday was the story in John's Gospel of the miracle at the wedding feast in Cana (an especial challenge when you could expect New Testament scholars James Dunn and C. K. Barrett to be in the congregation). But the story of the conversion of water into wine prompts us to expect something *new* to be in the offing and to be released from being hooked onto an imagined glorious past.[9] In early April at the CEC Presidium meeting in Istanbul we were also made aware of the passage of time: I had been in office nearly three years and it was already time to think of the next CEC Assembly due in 2003, and other new developments were afoot.

But it was also time for something else, unexpected and certainly unwanted. Just after that Presidium meeting I was diagnosed with bowel cancer. Surgery was required rather urgently, and fortunately the excellent University Hospital in Geneva was able to admit me a few days after Easter. The operation lasted several hours, but the tumor, on the verge of becoming invasive, was successfully removed. Margaret with the cooperation of sympathetic colleagues at UWE was able to rearrange her term-time schedule so as to be with me in Geneva for much of the month of May while I was recovering and convalescing. The recovery was good, and in fact for a while during the summer I was able to travel. I went to Iceland for the one-thousandth anniversary of Christianity there (which also provided time for wonderful bird-watching at historic Thingvellir). With Margaret, at the invitation of Berit Lanke, energetic

---

8. See above, chapter 1, p.11.
9. See "Unity: Hope for the Coming Glory", in Clements, *The Churches in Europe*, 100–104.

pastor of the Church of Norway and ever-cheerful supporter of CEC, in July I went to Trondheim for the annual St Olav Festival and preached in the great square in front of the Cathedral (Archbishop Anastasios was also attending, insisting on keeping a fatherly eye on my welfare). Then in August came the Eighth International Bonhoeffer Congress in Berlin where I gave a paper on "Integration, Conflict and the Ecumenical Quest. Bonhoeffer's Challenge to Twenty-First Century Europe". This last occasion witnessed a poignant absence: Eberhard Bethge had died in April. But while recovery from my operation had been good, there had to follow six months of chemotherapy which got progressively more challenging as the autumn wore on. My work was significantly interrupted and slowed down, and obviously increased demands were made on colleagues. I could only be thankful that eventually the recovery was judged complete, but I sensed that my energy level was never to be quite what it had been. Through it all I was surrounded and sustained by a wide fellowship of thought and prayer from people near and far around the world, which rather took me aback. So much so in fact that it prompted me some time later to deliver a small sermon in the Ecumenical Centre chapel, "On being prayed for", based on Philippians 1:19.[10] It is not always easy to welcome others praying for us, I suggested, because we like to think of ourselves as self-sufficient and essentially independent, not in need of others, whereas in the body of Christ we are members of one another in community. It is a bit like the adolescent who shrinks when being told that someone is keen on them. Perhaps if we feel embarrassed when people say "I'm praying for you" it means we're spiritually still in early adolescence, unlike Paul who had no inhibitions about asking for people's prayers. So this unwanted experience, too, became for me a lesson on where hope lies.

---

10. See Clements, *The Churches in Europe*, 46–49.

17

New Sign-Posts for Unity, New Challenges from War 2000–2003

FOR ALL THE SPECULATIONS that greeted the start of the new millennium in 2001, no-one actually foresaw just how the world look by 2003 when CEC held its Twelfth Assembly in Trondheim, Norway. Not that we were unaware of changes underway in certain directions, especially in European society and the EU, and in the relations between the churches, but these were developments that we were already well aware of and requiring our responses here and now, not possible challenges over the far horizon. It was a time of change within CEC too, not least at executive staffing level. In Geneva, Hans Schmocker and Robin Gurney both retired in 2001. Hans was succeeded in the finance office by Frenchman Jean-Daniel Birmelé, and Robin at the communications desk by Italian Luca Negro. Then in 2002 the Director of Church and Society and Associate General Secretary Keith Jenkins retired. Rüdiger Noll was appointed to the post and so transferred from Geneva to Brussels. Personnel in the CEC orchestra might change but the polyphony continued, with some new themes added to the score.

THE CHARTA OECUMENICA

Compared with travel to exotic places or war-torn locations, or with meeting Popes and Patriarchs and famous or infamous politicians, or even with writing the biography of a major ecumenical figure, the production of a thirteen-page document on cooperation between the churches of Europe might seem a dully mundane affair. Not so. The three-year process by which the *Charta Oecumenica. Guidelines for the Growing Cooperation among the Churches in Europe* took shape was as fascinating as it was challenging, and the eventual product a unique achievement in ecumenical life, in Europe or anywhere else. Nothing that happened during my time at CEC gave me more satisfaction or sense of accomplishment though of course it was not my work personally but that of many others in which I shared.

As related in the previous chapter the CEC-CCEE Joint Committee meeting at Rome in 1998 endorsed the recommendation of the Second European Assembly at Graz for a set of guidelines to be produced on how the churches of Europe should behave towards one another and grow further together in their common tasks in Europe. The Graz recommendation, it should be said, was made not in a state of euphoria such as can easily be generated at large gatherings of the likeminded but rather in a sober awareness that "the ecumenical fellowship is currently in a state of difficulties". The difficulties were not only on specific matters such as that of proselytism, or the intrusion into the canonical territory of one church by clergy or groups from another tradition, nor even the religious dimensions of conflict such as in the Balkans. There was also a general sense that within all traditions there was decreasing commitment to the ecumenical movement and in some cases a hardening attitude against it. To attempt what Graz had called for was inevitably and consciously to go against the stream that was rising in some parts of Europe at least.

The story of the actual production of the *Charta* can be told quite briefly. The CEC-CCEE meeting in Rome not only made a general recommendation but set out some desirable basic features of the text: relatively brief; neither dogma nor church law nor an international political statement; based on Holy Scripture and previous ecumenical and Roman Catholic statements; principles and criteria for promoting ecumenical commitment; promotion of a learning process towards an ecumenical culture and a culture of dialogue among the churches in Europe. What followed was a pattern of working which featured intensive work in small groups, larger consultations, the sharing of provisional results with the entire church constituency, then further revision. The text would be in three parts: first, an *indicative* section, based on Scripture, confessing our common faith and the inescapable call to ecumenism; second, an *imperative* section, on the churches and Christians of Europe committing themselves to live in ecumenical fellowship; third, a section on *concrete implications* on relations between majority and minority churches, proselytism, differences in approaches to ethical questions, dealings with history, and structures for dialogue between churches. A first draft was discussed at length at the next CEC-CCEE Joint Committee in Guernsey in March 1999 and received with the stern but wise recommendations that the final text be no longer than the present draft (as anyone who has attended church conferences or been involved in writing their reports, what begins as a sleek yacht tends to become an overladen barge by the end of the day). It was also proposed that the draft text be submitted just once to all the churches, in summer 1999, and the final version be adopted by the CEC-CCEE Joint Committee at its meeting early in 2001. But it was a wise move, also, to call for a larger consultation before the Cartigny draft was sent out to the churches and so a study conference of 50 persons took place over a weekend on Graz. All this, incidentally, was happening at the same time as we were trying to come to terms with the Kosovo crisis.

Part Four: Ecumenical Europe 1997–2005

At the end of June 1999 Viorel Ionita and I went to St Gallen for an overnight stay and meeting with Aldo Giordano and his assistant Sara Numico to tidy up the *Charta* draft in the light of the Graz discussion. Going to St Gallen was always a huge pleasure, for Aldo and his staff in their house at Arbon close by the shore of Lake Konstanz were so hospitable (one of the priests had been a professional chef before another vocation intervened), but this time there was additional satisfaction because we were now so well on with the *Charta* process and a critical point was being reached. Next afternoon on the train back to Geneva it was tempting simply to enjoy that wonderful rolling green scenery and wait for the marvelous view of Lake Geneva as the train emerged out of the tunnel near Montreux. Instead that landscape became an inspiring backdrop as I pulled out a writing pad and started composing the letter which would accompany the draft *Charta*. The draft went out in July to all the CEC member churches, the Catholic Bishops" Conferences and the Associated Organizations of CEC and CCEE, with the letter requesting that it be discussed thoroughly in their own contexts and for responses to be received by September 1 2000. There was thus over a year available for discussion and response. Besides the official languages of German, English and French it was translated even at this stage into at least sixteen other languages, and national councils of churches and ecumenical working groups were also wishing to take part in the exercise. By the end of September 2000 in Geneva we had received seventy-five responses from member churches and ecumenical organizations, and at St Gallen twenty responses and papers from bishops' conferences had arrived together with some fifty comments from various Catholic organizations and groups. There was evidence of widespread and serious discussion of the text in all traditions. Naturally there were many criticisms and suggestions for improvement and it was interesting how these sometimes contradicted each other or balanced each other out. Some felt the text to be too modest, others felt it not modest enough. Some Protestants felt it was too dominated by Orthodox language, while some churches from central and Eastern Europe found it to too western in ethos and too liberal in its underlying theology. A crucial meeting of the Working Group was held in the John Knox Centre, Geneva in October 2000 at which all the responses were looked at and also examined in three confessional groups—Catholic, Protestant and Orthodox. Throughout the *Charta* process, it was the intensive, searching exchanges at the personal level as we struggled together to find a common mind, going to the same sources of Scripture and the Trinitarian tradition of faith, persisting in trying to see and understand what the other was saying in his or her own terms, that I found most rewarding.. A revised text was eventually prepared to be submitted to the meeting of the CEC-CCEE Joint Committee in Porto, Portugal, in late January 2001.

This meeting of the Joint-Committee took place in an atmosphere of some uncertainty and indeed confusion. On August 6 the previous year the statement *Dominus Iesus* had been issued by the Vatican. A reiteration of standard Catholic teaching on the uniquely salvific role of Christ and on the universality of the Catholic Church, it caused offence to many outside the Roman and Orthodox worlds by declaring that those churches which did not in its view maintain the unbroken continuity with the church of the Apostles by recognizing the status of the successors of St Peter (in effect, Anglicans and all Protestants) should not be termed "churches" but "ecclesial communities". What did this betoken of commitment to ecumenical dialogue and what value would it place on a project like the *Charta*? When reporting to the CEC Central Committee at Iasi the previous October on reactions to the statement I had found a range of attitudes. Some were distinctly annoyed, especially as it seemed to set the clock back after the Lutheran-Catholic Agreement on Justification reached barely a year before *Dominus Iesus*. Others however warned against over-reacting. There was after all evidence that the declaration was largely the work of Cardinal Josef Ratzinger, head of the *Propaganda Fidei* and that it had equally annoyed others in the Vatican especially Cardinal Walter Kasper, now head of the Pontifical Commission for Promoting Christian Unity. At Porto it was equally clear that *Dominus Iesus* was just as much an embarrassment to some members of the CCEE delegation, notably Bishop Karl Lehmann who, while not openly critical of the statement, said that it demonstrated the need for deeper examination (by Catholics no less than others) of the nature of the unity we seek. In the midst of our discussions Bishop Lehmann was summoned outside to take a phone call. He returned and took his place again with what was presently shown to have been great self-control, for it was the news that he had been appointed a cardinal. Great was the acclaim.

The Porto meeting agreed on the final text of the *Charta* and approved it for transmission to the Ecumenical Encounter being to take place at Strasbourg just after Easter. This decision caused some dispute both within and outside the CEC governing bodies. Some, including on the CEC Presidium which met in Geneva in March, believed that it should still be open to further revision, even at the Encounter itself. But this was to mistake the nature and purpose of the *Charta*. It was not meant to be a kind of doctrinal statement commanding or claiming complete agreement by the churches. It was to be a set of guidelines *offered* to the churches formulated after the widest practicable consultation with them. It was, as Viorel Ionita insisted, a *basic text* that would be presented at Strasbourg after discussion but not further revision. It could be added to or adapted by churches as they saw fit in their own particular contexts, and would it was hoped stimulate a lot more thinking and action, but as a basic text it would stand as presently formulated.

So there it stood, its subtitle declaring that it comprised *Guidelines for the Growing Cooperation among the Churches in Europe* and, as stated in its preface, "a common commitment to dialogue and cooperation" and "fundamental ecumenical responsibilities". Its three short chapters were headed, respectively: "We Believe in One Holy Catholic and Apostolic Church"; "On the Way Towards the Visible Fellowship of the Churches in Europe"; and "Our Common Responsibility in Europe". This was somewhat different from the early conception of three sections in turn indicative, imperative and then concrete recommendations. Now, each section, after a Scriptural text, comprised descriptive statements of basic theology and ecumenical life, recommendations for action and, most importantly, *commitments*. For example, *we commit ourselves* to act together at all levels of church life wherever conditions permit and there are no reasons of faith or overriding expediency mitigating against this. *We commit ourselves* to work towards the goal of eucharistic fellowship. *We commit ourselves* to counteract any form of nationalism which leads to the oppression of other peoples and national minorities. *We commit ourselves* to support church environmental organizations in their efforts for the safeguarding of creation. In all there were twenty-five such commitments, covering the search for unity, evangelism, praying together, reconciling peoples and cultures, safeguarding creation, and relations with other faiths especially Judaism and Islam.

ENCOUNTER IN STRASBOURG

Meanwhile concurrently with the production of the *Charta Oecumenica* went the preparations for the Ecumenical Encounter which, as agreed by the CEC-CCEE Joint Committee, was to be held immediately after Easter 2001 under the theme "Lo, I am with you always, to the end of the age", and involving equal numbers of church leaders and people under thirty years of age. As a very first step a group was convened of representatives of the CEC-related youth organizations, i.e. the Ecumenical Youth Council in Europe (EYCE), the World Student Federation (WSCF) and the Orthodox youth organization Syndesmos, with representatives of Catholic youth organizations, to sound out their ideas and to listen to their concerns. The youth were also represented at the twice-yearly meetings of the full preparatory group. It is always a sensitive issue—certainly from the youth side—when youth are to be involved in such an event, as to whether their participation is genuine in the conception and implementation of planning decisions or whether they are being subtly and controlled and manipulated by the adult leadership. In the case of the Encounter such concern focused on the actual invitations to the event. On the CEC side it was decided that 50% of the youth delegates should be chosen by the youth organizations themselves with no questions asked, and 50% nominated by member churches of CEC but with the proviso that overall there should be a proper balance of confessions, regions and gender. On the CCEE side a greater measure of selection by the church authorities was evident.

During 1999 and 2000 planning was going well. It was also becoming evident that while originating independently the Encounter and the *Charta Oecumenica* could not only run in parallel but should appropriately converge, with the process of producing the *Charta* culminating at the Encounter. That, however, created a certain problem of its own in relation to the venue. The original idea was that it would be highly appropriate for a European event marking the start of the third millennium of the Christian era to be held at one of the most historically significant sites of the Christian mission to Europe, namely Thessaloniki in Greece where St Paul preached and founded a church soon after crossing from Asia, having seen a vision of the Macedonian man saying "Come over and help us" (Acts 16:9, 17:1–9). At first the idea was welcomed by the (Orthodox) Church of Greece. Presently however rumors began to reach us of certain anti-ecumenical voices being raised in that Church. With well under a year to go to Easter 2001, in June 2000 just as I was convalescing after surgery I heard by phone from Athens the news that the invitation to Thessaloniki could not now be confirmed. It was a deep disappointment, and a Plan B for the venue had urgently to be put into operation: Strasbourg, not as anciently significant as Thessaloniki but of great significance in the Reformation and recent ecumenical history, was moreover of very great contemporary importance as the seat of the European Parliament and other European Institutions. The Protestant Churches of Alsace and Strasbourg, and the Roman Catholic Church in France, nobly and readily agreed to take on the task of hosting the meeting at such short notice. It helped greatly that the CEC Deputy Vice-President, Jean-Marc Prieur, was a professor in the theology faculty of the University of Strasbourg in which the gathering would take place.

Strasbourg during April 19–22 2001 was cold and wet but this did not dampen the spirits of the two hundred people who came to the Encounter. It was preceded by meetings of the CEC Central Committee and the Council of CCEE, and a joint meeting of both, plus a preliminary youth event. The Encounter itself opened with a great service in Strasbourg Cathedral at which Professor Elisabeth Parmentier, a member of the CEC Dialogue Commission, preached on the Easter story (Matt. 28:1–10). Greetings were received from Pope John Paul II and the Ecumenical Patriarch Bartholomew. The following days were intensive, occupied with Bible studies, lectures and group discussions, and morning and evening prayers led according to different confessional traditions. The main theme was developed through sub-themes on successive days: "Who are you for me?"; "Where are you leading us?" and "Where are you sending us?" There was plenty of time, however for small round-table discussions with equal numbers of younger and older at each table. For many there were two main highlights. The first was an afternoon spent at the Council of Europe, where participants were welcomed by Bruno Haller, General Secretary of the Council of Europe Parliamentary Assembly, who said that with the *Charta Oecumenica* the churches had set an example for the politicians. Persons from different backgrounds including Cardinal Roger Etchegaray, Michael Weniger of the EU and a number of youth delegates spoke of what their personal faith meant to them and their commitment to working within the public sphere and politics. Later, Reinhard Frieling led a high-level scholarly presentation on the *Charta Oecumenica* which fed into the four working groups which met at the University next morning. The second highlight for many came next morning with the Emmaus Walk, a crucial part of the encounter between the generations. Following morning prayers at the St Paul's Church, each participant was given a card with a picture of the risen Jesus and the two disciples on the road to Emmaus. On the back of the card were questions to stimulate conversation about what

Part Four: Ecumenical Europe 1997–2005

Easter meant to the participants. All were then sent out in pairs, one young and one older, for the walk back to the University. Many found it an extraordinary experience. It was not just the older ones handing on the ecumenical commitment to the younger ones; it was equally the younger ones challenging and renewing the commitment of the older ones by their enthusiasm and questions. Finally, on the Sunday morning after worship in four different churches, all participants gathered for a final service in the St Thomas Church at which Archbishop Anastasios preached. He concluded: "Proceed with the certainty that 'all things' are under the power of the resurrected Lord, not only all humanity, but even the entire creation. Instead of an economic globalization which leads to the exploitation of many, let us struggle, each according to his or her abilities and opportunities, toward an ecumenical brotherhood that rests upon freedom, respect for one another, and love, which emanates from the cross and the life-giving tomb of the resurrected Christ." Following the service there came an unplanned but most affirmative moment when representatives of the youth delegates read out a message in which they committed themselves to support and to spread the *Charta Oecumenica*. Then came the climax of the whole Encounter as, to great and joyful acclaim, Cardinal Vlk and Metropolitan Jérémie signed the letter which would accompany the transmission of the *Charta* to the churches. Delegates were sent forth not only with a blessing but a mini-knapsack containing a copy of the *Charta*.

Signing of the *Charta Oecumenica*. L. to R: Viorel Ionita, Rut Rohrandt, Cardinal Vlk, Aldo Giordano, Reinhard Frieling, Metropolitan Jérémie, KC.

One journalist commented: "It is hard to say what weight the afternoon... at the Council of Europe will carry in ecumenical history. But to say that at the end the faces of all those present were radiant, without exception, does not require rhetoric." Elfriede Dörr, in dialogue with Cardinal Lehmann at the end, said of the encounter between the generations: "There was real listening and speaking, questioning and enquiring, getting to know one another and opening ourselves to being known." Another youth delegate said of the *Charta*: "It is really in the hearts of us young people. We have been looking forward to its signing, hoping that this word would 'become flesh'... for us as youth, ecumenical dialogue has absolute priority." Four weeks later, Aldo Giordano and I, together with Sara Numico and Viorel Ionita, met in Arbon to reflect on the Encounter, its strengths and shortcomings including those on the logistical side.

Following its launch at Strasbourg the *Charta Oecumenica* quickly took on a life of its own. By the end of 2002 it had been translated into thirty different languages. It was taken up and used in all areas of CEC's work—Church and Society, Inter-Church Service, Women's Desk, and in inter-faith relations too. It became a tool for use by churches, ecumenical organizations and theological seminaries, and special events on the *Charta* were being reported from Germany, Sweden, the Netherlands, Hungary, Slovakia and the Czech Republic. The Presidents of Churches Together in England (CTE) jointly signed it in the presence of Queen Elizabeth the Queen Mother (though the overall British reception of the *Charta* was lukewarm). Nor was its influence limited to Europe. In June 2001 the Council of the Lutheran World Federation decided to send the *Charta* to all its member churches throughout the world. It was also taken up in on-going bilateral dialogues between churches, in 2001 most notably in the dialogue meeting of the EKD and the Ecumenical Patriarchate. But no occasion stands more vividly in the memory than the sweltering afternoon evening of May 30 2003, when at the First Ecumenical Kirchentag in Berlin the heads of virtually all the German Churches, Roman Catholic and right across the Protestant spectrum and the Orthodox, solemnly signed the *Charta* to great applause. A moment of real thanksgiving and hope.

THE BALKANS AGAIN

The excitements of the Strasbourg Encounter and the follow-up on the *Charta Oecumenica* did not distract from the long-term concerns of CEC, especially in the Balkans. CEC and WCC had planned for a joint visit to Serbia in early 2001. In order to prepare for this, having just about got out of the chemotherapy regime, in December 2000 I sneaked a three-day visit to Belgrade Most of my time there was spent with Father Andreas Cilerdzic, the young priest who worked as secretary for external relations in the Orthodox Patriarchate and whom I had known well since our visits in 1999. We did not always see eye to eye on matters of the day but had become very good friends, His dedication and enthusiasm in the cause of opening up his church to the wider world were extraordinary in that closed-in nationalist atmosphere, and his round-the-clock energy seemed inexhaustible. But it came at cost. He had no assistance in his office, was barely surviving on the pittance of a wage from the church (he once dared to show me the dire state of his tattered jeans under his cassock), and he drove a worn-out banger of a car (supplied by friends in Germany). He received no petrol money from the Church, and like other visitors I was only too glad to include the fuel costs for our trips around and outside Belgrade in my travel expenses. The condition of his car, admittedly, came as no surprise to me when one afternoon we were driving out of town to visit his monastery for evening prayer and a meal. Suddenly without warning the car lurched off the road and down an embankment into a field. Noting my alarm he said, "Don't worry, this is just a short-cut to the monastery." Most of the people and places we visited in preparation for the CEC-WCC visit were of course familiar to me. But one scene was quite new: near the center of Belgrade, a camp for Serbian refugees from Kosovo. Their condition was quite pitiable. Expelled from Kosovo by Kosovar Albanian paramilitaries, they too had suffered ethnic cleansing if on a much smaller scale than their Albanian neighbors, and they were among the most forgotten victims. They included many young people; earlier that year Andreas had taken a party of them to Taizé, a world-opening, mind-blowing experience for them.

The CEC-WCC visit in February 2001, which included WCC General Secretary Konrad Raiser in the party, had good reason to feel that changes were under way in Serbia. Almost as soon as we arrived we found ourselves in an Orthodox Church where the new President of Yugoslavia, Vojislav Kostunica, was present as sponsor of two young women being baptized. Next day we had a substantial meeting with him on topics including the rights of religious minorities. We spent a morning with staff and students of the Orthodox Theological Faculty (which CEC had helped to fund during the communist time), and of course met with Patriarch Pavle and members of the Holy Synod. We also met some of the Reformed pastors in Vojvodina, one of whom now seemed to have a quite unreal notion of how and when the trouble began in Kosovo. I preached at Sunday morning service in the Baptist Church in Novi Sad.

From Belgrade some of us travelled on to Zagreb, and then to Skopje in Macedonia for a first consultation in the South-East Europe Ecumenical Partnership (SEEEP) programme being launched by the WCC, in which CEC had responsibility for the hub on peace-building and reconciliation[1], and for which Boris Peterlin of Zagreb had been seconded by the Baptist Union of Croatia to act as consultant. With CEC collaboration, in June the WCC convened a two-day meeting at Morges, under the moderatorship of Archbishop Anastasios, of representatives and leaders of the religious communities (Orthodox, Roman Catholic, Methodist, Muslim and Jewish) of Macedonia where there had been outbreaks of inter-ethnic violence. The meeting provided a striking and instructive demonstration of the dynamics involved whenever religious representatives are called to face the religious factor in conflict and violence. First of all, great mutual politeness, and strenuous denials that their respective faiths

1. See above, chapter 16, p.299.

are anything but peaceful and have anything to do with violence, and therefore are to be distanced from any of the scenes that have been reported. But then the Albanians started to talk of the destruction of mosques that had taken place, and the feeling that all along they were being treated as second class citizens. From the Catholic and Orthodox side came questions about the political agenda behind the Muslim protests. In what precise ways did the Albanians feel they were being mistreated? Was for example the language issue in the university for example really so serious? The discussion was now getting down to honest exchanges of pain on the one hand and anxiety on the other. The Jewish participant Viktor Mizrabi asked, "But what can we do to stop the war? We cannot as representatives of religions stop the war but at least we can stop it becoming a religious war." Then came a moment of acceptance of responsibility, when the Muslim Ljota Ruzli said, "We must put ourselves in each other's shoes"—the most "Christian" remark uttered up till then. Or, as Anastasios remarked soon afterwards, "It's not 'always some others' than ourselves who are the most dangerous people." (On another occasion I heard him remark to a gathering of Orthodox leaders, "Let us admit it: we have our own Taliban in our communities.") The immediate outcome of the meeting was a joint statement not only dissociating religion from the conflict but also calling for protection of civilians and respect for human rights. It was fast becoming clear that the acid test for religious integrity, as distinct from confessional chauvinism, was the commitment of faith leaders to human rights for all people regardless of religion. But very soon, in an unexpected way, the question of the role of religion in conflict and violence was suddenly to reach global dimensions.

SEPTEMBER 11 AND AFTER

On Tuesday September 11 2001 the CEC Budget Committee concluded a twenty-four hour meeting at John Knox House, Geneva. Returning to the Ecumenical Centre in the afternoon, I was standing in the CEC corridor when Robin Gurney emerged from the communications office holding a transistor radio to his ear and saying, "Someone's just flown an airliner into the World Trade Centre in New York... No, wait—a second plane has just gone in too." No-one knew what to say, until someone remarked "This is the end of politics". Back in the apartment, one could only watch on TV in disbelief at the scenes in New York, and hurriedly email friends there for any news of them. I emailed a letter of sympathy and solidarity to the National Churches of Christ. There was little chance to do more, for next morning Viorel Ionita and I were off to Sarajevo.

For a number of years the CEC-CCEE Committee had sponsored a joint committee on Islam in Europe. As well as an annual newsletter it made studies on Christian-Muslim relations in Europe, and produced materials on issues like mixed marriages and for use at inter-faith public events and joint commemorations. Up till now however it had not itself organized any Christian-Muslim encounters and on the CCEE side there had been reluctance about any direct dialogue with Muslims.

This international conference on "Christians and Muslims in Europe, responsibility and religious commitment to the plural society" was therefore a new venture and had been organized for September 12–16. The close concurrence of the occasion with the terrorist attacks in the USA seemed like an ironic—or providential—coincidence. In fact some of the seventy-eight participants had been travelling for over twenty-four hours and did not even hear of the events until they arrived in Sarajevo. The President of the Bosnia-Hercegovina Federation, Alijah Behmen, attended the first session. Most of the delegates were Christian but the Muslim contributors were from high-level academic institutions. A Christian and a Muslim voice introduced each of the three sub-themes: the challenges of living together in a largely secular and plural society; healing the wounds of Christian and Muslim memories so that we can commit ourselves to justice and peace for all; shared values through which our communities can contribute actively to constructing a better society. There was an interesting exchange between Professor Mehmet Aydin of the University of Izmkir and Archbishop Anastasios, the latter arguing against *too much* attention to history. Aldo Giordano and I jointly moderated the final session. A strong recommendation was made to focus on education especially in schools, to encourage pastors, priests, imams, and lay people to undertake interreligious dialogue, with exchanges between Christian and Muslim faculties and seminaries, and to maintain or set up in each European country institutions with the aim of interreligious dialogue on ethical, social, and political values in society. The events in the USA cast an inescapable shadow over all the proceedings and eventually it was decided to issue a statement. It was short and concise, expressing shock and sorrow, and pain for the thousands killed, injured and bereaved, unanimously condemning this act of violence "as well as any other destruction of human life as a violation of God's will and a sin against humanity" and, "recognizing the potential for violence that resides in all of us"; and praying that this senseless act would not provoke indiscriminate retaliation, and committing all participants at the conference to be instruments of justice, peace, and dialogue. Nothing more, and nothing less, could be said just then. On the final morning, a Sunday, I preached in the small Baptist congregation. Quite apart from what had happened in America five days earlier Sarajevo, a city fatefully associated with conflict and violence first in 1914 and then more recently as the besieged city of the 1990s, forced one to weigh one's words very carefully on the theme of reconciliation.[2]

The CEC Presidium, meeting in Palermo, Sicily early in October, endorsed what had been done thus far by CEC and after thorough discussion agreed that Metropolitan Jérémie and I should write to the CEC member churches, calling for increased interreligious dialogue and for serious reflection in relation to the attacks. Noting what the *Charta Oecumenica* said about the need for structures of peace the letter stated: "Responses to terrorist violence should be reflective, focused, measured

---

2. See sermon "After 11 September—a New Creation?" in Clements, *The Churches in Europe*, 117–121.

and proportionate . . . [T]hey should seek to produce a result which is more just after the event than before. Responses should also be in keeping with international law."

In November I flew to the USA, first of all for the annual assembly of the National Council of Churches of Christ in the USA (NCCCUSA), in Oakland near San Francisco at the invitation of the General Secretary of NCCCUSA Bob Edgar. He had taken charge of NCCUSA at the start of 2000 and I had met him at meetings of Regional Ecumenical Organizations and of the WCC. A minister of the United Methodist Church, he had also spent several years as a Democrat Congressman, among other things taking a key part in winding down the US military campaign in Vietnam and also serving on the commission which made the final report on the assassination of Martin Luther King. On one occasion during a presidential election he was dubbed by Ronald Reagan "the most dangerous man in this state". Quietly dynamic, he earned a reputation as a superb trouble-shooter who rescued several educational institutions from terminal decline, and was now doing the same for NCCCUSA which by 1999 had become directionless and was collapsing into severe financial and administrative disorder. He also had a weakness for ice-cream, jokes and excruciatingly awful puns. He was certainly needed at that time, for while he was pulling NCCCUSA around, at Oakland I found the member churches of NCCCUSA somewhat dispirited, not only by what had happened on September 11 but by their own evident failure thus far to make any impact in the public debate on the response to the attacks. Mainline Christianity was being marginalized. I was invited to speak and brought greetings from CEC. I said that now was the time for deeper partnership between churches region to region, and that a shared vulnerability was more important than self-protection and this must bring the churches of the world together in shared responsibility. But the USA at that time was still very jumpy. From San Francisco I flew to Denver, Colorado, for the AAR meetings and the Bonhoeffer Translation Editorial Board. The cabin was almost empty. For the moment, at any rate, it seemed Osama Bin Laden had won.

Soon after returning from the USA, for perhaps slightly different reasons I found uncertainty also at a four-day international consultation hosted by the WCC in Geneva at the end of November on "Beyond September 11: Assessing Global Implications" which drew together over twenty specialists from around the world. I was struck by how during the first day of discussion hardly any reference was made to the possibility of a specifically religious element or motivation in the attacks of September 11. The framework of the whole discussion was socio-political, and the imbalance of wealth and poverty in the world was the sole interpretative key. When I ventured to raise the religious question, a Latin American participant said, in effect, "Well, of course there is a religious element: the religious element is the idol of economic growth and economic oppression." That was a fair point, but it didn't address the question of why the terrorists of September 11 had copies of the Koran with them. There was something here too embarrassing and unsettling for the ideology which had assumed ecumenical dominance for so long. Anyway, the discussion was continued at various levels and in various places over the next few months. In December I wrote to the Belgian Prime Minister Guy Verhofstadt in view of the EU presidency being held the next half-year by Belgium, voicing two concerns: the prospect of extending the military "war on terror" to countries beyond Afghanistan; and the threat to human rights legislation in EU countries in reaction to terrorism. There was a meeting of Christian, Jewish and Muslim leaders in Brussels just before Christmas, invited by the Ecumenical Patriarch and the President of the EU Commission, and in January a brainstorming meeting convened by the CEC Church and Society Commission for informal talks on European political responsibility, with participants from the WCC, NCCCUSA and NATO. At the CEC central Committee in Morges in June 2002 Hans Ucko of the WCC Interreligious Relations and Dialogue desk addressed and led a discussion at a deliberative session on the issues raised by the attacks and their aftermath. All of which goes to show just how occupied we were with the implications of what had happened an ocean away from Europe, and what was now happening in the Middle East. Not that this absolved us from having address very concretely and in a practical way some long-running problems within Europe itself, as we shall now see.

SOLIDARITY

One of my favorite places to visit was the Church of Finland conference center at Järvenpää, about an hour's drive north of Helsinki. It stands by a large lake, a marvelous spot for bird-watching, being a major location for the migrating swans and geese in spring and autumn. Jan Sibelius, whose house still stands not far away as a shrine to his memory, also used to come here to watch the waterfowl. Whenever I listen to the opening movement of his first symphony I am transported back to that austerely beautiful waterside. One of the most important meetings held at Järvenpää was in late September 2001 just a fortnight after the terrorist attacks in America, the first and long-awaited truly pan-European Diaconal Forum, co-organized by the CEC Interchurch Service desk and the Church and Society Commission, Eurodiaconia, the European Contact Group (responsible particularly for urban and industrial mission), and the Churches' Commission on migrants in Europe (CCME). It brought together over one hundred and ten participants from twenty-six European countries for three days of dialogue, analysis and reflection on the new challenges which were being brought to the churches in a time of rapid change in Europe. Its sub-themes were the value of work and employment, migration and mobility, building sustainable communities and seeking quality of life for all. Three round tables focused on the relationship between diaconic work and the churches, between diaconia and civil society, and the tasks of diaconia in the context of the changing role of the state and the European Institutions. It identified main priorities in all these areas. In my opening address I could not avoid mentioning the attacks in the USA and the disturbing effect that they had on all people concerned for social welfare because of course they prompted the question, "What if something like that also happens here?" I pointed to the way in which the Letter to the Hebrews, written at a time of evident uncertainty and threats to the early church, enjoined the building of community and the welcome to be given to outsiders: "Let mutual love continue. Do not neglect to show hospitality to strangers, for by doing that some have entertained angels without knowing it. Remember those in prison, as though were in prison with them . . . " (Hebs 13:1–3). I have to say that finding an ecumenical pattern and framework for the whole range of diaconal work was the hardest organizational task we faced during my time in CEC and, in terms of results, the aspect I was least happy with. We had failed to find a workable structure for a "Commission on Solidarity", due in large part to the disparity of the constituent parties and their felt needs. The Diaconal Forum was a great step forward. It was not really able, however, to address the underlying g questions of the relationship between the organizing bodies, which included of course their relationship to CEC. Keen to fulfil their diaconic role, such organizations can be as competitive as they are, on paper, cooperative. Tension arose particularly over the claim increasingly made by Eurodiaconia that it, and not CEC, should be main coordinating group for diaconal work in Europe as a whole. An even more protracted and intractable problem was that of the relationship of the Churches Commission on Migrants (CCME), very ably led by Doris Peschke, to CEC. For some time it had been an associated organization of CEC, but there were clear advantages if it became a commission of CEC no less than Church and Society or the Dialogue Commission. This would give solidity to it, and even more important, ensure that its vital work with refugees, migrants and asylum-seekers would be brought into the heart of CEC and adopted as a responsibility of all the churches. An arrangement was worked out whereby a three-way partnership between the CEC Interchurch Service desk, CCME and the WCC would cover much of the work in this area but it never proved satisfactory. As far as CCME becoming a commission of CEC, an inherent difficulty was that a significant part of CCME's constituency and membership did not coincide with that of CEC—for example some of the African independent churches and migrants' organizations. It would be a tricky marriage from that point of view. Working group after working group struggled with this but it was still not wholly resolved by the time I left CEC, and I felt bad about that.

THE LARGER EUROPE AND AN ENLARGING EU

In February 2002 the staff from all three CEC offices in Geneva, Brussels and Strasbourg met for a two-day residential meeting. Much of our time was spent on plans for the CEC Assembly in Trondheim the following year. The discussion inevitably led on to "CEC post-Trondheim", which in turn led to reflection on the changes taking place in Europe just then. Not least, the European Convention process set up by the Heads of state and governments in 2001 was already generating intense debate on the nature and scope of a new constitution for the EU—while at the same time applications for EU membership were in train from ten countries in Eastern Europe. What I most vividly recall from this discussion was a warning from Keith Jenkins against assuming that the future of the EU was going to be a smooth, guaranteed ride of progress, peace and prosperity. There could even be derailment. There were inbuilt ambiguities and tensions in the European project, promising consumerist freedom while at the same time requiring solidarity among and between peoples. Moreover there was increasing popular suspicion and skepticism about all institutions and what they could deliver. For the churches therefore a prime concern was whether Europe and in particular the EU was also a community of common values. The Church and Society Commission's Working Group on the European Integration Process had published in 2001 a text, *Churches in the Process of European Integration* which was circulated to all CEC member churches. The Commission then turned its close attention to the Convention Process in close cooperation with the (Roman Catholic) Commission of the Bishops' Conferences of the European Community (COMECE), organizing a number of meetings with individual members of the Convention and making submissions to the Convection as a whole. Relevant to this discussion was also the continuing work on reconciliation in Europe, not only in the Balkans but wherever the wounds of past conflicts and their memories still needed healing. The Dialogue Commission, for example, meeting in Trondheim in May 2002 included a workshop on the healings of memories in Northern Ireland, on the relation of the Sami indigenous people and Roma in relation to church and nation in Norway, on relations between Germany and Poland since the Second World War, and between Germany and the Czech people.

GEORGIA: HEAD IN EUROPE, BODY IN ASIA

For myself, one of the regions where the issue of common European values and ecumenical fellowship came alive most sharply was on the European eastern fringe: the vulnerable and fragile Caucasus. There was for a start the war being waged in Chechnya by Russian forces and Chechnyan rebels. Already in the winter of 1999–2000 Konrad Raiser and I had written on behalf of the WCC and CEC to Patriarch Alexei in Moscow, expressing concern over the way the war was being waged, the extent of suffering of civilians and the numbers of refugees. In May 2001 I attended part of the Dialogue Commission meeting in Armenia, and so was able to visit historic Yerevan, to experience rural life still dragging itself out of post-USSR poverty, and to witness the reviving life of the Armenian Church and not least in its monasteries and seminaries. Then in June 2002 I visited Georgia at the invitation of the Lutheran Bishop Dr Gert Hummel and the Baptist leader Bishop Malkhaz Songulashvili whom I had met several times in the Baptist World Alliance, and was well-known for his adoption of Orthodox dress and, in worship, symbolism. There was special sensitivity in this visit as the (Orthodox) Church of Georgia had in 1997 withdrawn its membership from both CEC and the WCC largely, it was believed, because of strongly nationalist and anti-ecumenical elements fostering discord within the Church. There had also been widely-reported incidents of violence and intimidation being committed by some of these elements, especially one led by the fanatic ex-priest Vasili Mkalishhvili, against non-Orthodox churches particularly the Baptists. Church buildings had been attacked, services disrupted, and the store of Bibles at the joint premises of the Baptist Church and the United Bible Societies had been publicly burnt—all with apparent impunity.

My first two days in Tbilisi were packed with meetings and sight-seeing. There is so much history to acknowledge in Georgia, centering on the shrine of St Nina, first bearer of the gospel to the country in the fourth century. There was also, it seemed, so much to eat and drink and the summer heat made the hospitality strenuous as well as delightful. I had long discussions with the Baptists, Lutherans, Roman Catholics and Armenian Orthodox, plus an ecumenically-minded Georgian priest Farther Zaza Tervzadze who had just returned from language study at Selly Oak, sponsored by the Church Mission Society. I found real interest and desire to know about ecumenism. The *Charta Oecumenica* had already been translated into Georgian, and we discussed at length how CEC and the WCC might help supply information and study materials. At that time the only ecumenical structures of any kind were the United Bible Society and the Ecumenical Study Group. The Orthodox were not part of the Study Group apparently because encounter with the Roman Catholics would have presented difficulties for them. For the Orthodox in particular it was clear that to be known as ecumenical meant a real and potentially costly commitment. One Orthodox priest who attended the ceremonial launch of the *Charta Oecumenica* in Tbilisi in his vestments was visited in his church a few days later by some other priests and aggressively criticized for doing so (I recalled this story whenever snooty voices in the West were dismissive of the *Charta* as "insignificant"). Truly inclusive ecumenism in this context had necessarily to be informal in nature. In it all, the churches of all traditions were vitally and imaginatively engaged in all kinds of diaconic work, with community centers, church restoration projects, and cultural and educational programs. None were driven into survival-only mentality. One of my cherished memories is of Malkhaz Songulashvili talking at length with street children in the center of Tbilisi. I met also the Chief Rabbi, the American Chargé d'affaires, a number of politicians and government officials and the British Ambassador Deborah Barnes Jones (who took a keen interest in the church scene and was very supportive of the Baptists), and the Human Rights desk person at the OSCE offices in Tbilisi. Human rights and religious freedom were main topics at the political level, particularly as new legislation in draft form, *On Freedom of Conscience and Religious Entities* would shortly be going through Parliament. The non-Orthodox, including the Baptists, with whom I discussed this regarded it as on the while unexceptional. The only problems foreseen lay with the ambiguities of such terms as "improper proselytism" which implied the offer of material or social benefits or the application of psycho-social influence as inducements or pressures to join a religious entity. Of more concern to evangelical minorities was the failure of the legal system to deal with the fanatics.

Three occasions stand out as highlights. The first was the late afternoon ecumenical service in the Tbilisi Central Baptist Church at which I had been invited to preach. On arrival the first thing on view was a large police presence outside the church. This had not been asked for but on being informed of the service and of my visit the authorities on this occasion at least, wanted to forestall any trouble by the extremist groups. So I can at least say I have preached under police guard. There was a large congregation even though it was during working hours, with a significant presence of younger people and children. Guests included a number from the political sphere including parliamentarians such as Mikhail Naneichvili, incoming chair of the Committee on Human Rights. In keeping with Malkhaz Shongulashvili's style the service was by most Baptist standards very liturgical: vestments, a procession led by a censer, candles, and conducted in great dignity (despite the heat I acceded to Malkhaz's request to wear a Geneva gown). A small choir sang Orthodox-type chants while a youth choir contributed more western-style items. A group of young women danced beautifully on the theme of the ascension (unfortunately during the service the electricity supply failed—a frequent occurrence in Tbilisi—depriving them of the background music they needed for the second dance). I preached, through an interpreter, on "Staying with Christ", based on John 6:67–68.[3] In it, and not only for the benefit of the politicos listening, I emphasized that for CEC in the Europe of today respect for human rights and the rule of law must be the duty of every government, without exception. When I returned to my velvet-cushioned seat I found it now occupied by a liturgically-minded young cat who proved reluctant to move but deigned to sit on my lap for the next part of the service in face of disapproving stares from some members of the congregation. The service concluded with the eucharist presided over by Malkhaz assisted by Bishop Hummel and myself. The whole occasion was impressive and inspiring, above all because of the warmth of the welcome and appreciation of the worshippers themselves.

---

3. See sermon "After 11 September—a New Creation?" in Clements, *The Churches in Europe*, 117–121.

Eye to eye across the table with Eduard Shevardnadze

The second was the forty-five minute meeting I had with State President Eduard Shevardnadze. Minister of State for Foreign Affairs during the last years of the Soviet Union and one of Mikhail Gorbachev's right-hand men in bringing about the eventual changes (I had heard him lecture on this at Chatham House during my time at CCBI), he had returned to his native Georgia as President in 1992. Our meeting was open and cordial. He presented me with a copy of his decree of May 17 2002, "About the Measures on the Strengthening of Human Rights in Georgia", and in turn I presented him with the Georgian version of the *Charta Oecumenica*. We discussed both the evident failure to prosecute the likes of Mkalishhvili and his gangs and, at greater length, the new draft religious legislation. He expressed his commitment to ensure the progress of democratization and the establishment of human rights in Georgia. He reiterated that Georgia was on the road to being a fully democratic society and it was reassuring to hear him say that the rule of law would be established in the Mkalkasvili case where one of the main obstacles to bringing him to court had been the failure to ensure the safety of witnesses. He said, with a rueful smile, that in the "old days" the government would of course have had much more direct control of the courts! There was, I felt still a lack of will to act. It was all very well saying that much depended on gradually changing the climate of public opinion. Equally, it had been shown in many countries that enforcing the law could itself be a powerful factor in changing that climate.[4]

---

4. In January 2004 Shevardnadze was removed from office in the "Rose Revolution" and succeeded by the more pro-Western Mikheil Saakashvili. In March 2004 Mkalishhvili was arrested, brought to court and sentenced to prison. Giving evidence as a witness in court, Malkhaz Shongulashvili was

Third, on my final evening came what ecumenically was the most important meeting of all, with His Holiness Catholicos Patriarch Ilia II. With him was Archbishop Abraham Chiatura, Head of the Foreign Affairs Department of the Church. Malkhaz Shongulashvili interpreted for us. We had about an hour together. The Patriarch was at pains to explain that the factors which had led to the withdrawal from CEC and WCC in 1997 still operated, but equally he was anxious to avoid isolation while Georgia was in a "phase of transition" and he wished to know about CEC's recent and current activities. The Church was also pursuing bilateral relationships with several other churches. I pointed out in turn that the place on the CEC Central Committee which would have been allocated to the Church of Georgia was in fact being occupied pro tem by a representative of the Ecumenical Patriarchate until the next CEC Assembly and would be offered back to the Church if it wished to re-join CEC during that time. I was impressed by how genuinely eager was the Patriarch to hear news of CEC's activities. He specially mentioned problems in the areas of bioethics and environmental issues, and the need for a new approach to interreligious relations. We might have been a long way from Geneva or Brussels but there was no mistaking his serious attention to the issues being dealt with there. Ecumenism in cases like this means hanging in there and waiting.

"Our head is in Europe, but our body is in Asia" is how one person summed up the Georgian mentality for me. Socially and culturally at that time Georgia had an image-problem in the West: corruption, gangsterism and only half-hearted commitment to democratic values. But what was undeniable and impressive was the presence, in all the church communities I visited, of people determined that this should not be so, and who were working hard towards both serving the needs of their society with humanity and compassion, and to make the life of their churches and their relations with one another pointers towards what true community is all about.

WAR ON IRAQ: THE ECUMENICAL RESPONSE

At the end of January 2003 the CEC-CCEE Joint Committee met in Bucharest. There was much to talk about: progress of the *Charta Oecumenica*, prospects of an encounter in 2004 between church and European political leaders, the Islam in Europe Committee and so forth. Among the CEC delegation there was a good deal of corridor talk about the forthcoming assembly in Trondheim and on who might be suggested as the next President of CEC. There was however also an intervention by Antje Heider-Rottwilm of the EKD asking whether the committee should not make a statement on the growing crisis over Iraq. Cardinal Murphy O'Connor and others supported this. The meeting did not have time to deal with this adequately but it was clearly felt to be a matter to take back to the delegates' churches. Much was in fact already happening among the churches nationally and internationally, and I reported that within a very

---

conciliatory and forgiving.

few days there would be a meeting in Berlin of church representatives from across Europe, from the USA and the Middle East, convened by the WCC, which I would be attending. In the meantime as soon as the Bucharest meeting was over Viorel Ionita, Aldo Giordano, Sara Numico and I had to drive north to Brasov for a two-day roundtable of the Romanian churches on the *Charta Oecumenica*. It was a useful meeting and the snow-clad forests glistening in the sun made for a beautiful setting but my mind was elsewhere a lot of the time. For months now the pressure by the USA for military action against Saddam Hussein, encouraged by Tony Blair in London, had been building up. The previous November at the AAR meetings in Toronto I was shocked to hear from American friends that it was a popular assumption in the USA that Saddam Hussein was "somehow" connected with the terrorist attacks of September 2001, and that all the Arab world was somehow tarred with the Osama bin Laden brush so "they" needed to be taught a vengeful lesson. But any pre-emptive military action ran clean counter to all that had been said ecumenically about justice, peace and the integrity of creation over the past decade or more, and to all that had been said at the Basel and Graz Ecumenical Assemblies about promoting a culture of peace, and to what I had said to the EU Presidency in December 2001 about not extending the "war on terror" from Afghanistan to elsewhere. Not that anyone, least of all those who had actually been to Iraq since 1991, held any brief for Saddam Hussein and the brutality of his regime. But the churches did have a brief for the wider Middle East and the likely consequences, political and humanitarian, of a further all-out war. On Tuesday morning February 4 we drove back to Bucharest, and there began the most intensive six weeks of my time at CEC.

From Bucharest I flew via Frankfurt to Berlin, arriving just in time for the start of the meeting in the Allegra Hotel. Some twenty people were there including of course Konrad Raiser of the WCC, together with Bishop Manfred Kock, president of the Council of the EKD, and others from France, Austria, Switzerland, Sweden, Norway, Finland, Denmark and the Netherlands. Alison Elliot from Scotland (a member of CEC Central Committee) was the sole UK representative. Notably absent was any Anglican presence. Such vapors as had wafted from Lambeth Palace and Church House were distinctly aloof, claiming that the Church of England's position was already well enough known (as if that precluded them now collaborating ecumenically). Dr Nuhad Daoud Tomeh came to represent the Middle East Council of Churches, and there were three from the USA: Bob Edgar from NCCCUSA, James Winkler from the United Methodist Church and Rebecca Larson from the Evangelical Lutheran Church. We knew that in New York US Secretary of State Colin Powell was just then presenting a report to the UN Security Council making the Bush Administration's case for war. We worked hard, in groups and in plenary, and by mid-morning next day had agreed on a statement. As it formed the basis of much that was undertaken in the coming weeks, and is also still of interest in light of what happened in and to Iraq and the region in the months and years that followed, it is worth quoting in full.

Part Four: Ecumenical Europe 1997–2005

1. As European church leaders, in consultation with councils of churches in the USA and Middle East, we remain extremely concerned with the continued calls for military action against Iraq by the US and some European governments. As people of faith, our love of neighbor compels us to oppose war and to seek peaceful resolution of conflicts. As churches we pray for peace and freedom, justice and safety for the people of Iraq and in the Middle East as a whole. Such prayer obliges us to be instruments of peace.

2. We deplore the fact that the most powerful nations of this world again regard war as an acceptable instrument of foreign policy. This creates an international culture of fear, threat and insecurity.

3. We cannot accept the stated objectives of a war against Iraq, as laid out by these governments, in particular the US. Pre-emptive military strike and war as a means to change the regime of a sovereign state are immoral and in violation of the UN Charter. We appeal to the Security Council to uphold the principles of the UN Charter which strictly limit the legitimate use of military force and to refrain from creating negative precedence and lowering the threshold for using violent means to solve international conflicts.

4. We believe that military force is an inappropriate means to achieve disarmament of any Iraqi weapons of mass destruction. We insist that the carefully designed mechanisms of the UN weapons inspections be given the time needed to complete their work.

5. All UN member states have to comply with binding UN resolutions and resolve conflicts by peaceful means. Iraq can be no exception. We call on the government of Iraq to destroy any weapons of mass destruction and related research and production facilities. Iraq must cooperate fully with UN weapons inspectors, and guarantee full respect of the civil and political, economic, social and cultural human rights for all its citizens. The people in Iraq must be given hope that there are alternatives to both dictatorship and war.

6. A war would have unacceptable humanitarian consequences, including large-scale displacement of people, the breakdown of state functions, the possibility of civil war and major unrest in the whole region. The plight of Iraqi children and the unnecessary deaths of hundreds of thousands of Iraqis over the past 12 years of sanctions regime weighs heavily on our hearts. In the present situation, we strongly affirm the long-standing humanitarian principles of unconditional access to people in need.

7. We further caution against the potential social, cultural, and religious as well as diplomatic long-term consequences of such a war. Further fueling the fires of violence that are already consuming the region will only exacerbate intense hatred strengthening extremist ideologies and breeding further global instability

and insecurity. As church leaders in Europe we have a moral and pastoral responsibility to challenge xenophobia in our own countries as well as allay the fears of many in the Muslim world that the so-called Western Christianity is against their culture, religion and values. We should seek co-operation for peace, justice and human dignity.

8. All governments, in particular the members of the Security Council have the responsibility to consider the whole complexity of this issue. All peaceful and diplomatic means to compel Iraq to comply with the UN Security Council resolutions have not been exhausted

9. For us it is a spiritual obligation, grounded in God's love for all humanity, to speak out against war in Iraq. Through this message we send a strong sign of solidarity and support, to churches in Iraq, the Middle East and in the USA. We pray that God will guide those responsible to take decisions based on careful reflections, moral principles and high legal standards. We invite all churches to join us in this act of witness and to pray for and encourage participation of all people in the struggle for a peaceful resolution of this conflict.

After lunch we resorted to the Französische Kirche, familiar to me as the main meeting-place for the Bonhoeffer Congress in 2000, first for a televised prayer service in which several of us including myself took short parts, and then for a press conference. Most of the press conferences I've been involved in for church-related events have been fairly tame affairs, three or four journalists dutifully nodding over their notepads, and a photographer or two if you were lucky. This time on entering the room I was staggered. Over forty reporters were there, with ranks of fourteen television cameras, and many photographers. Such media interest was far more than we had expected or even hoped for. A small panel including Konrad Raiser, Manfred Kock, and myself were deputed to comment and field questions after presentation of the statement. I was allotted paragraphs six and seven and stressed especially the humanitarian consequences that were foreseen and the impact upon the fragile Middle East as a whole. One questioner asked why it was that the political leaders involved (especially in the US) were adopting such a high moral tone in favor of war with an implied undergirding of religion. How were the churches reacting to this? I commented that it was indeed striking how in this case the usual roles of politicians and church representatives were to some extent reversed. Typically it is the politicians who respond to moral appeals for some kind of action by saying, "Look at the consequences. You theologians don't understand what a complex issue this is". Now, it was the churches who were saying exactly that to Bush, Blair and company; and we were saying it through what we actually knew of the Middle East and through the eyes of our church partners there. Such a level of media interest in a church position as we found in Berlin I had never met excepting possibly the launch of the *Kairos* document in Johannesburg eighteen years earlier. The parallel was not fortuitous, for the European churches were more united in opposition to this war than on any other issue since apartheid.

Those of us on the panel then walked to the Reichstag building where we met with Chancellor Gerhard Schröder for a whole hour. Again there was a division of labor among us in presenting our statement, and I was asked to lead off on the humanitarian aspect. Schröder was all attention, and made clear his objective to maintain Germany's stance that there was no compelling reason to rush to war. He was no pacifist, he emphasized, but equally Germany believed that war should not be just one more tool to be used routinely. Meeting in the very place where a somewhat different kind of speech had routinely been made seventy years before, lent historical poignancy to what he was saying. He had in fact changed post-war German foreign policy to allow ten thousand troops to be deployed to the Balkans and Afghanistan, but his government did not think the use of military force would be useful in the Iraqi case. Nor was he, he said, taking an anti-American position, nor did he lack a commitment to fighting terrorism. It was pragmatism: Germany simply disagreed on the necessity of going to war with Iraq. The meeting over, before joining the group dashing to Tempelhof airport for the flight back to Geneva I gave a short radio interview on the BBC World Service. The interviewer pressed me on why we laid such emphasis on the UN. Next day an email was forwarded to me from a listener in New Zealand, thanking me for not giving way on this.

SPEAKING TRUTH TO POWER: DOWNING STREET AND THE KREMLIN

As well as joining in the Berlin meeting, the US church and ecumenical leaders wished over the coming weeks to visit the European governments in Paris, London, Moscow and Rome, and CEC was glad to cooperate and, where necessary, to help facilitate these. Their visit to London to meet with Tony Blair took place February 17–18, and their delegation comprised Bishop John Bryson Chane (Episcopal Diocese of Washington), Bishop Melvin Talbert (Ecumenical Officer, Council of Methodist Bishops), Clifton Kirkpatrick (Secretary of the Presbyterian Church USA), Dan Weiss (former general secretary, American Baptist Churches in the USA), and Jim Wallis (leader of the radical evangelical Sojourners movement). It was augmented by three Anglicans from overseas: Njongonkulu Ndungane (archbishop of Cape Town), Clive Handford (bishop of Cyprus and the Gulf), and Riah Abu El-Assal (bishop of Jerusalem). I joined the party over dinner on the evening of February 17 to find Peter Price, then bishop of Kingston-on-Thames, also present. There were evidently a number of dynamics at work here. First, among the Americans in NCCCUSA there was some anxiety that it was being presented as largely the work of Jim Wallis and his Sojourners. Community.[5] Second, on the UK

---

5. But see Wallis's own account of the visit in his *God's Politics*, 133–136, in which he recognises NCCCUSA was a partner.

ecumenical side there was feeling that the Anglicans wanted it to be largely their show, though CTBI general secretary David Goodbourne and Paul Renshaw, my successor at the International Affairs desk, were present. But also there was some unease within the Anglican fold too, as became clear at a preliminary briefing meeting in Lambeth Palace next morning. It still seemed that the Church of England was reluctant to be in the ecumenical boat. One senior bishop had apparently thought that the Berlin statement was "wild". Rowan Williams himself however was concerned at the military option and at the accusations of "appeasement" being levelled at any who opposed it. Discussion continued at Inter-Church House, then after lunch we gathered at the office of Clare Short MP, Secretary of State for International Development, just off Whitehall. By now the group was growing with, in addition to the names already mentioned, the presence of John Gladwin (bishop of Guildford), David Coffey (general secretary, Baptist Union), and John Waller (moderator, United Reformed Church).

Clare Short accompanied us to Downing Street. At Number Ten we were led upstairs to a smallish room which Tony Blair informed us had been used by Margaret Thatcher as her library. He warmly greeted us each in turn. We had been promised fifteen to twenty minutes of his time. In fact he gave us fifty, listening carefully and responding candidly. Quite properly we left the Americans to do most of the talking. Their approach was interesting: less of a frontal assault on his support for war, rather (and not necessarily just a polish to his ego) a suggestion that *he* was perhaps the one person in the world who could bring pressure on George Bush and offer him an alternative route to take. They recognized that Blair as a practicing Christian was seeking to bring moral concerns into the debate and agreed with him that terrorism and the threat of weapons of mass destruction (WMDs) were crucial moral and theological issues, and that Saddam Hussein was a real threat to his own and other peoples. But they made clear that American church leaders had never before in their history been so united in opposition to a war, and that the consequences of this war were unpredictable and could be unthinkable. It might well increase, not eliminate, the threat of terrorism, and it would be seen as an anti-Muslim Christian crusade. As Jim Wallis said afterwards, "We told the prime minister that the answer to a brutal, threatening dictator must not be the bombing of Baghdad's children."[6] Then there were the attendant issues. Bishop Riah pointed out that "The road to Baghdad leads through Jerusalem." I felt that Blair genuinely listened, never glancing at his watch despite the frequent intrusions by aides with papers for him to sign. But fundamentally he gave no ground. He was still hoping for UN approval. He also felt, he said, accountable to the Iraqi opposition groups inside and (mostly) outside Iraq who wanted an end to Saddam Hussein's rule. Towards the end, with Clare Short's support, we did point out to him that while these American church leaders were being received in the capitals of Europe, the one government or head of state that was apparently unwilling to meet them was their own, and we asked if he could not use his good offices to persuade George Bush to listen to them himself. On the

6. Ibid., 134.

way downstairs afterwards, noting the pictures of former prime ministers adorning the walls, one could not help wondering if any person living daily with these daily reminders of such predecessors as Lloyd George, Winston Churchill and Margaret Thatcher could feel justified in holding office without a war by which to prove themselves on the world stage. But the meeting also signaled to me the enormous mental and physical strain which the job entailed. One could see the look of relief on the face of one of his staff when at last he brought the meeting to a close to return to the next urgent task on the table. The very thought of such pressure suddenly made me feel weary. Maybe that was signaling a warning to myself.

Academically-minded people frustrated by the world around them typically resort to writing, and quite often writing a letter. The day after the London meeting with Tiny Blair I sat down and wrote an open letter on behalf of CEC to the US President. I described to him the visits by the American churches leaders that had been, and would be taking, place, including that to Tony Blair, and continued:

> The fact that these visitors are being received in such high places is an indication of how seriously their views are being listened to all across Europe, including those governments which are closest in position to the stated policy of the United States on Iraq.
>
> This brings me, Mr President, to the burden of my letter: It is my understanding that several approaches have been made by the General Secretary of NCCCUSA, Dr Robert Edgar, and his colleagues, for a meeting with yourself similar to those which are being accorded by heads of government in Europe, but that so far no response has come from your office. To us in Europe, it would seem to be a paradox if those who are being granted hearings in the highest circles on our continent were not to be accorded a corresponding attention at home, and therefore in all sincerity I express the hope that their requests for a meeting with yourself be sympathetically considered and granted.
>
> Two considerations, Mr President, make me especially hopeful of your sympathy here. The first is, that those who have been taking part in these delegations, far from giving an impression of being "unpatriotic" Americans who will protest for the sake of protest, have conveyed a sense of profound love of their country, of respect for its democratic and freedom-loving traditions, and desire for the advancement of its real and long-term interests in the world, interests which they seriously believe will be threatened by war.
>
> Second, I write to you Mr President, knowing you to be a person of Christian faith. The United States, as the world knows to its credit, is a country rejoicing in religious freedom with many expressions of Christian faith and church life. The churches represented in NCCCUSA would not claim to be representative of the entire spectrum of Christianity in your country, but they do embody a very significant part of it. I do not doubt that there any many people who wish to advise and counsel you out of their particular religious perspective. All I would ask is that due respect and attention also be paid to the views of the member

churches of NCCCUSA which merit communicating to you no less than those of others. As you know, the Biblical faith does not lead us to expect that Christians will always agree with one another, but rather enjoins us in all humility to "test the spirits to see whether they are from God" (I John 4.1).

One copy of the letter went via the US embassy in Geneva. I never seriously thought it would get a reply, but it was a ruse to publicize further the fact that in the White House George Bush was surrounding himself by fundamentalist religious guests and tele-evangelists like Pat Robertson who would doubtless prove supportive court prophets, while there was an alternative Christian voice in the USA embracing all the mainstream churches, Catholic, Protestant and Orthodox and many evangelicals. In fact the letter got quite a lot of publicity, aided by its appearance in the Newsletter of the International Bonhoeffer Society which was published in the USA. One Catholic friend there, however, while very appreciative told me in very earthy terms what likely use George Bush would make of a letter like that.

The next and final visit in which I shared was the one to Moscow, March 3–5. I went via Oslo, where I was scheduled to give a lecture on "Ecumenism and the New Paradigm of Healing" for a seminar marking the Fiftieth anniversary of the Church of Norway's Council of Ecumenical and International Relations. After the lecture I was taken to a nearby church to be filmed for TV, commenting on the churches' advocacy of an alternative to military action on Iraq, and lighting a candle for peace. Then to the airport for the late evening Aeroflot flight to Moscow. It proved a nightmare traveler's tale. We were kept in the plane for nearly four hours while a technical fault was sorted out, with nothing to eat or drink, and eventually arrived in Moscow in a grey dawn. I had hardly slept and the first meeting in the Kremlin was set for mid-morning. At the Danilov Hotel (owned by the Orthodox Church and familiar to me by now), I managed about forty-five minutes' sleep before being roused to meet Bob Edgar and Leonid Kishkovsky who had arrived from the USA the day before. At the Kremlin we met with a deputy from the Foreign Ministry and had a good meeting ranging over the need for multilateral mechanisms to settle disputes, the problems of verifying the weapons of mass destruction in Iraq, the need for Security Council approval for any action proposed, and the phenomenon of government going to war while great sections of their people were opposed to it. There was time to get some more sleep after this meeting, and at five in the afternoon we returned to the Kremlin for a session with Yevgeny Primakov, a very senior figure, sometime head of the KGB, who had been Mikhail Gorbachev's special envoy to Iraq at the time of the first Gulf War, had been Prime Minister of Russia under Boris Yeltsin and Minister of Foreign Affairs 1996–98, and now under Vladimir Putin was again in an envoy role to Iraq. His personal view was that Bush was making a big mistake but that no force in the USA was able to stop him. He was again dividing East from West. Even moderate Arab states would be opposed to Bush. The century of super-powers was over, and any talk of "super" should imply not the quantity but the quality of power. The danger now was that the Cold War was going to be replaced by a division between civilizations or confessions. His own interpretation of Iraq, after recent visits, was that Saddam Hussein did not understand what he was faced with—or perhaps was actually wanting the role of martyr. If the US got no support from the UN Security Council when it brought a resolution in two days' time, he would not exclude the possibility that the US will start bombing Iraq regardless. "The US Administration has no power to replace Saddam Hussein if the war is successful. But I do not understand how the Administration will act in Iraq." Kishkovsky and Edgar both stressed the strength of church opposition to the war in the USA, and I likewise at the international level. Obviously as a politician and diplomat Primakov was thinking pragmatically and we could only hope that he would feel encouraged by us to persist in this way. (We did not of course know at the time that Primakov was suggesting to the Iraqis that any WMDs should be handed over to UN control).

Next morning in the Patriarchate we met with Metropolitan Kirill who some months before had visited Iraq and had spent two hours with Iraqi Foreign Minister Tariq Aziz (a Chaldean Catholic Christian) in the presence of the Russian Ambassador. At the end he thought he had convinced Aziz that this was "the last chance". Aziz had claimed to have no fear of weapons inspections as such—only a fear of them being used for spying. Kirill himself did not believe Iraq had any WMDs. He also spoke of growing Anti-Americanism in Russia. believe

WITNESS-"BUT WHAT IF IT DOESN'T WORK?"

It was also about this time that I hatched a plot with a couple of other people in Geneva for the leaders of the Christian world communions to form a delegation and visit both Washington and Baghdad to make a final appeal to both sides not to go to war. It was a *very* long shot of course, but we found interest in circles of the Ecumenical Patriarchate, the Roman Catholic Church (at least the Pope, we were told, would be willing to send a representative of his choosing), and the Lutheran and Reformed world organizations. I then phoned Lambeth Palace. Unfortunately I was not able to speak directly to Rowan Williams and anyway could not be sure what his reaction would have been, but was nonplussed by the staff person I spoke to who asked, "But what if it doesn't work?" An interesting assumption in high places (of a "faith" community at that!) that one should only do what could be guaranteed in advanced to be successful, in this case actually stopping the war, and do nothing that might damage the standing of the leaders in the eyes of the world. Nothing could be further from what I understood to be true *witness* to peace and justice, come what may, and from Bonhoeffer's declaration that the church believes in the mercy of God and can allow God in the end to make use of such witness, even a fallible and broken one, as God sees fit.[7]

7. Cf Bonhoeffer in 1932 addressing the ecumenical youth conference in Czechoslovakia where he states that the church in engaging with issues like war and peace cannot indulge in generalities but must choose either a "qualified silence" or take the risk of speaking specifically and decisively to the

On March 17 I wrote again, not a letter this time but a short reflection for friends and colleagues in Geneva. I pictured George Bush visiting Baghdad in 2004 to see how the destroyed city was being rebuilt by American-owned construction firms. He visits the home of a Mrs Mitri whose young son had been killed in the bombing in 2003. The President expresses his regret at the "collateral damage". She asks what he means and the conversation continues:

> "The collateral damage. It's a phrase we use to describe the side-effects of attacking legitimate targets. Unfortunately it's what we had to do to rid your country of Saddam Hussein."
>
> "So my Hassan's death was a side-effect? It might be a side-effect to you, Mr President, but it was a direct hit on Hassan and on my life as his mother."
>
> "Democracy and the rule of law never come without sacrifice. I say to you, dear Mrs Mitri, that you have truly made the greatest sacrifice anyone can make for these great and precious human values. And here and now I want to pay tribute to you for making such a sacrifice. The whole free world is grateful to you. You have given so much for democracy!"
>
> "What is democracy, Mr President?"
>
> "It's the freedom of people to choose the government they want. The freedom of people to walk their streets without fear. The freedom to . . . "
>
> "Make sacrifices?"
>
> "Sure, that's part of it."
>
> "But Mr President, you didn't give me the freedom of choice to make a sacrifice. You imposed it on me, your pilot literally dropped it on me from however many thousand meters. Still less did little Hassan have any choice about it!"
>
> "Well, that's a point of view I suppose. And I appreciate your feelings. But at least you know that with the protection of the US you are now in a free and democratic society where you can say whatever you wish about the government without fear."
>
> "That's true, Mr. President. But I would still much prefer to be able to say 'Hassan! Come in now, your supper's ready.'"

Of course it didn't *quite* work out like that. But neither did "Operation Enduring Freedom", which began the next night in "shock and awe", work out as its instigators had planned; whereas our Berlin statement's warnings on humanitarian disaster, damage to interfaith relations and the likelihood of the rise of extremism were fulfilled in just about every respect. Over the next two years I several times referred to the story of Paul's ill-fated departure by boat from Crete to Rome: "Paul advised [the centurion and the pilot] saying, 'Sirs, I can see that the voyage will be with danger and much heavy loss, not only of the cargo and the ship, but also of our lives.' But the centurion

---

situation, "out of the clear recognition that it is possible therewith to take the name of God in vain, that the church is in error and is sinful, but it may speak it in faith in the forgiveness of sins that holds true for the church as well." Bonhoeffer, "On the Theological Foundation of the Work of the World Alliance", in *Ecumenical, Academic and Pastoral Work*, 361.

paid more attention to the owner of the ship than to what Paul said" (Acts 27:11). An American friend bewailed the fact the churches had not been able to prevent the war and therefore "we failed". On one level that was so. On another level however it was the case that the word which the churches had uttered held good. Prophecy sometimes has to wait. There is no more haunting phrase in the Bible than "Thus it came pass, that which was spoken by the prophet . . . "

TRONDHEIM: JESUS CHRIST HEALS AND RECONCILES: OUR WITNESS IN EUROPE

However much time and effort was devoted to confronting the build-up to the Iraq war, it could not be allowed to distract from the on-going work of CEC, its commissions and committees, and above all the preparations for the Twelfth Assembly June 25—July 2 2003. In fact the preparations had begun three years previously in 2000 at the Presidium in Istanbul. Fairly soon the venue—Trondheim in Norway—and the theme *Jesus Christ Heals and Reconciles: Our Witness in Europe*, were decided upon. Thereafter it was the task of committees on programme, worship, youth and stewards, housing and all the innumerable items that an Assembly requires. Which meant of course a lot of work for staff and people from the member churches appointed to the various committees and working groups and committees. Fortunately there was an excellent local committee in Trondheim. The Church of Norway, the Christian Council of Norway and the city of Trondheim were generous hosts, and moreover the Norwegian government was generous in its financial support. Especially important to us were Finn Wagle Bishop of the diocese of Nidaros (Trondheim), Lutheran pastor in Trondheim Berit Lanke (whose husband Ola was an MP), and Stig Utnem of the Church of Norway and Christian Council of Norway in Oslo.

A CEC Assembly had to be held every six years. It was required to carry out several main tasks: to review the work of CEC since the last assembly, to set out main guidelines for its future priorities and ways of working, to agree a new financial framework and to elect a new Central Committee; but no less important, to provide inspiration and fellowship through celebration, prayer, worship, study and encounter. Trondheim brought together some eight hundred participants including two hundred and seventy official delegates from the member churches. It was quite an event to organize and quite an event to participate in—and even more so to lead it. It was also for myself a timely moment to reflect on how my mind had been working these past six years, and to this end I garnered up twenty-one sermons, lectures and other pieces I had produced since coming to CEC, published by WCC in time for the Assembly as *The Churches in Europe as Witnesses to Healing*.

I cannot say much more for the purpose of this book than to say that the Assembly did happen, and that it largely fulfilled its constitutional tasks.[8] I say "largely" because with all such events there is always some unfinished business that has to be picked up by the new governing bodies afterwards, and always some matters that could have been handled better. But happen it did. We had decided that early on we needed a voice from outside Europe, and on the first full day Kenneth Kaunda, former President of Zambia, gave the keynote address on the Assembly theme of healing and reconciliation, speaking powerfully on the need for Europe to have a new relationship to others and to work in partnership with Africa and other regions to face the global challenges: "Our big challenge is not to find solutions, but to humble ourselves, listen and share views and appropriate solutions from our brothers and sisters in God."[9] The Ecumenical Patriarch Bartholomew preached at the opening worship in Nidaros Cathedral. There were other outstanding preachers from all the main traditions and some superb presentations in plenary especially on the churches and the integration process in Europe. Youth made an imaginative presentation on reconciliation. There was a whole session devoted to the *Charta Oecumenica*. We had a number of guests from overseas including Bob Edgar who spoke gratefully of our collaboration over the Iraq war, and Riad Jarjour, secretary of the Middle East Council of Churches. A major feature was the *Tørg* or marketplace in one of the main halls, in which many groups and organizations could display and invite discussion on how they were tackling some of the main aspects of the Assembly theme, whether migrants, minority communities, economic justice, youth, Europe, new forms of church, etc. It was opened by Norwegian Prime Minister Kjell Magne Bondevik in the presence of King Harald V. Under our moderator Jean Arnold de Clermont (Reformed Church of France) and co-moderators Katerina Karkala-Zorba (Church of Greece) and Dr Bela Harmati (Evangelical Lutheran Church of Hungary) the official business was managed though with something of a struggle at times, as in such a large and varied gathering there can be differing views and expectations on style and rules of procedure. I was glad to have been told, some years before, by Eric Fenn who was J. H. Oldham's assistant at the pivotal 1937 ecumenical conference on "Church, Community and State" in Oxford, how one day during the conference he came across the eminent Dutch missiologist Hendrik Kraemer, and complained to him how badly he thought it was all going. "Never mind," said Kraemer putting his arm around the younger man's shoulder, "it's all the same with these big conferences—99% of them is rubbish—our job is to find the 1% that is gold." In fact there was quite a lot of gold at Trondheim, not just in the main addresses but in the reports made and accepted and the decisions taken. And as always, there were the countless personal encounters and friendships made, and the encouragement given to people who most of the time lived and worked in isolation. During the celebrations of the one thousandth anniversary of Christianity in Iceland

---

8. See Luca Negro (Ed.) *Trondheim Report*.
9. Ibid, 57.

in 2000, a young woman Lutheran pastor came up to me and said "You don't know me but I know you. I was at Graz. My parish is in a very remote part of Iceland. You've no idea what these occasions mean to people like me." Sometimes it is the odd, seemingly trivial thing that sparks off a conversation. Margaret was at Trondheim for most of the Assembly, and being a keen needle-worker spent time each day with her embroidery, seated on some steps near the office of the general secretariat. A Hungarian participant noticed this, and told her about his wife's devotion to the same craft. It was a good two years' later that I was at the annual meeting of the European Churches Environmental Network (ECEN) in Basel, when the same man (whom I had forgotten about completely) came up to me and asked what was she working on now!

Festive lunch at Trondheim. L. to R: Margaret, KC, Ecumenical Patriarch Bartholomew, King Harald.

In the months leading up to Trondheim one particular concern had weighed on our thinking, namely, the participation from the Orthodox Churches. The WCC Special Commission on Orthodox Participation had highlighted two concerns of special significance for ecumenical gatherings: common worship and the method of decision-making. On worship, some Orthodox ruled out of court any Orthodox meeting with "heretics" even for prayer. This was an extreme view, but many Orthodox were not happy with ecumenical styles of worship which seemed to manifest a pick-and-mix approach to worship whereas greater respect should be paid to the distinct and identifiable forms of worship characteristic of each Christian tradition. On decision-making, it was not only the Orthodox but also a substantial body of opinion from other churches which wanted a more consensus-seeking style rather than simple majority/minority counting of votes.

As far as worship was concerned, Trondheim's sessions of morning and evening prayer won almost universal appreciation. It was sensitively prepared and movingly presented, with superb and varied music reflecting the range of the constituency. As for decision-making, this proved to be a non-issue when it came to the Assembly sessions. Central Committee had labored long and hard to agree some rules to implement the requirement for consensus-seeking but as far as I can recall this was never requested during the Assembly itself. There was here something of a mystery. For all the concern expressed by and about the Orthodox, the Orthodox themselves when pressed never seemed as worried about what CEC did as compared with the WCC. Perhaps it was because in CEC they were never as much in a minority as in the WCC, and in Europe they were always playing at home. Sometimes when I was trying to prompt discussion on the issues in Central Committee Orthodox voices were raised asking "Why are we discussing this *here*?" The same applied to long discussions in a working group on membership. There were worries about the danger of admitting too many numerically smaller churches into CEC which might have the effect of diluting the Orthodox presence. When it came to receiving the report of the working group on membership, however, what was chiefly asked for was not a criterion of size but of quality of commitment to seeking unity with other churches. There had been an underlying assumption that "smaller" implied "schismatic".

Not all the Orthodox at Trondheim stayed away from the regular worship sessions though some did. At the same time there were some disagreements among themselves. In his sermon at the opening service Patriarch Bartholomew expressed gratitude for the great progress that had been made in inter-church relations, but warned that for the present the Orthodox could not agree to intercommunion. One of the Sunday morning services however was a eucharist presided over by Archbishop Vosgan Kalpakian of the (Oriental Orthodox) Armenian Apostolic Church. At the end he invited all, of whatever tradition, who wished to communicate to do so. This caused something of a furor among other Orthodox but in fact the archbishop was only acting according to the custom of his church which permitted this especially as a gesture of hospitality to those away from home or travelling. Other incidents caused problems the other way. In one plenary session the Russian Father Hilarion Alfayev made an outspoken attack on what he considered to be the theological and ethical libertinism of the western churches, which some regarded as uncalled for and offensive. There had indeed been a change in attitudes since Graz six years earlier. But right at the end there was a gesture which I found rather ironic. One of the organizations with a stall in the *Tørg* was from Sweden, which sought to provide pastoral care and support for gays and lesbians in the church, civil service, and the armed services. On the final evening, in fact just as the *Tørg* was being closed down, I was presented by several of the Russian contingent with a letter protesting at the presence of such a group. The fact that they had left this to the very end, when it was now too late for the Assembly to do anything about it even if it had wished to do so, led me to believe that they had not seriously wished to make a public protest, but it would be enough to be able to tell their authorities back in Moscow that they had made a stand.

The closing service was held in the open air by the River Nidelva, and the symbol of water was put to simple but moving effect as the Orthodox and Armenian bishops blessed the waters of the river. Archbishop Rowan Williams preached on the theme "Let us swim in the water of God's gift", based on John 4:1–14, the story of Jesus and the woman at Jacob's well: "Who we are is a mysterious gift, not something we possess, defend and manipulate. We find ourselves when we understand that we don't know and need to be told who we are—when we come to drink of the waters of God's love poured out for us. And this triggers a new receptivity to each other . . . "[10] Afterwards I walked back with him to the Cathedral to disrobe. As we entered the nave a guide was speaking to a party of Americans about the Cathedral's history. On hearing her say " . . . and then in the sixteenth century Catholicism was abolished", the scholarly archiepiscopal voice boomed out "No, it was *reformed*!"

For most, I imagine, the most abiding memory of the Assembly would have been the beauty of Trondheim itself and the blessing of glorious weather with the midsummer sun lasting not quite but nearly till midnight. I was particularly glad of that because like some of our staff I had to stay on for a couple of days longer and I felt totally exhausted. Including the work needing to be done immediately before the Assembly started, it had been ten days of non-stop concentration and, at times, hectic trouble-shooting, and always concern about what was going to happen next. But I had learnt to tell myself that whenever one thinks in the small hours about the things that could go wrong there is never enough time for *all* of them to happen. On the third day after the close I flew north to (literally) chill out in the arctic, on the island of Svalbard (Spitzbergen) for three days of rest and bird-watching.

---

10. Ibid., 44.

18

Mission, European Integration, Dreams, and Commemorations 2003–2005

ARCHBISHOP ANASTASIOS WAS NOT a man to be easily startled. But he was rather taken aback when, a few days after returning from Trondheim and the arctic, I confided to him that I intended to retire from CEC in just over two years' time, at the end of 2005. Margaret and I had gone to Albania to attend the annual assembly of Syndesmos, the Orthodox youth organization which was being hosted at the seminary in Durres and we were sitting with Anastasios at lunch. I explained that while I was not due to retire until I reached age sixty-five in 2008 (my contract had been renewed by the Central Committee in 2002), for a number of reasons I felt it would be better both for CEC and myself if I left before then. This was not a sudden decision, and in fact I had come to it some weeks before Trondheim. I was conscious that my energy level had not really recovered following my illness and treatment in 2000, and a very great deal of energy indeed would be required over the next few years especially with a Third European Ecumenical Assembly (EEA3) now on the horizon for 2007. A number of times in my life I had witnessed heads of organizations starting to coast if not actually slow down in the years immediately before retirement. I believed CEC deserved better than that, and that a new general secretary should be brought in in time to have a run up to the EEA3 and in view also of the organizational challenges that were in the offing. Anastasios was sincerely regretful, as he was when I made public my decision at the CEC Central Committee meeting in Geneva in December that year. At that meeting Jean Arnold de Clermont (French Reformed Church) was elected President, with Anastasios as Vice-President and Margarethe Isberg (now Dean of Västeras Cathedral, Sweden) Deputy Vice-President. As expected, the Trondheim Assembly had produced a substantial list of recommendations for CEC's work over the next six years and these needed to be addressed especially through the Dialogue and Church and Society Commissions. Up to my leaving at the end of 2005, and beyond, there was intensive work on CEC's structure which involved attempting to find a way of recognizing the diverse roles of the three commissions while bringing them into coherent relationship with each other. Discussions on the integration of CCME with CEC continued unabated. The taxing question of whether CEC should continue with three offices in Geneva, Brussels and Strasbourg or whether work should be concentrated in Brussels, was looked at afresh yet again, as it had been repeatedly over ten years or more. These were the issues that continuously engaged our attention as well as the regular business of the Presidium and Central Committee. But there was also much that thankfully was an antidote to navel-gazing, the world being as it was.

A NEW VENTURE: MISSION CONSULTANCY

Almost from the time I started at CEC I felt there was a certain lack in the mind of CEC and its programs, namely in the area of mission and its specifically evangelistic aspect. I was aware, too, that this feeling was shared in a number of Protestant and Anglican churches. At the Graz Assembly one speaker from the (Anglican) Church Mission Society, Mark Oxbrow, called for CEC to facilitate the coordination of mission efforts and agencies in Europe. At the time, while I believed that this was a necessary task I was not sure it had to be done by CEC, although the Assembly's Policy Reference Report stated that CEC should "seek to continue to promote cooperative, rather than competitive mission", and that a number of issues had been identified where CEC could usefully assist in "sharing good experiences of churches in common mission". Steadily during 1999–2001 my own mind moved on in this area. For one thing it became clear in reading the responses of churches to the draft of the *Charta Oecumenica* that there was a widely shared concern for more emphasis on the common task of communicating the gospel in Europe. Accordingly the final version of the *Charta* stated that "The most important task of the churches in Europe is the common proclamation of the Gospel, in both word and deed, for the salvation of all", and set out a commitment by churches "to discuss our plans for evangelization with other churches, entering into agreements with them and thus avoiding harmful competition and the risk of fresh divisions". The wording of this commitment was clearly with an eye to the debates about "proselytism"; but equally it presupposed an evangelistic commitment by *all* churches in the first place. Since the subject of common mission at a theological level fell within the Dialogue Commission it was to Viorel Ionita that early in 2000 I first mooted the idea of CEC appointing a "consultant on mission" to promote both the strategy and theology of common mission with a particular focus on evangelism in contemporary Europe. Viorel was supportive of the idea which had come at a timely moment because of the forthcoming conference "Giving Account of the Hope Within Us" convened by CEC and the Evangelical Church of Baden, Germany, to take place at Bad Herrenalb March 13–17. I was able to attend part of this conference and was impressed especially by how the substantial group of younger theologians there, from both eastern and western Europe—and including Orthodox—were engaging with the theme of communicating the faith in an increasingly secularized Europe. The conference laid down a particular challenge to CEC: as well as promoting cooperation with other ecumenical partners, mission councils and national councils of churches, and stimulating thinking on how this cooperation might be redeveloped, CEC should "develop a programme of ecumenical missionary work in which both majority and minority churches are involved, and which is oriented towards the younger regeneration"; help its member churches to confront the issues of their societal context from a missionary viewpoint; and support model projects in local contexts for example developing a programme of training for "ecumenically responsible mission" and organization of local initiatives. The conference called on CEC's member churches and other partners to support CEC in this through making finance and personnel available. By this time I had already prepared a recommendation, to be discussed at the CEC Presidium in Istanbul in three weeks' time, that as General Secretary I should "explore with appropriate persons in church mission departments and church-related mission agencies, and with bodies such as the European Coordinating Group and the European Federation if Mission Councils" how closer and more effective cooperation between them and CEC could be ensured. As background to this I had referred in my General Secretary's report to CEC's involvement in recent consultations on mission in Europe:

> These are greatly to be welcomed. There has always been a danger of polarization between "ecumenism as inter-church relations" and "ecumenism as mission"; and within "ecumenism as mission" moreover there can be very different emphases on the diaconal, prophetic (socio-political) and evangelistic aspects of "mission". In some quarters, CEC itself has over the years been viewed as relatively uninterested in the goal of "mission in Europe", as compared with promoting dialogue between the churches, cooperation in diaconal work and engaging with the European institutions.

When the Preamble to the CEC Constitution speaks of CEC's objectives as including the strengthening of the churches "common witness", I said, "witness" must surely be understood to include the specific task of communication of the gospel, in word and action, to the contemporary world so that "the claims of the transforming truth of Jesus Christ are presented to individuals, communities and powers for response and action". The Presidium agreed that I pursue the enquiry with the proviso that no scheme be suggested which would make further demands on CEC's budget. I was quite clear on this: Bad Herrenalb had requested CEC's involvement and at the same time had challenged the churches and various mission agencies to resource CEC financially and in personnel at this point. CEC was therefore fully entitled to put that challenge back to the mission constituency.

Because of my illness and treatment in the ensuing weeks the follow-up on this was delayed. But to cut a long story short a scheme was worked out whereby the Church Mission Society (CMS) would, with CEC, recruit a suitable Mission Partner who would then be seconded to CEC as a researcher in mission, financially supported by CMS and certain other agencies. The emphasis would be on observing where creative experiments and projects in mission and evangelism were taking place in Europe and how these could be learning experiences for the whole ecumenical fellowship. There was long and at times skeptical discussion of this at CEC Central Committee in

Morges in June 2002. The skepticism, interestingly, did not come from the Orthodox (Metropolitan Daniel for example gave it his strong support) but mainly from some in the EKD and the larger Scandinavian churches. There was evidently some misgiving as to what the implications might be for the *Volkskirche* of talk of mission if it implied a critique of the historic standing of the church in society and its hold on the people. But eventually it was agreed. In 2003 Darrell Jackson, English Baptist minister and Mission Adviser to the Baptist Union of Great Britain, was appointed to the post, and with his wife Beth was settled in Budapest, his office being located within the Institute for Protestant Mission Studies. From late 2003 he made a fine and stimulating contribution to European mission studies in ecumenical context, ably supported by a small and ecumenically representative reference group and, in relation to CEC structures, reporting to the Dialogue Commission, and he also contributed well to the World Mission Conference at Athens in May 2005.

I believe this was a positive and creative development, employing a useful methodology of partnership with an associated organization of CEC and networking across and beyond the normal range of CEC's constituency. It should also be said that during these post-Trondheim years I had a number of informal and friendly meetings with the General Secretary of Evangelical Alliance Europe (EAE), Gordon Showell-Rogers. He had taken the initiative for starting the conversation, believing that the Alliance had much to gain from developing its ecumenical contacts, and in turn I believed that EAE could help further the missionary concern of CEC. Moreover, when we compared the range of social concerns of CEC and EAE we were struck by how far they coincided. As far as the EAE was concerned the days when "evangelical" and "social dimension of the gospel" were seen as inimical were long past. Gordon Showell-Rogers would very much have liked EAE to become an associated organization of CEC but was uncertain whether a majority on his board would agree with him. Evidently his doubts were confirmed, but it was a positive and useful dialogue. Then too, from 2003 there were a number of meetings with representatives of some of the African-originated churches now present and active in Europe.

THE EUROPEAN PROJECT: WHERE TO PUT GOD IN IT?

In Brussels the huge Berlaymont building, home to the European Commission in its fourteen stories of glass and steel, makes everything else in the neighborhood look (or feel) puny, hence one of its nicknames: "the Berlaymonster". About five minutes' walk away, on the Rue Joseph II, is a much more modest row of nineteenth-century buildings, formerly private dwellings and now mostly offices. Among them is one where for many years the European Ecumenical Commission for Church and Society (EECCS) which subsequently became the Church and Society Commission of CEC, was located.[1] The contrast between the towering Berlaymont and the relatively minute set of ecumenical offices[2] might seem an appropriate reflection of the overwhelming power of the secular European political and economic project and the marginal place of the churches in public affairs today. But CEC and its Church and Society work are representative of church communities right across Europe. Ever since Christian laypeople, in the 1950s and 1960s, working in the offices of the then newly formed European Economic Community, began to meet and consider how their work and their faith should bear on each other, an interest out of which EECS eventually grew, there has been a tenacious ecumenical presence in Brussels—and in Strasbourg too— maintaining a dialogue with the EU and the other European Institutions. In turn it has sought to keep the churches informed of European developments which affect human welfare and society at every level and require ethical reflection. It has meant a challenge alike to easy-going secularism, which sees no relevance of faith or religion in the public forum (except to be a nuisance), and equally to the ghetto-like version of faith which prefers not to relate at all to the world in its complexity and uncertainties. At one of the plenary assemblies of the Church and Society Commission participants were invited to bring one or more items which for them symbolized Europe and the work of the Commission. I brought along two: a copy of the daily *Watchwords* of Bible verses produced by the Moravian Church, and a copy of the *Economist*. Rather as Karl Barth enjoined reading the Bible in one hand with the newspaper in the other, we somehow had to make that link between faith and Christian tradition on the one hand, and the world of harsh political and economic realities on the other. Both sides require a good deal of study and reflection. Rarely does the Bible give instant answers to present-day situations, as the likes of J. H. Oldham well knew. (Occasionally, it has to be said, there is an apposite or amusing coincidence of the day's text in the *Watchwords* with a burning topic of the day. When the global financial system crashed in September 2008 the New Testament text for the day was 1 Timothy 6:17: "As for those who in the present age are rich, command them not to be haughty, or to set their hopes on the uncertainty of riches . . . ")

In 2003 a major part of the Church and Society work came to fruition. The years 2000–2003 were critical for the development of the EU for two main and related reasons. First, over the course of decades the legal framework of the EU had been progressively built up by a succession of treaties, not all of which were relevant to present needs nor devoid of inconsistencies, and there was now a felt need for an overall treaty and if possible an actual constitution for the EU. Second, enlargement of the EU was now an imminent reality with ten states from Eastern Europe applying for membership. The CEC Church and Society Commission, through its Working Group on European

---

1. In 2014 the CEC secretariat and headquarters was also relocated there from Geneva.

2. The building has for many years also housed the offices of closely related ecumenical organisations such as the Churches Commission on migrants in Europe (CCME) and the Ecumenical Youth Council for Europe (EYCE)

Integration, was already in 2000 working on this and in 2001 published its text *Churches in the Process of European Integration*. Meanwhile the European Council at its meeting at Laeken in December 2001 opted for the creation of a Convention to bring about reform of the EU, which would work towards a new treaty and, it was hoped, a Constitution. The Convention represented a new departure for the EU's method of working. Chaired by Valéry Giscard d'Estaing, former President of France, it would be a far more open process than anything the EU had launched before. It would consist not only of negotiations between governments, civil servants and EU bureaucrats but would in its first phase be open to all parties with serious interest in the future of Europe, including groups in civil society. The Church and Society Commission, together with its Roman Catholic counterpart the Commission of the Bishops' Conferences of the European Community (COMECE) seized the opportunity presented by this wish for openness and transparency and made representations to the Convention. CEC's Church and Society Commission in fact held a number of seminars, including one for youth in August 2001 (the Convention itself held a Youth Convention in July 2002), and produced a study pack on the Convention. It is quite clear that far from merely reacting to what the EU was doing, in this case the churches through their ecumenical instruments were well up with the game and in some respects ahead of it, and great credit for this must go to the then Director of the Church and Society Commission Keith Jenkins and his Catholic counterpart Noel Treanor of COMECE.

There was controversy in some quarters, both church and secular, over whether the Preamble to the new Constitution should make specific reference to the historic role of Christianity in Europe and its identity, or whether it might even speak of belief in God as the foundation of European values. In CEC we were relieved not to be pressed on this issue, since opinions differed so widely among not only among the countries but also the churches within the present and future EU. On the one hand there were thoroughly secular states like France where the doctrine of *laïcité* and the strictest separation of church and state would vigorously forbid any specifically religious reference, while countries like Catholic Poland or Orthodox Greece would welcome a full affirmation of the deity. (Even in France there were Catholic circles campaigning for this. While holidaying in the Pyrenees Margaret and I came across in a village *boulangerie* a petition being drawn up with signatures calling for *le nom de Dieu* to feature in the Constitution). A number of the Protestant churches in Western Europe would have been content to have a clear recognition of the role and influence of the Christian churches. What did eventuate under the pen of M. d'Estaing was a rather nebulous sentence about drawing inspiration "from the cultural, religious and humanist inheritance of Europe". This however was not the whole story. CEC and COMECE together submitted a proposal to the Convention which resulted in the inclusion in the actual text of the draft Constitution an article on the "Status of Churches and Non-Confessional Organizations" which, recognizing their identity and specific contributions, committed the Union to "maintain an open, transparent and regular dialogue with these churches and organizations". Quite apart from the fact that the Preamble itself has no legal status vis-à-vis the Constitution, this article in the actual text was arguably far more significant than any specifically religious statement in the Preamble would have been.

I stressed this point in a sermon I preached in the Chapel of the Resurrection in Brussels, during a conference in October 2003 on "The Churches and the EU Constitution". The sermon was titled "Trustworthiness—more than preserving the past" and was based on Jesus' parable of the talents in Matthew 25:13–40. In the story, the third servant is roundly rebuked for simply burying his master's money in the ground for safe keeping, rather than taking the risk of trading it on the market.

> For many of us gathered here, it would be great if the Preamble to the European Constitution were to include mention of God. Others would be satisfied if a specific reference to Christianity as foundational to Europe was made. Let that debate go on. But let us also be careful. Suppose our aspirations for the wording of the Constitution were indeed met—what then? Would we then say, "Ah! We've got it in! It's safe now!"? If that's all we feel at that point, we might be the third servant, the hesitant one, the one who is concerned only not to lose the master's treasure; *and the Constitution would simply be the ground in which we bury it for safe keeping.*

In contrast, the substantive text of the Constitution provided the means and the encouragement to venture onto the European marketplace with our faith and commitment to justice and the common good, in risk and hope.

EVANGELIST FOR THE EU

During these years I tried to be an evangelist for the EU as a field of Christian responsibility, never wholly uncritically but as an area requiring Christian discernment. In July 2004 I addressed the Church of England General Synod in York. By then, as I pointed out to the gathering, "Europe" (meaning the EU) was becoming something of a swear-word to some circles in Britain. Part of the problem, I suggested was that "Europe" was just over the channel and therefore foreign, but it was not as far away as the continents and places which were thought to be more interesting and romantic, perhaps exotically so. It's the near neighbors, not the people at home or those far away, whom we're most suspicious of. In the same way in Jesus' time it was Samaria, not Rome, which was the worst swear-word to many Jews of Jerusalem. When in March 2005 I spoke to the Baptist Union Council I was heartened by how much real interest there was in the EU—but taken aback at the confessed ignorance of so many regarding its origins and subsequent story as a force for peace and stability, and the churches' ecumenical involvement in it. The most positive view of the EU was given to me outside Europe, in fact in the office of UN Secretary-General Kofi Annan in

May 2004. I was in a group of church representatives from the USA, Canada, the Middle East, Africa and Europe organized by Bob Edgar of NCCUSA and invited at short notice to meet with Annan, for two main purposes. The first was to provide a kind of pastoral support and appreciation for him personally at a time when the UN was under continual pressure from the USA either to do its bidding or be side-lined. Second, to lend support for a greater role of the UN in Iraq, still occupied by the coalition that had invaded in 2001. The group comprised twelve people, a number of whom I knew like Bob Edgar himself, Clifton Kirkpatrick, Leonid Kishkovsky, James Winkler, Karen Hamilton of the Canadian Council of Churches, and Paul Renshaw of CTBI. Annan, gentle and dignified as always, was genuinely pleased to see us. I was asked to lead off after Bob Edgar's introduction, and I spoke of the "deep longing for a multilateral approach that has marked Europe since World War II", how "it has been deeply frustrating for us that the UN has not been allowed to play its role in Iraq" and how in Europe there was tremendous support for such a UN role. Our discussion ranged over these and other major issues, including the role of religion in conflict on which as churches we had to confess that a frequent negative role had been played. "The problem", commented Annan with a smile, "is not so much the faiths as some of the faithful." Members of the group stressed that churches wished to play a part in peace-building. But what Impressed me most was what he said, turning to me: "In Europe you really have developed a multilateral approach among yourselves, and that is an example for the rest of the world." When I recall this now, writing as I do just days after the UK voted in a referendum to leave the EU, that decision in the light of what Kofi Annan said seems tantamount to sacrilege.

"KOSOVO MUST NOT BE FORGOTTEN"

It is a grey, freezing day and our two cars trundle slowly along the rutted roads led and followed by two armed UNMIK (United Nations Interim Administration in Kosovo) vehicles. This is February 2005, and our four-person CEC delegation—Bishop Athanasios (Church of Greece), Mariela Mihaylova (Bulgarian Methodist Church), Matthew Ross (Executive Secretary of the Church and Society Commission) and myself—are on a four-day visit hosted by the Serbian Orthodox Church to Serbia and Kosovo. We have been in Belgrade and Novi Sad, and now are touring Kosovo for a day and half, visiting the historic sites of Serbian Orthodoxy there: the monastery of Gracinica, the ancient churches of the Patriarchate of Pec, and the monastery of Decani, all of them under the armed protection of UNMIK troops. In March the previous year there were outbreaks of violence and destruction of churches by groups in the Albanian population. What is now the small minority of Serbs feel very vulnerable. Kosovo was still extremely fragile, nearly five years after the war of 1999.

This was a visit to try and assess at first-hand the situation of the CEC member churches in Serbia and Kosovo—not just the Orthodox but also in Vojvodina the Protestant churches. We met in turn with Bishop Artimije at Gracinica and with Bishop Theodosije at Decani. Neither breathed any optimism about the immediate future, there being so little trust between the remaining Serbs and Albanians, even though some of the Orthodox monasteries and churches had given refuge to Albanians during the war. In Pristina, capital of Kosovo, we had nearly an hour with Søren Jessen-Petersen, Special Representative of the UN Secretary-General in Kosovo, and his staff, and during which we discussed the need for security to be maintained, for confidence to be rebuilt among the communities in Kosovo, the prospects for return of refugees and displaced persons, and the role which the church might play in the processes of reconstruction. It did seem like a chicken-and-egg situation: no security without return of refugees, and no return of refugees without security. One could only admire the tenacity shown by such people, working in such a bleak situation where hope could only grow, if at all, step by minute step.

There was a little more hopefulness in Vojvodina this time, where some sort of ecumenical dialogue at least between the Orthodox Church and the Protestant communities was being maintained and where the work of the Ecumenical Humanitarian Organization (EHO) led by Karolj Beres and his faithful staff was still strong. In Novi Sad however the bridges across the Danube still lay broken-backed from the NATO bombing in 1999. The same nearly applied to me on Sunday morning for as we approached the Church of the Three Hierarchs I slipped and fell flat on the ice. At the end of the liturgy some of us were invited to bring a short message to the congregation. I had been handed a small brass crucifix which I lifted up and said, "This is the one bridge that can never be broken, and by it what is broken can be healed." But it was in Belgrade that the most evident signs of hope were springing up. It was not just at the theological faculty, nor at the Orthodox diaconic organization Philanthropy both of which I had seen before and were doing well. Rather, something new was in the air which I did not recall even on my last visit in 2001. It was the emergence of a new generation, especially among students and recent graduates, not wishing to fight yet again the battles of the past but instead eager to find their roles in a new world, and looking westwards to be part of the new Europe. This was especially evident at the Christian Cultural Centre led by Professor Radovan Bigovic, where a dozen or so young people—including linguists, theologians, engineers, project managers, philosophers—told us of their hopes of making a contribution to a society "in which people can live side by side". Among them was a young graduate, Elizabeta Kitanovic who eagerly told me of the thesis she was now working on: the role, no less, of CEC in relation to European integration. If asked, I would still have thought it incredible that a Serbian Orthodox would ever be at the Human Rights desk of CEC in Brussels, but Elizabeta proved me wrong. In 2007 she was appointed to that post. On our final morning in Belgrade we had a lengthy meeting with the Serbian Minister of Faiths, Milan Raduvic, focusing on a proposed new Religious Law for Serbia. We were indeed in a time of transition. Mr Raduvic was obviously casting eyes towards eventual

Serbian membership of the EU, but at the same time the proposed new law remained ambiguous on the position of minorities such as the Methodists and Baptists which were not recognized as "traditional" churches. Elizabeta sat in on that meeting. In retrospect perhaps it was part of her training for the Brussels post.

Meanwhile the work of the South-East Europe Ecumenical Partnership (SEEEP) continued, and there were many interested actors from the wider world. At the end of September 2003 there was a memorable meeting of the European Council of Religious Leaders for Peace (ECRL) in Sarajevo, with representatives from the World Conference of Religions and Peace, which drew together Christian, Muslim and Jewish thinkers. My notes do not record who actually said it (it might even have been myself but I doubt it), or from which faith tradition it came, but I was grateful for some remarks right at the end of the concluding session, on whether faith representatives would be taken seriously by political leaders. The remark was to the effect that we must maintain a twofold approach: it depends on our offering whatever expertise we genuinely have on particular topics; and that we must "dare to be weak". In the Balkans there were still so many different frontiers of peacemaking to be advanced, and some of them not even in that theatre itself. During the violence in Kosovo of March 2004 Patriarch Pavle had written to me pleading that CEC raise the issue with the UN. I sent a letter of regret and solidarity to Pavle himself, and to the UN a letter underlining the need for effective protection for Serbs as for all people in Kosovo. This was made public and prompted a furious letter from a Serb in the USA accusing me of sheer hypocrisy, asking what right had I to express such sympathy when CEC had expelled the Serbian Church from membership? Where had I been during the bombing of Belgrade by NATO? And so on. I replied as factually and reasonably as I could that it was at Patriarch Pavle's personal request that I had written on his behalf; that the correspondent had been sadly misinformed since CEC had not expelled the Serbian Orthodox Church from membership and Bishop Irenij remained a member of our Central Committee; and that during the bombing of Belgrade I myself had been there twice. I received a somewhat contrite reply admitting that what I said was "in the main" correct. But this conflict had been, and still was, a propaganda war where disinformation created a minefield of mistrust. And the trouble with mines is that each one has to be dealt with individually and carefully.

RELATIONS WITH ROME

During my last two years in CEC our relations with the Roman Catholic Church brought about a strange mixture of assurance and doubts, affirmations and hesitations. On the one hand there were the friendliest personal relationships between ourselves on the CEC staff and Aldo Giordano and others in CCEE, as also between the Church and Society staff in Brussels and the COMECE headquarters. But as with the case of *Dominus Iesus* in 2000, and the chilly response of the Vatican to the Ecumenical

Kirchentag in May 2003, one also had the impression that brakes were being applied from the Curia. During the Trondheim Assembly there was published by the Vatican the Pope's "Post-Synodal Exhortation" *Ecclesia in Europa*, the long-awaited official comment on the deliberations of the Synod of European Bishops in October 1999, which I and two others had attended on behalf of CEC. It was with deep disappointment that, despite several paragraphs stating the importance of ecumenism, nowhere was there mention of any specific event, programme or organization featuring in the recent and contemporary ecumenical journey in Europe: nothing on CEC and its cooperation with CCEE, the Basel and Graz Assemblies, the CEC Church and Society collaboration with COMECE and—especially disappointing—no reference to the *Charta Oecumenica*. I wrote to Cardinal Walter Kasper, head of the Pontifical Commission for Christian Unity expressing our thoughts. There came a friendly and sympathetic reply. The following January I was able to meet with him while visiting Rome in connection with the International Bonhoeffer Congress being planned for later that year. In person as in writing, he was open and sympathetic, and was clearly trying diplomatically to distance himself from positions being taken, or interests advanced, by other quarters in the Vatican, most notably by Cardinal Joseph Ratzinger of the *Propaganda Fidei*. Then, also in contrast to the conservative and traditionalist mode, came an experience during the annual international meeting of the St Egidio Community in Aachen in 2004. Meetings of the St Egidio Community—that largely lay-based and lay-led movement founded in Rome by younger Catholics seeking to implement the outcomes of the Second Vatican Council in service and witness to the world—were always in themselves ecumenical and inter-faith occasions. At Aachen I was asked to moderate a whole morning session on the outcomes of the 1999 Lutheran-Catholic Accord on Justification. The two speakers were Ishmael Noko, general secretary of the Lutheran World Federation whom I knew well in Geneva, and Paul-Werner Scheele, former bishop of Würzburg whom I had first met at the Faith and Order consultation there in 1989. The discussion with questions from the floor ranged far and wide but became especially interesting on the understanding of the eucharist. I put the question to both speakers: "Do you believe differently about what *happens* in the eucharist?" The emphatic answer from each was "No".

At the end of January 2004 the CEC-CCEE Joint Committee met in Opole in the Silesian region of Poland. Both delegations were new, and there seemed more hesitancy than I had previously experienced. "What has happened to the cross in our ecumenism?" asked Archbishop Anastasios at one point., But very first steps were taken to launch preparations for the Third European Ecumenical Assembly (EEA3) which this time, it was eventually decided, would take place in an Orthodox context, namely Sibiu in Romania, in 2007 under the theme "The light of Christ shines upon all—Hope for renewal and unity in Europe". Shortly afterwards I was back in Poland again, this time in Gniezno, the ecclesiastical capital of Poland, for a large convention on "Europe of the Spirit". Aldo Giordano and I had both been invited to speak on "Europe as a Common

Task of Christians", and I spoke of the EU—of which Poland was now a member—as an enterprise fully compatible with the gospel and a means of fulfilling Christian responsibility. One evening there was a huge procession of prayer and commemoration around the city, joined by many citizens, with chants and hymns. One felt the immense power of popular, communal Catholicism. But here and there during the convention it there were undercurrents that made one uneasy, with an agenda of very traditionalist and nationalist values at work. After my address someone queried my advocacy of what he called "western political correctness" which is how he had interpreted my description of the EU and the *Charta Oecumenica*. From Gniezno I went to Warsaw to stay in the Baptist seminary, meeting next day with the Polish Ecumenical Council, and then by train to Katowice where I was hosted by the Lutheran Church. On my final day I visited Auschwitz. Aldo Giordano and I were together again early in October in Trento, Italy, for a two-day ecumenical celebration of the twentieth anniversary of the seminal CEC-CCEE Ecumenical Encounter at nearby Riva del Garda[3] which was a very happy and positive experience. Trento seemed a defiant outpost of ecumenism where Vatican II still reigned, with a lot of lay people, and priests too, on the Catholic side impatient for more ecumenical advance. A quite incidental illustration of the latter attitude—or at any rate a casual side-stepping of official obstructions to progress—came at the end of that month in, of all places, Salisbury. I had gone to share in a weekend conference at Sarum College on "Generosity and Imagination—What Values for the New Europe?" and had been invited to preach at the Sunday morning Choral Eucharist in the Cathedral. It so happened that the Cathedral choir was having its half-term holiday break, and the choir stalls were filled instead by a visiting choir of men and boys from a Catholic school in Liverpool. In my sermon I remarked that at the same as we were worshipping, in Augsburg in Germany there was taking place an ecumenical celebration marking the Fifth anniversary of the Lutheran-Catholic Accord on Justification. When it came to communion, it seemed that nearly the entire choir came forward to receive the sacrament.

WHICH POPE?

For me, much of the ambiguity in current Catholicism centered on the figure of Pope John Paul II himself. In 2001 I had reviewed George Weigel's *Witness to Hope: The Biography of Pope John Paul II*. I felt that the account of his pontificate left me wondering if there was not, for all his efforts to reach out to others, a much more harshly authoritarian streak in John Paul II than was usually acknowledged. I was reluctant to buy this:

> But my refusal has a price. For it will then have to be surmised that the one who stood out against totalitarian oppression in eastern Europe tried but was unable to prevent his own church, more particularly his own staff in Rome,

---

3. See above, chapter16, p.283.

from reverting to a centrist authoritarianism which has hurt many of the Church's most devoted and creative members and leaves many of the rest of us uncertain about the future. Whether that is more a comment, for all his greatness, upon Karol Wojytla's limitations, or upon the formidable power of conservatism in the Vatican machinery, is the open question.[4]

I was in Thailand attending the Assembly of the Christian Conference of Asia when the death of John Paul II was announced on April 2 2005. In public statements I saluted his undoubted achievements and greatness in so many respects, not least his passionate concern for peace in the world, while pointing to the frustrations of the ecumenical journey in recent years. As it did to many (especially in Geneva) the election of Joseph Ratzinger came as a shock. Was the ecumenical winter to freeze still further? But despite the disapproval from one or two senior Protestant figures in CEC churches I had no hesitation in attending his installation in Rome on April 24. If being ecumenical means opening doors and keeping them open as far as possible then that is what we have to do. If doors are to be closed, let others do the shutting and bolting, not us. In fact I found the inaugural mass an extraordinarily impressive occasion. We ecumenical guests had to sit for what like seemed like hours beforehand in the warm sunshine in front of St Peter's. Playing spot the faces helped to while away the time. To my left sat the Catholic bishops, a sea of purple. Two rows in front of me was Rowan Williams, immediately behind me the representative of the Billy Graham Evangelistic Association. The most moving feature of the actual service for me came in the Gospel reading, the story of the risen Jesus meeting Simon Peter by the lakeside and bidding him "Feed my sheep". It was read by several young people in turn, each in a different language. The air was perfectly still, breathless—how could a million people in St Peter's Square keep such silence? The only sound was the very, very distant drone of a police helicopter. It was one of those instances when time and space slip away, we were all by the lakeside again, and the Lord himself was speaking. An unforgettable moment.

The anxiety side of the relationship mounted for a time during the summer of 2005. A lot of hard work was already being put into planning the EEA3 for Sibiu in 2007, but when Aldo Giordano arrived as guest at the CEC Central Committee in Hagios Nikolaios, Crete, in early June he had been preceded by some unwelcome news. The Council of CCEE had just been meeting and had seen fit to raise some questions about the desirability and feasibility of another large ecumenical gathering even though it was just over two years hence. Members of the CEC Central Committee expressed severe annoyance at this, and when Aldo arrived to meet with Jean Arnold de Clermont, Viorel Ionita and myself there were strong if diplomatic exchanges before we convinced him that CEC was determined to go ahead. Thankfully by later in the year things were back on track.

---

4. See *Epworth Review* Vol. 29, 3 (July 2002), 92.

In retrospect it is significant that by my reckoning I spent at least as much time in communication with the CCEE office in St Gallen as with any single one of our CEC member churches. But the relating was not all in formal or official ways. Ecumenism depends a great deal on friendship, and on some occasions Aldo Giordano and I represented each other or deputized for one another at ecumenical meetings. One such was the St Egidio meeting in September 2005 in Lyon, when I was on a panel discussing "Europe: what vision for the future?" along with others including Rowan Williams and the Vice-President of the German Bundestag. I claimed that I was really Aldo Giordano in disguise as a Baptist. Later, shortly before I retired from CEC, Aldo wrote to me:

> A few days ago in Rome, I met the French Ambassador to the Holy See: straight away he told me that in your intervention at a round table discussion during the S. Egidio meeting in Lyons you spoke, and in my name too, about the ecumenical situation in Europe: he was surprised at the fact that it was so normal for a Baptist minister to speak also on behalf of a Catholic priest, the CCEE General Secretary! And this has happened mutually on a number of occasions. It is a sign that true friendship and fraternity exists between us. We are also aware of the difficulties we have met: the ecumenical route requires a good dose of courage, but I believe that we have never once wanted to turn back. We have experienced the joy of mutual hospitality and together borne worries and suffering. At this moment, in my heart I wish to give back to the Eternal Father all that we have shared, all the plans we have carried out and our limits, too: thus, he will be able to bring to completion the plan He had for our common task.

The notion of standing in for one another was already a seed-thought which within a short time of my leaving CEC moved to the center of my thinking on what "being ecumenical" was all about.

THE ORTHODOX

The problems anticipated with the Orthodox at Trondheim, and for the most part not realized, seemed strangely irrelevant by the time 2004 arrived. In January Jean Arnold de Clermont came with me to Constantinople to make his first visit to His Holiness Bartholomew, and this went well. In October that year under the auspices of the CEC Dialogue Commission and the Council of Protestant Churches in Europe (CPCE)[5] a very constructive two-day dialogue between Orthodox and Reformation Churches took place in *Lutherstadt* Wittenberg. In January 2005 Jean Arnold de Clermont and I went on pilgrimage again, this time to Moscow. This enabled him to see at first hand a lot of the diaconal and cultural work of the Orthodox Church, and we attended the opening by Patriarch Alexei of an exhibition, "Orthodox Russia". We had lengthy discussions with staff at the Church's Department of External Relations, and of course met with

---

5. Formerly the "Leuenberg Fellowship".

Patriarch Alexei himself. A number of senior political figures were there too, including the Minister of Culture Alexander Sikholov. We also met with the Baptist leaders and, at a reception, the bishop of the Ingrian Lutheran Church. Underlying it all, however, was the barely hidden agenda of procedure for the appointment of my successor as General Secretary. It was common knowledge that among the Orthodox the Russians, at least, would not countenance a woman in that post. But the CEC central Committee had also made clear that in short-listing candidates gender must not be a criterion and this needed to be reaffirmed by us, as it was apparent that some names of applicants had leaked out despite all the instructions on confidentiality by the nominating committee.

The temperature in Moscow during that visit plunged to minus 20 Celsius. But memories of Orthodoxy also involve summer sun and Mediterranean sea. In May 2005 the WCC World Mission Conference was held just outside Athens. It was the occasion of some amusement for me at one point. Darrell Jackson, CEC Researcher in Mission, was naturally there. Perhaps presumptuously, I had expected also to be invited to attend as General Secretary of the ecumenical organization of the region in which it was taking place. But no invitation came, and on enquiring I learnt from the CWME powers-that-be that my attendance was not required. Sam Kobia, WCC General Secretary, however, was persuaded to ensure that I was invited, to some people's annoyance. On the first full day of the conference I was wandering around in appropriately very casual gear because of the heat, when one of the Church of Greece staff came looking for me urgently. His Holiness Christodoulos, Archbishop of Athens and All Greece, whom I had met several times before, had just arrived with his entourage. Ceremonially sitting down in the reception room and attended by WCC eminences he had looked round and boomed out, "And where is *Clements*?" There was no time to change and, as was proved by his warm greeting, no need to apologize. Then in early October came one of those events which were somewhat baffling then and still is in recollection, a large conference on the Greek island of Rodos to which I was invited, on "Dialogue of Civilizations". The main ecclesiastical player in this was the Russian Orthodox Church and the main financial resources for it were evidently Russian too, though from what quarters was never clear. There were other church figures and representatives of other faiths there, and political people mainly from Eastern Europe, some academics and lots of affluent looking businessmen, bankers and the like, and their wives, including from the USA. At the opening plenary I had to make a brief presentation on Europe in Christian perspective, and next day with Seva Chaplin of Moscow chaired a seminar on interfaith relations and national identities. It was all good fun, the sea-front hotel accommodation was lavish and so was the night-time entertainment with alfresco dining, a dance floor so crowded that no one could tell if you were actually dancing or not, and a rumbustious firework display. I have still no idea what it was all about. All I know is that in the Orthodox world you must be prepared for anything and enjoy what is on offer.

PART FOUR: ECUMENICAL EUROPE 1997–2005

Taking a break: Margaret and Donata Coleman at the Orthodox Academy, Crete.

THE ECUMENICAL MOVEMENT: AS IT IS AND AS IT MIGHT BE

"Reconfiguration of the ecumenical movement" would seem to be a yawn-inducing term. Be that as it may, it signified a debate which dominated much of the agendas of ecumenical bodies, including CEC, from 2003 onwards. It was initiated in 2002 by Konrad Raiser, then General Secretary of the WCC, who pointed out important changes taking place on the ecumenical scene at large: the increasing importance of Christian World Communions, the rising profile of the Pentecostal Churches, the explorations of what a Global Christian Forum might be and do, the ambiguous relations between ecumenical bodies and funding agencies in the north, and so forth. In all this, the increasing financial burden being felt by churches was raising questions about the sustainability of what seemed to many of them an unwieldy number of ecumenical bodies claiming their support. In my report to the Trondheim Assembly in 2003 I welcomed the opening up of this debate and called on CEC to make its own contribution to it, for of course the relationship between the WCC and the Regional Ecumenical Organizations (REOs) was a key factor. The Assembly's recommendations for future CEC policy firmly endorsed CEC's participation in the discussions, calling for the new Central Committee to "define the mandate and function of CEC itself within a new configuration of ecumenical and denominational organizations which work in Europe". What transpired in CEC during 2003–2005 was a peculiarly intense examination since at the same time as the wider ecumenical debate we were committed to a looking anew at our own internal structure, including the long wished-for integration of CCME with CEC. The new CEC Central Committee at its first full meeting in Geneva in December 2003 resolved to appoint an ad-hoc group to deal with the organization and ecumenical role of CEC within the overall process of reconfiguration of the ecumenical movement, and asked that a consultation be started also with bodies like the Communion of Protestant Churches in Europe (CPCE).

The Working Group met several times during 2004 and reported to the Presidium and Central Committee. Almost the first recommendation it made was to drop the term "reconfiguration" itself as too abstract, static and giving the impression that the debate was purely about structures and organization, when in fact it was surely about vision and dynamic relationships. This was well conveyed in the paper "Our Common Way" which was brought to the Central Committee in Prague in October 2004 and set out the *values* which should take precedence over and inform whatever structures were deemed necessary, in line with the *Charta Oecumenica*. Reconciliation, dialogue, solidarity and partnership had to be central to its life, in line with CEC's founding role as a bridge-builder between churches in different parts of Europe. Setting the whole discussion within a vision of values and relationships was to prove vital in helping CEC to find its own format and its role in the wider ecumenical scene in the coming years.

The matter of reconfiguring was, I believe, much more a matter of re-learning than just re-organizing. It was a matter of living relationships and mutual attitudes. Several times for example I was taken aback when listening to WCC discussions when I realized the presuppositions s people had about the REOs. I have already mentioned[6] what I had to counter during the WCC Assembly in Harare in 1998, namely the assumption that the REOs might simply pick up work which the WCC could no longer afford. In 2002 during the WCC Central Committee lively debate on the results of the Special Commission on Orthodox Participation there was a suggestion from the floor that forms of worship for ecumenical meetings might first be "tried out" in the REOs before being used in the WCC. This brought me to the microphone to say very firmly that CEC, for its part, would carry on with ecumenical worship as it had always done and according to its lights, thank you very much. We were not just a testing ground for the "real" ecumenical body. I was also arguing both within CEC itself and in the annual meetings of the REOs that as regional bodies we should be taking more initiative in how we related to one another in the normal course of our work. In fact we were already beginning to put flesh on this idea, with the start of a very fruitful programme of joint encounters with the Latin American Council of Churches on shared mission, which on our side was handled by the CEC Dialogue Commission, and also on matters of economic justice, with the involvement of our Church and Society Commission. During my last year we were also starting to explore how CEC might work together with the Middle East Council of Churches and the All Africa Conference of Churches in shared concern on the area we had in common—the Mediterranean. In view of

---

6. See above chapter 16, p.290.

what is now happening there and the way in which the sea is now a sea of refugees, this was not a fanciful but a prophetically sensible idea.

The WCC's own exploration of "reconfiguration" (I still preferred CEC's notion of "our common way") involved a consultation at Antelias, Lebanon, in November 2003 followed by a wider process of reflection among the member churches and related organizations, which culminated in a further consultation, on "Ecumenism in the 21st Century" held near Geneva November 30—December 3 2004. As part of the preparation for this thirty people from around the world, myself among them, had been invited to write their reflections on the future of the ecumenical movement, and these were published before the meeting as *Reflections on Ecumenism in the 21st Century*. My own reflection did not set out a plan or programme or even a list of priorities but rather let my mind run, gathering impressions, scenes and memories influences upon me which encouraged my dream of what ecumenism meant. I wrote:

> In the dream these voices and images coalesce into something greater than the sum of the parts: a dynamic scene of churches and Christians being together, staying together and journeying together for the sake of the world as God wants it to be. It is a ballet of communities of love indwelling each other, drawing from each other, giving to each other, suffering with each other in a way that spills over to embrace the entire world in its need and suffering and divisions. It is evangelical not so much because it deliberately "evangelizes" but rather because the world actually longs to grab what is seen there, like starving people for bread. It is catholic not because it imposes an external claim to universal authority but because all people, as on the day of Pentecost, recognize their language spoken here, their deepest longings for peace, justice and reconciliation, and life in all its fullness, being met. It is orthodox, not because it defends the tradition but because the tradition speaks for itself in new, creative and empowering ways.
>
> What I think my muddled dream, both in its connections with reality and in its flights of fancy, is essentially about is a new quality of mutual relationships, focused on belonging to Jesus Christ and at the same time enabling a strange new sense of belonging to the whole world. It is also about future-orientation, a hopeful expectancy born out of prayer in the Spirit which opens up to still more breathing-in from that Spirit.
>
> I have to be honest: no ecumenical organization as such—not even CEC!—appears in this view of the scene. Maybe that is where self-indulgent romanticism is taking over. Or, maybe, the organization or institution is invisible because it is not itself an actor but the self-effacing stage, the space for the drama. In which case, the question is, what kind of service needs to be provided to assist or enable the scene to come on stage?[7]

Enough said? Or too much?

---

7. Clements, "The Ecumenical Movement: My Vision", in *Reflections on Ecumenism*, 24.

Mission, European Integration, Dreams, and Commemorations

REMEMBERING AND COMMEMORATING

My visit to Poland in March 2004 concluded with a day spent at Auschwitz. My first really serious thought about the Holocaust and its implications had begun in 1972 with reading Elie Wiesel's *Night*, the account of his own experiences at Auschwitz-Birkenau, including his nightmarish description of the slow hanging, before the assembled prisoners, of a Jewish boy which prompted the question among the onlookers, "Where is God?" and the answer that came, "He is there, hanging on the gallows". Since then I had read a good deal more, seen the requisite documentaries and film dramas right down to *Schindler's List*, visited Buchenwald, Sachsenhausen and Flossenbürg, and in 1988 gave a course of lectures at Bristol University on Theological Responses to the Holocaust. The visits to these sites of brutality and extermination had produced their own kinds of emotional reaction and I wondered what might be unleashed within me by exposure to this, the ultimate scene in the theatre of Nazism. Strangely, it produced no tearful turmoil, no gut-wrenching sickness mental or physical, not even a the cry of from the heart, "God, why?", no pretext to show by any such displays of horrified sensitivity how humane one was in contrast to the evil Nazis. Auschwitz was too vast in its cold, inhuman emptiness to do anything except deaden the spirit. Even prayer is difficult in Auschwitz. One can only reflect there. Even more than stepping inside the one remaining gas-chamber, the most abiding memory for me remains that of just standing on the single rail track as it enters the gates under the guardhouse. It was hard to realize that one was actually standing on this, the most infamous piece of railway in the world—and then to comprehend that it connects with all the other railway lines in Europe. The implications are haunting.

In 2005 came the sixtieth anniversary of the end of the Second World War. To commemorate the ending of the conflicts in both Europe and the Far East, in June the BBC recorded a service during the biennial International festival of Church Music which that year was taking place in Bern, and I was asked to preach the sermon. The festival choir comprised singers from many different regions including Africa and Asia with a large contingent from the USA so there was a ready-made cosmopolitan atmosphere when I preached on the text *We went through fire and through water, yet you have brought us out to a spacious place* (Ps.66:12). We did well, I said, to express gratitude for that deliverance, but had we made full use of the "spacious place" in the following years? As of today spending on armaments far exceeded that on development. Racism and xenophobia were abroad again especially in Europe. I pointed to the significance of Jesus' parable about the man who had an evil spirit cast out of him and the spirit comes back later to find that person's life empty, like a room swept clean, and so brings seven even worse demons to set up home there. That could be a warning for today. But it was an appropriately joyful occasion and service, and an added bonus was that the musical director of the Festival was none other than (Sir) David Willcocks, as sprightly in his mid-80s as he was forty years earlier at King's. It was also appropriate that the service as broadcast included some of his own reminiscences of serving in the war, but it was also typical of his modesty that the producer Mark O'Brien was not aware, until I told him, that David Willcocks had actually been awarded the Military Cross during the Normandy campaign. Following the service recording, I sat in on the rehearsal for the evening concert, the main item of which was to be Mendelssohn's *Hymn of Praise*. After about twenty minutes of attention to pitch and detail David Willcocks said that that would be enough, but before dismissing the choir he asked, "Now, as you walk around Bern during the day, and you get talking to people and say why you're here, if they ask what you will be singing tonight what will you say?" Several Texan voices drawled, "A Hymn of Praise." "No!" said Sir David almost leaping up and exclaiming, "you say, a Hymn of *Praise!*" We walked back to our hotel together, reminiscing about King's and Alec Vidler, and I took the opportunity to say that after all these years what I still most appreciated from King's Chapel was the singing of the Psalms. The service was due to go out on Sunday morning July 10, but three days earlier something happened in London which left fifty-two people dead and hundreds injured. Obviously, a present-day terrorist attack and its traumas had to take precedence over a sixty-year old war as the theme of a service that day, and the recording was put on hold. It was broadcast on Remembrance Sunday later that year.

In August Margaret and I yet again went on holiday for a week at Argelès-sur-Mer, followed by a few days in the Pyrenees. On the morning of August 17 I was loading the car for departure from the hill village of Les Rochers when Viorel Ionita called me in some distress. Roger Schutz, founder and leader of the Taizé Community, had been stabbed to death by a mentally ill Romanian woman at prayers in the chapel at Taizé the previous evening. It was hard to believe that this embodiment of the quest for Christian unity and peace in the world, who had seemed such a fixture of ecumenism ever since the Second World War, could have been taken, in his ninety-first year, in such a brutal way. A week later back in Geneva we were having a joint CEC-CCEE planning group for the EEA3. Aldo Giordano was present for that, and it was agreed that it would be fitting for us both to leave the meeting early so that we could drive over to Taizé and attend the funeral together. On arrival at Taizé we were invited to pay our respects to Brother Roger's body in his open coffin and accompany the cortege to the church which was packed with worshippers, while in the fields outside thousands were able to watch the televised service on huge screens. As well as many church dignitaries the President of Germany Horst Kohler and Nicholas Sarkozy, at that time French Minister of the Interior, were present. Schutz lived and died a Protestant pastor but it was Cardinal Walter Kasper who presided at the eucharist, and Brother Roger's successor Alois Loser prayed for the forgiveness of his assailant. It was thus a fitting if sad farewell, as much an affirmation of all that Roger Schutz and Taizé stood for as a mourning of his loss.

There was one more commemoration to be observed before I left CEC, perhaps less dramatic but of great significance in the story of post-war reconciliation. In October 1945 in the shattered city of Stuttgart a meeting took place in the Markuskirche, one of the few churches not wholly bombed out of usability. It was an encounter between representatives of the German Evangelical Church, including some who has suffered for their witness in the Confessing Church such as Martin Niemöller, Hans Lilje and Hans Asmussen on the one hand, and representatives of the ecumenical movement outside Germany, led by W. A. Visser't Hooft, secretary of the infant WCC, and including Bishop George Bell of England, Pastor Paul Maury of France, and two representatives from the USA on the other. It was the first attempt to restore relationships between the German Protestants and the wider fellowship, and there was much anxiety—on both sides—about how this could be done given the enormity of the evils committed by Nazism. During and just after the First World War there had been much recrimination between Germany and the allies, and in some cases between the respective churches on both sides too. At Stuttgart however the tension was broken as the Germans made admission of their failures and confessed that "through us" great violence and suffering had been unleashed upon the world: "We accuse ourselves, for not witnessing more courageously, for not praying more faithfully, for not believing more joyously, and for not loving more ardently". Both Visser't Hooft and George Bell believed that behind the Stuttgart Declaration, as it was called, lay the influence of Dietrich Bonhoeffer's wartime writings that had become known to some of his German colleagues, on the calling of the church to lead the confession of guilt on behalf of the people at large. It was striking how it was figures who themselves had significantly challenged Nazism and suffered for it, who made the confession and who were therefore not trying to distance themselves self-righteously from their fellow-Germans. Within Germany the Stuttgart Declaration drew fierce criticism: why should we Germans be made to feel guilty when we too have suffered so much—look what the Russians did to us? On the other hand, outside Germany it was criticized, the more so as time went on, for not saying enough and not specifically enough about German misdeeds: in particular there is nothing said about the crimes committed against the Jews. Yet in its time and place the Stuttgart Declaration was important in establishing a bridge between Germany and its churches with the outside world. As the statement said, "Now a new beginning is to be made". Sometimes, the first bridge to be built can only be a frail structure, but at least if people can walk across it that is a vital beginning.

To mark the sixtieth anniversary of the Stuttgart Declaration the Church of Württemburg organized a conference and commemoration service in the very same church in Stuttgart where the meeting had taken place in 1945 and where the Declaration was made and received. I was invited to come and deliver a message of behalf of CEC during the Sunday morning service and Margaret came with me. I pointed out that while the Stuttgart Declaration predated the birth of CEC by about fifteen years, CEC could well be considered to be one of its children, dedicated as it was to reconciliation, peace and Christian unity in Europe. Indeed, Hans Lilje who was in the German delegation at Stuttgart was one of the first presidents of CEC, and Gordon Rupp, who as a young English Methodist was accompanying George Bell at

Stuttgart, was involved in CEC in its early days. But I also used the occasion to reiterate my concerns about the contemporary reconfiguration debate, and warned:

> In all this the actual spirit and goal of ecumenism are easily lost sight of. Stuttgart 1945 was not about organizations and structures, but about relationships and especially the healing of broken relationships. It was not so much about membership of an organization . . . but learning to become again *members of one another*. It was not about finances, but about what is costlier than any amount of money, namely, confessing guilt before God and before each other. It was about—to use that delightful misquotation of the Apostles' Creed— "The communion of sins and the forgiveness of saints". It was, in short, about reconciliation . . . The ecumenical movement must continually ask itself whether it is enabling or hindering the building of relationships as the core of its life. If it does not, it loses its soul.

BONHOEFFER

While over the years I had visited many sites associated with Dietrich Bonhoeffer's life and career, I had not so far viewed the scenes of his last days and hours on earth, in Bavaria. In September 2002 there was a weekend meeting near Augsburg on the *Charta Oecumenica*. With a couple of days to spare beforehand I had driven up from Geneva and spent a night in hotel near Munich, and next day made the pilgrimage to Flossenbürg and meditated on the very spot where on April 9 1945, barely four weeks before the end of the war, he and five other remaining conspirators were put to death in a sadistically prolonged way.

As far as time allowed I had kept up my involvement in Bonhoeffer studies all through my time in CEC. The Eighth International Congress in Berlin[8] was followed by the Ninth in Rome in 2004, at which I preached at the opening service and in the final session chaired a panel with three speakers: Cardinal Walter Kasper, Bishop Margot Kässmann of Hanover, and Ishmael Noko, General Secretary of the Lutheran World Federation. By that time I was deep into the editing of Volume 13 (Bonhoeffer's London period 1933–35) of the English editions of Bonhoeffer's works. I had finally decided that it would be more effective to use just one translator and Isabel Best, who had been assistant in the CEC Communications office until 2001, did a first-rate job. Martin Conway, former President of the Selly Oak Colleges, gave invaluable service as consultant to us both. Isabel proved so able and enthusiastic a Bonhoeffer translator that later she also took on much of the translation of Volume 8 (the famous prison writings), and eventually for good measure translated Ferdinand Schlingensipen's fine biography of Bonhoeffer. By that time Isabel had returned to her native USA with her husband Tom Best who had worked for many years in the WCC Faith and Order

---

8. See above chapter 16, p.303.

Commission. Finally she edited her own selection of Bonhoeffer's sermons, which was published by Fortress press in 2012. As a spin-off from my work on Volume 13 I started also to collect material for a shorter book which I had had in mind for some time—an account of Bonhoeffer's times in England and his connections with Britain. In addition to all this, I continued to receive invitations to lecture on Bonhoeffer. A very memorable occasion was a conference in July 2004 marking the sixtieth anniversary of the July Plot of 1944, in the former home at Imshausen in Hesse of Adam von Trott, one of the outstanding members of the resistance executed in 1944. I gave a paper on Bonhoeffer as both ecumenist and resister, and the relation between these two aspects of his life. In November I gave a slightly adapted version of the paper at Westminster College, Cambridge. It was also good and necessary to keep in touch with the wider circle of Bonhoeffer scholars and enthusiasts, particularly the Editorial Board which met during the American Academy of Religion gatherings each November. Eberhard Bethge was of course greatly missed since his death in 2000 but Renate remained active during this period. From the Stuttgart commemoration meeting in October 2005 Margaret and I went to stay with her for two days at Wachtberg-Villiprott. John de Gruchy's biography of Eberhard, *Dear and Trusting Spirit*, had just been published and it was very moving to begin reading it in that quiet house where so many conversations with Eberhard had taken place. It felt like they were continuing.

FAREWELLS

The CEC Central Committee met in Hagios Nikolaios, Crete, early in June 2005. It was a fairly tough agenda. An important decision was made on gender-related issues, with the intention of securing an executive post to ensure that this subject was mainstreamed in all areas of CEC's work. Reports were received on progress towards a new structure for CEC, and on youth participation, and there were thematic sessions on migrants and on mission. Most important of all, my successor was appointed: Colin Williams, Anglican priest and archdeacon of Lancaster. Suddenly it really felt that I would be leaving at the end of the year. The Central Committee presented me with a fine Greek ikon of Jesus, to be placed alongside one of the *Theotokos* and child that Archbishop Anastasios had already presented to Margaret and myself. The meeting ended with much conviviality under the Aegean night sky. The actual retirement ceremonies took place in Geneva at the beginning of November. There was a service in the Ecumenical Centre chapel at which John Arnold preached, attended by many friends in Geneva as well as all the CEC staff from all three offices, followed by a reception where many kind words were said and Margaret was presented with an enormous bouquet. There was a CEC staff dinner at John Knox Centre in the evening at which I was given, as an aid to retirement, a field telescope with my bird-watching in mind.

Then came all the practicalities of moving. A good deal of furniture and household items had to be shipped back to Bristol. Not to mention *some* of the books for which space could be found. Having decided which ones I certainly wished to keep, I gave the WCC library the first option on the rest, followed by the CEC staff, and then finally shifted the remainder into the corridor for Ecumenical Centre staff as a whole to browse through and help themselves. It was amusing to see that it was the paperback fiction that went far sooner than theology. In December I took Colin Williams to Istanbul with me for his introduction to Patriarch Bartholomew. Colin stayed on for an extra day or two. On boarding my flight back to Geneva I received a text message saying that our first grandchild had arrived safely, Oliver Anthony, born to Laura and Peter, now living at Uppingham where Peter was teaching at Uppingham School. Already one felt the new stage of life, and with it a new status.

But roots had gone down deep in Geneva and in CEC circles. It helped that a book of farewell messages was compiled for me, from friends and colleagues far and near. It contained messages both kind and wise, many of them reflecting on the difficult as well as joyful times. I cherish none more than the letter from one of the minority churches in Serbia-Montenegro, struggling with the prospect of a new law on freedom of belief, and who had asked for my help:

> Busy as you must have been, you could have thought about who could do what to ease the situation... Knowing many very important people you could have thought about whom to contact in order to comfort us.
>
> But we experienced that you are obviously a man belonging to those doing something. You did not try to solve the problem from Geneva but came to stand by our side working towards justice in our country. This was a very impressing experience for us, and although the sun has not yet risen, we are deeply grateful for your concern and for your faith that makes you love others. You gave us the feeling to belong to a worldwide Ecumenical family. This we will treasure in our hearts.

Inevitably at such a time one ponders all the plusses and minuses of one's efforts and their outcomes. I am always grateful for the wisdom of Reinhold Niebuhr, who once said that very rarely are the most important things accomplished completely in one person's lifetime let alone by one person. The most significant work most of us do, is either completing or carrying on what others have begun before us, or starting something which will only be brought to fruition long after us.

I wrote a letter of farewell to all the CEC member churches and associated organizations, reviewing what I thought were both highlights and difficulties of the last eight years. Among the former of course were the CEC-EECCS integration, the *Charta Oecumenica* and our work for reconciliation in South-East Europe, together with the development of theological education networks and the new project on research in mission. We had had difficulties in sustaining the Solidarity work adequately but the Central Committee meeting in Crete had been able to take this forward. We had had the major financial crisis in 1998 but thanks to due diligence CEC was now in credit again. I referred to the tragic events of September 2001 and their implications, which in fact had created a fresh consciousness of the urgency of finding a new way of being one human family on this planet. "There keeps coming back into my mind the text on which I preached one of my very first sermons while a student in Cambridge in 1965, Psalm 24:1: 'The earth is the Lord's, and all that is in it, the world, and those who live on it.'" I referred to the positive developments in Europe too, among which enlargement of the EU ranked very high, and the EU itself as something to be valued as a new way of being a community of nations in a world which in so many areas was in deepening conflict. I referred to the changes coming about in ecumenism at a world level, both positively yet also as raising serious questions: "What continually gives me hope is the continuing commitment among so many of the people of God, the *Laos*, at grassroots level in Europe, for the ecumenical journey."

"What continually gives me hope . . . " In my eight years in CEC I had seen, despite difficulties, setbacks and disappointments, so much which could only be ascribed to the Holy Spirit, giver of life and igniter of community. I could only look back in hope as well as gratitude, and concluded my letter with my favorite Pauline benediction: *May the God of hope fill you with all joy and peace in believing, so that by the power of the Holy Spirit you may abound in hope* (Rom. 15:13).

PART FIVE

Old Interests, New Horizons 2006–2016

On Victoria's Great Ocean Road

19

A Full Life—At Our Own Pace

"I THINK IT'S A job for a younger man," Morris West had joked to me, so busy had he become after two years into his retirement. But then he was fond of committee work. I had no grand or precise ideas on leaving Geneva beyond the wish somehow to make myself available for some theological teaching and to contribute to the ecumenical movement in Britain, and to do some writing. I was expecting an obvious change in daily life but also hoping for some continuity. That blend seemed symbolized at the family level too, since the return to England meant a much more normal family life while at the same the birth of our first grandchild Oliver, just days before I left Geneva, brought a joyous new dimension into the domestic scene. For her part Margaret, who had retired from full-time work at UWE in 2002, my permanent return to the Bristol home accompanied by innumerable cartons of books and some of the furniture and household items we had acquired in Geneva, felt like a kind of invasion.

Retirement can be rather like after years of relying on timetables suddenly discovering that there no longer is one. By conferring the freedom to do what one wishes to do whether or not one is paid for it, retirement thereby also forces the question, "What do you *really* want to do?" In this respect I had a fairly soft landing, since during the first few months of 2006 I was occupied with engagements already decided upon before I left Geneva, or completing work which was already underway. Thus early in February I gave a lecture at St Martin-in-the-Fields in London, on a Christian view of Europe, and three days later flew to Porto Alegre in Brazil for the Ninth Assembly of the WCC. There I worked as a co-opted staff member in the assembly communications office, my main assignment being to write a daily column under the heading "By the way . . . " for the nine issues of the assembly newspaper over the pen-name "Angelos", commenting on main themes and challenges of the assembly in the light of the longer ecumenical story. In March, in St Martin-in-the-Fields again, my book *Bonhoeffer and Britain* was launched by CTBI at a lunchtime meeting in the crypt, together with a compilation of correspondence of Bishop George Bell edited by Peter Walker, former bishop of Ely. John Arnold made the commendatory speech, and well-deserved thanks was paid to my friend Michael Bray who had not only taken a large number of the photographs of Bonhoeffer-related sites in London and elsewhere but had done most of the editing and preparation of other pictures for the publication. A very pleasing touch was the presence at the launch of two people who had a personal connection with Bonhoeffer the London pastor of 1933–35: Sir Michael Neubert who as an infant was baptized by Bonhoeffer at the St Paul's Church in Aldgate; and Mrs Rita Coleman the daughter of Frank and Doris Goetz whose wedding Bonhoeffer conducted, also at the St Paul's Church. She was able also to bring the Bible, complete with Pastor Bonhoeffer's signature, which he had presented to the couple at the service. A few days later we had a second launch party at Sarum College, Salisbury. In fact the first half of 2006 was busy with Bonhoeffer events, since February 4 saw the centenary of his birth. There was a major commemoration at Westminster Abbey at which Margot Kässmann, bishop of Hanover, preached. I gave lectures on Bonhoeffer in Bristol, Oxford, Lincoln and London. At the same time there was the final editing and proof-reading to do for Volume 13 of the English Dietrich Bonhoeffer Works series, *London 1933–1935*, which Fortress Press brought out in 2007, and for which *Bonhoeffer and Britain* was intended to serve as a kind of popular companion.

WITH OLDHAM—AND OTHER OLD FRIENDS-AGAIN

In 2006 I was also able to start a project which I had had in mind ever since the publication of my biography of J. H. Oldham in 1999, and which was to be my main literary preoccupation for the next four years, namely, to edit for publication the minutes and associated papers of the Moot, Oldham's discussion group of theologians, philosophers sociologists and literati that had met from 1938 to 1947 including Karl Mannheim, T.S. Eliot, John Baillie, Alec Vidler, H.A. Hodges and John Middleton Murry. This would prove quite an undertaking since the surviving minutes alone comprised verbatim records of the twenty two-or three-day meetings, which together with the many papers prepared for discussion (Mannheim and Hodges were the most prolific writers), and correspondence, made for a formidable array of material. But I believed that making available all this material, at present housed with the rest of the other Oldham papers in the library of New College, Edinburgh, would be a very significant contribution to the study of Christian intellectual and social thinking in the mid-twentieth century. Duncan Forrester, who had originally recruited me to write the Oldham biography, strongly agreed with me, and he facilitated an ad hoc advisory group of academics at New College who met with me several times, under the chairmanship first of Professor David Fergusson and then of Professor Larry Hurtado. Such a piece of work required both moral and financial backing from a solid academic institution and this, as well of course as access to all the papers, New College certainly provided, and terms were agreed with the publishers T. & T. Clark for publication in 2010. The editorial work was itself challenging on two levels. First of all the transcribing of seventy-year old, fading cyclostyled typescripts on foolscap paper into digitally usable form was a labor in itself even with the aid of a scanning machine in Margaret's university office. Second, the actual editing of the content meant supplying numerous notes and references to the minutes themselves, in order to explain and illuminate what was being said in the Moot discussions, and what was happening in the world at large of the time. In addition, there had to be an introductory chapter to the collection as a whole, with summary biographies of the overall twenty-three members of the Moot (Karl Mannheim I felt, also merited a special chapter as an extended note on his special role and significance in the group), and notes setting each meeting in context. Not all the discussion papers could be included in full, otherwise the book which eventually totaled over seven hundred pages, would have become impossibly unwieldy. Overall, it was a fascinating enterprise that I had set myself, using the experience acquired in the editing of Volume 13 of the Bonhoeffer works. Not least, I learnt an immense amount of detail about the intellectual and social milieu of Britain—including in wartime—in the years 1938 to 1947, much of which went into the footnotes. The work was finished in 2009 and the launch of *The Moot Papers: Faith, Freedom and Society* 1938–1944, published by T. and T. Clark, took place in March 2010, marked by a public lecture which I gave at New College, Edinburgh. It has taken its place in the new wave of interest in British intellectual life in the mid-twentieth century, and among the unexpected but gratifying uses that have been made of it is as a background resource for the new edition of the works of T. S. Eliot being published by Faber & Faber.

But retirement could also make time and space for the unplanned and unexpected engagement. Robert Bradnock, friend since Cambridge days, was now a noted geographer on the staff of the School of Oriental and African Studies, and an authority on India, glaciers, climate change (on some aspects of which he took an independent line) and much else on the global scene. He had become a frequent guest lecturer on the noted Swan Hellenic cruises which catered mainly for an educated clientele wanting still more education, and in May 2006 he called me to say that Swan Hellenic were still looking for a clerical lecturer for their forthcoming cruise in July to the Norwegian fjords and Spitzbergen, on which he (as a lecturer) and his brother Christopher and their wives would be going, together with other friends including another Cambridge Robert Hall Society contemporary, Richard Brown and his wife Phyllis. I needed little encouragement to be proposed, not least because as was customary with Swan Hellenic both Margaret and I would have free board and passage (with privileges at the bar too), and was accepted. So at the beginning of July we boarded *Minerva II* at Dover and four days later were watching the ice floes slipping by us north of the Arctic Circle. Like the other speakers (as well as Robert, there were two ornithologists and an art historian), I had to give four lectures. Mine were on the earlier story of Christianity in Norway, on the contemporary Norwegian churches, on the churches and the résistance in Norway during the Second World War, and on the churches and environmental issues. There were also two Sunday communion services to take. On

Spitzbergen it was good to meet up again with the Lutheran pastor of Longyearbyen, Jan Höftödt, whom I had met on my visit there in 2003. And throughout the cruise the bird-watching was magnificent, the best sea-watching since my voyage on *Weather Monitor* forty-five years earlier.

FINDING A NEW USE: AUSTRALIA

I have to be honest and admit to a feeling during these first months back in England of being almost totally ignored on the UK Baptist scene. David Coffey, who had been warmly enthusiastic about my appointment to CEC nine years earlier, was now nearing the end of his time as General Secretary of the Baptist Union, and in 2003 out of courtesy I had apprised him of my intention to retire before it was made public. But there had been no acknowledgment (and from among the British churches only Cardinal Murphy O'Connor, the Methodist Church, and Cytun in the person of Gethin Abraham-Williams, made any response to my farewell letter from CEC). I was puzzled as to why, if the BU had regarded such an appointment so highly, they now seemed not interested in using me in any capacity, consultative or advisory or whatever, in ecumenical matters, and in which I would have been glad to be involved. I had the growing feeling, however, that the lack of interest was not so much towards me as to ecumenism generally. Apart from taking on the supervision of a PhD student, Paul Spanring, at Bristol Baptist College for his study of the German Baptist Arnold Koester in comparison with Bonhoeffer, and some other duties for the College, and of course preaching here and there in local churches, I seemed to have dropped off the Baptist radar. More than compensatory however were the invitations from non-Baptist or ecumenical circles: Sarum College, the Wyndham Place Charlemagne Trust, the Society for Ecumenical Studies and, most substantially of all, the Council of the Keston Institute, successor to Keston College. During the Cold War Keston, under its Director Michael Bourdeaux, had done so much to gather and disseminate information on the situation of religion in communist countries and was now promoting the scholarly use of its immense archive of materials. I was also pretty soon reviewing books for journals such as *Theology*, *Ecclesiology* and *Ecumenical Review*. So all told I was not actually short of things to do.

There was moreover however, one quite unexpected invitation prompted by a letter I had written to Baptist theological colleges, including several overseas. Frank Rees, acting principal of Whitley College, Melbourne, responded with an enthusiastic—almost begging—plea for me to visit Whitley for several weeks so that together we might weigh up form on how I might be put to use there. Hitherto I'd had no contact with Whitley except through Ken Manley, the recently retired principal with whom as a student I had overlapped for a year at Regent's Park College (at cricket we had crouched alongside each other, he at slip and myself keeping wicket) and with whom I had since met up several times at BWA meetings. This seemed too good a chance to miss and so in late August

2006 Margaret and I took off from Heathrow and after a brief stop-over in Singapore had our first experience down under. It was two months of unalloyed pleasure. Melbourne as a city delighted us with its welcoming and cosmopolitan atmosphere, its restaurants, art galleries, concert venues and riverside walks. Whitley College is situated in the pleasant, green and leafy university area of Parkville, about twenty minutes' tram ride from downtown Melbourne. Originally wholly intended for Baptist ministerial training, its residential building (a circular building known affectionately as the "doughnut") now serves as a university student hall of residence while the theological teaching takes place across the cobbled Mile Lane in the non-residential Mervyn Himbury Centre, named after a former principal, a Welshman of colorful personality (stories are still current of memorable exchanges between him and G. Henton Davies). We were provided with a flat next door to the college. Possums could be heard scuttering across the roof at night. Frank Rees, whose appointment as Principal was soon to be made permanent, and his colleagues made us more than welcome. I agreed to take a number of small seminars, some for graduate or research students, on the doctrine of God, on Bonhoeffer-related topics, and on theology in the public square. Apart from that I was left largely to my own devices, and to read and write. It was wonderful to be living right next door to a good theological library, while ten minutes' walk away next to Ormond College was the Dalton McCaughey Library, the finest theological library I have ever seen after that in Union Seminary, New York. By coincidence, in the middle of our stay Whitley College hosted a weekend Bonhoeffer conference organized by a group of Australian Bonhoeffer scholars and enthusiasts at which I gave a paper on "Bonhoeffer the Ecumenical Troublemaker"[1]. I was delighted to find that John de Gruchy was the other overseas contributor. But the star catch of the conference was Kevin Rudd, up and coming Labor Party politician and Shadow Cabinet Minister for Foreign Affairs. Known to be a Bonhoeffer enthusiast he was scheduled to speak at the Saturday night dinner and turned up at our table just as the meal was being served. He was a fascinating conversationalist (including on China which was his special interest) and his address was a forthright, at times caustically anti-government, statement of his political beliefs, making clear how much his concern for justice, peace and human rights had been inspired by Bonhoeffer. His address "Faith in Politics" received wide press coverage both in Australia and overseas.[2] On the Sunday morning I preached at the closing eucharist.[3] A few weeks later Rudd became leader of the Labor Party and in 2007 brought the party to power in a landslide victory for the first of his two terms as Prime Minister.

Melbourne, however, also had some special personal significance for us. It was while living here in the late 1920s that my mother felt the call to become a missionary to China and trained at what was then the Melbourne Bible Institute. It was from Collins Street Baptist Church that she was valedicted for what would prove to be the

1. See Preece and Packer (Eds), *Bonhoeffer Down Under*, 193–211.
2. Ibid., 223–236.
3. Sermon "Not a Spirit of Cowardice", ibid. 237–242.

real prelude to my own history, and so it was poignant for us to worship there one Sunday morning. Moreover, just a day's sailing from Melbourne lay Tasmania, the scene of some years of her childhood during 1912–14, and then again after the First World War for her teenage and young adult years. We took the *Spirit of Tasmania* to Devonport and hired a car for our three-day stay. First we made a bee-line for the tiny village of Bagdad (*sic*) where my grandmother, her two daughters and her parents had settled on their 1912 migration. Never a hive of activity, it still seemed well off the beaten track. The old railway line to Hobart was rusted and overgrown. We located the house where they had lived, identified from old family photographs, and visited the school (twice burnt down in its lifetime) which my mother and her sister Madge had attended. Then on to Hobart and to Franklin on the Huon River. We had with us a photograph of the house where my Aunt Madge and her orchardist husband Arthur and their children had lived in Franklin during the 1930s, and where my parents and their first son John had stayed on their furlough from China in 1937. Driving into the quiet, straggling row of buildings that was Franklin we had no idea where to look. We stopped by a woman selling fruit on the roadside. Margaret showed her the photograph. "Oh yes", she said, "Hillcrest!", and pointed towards an unsurfaced road going up the hillside. The young couple who were now living there were intrigued when we knocked on their door and explained our interest—and what's more were keen to have a copy of the photograph emailed to them later as they were planning to restore the house to as nearly its original style as possible. From Hobart we visited among other places the (in)famous historic convict settlement at Port Arthur. Margaret ironically observed how closely the grim stone prison buildings resembled Shepton Mallet gaol where she took Open University tutorials; only, whereas Australia had long since closed its pre-Victorian edifice Shepton Mallet's even older buildings were still deemed fit for purpose. In the rather chilly and rainy Hobart spring, we concluded that my mother's picturing of Tasmania as perpetual warmth and sunshine was, to say the least, somewhat romanticized but the charm of the island was undeniable.

Of course there was much to see on the mainland too. We explored the wonders of the Great Ocean Road and Wilson's Promontory National Park, watched the Little Penguins make their evening invasion up the beach on Phillip Island, were captivated by Crimson Rosellas, Fairy Wrens and a multitude of other birds, and had friendly encounters with Wallabies and more distant ones with Kangaroos. But above all Melbourne became a place of friends, first of all at Whitley of course with Frank Rees and his staff, and close associates such as Ken and Margaret Manley, and recently retired tutor Colin Hunter and his wife Jenny, all of whom were given to hospitality. An additional bonus was that our old Cambridge medical friends Colin and Ruth Morley were still in Melbourne after some years working there, Colin as a world-esteemed pediatrician, Ruth as an epidemiologist. Among other things they introduced us to the best eateries on Lygon Street, and when they went away for a week or so loaned us their car. Then there were contacts through the wider network into which the

Bonhoeffer conference led us, in particular Rod Horsfield, a minister of the Uniting Church who had been much involved in that conference, and his wife Beth; and Tom and Mary Williams, radically anti-hierarchical Catholics whose dinner table chattered with subversive hilarity. A contact with whom I had corresponded years before in my research on Ronald Gregor Smith was Harry Wardlaw, former professor of philosophy at Ormond College, who as a student had actually heard Ronald Gregor Smith give his seminal lectures on *The New Man* there in 1955, and subsequently went to Glasgow University to write his thesis under him. He described Gregor Smith to me as the person who, more than any other he knew, showed what it meant to live by grace. Harry and his wife Ruth in turn introduced us to Jean McCaughey, widow of the late Davis McCaughey, former Master of Ormond College and then Governor of Victoria 1986–91, one of Australia's most renowned churchmen. Advanced in years, somewhat frail but with a sharp mind and vivid memory she delighted us with her memories of Ronnie and Käthe Gregor Smith on their visit to Ormond in 1955 (Ronnie found it hard to cope with the rumbustious McCaughey children), and no less amusing (and revealing) were her accounts of entertaining the Queen and other members of the royal family in Government House on their visits to Victoria over the years.

In late October Margaret flew home a week earlier than I did, to begin teaching her MSc course at UWE. Frank Rees and I sat down to think out the next step in my relationship with Whitley, and it was agreed that I should come in 2008 to teach an elective intensive course on "Bonhoeffer's Theology in Historical Perspective". So began a happy and most fulfilling pattern of visits and engagements for the next decade.

The next year, 2007, proved very busy on several counts. In March I went to Herrnhut in Germany, historic home and headquarters of the Moravian Church, to give a lecture on "Community: promise or danger?" at the annual conference of Moravian clergy in Europe.[4] The invitation had come via Sarah Groves, a Moravian minister who had studied at Bristol Baptist College during my time there. It was interesting to see the actual iron basket out of which the biblical texts are taken by lot for the coming year's daily *Losungen* ("Watchwords") which I myself had used over many years. It was, also, moving to walk up to the Moravian cemetery on a gentle hill overlooking the village. On the crest of the hill there was a memorial to the war dead of 1914–18. Beside it lay a later memorial, a great stone slab brutally fractured down the middle and engraved simply "1933–1945", a sober, repentant commemoration of Germany's most fateful years. Early in May I gave the Adam von Trott Memorial Lecture to a dauntingly distinguished audience at the German Embassy in London, on "Faith, European Values and the American Dream: Echoes from the German resistance for today"[5]. Later that month there was a Bonhoeffer seminar in Berlin. For a week in September Margaret and I were on Iona, which for all the many contacts I

---

4. Published as chapter 10 in my *Ecumenical Dynamic: living in more than one place at once* (Geneva: WCC Publications, 2013).

5. Published in *Humanitas. Journal of the George Bell Institute*, Vol. 11, 1 (October 2009), 34–55.

had had with members of the Iona Community was my first actual visit to the island. Murdoch Mackenzie, ardently ecumenical minister of the United Reformed Church, had organized one of the regular Iona conferences on ecumenism for young people at which I spoke, and I preached at the Sunday morning service in the Abbey. Then throughout the year it seemed that I was constantly visiting Prague, mostly for meetings of the planning committee for the next International Bonhoeffer Congress to take place there in July 2008, and of which I was chairperson, but also for a memorial service for Milan Opocesnky, former General Secretary of the World Alliance of Reformed Churches and a good friend and colleague in Geneva; and also for the oral examination of Keith Jones, Rector of the International Baptist Seminary, on his doctoral thesis on the European Baptist Federation.

Margaret and I celebrated our ruby wedding in September with a party of family and close friends at home. At the end of that month there was a reunion in Cambridge for King's alumni of my year, in the middle of which Jonathan called me to announce that he and Ginny Sandringham, who worked for Channel Four News, had become engaged, and we were glad.

MOVE TO THE SEA

The most strenuous item in 2007 however was of another order: moving home. We had lived in Westbury Park for thirty years. Both sons had grown up there, the house had served us very well and we had expended a good deal on improving it. Roots were there. But Margaret and I both felt that a move out of the city and the continual Bristol traffic hum would be a good thing. Also I maintained that having lived for several years in Geneva with a sixth-floor vista of the Alps and the Jura, I wanted to retire to a place with a view other than that of next door's garage. Margaret did not object to this wish, but where to? There the arguments began. For a while I maintained that a really clean break from Bristol and a new start elsewhere was needed, for example the edge of the Lake District. Margaret was far from convinced and pointed out that both Peter and Jonathan were already three hours' drive away from where we were living and that would be increased by a move to the north-west of England of which, admittedly, we were very fond and where we had a number of connections. (I also received stern advice from Edwin Robertson, who urged against joining the habitual exodus of retired academic clergy into oblivion in the Lake District.) Eventually Margaret and her wisdom prevailed and we began looking for somewhere that would both satisfy my wish for a view and still be within range of Bristol where most of our live contacts were. We settled on Portishead, about ten miles out of Bristol, at the mouth of the Avon where it runs into the Bristol Channel. We found a suitable and affordable house at the Redcliffe Bay end of the town, standing on a bluff commanding stunning views over the Bristol Channel to the Welsh hills beyond—not Mont Blanc but as good as a vista as anywhere in England. Honor satisfied all round, after the usual traumas of selling-and-buying we moved in late September. During the year we had scrabbled together several short holiday breaks, including Mallorca and the Yorkshire Dales, but by late autumn felt in need of a more exotic trip. In November I attended the AAR meetings in San Diego, California, going there via Rockford near Chicago to give some public lectures on Bonhoeffer and church-in-society topics. From San Diego I flew with Pat Kelley. veteran of the Bonhoeffer Society, to Nashville, Tennessee where Margaret joined us and we had the all-American experience of Thanksgiving Day with Pat and his wife Connie and friends in the little university town of Sewanee. Just before Thanksgiving itself Pat got me to take a seminar on the churches and reconciliation in Europe for his ethics class. Our stay was a real Appalachian experience, revealing too of the existence of real poverty in this rural scene. From Nashville Margaret and I flew down to Florida for a glorious week of warmth at Bradenton on the Gulf Coast.

A NEW LIFE IN PORTISHEAD

From early 2008 life in a new home took on a new regular pattern. We quickly felt at home in Portishead, a small (some twenty-five thousand population) but fast-growing town, in part a dormitory for Bristol. Formerly a port importing fertilizer, and fuel for its two power-stations (finally demolished in 1992), and still with strong links to the sea, its former docks were now converted into a marina. Ships of all shapes and sizes plying to and from the docks at Avonmouth and Portbury pass our house close inshore for our daily entertainment, while the steeply sloping wood adjoining the rear of our garden is home to a host of species of birds including nesting Buzzards and Sparrowhawks. So far we have a tally of fifty species seen in or from our garden alone. We continue in membership at Tyndale Baptist in Bristol but also regularly attend St Nicholas Church, literally five minutes' walk down the hill from us, one of the two Anglican churches in Portishead parish, and I preach from time to time for the United Reformed congregation which also meets there. Margaret has plied her needle with a group of women producing new altar frontals and vestments at St Nicholas as well as continuing as a deacon at Tyndale. She is also a National Trust volunteer guide at Tyntesfield House. We sing in the local choral society, the first time we have been able to be so involved since our student days. In 2010 I started a theological reading group, with about twelve people, mostly lay and retired, Anglican, Baptist, Quaker and Roman Catholic in membership and including lay readers, scientists, a doctor and a psychiatrist. This meets once a month and we work chapter by chapter through a recent book of serious but not too heavily academic theology (Rowan Williams's *Lost Icons*, Paula Gooder's *Heaven*, and John de Gruchy's *Led into Mystery* for example). I had long wanted to do something like this, encouraged by Alec Vidler's example of hosting a Bible-study group when he retired to Rye in Sussex, and his conviction that the Christian academic has a continuing duty to serve the local church community.

PART FIVE: OLD INTERESTS, NEW HORIZONS 2006–2016

The Portishead Theological Reading Group meets in our living room.

Two years out of three, the highlight has been the five-week stint at Whitley College in Melbourne, one year (2008, 2011, 2014) for the intensive course on Bonhoeffer, the next (2009, 2022, 2015) a course on the churches and peacemaking. But rather than tediously attempt to chronicle all that has happened in these years is better just to focus on where my main concerns and engagements have lain and to link other matters and events to them as appropriate.

ECUMENISM: WHAT NOW?

The WCC Assembly at Porto Alegre in February 2006 had about it an air of buoyancy and optimism compared with that in Harare eight years earlier when, particularly, anxieties and quarrels about Orthodox participation in the ecumenical movement had a somewhat dampening effect on the atmosphere. Among other things, at Porto Alegre I was glad to see a text on ecclesiology, "Called to be the One Church" adopted by the Assembly. In effect it was a distillation of the work of Faith and Order over the past twenty-five years which had seen close convergence in so many areas of faith and practice. The text called upon the churches to engage in even deeper dialogue, mutual recognition, partnership and solidarity, and to face the issues that still divide them. It was, I thought, good to remind people (or in many cases inform them in the first place) that this work and its reception in the churches had a long history. I had after all since the mid-1970s been involved in some of the major Faith and Order programs including the "Giving Account of Hope" project, the promotion of *Baptism, Eucharist and Ministry* (1982), the Apostolic Faith Today study and the discussions on *koinonia* at the Fifth World Faith and Order Conference at Santiago Compostela in 1993. But what now? Under the heading "Time to let fly" I commented in my sixth "By the way . . ." column in the Assembly newspaper that the document resembled the arrowhead of the contemporary challenge mounted on a long shaft of previous work and prayer for unity, and concluded: "But the arrow will not fly by itself, however carefully shaped and sharpened. A few years ago a veteran of nearly forty years work with Faith and Order caused surprise when he declined to serve on yet another national study group on baptism. There had been enough study, he said. Now was the time for action by the churches. The risk has to be taken of drawing the bow and letting go." The veteran was in fact Morris West. Another seasoned theological participant, Jürgen Moltmann, had said much the same thing *twenty years earlier* in 1977 on the fiftieth anniversary of the start of Faith and Order: "The time for non-committal ecumenical efforts, for committees and working papers is coming to an end. The time of conclusive action in reciprocal recognition and growing mutual fellowship must now begin."[6]

Back home in the UK, far from being held taut and ready to release, the bow-string was hanging limp and loose. I was just not prepared for the dismally non-ecumenical church scene that seemed to have taken over during my eight years in Geneva. Of course I knew about the large-scale downsizing of CTBI that had taken place soon after 2000, ostensibly for financial reasons, meaning it was now in effect an agency offering services to the churches instead of a platform on which the churches acted jointly. This was reflecting the growingly isolationist ethos of the British social and political scene as a whole. But, I had been assured, this did not mean that at four-nation level the churches were any less committed to working together. Moreover in England at any rate, I was told, the principles that had inspired the Swanwick Declaration of 1987 were still animating Churches Together in England (CTE) which if anything had grown stronger (perhaps at CTBI's expense). Not everywhere, though. Someone I met in the diocese of Chichester told me that in one town the clergy had decided there was no need for a local "Churches Together" since they themselves met together from time to time. Indeed overall it seemed that what passed for ecumenism was being clericalised. In practice few people seemed bothered anymore. I heard complaints from people in Local Ecumenical Projects (LEPs) that they felt disowned by the various denominational headquarters. There was even less interest in what was happening on the wider scene as was apparent when Mary Tanner, David Carter and I set up a short residential conference at Sarum College, Salisbury, on the outcomes of the Porto Alegre Assembly and their significance for churches in Britain. But the take-up was almost zero and we cancelled it.

Just before Christmas 2006 there was prominent press and television coverage given to a visit to the Holy Land by the archbishop of Canterbury, Rowan Williams,

6. *Fifty Years of Faith and Order*, in Kinnamon and Cope (Eds), *The Ecumenical Movement*, 210.

and the archbishop of Westminster, Cardinal Murphy O'Connor. Much was made of the impressive sight of the Anglican and Roman Catholic leaders visiting together the sites associated with the nativity and showing solidarity with the Christian churches in the troubled context of Israel-Palestine. But this was very misleading. Two other church leaders were also on the visit: the Baptist Union general secretary David Coffey, and Bishop Nathan Hovhanissian of the Armenian Church. All four went as Presidents of CTE. Scarcely any mention in the media was made of Coffey or Hovhanissian, and there was no reference to CTE at all. The non-Anglican and non-Catholic presence was airbrushed out, and the very existence of the ecumenical body was not acknowledged. It was no answer to say (as was said) that this was the typical fault of the secular media who are not interested in anything but the simplest ideas and the most telegenic images. If the Anglicans and Catholics were truly concerned for the ecumenical cause (I am thinking less of the archbishops themselves than of their respective entourages) they would have insisted that the other two leaders also be on view, in the same way that during the 1980s on Merseyside whenever the ecumenical trio of Bishop David Sheppard, Archbishop Derek Worlock and the Methodist John Newton appeared at public events the Anglican and Catholic prelates always insisted that their Methodist brother sat between them to ensure that the properly ecumenical presence was noted (and photographed).[7]

This might have been a relatively unimportant episode but it was symptomatic of what I felt to be a growing trend. Just after Christmas I wrote to a number of friends and former ecumenical colleagues to share my impressions that in England at any rate both the ecumenical movement and the Free Church presence were being side-lined by the two largest churches and in the media. At the same time the Free Churches themselves seemed to be acquiescing in their own marginalization. Replies to my letter largely confirmed these impressions and anxieties as well as detailing certain factors in what was quite a complex scenario. What also came across, however, was a lot of ill-feeling about how the massive downsizing of CTBI had been engineered. I knew of course about the review of CCBI that was conducted during 1996–97 by Raymond Clarke of the United Reformed Church and which reported in early 1997 while I was still at CCBI. The report was very thorough and I felt that those of us who worked in CCBI came out of it rather well. It was, however, a review of CCBI as an organization, and less a review of the member churches' attitudes and their own commitment to using it as their ecumenical instrument. Thus an ambiguity hovered around its future. What finally emerged in February 1999 was a somewhat diminished "Churches Together in Britain and Ireland" (CTBI) though still like its immediate predecessor in operating on the principle of enabling the churches to work together. But more was in store, not least threats from the financial quarter. It was at a later CTBI Church Representatives' Meeting in Swansea that the Roman Catholic Bishops' Conference in England and Wales announced that it no longer could or would support CTBI

---

7. George Carey confesses that overlooking of the smaller churches had similarly occurred when he was Archbishop of Canterbury and a President of CTE in the 1990s. See Carey, *Know the Truth*, 334f.

financially. This prompted the Church of England to follow suit, confirming suspicions in some quarters that it had never felt wholly comfortable in the four-nation body and much preferred to hold sway in the English-only CTE. By the time I returned from Geneva CTBI was basically a small agency offering ecumenical projects to the churches—of a very high quality it should be said and most imaginatively led by its new general secretary Bob Fyffe of the Scottish Episcopal Church.

What had become of the vision generated at Swanwick in 1987 and manifested in the great celebration and march along Hope Street in Liverpool in September 1990? Was there any equally public manifestation, now, of regret (not to mention repentance) at the churches' unfaithfulness to the solemn commitments made then to journey ever more closely together on the way to visible unity? No, not a word. Was anything said of gratitude or even acknowledgement of the hard and in some cases sacrificial work put in by staff from 1990 onwards, who had given much of the best of their lives to the enterprise? I had not heard any, and was tempted to feel that seven years of my life as that of others had been discounted if not wiped from the record. What Gillian Paterson and I had written in our 1994 "Leviathan" papers[8], of the need to acknowledge the role of staff in maintaining the prophetic ecumenical vision, had now proved all too true—by being ignored. This act of sheer vandalism of the ecumenical instrument, purely out of ecclesiastical self-interest, was a shameful betrayal of what had been launched in faith, hope, and love of the ecumenical enterprise in 1990. What made it feel worse was that a main reason for designing the "churches together" model had been precisely to accommodate the Catholic wish for that kind of body rather than the old British Council of Churches structure—and now this too had been jettisoned. The Free Churches had welcomed the CCBI vessel in 1990 and gladly got on board. Its effective torpedoing by the Roman Catholics and Church of England, who could now look forward to doing things together on their own terms or in the closer confines of CTE, *ipso facto* meant the marginalizing of the Free Churches and other minorities.

I made these points in an article headed "Where are the Free Churches?" published in the *Baptist Times* on March 15 2007, and again in a paper "The Free Churches and the Future of Ecumenism" which I gave to the annual meeting of the Protestant Dissenting Deputies in London in November that year. It seemed to me that Christopher Driver's prophecy made in 1962[9] that there was no future for the Free Churches apart from reunion with the Church of England—although a significantly reformed Church of England—was now coming true. But who was really interested in that possibility now? Church leaders seemed content with a superficial ecumenism of mutual bonhomie whereas the times called for a serious debate, indeed fierce argument if need be, on what kind of church was needed in contemporary Britain. I was aware that I was on somewhat shaky ground here if I was hoping for prophetic input from the Free Churches and not least from my own Baptist constituency which, as

8. See above, chapter 8, p.80f.
9. See above, chapter 2, p.40.

one religious journalist put it to me, seemed to have opted for a "soft evangelicalism" rather than any theology with a real cutting edge. The Methodists had some sort of covenant with the Anglicans and were in renewed conversations with them, though few Methodists to whom I talked set any great store by it; one Anglican diocesan ecumenical officer told me, "The Methodists fear a take-over by the Anglicans; the Anglicans assume it". Meanwhile the Anglican ship itself appeared to be an increasingly leaky vessel, both numerically and in strength of its parish infrastructure despite the injection of new life brought by the ordination of women. It was moreover capable of the most arrogant gestures as in its much publicized report *Mission-Shaped Church* (2004), which was dismissive of Local Ecumenical Partnerships, indeed of ecumenism as such, and presented a curious argument that, being the "national church", it could view mission as its special prerogative without regard to other denominations. I strongly agreed with the trenchant criticism of the report made by the United Reformed theologian John Hull.[10]

WHERE ARE THE LEADERS?

A year went by, and towards the end of 2008 I felt it would be useful to engineer some public statements by leaders of the mainstream churches in England, to reveal what they saw as the goals and priorities of the ecumenical movement. Mark Woods, one of my former students at Bristol Baptist College and now editor of the *Baptist Times*, was sympathetic to the idea and organized a syndicated article to appear in several of the religious weeklies during the Week of Prayer for Christian Unity in January 2009. It comprised statements from Archbishop Rowan Williams, Cardinal Murphy O'Connor and the general secretaries of the Baptist Union (Jonathan Edwards), the Methodist Church (Martin Atkins) and the United Reformed Church (Roberta Rominger). The result[11] was not exactly unexpected but still revealing. Only Rowan Williams dared to ask that the goal of visible unity be kept in view and prayed for. Otherwise the "visions" consisted of bland and incontrovertible generalizations about "the unity of the church for the sake of the kingdom of God", or "to put Jesus first and to be the Church that he has called us to be" with the overall impression that "we have to work with denominational situations as they are". There is of course nothing wrong with a sober realism. No one could pretend that denominational structures would simply go away (though the same might be said of Stonehenge), but where was the vision in all this? At least it supplied the pretext for a rejoinder from me which appeared in the *Baptist Times* a few weeks later. I pointed out that the "new" ecumenical instruments that were inaugurated in 1990, now largely de-funded and evidently thought not worthy of real support, had *not* as often alleged been imposed on the churches from above. They had arisen as the fruit of wide-ranging study, debate and prayer across all the churches and denominations in the Not Strangers

10. J. Hull, *Mission-Shaped Church: A Theological Response*.
11. See e.g. "Ecumenical Encounters", *Baptist Times* January 22 2009.

but Pilgrims process in which it had become clear that people wanted a means by which the churches could journey onwards in mission and service to the world and in deepening fellowship with each other. "But this put an extremely high premium on the role of church leaders both to embody this deepening of commitment and relationships among themselves and to generate the enthusiasm for the onward journey in their local constituencies. What has happened to that commitment?" For all the generalized talk of mission, no one seemed to be asking what this or the kingdom of God meant specifically in and for contemporary Britain. I continued:

> Our society is undergoing profound transformations, socially, culturally and religiously, as is the wider world. Britain is far from clear what its own place and role in that wider world are, and what kind of community it aims to be in itself., It is surely the calling of the churches to serve our generation by forming a mind on these issues in the light of God's purpose, to make our discernment of God's kingdom a common venture and to ask what kind of common Christianity is needed for the next stage of our people's history. It is by daring to place ourselves *there* that the quest for unity will become meaningful again.[12]

Paul Ballard, who had taught pastoral theology and ethics at Cardiff University for many years and whose ecumenical commitment went back still further than mine, also expressed disappointment with the church leaders in the *Baptist Times*.

CALL TO BE ONE?

We were not actually alone. Nor was it the case that *nothing* was happening ecumenically in Britain. There was now the Joint Public Issues Team formed by the Baptist Union and the Methodist and United Reformed Churches which over the next few years was to provide informed and critical reflection on social issues. There were still the LEPs and quite a few individuals who shared the feelings of disappointment and frustration. But all such felt they were the exceptions to the prevailing ethos, and receiving little or no encouragement from official church leadership. At the very least there was a need to gather such malcontents together. David Carter, Gethin Abraham-Williams and I met together and organized a twenty-four hour residential meeting at Wesley College, Bristol for November 12–13 2009, inviting personally some thirty participants to discuss the theme "Called to be One—What Now?". Not only was such a meeting urgent, we felt, but it would also be timely in that next year would see the centenary of the 1910 Edinburgh World Missionary Conference, widely recognized as the birth of the modern ecumenical movement. All the main denominations and confessions were present in some form at the meeting, including the minority ethnic churches as represented by Joe Aldred, secretary for Minority Ethnic Affairs in CTE, and the English, Scottish and Welsh nations. Ecumenical workers of long-standing

---

12. "The Ecumenical Landscape Today", *Baptist Times* February 19 2009.

were present, like Myra Blyth, Martin Conway, Roger Nunn, Murdoch Mackenzie and John Johansenberg, together with Bob Fyffe and David Cornick, general secretaries of CTBI and CTE respectively. The radical wing was represented by Simon Barrow of *Ecclesia* and Hilary Topp of SCM. David Hawtin, my old Lytham schoolmate, now retired from being bishop of Repton, came, as he put it, as part of his mission to counter Anglican assumptions of effortless superiority. It was a great pity that for family reasons Mary Tanner was unable to attend at the last minute. The discussions were both searching and wide-ranging, covering current attitudes in the churches, willful independence, unity and diversity, denominationalism and local ecumenism, power, the role of the ecumenical instruments, church leaders ... and much else. It was by no means just a matter of grumpy old veterans lamenting the loss of vision. Whether liked or not, circumstances had changed. For example ecumenical activity had in many cases fallen victim to critically reduced finances and staffing in the churches, together with a lessening attachment to structures in favor of single-issue campaigning. As one participant out it: "We need to look back to the past and see where things were exciting—and where we were deluded. Can we read our current situation with this hindsight?" Nevertheless, as another person said, "In the 1960s and 70s I really did believe that the Holy Spirit was at work in the ecumenical movement. Am I now to jettison that belief?" Indeed we all had to ask about the biblically-based imperative that only a reconciled church could adequately witness to the gospel of reconciliation. Was that an enduring imperative, or only a passing fad? Nothing was more revealing, I felt, than the comment made that CTE had offered training, or at least briefing, on ecumenism for new newly appointed church leaders but the offers had all been ignored. Nevertheless in some areas there was still real ecumenical life. Someone summed it up by saying we were all both pessimists and optimists. A full report *Called to be One—What Now?* was produced online which as well as calling for a renewed vision specified some small but concrete steps that churches could take even now, in obedience to that vision.

As agreed by the meeting, in January 2010 on behalf of the participants and as a supplement to the online report, I wrote an open letter to all the churches in Britain and Ireland. It called attention to the centennial anniversary of Edinburgh 1910 and the twentieth anniversary of the "new" instruments formed in 1990, and summarized the thinking of the Bristol meeting, its hopes for a renewed commitment to the ecumenical cause, with its suggestions that further meetings of the same kind be organized regionally and locally. Not one acknowledgment or reply was received. It had indeed been a good meeting, it meant a lot to those who attended and it helped to raise morale among those determined to keep the ecumenical flag flying. But, it had to be admitted, our impact on the churches was virtually nil. As a further gesture to mark the centenary of Edinburgh 1910 Stephen Plant the editor of *Theology* invited me to organize the contents of the November/December 2010 issue of the journal around the theme of ecumenism. Mary Tanner wrote on "Celebrating Edinburgh 1910:

Reflections on visible unity", David Carter on "Unity in Reconciled Diversity: Cop-out or Rainbow Church?", Donald Norwood on "'United Nations', 'United Church'"; and I myself on "Free Church, National Church: Dropping Pretences for Unity".

ECUMENICAL DYNAMIC

Perhaps if I had continued to focus entirely, and vainly, on responses from official church and denominational leadership I would have wandered into a Slough of Despond. But there were other voices beckoning along the pilgrim way which led, if not to the Delectable Mountains then at any rate to unexpected and promising pathways. Surprisingly at first, I found myself increasingly being invited to speak in Anglican contexts. In 2011 I was invited by Jeremy Morris, at that time dean of King's, Cambridge, to address a conference of the Old Catholic Church and Anglicans, at Neustadt in Germany. My paper "Believing and Belonging: Perspectives on Christian Developments in Europe Today" which addressed the changing nature of Christianity in a more secular and pluralistic Europe seemed to ring bells not only with the gathering as a whole but in particular with Geoffrey Rowell, bishop of the Diocese of Gibraltar in Europe. Geoffrey in turn invited me to speak similarly to the Synod of the diocese at its annual meeting near Cologne in 2012, which in turn prompted two further invitations, to address the archdeaconry synods of France and of North-West Europe in 2013.[13] What I found refreshing was that, set in contexts other than Britain and denuded of the pretensions of being a "national church", Anglican communities were looking at their ecumenical relations and at society in ways that were often far more creative than back in England. I very much hoped that they would feed their thinking back into the Church of England at home. I made another sally at the Church of England in May 2012 as the process got underway for appointing a successor to Rowan Williams as archbishop of Canterbury. An editorial in the *Times* offered a catalogue of desired qualities and aspirations for the new incumbent but made no mention of ecumenical interest and involvement. I wrote a letter, which was published soon after, pointing out this omission, saying that Rowan Williams as a Christian and a thinker was probably appreciated outside his communion at least as much as within it, and hoping that whoever was appointed would carry on the best of the tradition of Anglican archbishops who had shown ecumenical leadership. It is not for me to say, yet, whether this advice was really heeded. But it was apparent that interest in ecumenism and the need for a united voice of the churches in public affairs was found more readily beyond rather than within the shores of the United Kingdom. I was able to attend the assemblies of CEC in Lyon (1909) and Budapest (2013) and so see at first hand the changes in its structure now being envisaged which if questionable in some aspects at least betokened a continuing commitment by the churches at

---

13. Published as "Christian Faith in Europe: residual or potential?". *International Journal for the Study of the Christian Church*, Vol 13, 1, (February 2013), 3–15.

continent-wide level (I also found myself still being rebuked by Archbishop Anastasios for having retired when I did). I also found eager audiences in the USA, including at Rockville near Chicago in 2007, and more surprisingly perhaps at Baylor University in Texas in 2011 when I addressed a crowd (yes) of first-year students. Maybe the very fact that they mostly came from a conservative Southern Baptist background generated a genuine curiosity in what was a wholly new area to them.

At home, the sense that ecumenism was now a minority interest was confirmed repeatedly. In August 2010 Margaret and I attended the annual conference of the Association of Inter-Church Families (AIF), at Swanwick, at which I had been invited to be on the panel of speakers. The British AIF dates from 1968 (other countries were in the game earlier) and exists to offer support and guidance to families where the partners are of different Christian traditions (the great majority being Anglican-Roman Catholic marriages). I knew quite a lot about the AIF since its cofounders were, appropriately Martin (Anglican) and Ruth (Roman Catholic) Reardon, both familiar figures on the ecumenical scene, Martin as I have related being general secretary of CTE while I was at CCBI. Margaret and I found the Swanwick gathering a real blessing, welcoming, affirming and joyous—so much so that I joked it was almost tempting for either Margaret or myself to turn Catholic for the privilege of joining the AIF. But there was no mistaking, either, the deep frustration and indeed anger that while so many real advances had been made over the years there was still blockage on the central and most sensitive issue of communion. Why in accordance with official Catholic teaching were couples bound together in holy matrimony debarred from taking communion together? This was not a matter of abstract theology and church law, it was directly affecting their children for whom a church quarrel sundering the family was not a good advert for the faith, and was having adverse pastoral and indeed evangelistic consequences. At church leader level Roman intransigence was blending with Anglican acquiescence. The same disparity between leaders and people was to be found in the Free Churches. In January 2011 the Joint Public Issues Team (JPIT) of the Baptist Union, the Methodist Church and the United Reformed Church held a remarkably good day conference in Birmingham on "Poverty of Ambition? Churches and a politics of hope". The main presenter was the social affairs journalist and commentator Will Hutton. Some 200 people attended but no senior church figure, as I recall, was there. And as far as Baptists went I was appalled that fewer than ten attended. Meanwhile in Scotland the Scottish Friends of Ecumenism in February 2013 held a lively brainstorming weekend in Perth which I was invited to attend as an outside commentator.

Ecumenists were no longer riding a wave but swimming against the slow tide of indifference or even outright hostility. I tried to give a shot in the arm for the swimmers in my book published by the WCC in 2013, *Ecumenical Dynamic: living in more than one place at once*. This was to a large extent a collation of lectures or papers I had written since returning from Geneva, on the modern ecumenical story and certain contemporary challenges as I saw them. It included personal reflections on my own ecumenical journey from Cambridge days onwards, and how my sense of "living in more than one place" had been fostered by my China birth and missionary background. There was a good deal on such as J. H. Oldham (including his "middle axioms" as an ingredient in social ethics) and George Bell but I also challenged the conventional attribution of the start of the ecumenical movement to Edinburgh 1910 at the expense of the Anglo-German churches' peace exchanges of 1908–09. I also sought to lay a biblical foundation for the concept of ecumenism as "living in more than one place at once", and my final chapter "Who are we? Continuing Ecumenical Quest" was essentially an attack on what I saw as the churches' current obsession with denominational or confessional "identity". Many supposed identities, especially when they are accorded a kind of inherently sacral or mystical status, are manufactured in the interests of maintaining the autonomy of the institution and serve as safeguards against entering into deeper relationships with other communities. Hence ecumenical advance gets no further than dialogue. Of course there is a continuing need for dialogue but something more is required if we are to reach genuine *koinonia*. If dialogue means "exchange of words" then in faithfulness to the *incarnate* Word should there not also be an exchange of *life*? For example, what about the churches, meeting in conciliar fellowship, commissioning an order of persons assigned for a time the mission of sharing to the full the life of churches other than their own, whereby "the integrity of the different churches would be maintained while at the same time a form of *koinonia* would be enabled that could fructify ecumenical encounter with quite unforeseen possibilities."[14]. Admittedly we do not yet have a word to convey what I was driving at. So I suggested that, following John 1:14 which testifies that the Word was made flesh ". . . . and lived among us" we should look at the Greek verb for "lived" as used here, which is *eskēnōsen* and literally means "pitched his tent". Out of that we could make a new English term. "[T]he image is deeply suggestive of 'living in' and sharing all the conditions of skin-thin tented life and human vulnerability. To live authentically in response to such incarnate love will mean a parallel readiness to pitch one's tent where others are, even to exchange tents if called for. This would mean going beyond dialogue to—let us invent the new word—*diaskeny*, exchange of living residence."[15] I don't know what, if anything, scholars of New Testament Greek make of this, or if anyone else has taken up the suggestion. Maybe it has to be just a seed left in the ground which will germinate if and when the time is right.

WAR AND PEACE

Another avenue of ecumenical activity, this time in historical commemoration and its contemporary significance, began to open up one day in 2006 while on a brisk walk around the Bristol Downs. It occurred to me that 2008 would see the one

14. *Ecumenical Dynamic*, 212.
15. Ibid., 213.

hundredth anniversary of the visit in May 1908 of over a hundred German church leaders, theologians and distinguished laymen to Britain, followed the following year by a return visit of like British figures to Germany. At a time of rising tension between Britain and Germany and the acceleration of the naval arms race, this was a venture in promoting a culture of peace between the two nations, and was a major stimulus to the formation of the World Alliance for International Friendship through the Churches—although with supreme irony that came about only on the outbreak of war in August 1914. It was a therefore a very significant event in the modern ecumenical story, in my view rivalling the claim of the 1910 Edinburgh Missionary Conference (*pace* the role in it of my hero J. H. Oldham) to be the genesis of the movement. For me this also represented a return to the piece of history that I had first researched in my early days in ministry, on the churches' early peace movement and the First World War.[16] I quickly contacted Bob Fyffe, general secretary of CTBI, his German counterpart Barbara Rudolph, secretary of the Arbeitsgemeinschaft Christlicher Kirchen in Deutschland, and other figures in the German churches, all of whom who soon gave their enthusiastic support for an ecumenical delegation from Germany to visit England in May 2008. This would include a conference with British church people in London, followed by a visit to Cambridge next day, where on that exact date in 1908 the German visitors had been received by the University. For this we secured Jürgen Moltmann as a main speaker. It would obviously be a smaller-scale event than that which it was commemorating (though we could have done without the world-weary response from Church House, Westminster, that it did not merit much attention by the Church of England and that in any case there were enough anniversaries being marked just then). The London conference at St Katherine's House, Limehouse, was quite intense with an honest look at certain anti-German prejudices still evident in Britain ("We had to bomb German cities in World War II"), but also the solid work of reconciliation that had gone on, not least through the churches, and the need for continued partnership in addressing peace and justice issues in the wider world today. Next day in Cambridge was especially memorable. In the morning Jürgen Moltmann addressed the packed main lecture theatre in the Divinity School, on the relationships between German and British theology over the past hundred years, reiterating his moving tribute to what he himself owed to help and encouragement in his faith and theological vocation while a prisoner-of-war in Scotland and England.[17] In the afternoon Richard Bauckham, biblical scholar and theologian, focused on German and British New Testament scholarship. It was, all told, a worthy occasion. The day concluded with evensong in King's Chapel sung by the men's voices of the choir, a moment of beautiful poignancy because on the visit in 1908 a high point of the day in Cambridge, and indeed the whole German visit, came when the Germans, assembled in the chapel, were so entranced by what they saw around and above them that they

16. See above, chapters 4 and 5.
17. See Moltmann *A Broad Place,* chapter 3.

burst into a spontaneous and vigorous rendition of the hymn *Grosser Gott wir loben dich*, a detail which the chaplain of King's, Richard Lloyd Morgan, included in his welcome at the start of the service.

In June the following year the Theology Faculty at Heidelberg University hosted an ecumenical forum in commemoration of the British churches' visit to Germany in 1909, on the theme *The Triune God—a God of Peace and Dialogue?* A prime mover at the Heidelberg end was Professor Friederike Nüssel whom I knew from her membership of the CEC Dialogue Commission. Most of the presentations were by Germans. I gave a paper on "Whose is the Kingdom, the Power and the Glory? Britain, Germany and God since 1909". The other British lecturer was Nicholas Sagovsky, on "The Triune God—a God of Peace, Justice and Dialogue". It was a nice surprise to find also present Father Andreas Cilerdzic, last seen in Belgrade, now pursuing a doctorate in Germany. There was also a good contingent from the Irish School of Ecumenics in Dublin. Margaret joined me midway through the event and afterwards we spent a couple of days with our friends in Frankfurt Henry and Barbara Jakob.

With 2014 of course there came all kinds of commemorations of the outbreak of war in 1914. I was anxious that the war should be seen not just as a demonstration of British heroism and sacrifice, but as a disaster and tragedy for the whole of Europe and to be marked as far as possible on a Europe-wide scale. Invitations came to lecture to the churches at Wallingford near Oxford, to the Worthing Theological Society, to the Protestant Dissenting Deputies in London, and to a Baptist Anglo-German historical conference at Regent's Park College, Oxford. But my main contribution came at the request of Bob Fyffe at CTBI, to write an E-book of reflections on the war and the churches' reactions to it at the time, reflecting the whole range of perspectives from militarist to pacifist, and to include both British and German testimonies of loss, grief and enduring faith and to recall too the experiences of those enlisted from the Indian sub-continent. We called it simply *We Will Remember*.

BONHOEFFER—AND OTHERS—DOWN UNDER

Beyond seeing to the launch of *Bonhoeffer and Britain* and Volume 13 of the English series of the Bonhoeffer Works, when I returned from Geneva I had no particular plan in mind, or any ambition, for further work on Bonhoeffer. As it turned out, the 2006 commemorations of the centenary of his birth marked only the beginning of a continual stream of lecturing engagements and writing, nearly all in response to requests and invitations. First and foremost has been the series of two-week intensive courses on "Bonhoeffer's Theology in Historical Context" which as mentioned earlier I have taught at Whitley College, Melbourne, in the month of February in 2008, 2011 and 2014 (in fact we have usually spent four to five weeks there each time). The classes have been a delight to teach, drawing students from a wide range of ages and denominations (Anglican, Baptist, Church of Christ, Uniting Church, Roman Catholic, and Salvation Army) and also reflecting Melbourne's cosmopolitan population: anything from South Korea, El Salvador, Hong Kong, mainland China, and Indonesia. . . . as well as Australian-born. Some memorable moments have occurred seemingly by chance. During the second week of the 2008 course we were at the point of looking at themes in Bonhoeffer's *Ethics* and in particular that of responsibility in society and the acknowledgment of historical guilt. That very morning, Prime Minister Kevin Rudd was making his outstanding "Sorry" speech acknowledging the wrong committed to Australia's indigenous people by the earlier policies of removing their children for upbringing in white communities. We spent the first half of the morning class watching him make his speech live on TV. Then in 2014 one member of the class happened to mention that his grandmother, now living with his family in Melbourne, was German-born and had spent her girlhood in the Third Reich. I arranged for him to bring her to the class the first morning of the following week. A somewhat frail white-haired lady in her eighties, rather diffident at first despite her good English, she held the class spellbound as for an hour she spoke and answered questions on what it was like to be a village child under the Swastika, a member perforce of the Hitler Youth and permitted to attend her (Catholic) church only so long as the priest did not say that Jesus was a Jew. She told how she had a picture of Hitler on her bedroom wall, and how the day after the failed plot of July 20 1944 all the school had to parade down the street singing songs in praise of the *Führer*. She made clear she was now an admirer of Bonhoeffer but her account of her life in those days was totally honest, not glossing over uncomfortable details, and for that very reason compellingly moving. This was history come alive for the class.

With Whitley College staff and students on retreat. Frank Rees is front row, center.

Each year following that of the Bonhoeffer course I have taught at Whitley a class on "The Churches and Peacemaking" and this too has been enriched by the diverse contexts from which many students have come, especially countries and situations that have experienced conflict such as Burma, East Timor and the stand-off between South and North Korea, as well as Australia's history of mistreatment of its indigenous people. Going to Australia two years out of three has enabled Margaret and me to extend still further our experience of the country and the circle of friends we made first in 2006. Harry and Ruth Wardlaw made a habit of loaning us their cottage at Airey's Inlet on the Great Ocean Road for a weekend. We have visited Sydney, Adelaide and the South Australia coast, revisited Tasmania and in 2009 spent several days on the Queensland coast based in Cairns. From Cairns we spent a day on Green Island which enabled me to indulge an afternoon snorkeling. That particular visit was put in jeopardy when towards the end of our time in Melbourne Margaret was rushed into hospital with appendicitis. This was on the Tuesday, she would be operated on that night and we were due to fly to Cairns on Friday. We looked anxiously at the surgeon. "Fly to Cairns on Friday—what's the problem?" was his reaction. We were in a country where people often *have* to fly great distances and health-and-safety considerations are relativised. Mind you, sensitivities of various kinds are also relative. Would you expect to see in Britain, as we did in Melbourne, adverts for undertakers in the hospital lifts? What could never be relativized, however, was the kind of tragedy that had engulfed the countryside just north of Melbourne halfway through that 2009 visit, with the bush fires that swept through eastern Victoria on "Black Saturday", February 7. Fires were already alight in the bush but on that Saturday with forecasts of temperatures soaring above 40 C people in Melbourne, if they didn't have air-conditioning were warned to find a convenient shopping mall to hole into. That applied to us in our flat at Whitley but Colin and Jenny Hunter took us into their home for the day. We were more than grateful, for by mid-afternoon the thermometer was indeed showing the mid-forties, and clouds of smoke were drifting across the city from the north-east. Then, the wind changed to southerly, the temperature began to drop and the overhead pall of ash thinned. We greeted this with relief but little did we know that this was when the real disaster began for those small towns to the north, many of which we knew from visits, as the wind drove the fires with increased ferocity north-eastward. Next day, Sunday, it began to emerge that nearly two hundred people had died, and over two thousand homes had been destroyed. Next day in my class a minister told us that he had had an orphaned boy in his Sunday morning congregation. Another member of the class, a postal worker, was absent as he had gone north to help with his trade union's welfare work among the victims. To have been so close to such a tragedy was sobering. But equally it was moving and inspirational to witness the huge outpouring of generosity and solidarity in the Victorian community as a whole, and we felt privileged to be among such people.

Bonhoeffer continued to occupy much of my time at home—and abroad. The Tenth International Bonhoeffer Congress was scheduled to take place in Prague in July 2008 and I had been appointed chairman of its planning committee which would also mean being President of the Congress itself. This meant a good deal of work, and travelling to Prague, from 2006 onwards. Jürgen Moltmann and Martin Marty had been signed up as keynote speakers and despite some real anxieties about the finances (which were to come all right in the end) by the spring of 2008 everything seemed to be on track. Unfortunately I had to withdraw from involvement at fairly short notice when June Margaret after a routine mammogram was diagnosed with breast cancer. Naturally this came as a shock and anxiety and the Congress slipped down the table of priorities. Her surgery in any case fell during the time of the Congress itself. My good friend and Lutheran pastor from Minneapolis John Matthews took over the presidency. Margaret's surgery had to be followed up with radiotherapy but prior to that there were complications with the results of the surgery. We did manage to get away to holiday in France in late August though not before, somewhat to general bemusement, my being given some basic nursing training at the Medical Centre in Portishead, on how to dress daily a persistent wound with special antiseptic material. So now both of us had had an encounter with cancer within eight years.

BONHOEFFER AND THE NEW GENERATION

The writing and speaking continued. I contributed to SPCK's series on significant modern theologians with *The SPCK Introduction to Bonhoeffer* which was published in 2010. In November 2011 the completion of the Dietrich Bonhoeffer Works English Edition was marked by an international conference at Union Seminary, New York, on "Bonhoeffer for the Coming Generations". As well as from the USA, scholars from the UK, Germany, South Africa, Brazil and Japan attended. I was asked to speak on "Public Ethics and the Reception of Bonhoeffer in Britain".[18] It was a worthy and encouraging occasion, not just celebrating the completion of a twenty-five year project but also inaugurating a new era in Bonhoeffer studies in which all Bonhoeffer's works could be studied as a whole and as never before. Sadly, it proved to be the last time I was with Isabel Best. She had been suffering with a respiratory and heart condition for some time, and she died in 2013. At the same time I was working on an interesting assignment at the request of Bob Fyffe, secretary of CTBI. Each year CTBI produced a Lent series of studies in conjunction with BBC Religious Programs, and for 2012 Bob invited me to write the on-line study using Bonhoeffer as a resource. This I did, and it was called *The Way to Freedom* as we had decided to build it around Bonhoeffer's poem written in prison, "Stations on the Way to Freedom". The Sunday morning broadcast services during Lent followed the theme through as well with a variety of

---

18. See Green and Carter, Guy, *Interpreting Bonhoeffer* 25–33.

preachers, including Rowan Williams, and I myself preached at the service on Passion Sunday, broadcast from Manchester.

At the academic level of Bonhoeffer studies, a younger generation of theologians and historians was making its presence felt, using new tools of literary and sociological analysis and offering quite new perspectives on the development of Bonhoeffer's theology. That became even more evident at the Twelfth Bonhoeffer Congress held in July 2012 in Sweden, which under the title "A Spoke in the Wheel" focused on the political elements and implications of Bonhoeffer's thought. That it took place in Sigtuna, the small and beautiful lakeside town where in 1942 Bonhoeffer had his clandestine meeting with Bishop George Bell to inform him fully about the conspiracy against Hitler, lent extra significance. Such was the interest generated by the Congress and its theme that far more proposals for seminar papers had been received than could be accommodated in the programme.[19] Far from being tired and worn out, the Bonhoeffer industry was thriving as never before, and ever more widely throughout the world. Quite apart from my experience of lecturing at Whitley College I found this to be true in Australia as well. There is a lively Bonhoeffer interest group based mainly in Melbourne and Sydney which had organized the 2006 conference at Whitley and publishes its own journal. For the Australasian journal *Pacifica*, edited by a former Bristol College student Sean Winter, I wrote an account of the Bonhoeffer Works project and its importance.[20]

But the home scene of Bonhoeffer studies was also encouraging, with a constant stream of PhD theses emanating especially from Cambridge (where Stephen Plant has been very influential), Oxford, Durham, and Aberdeen. At Bristol I supervised the comparative study made by Paul Spanring, Austrian-born Baptist minister, of the German Baptist pastor Arnold Köster, one of the very few Baptists who preached and taught against Nazism, and Dietrich Bonhoeffer, and wrote the preface when his thesis was published.[21] The individual pieces of writing and speaking engagements overall are just too numerous to be detailed here, but two I must mention. First, the Student Christian Movement (SCM) was by now in something like revival mode and among its activities was the "Bonhoeffer Project" which owed much to former SCM people hailing from the radical heydays of the 1960s and earlier, who wished to re-link faith and social action drawing upon Bonhoeffer as a mentor. Central to the project are the placements of a small number of students or recent graduates each year in challenging contexts of social responsibility, with the encouragement to learn something of relevance from Bonhoeffer and to offer their findings and reflections to the churches.

---

19. For the symposium of papers at the Sigtuna Congress see Nielsen, and. Zimmermann, *A Spoke in the Wheel*. This includes (109–119) my own paper "Between a Confessing Church and Contextual Ethics. Bonhoeffer: The Bruay Conference (1934) and the Continuing Ecumenical Quest for a Public Theology".

20. "Bonhoeffer for the Coming Generations: The New English Works", *Pacifica* 25, 2 (June 2012), 105–121.

21. Paul Spanring, *Dietrich Bonhoeffer and Arnold Köster. Two Distinct Voices in the Midst of Germany's Third Reich Turmoil* (Eugene, Oregon: Pickwick Publications, 2013)

At the annual meeting of the project at Friends' House in London in November 2012 I was invited to lead a day of study on Bonhoeffer and heard the reports from two of those now in the scheme—a woman working for a small-scale overseas development agency based in Herefordshire, and a man engaged with a scheme for delinquent young adults in south London. It was inspirational. Second, I had revived my long-standing interest in Thomas Traherne[22] and joined the Traherne Association. Stimulated by reading an account of Traherne in Melvyn Matthews' study of spirituality and mysticism *Awake to God*, in August 2013 our Portishead theological reading group made had an outing to Hereford, viewing the beautiful windows in honor of Traherne in the cathedral, and to Traherne's nearby parish Credenhill. Then the organizers of the 2013 Traherne Association's annual festival at Credenhill invited me to give one of the lectures, and I chose to speak on a theme that had long intrigued me, namely the strong and positive "worldliness" in both Traherne and Bonhoeffer, and the affinities between them notwithstanding their being separated by three centuries and living in very different contexts.[23]

SOUTH AFRICA AGAIN

The Bonhoeffer Works Editorial Board wound itself up at the AAR meetings in Baltimore in 2013, following which there was no call for me to cross the Atlantic each November. Participation in the International Bonhoeffer Society and working with colleagues in the network continued in various ways however, and in this regard South Africa and John de Gruchy continued to be a major draw. In August 2009 Margaret and I holidayed for two weeks in the country, and after spending some time in a safari camp in a corner of the Kruger National Park, where we both viewed and were viewed by lions close-up, we flew to the Western Cape and stayed with the de Gruchys in their home in the Volmoed community near Hermanus. We then went with John to Stellenbosch for a conference on John Calvin and his contemporary significance, to mark the five-hundredth anniversary of the reformer's birth. The following year I went to South Africa again. The centenary of the 1910 Edinburgh Missionary Conference and the fiftieth anniversary of the Cottesloe Conference, a defining moment in the anti-apartheid struggle, were being observed. The main event was the annual conference of the Theological Society of South Africa at Kimberley, at which I gave the opening address, on the affinities between Edinburgh 1910, Cottesloe 1960 and their significance for contemporary ecumenism. I also gave seminars at Pietermaritzburg and, accompanied by Louis Kretzschmar, at the University of South Africa in Pretoria, as well as spending time with the de Gruchys at Volmoed. It was however a year overhung with tragedy, as in February John and Isobel's son Steve, himself an extraordinarily

---

22. See above, chapter 3, p.55; chapter 6, p.128.

23. Unpublished lecture, "Centuries apart yet neighbours in spirit? The Worldly Holiness of Thomas Traherne and Dietrich Bonhoeffer."

able theologian, had tragically drowned in a river rafting accident. Then in 2014 John celebrated his seventy-fifth birthday. Margaret and I flew to Cape Town for two of the main events. First, at Volmoed there was a two-day seminar on Bonhoeffer's legacy attended by John's research students. Larry Rasmussen and Clifford Green came from the USA and we each gave presentations, with Graham Ward of Oxford as interlocutor, mine being on the significance of Bonhoeffer's legacy for ecumenism. We then transferred to a larger conference at Stellenbosch on the theme which was evocative of John's interests and style, "Theology on the Edge", again with a strong international element including figures from Germany (Wolfgang Huber) and the Netherlands (Fritz de Lange) as well as South African veterans such as Allan Boesak, Denise Ackerman, and Dirkie Smit. As in the 2012 New York conference, however, it was very much an encounter between generations. I was glad to be on a panel commending John's autobiographical collection of writings *A Theological Odyssey*. After this memorable conference Margaret and I took off for ten days' genuine holiday driving around Namibia, enjoying the huge emptiness of the country, its plains and mountains, the massive sand dunes on the coast at Sossvulei, the quaintly Germanic life of Swakopmund and the teeming wildlife of the game reserves, especially at Etosha where we had suddenly to reverse the car at full throttle and beat a hasty retreat when a group of elephants decided to take exception to a small pride of lions—and we were in the way.

Like the 2012 Sigtuna Congress and the New York conference these South African Bonhoeffer-related meetings were very much inter-generational encounters. There was about them all a sense of both completion and new beginning, of appreciation for the past and of the opening up of new chapters by younger scholars. As far as the former aspect was concerned, earlier in 2014 a happy occasion, which several of us had hoped and planned for, took place at the University of Aberdeen. Clifford Green was awarded an honorary DD in recognition of his outstanding role as Executive Editor of the Dietrich Bonhoeffer Works English Edition, and as a way of highlighting the importance of that whole project for theology in the English-speaking world. Degree ceremonies the world over have their distinctive rituals, but the Scots combine in a unique way the dignified procession, speech-making, music of all kinds (bagpipes included of course) and rumbustious student hilarity. Clifford obviously enjoyed it too.

By this time I myself was completing what I intended to be my last substantial work on Bonhoeffer and this too would combine a look at history with questions for the future. During a visit to Geneva about a year before *Ecumenical Dynamic* was published Michael West, Editor of WCC Publications, asked me if I would like to write a book on Bonhoeffer and the ecumenical movement. I quite readily agreed, rather presumptuously thinking that I already knew a lot about Bonhoeffer's ecumenical engagements and his posthumous influence on the movement and that it would not therefore cost a lot of effort. That proved not to be the case at all, for while Eberhard Bethge and, more recently, Ferdinand Schlingensiepen in their Bonhoeffer biographies had laid a solid foundation for such a study I soon found that there was a great deal more to be uncovered about the precise contexts in which Bonhoeffer had worked for international Christian unity and peace, and how he related to them. He took the ecumenical organizations of his time so seriously yet equally could be severely critical of them. I had the benefit now of course of the completed English Works Edition which enabled a much more complete picture of Bonhoeffer's lifelong activity and thought, but I also could turn to the archives of the WCC and other sources—Victoria Barnett of Washington DC was very helpful here—for eyewitness accounts of meetings and encounters in which Bonhoeffer was engaged in the 1930s, notably for example the dramatic conference on the island of Fanø, Denmark, in 1934. Moreover I searched in vain for an "ecumenical theology" in Bonhoeffer until I realized that he did have one, namely, none other than his doctrine of the church as "Christ existing as community", a community bound together by the Christlike, loving "vicarious representative action" of its members towards one another. Bonhoeffer simply extended this understanding of the *sanctorum communio* beyond the local parish or congregation to all churches and communities, in all nations of the *oikoumene* that confessed Christ as Lord and head of his body. I also looked hard at his crucial 1935 paper "The Confessing Church and the Ecumenical Movement" which sets out a challenge for ecumenism, and all churches, which still awaits answers today, and is designed to keep the ecumenical quest both humble and hopeful under the command and promise of God.[24] There were also further avenues to be explored on the relation between his ecumenism and his role in the wartime resistance. Each intensified the other. Here one of the—to me—real discoveries was at this how in the resistance he was increasingly involved with Roman Catholics and given cause to ponder the future relations between Protestants and Catholics. The more I worked on the material, the more my target readership became clearer to me: those admirers of Bonhoeffer who looked askance at his ecumenical work as a mere sideshow to his radical theology and political engagement, and on the other hand those ecumenical enthusiasts who beyond regarding him as a kind of martyr figure were largely uninterested in what he had to say about the ecumenical movement itself. Moreover, I believed, there were really important implications in his prison writings on "religionless Christianity" for the ecumenical movement as the call for the churches are to identify with the whole world, the *oikoumene*, before God. So took shape *Dietrich Bonhoeffer's Ecumenical Quest*. The book concludes:

> In the coming years, ecumenical structures at any level may well change, perhaps hardly recognizable to those of us who have inhabited the forms established since 1948. That, of course, will not mean the end of ecumenism but merely that its living reality has to be rediscovered and re-embodied again and again. Dietrich Bonhoeffer, precisely because he sits loose to particular ecumenical forms while utterly committed to their theological purpose, will

24. It is good to learn that Bonhoeffer's essay is to be included in a new edition of Kinnamon and Cope (Eds), *The Ecumenical Movement*.

remain ahead of us for a very long time to come. [As he stated of the ecumenical fellowship] "It is not an ideal that has been set up but a commandment and promise—it is not high-handed implementation of one's own goals that is required but obedience".

Dietrich Bonhoeffer's Ecumenical Quest was launched in March 2015 at a half-day seminar in Geneva, at which I was joined by Victoria Barnett and Stephen Brown (ecumenical historian and now working for the Global Ethics Forum), to discuss themes and issues raised by the book. This was not quite a conclusion to Bonhoeffer engagement however. Early in 2014 I had been invited by Gary Blount, psychiatrist in Minnesota, USA and Bonhoeffer enthusiast, to join a team being assembled by him and his wife Lee to make a docu-drama film about Bonhoeffer and the last days of the resistance to Hitler, interwoven with Sefton Delmer's "Black Propaganda" BBC transmissions to Nazi Germany. This was an intriguing project and it came to successful fruition in January 2017 with its premiere showing in Loma Linda, California, attended by some two thousand people, the day after Donald Trump's inauguration as US President.

A FULL LIFE—AT OUR OWN PACE

Life since Geneva has certainly been full, though without the demands and pressures imposed from outside. In retirement one can and should walk at one's own pace, doing the things one really wants to do whether or not one is paid for it. Enrichment has come in several ways as will be already be apparent from this chapter. The family circle has grown. Jonathan and Ginny Sandringham married in January 2008, their wedding taking place at the historic St Alphege Church in Greenwich. The service was conducted by Ginny's aunt Linda Dean who is an Anglican priest, and I gave the address. Jonathan continued working for the *Daily Mirror*, having survived among other things a stint in Lebanon in July 2006 covering the horrors of the Israeli air-strikes on Beirut and other sites. Then in 2011 he turned to television, joining ITN as crime correspondent. This was going very well but in late 2012 he was suddenly made redundant in a major restructuring of the organization. He rose to the challenge however and over the course of the following year with some friends set up a consultancy in publicity and media relations which soon became very busy. Meanwhile he and Ginny supplied us with two more grandchildren, Bess born in 2009 and Tom in 2011. Bess has disconcerted her father and delighted "Grandma Bristol" in showing both skill and delight in maths. At Uppingham their cousin Oliver, now eleven at the time of writing, has inherited his parents' musicality and is flourishing on the violin. So life flows on, even as the older generation lets go of responsibilities. Margaret finished working part-time for the University of the West of England in 2010 but continued with the Open University well beyond the time when she would have been expected to have been shown the door, probably because she was always willing to take tutorials inside HM prisons. Finally in 2014 she did retire after forty years as tutor—well-nigh a record and this was recognized by the OU inviting her to attend the South-West degree ceremony at Torquay and receiving special mention in the pro-vice-chancellor's speech.

Seventieth birthday family gathering, Cambridge 2013.
L. to R.: Keith, Oliver, Jonathan, Tom, Peter, Laura, Margaret, Bess, Ginny.

Reaching the biblical three-score years and ten obviously requires some special note to be taken. We celebrated Margaret's anniversary with a family gathering and lunch near Uppingham, and mine in Cambridge (King's Fellows' Garden proved a marvelous adventure playground for small children). Margaret and I thought a joint exercise was also needed and we decided this would be an overseas trip to somewhere neither of us had been before. So in February 2013 we headed off for a fortnight to Kerala in south-west India and Sri Lanka. The highlight in Kerala, together with the rich history of its varied cultures including the ancient St Thomas Christian tradition, was the three-day excursion by houseboat on the inland waterways: sheer, tranquil enjoyment of nature, ancient temples, churches, and bird-watching. We likewise enjoyed Sri Lanka and saw most of the celebrated temples and rock-carvings in the interior, but what was also special was being able to visit the headquarters of the Sri Lankan Baptist Sangamaya (Union) in Colombo. Now an office on the leafy Kinsey Road, it was where my parents had lived during in 1969–72. We spent a morning there as I had been invited to lead a seminar on ecumenism for ministers and part-time theological students. We had always regretted not being able to get to Sri Lanka while my parents were there, and this at least was some compensation.

But these years also have us opportunities for maintaining or picking up and renewing old friendships, and making some quite new ones. The friendship with Mike and Liz Jackson, now retired to Cumbria, is as warm as ever, the more so as we grow older and we exemplify the truth that in any meeting or phone conversation the first ten minutes is an organ recital. In chapter 2 I remarked that when I was about to leave Cambridge in 1965 I had said that what I most appreciated in my time there was "friends". A surprising number of student friendships are still very much alive and in some cases flourishing even more during these last years. King's friend Alwyn Thompson and his wife Sue now live in Cheltenham and we visit each other at least twice a year. David Carter lives in Bristol and we meet at regular intervals for a pub lunch, to reminisce about Alec Vidler and put the contemporary world (and church) to rights. Nor is distance always an impediment. Another 1962 Kingsman, Welshman Griff Lewis, toured the world for a gap year after graduating, got to Australia, met Carole and went no further, marrying and settling there to work for the government on indigenous peoples' issues. Twice on our Australian visits we have been guests of Griff and Carole in their home up in the Blue Mountains just inland from Sydney. In September 2015, Griff still being a stalwart follower of Welsh rugby, they came over for an extended visit during the World Cup Series, and Margaret and I were glad to host a mini-reunion for them with a number of Kingsmen of our year, and their wives, who live in the Bristol area. On such occasions there is always plenty of food for thought on how we now view the Cambridge experience, with what perspectives we now see those who tried to teach us, what has lasted, what we appreciate, what we don't, and what remains of value. Then there were the friendships made through the Robert Hall Society. We still keep in close touch with Christopher and Robert Bradnock and their older brother James, and see from time to time Michael and Anne Bowker, David Thompson (now a professor emeritus in Cambridge), Colin and Ruth Morley, and others of our years. In September 2010 a number of us organized a reunion in Cambridge of people who had been in RHS at some time during the period 1960–66, and their spouses (in some cases of course, as with Margaret and myself, the spouseification was owed to RHS itself). Some seventy people came for a sunny, convivial yet also at times movingly reminiscent day at Fitzwilliam College. Life-stories were shared, tragedy as well as success. In some cases they revealed how far people had travelled from the way they expressed their faith all those years ago, but always appreciative for what that transient yet fruitfully diverse fellowship (like a compost heap, said one) had given them. One person declined to come, saying that it was more important to live in the present and look forward than to look back. That is true of course, but no one was suggesting that we were offering a permanent return to the past, merely that, as T.S. Eliot observes somewhere, there is a time for an evening with the photograph album. Such moments remind us that we live in time, that it is enriching to trace the continuities that thread our moments together in ongoing community, and also sometimes to discover the long-forgotten encounters that have helped to shape us. In other words, to be aware of grace then and now—and tomorrow.

Sometimes it is not so much a case of us revisiting the past, but the past unexpectedly visiting us. In late May 2012, a few days after my *Times* letter arguing that

Part Five: Old Interests, New Horizons 2006–2016

Rowan Williams's successor as archbishop should have ecumenical credentials, a letter arrived in the post from a woman whose married name I did not recognize. She wanted to know if the writer of that letter, the "Revd Dr Keith Clements", was by any chance the Keith Clements she recalled as a teenager when holidaying with her parents and brother at a Christian guest house in Llandudno fifty-three years ago. It was Janet, the girl I had fallen for so helplessly but too coyly on that holiday. There was mutual amusement and an exchange of correspondence as we caught up on our very different life-stories and family affairs, and Margaret and I have twice visited her and her husband at their home in Buckinghamshire.

Among preaching invitations have been those from churches with very long associations for me. In 2008 Margaret and I returned to Ferryhill in County Durham for the centenary weekend of the chapel which my father had pastored part-time while minister in Darlington, and where my brother John and his family still live. For similar purposes four years later we went back to Wallasey for the anniversary of what is now Serpentine Road Family Church, in a completely new building, the Egremont Baptist Church where I had been baptized having united with the nearby United Reformed Church. It is good to meet old friends again but, in a church, it is even better to see new faces that have arrived. Then there is King's, as a college revisited often enough for reunions and other reasons but whose chapel above all has as unique a place in my affections as it did more than fifty years ago. In 2009 Margaret and I returned for the Advent Sunday service. Leaving through the antechapel afterwards we found someone there who had even more cause to look back with gratitude. An elderly but very upright, begowned figure was standing still, gazing eastwards at the organ screen. It was David Willcocks. We greeted him and he and I recalled our previous meeting in Bern in 2005. Then he told us why he was there. It was seventy years before, in 1939, that as organ scholar he had first played for the Christmas Eve service, before leaving to serve in the army for the duration of the war. One could only guess at the memories. Two years, later in October 2011, invited by Jeremy Morris the dean I preached at sung Matins in King's. No preaching engagement could have meant more to me. To preach in King's is of course a special challenge, not just because of the resonant acoustic but because you suspect that the expressions on the faces in the congregation are saying, "It's not *you* we've come to hear!" The appointed New Testament reading was Luke 13:22–30 and I based the sermon on verse 29: "And they shall come from the east, and from the west, and from the north and from the south, and shall sit down in the kingdom of God." The gist of the sermon was that the kingdom of God inaugurated by Jesus means the end of tribalism of every kind, that this was the essence of the ecumenical movement too, and I spoke about the roles King's itself had played in that movement. I spoke about how in 1908, in the very place where we were gathered, the German church guests' rapturous reaction to its beauty had been a highlight of their whole visit to England out of which an important strand of the ecumenical movement for peace had been born. I mentioned, too, what Eberhard Bethge once told me how during the war, in the years before his imprisonment, Dietrich Bonhoeffer had always loved to tune in to the BBC overseas broadcast of the Christmas Eve service, a token of the international fellowship that was so dear to him. Every act of worship in praise of the one God of all the peoples is a subversion of tribalism. I need not have worried about interest taken by some at least of the congregation, for by wonderful chance there was present that morning another party of Germans, Rotarians from Essen. Stephen Cleobury, the director of music, told me that knowing how Bonhoeffer had listened in each year would now make conducting the Christmas Eve service mean even more to him. That morning was an occasion in which so many strands of one's life came together in a moment of grace.

At Christmas 2014 our annual letter to family and friends included a photograph of Margaret's great-grandparents and great-uncle-and-aunt, taken in a sitting-room in Halifax. The scene has a certain poignancy, for it was actually taken on Christmas Day 1914, the first Christmas in the war to end all wars. Our letter concluded assuringly, "Life did, and does, go on." There was no reason to doubt the continuity of our own life. It was even possible to claim some kind of fulfilment in worthwhile things done, or at any rate attempted, and gifts that had been experienced. Growing yet older need not present any real problems or set-backs. Unwelcome events during the next two years, however, were to challenge that assumption.

20

Two Troubling Years

THE FIRST FOUR MONTHS of 2015 looked set to be rewarding, and indeed all went according to schedule. Margaret and I flew to Australia in late January, stayed with Griff and Carole Lewis in the Blue Mountains and then drove down to Melbourne. At Whitley College the intensive course on the churches and peacemaking went as planned. In addition, towards the end of our four weeks in Melbourne I flew to Canberra for an overnight visit and gave the lecture for the opening of the new academic year at St Paul's (Anglican) Theological Centre, on "Life Together in a Digital Age". Three days after arriving home in Portishead, on March 4 I was at the WCC in Geneva for the launch of *Dietrich Bonhoeffer's Ecumenical Quest*. Ten days after that we were on the move again, to Sri Lanka, as I had been invited to lecture for the second time on a two-week Swan Hellenic cruise, this time from Colombo to Muscat in Oman via the Malabar coast. It was a delight to see Colombo and the Kerala coastal towns again, stopping also at Mumbai and Porbandor, the birthplace of Mahatma Gandhi. I gave four lectures on interactions between Christianity and India over the centuries, and conducted two Sunday communion services. The other lecturers were writer and broadcaster Lord John Julius Norwich, Oliver Everett (former Librarian of the Royal Windsor Library), and retired diplomat Sir Adrian Beamish. By chance among the passengers were friends Win and Hugh Burton of Oxford, both of whom had worked in Brussels, and I had known Win from her work on the Soul for Europe programme in the Ecumenical Centre there. Also on the passenger-list were the husband and wife actors Timothy West and Prunella Scales. Timothy volunteered himself as a lesson reader for the first of the communion services (Margaret said she had never heard a chunk of the Epistle to the Romans read so understandably). The second service fell on Palm Sunday for which at my request he read G. K. Chesterton's poem *The Donkey*, again to great effect. Back home, the next engagement was on April 9, the seventieth anniversary of Dietrich Bonhoeffer's death at Flossenbürg, and I gave the commemorative lecture "A Pastor to the Very End", at the German Church in Sydenham where he had been pastor 1933–35.

CANCER AGAIN

So, a very full, and fulfilling, three months. But it was also a grim time physically. Since Christmas I had been plagued with excruciating sciatic pain in the lower back and down the left leg. Neither Marion, our excellent physiotherapist in Bristol, nor the one I visited in Melbourne were able to provide more than temporary relief. In April Marion strongly advised going to see a neurosurgeon for an MRI (magnetic resonance imaging) scan. I duly did so. This revealed not the slipped disc that both she and the neurosurgeon had been expecting, but a tumor on the spine. Further tests showed that in fact I had prostate cancer, previously unsuspected, which had metastised to the bones, and nodules were also showing up in the lungs. The National Health Service in Bristol went into action in double-quick time with hormone injections, and surgery on the spine in late May which instantly and wonderfully relieved the pain, followed by a shot of radiotherapy. Obviously all this was disruptive of engagements, for example I had to cancel a lecture in Finland. But by the beginning of July I was getting mobile again and was able to give a lecture on the churches and the approach to war in 1914, at the URC History Society's annual meeting in Cambridge; and in early September another lecture at a conference on Bonhoeffer at the Community of the Resurrection in Mirfield. After which there would be a programme of chemotherapy starting in October, not a welcome prospect but necessary.

This however was but half the story. The previous November Margaret was found to have a mole on the retina of her right eye. Tests at St Bartholomew's (Barts) Hospital in London, one of the few centers in the country with the specialism to deal with such conditions, at first indicated it not to be harmless. But at her third examination in July it was proving to be cancerous. She had to spend a week of August at Barts in solitary confinement with a radioactive disc over the offending eye. Follow-up examinations indicate that the cancer has been stopped, and shows no sign as yet of spreading elsewhere.

So there we were, both of us with cancer for the second time round. My chemotherapy, six sessions in all at three-weekly intervals, began in October and finished in early February, and was not too troublesome except for the three or four days of heaviness and tiredness following each session of treatment, and I was able to keep to a number of engagements. My PSA blood reading dropped from the astronomically high to the nearly-normal and the post-chemotherapy MRI scan showed the cancer in the bones to have been halted (it can never be removed) and the lungs to be clear. So for the time being, in medical language it is "stabilized", and apart from stiffness in the back and some joints I'm living as normal a life as can be imagined at my age. At some point within months or a year or so the cancer is likely to be on the move again, and another form of slowing-it-down therapy might be on offer. As when I had my first bout of cancer when in Geneva, I dislike talk of "battling cancer". Rather, I would say, I have cancer and I have a life still to be lived as fully as possible. Of course, despite all the extraordinary advances in therapies that we are blessed with in our generation, cancer arrives with a sharp reminder of our human fragility. One's reaction is "I've always known I'm mortal, but not as mortal as *that*." One day, no doubt, this particular cancer will prove unstoppable and the body will eventually cease to function. But that was always going to happen sooner or later anyway, and it will not mean that cancer has won. It will simply mean that the temporal boundary has been reached for my living the life that God has given me to live, and I hope that what will be observed will be not what cancer has done to me but whether and how grace has triumphed in the life that was given me.

In short, life for both of us became a lot more uncertain than we could have imagined two years earlier. At least, that provided a spur for writing this book. The sudden, sharper awareness of mortality prompts a recall and some attempt at an evaluation of one's life as whole before, humanly speaking, it has gone for good. What I have been writing is essentially a way of trying to sum up what I have been grateful for, together with measuring how far what I have experienced leaves me with hope for the wider human story of which I have been part. Left to itself, the onset of cancer at my age has little bearing on that bigger question since I feel my allotted years have been so filled with good things that I am not owed anything more (though of course I would still *like* to have more—another Christmas, another visit to Australia, our golden wedding, the chance to see our grandchildren grow up further). Well might I say with the seventeenth-century Thomas Traherne:

> He that is in all, and with all, can never be Desolat. All the Joys and all the Treasures, all the Counsels and all the Perfections, all the Angels and all the Saints of GOD are with Him. All the Kingdoms of the World and the Glory of them are continually in his Ey: The Patriarchs, Prophets and Apostles are always before Him. The Counsels and the fathers, the Bishops and the Doctors minister unto Him. All Temples are Open before Him, the Melodies of all Quires reviveth Him, the Learning of all Universities doth employ Him, the Riches of all Palaces Delight him. The joys of Eden Ravish Him, the Revelations of S. John Transport Him, the Creation and the Day of Judgment pleas Him. The Hosannas of the Church Militant, and the Hallelujahs of the Saints Triumphant fill Him, the Splendor of all Coronations entertain Him, the Joys of Heaven surround Him, And our Saviors Cross, like the Centre of Eternity is in Him. It taketh up his Thoughts, and exerciseth all the Powers of his soul, with Wonder Admiration Joy and Thanksgiving. The Omnipotence of God is His Hous, and Eternity his Habitation.[1]

The real challenge is that the unexpected, likely foreshortening of life has also been accompanied by a turn of events in the public sphere which, depressing enough in itself, puts a question-mark against the value of so much that I have lived and worked for my whole adult life long. On June 23 2016 a majority of British people voted for their country to leave the European Union.

---

1. Traherne *Poems, Centuries, and Three Thanksgivings*, 188.

BRITAIN AND EUROPE

No surprise, I was a firm "remainer". I share the view that the referendum was an ill-conceived political ploy by Prime Minister David Cameron to head off conflict within his own party, a gamble relying on overall support in the country at large but undertaken with no real commitment or argument, and no vision beyond narrowly-viewed British economic self-interest. Nor was the Labour Party leadership, now under Jeremy Corbyn, more than lukewarm—again, I believe, for being captive to sectional interests in the camp. This meant that the referendum campaign—and indeed the debate on Europe that had been running for months and even years before that—was always hostage to the vicious, poisonous and often downright mendacious anti-Europeanism of the right-wing press. I do not buy any of the single-cause explanations of the majority vote, except to say that it revealed a widespread underlying British fear about the world we are now living in, and a childish wish to revert to a mythical time when "Britain was great" and strong enough to "stand on her own" against the world (the sentiments evoked by the current First World War commemorations and Second World War nostalgia were easily conscripted into "Brexit"). I agree that migration was an important factor and would criticize the mainstream political leadership on their approach to this—but not for the reasons generally stated. The starting point for truly statesmanlike political leadership is not to see migration as a problem that can somehow be solved by tougher measures by our own country. The starting point is surely to look at the big picture, however unwelcome, and face the truth that we all live in *a migratory world* as never before, and no measures taken by any one country on its own are going stop that. At least the EU for all its faults, offers the means of collective action which is both just and practicable. On this issue the leave vote had a great deal of fancifulness in it, while at the same time legitimizing racism and xenophobia on an unprecedented scale.

For myself and others like me the EU was not an issue suddenly confronting us for decision in June 2016, nor was the vote a matter on which one might simply express disagreement with the result and go on my way with a shrug of the shoulders. Europe for me meant a commitment to values I had held since the late 1960s, and the referendum result felt like a total rejection of these. As minister at Downend in June 1975, just before the referendum held by Harold Wilson to endorse continued British continued membership of what was then the European Economic Community (EEC), I had preached on the issue, basing my sermon on Psalm 127:1, "Unless the Lord builds the house, its builders will have labored in vain".[2] I tried to make clear that I was not actually telling my congregation how to vote but that nevertheless there were certain factors and basic issues which for Christians should be crucial: that the church as a community in Christ is transnational in its very nature, and that British Christianity owed so much to our European Christian partners; that (perhaps strangely to people of faith) God calls us to acknowledge certain realities in the world as it is, not as we

---

2. See above, chapter 5, p.109.

would fondly like it to be; that Christ is our peace, and the EEC owed its origin to a Christian-inspired vision to build peace and reconciliation in a shattered Europe after World War II, and therefore we must ask how our country, "in" or "out" is to be a more effective agent for peace and for justice in a world of increasing divides between rich and poor; and that we need to look carefully at what "sovereignty" means in a world over which God alone is the truly sovereign one.

Thirty-one years later, more might need to be added but very little change, it seemed, was needed in the basic content of what had I had said then. The European Community in its development through the 1980s and early 1990s into the Single Market and the European Union, and its dramatic enlargement after the end of the Cold War, was whatever its faults a force for peace, stability and cooperation, not itself the kingdom of God on earth but much more reflective of the values of that kingdom than free-for-all competitiveness and nationalistic self-aggrandizement could ever be. It was an enterprise, moreover, which had been accompanied closely by the churches in the development of the European Ecumenical Commission on Church and Society (EECCS) in Brussels and Strasbourg, and the Commission of the Catholic Bishops' Conferences in the EU (COMECE). The churches therefore had a very long-standing commitment to monitoring the EU and the other European Institutions and engaging in dialogue with their staff. My time as general secretary of CEC coincided with the integration of EECCS and CEC and therefore I was as concerned as anyone to maintain a Christian presence at the heart of the European project. In June 1998 the EU annual summit took place in Cardiff, and on the day before it opened I preached at the Sunday morning BBC broadcast service held in the Norwegian Sailors' Church in Cardiff, and conducted by my ecumenical and fellow-Baptist friend Gethin Abraham-Williams. Based on the gospel story of Jesus and his disciples faced with the hungry five thousand in the wilderness ("*You* give them something to eat"), I took as my theme "Europe is Meeting"[3]. As I frequently did in those days, I likened post-Cold War Europe as a place where people, having formerly complained about the walls separating them from their neighbors, now that the walls were coming down were instead complaining about their neighbors: a Europe that had not only witnessed ethnic cleansing but where on the borders people were finding it ever harder to find refuge and asylum; a Europe that had to find its role in making the world a more just and peaceful place. "If you turn away your neighbors you will one day have no neighbor to care for you. In the long run we cannot have a peaceful world if it's an increasingly unjust or unequal world."

I reiterated the message many times during my years at CEC. The EU, and the other institutions such as the Council of Europe represented a form of cooperation. Europe was making a bold experiment in the direction of what Karl Barth called "co-humanity" and as such was to be valued however just the criticism of it was at times. In 2001 at a Methodist conference on mission at Swanwick, in advance of the forthcoming debate on the constitution of the EU I pointed to the uncertainties ahead

3. Clements, *The Churches in Europe*, 25–28.

"But some sort of integration involving the word 'federalism' is before us. I do not see how any Christian mind can be opposed to this in principle. We are gloriously privileged to live in a time of opportunity for Europe to overcome both the divisions which have plagued it in the past, and which have generated devastating wars from the seventeenth century inwards, and the rivalries that, moreover, have been exported with tragic consequences for the rest of the world . . . "[4] But also, underlying all that I had been thinking and saying since the early 1980s, was what I had set out in *A Patriotism for Today*: the distinction between a genuine love of one's country within the community of peoples as a whole, and the spurious national self-glorification that masquerades as patriotism and functions as an idolatrous substitute religion.

On returning from Geneva at the end of 2005, I felt increasingly uneasy about the quality of political debate about Britain in Europe. Tony Blair was certainly pro-EU but never, it seemed, advancing the case beyond "what is best for Britain". Once this stance became the basis for discussing Britain's future and the EU, the die was essentially cast: the EU was implicitly seen negatively. No leading politician in either main party seemed prepared to begin with the question, "What is good for Europe as a whole, and therefore for Britain?" The vision stopped at the white cliffs of Dover. The debate was always prey to the endemic isolationism in many British people (or rather especially the English since Scotland was a rather different case). One only had to look at the very language used to demonize Brussels as if the EU was an external but intrusive and dictatorial power over the UK, ignoring the fact that *we*, the UK, were actually "Brussels" too and as involved in deciding EU legislation as much as any other body or country is. The case for partnership and cooperation as alternative avenues to either independence or enslavement was never put.

AND THE CHURCHES?

Sitting in front of the television in the early hours of June 24 as David Dimbleby declared "Britain will leave the European Union" therefore felt like a rejection of so much that I had believed in, preached on and worked for since student days. But that was not all. Where had the British churches been in all this sorry business? The sad answer: mostly, nowhere of any consequence. I suppose that any return home to Britain from the European church scene would have seemed a bit of a come-down, but as the years rolled on and talk of an EU referendum grew I was genuinely puzzled as to why there seemed so little discussion within the churches apart from special-interest groups like Faith in Europe. It was a far cry from the 1970s when, for example, the British Council of Churches had produced the booklet *Christians and the Common Market* which usefully set out the main issues. In early January 2015 I wrote to a number of friends and colleagues in the churches and ecumenical bodies who I knew were

---

4. *The Churches in Europe*, 7.

concerned with European themes, asking where, if anywhere, was this discussion taking place in the churches and how was it envisaged being brought into the public domain. The answers I got, as expected, shared my concern. But nothing more seemed to happen. In the autumn a website was opened by the Church of England and Church of Scotland called "Reimagining Europe" which provided an online discussion point. But the very title suggested pipe-dreaming rather than prophetic vision, and while it is always good to provide a means of exchanging views it still seemed evasive of the churches and their leadership not to declare more fully their hand. On New Year's Day 2016 the *Times* greeted the year of the referendum with an editorial on the issues to be debated. I felt moved to write a letter:

> Your leader on the wider issues of "The European Question" (January 1) prompts the observation that one quarter which has been notably silent in the current debate is that of the churches. From the end of World War II the British churches and their leaders played a major role in advocating reconstruction and reconciliation in Europe, and both before and after Britain joined the European Economic Community they followed closely, though never wholly uncritically, the development of what is now the EU. Today in Brussels and Strasbourg they share in the well-established ecumenical bodies which engage in regular dialogue with the European Commission and the other European Institutions on policy matters affecting every aspect of human welfare. Further, at many levels, from official inter-church agreements to parish and congregational partnerships, churches of all denominations in this country are part of a Europe-wide network.
>
> One would hardly guess this, however, from the continued silence of church leaders or representative bodies and their apparent unwillingness to enter the public forum with the questions which too many of our politicians and commentators, on either side of the in/out debate, ignore: questions about what just, peaceable and creative relationships between peoples now require in a rapidly changing world in which any one nation's welfare is inextricably bound up with that of others, in Europe and beyond. A voice is required alternative to both isolationist fantasies and narrowly-conceived immediate economic self-interest. If the churches do not help to provide such a voice they are forgetting their historic role and evading their present responsibility.

The letter, in slightly shortened form, appeared on January 4, and as with the letter a year earlier I had also circulated it to a like-minded circle. Virtually all responses were highly positive, although the bishop of Leeds Nick Baines took me to task over the alleged silence of the churches, saying that he had spoken on Europe in the House of Lords (one non-church person in Portishead, who had seen my letter in the *Times,* commented to me that this was not so very different from staying silent). Tony Peck, secretary of the European Baptist Federation but based in Bristol, and I sat down to try and see if the Free Churches at least could be prompted to do more. Even the Joint Public Issues Team (Baptist, Methodist, and URC) which had such a good track record on social issues, evidently felt intimidated, as did the social responsibility departments of the churches generally, by the "politically divisive" nature of the issue. Eventually the JPIT did, in conjunction with the Church of Scotland, set up a useful online resource but it was very late in the day and still very much an intra-church affair rather than right out there in the public forum. As for *corporate* stands taken by the churches officially, these were almost totally lacking. The two brilliant exceptions were the Quaker Council of European Affairs which "discerned" (no doubt quietly) that Britain should remain a member of the EU; and the Church of Scotland General Assembly which overwhelmingly (and noisily) reaffirmed its support for continued UK membership. Otherwise it was a sorry picture of individuals and church leaders giving what were essentially their personal views. The archbishop of Canterbury Justin Welby for example gave an interview for the Parliamentary in-house magazine. Hardly the platform for prophetic utterance in the public sphere. His accusations, in the last few days before the vote, of UKIP leader Nigel Farage making racist remarks resembled aiming a pea-shooter at an elephant that for days had been rampaging round the village. It was all too little, too late, too light-weight, too individualistic.

What should the churches have been saying? For my own part I wrote a short piece, "The EU Debate" and the Gospel" which appeared on the website of Faith in Europe and the Baptist Union, and in fact was first published in the magazine of Tyndale Baptist Church. I took issue with those who said that the EU vote was a purely political matter and had nothing to do with faith. Our faith and the EU were both about *relationships*, and that means doing justly, loving mercy and walking humbly with God, at every level of life.

> How we are going to live together with our neighbors, peaceably, fairly and creatively is the paramount concern prompted by the gospel, and the key issue in the referendum debate is whether we think staying in or coming out of the EU is the better of way of serving *that* concern. That of course still leaves room for sincerely held opinions to differ on whether the EU is in fact a serviceable instrument for God's purpose of justice and peace in the world.

Whatever else, I argued, the EU had been a means of building peace in the world. Yes, let all the criticisms possible be made against it but it was against *that* paramount concern that they had to be weighed. Surely the church leadership, as loudly and clearly as possible, could have said something like that together, and on that basis challenged the superficiality, opportunistic self-centeredness and untruthfulness of much of the public debate—and would have addressed the confusion and uncertainty in their own constituencies (UKIP evidently had a lot of support among church members as elsewhere). But what if, nevertheless, the vote had still been for "leave"? No matter; the basic values would have been stated. Truth would have been told, and reality would still have to be faced in the coming days. "There are fundamental truths in human life to which it always returns sooner or later" (Bonhoeffer).[5]

It is no accident that my disappointment over Britain's vote on Europe is in parallel with my frustration at the state of ecumenism, for the two issues are closely related. Both represent a preference for a supposed autonomy and a clinging to ill-defined identities, over against a relational, community-building ethos. Moreover, the failure of the UK churches to address adequately the European issue in the public forum is a direct consequence of the downsizing and weakening of the ecumenical bodies. In particular, with the ending of CTBI in its former status there is no longer any inclusive, four-nation forum for all the churches to meet and seek a common mind on the major public issues of the day. That has proved disastrous in the Europe debate, in which the churches consigned themselves to virtual invisibility and silence. The churches are now totally marginalized and can no longer expect, unless something really dramatic occurs, to be taken seriously in the public sphere. It may be, of course, that they no longer really *want* to be taken seriously there—at any rate as corporate entities as distinct from certain individuals in front of the microphone or the TV cameras. This brings us to a still deeper question: do the churches really regard themselves as distinctive *communities of faith* any longer, or does Christianity now simply comprise a list of individuals who somehow belong to different churches but are otherwise indistinguishable from society as a whole? What does it mean to be the *body* of Christ in the world today? There is little point in talking about Christian unity if in the first place all semblance of a corporate common life and mutual accountability has dissolved into a sea of religious individualism.

All this, written in late 2016, no doubt reads pessimistically. Am I disappointed? Yes. Angry? Yes. Combined, cancer and this debacle over Europe certainly don't provide a happy ending. Have I stopped hoping? Actually, no.

---

5. Bonhoeffer, *Letters and Papers*, 385.

Postlude: Still Hoping

IN OUR LIVING ROOM in Portishead still stands the Indian water jar which my parents kept in their baggage as a souvenir of the wartime journey from China to England. Someone once suggested to me that the story with which I began this memoir was responsible for making me into an incorrigible optimist; or possibly I had simply inherited the genes of hopefulness from my parents who had decided to set out on that journey. Either might be true. Certainly I have often reflected on that tale and what it says about travelling together, embracing uncertainties and risk, about unexpected encounters, about helping others along the way and in turn being helped by strangers and even enemy aliens—and persisting to the very end. So it was tempting to use journeying as the unifying metaphor for this memoir as so many others have done in writing their life-stories. But I was reluctant to do this, for three reasons. First, the journey from China had from the start a very definite goal, England, whereas while I hope my career was never aimless it took in a variety of destinations, a good number of them quite unforeseen, and so the parallel with the family saga doesn't quite hold. Second, I wanted to highlight the things I have seen and learnt along the way, and not just the route itself. Third, the last thing I wished to imply was that somehow the way had always been planned for me in advance. That would involve a rather specious and self-justifying understanding of providence. My own conception of providence is rather of how the Spirit, the Lord and giver of life, is able to create out of the seemingly random, coincidental, even trivial and disappointing happenings and encounters, the most extraordinary outcomes and new possibilities of grace-filled life. So the water-jar still stands in all its simple fragility, from a very different place and a very different world to the one I live in now, but still speaking of what matters most in life today as much as seventy years ago, and of unforeseen possibilities that lie before us.

It is certainly possible to discern some continuities, if not always in one's own life then in the wider life of which it is a part. On occasion in this account I have used the term "web of grace". It was coined by Ronald Gregor Smith to describe how both in the Hebrew Scriptures and the New Testament God is encountered in historical events, and how this encounter releases people by faith into a fresh entry into history, empowered by grace and channeling that grace in new and creative directions. He says for example of St Paul that the center of his story "lies . . . in the *web of grace* in which he is caught, in the history which he now sees as completed, in the work which nevertheless remains to be done, as he presses on to the goal which has already been established for the whole of history in that same divine self-disclosure"; and that the biblical personalities "launched all the force of their convictions in the direction of that hidden yet most real world, that *structure of grace* which permeates the whole of history, and so disclosed and drew out the meaning which lies in the simplest happening".[1] This answers to my own sense that for me faith has meant being caught up into a movement of grace in the world which began long before me, and was spun around me by many people including my parents and so many of the people who have featured in this story, some famous, others scarcely known beyond myself, but all of them living by grace and in turn challenging and directing the life around them towards compassion, justice, peace and community—what in *Learning to Speak* I called "God's alternative history". I think especially of that ecumenical network of twentieth-century figures who were linked in diverse ways over time, personally or indirectly—like J. H. Oldham, Dietrich Bonhoeffer, Eberhard and Renate Bethge, Alec Vidler, Clifford Cleal, Oliver Tomkins, Ronald and Käthe Gregor Smith, Morris West, Duncan Forrester, Lesslie Newbigin, Kathleen Bliss, Peter and Donata Coleman, Elizabeth Salter—and into whose life, thought and influence by some means or other I was caught up, in an ongoing web of endeavor and witness for the good of the world. To all such I owe the encouragement to continue in the same direction, to spin another strand of the web however fragile.

1. *The New Man*, 25–26. My emphases.

The ecumenical calling that embraced me first at Cambridge is what I have sought to live out. I cannot claim to have lived it faithfully but I hope my account has portrayed people and communities who highlight what it means.

To speak of the web of grace within human history, or the alternative history, does not lead to a glib optimism. Rather it conveys a tenacious insistence that another way than the way of the present world is on offer—even if the offer is refused. I have seen so much that has encouraged and inspired me to believe that notwithstanding all that is wrong in the world, fearful, evil, or just plain stupid, this world is embraced by a Spirit, wholly other yet wholly self-giving to the world, which is making its presence known. "Yet always there was hope."[2] It is a hope ultimately underwritten by the once-for-all yet ever-to-be re-enacted story of incarnation, cross, resurrection and Pentecost. It is a worldly story. We cannot have God without the world, nor the world without God, says Bonhoeffer. In one respect that makes finding hope rather difficult. It would be easier to have a hope which was simply a nebulous looking to what lies beyond this world and outside human history with all its messiness and suffering, a hope attached to a parallel universe unaffected by pain and tragedy. Instead, the hope given by Christ crucified and risen always arises, paradoxically, in conjunction with what seems to deny it, in the besetting injustices and cruelties of the world and the fact of death. It has meant so much me, to see where and how people and communities have reacted to the darkness around them not by denial, evasion or escape, but by claiming right there and then that Christ seeks to take form in the world. I look back on these in hope, for they represent God's purpose and God's promise. In themselves they may not have changed the world perfectly or permanently (see South Africa today, for example) any more than did the deliverance of the Israelites at the Red Sea. But like that event, they were moments when liberating grace broke through, revealing what the whole story is about, then, now, and in days to come, until the end is reached

Margaret and I have just returned from a week's rest and relaxation in that most beautiful (in every sense) place we have come to know over the years, and which has already featured in this account: the Orthodox Academy of Crete. Set on a rocky bluff over the sea near Chania at the western end of the island, it is loved by all its visitors for its serenity and hospitality, set in the most stunning natural surroundings. Yet its story for me also sums up so much of why as an ecumenical Christian I still hope. It was born out of the death brought by war, destruction and hatred. From its terrace one sees across the bay the strip of coast where in 1942 some of the bloodiest fighting of the Second World War took place between the airborne German invaders and the defending allied troops, leading to the allied defeat and three grim years of occupation. Partisan Cretan resistance was met with brutal retribution. For example in 1943 the village of Livadas was totally razed by the Germans. One of its children, a ten-year old boy called Alexandros Papaderos whose family was involved in the resistance, was transported to a concentration camp in Chania, an experience which marked him for

2. Romans 8:20 (New English Bible 1961 version).

life but not in the way that might have been expected. After the war and schooling he studied theology, not for the priesthood for his main interest was in social and diaconic work. At ecumenical work-camps organized by the WCC during the 1950s he met German, British, French and American students. He went on to study and research in social sciences in Germany. He could have stayed abroad as yet another gifted member of the Greek *diaspora* with an assuredly successful academic career. But he felt called back to Crete, to its endemic rural poverty, moreover still carrying the wounds of war. Inspired by the burgeoning Evangelical Lay Academies in Germany, in partnership with the Metropolitan Bishop Irineos of Kisamos he set up the Orthodox Academy on land owned by the monastery of Gonia at Kolympari. This became a center for lay people (and clergy as appropriate) to address through conferences and seminars the urgent needs to improve agriculture, education, healthcare, and to apply the sciences to human welfare—and to build peace in the world. It became a living example of reconciliation between nations, communities and religious traditions, not least because the bulk of the academy's funding was provided by the Evangelical Church of Germany, and much of its work continues to be in closer partnership with the churches and institutions of Germany than with any other country. Dialogue is its watchword, which became a dangerous word during the dictatorship of the colonels in the 1970s when the academy continued its work regardless. Today the academy is a world-renowned center bringing together people of all backgrounds and religious persuasions (or none) in study and debate on the common ethical concerns of humanity, especially the environment and the life-sciences. Pugwash scientists, Prince Philip, Stephen Hawking, famous novelists, poets, artists and musicians have all felt at home here. It is where the Magi of the contemporary world can come with their gifts for the good of the whole *oikoumene*. Yet the academy has never lost its Orthodox foundation and ethos. It is a church-sponsored, church-accountable organization. It has found a way of using its distinctive theology and spirituality in service to the whole human community. Such a community is for me a living example of Bonhoeffer's "church existing for others", and as such a sign of grace and hope.

But elsewhere too, as I have recounted, I have seen time and again candles in the dark both metaphorically and literally; sometimes just persistent glimmers of hope, at other times creative, breakthrough developments in life and thought; sometimes instances of high drama on the international scene; above all in the extraordinary people and communities whom I have met, served with and been befriended by. Sometimes these have included very eminent people but more often so-called ordinary individuals, their real significance hidden from public view and in some cases unknown even to themselves.

I look back in hope because those stories point to the great story that is not over. The Spirit is eternally persistent. Grace is always looking for a chance to break through. We continually pray "Your kingdom come" as a way of saying "We are ready to be surprised". That is true in the ecumenical movement itself as a witness to the new humanity.

Postlude: Still Hoping

Towards the end of his life Wim Visser't Hooft in his book *Has the Ecumenical Movement a Future?* wrote of the importance of prophecy which is a continual possibility as a gift to God's people: " . . . prophecy knows of a dimension of human life which the world does not know of itself: the dimension of God's actions. Prophecy bears witness to that which God has done, to what God does and to what He will do."[3] Prophets there have been, prophets there will surely be. Even the result of the EU referendum is not the end of the story. People may have turned their back on "Europe" but in reality there is no other way forward for the world of today than the way of cooperation and interdependence, by one means or another. It will be hard and uncomfortable realities that will bring that message home, and it is the prophets who will interpret this discomfort as a means of judgment and grace. The prophets will be addressing the dramatic changes that are even now coming upon the world, especially the seismic upheavals brought by the huge expansion of Asian power and the diminishing status of the West. The water-jar may thereby acquire a new symbolic significance. Perhaps too the work of my parents and their generation in China, and in my own birthplace Gulin, will be transformed in meaning with the dramatic growth of the church in what could, in my grandchildren's lifetime, become the most powerful nation on earth.

So I look back—and therefore forwards too—in hope. But what can I really look forward to for myself? Cancer is waiting at the door. It's often said that when faced with the finality of death or at least a major uncertainty about how long one has to live, the thing to do is to live as fully and intensely as possible, each day. To a great extent I agree with that. But to make it an absolute rule is fanciful. There are things that have to be done which are just mundane or boring, like cutting the grass, washing dishes or filling in the tax return. I don't wish to feel ecstatic when doing any of them, merely to do them competently and cross them off the list. I cannot determine or control just how intensely I can live at any one time. I don't have a regulator or switch that I can turn to ratchet up the excitement. It's more important, as well as more realistic, to find a *meaning* than a feeling in the life one is living. What really matters is to accept that one's life is necessarily of short duration, and therefore to find a meaning by placing it in a larger whole, by seeing it as one story within the grand narrative of what is ultimately going on, the web of grace, and as having a part—however fragmentary it may seem—within that epic. So Paul for example speaks of his ministry, including all its set-backs and disappointments as well as achievements and advances, as a sharing in the filling up of Christ's sufferings that are still outstanding, as part of God's plan for the fullness of time, which is to gather up all things in Christ (Eph. 1:10). I trust that Paul is glad have the agreement of Bonhoeffer who from his prison cell, knowing what fate, humanly speaking, awaited him, using a musical analogy could write:

> What matters . . . is whether one still sees, in this fragment of life that we have, what the whole was intended and designed to be, and of what material it is

---

3. Visser't Hooft, *Has the Ecumenical Movement a Future?*, 92.

Postlude: Still Hoping

made . . . If our life is only the most remote reflection of such a fragment, in which, even for a short time, the various themes gradually accumulate and harmonize with one another and in which the great counterpoint is sustained from beginning to end—so that finally, when they cease, all one can do is sing the chorale "Before Your throne O God I come"—then it is not for us, either, to complain about this fragmentariness, but rather even to be glad of it.[4]

"And now, O Lord, what do I wait for? My hope is in you." (Ps. 39:7). I have all the misgivings and fears natural to anyone in my condition, not just about what pain and physical debilitation may await me, but more poignantly the suffering that my parting from them will bring to those whom I love and by whom I am loved; above all the thought that Margaret if her cancer returned would not have me with her. Nothing can ameliorate the ultimate challenge of letting go of all that is most precious to us in life. But that is precisely when the hope of utter newness is given to us. Bonhoeffer again: "Only when one loves life and the earth so much that with it everything seems to be lost and at its end may one believe in the resurrection of the dead and a new world."[5] And a new world and everlasting life in all its fullness there certainly will be. The fact that we cannot at present really envisage it is itself reason for joy. If with my present puny mind I could picture it, it would hardly be worth getting excited about. "*Then* I shall know, even as I have been fully known", says Paul (1 Corinthians 13:12); and "We are God's children now", says John, "what we will be has not yet been revealed. What we do know is this: when he is revealed, we will be like him, for we will see him as he is" (1 John 3:2). There is joy in not knowing, if we trust the Giver.

"Stop writing now!" The invigilator sounds the end of the exam. Put down the pen. No more scribbling, revisions or deletions from the record. Too late for any more attempts at self-justification. Let it be. Hand the life in for a judgment not your own, a grace not of your enabling, and a future still beyond your power to imagine.

---

4. Bonhoeffer, *Letters and Papers* Works Vol. 8 version, 306.
5. Ibid., 213.

Bibliography

Archbishops' Council. *Mission-Shaped Church: Church Planting and Fresh Expressions of Church in a Changing Context*. London: Church House, 2004.
Barth, Karl. *The Epistle to the Romans*. Oxford: Oxford University Press, 1933.
Best, Thomas (Ed.), *Faith and Renewal: Reports and Documents if the Commission on Faith and Order, Stavanger 1985, Norway*. Geneva: WCC, 1986.
Bonhoeffer, Dietrich. *Ecumenical, Academic and Pastoral Work 1932 (Dietrich Bonhoeffer Works Vol. 11)*. Minneapolis: Fortress, 2012.
———. *Ethics (Dietrich Bonhoeffer Works Vol. 6)*. Minneapolis: Fortress, 2005.
———. *Letters and Papers from Prison*. London: SCM, 1953.
———. *Letters and Papers from Prison (Dietrich Bonhoeffer Works Vol. 8)*. Minneapolis: Fortress, 2010.
———. *London 1933–1935 (Dietrich Bonhoeffer Works Vol. 13)*. Minneapolis: Fortress, 2007.
Booth, Alan. *Not Only Peace*. London: SCM, 1967.
Butler, Barbara (Ed.). *Open Hands. Reconciliation, justice and peace around the world*. Bury St Edmunds: Kevin Mayhew 1998,
Carey, George. *Know the Truth. A Memoir*. London: HarperPerennial, 2005.
Cleal, Clifford. "The Role of the Ordained Minister Today". *Baptist Quarterly* 25, 5 (January 1974) 194–203
Clements, Keith. "Baptists and the Outbreak of the First World War". *Baptist Quarterly* 26, 2 (April 1975) 74–92.
———. *Bonhoeffer and Britain*. London: CCBI, 2006.
———. *The Churches in Europe as Witnesses to Healing*. Geneva: WCC, 2003.
———. "A Conversation About Hope". *Study Encounter* 11, 2 (1975), 10–16.
———. "The Covenant and Community". In Fiddes, Paul et al. *Bound to Love. The Covenant Basis of Baptist Life and Mission*, 50–62. London: Baptist Union, 1985.
———. *Dietrich Bonhoeffer's Ecumenical Quest*. Geneva: WCC, 2015.
———. *Ecumenical Dynamic: Living in More than One Place at Once*. Geneva: WCC, 2013.
———. "Facing Secularism". In Clements et al. *A Call to Mind. Baptist Essays Towards a Theology of Commitment*, 9–21. London: Baptist Union, 1981.
———. *Faith*. London: SCM, 1981.
———. *Faith on the Frontier. A Life of J. H. Oldham*. Edinburgh: T and T. Clark, 1999.
———. "God at Work in the World: Old Liberal and New Secular Theology". *Baptist Quarterly* 24, 7 (July 1972) 345–360.

BIBLIOGRAPHY

———. *God's Angry Love. The theological case for sanctions against South Africa*. London: Christian Concern for Southern Africa, 1990

.———. "God's Concern." *Expository Times* 81, 7 (April 1971) 207–8.

———. "An Interview with Beyers Naudé". In Hansen, L. and Vosloo, R. (Eds), *Oom Bey for the Future: Engaging the Witness of Beyers Naudé*, 167–172. Stellenbosch: Sun Press, 2006.

———. *Learning to Speak. The Church's Voice in Public Affairs*. Edinburgh: T. and T. Clark, 1995.

———. (With Chandler, Alan). "A Live Bishop Bell in 1994? A Response to Adrian Hastings", *Theology* Vol. 98, 781 (January/February 1995), 9–15.

———. *Lovers of Discord. Twentieth Century Theological Controversies in England*. London: SPCK, 1988.

———. (Ed.) *The Moot Papers. Faith, Freedom and Society 1938–1947*. London: T. and T. Clark, 2010.

———. *A Patriotism for Today: Love of Country in Dialogue with the Witness of Dietrich Bonhoeffer* London: Collins, 1986.

———. "A Plea for Conservation." *The Lidunian*. Spring Term 1961, 23–25.

———. *The Theology of Ronald Gregor Smith*. Leiden: E. J. Brill, 1986

———. *What Freedom? The Persistent Challenge of Dietrich Bonhoeffer*. Bristol: Bristol Baptist College, 1990.

Cox, Harvey. *The Secular City*. London: SCM, 1965.

De Gruchy, John W. *Bonhoeffer for a New Day. Theology in a Time of Transition*. Grand Rapids: W. B. Eerdmans, 1997.

———. *Dear and Trusting Spirit. Bonhoeffer's Friend Eberhard Bethge*. Minneapolis: Fortress, 2005.

———. *I Have Come a Long Way*. Cape Town: Lux Verbi, 2015.

Driver, Christopher. *A Future for the Free Churches?* London: SCM, 1962.

Falconer, Alan (Ed.). *Faith and Order in Moshi. The 1996 Commission Meeting*. Geneva: WCC, 1998.

Hull, John. *Mission-Shaped Church: A Theological Response*. London: SCM, 2006.

Institute for Contextual Theology. *The Kairos Document. Challenge to the Church. A Theological Statement on the Political Crisis in South Africa*. London: CIIR and BCC, 1985. Available online at ujamaa.ukzn.ac.za/Libraries/manuals/The_Kairos_Documents.sflb.ashx.

Inter-Church Process. *Churches Together in Pilgrimage. Including Definitive Proposals for Ecumenical Instruments*. London: British Council of Churches and Catholic Truth Society, 1989.

Kinnamon, Michael, and Cope, Brian E. (Eds). *The Ecumenical Movement. An Anthology of Key Texts and Voices*. Geneva: WCC, 1997.

Lack, David. *Swifts in a Tower*. London: Methuen, 1956.

Mehta, Ved. *The New Theologian*. London: Pelican, 1968.

Moltmann, Jürgen. *A Broad Place. An Autobiography*. Minneapolis: Fortress, 2008.

Negro, Luca (Ed.). *Trondheim Report: Jesus Christ Heals and Reconciles*. Geneva: Conference of European Churches, 2004.

Newbigin, Lesslie. "Editorial". *International Review of Missions* 54, 216 (October 1965), 421–2.

Nielsen, Kirsten,Busch et al (Eds). *A Spoke in the Wheel. The Political in the Theology of Dietrich Bonhoeffer* .Gütersloh: Gütersloher Verlagshaus, 2013.

Oldham, J. H., and Visser't Hooft, W. A. (Eds). *The Church and Its Function in Society.* London: George Allen and Unwin, 1937.

Preece, Gordon, and Packer, Ian (Eds). *Bonhoeffer Down Under. Australian and South African Essays Celebrating the Centenary of Dietrich Bonhoeffer's Birth.* Adelaide: ATF Theology, 2012.

Sampson, Anthony. *Anatomy of Britain.* London: Hodder & Stoughton, 1962.

Smith, Ronald Gregor. *The Doctrine of God.* London: Collins, 1970.

———. *The New Man. Christianity and Man's Coming of Age.* London: SCM, 1956.

———. *Secular Christianity.* London: Collins, 1966.

Ting, T. K.. *A Chinese Contribution to Ecumenical Theology. Selected Writings of Bishop K. H. Ting.* Edited by Janine and Philip Wickerei. Geneva: WCC, 2002.

Traherne, Thomas. *Poems, Centuries, and Three Thanksgivings.* Edited by Anne Ridler. London: Oxford University Press, 1966.

Vidler, Alec R.. *Christ's Strange Work.* London: SCM, 1963.

———. (Ed.) *Objections to Christian Belief.* London: Constable, 1963.

———. *Scenes from a Clerical Life. An Autobiography.* London: Collins, 1977.

———. (Ed.) *Soundings. Essays Concerning Christian Understanding.* Cambridge: Cambridge University Press, 1962.

Visser't Hooft, W. A. *Has the Ecumenical Movement a Future?* Belfast: Christian Journals, 1974.

Wallis, Jim. *God's Politics.* New York: HarperCollins, 2005.

World Council of Churches. *Ecumenism in the 21st Century.* Geneva: WCC, 2004.

Index of Subjects and Places

Adam von Trott Memorial Lecture, 367
"Africa, Listening to", 220, 222–23
Albania, 283–84
Anglican-Methodist reunion scheme, 76–77
Anglo-German Churches' 1908–9 peace
    exchanges, 83, 392
    commemorations 2008–9, 379–81
Angola, 19
Ann Frank House, 41
Association of Inter-Church Families, 378
Auschwitz, 351

Balkan region, survey for reconciliation, 219
baptism, 34
Baptism, Eucharist and Ministry, 148
Baptist Churches (England)
    Ansdell, 12, 14–15
    Cross Street, Chesterfield, 64
    Downend, 85, 88–90, 107–8
    Egremont, Wallasey, 21, 392
    Ferryhill, 8, 392
    Geneva Road, Darlington, 7, 7–8, 47
    New Road, Oxford, 51
    St Andrews Street, Cambridge, 27–28
    Tyndale, Bristol, 110, 157, 369
    West Malling, 9
    Woodstock, 48, 54–55
    See also Mid-Cheshire Fellowship of Baptist
    Churches
Baptist Concern for South Africa, 142–43,
    144–46
Baptist Convention of South Africa, 139, 143
Baptist Historical Society, 115
Baptist Hymn Book, new, committee, 133
Baptist Missionary Society, 19, 82
Baptist Student Federation, 40, 48, 57–58
Baptist Union of South Africa, 139, 143

Baptist World Alliance, 133, 142, 143, 146, 173,
    174, 174
Barnton, 68, 72–74
Baylor University, 378
Beirut, 163
Belgrade under NATO bombing (1999), 289–
    90, 292–95
Beyond the Fringe, 23
Bible, study of, 31, 33
bird-watching, 16–17, 20, 41, 161, 245, 298,
    332, 363, 369, 390
Bonhoeffer and Britain, 361–62
Bonhoeffer Society, International, 115, 128, 184,
    299, 354, 368, 384, 385
Bonhoeffer translation project, 152, 183, 184–
    85, 312, 354, 362, 384, 386
Bosnia-Hercegovina, 177, 208, 209–10, 215–18
Bristol, 88, 110–11
Bristol Baptist College, 65, 91, 107, 109–10,
    111–13, 114–15, 159, 364
    Lay Training Program, 94–96
Bristol Cathedral, 111
Bristol Council of Churches, 97, 14
British Council of Churches, 57, 62, 148, 156,
    159, 165
broadcasting, 113–14, 117, 132, 151, 152–53,
    179–180, 249, 257, 259, 281, 384–85
Buchenwald, 122–23
Buenos Aires, 174

CAFOD, 169, 174
"Call to the North", 74–75
Cambridge, 23–47
    Cambridge Inter-Collegiate Christian
    Union, 26
    Clare College, 47, 161,185
    Great St Mary's, 28, 37, 38, 186–87

Index of Subjects and Places

Cambridge (*continued*)
   King's College, 20, 21, 23–26, 43, 391
   King's College Chapel, 35–36, 46–47, 392, 392–93
   Robert Hall Society, 26–28, 33, 38, 40, 391
Canada, 188–89
cancer, 298, 384, 395, 396, 402, 407
CEC-CCEE Islam in Europe Committee, 309
   Christian-Muslim Conference, Sarajevo 2001, 309,
CEC-CCEE Joint Committee meetings, 278–81
Charta Oecumenica, 280, 283, 300–302, 303–4, 305–7, 343,
Chatham House, 169
China, birth in, xviii
   CCBI visit 1994, 251–58
   Fuh-in-wan, 10, 254–56
   future, 407
   Gulin, xvii-xviii, 6, 252–54 (return to)
   journey from to England, xvii-xxi
China Inland Mission (CIM), xvii, 4, 10–11
China, "memories" of, 6, 10, 250, 252
China Christian Council, 251, 256
Christian Aid, 169, 174
Christian unity
   Baptists and, 57–58, 75–76, 102–3
   Nottingham Conference 1984, 38, 58, 58–59
Church of England Diocese of Gibraltar in Europe, 377
Church of Scotland, 173, 198, 401
Churches' Commission on Migrants in Europe, 313
Churches Together in Britain and Ireland, 371, 384
Churches Together in England, 371
coal strike 1984–85, 131
Commission of the Bishops' Conferences of the European Community (COMEC), 338, 342
Conference of European Churches, 173, 207
   appointment to, 260–62
   Central Committee meetings, 270–71, 281, 282–83, 355
   Church and Society Commission, 281, 312, 314, 336–38, 342
   Mission Consultancy, 334–36
   Presidium meetings, 277–78, 298, 310
   Solidarity (diaconal) work, 312–13
   staff, 271–72, 274, 300
   11th Assembly Graz 1997, 266, 270
   12th Assembly Trondheim 2003, 267, 313, 328–32
   13th Assembly Lyon 2009, 377
   14th Assembly Budapest 2013, 377

Confessing the One Faith, 151
Conservation, 17, 79–80
Coventry Cathedral, 37, 185
Corrymeela Community, 156
Council of Churches for Britain and Ireland, 160, 165–67, 178–79
   international affairs work, 168–70, 171–73, 176–77, 263
   arms trade, 176–77
   Former Yugoslavia, 210–16
   Gulf War (1990–91), 170–71, 190–91, 200–201
   See also Churches Together in Britain and Ireland
Council of Episcopal Conferences in Europe, 207, 342
Council on Christian Approaches to Defence and Disarmament, 169
Cry, the Beloved Country, 9

Darlington, 7–12
Dietrich Bonhoeffer's Ecumenical Quest, 387–88
Dominus Iesus, 302–3,
Durham Cathedral, 11, 298

Ecumenical Encounter, Strasbourg 2001, 280, 304–7
ecumenism in UK post-2000, 371–75
   "Called to be One—What Now?" conference 2009, 375–76
   Church of England's role, 374
   Free Churches, 373–74, 378
   Methodists, 374
Ecumenical Centre, Geneva, 269
Ecumenical Dynamic, 378–79
Ecumenical Order of Teachers, 96
Ecumenical Patriarchate, 274–75, 356
English-Speaking Lutheran Church, Geneva, 273
European Common Market, 79
European Convention Process, 314, 338–39
European Union, 281, 314, 340, 361
   UK referendum vote to leave, 396–99
   churches and, 399–402
European Ecumenical Commission on Church and Society, 277, 278, 337
   integration with CEC, 277, 278
Evangelical Alliance Europe, 399

Faith, 117–18
Faith Freedom and Society: The Moot Papers. 363
Faith on the Frontier, 217

Index of Subjects and Places

Faith and Order Commission, 101–2, 133, 147–48, 160, 174–76, 371–72
    World Conference 1993, 174–76, 372
Fellowship of Concerned Baptists (South Africa), 139, 142, 145, 147
Flossenbürg, 354
European Ecumenical Assembly, First, 264–65
European Ecumenical Assembly, Second, 264–66
Free Churches and unity, 39–40

Geneva, life in, 266, 269, 273
Georgia, 314–18
German Democratic Republic, 119–24
Gloucester Cathedral, 160
Gulin, xvii

Herrnhut, 367
Holocaust, 133
Honest to God, 32, 69
Hong Kong, 251, 259

Iceland, 298
Imperial Chemical Industries (ICI), 67, 68, 77, 94–95
Imshausen, 355
India, xx
Iona, 367–68
Iraq 1994, 201–5
Iraq War 2003, 318–28
Irish churches, 156, 199
Israel-Palestine 1991, 199–200

Kairos Document, 136–38, 139–40, 140
Kerala, 390
Kirchentag
    Frankfurt 1975, 99–100
    Berlin 2003, 307
    Munich 1993, 173
    Hamburg 1995, 173
    Ruhrgebniet 1991, 173
Keston Institute, 364
Kosovo 1999, 286–96, 301
Kosovo 2005, 340–42

Laity, role of, 69–70, 93–94
Learning to Speak, 183, 286
Lebanon, 191–98, 389
Lovers of Discord, 133
Lytham St Anne's, 12–22

Macedonia 2001, 308–9
Malawi crisis 1992, 220–21

Mangotsfield and District Council of Churches, 88, 106–7
Melbourne, Victoria, 364–67, 394
    Whitley College, 364–65, 367, 370–71, 382–84
Mass in B-Minor, 36
Mid-Cheshire Fellowship of Baptist Churches, 60–62, 64, 68–69, 70–72, 77–79, 86
    Anderton, 68, 70, 72–74, 77, 85, 86
    Little Leigh, 68,
    Milton, 68
    Runcorn, 71
    Tarporley, 64, 68, 79
Middle East Council of Churches, 191
Mirfield, Community of the Resurrection, 52, 395
Montego Bay, 174
Moscow, 153–56
Mosul, 202–4, 205

Namibia, 387
National Council of Churches of Christ in the USA, 174, 311
New College, Edinburgh, 180, 181, 185, 264, 297, 362, 363
Nicaragua, 175
Northern Ireland, 156
Northwich, 67
Northwich Council of Churches, 74
Nuclear warfare, 18, 19, 57, 156

Oldham biography (*Faith on the Frontier*), 180–82, 217, 264, 297–98
Oriel College, Oxford, 185
Orthodox Academy of Crete, 278, 404–5
Orthodox Church, 149–50, 185
Orthodox churches and CEC, 270–72, 286, 318, 330–32, 346–48,
Oxford, 48–64
    Regent's Park College, 48–52, 159

A Patriotism for Today, 125–27, 128–29, 130, 132
Portishead, 368, 369
    St Nicholas Church, 369
    Theological Reading Group, 369–70
    United Reformed Church, 369
Prague, 368, 384

Quaker Council on European Affairs, 401

"Reconfiguring" ecumenical movement, 349–51
Reeth, 64

Index of Subjects and Places

Roman Catholic-CEC relations 2003–5, 342–44, 346
Romania 218–19
Rugby, 42
Russian Orthodox Church, Moscow Patriarchate
  visits, 276–77, 347
Rwanda and Burundi 1995, 223–31

St Giles Cathedral, Edinburgh, 185
St Egidio Community, 343
St Mary-de-Crypt, Gloucester, 131–32
Salisbury Cathedral, 344
Second Vatican Council, 37, 58, 74, 165
September 11 attacks and aftermath, 309–12
Serbian Orthodox Church, 213–16, 275, 293, 307–9
Sewanee, 369
South Africa,
  anti-apartheid activity 80–81
  Baptist Union of Great Britain and, 80–81, 144–47
  changes 1988–90, 157–58
  Ecumenical Monitoring Programme, 238, 243, 246
  ending apartheid, 232–38, 247
  Sharpeville massacre, 18
  student protests, 56
South Africa, visits to, 134–42 (1985), 233–38 (1992), 239–43 (1993), 243–46 (1994), 248–49 (1996), 386 (2009), 386–87 (2010), 387 (2014)
South Korea, 161
schools
  Ansdell County, 12–13
  Dodmire, Darlington, 7, 11–12
  King Edward VII, Lytham, 13, 16, 17, 18–19, 20. 22
  Ryarsh, 7
"secular theology", 53, 83, 90–91
South African Council of Churches, 134, 135–36, 140
South West Ecumenical Congress, 97–98 (1973), 100–101 (1976),

Sri Lanka, 82, 390
Student Christian Movement, 27–28, 385–86
Stuttgart 1945 commemoration, 352–54
Swan Hellenic Cruises, 363 (Norway 2006), 394 (Sri Lanka to Muscat)

Tasmania, 366
The Theology of Ronald Gregor Smith, 117
Taizé Community, 97, 291, 308, 352
Timisoara, 218
Treasure Island, 8
Trondheim, St Olav Festival, 299
Tyntesfield House, 370

United Nations, 174, 176–77, 208, 340

Wars
  Arab-Israel 1967, 57
  Biafran, 79
  Falklands/Malvinas, 125–26, 127
  World, First 18, 83, 91 (churches and) commemorations 2014
  World, Second, 18, 77–78, 132
  Vietnam, 57, 79
The Way to Freedom, 384–85
War Requiem, 36
"web of grace", 404–5, 407
West Malling, 5–7
Westminster Abbey, 185
Worcester Cathedral, 185
World Council of Churches, 37, 62, 74, 102, 173, 199, 219
  Program to Combat Racism, 81, 239–40
  8th Assembly Harare 1998, 272, 285–86
  9th Assembly Porto Alegre, 2006, 361, 370–71, 371
  See also Faith and Order Commission
World Mission Conference, Athens 2005, 347

Yugoslavia, break up of, 206–9

Zimbabwe 1993, 222

Index of Names

Abraham-Williams, Gethin, 364, 375, 398
Abu El-Assal, Bishop Riah, 322
Ackerman, Denise, 249, 387
Akhtal, Shabbir, 210
al-Assad, Hafez, 19
Aldred, Joe, 375
Alexander, Stella, 207
Alexei, Patriarch, 276, 314, 346–47
Alfayev, Hilarion, 276, 291, 292
Anastasios, Archbishop, 283, 284, 285, 290, 299, 306, 308, 309, 310, 333, 333, 343, 355
Annan, Kofi, 339–40
Annan, Noel, 23
Arnold, John, 261, 264, 274, 278, 298, 355, 361
Artimej, Bishop, 288
Askola, Irja, 272, 280, 297
Athanasios, Bishop, 340
Atkins, Martin, 374
Attfield, Robin, 49
Augustine, 132
Aydin, Mehmet, 310
Aylward, Gladys, 250

Bailey, Sydney, 169, 170
Baillie, John, 185–86
Baines, Nick, 400
Ballard, Paul, 375
Banda, Hastings, 220, 221
Barclay, Enid, 14
Barnett, Victoria, 388, 389
Barrington-Ward, Simon, 232
Barth, Karl, 45, 52–53, 56, 71, 132, 152–53, 337, 398
Bartholomew, Ecumenical Patriarch, 275, 305, 312, 329, 330, 331
Bataringaya, Pascal, 229
Battle, John, 176

Bauckham, Richard, 156, 380
Beach, Hugh, 156, 176
Beamish, Adrian, 394
Beasley-Murray, Paul, 41
Beeching, Richard, 37
Beeson, Trevor, 54, 119, 128
Behmen, Alijah, 310
Behr, Nicolas, 101, 150
Bell, George, 297, 353, 379
Belopopsky, Alex, 283, 289
Benedict XVI, Pope, *see* Ratzinger
Benn, Tony, 115
Beresford, Bob, 172
Best, Isabel, 275, 384
Bethge, Dietrich, 297
Bethge, Eberhard, 84, 103–5, 125, 126, 128, 129, 151–52, 179, 188, 297, 387, 392, 404
Bethge, Renate, 103–5, 128, 129, 151–52, 297, 299, 355, 404
Bezzant, J. S., 29
Bichkov, Alexei, 155
Bidawi, Mar Raphael, 202
Biggs, John, 210, 212
Bigovic, Radovan, 341
Biko, Steve, 109
Birmelé, Jean-Daniel, 300
Bishop, Dale, 201
Black, Cyril, 80–81
Black, Donald, 119, 134, 142, 143, 146, 146, 170, 171
Blair, Tony, 281, 294, 322, 323–24, 399
Bleakley, David, 208
Bliss, Kathleen, 180, 182, 404
Blount, Gary and Lee, 390
Blyth, Myra, 376
Boesak, Allan, 138, 142, 387
Bond, Alice, 184

Index of Names

Bonhoeffer, Dietrich, x, 30, 31–32, 33, 37, 51, 53, 83–84, 103–4, 124, 125, 128, 129, 136, 151–52 , 157, 183–85, 186, 226, 229, 248, 294, 297, 299, 326, 353, 354–55, 361–62, 364, 365, 367, 369, 381–82, 384–86, 386–89, 393, 402, 404, 405, 407–8, 408
Bonino, Miguez, 174
Booth, Alan, 91
Bordeaux, Michael, 364
Borden, Jenny, 172
Bosanquet, Mary, 125
Bossoff, Karl, 140
Botha, P. W., 134
Bowden, John, 117, 117–18, 127
Bowker, Michael, 27, 391
Boyd, Caroline, 212, 213
Bradnock, Christopher, 27, 41, 64, 363, 391
Bradnock, Robert, 27, 38, 363. 391
Brain, Peter, 172
Bray, Michael, 361–62
Brookes, Albert, 73, 78
Brown, Alan, 27
Brown, Brian, 134, 135
Brown, George (Catholic priest), 71
Brown, George (politician), 28
Brown, Stephen, 389
Burrows, Edward, 49
Burton, Win and Hugh, 394
Bush, George, 323, 324–25, 327
Butler, Dom Christopher, 38
Byrne, Lavinia, 168

Caird, George, 50, 63
Caligiorlis, Jérémie, 271, 275, 278, 288, 305, 310
Cameron, Bruce, 222
Cameron, David, 397
Campbell, Joan Brown, 198
Campbell, R. J., 112, 133
Carah, Peter, 12, 16, 18
Carey, George, 209, 216, 257–58, 372n
Carter, David, 28, 30, 41, 45–46, 47, 76, 371 375, 377, 391
Cassidy, Edward, 296
Castro, Emilio, 173, 209
Cé, Marco, 151
Chadwick, Owen, 45
Champion, Leonard, 88, 118
Chapman, Sue, 128
Chernomyrdin, Viktor, 294
Chikane, Frank, 185, 232–33, 234–35, 240, 249
Christodoulos, Archbishop, 347
Chung Hyan Kyung, 185
Cilerdzic, Andreas, 289, 307–8, 381

Clark, Andrew, 172
Clark, Neville, 34, 112
Cleal, Clifford, 60–62, 68, 69–70, 71, 75, 82, 83, 85, 94, 404
Cleal, Rene, 68, 79
Clements, Bess, 389
Clements, Brian, xvii, 6, 11, 12, 82
Clements, Fay, xvii–xix, 4, 6, 7, 17, 61, 82, 89–90, 111, 186, 365–66
Clements, Ginny (Sandringham), 368, 389
Clements, Harry, xvii–xix, 4, 6, 8, 17, 22, 34, 82, 89–90, 111, 159, 250
Clements, Jonathan, 107, 111, 129, 141, 151, 160, 177, 188, 189, 368, 389, 390
Clements, John, xvii, 5, 6, 12
Clements, Laura (née Epton), 188, 297, 356, 390
Clements, Margaret (née Hirst), 46–47, 49, 61–63, 73, 85, 86, 90, 110, 113, 151, 159,160,187, 260, 262, 263, 264, 267, 273, 298, 330, 348, 353, 355, 361, 369, 381, 384, 389–90, 395, 405
Clements, Oliver, 356, 390
Clements, Peter, 89, 100, 107, 111, 129, 140, 161, 187, 187–88, 188, 264, 297, 356, 390
Clements, Tom, 389, 390
Clifford, Paul Rowntree, 102
Clinton, Bill, 292, 293
Cockrell, Patricia, 210, 213
Coffey, David, 222, 323, 362, 371
Coleman, Donata, 97, 148, 348, 404
Coleman, Peter, 97, 97–98, 148, 404
Collins, Lady, 117
Conway, Martin, 102, 149, 264
Cook, Robin, 288
Corbyn, Jeremy, 397
Corneanu, Nicolae, 218
Cornell, Margaret, 135, 138
Cornick, David, 376
Cowley, Ronald, 103
Cox, Harvey, 53, 90
Craig, Maxwell, 172
Cressy, Martin, 175
Crow, Paul, 149, 298
Crowe, Philip, 170, 170
Cupitt, Don, 133
Cvicc, Chris, 207

d'Estaing, Valéry Giscard, 338
D'Oliveira, Basil, 80
Dammers, Horace, 96, 132
Daniel, Metropolitan, 270–71, 275, 278, 336
Dante, x
Daries, John, 142–44, 146, 244, 246, 248

Index of Names

Davey, Colin, 168
Davidson, Robert, 221
Davies, Gwyn Henton, 43, 50, 52, 60, 64, 85, 153, 365
Davies, Myriel, 172, 177
Davies, Noel, 172
Davies, Rupert, 88, 96, 102
de Blank, Joost, 37
de Clermont, Jean Arnold, 329, 333, 345
de Gruchy, Isobel, 125, 128. 233, 244-45, 365, 386
de Gruchy, John, 125, 128, 138, 151, 157-58, 184, 233, 244-46, 247, 355, 365, 386, 387
de Gruchy, Steve, 386-87
de Klerk, F. W., 232, 233, 234
Dixon, Bill, 87, 89
Dixon, Malcolm, 41
Doling, Ruth, *see* Morley
Dörr, Elfriede, 270, 307
Doyle, Graham, 208, 210
Driver, Christopher, 39-40
du Toit, Eliane, 225

Edgar, Bob, 311, 319, 325, 326, 329, 340
Edwards, David, 298
Edwards, Jonathan, 374
Elliot, Alison, 319
Elliot, Donald, 168-69
Ellis, Marc, 239
Ellison, Gerald, 75
Epton, Laura, *see* Clements
Everett, Oliver, 394

Fairburn, Norman, 81
Falconer, Alan, 175
Farage, Nigel, 401
Farquhar, Tony, 199, 200
Fenn, Eric, 181, 329
Fergusson, David, 362
Fiddes, Paul, 118, 133, 159
Fielding, Harry, 14-15
Firth, Peter, 94, 113, 132
Fischer, Jean, 195, 210, 215, 275, 281
Fisk, Robert, 192
Fison, Joe, 28
Fitzgerald, Michael, 202
Fledelius, Karsten, 287
Forrester, Duncan, 149, 152, 180-81, 264, 297, 362, 404
Forrester, Margaret, 181
Forster, E. M., 24, 43
Forsyth, P. T., 44, 82, 132, 182, 185
Francis, Arthur and Thea, 111

Frieling, Reinhard, 296, 305, 306
Fuhrmann, Klaus, 120, 123-24
Fung, Raymond, 259
Fyffe, Bob, 373, 376, 380, 381, 384

Galloway, Alan, 117
Garnett, John, 71
Gassmann, Günther, 149, 151
George, Raymond, 102
Georgevitch, Armand, 195
Gibbs, Mark, 94, 98-99, 100
Gibson, Alan, 94
Gill, Adrian, 27, 33-34
Gilmore, Alec, 34
Giordano, Aldo, 278, 280, 296, 302, 306, 307, 318, 342, 343, 345, 352
Godsey, John, 125
Gohde, Jürgen, 291, 292
Gorbachev, Mikhail, 154, 156
Grace, W. G., 87
Graham, Billy, 20
Gray, Gordon, 199, 200
Grayston, Kenneth, 96, 115
Green, Barbara, 184
Green, Bernard, 144-45, 146
Green, Clifford, 125, 184, 387
Gruber, Pamela, 171-72
Gurney, Robin, 271, 273, 277, 300, 309

Habgood, John, 170, 176, 177, 190-91
Habib, Gabi, 191, 197, 198
Hackel, Sergei, 172, 264
Hani, Chris, 234, 239-43, 247
Hanmer, Jean and James, 88
Harald V, King (Norway), 329, 330
Harmati, Bela, 329
Harper, Malcolm, 177
Harris, Jim, 243
Haslam, David, 168
Hastings, Adrian, 217-18
Hastings, Gordon, 81
Hawtin, David, 13, 52, 165, 376
Hayden, Roger, 118
Haymes, Brian, 118
Healey, Denis, 28
Heaney, Carmel, 168, 208
Heath, Edward, 37
Heaton, Eric, 50
Heider-Rottwilm, Antje, 274, 278, 318
Henkys, Jürgen, 120
Herbert, George, 36
Hicks, Douglas, 59-60
Hill, Maurice, 41
Hirsekoorn, Heinz-Dieter, 121

Index of Names

Hirst, Margaret, *see* Clements
Hodosy, Imre, 211-12
Hofmeister, Desmond, 235
Honecker, Erich, 121
Horsfield, Rod and Beth, 367
House, Francis, 75
Hovhanissian, Nathan, 372
Huddleston, Trevor, 30-31, 241, 294,
Hull, John, 374
Hume, Basil, 165, 166, 176, 177, 209, 264
Hummel, Gert, 314, 316
Hunter, Colin and Jenny, 366, 383
Hurd, Douglas, 171
Hussein, Saddam, 167, 170, 319
Huxley, Julian, 21

Ilia II, Patriarch (Georgia), 318
Ionita, Viorel, 271, 302, 306, 307, 319, 334, 345, 346, 352
Irenaeus, 51
Irenij, Bishop (of Novi Sad), 275, 342
Isberg, Margarethe, 274, 333

Jackson, Darrell, 336, 347
Jackson, Michael and Elizabeth, 82, 390-91
Jakob, Henry and Barbara, 100, 129, 188, 381
Jakobsen, Wilma, 248, 248
Jarjour, Riad, 329
Jenkins, Daniel, 182
Jenkins, David, 133
Jenkins, Ivor and Karin, 146
Jenkins, Keith, 300, 314, 338
Jestice, Arthur, 27, 43
John Paul II, Pope, 278, 279, 296, 305, 344-45
John XXIII, Pope, 37, 154, 165
Johns, Paul, 216
Johnson, Tilewa, 220
Jones, Keith, 260, 368
Jones, Norman, 60, 81, 111
Jones, Ron, 75
Jones, Roy, 71

Kafity, Samir, 199
Kalpakian, Vosgan, 331
Karkala-Zorba, Katerina, 329
Kasper, Walter, 303, 343, 352
Kaunda, Kenneth, 329
Kelley, Pat, 125, 184, 369
Kelly, Geff, 125, 184
Kendal, Elliott, 158
Kidd, Richard, 118
King, Martin Luther, 42, 79
Kirby, Ermal, 168
Kirill, Metropolitan, 291, 292-94, 326

Kishkovsky, Leonard, 292, 293, 325, 326, 340
Kisitu, Eva, 168, 263
Kitanovic, Elizabeta, 341-42
Knight, Jack, 85, 89
Kock, Manfred, 319, 321
Koppe, Rolf, 291
Kraemer, Hendrik, 70, 94, 329
Krtezschmar, Louise, 235, 243
Kuharic, Cardinal, 207, 210, 212
Kühn, Ulrich, 150, 151
Küng, Hans, 99, 152
Kwok Nai Wong, 259

Lack, David, 21-22
Lake, Frank, 30
Lake, Robert, 43
Lamola, John, 147, 234
Lampe, Geoffrey, 45
Lanke, Berit, 298-99, 328
Lassila, Olli-Pekka, 289
Lawrence, T. E., 4
Le Grange, Louis, 140
Lehmann, Karl, 280, 303, 307
Lewis, C. S., 21
Lewis, Griff, 25, 391, 394
Lilje, Hans, 353
Limouris, Gennadios, 149
Linden, Ian, 147, 183
Lochman, Jan Milic, 152, 153
Lockes, Geoffrey, 144-45, 146
Long, Eugene, 117
Lotz, Denton, 155
Luther, Martin, 124, 132
Lyttle, John, 191

MacCaughey, Jean, 367
Mackenzie, Murdoch, 368
Mackinnon, Donald, 29, 45-46, 182
Macleod, George, 30, 33
Macleod, Norman, 94
Macquarrie, John, 82, 104, 106, 117. 132
Madolo, Diba, 233, 234
Major, John, 209
Makhanya, Gideon, 146, 147, 174, 233
Mandela, Nelson, 158, 232, 241, 242, 243, 248, 286
Manley, Ken, 364, 366
Mann, Chris, 117
Marsh, Charles, 226
Marsh, Richard, 210, 216, 291, 294
Martini, Maria, 296
Mathews, J.C., 12
Matthews, John, 184, 384
Matthews, Stanley, 12

Index of Names

Maxian, Françoise, 272
Mayland, Jean, 168n
McIntyre, Ian, 124
Mehta, Ved, 46n
Mhxlope, Peter, 146, 147
Migliore, Celestino, 291
Mihaylova, Mariela, 340
Milosevic, Slobodan, 287, 291, 292–95
Milroy, Arthur, 88
Mkapa, Benjamin, 175
Moltmann, Jürgen, 82, 101, 116, 152, 161, 371, 380, 384
Montefiore, Hugh, 28, 37, 183
Moon, Norman, 111–12
Morgan, Philip, 135, 136
Morgan-Wynne, John, 50, 159
Morley (*née* Doling), Ruth, 41, 366, 391
Morley, Colin, 41, 366, 391
Morris, Colin, 179
Morris, Harry, 14
Morris, Jeremy, 377, 392
Morton, Ralph, 94, 98
Mosala, Itemelung, 239
Mott, John R., 93, 277
Moule, C. F. D., 45
Mowvley, Harry, 95, 112, 159
Mozart, W. A., 151
Mugabe, Robert, 286
Mulyungi, Josphat, 220
Murphy, Tommy, 251, 255

Nahhal, Mike, 192, 193, 198, 202, 204, 205
Naphy, William, 181
Napier, William, 235
Naudé, Beyers, 99, 134, 135, 136, 185, 249
Negro, Luca, 300
Neill, John, 210, 212
Neill, Stephen, 55
Nelson, Burton, 184
Nevile, Mildred, 135, 136
Newbigin, Lesslie, 55–56, 182, 404
Newton, John, 165, 372
Nicholls, Vincent, 278, 280
Nicholson, Gisela, 146–47, 235, 242
Niemöller, Martin, 19, 37, 353
Nineham, Dennis, 45
Nkbantungany, Silvestre, 225
Norwich, John Julius, 394
Noko, Ishmael, 343
Nolan, Albert, 138
Noll, Rüdiger, 271–72, 280, 295, 300
Norwood, Donald, 377
Nourse, Errol, 139, 142
Ntoni-Nzinga, Daniel, 224

Nunn, Roger, 75
Nüsserl, Frederike, 381

O'Brien, James, 221
O'Connor, Murphy, 318, 364, 371, 374
Oestreicher, Paul, 30, 120, 135, 157
Oldham, J. H., 44, 93–94, 132, 180–83, 185, 197–98, 337, 362–63, 379, 404
Oliver, Stephen, 152, 158
Opocensky, Milan, 368
Ortega, Daniel, 174

Pannenberg, Wolfhart, 101, 149, 175
Papaderos, Alexandros, 261, 262, 405–6
Paterson, Gillian, 169, 178–79, 251, 373
Paton, David, 132, 250–51
Paton, William (Bill), 132
Patterson, Morgan, 58
Pavle, Patriarch, 207, 211, 214, 216, 289–90, 293, 308, 342
Payne, Ernest, 59, 80, 83, 91, 110, 119
Pearce, Gordon, 50
Peschke, Doris, 313
Peterlin, Boris, 212, 213, 308
Pityana, Barney, 238, 239
Plant, Stephen, 376
Polack, Kenneth, 24
Potter, Philip, 100, 269, 298
Powell, Enoch, 28, 79, 125
Poyntz, Sam, 199, 200
Preston, Ronald, 181–82
Price, Ray, 88
Priestland, Gerald, 135, 138, 140
Prieur, Jean-Marc, 271, 275, 305
Primakov, Yevgeny, 325–26
Pritchard, John, 251, 258

Raiser, Konrad, 185, 244, 308, 314, 319, 321, 348
Ramsey, Michael, 37, 76, 98, 157
Rasmussen, Larry, 174, 184, 244–45, 387
Ratzinger, Josef 303, 343
Raven, John, 20
Ray, Ernie, 132, 152
Reagan, Ronald, 156, 311
Reardon, John, 168, 251
Reardon, Martin, 173, 378
Reardon, Ruth, 378
Rees, Frank, 364–65, 367, 382
Reeves, Ambrose, 37
Reeves, Marjorie, 181–82
Reeves, Paul, 174, 243
Renshaw, Paul, 238, 243, 246, 323, 340
Richards, Reuben, 265

Index of Names

Riding, Harold and Amy, 77–78, 85
Robertson, Edwin, 102, 125, 368
Robinson, Debbie, 239, 242
Robinson, John A. T., 32, 37, 53
Rohrandt, Rut, 271, 275, 306
Rominger, Roberta, 374
Root, Howard, 37–38
Rosen, David, 199
Ross, Matthew, 340
Rowell, Geoffrey, 377
Roy, Kevin, 145
Rubeiz, Ghassan, 191, 198
Rudd, Kevin, 365
Rudolph, Barbara, 380
Runcie, Robert, 92, 165
Rupp, Gordon, 353–54, 382
Rusama, Jaako, 221
Russell, Horace, 149
Russell, Philip, 138–39

Sabbah, Michael, 199
Sagovsky, Nicholas, 381
Salt, George, 24
Salter, Elizabeth, 135, 173, 198, 261–62, 282, 404
Sandringham, Ginny, *see* Clements
Sansbury, Kenneth, 74
Santer, Jacques, 283
Santer, Mark, 221
Sava, Father (Janjic), 288
Scheele, Walter, 343
Schlingensiepen, Ferdinand, 387
Schmidt, Helmut, 100
Schmocker, Hans, 271, 273, 282, 300
Schneider, Paul, 123
Schofield, J. N., 27
Schönborn, Archbishop Christoph, 292
Schönherr, Albrecht, 121, 124, 128, 184
Schröder, Gerhard, 322
Schutz, Roger, 352
Scott-Joynt, Michael, 26, 47
Sharpe, Eric, 51
Sharpe, Gwen, 51
Sharpe, Sam, 174
Shaw, Gordon, 169
Sheppard, David, 80, 165, 372
Sherman, Franklin, 51
Sherrington, Charles, 21
Shevardnaze, Eduard, 317
Shkeiban, Lamia, 195
Short, Clare, 323
Showell-Rogers, Gordon, 336
Sidoroff, Matti, 218, 219
Siegrist, Roland, 261

Simpfendörfer, Werner, 9
Simpson, John, 289
Sisulu, Walter, 241
Smit, Dirkie, 387
Smith, Dinah, 244
Smith, Käthe Gregor, 104–5, 117, 404
Smith, Nico, 235
Smith, Philip, 142
Smith, Ronald Gregor, 53, 82–83, 104–6, 116–17, 118, 132, 185, 367, 404, 404
Songulashvili, Malkhaz, 314
Soutar, Douglas, 192
Spanring, Paul, 364, 384
Sparkes, Douglas, 154
Stacey, Nick, 54
Stephens, David, 172
Stephens, Rachel, 170, 261, 264
Stewart, Jacques, 210, 291
Stewart, James, 37
Stockwood, Mervyn, 28, 37
Stunell, Andrew, 75–76
Suenens, Cardinal, 98
Swart, Trevor, 143

Tagg, Chris, 13
Tang, Edmund, 169, 251, 255
Tanner, Mary, 102, 148, 149, 244, 371, 376, 377
Tatham, David, 192–93
Taylor, (Bishop) John, 135, 136, 139, 169,
Taylor, John, 272, 282
Taylor, Michael, 76, 85, 99, 233
Taylor, Ray, 95, 96
Terrill, Edward, 114, 115
Thatcher, Margaret, 107, 125, 131, 156
Thompson, Alwyn, 25, 43, 391
Thompson, David, 27, 38, 391
Tillard, Jean, 149, 151
Ting, K. H., 256–57, 259
Tökes, Lazlo, 218
Tomkins, Oliver, 88, 149, 181, 404
Torrance, T. F., 82, 152
Traherne, Thomas, 6, 22, 54, 126, 386, 396
Treanor, Noel, 338
Treu, Hans, 122
Trotman, Willie, 107–8
Tutu, Desmond, 97, 136, 175, 176, 185, 235, 242, 243, 247–48

Utnem, Stig, 328

van Beek, Huibert, 219
van Buren, Paul, 53
Varah, Chad, 28
Verhofstadt, Guy, 312

Index of Names

Vidler, Alec, 23, 28–29, 38, 41, 43–45, 47, 94, 132, 181, 369, 404
Villa-Vicencio, Charles, 138, 157, 239, 249
Visser't Hooft, W. A., 37, 93, 353, 407
Vlk, Miloslav, 278, 279, 306
Vogel-Mfato, Eva-Sybille, 297

Wagle, Finn, 278, 328,
Waite, Terry, 191
Walker, Paul, 142
Walker, Terry, 106–7
Walley, Derek, 68
Walley, Jean, 68, 79
Wallis, Jim, 322, 323
Walters, Norman, 27
Ward, Graham, 387
Wardlaw, Harry and Ruth, 367, 383
Ware, John, 96
Ware, Timothy (Kallistos), 51
Weatherhead, Leslie, 37
Webb, Pauline, 100, 128, 222
Weide, Helmut, 282
Welby, Justin, 401
Welch, Elizabeth, 244
West, Michael (WCC), 387
West, Mike, 100, 120, 123
West, Timothy, and Scales, Prunella, 394
West, W. M. S. (Morris), 34, 88, 91, 92–93, 94, 101–2, 111, 114, 115, 127, 133, 148, 159, 361, 371, 404

White, Barrie, 50, 159
Wiesel, Eli, 123, 351
Wigglesworth, Chris, 170, 172
Wilcox, David, 49
Wiles, Maurice, 118
Wilkie, Jim, 135, 221
Wilkinson, Alan, 128
Willcocks, David, 35, 36, 351–52, 392
Williams, Colin, 355
Williams, Harry, 29
Williams, Rowan, 175, 264, 323, 326, 331, 345, 371–72, 374, 377
Williams, Tom and Mary, 367
Williamson, Roger, 120, 121–22, 176, 177
Wilson, Richard, 16
Winter, Derek, 115,
Winter, Sean, 385
Winward, Stephen, 34
Wolf, Christian, 120
Woods, Mark, 374
Wooldridge, Mike, 137
Worlock, Derek, 165, 372
Wotton, Michael, 159
Wright, John, 83–84

Yang, Grace, 10, 252
Yonge, Gary, 247
Young, Frances, 175

Zahrnt, Heinz, 99

www.ingramcontent.com/pod-product-compliance
Lightning Source LLC
Chambersburg PA
CBHW081146290426
44108CB00018B/2449